LABOUR ARBITRATION
IN CANADA

Morton Mitchnick
and
Brian Etherington

Lancaster House

All rights reserved. No part of this publication may be reproduced or transmitted in any form or by any means, electronic or mechanical, including photocopy, recording, or any information storage system, without permission in writing from the publisher.

© Lancaster House 2006

National Library of Canada Cataloguing in Publication Data

Mitchnick, M. G.
  Labour Arbitration in Canada / Morton Mitchnick and Brian Etherington.

Includes bibliographical references and index.
ISBN 0-920450-29-6

  1. Arbitration, Industrial—Law and legislation—Canada. I. Etherington, Brian II. Title.

KE3206.M48 2006   344.7101'89143   C2006-903327-7
KF3424.M48 2066

Lancaster House

17 Dundonald Street, Suite 200
Toronto, ON M4Y 1K3
Customer Service: (416) 977-6618
Email: Lan@lancasterhouse.com
Website: www.lancasterhouse.com

 PRINTED IN CANADA

ABOUT THE AUTHORS

Mort Mitchnick, a graduate of McMaster University and the University of Toronto, is national counsel to the law firm Borden Ladner Gervais. Formerly Chair of the Ontario Labour Relations Board, as well as a senior arbitrator and mediator, he lectures and writes extensively on labour law and labour arbitration. His writings include *Union Security and the Charter*, and "Recent Developments in Compulsory Unionism", published in the International Labour Review. During his tenure as an arbitrator, Mr. Mitchnick was a member of the National Academy of Arbitrators, and served on standing panels of arbitrators under numerous collective agreements, including the salary arbitration panel for Major League Baseball.

Brian Etherington is a graduate of McMaster University, Queen's University and Yale. He now teaches labour arbitration, labour law, individual employment law and criminal law at the University of Windsor. Professor Etherington has frequently written about, and acted as a consultant on, administrative, constitutional, criminal and trade law, as well as labour and employment law. Editor-in-chief of the Canadian Labour and Employment Law Journal between 1995 and 2004, he also acts as an arbitrator and mediator. He is co-author of *Labour Law in Canada*, a division of the *International Encyclopedia of Labour Law*, and a member of the Canadian Labour Law Casebook Group.

TABLE OF CONTENTS

CHAPTER 4.   PRE-HEARING PROCEDURE

CHAPTER 5.   PROCEDURE AND PROOF AT THE HEARING

CHAPTER 6.   ADMISSIBILITY OF EVIDENCE

CHAPTER 9.   DUTY OF FAIR REPRESENTATION

PART 2.   DISCHARGE AND DISCIPLINE

CHAPTER 10.   GENERAL PRINCIPLES

CHAPTER 14.   NON-DISCIPLINARY DISCHARGE

CHAPTER 15.   OTHER FORMS OF SEPARATION

PART 3. CONTRACT INTERPRETATION

CHAPTER 16. INTERPRETING THE COLLECTIVE AGREEMENT

ABBREVIATIONS AND CITATIONS

STATUTES

S.C./R.S.C.	Statutes/Revised Statutes of Canada
S.A./R.S.A.	Statutes/Revised Statutes of Alberta
S.B.C./R.S.B.C.	Statutes/Revised Statutes of British Columbia
S.M./R.S.M.	Statutes/Revised Statutes of Manitoba
S.N.L./R.S.N.L.	Statutes/Revised Statutes of Newfoundland and Labrador
S.N.B./R.S.N.B.	Statutes/Revised Statutes of New Brunswick
S.N.S./R.S.N.S.	Statutes/Revised Statutes of Nova Scotia
S.O./R.S.O.	Statutes/Revised Statutes of Ontario
S.P.E.I./R.S.P.E.I.	Statutes/Revised Statutes of Prince Edward Island
S.Q./R.S.Q.	Statutes/Revised Statutes of Quebec
S.S./R.S.S.	Statutes/Revised Statutes of Saskatchewan
Reg./R.R.	Regulation/Revised Regulations

COURTS AND TRIBUNALS

B.C.C.H.R.	British Columbia Council of Human Rights
Bd. of Inquiry	Board of Inquiry
C.A.	Court of Appeal
C.R.O.A.	Canadian Railway Office of Arbitration
Div. Ct.	Divisional Court
F.C.	Federal Court
F.C.A.	Federal Court of Appeal
Gen. Div.	General Division
H.C.J.	High Court of Justice
H.R. Trib.	Human Rights Tribunal
I.R.B.	Industrial Relations Board
I.R.C.	Industrial Relations Council
K.B.	Court of King's Bench
L.R.B.	Labour Relations Board
Ont. G.S.B.	Ontario Crown Employees Grievance Settlement Board
P.C.	Judicial Committee of the Privy Council (U.K.)
P.S.L.R.B.	Public Service Labour Relations Board (after 2005)
P.S.S.R.B.	Public Service Staff Relations Board (to 2005)
Q.B.	Court of Queen's Bench
S.C.	Supreme Court (Provincial)
A.D.	Appellate Division
T.D.	Trial Division

S.C.C.	Supreme Court of Canada
Sup. Ct. J.	Superior Court of Justice
Trib.	Tribunal
W.C.B.	Workers' Compensation Board

CANADIAN LAW REPORTS

Admin. L.R.	Administrative Law Reports
Alta. L.R.	Alberta Law Reports
A.R.	Alberta Reports
B.C.L.R.	British Columbia Law Reports
Can. L.R.B.R.	Canadian Labour Relations Boards Reports
C.C.E.L.	Canadian Cases on Employment Law
C.H.R.R.	Canadian Human Rights Reporter
C.L.L.C.	Canadian Labour Law Cases
C.L.R.	Construction Law Reports
di	decisions/information (Canada Industrial Relations Board)
D.L.R.	Dominion Law Reports
F.C.	Federal Court Reports
F.T.R.	Federal Trial Reports
L.A.C.	Labour Arbitration Cases
Man. R.	Manitoba Reports
N.R.	National Reporter
N.B.R.	New Brunswick Reports
Nfld. & P.E.I.R.	Newfoundland & Prince Edward Island Reports
N.S.R.	Nova Scotia Reports
O.A.C.	Ontario Appeal Cases
O.L.R.B. Rep.	Ontario Labour Relations Board Reports
O.R.	Ontario Reports
P.R.	Ontario Practice Reports
QL	Quicklaw
Sask. R.	Saskatchewan Reports
S.C.R.	Supreme Court Reports
U.M.A.C.	Union-Management Arbitration Cases
W.W.R.	Western Weekly Reports

U.K. LAW REPORTS

A.C.	Appeal Cases
All E.R.	All England Reports
Ch.	Chancery Division
E.R.	English Reports
K.B.	King's Bench Division

Q.B.   Queen's Bench Division
R.   The Reports

U.S. LAW REPORTS

ARB   Labour Arbitration Awards
L.A.   Labour Arbitration Reports
N.L.R.B.   National Labor Relations Board Decisions
S. Ct.   Supreme Court Reporter
U.S.   United States Reports

QUICKLAW (QL) CITATIONS

A.G.A.A.   Alberta Grievance Arbitration Awards
A.J.   Alberta Judgments
B.C.C.A.A.A.   British Columbia Collective Agreement Arbitration
                  Awards
B.C.C.H.R.D.   British Columbia Council of Human Rights Decisions
                  (to 1997)
B.C.H.R.T.D.   British Columbia Human Rights Tribunal Decisions
                  (after 1997)
B.C.J.   British Columbia Judgments
B.C.L.R.B.D.   British Columbia Labour Relations Board Decisions
C.H.R.D.   Canadian Human Rights Tribunal Decisions
C.I.R.B.D.   Canada Industrial Relations Board Decisions
C.L.A.D.   Canada Labour Code Arbitration Awards
C.P.S.L.R.B.   Canada Public Service Labour Relations Board Decisions
                  (after 2005)
C.P.S.S.R.B.   Canada Public Service Staff Relations Board Decisions
                  (to 2005)
D.A.T.C.   Arbitrage en relations de travail
F.C.J.   Federal Court Judgments
J.Q.   Quebec Judgments
M.G.A.D.   Manitoba Grievance Arbitration Decisions
M.J.   Manitoba Judgments
N.B.J.   New Brunswick Judgments
N.B.L.A.A.   New Brunswick Labour Adjudication Awards
N.J.   Newfoundland and Labrador Judgments
N.L.L.A.A.   Newfoundland and Labrador Labour Arbitration Awards
N.S.J.   Nova Scotia Judgments
N.S.L.A.A.   Nova Scotia Labour Arbitration Awards
N.W.T.L.A.A.   Northwest Territories Labour Arbitration Awards
O.G.S.B.A.   Ontario Grievance Settlement Board Decisions
O.H.R.T.D.   Ontario Human Rights Tribunal Decisions

O.J.	Ontario Judgments
O.L.A.A.	Ontario Labour Arbitration Awards
O.L.R.D.	Ontario Labour Relations Board Decisions
P.E.I.J.	Prince Edward Island Judgments
P.E.I.L.A.A.	Prince Edward Island Labour Arbitration Awards
S.C.J.	Supreme Court of Canada Judgments
S.J.	Saskatchewan Judgments
S.L.A.A.	Saskatchewan Labour Arbitration Awards
Y.L.A.A.	Yukon Labour Arbitration Awards

TRADE UNIONS

A.A.H.P.O.	Association of Allied Health Professionals: Ontario
A.C. & T.W.U.	Atlantic Communication and Technical Workers' Union
A.C.T.R.A.	Alliance of Canadian Cinema, Television and Radio Artists
A.C.T.W.U.	Amalgamated Clothing and Textile Workers Union
A.F.G.M.	American Federation of Grain Millers
A.M.A.P.C.E.O.	Association of Management, Administrative and Professional Crown Employees of Ontario
A.P.O.C.	Association of Postal Officials of Canada
A.P.U.O.	Association of Professors of the University of Ottawa
A.T.A.	Alberta Teachers' Association
A.T.U.	Amalgamated Transit Union
A.T.W.U.	Amalgamated Textile Workers' Union
A.U.C.E.	Association of University and College Employees
A.U.P.E.	Alberta Union of Provincial Employees
B.A.C.	International Union of Bricklayers and Allied Craftsmen
B.B.F.	International Brotherhood of Boilermakers, Iron Ship Builders, Blacksmiths, Forgers and Helpers
B.C.G.E.U.	British Columbia Government and Service Employees' Union
B.C.N.U.	British Columbia Nurses' Union
B.C.T.	Bakery, Confectionery and Tobacco Workers International Union
B.C.T.F.	British Columbia Teachers' Federation
B.L.E.	International Brotherhood of Locomotive Engineers
B.M.W.E.	Brotherhood of Maintenance of Way Employees
B.R.A.C.	Brotherhood of Railway, Airline and Steamship Clerks, Freight Handlers, Express and Station Employees
B.S.O.I.W.	International Association of Bridge, Structural, Ornamental and Reinforcing Iron Workers
C.A.C.A.W.	Canadian Association of Communications and Allied Workers

C.A.I.M.A.W.	Canadian Association of Industrial, Mechanical and Allied Workers
C.A.L.D.A.	Canadian Air Line Dispatchers' Association
C.A.L.F.A.A.	Canadian Air Line Flight Attendants' Association
C.A.L.P.A.	Canadian Air Line Pilots Association
C.A.S.A.W.	Canadian Association of Smelter and Allied Workers
C.A.T.C.A.	Canadian Air Traffic Control Association
C.A.U.T.	Canadian Association of University Teachers
C.A.W.	Canadian Auto Workers
C.B.R.T. & G.W.	Canadian Brotherhood of Railway, Transport and General Workers
C.E.P.	Communications, Energy and Paperworkers
C.G.A.	Canadian Guards Association
C.J.A.	United Brotherhood of Carpenters and Joiners of America
C.L.A.C.	Christian Labour Association of Canada
C.M.S.G.	Canadian Merchant Service Guild
C.O.P.E.	Canadian Office and Professional Employees Union
C.P.A.A.	Canadian Postmasters and Assistants Association
C.P.U.	Canadian Paperworkers' Union
C.S.A.W.U.	Canadian Seafood and Allied Workers' Union
C.T.C.U.	Canadian Textile and Chemical Union
C.T.E.A.	Canadian Telephone Employees' Association
C.U.O.E.	Canadian Union of Operating Engineers and General Workers
C.U.P.E.	Canadian Union of Public Employees
C.U.P.W.	Canadian Union of Postal Workers
C.U.T.E.	Canadian Union of Transportation Employees
C.W.A.	Communications Workers of America
C.W.C.	Communications and Electrical Workers of Canada
D.F.A.	Dalhousie Faculty Association
E.C.W.U.	Energy and Chemical Workers' Union
G.C.I.U.	Graphic Communications International Union
G.S.U.	Grain Services Union
G.V.R.D.E.U.	Greater Vancouver Regional District Employees' Union
H.E.R.E.	Hotel Employees and Restaurant Employees International Union
H.E.U.	Hospital Employees' Union
H.S.A.A.	Health Sciences Association of Alberta
H.S.A.B.C.	Health Sciences Association of British Columbia
I.A.F.F.	International Association of Fire Fighters
I.A.M.	International Association of Machinists and Aerospace Workers
I.A.T.S.E.	International Alliance of Theatrical Stage Employees and Moving Picture Machine Operators of the United States and Canada

I.B.E.W.	International Brotherhood of Electrical Workers
I.C.T.U.	Independent Canadian Transit Union
I.L.A.	International Longshoremen's Association
I.L.G.P.N.W.U.	International Leather Goods, Plastics and Novelty Workers' Union
I.L.G.W.U.	International Ladies' Garment Workers' Union
I.L.W.U.	International Longshore and Warehouse Union
I.M.A.W.	International Molders' and Allied Workers' Union
I.T.U.	International Typographical Union
I.U.E.	International Union of Electronic, Electrical, Salaried, Machine and Furniture Workers
I.U.E.C.	International Union of Elevator Constructors
I.U.O.E.	International Union of Operating Engineers
I.W.A.	International Woodworkers of America
I.W.A. – Canada	Industrial, Wood and Allied Workers of Canada
L.C.U.C.	Letter Carriers' Union of Canada
L.I.U.N.A.	Labourers' International Union of North America
M.G.E.U.	Manitoba Government and General Employees Union
M.O.N.A.	Manitoba Organization of Nurses' Associations
M.T.S.	Manitoba Teachers' Society
M.U.A.	Métallurgistes unis d'Amérique (U.S.W.A.)
N.A.B.E.T.	National Association of Broadcast Employees and Technicians
N.A.P.E.	Newfoundland and Labrador Association of Public and Private Employees
N.B.P.E.A.	New Brunswick Public Employees Association
N.B.T.F.	New Brunswick Teachers' Federation
N.R.P.A.	National Radio Producers' Association
N.S.G.E.U.	Nova Scotia Government and General Employees Union
N.S.N.U.	Nova Scotia Nurses' Union
N.S.T.U.	Nova Scotia Teachers Union
N.S.U.P.E.	Nova Scotia Union of Public Employees
O.E.C.T.A.	Ontario English Catholic Teachers' Association
O.L.B.E.U.	Ontario Liquor Board Employees' Union
O.N.A.	Ontario Nurses' Association
O.P.E.I.U.	Office and Professional Employees International Union
O.P.P.A.	Ontario Provincial Police Association
O.P.S.E.U.	Ontario Public Service Employees Union
O.P.S.T.F.	Ontario Public School Teachers' Federation
O.S.S.T.F.	Ontario Secondary School Teachers' Federation
P.A.C.E.	Paper, Allied-Industrial, Chemical and Energy Workers International Union
P.A.N.S.	Police Association of Nova Scotia
P.A.T.	International Brotherhood of Painters and Allied Trades

P.I.P.S.	Professional Institute of the Public Service of Canada
P.S.A.C.	Public Service Alliance of Canada
R.W.D.S.U.	Retail, Wholesale and Department Store Union
S.C.F.P.	Syndicat canadien de la fonction publique (C.U.P.E.)
S.E.I.U.	Service Employees International Union
S.G.E.U.	Saskatchewan Government and General Employees Union
S.I.E.P.B.	Syndicat international des employées et employés professionels-les et de bureau (O.P.E.I.U.)
S.M.W.	Sheet Metal Workers' International Association
S.O.R.W.U.C.	Service, Office and Retail Workers' Union of Canada
S.T.E.C.	Syndicat des travailleurs de l'énergie et de la chimie (E.C.W.U.)
S.U.N.	Saskatchewan Union of Nurses
T.C.U.	Transportation Communications International Union
T.P.E.A.	Thompson Products Employees' Association
T.U.A.	Syndicat international des travailleurs unis de l'automobile de l'aérospatiale et de l'outillage agricole d'Amérique (U.A.W.)
T.U.A.C.	Syndicat international des travailleurs unis de l'alimentation et du commerce (U.F.C.W.)
T.W.U.	Telecommunications Workers Union
U.A.	United Association of Journeymen and Apprentices of the Plumbing and Pipe Fitting Industry of the United States and Canada
U.A.W.	International Union, United Automobile, Aerospace and Agricultural Implement Workers of America
U.B.W.W.	United Brewers' Warehousing Workers' Provincial Board
U.E.	United Electrical, Radio and Machine Workers of Canada
U.F.A.W.U.	United Fishermen and Allied Workers' Union
U.F.C.W.	United Food and Commercial Workers International Union
U.I.E.S.	Union internationale des employés des services (S.E.I.U.)
U.M.W.	United Mine Workers of America
U.N.A.	United Nurses of Alberta
U.N.I.T.E.	Union of Needletrades, Industrial and Textile Employees
U.P.G.W.A.	United Plant Guard Workers of America International Union
U.P.I.U.	United Paperworkers International Union
U.R.W.	United Rubber, Cork, Linoleum and Plastic Workers of America
U.S.W.A.	United Steelworkers of America
U.T.U.	United Transportation Union
U.T.W.	United Telegraph Workers
U.T.W.A.	United Textile Workers of America

U.W.C.	Utility Workers of Canada
V.M.R.E.U.	Vancouver Municipal and Regional Employees' Union
Y.U.S.A.	York University Staff Association

ILLUSTRATION OF STATUTORY CITATION

Canada Labour Code, R.S.C. 1985, c. L-2

| statute title | volume and jurisdiction | year | chapter number |

ILLUSTRATION OF CASE CITATIONS

Edmonton (City) and A.T.U., Local 569 (2003), 121 L.A.C. (4th) 289 (Ponak)

| case name | year of decision | title and volume number of report | fourth series | page number | name of arbitrator |

Haydon v. Canada, [2001] F.C. 82 (T.D.)

| case name | year of report | title of report | page number | name of court |

PART 1
EVIDENCE AND PROCEDURE

CHAPTER 1

THE ARBITRATION PROCESS

1.1 THE RULES OF NATURAL JUSTICE

1.1.1 General

Labour arbitration in Canada exists primarily as a process of rights adjudication mandated by statute for the determination of workplace disputes arising under a collective agreement. It was, and is, designed as a substitute for the withdrawal of services, which is prohibited by statute, and by most collective agreements, while the collective agreement is in operation. Arbitration, the Supreme Court has said in *Parry Sound (District) Social Services Administration Board v. O.P.S.E.U., Local 324* (2003), 230 D.L.R. (4th) 257 (S.C.C.), possesses both a private and a public function, namely, the peaceful resolution of labour disputes, and for that reason arbitrators have the authority to apply the provisions of legislation in reaching a decision. Arbitrators are vested by statute with the authority to make a final and binding disposition of the parties' legal rights, but the courts retain a residual supervisory jurisdiction and the arbitration process itself is recognized to be "quasi-judicial". This means that, in discharging his or her functions, an arbitrator must adhere to the principles of natural justice, *i.e.* procedural fairness, failing which the courts may overturn the award on an application for judicial review. In British Columbia, while review by the courts is available where the case raises a matter of "general law", the *Labour Relations Code*, R.S.B.C. 1996, c. 244, assigns jurisdiction to the Labour Relations Board to review arbitration awards if an issue arises of consistency with the *Code*'s principles or with the fairness of the hearing.

1.1.2   *Audi Alteram Partem*: The Right to Respond

A fundamental principle of "natural justice" is captured in the Latin legal maxim *audi alteram partem*, the meaning of which was explained in *Williams v. Roblin* (1858), 2 P.R. 234, at p. 237: "Neither side can be allowed to use any means of influencing the mind of an arbitrator which are not known to and capable of being met and resisted by the other". A modern Canadian restatement of the same principle is found in *St. Patrick's Mercy Home v. C.U.P.E., Local 879* (1982), 139 D.L.R. (3d) 740, a decision of the Supreme Court of Newfoundland. In that case, an arbitration board, after issuing a decision on the merits, purported to reconvene the hearing at the union's request and to issue a supplementary ruling on a new issue, without giving the employer notice or an opportunity to be heard. Quashing the supplementary award, the Court declared, at p. 744: "The board, and in fact any quasi-judicial or judicial tribunal, must comply with all of the rules of natural justice, except to the extent that they or any of them may be excluded or varied by express agreement between the parties or by statute".

At the same time, a recent decision of the Federal Court of Canada confirms that the right to be "heard" does not necessarily confer a right to an oral hearing, as long as each party's representations have reached the decision-maker in an unedited form. "[A] party whose rights are to be affected must be given a chance to be heard", the Court noted, "though not necessarily in person": *Rockman v. Canada (Attorney General)* (2000), 182 F.T.R. 240, at p. 248.

The principle of *audi alteram partem* extends to the reliance by a board of arbitration on material obtained through its own devices. It has, for example, been held to prohibit recourse to caselaw which has not yet been reported, and which is therefore not readily available to both parties at the time of the hearing. This was the situation in *Gates Rubber of Canada Ltd. v. U.R.W., Local 753*, where the Court quashed the award of an arbitration board which had purported to apply a recent judicial decision without first giving the parties an opportunity to make submissions on the matter: see [1980] O.J. No. 25 (QL) (Gen. Div.). More recently, a decision of the Nova Scotia Workers' Compensation Appeals Tribunal was quashed because the Tribunal founded its decision on a point that had not been put to the parties: *MacNeil v. Nova Scotia (Workers' Compensation Appeals Tribunal)*, [2001] N.S.J. No. 4 (QL) (C.A.).

1.1.3   The Rule Against Bias

As Chief Justice Lamer put it in *Matsqui Indian Band Council v. Canadian Pacific Ltd.* (1995), 122 D.L.R. (4th) 129 (S.C.C.), it is a principle of natural justice that a party should receive a hearing before a tribunal which not only *is* independent, but *appears* independent as well. At the same time, however, the courts have made it clear that the test is an objective one, that is, there must be a *reasonable* apprehension of bias on the part of the party mounting an objection. In *Committee for Justice and Liberty v. Canada (National Energy Board)* (1976), 68 D.L.R. (3d) 716 (S.C.C.), Justice de Grandpré explained the nature of the applicable test:

> [T]he apprehension of bias must be a reasonable one, held by reasonable and right-minded persons, applying themselves to the question and obtaining thereon the required information. In the words of the Court of Appeal, that test is "what would an informed person, viewing the matter realistically and practically — and having thought the matter through — conclude. Would he think that it is more likely than not that [the appointee], whether consciously or unconsciously, would not decide fairly?"

Where a party objects to the appointment of a member of an arbitration board on the basis of a reasonable apprehension of bias, it is obligated to make its position known immediately. The decision in *Vancouver Wharves Ltd. and I.L.W.U., Local 514* (1995), 47 L.A.C. (4th) 210 (Thompson) affirms that a party which has been fully apprised of the facts must bring its motion to disqualify the nominee prior to the commencement of the proceedings.

NEUTRALS

In the case of a neutral chair of an arbitration board, or sole arbitrator, a reasonable apprehension of bias can arise in a variety of situations. In *Camp Hill Medical Centre and N.S.N.U.* (1995), 51 L.A.C. (4th) 164, Arbitrator Slone reviewed the caselaw on bias, and outlined the grounds for removal of an arbitrator as follows:

(1) "Demonstrated" bias, based on something done or said in the course of the proceedings.

(2) Prior or present involvement in the same case.

(3) An ongoing client relationship with one of the parties.

(4) A family or other personal relationship with one of the participants.

(5) Prior professional associations not separated by a "respectable period of time".

The arbitrator emphasized that the mere discomfort of the objecting party is not a sufficient ground on which to disqualify an appointee. In each case, it is the "reasonableness" of the asserted apprehension which must be assessed.

PARTY NOMINEES

The question of the precise standard of independence expected of employer or union nominees to a board of arbitration (as opposed to the chair of the board) has been the subject of judicial comment. In *General Truck Drivers Union, Local 938 v. Hoar Transport Co. Ltd.* (1969), 4 D.L.R. (3d) 449, the

Supreme Court of Canada held that a nominee is an agent of the nominating party for the purpose of establishing the board; but, once the board has been constituted, it is deemed to act in a "quasi-judicial" capacity. However, as the Court emphasized in *Committee for Justice and Liberty, supra*, there is no single code or standard of independence applicable to all administrative bodies, and the particular circumstances in which each tribunal functions must be considered.

With respect to a nominee's ongoing involvement in the labour relations of his or her nominating party, the courts have recognized a distinction between rights arbitration and interest arbitration. In *Gypsumville District Teachers' Ass'n No. 1612, M.T.S. v. Gypsumville Consolidated School District No. 2461* (1979), 103 D.L.R. (3d) 672 , where both the employer nominee and the union nominee were well known for their opinions on labour relations, a majority of the Manitoba Court of Appeal strongly affirmed that total impartiality is not expected. Each party, Justice Monnin ruled, was entitled to nominate a person who was familiar with its concerns and whose philosophy was in accordance with its own. The Court of Appeal's decision was upheld on appeal, without reasons: (1980), 121 D.L.R. (3d) 509 (S.C.C.).

Subsequently, however, in *Simmons v. Manitoba* (1981), 129 D.L.R. (3d) 694, a differently constituted majority of the Manitoba Court of Appeal expressly limited the principle expressed in *Gypsumville Consolidated School District* to interest arbitration. *Simmons* involved the discharge of a provincial government employee. The Court ruled that, in the context of rights arbitration, including the adjudication of a discharge grievance, all members of an arbitration board "are required to act with impartiality, as would a court of law" (at p. 703). The fact that the employer's nominee had been appointed to a part-time position with the government, albeit in a different department, was therefore held to give rise to a reasonable apprehension of bias.

The Alberta Court of Appeal has also emphasized the distinction between rights arbitration and interest arbitration. The Alberta *Labour Relations Code*, R.S.A. 2000, c. L-1, has for years limited the grounds on which a party's nominee can be disqualified, expressly prohibiting the appointment of an individual who is "directly affected by the difference or has been involved in an attempt to negotiate or settle the difference". The province's Court of Appeal has nonetheless ruled that, in a rights arbitration, as opposed to an interest arbitration, there is a general requirement for independence as well as an appearance of independence (even though partiality towards a nominee's appointing party is to be expected): *Foothills Provincial General Hospital Board v. U.N.A., Local 115* (1986), 27 D.L.R. (4th) 665 (Alta. C.A.), affirming *Bethany Care Centre v. U.N.A., Local 91* (1983), 5 D.L.R. (4th) 54 (Alta. C.A.). Thus, it was held that an individual in an employment relationship with one of the parties could not sit as its nominee on a grievance arbitration board in the face of an objection by the other party.

The same issue came before a Newfoundland and Labrador arbitration board chaired by James Oakley in *Abitibi Consolidated Inc. and C.E.P., Local 60N* (2004), 130 L.A.C. (4th) 129. At the outset, responding to the employer's argument that the board lacked jurisdiction to rule on the issue of its own bias, the board concluded that the process was better served by entertaining evidence and submissions relating to the objection at the arbitration hearing itself, without awaiting an application for judicial review. On the substantive question, the board found that the courts in Newfoundland and Labrador have adopted the "legal" model (applicable to commercial arbitration) rather than the more permissive "labour relations" model (followed in British Columbia) to grievance arbitration and that, accordingly, a stricter standard of independence was required. Ontario arbitrators have taken a similar position, and required individuals in an employment relationship with the nominating party to step down if challenged; while nominees to a board of grievance arbitration are not expected to be impartial, the Chair stated, they are required to exercise, and appear to exercise, independent judgment: *Centenary Health Centre and O.P.S.E.U.* (1996), 60 L.A.C. (4th) 21 (Whitaker).

As indicated, the view in British Columbia is markedly different. In *West Coast General Hospital and B.C.N.U.* (1999), 83 L.A.C. (4th) 183 (Larson), affirmed [2001] B.C.L.R.B.D. No. 188 (QL), the nominee of the employer worked for its accredited bargaining agent. Noting the pragmatic approach taken by the British Columbia Labour Relations Board, Arbitrator Larson found that even a *direct* employer-employee relationship was not a sufficient disqualifying factor, unless the nominee had played a role in the very matter at hand. Indeed, in the absence of the latter element (which is similar to the exclusionary consideration under Alberta's *Labour Relations Code*), the arbitrator suggested that there may be "distinct advantages" in having nominees who are "familiar with the work setting".

The extent to which the existence of a marital relationship gives rise to a reasonable apprehension of bias was considered in *Newfoundland (Treasury Board) v. N.A.P.E.* (1999), 184 Nfld. & P.E.I.R. 237 (Nfld. S.C.). There, the spouse of the employer's nominee was a government lawyer who had on occasion advised the employer. At no time, however, had she offered advice with respect to the matter at issue. Ruling that the union's concern over "pillow talk" was anachronistic, Chief Justice Hickman concluded that a spousal relationship did not lead to a reasonable inference that the nominee was incapable of exercising independent judgment.

Additional Reading

D.C. McPhillips, "The Role of the Nominee at Grievance Arbitration" in W. Kaplan, J. Sack & M. Gunderson, eds., *Labour Arbitration Yearbook 1993*, p. 45.

T. Kuttner, "Bias and the Arbitral Forum" in W. Kaplan, J. Sack & M. Gunderson, eds., *Labour Arbitration Yearbook 1991*, vol. 1, p. 23.

1.1.4   Death/Resignation of a Board Member

If a party's nominee dies or becomes incapacitated before the board has completed its work, it becomes necessary, in the absence of some other consensual arrangement, to reconstitute the board and to begin the proceedings anew: *Canadian Press Broadcast News Ltd. and Canadian Wire Service Guild, Local 213* (1977), 17 L.A.C. (2d) 7 (Kennedy). However, the view expressed in the latter decision has been questioned, and Arbitrator Weatherill has expressly declined to follow it, ruling that the death of a party nominee after a draft award had been issued did not render the proceedings null and void: *Scarborough (City) Public Utilities Commission and Utility Workers of Canada, Local 1* (1986), 23 L.A.C. (3d) 295.

Where the impediment results from an act within the nominee's control, as in a refusal or failure to attend at the hearing, arbitrators have ruled that a majority of the board can proceed in his or her absence, pointing out that a party does not have the unilateral right to frustrate the process: see, for example, *Raney-Brady and C.J.A., Local 38* (1972), 1 L.A.C. (2d) 269 (O'Shea). The decision in *Newfoundland v. N.A.P.E.* (1999), 177 Nfld. & P.E.I.R. 345 (Nfld. S.C.), however, appears to cast doubt on the validity of this reasoning. In a decision reported at (1999), 82 L.A.C. (4th) 33, Arbitrator Oakley held that the resignation of the employer's nominee in the middle of the hearing did not deprive the Chair and the union nominee of jurisdiction to continue the proceedings. On an application for judicial review, the Newfoundland Supreme Court quashed the award, ruling that the board was without jurisdiction if any of its members "were not exposed to the countervailing points of view" (at p. 347). On the other hand, the Court indicated that the result would be different if the resignation had taken place after the case had been heard, so that the majority could render an informed decision.

1.2   SOURCES OF JURISDICTION

1.2.1   The Collective Agreement

It has long been recognized that arbitrators derive their jurisdiction, either explicitly or by necessary implication, from the collective agreement under which they are appointed. Arbitrators have repeatedly echoed Harry Arthurs' observation in *Toronto (City) and Civic Employees Union, Local 43* (1967), 18 L.A.C. 273 that "we must ultimately trace all enforceable claims back to the collective agreement". The fact that Canadian labour relations legislation requires collective agreements to be in writing is also frequently invoked in arbitral decision-making. This emphasis on the collective agreement as the root of jurisdiction typically arises when one party attempts to compel the continuation of a past practice which has not been reduced to a contractual obligation. An often-cited example is *Brampton Public Library Board and C.U.P.E., Local 1776* (1976), 13 L.A.C. (2d) 57 (Johnston). The same collective agreement-focused approach to jurisdiction has been articulated in other decisions, as, for example, in *York Region Separate School Board and O.E.C.T.A. (Phillips)* (1995), 52 L.A.C. (4th) 285 (Kaplan).

Whether and to what extent arbitrators possess jurisdictional competence beyond the "four corners of the collective agreement" has consistently been a contentious issue attracting the intervention of the courts: see Chapters 1.2.3 and 1.2.4, respectively, on the power of arbitrators to apply statute law and the *Charter of Rights and Freedoms*; Chapter 16.2.2 on the "general" duty of fairness; Chapter 16.3 on the rules relating to the doctrine of necessary implication; Chapter 16.4.2 on the problem of ambiguity and the use of extrinsic evidence; and Chapter 16.5 on estoppel.

1.2.2 Ancillary or Side Documents

Although collective bargaining statutes in Canada invariably require that there be only one collective agreement, it is well established that the agreement can consist of more than one document. That is, there may be any number of "ancillary" documents in the form of letters of understanding or supplementary agreements which the parties have recognized as forming part of their collective agreement. In *Canada Bread Co. Ltd. and Bakery & Confectionery Workers' Int'l Union, Local 322* (1970), 22 L.A.C. 98, the seminal case in this area, Arbitrator Christie held that one of the consequences of the statutory definition of "collective agreement" is that an ancillary document must be in writing and signed by both parties. Furthermore, he ruled, "whether a document will be treated as part of the collective agreement must depend, in the final analysis, on whether the parties have manifested an intention to make it part of the agreement" (at p. 103). Such an intention can be indicated in a number of ways, including, most commonly, by inclusion of the letter or ancillary document in the collective agreement booklet; specific reference in the document to the collective agreement provision that it is modifying or amplifying; or incorporation of the document by reference within the main body of the collective agreement.

However the connection to the collective agreement is established, the next issue that arises, as *Canada Bread* notes, is the length of the period during which the ancillary agreement continues in effect. Assuming there is no clear indication on the face of the document itself, the cases identify three possibilities:

(1) The letter is operative only during the term of the collective agreement of which it was originally made a part.

(2) The letter continues to be operative until one party gives notice that it will expire with the current collective agreement.

(3) The letter continues to be operative until the parties jointly agree to its modification or termination.

In *Canada Bread*, Arbitrator Christie was of the view that it flowed "inevitably" from a finding that the letter had been made part of the collective agreement that it was of no force and effect beyond the termination of the agreement under which it arose, unless specifically revived by the parties in the ensuing round of bargaining.

Arbitrator Christie's assumption that the terms of a supplementary agreement had to be expressly revived, unlike any of the other terms in a collective agreement, as well as his requirement for joint signatures, has been firmly rejected by more recent arbitrators, most consistently in British Columbia. First, in *United Grain Growers Ltd. and Grain Workers' Union, Local 333* (1986), 24 L.A.C. (3d) 226, Arbitrator Munroe questioned the proposition that a document, to be incorporated as part of the collective agreement, must be signed by both parties. Arbitrator Munroe did agree with Arbitrator Christie, however, that the critical focus in determining whether a document has been incorporated into the collective agreement is the intention of the parties.

Arbitrator Munroe also rejected the conclusion in *Canada Bread* that, without specific indications to the contrary, an ancillary document expires with the collective agreement under which it arose, unless expressly renewed in later bargaining. On this view, like any other term of the collective agreement, a side-letter generally "rolls over" into the renewal agreement unless the parties specify otherwise, or unless it is stated on the face of the letter that it will lapse upon the expiry of the collective agreement. The real question, therefore, is whether side-letters or agreements are any more subject than provisions in the main body of the collective agreement to being terminated, at the expiry date of the agreement, by the mere giving of notice by one party to the other. In other words, what is the "default mode" for such letters or agreements, once notice to alter or terminate has been given: Do they automatically cease to have effect, unless the parties agree to renew them? Or do they continue into the next collective agreement, unless the parties agree to alter or terminate them (as would be the case with any other term in the main body of the collective agreement)? Arbitrator Munroe addressed this issue more fully in a subsequent case, *Eurocan Pulp & Paper Co. and C.E.P., Local 298* (1998), 72 L.A.C. (4th) 153, where he again stated that the real test was the parties' true intention or expectation, which in each case falls to be determined as a matter of *fact*. The arbitrator went on to observe that, based on the norms of industry practice, the "general rule [in British Columbia] is that collateral, ancillary or subsidiary agreements can be brought to an end by one side giving notice to the other effective the expiry of the subsisting collective agreement" (at p. 163). He added, however, that there may be cases, particularly where the document contains mutual covenants which have already been acted upon, in which the intention of the parties was that the document could be altered or terminated only through mutual agreement.

Reviewing the caselaw in *Telus and T.C.U.*, [2004] C.L.A.D. No. 179 (QL), Arbitrator Germaine affirmed that, in British Columbia, the general rule is that set out by Arbitrator Munroe in *Eurocan Pulp & Paper*: there is a (rebuttable) presumption that side-letters or agreements differ from provisions included in the main body of the collective agreement in that they may be terminated upon notice by one party to the other before the next round of bargaining.

All of these awards, it should be noted, deal with bilateral side agreements, whether signed by both parties or otherwise, that are considered part of the collective agreement under which they were negotiated. They are enforceable in their own right, at least during the period in which they are in effect. Such agreements are to be distinguished from a long-standing but unilaterally promulgated statement of employer policy. Arbitrators have held that such a document will go no further than to establish a past practice, not enforceable unless to give meaning to some other provision of the collective agreement. A good example can be seen in *Long Manufacturing Ltd. and C.A.W., Local 1285* (1995), 48 L.A.C. (4th) 208 (H.D. Brown). Unilateral documents may, nevertheless, form the foundation of an argument based on estoppel, *i.e.* that in the face of a representation contained in such a document, that has been relied upon to a party's detriment, an explicit provision of a collective agreement cannot be enforced: see Chapter 16.5.3.

1.2.3 Legislation

Since the Supreme Court of Canada's judgment in *McLeod v. Egan* (1974), 46 D.L.R. (3d) 150, it has been clear that labour and employment legislation forms a potentially relevant background for an arbitrator in interpreting or applying a collective agreement. Indeed, in language reminiscent of Lord Denning's comment in *David Taylor & Son Ltd. v. Barnett*, [1953] 1 All E.R. 843 (C.A.) that "[t]here is not one law for arbitrators, and another for the court, but one law for all", Chief Justice Laskin ruled that an arbitrator must construe a statute that bears on the collective agreement issue which has been submitted for determination.

In what is usually cited as the seminal arbitration decision, *Denison Mines Ltd. and U.S.W.A.* (1982), 5 L.A.C. (3d) 19, Arbitrator Adams identified the various ways in which a statute can bear upon or become relevant in interpreting a collective agreement:

(1) A collective agreement may expressly or impliedly incorporate the provisions of a statute.

(2) A statute may provide an aid to the interpretation of a collective agreement.

(3) A statute may render unlawful a provision of a collective agreement, with the consequence that an arbitrator is obligated to refuse to enforce the offending provision.

(4) A statute may speak to the very issues addressed by a collective agreement, but provide superior benefits.

The award in *Denison Mines* also affirmed the principle that an arbitrator has no jurisdiction to apply and enforce external legislation in the absence of some "nexus" in the collective agreement. That is, unless the statute in question affects the interpretation or application of a specific provision in the collective agreement, other than a standard statement of management's rights, the matter will be deemed inarbitrable.

In ruling that he lacked jurisdiction to apply legislation where the collective agreement was silent with respect to the subject-matter of the statute, Arbitrator Adams expressed a consensus of long standing in the arbitral community. It was subsequently held, for example, that while an arbitrator can "read up" the collective agreement in order to provide employees with a benefit to which they are entitled pursuant to statute, the authority to do so arises only if an express provision in the agreement conflicts with the legislation: *Haldimand-Norfolk Police Services Board and Haldimand-Norfolk Police Ass'n* (1993), 36 L.A.C. (4th) 246 (Jackson).

The prevailing consensus was largely unchanged by the enactment, in several jurisdictions, of amendments to the applicable labour relations legislation specifically empowering arbitrators to take relevant statutes into account in resolving collective agreement disputes. A typical example of such enactments is s. 48(12)(j) of Ontario's *Labour Relations Act*, S.O. 1995, c. 1, Sch. A, authorizing arbitrators

> . . . to interpret and apply human rights and other employment-related statutes, despite any conflict between those statutes and the terms of the collective agreement.

(Compare s. 89(g) of the British Columbia *Labour Relations Code*, R.S.B.C. 1996, c. 244, and s. 43(e) of the Nova Scotia *Trade Union Act*, R.S.N.S. 1989, c. 475.) In *Cargill Foods Ltd. and U.F.C.W., Local 175/633* (1996), 57 L.A.C. (4th) 21, Arbitrator O'Neil rejected the proposition that the Ontario provision gave arbitrators "stand-alone" jurisdiction to address alleged violations of any employment-related statute, even in the absence of a nexus to the collective agreement. In her opinion, the primary responsibility for enforcing a statute remains with the specialized tribunal created expressly for this purpose (such as a labour relations board or a human rights board of inquiry), and it is only through such a tribunal that unionized employees can obtain "direct access" to the statutory enforcement machinery. In other words, an arbitrator acquires jurisdiction over the subject-matter of the statute only in the context of otherwise having to deal with an arbitrable dispute under the collective agreement.

Consistent with this approach, from a remedial standpoint, is *Cambridge Brass and U.S.W.A., Local 4045* (1999), 82 L.A.C. (4th) 284 (Beck), where it was held that s. 48(12)(j) of the Ontario *Labour Relations Act* obliges arbitrators to consider granting any remedy that would be available under an external statute, provided, however, that a nexus has been established between the statute and the collective agreement.

The validity of this analytical framework, though, has been thrown into doubt by the Supreme Court of Canada's recent pronouncement in *Parry Sound (District) Social Services Administration Board v. O.P.S.E.U., Local 324* (2003), 230 D.L.R. (4th) 257. Taking *Parry Sound* at face value, the Court appears to have determined that, whether or not the subject-matter is addressed in the collective agreement, an arbitrator has at least concurrent jurisdiction with the statutory tribunal to entertain claims alleging a breach of an employment-related statute. To quote the opening words of Justice Major's dissenting judgment, the majority of the Court held, in essence, that "all employment and human rights statutes [are] incorporated into every collective bargaining agreement" (at p. 287).

Parry Sound involved the grievance of a probationary employee who alleged that she had been discharged because of her absence from work on maternity leave, contrary to the Ontario *Human Rights Code*, R.S.O. 1990, c. H.19. The collective agreement did not in express terms prohibit the employer from discriminating against employees on prohibited grounds, and barred probationers from challenging their discharge through the grievance and arbitration procedures. The agreement also provided that a "probationary employee may be discharged at the sole discretion of and for any reason satisfactory to the Employer". On the basis that it was required, under s. 48(12)(j) of the Ontario *Labour Relations Act*, to interpret the collective agreement in a manner consistent with the *Code*, an arbitration board asserted jurisdiction over the "narrow question of whether discrimination was a factor in the [grievor's] discharge": see [1999] O.L.A.A. No. 76 (QL) (Knopf).

While upholding this ruling, the Supreme Court took a far more expansive view of the grounds on which the arbitration board was entitled to inquire into the dispute. According to the Court, its prior decision in *McLeod v. Egan, supra*, established the proposition that an employer's right to manage the enterprise and direct the workforce is subject not only to the express provisions of the collective agreement, but also to the statutory rights of employees, including the right to equal treatment in employment without discrimination. This was true, the Court suggested, whether or not the governing labour relations legislation contains a provision, comparable to Ontario's, empowering arbitrators to "interpret and apply human rights and other employment-related statutes". Thus, the Court held, "an alleged violation of the *Human Rights Code* constitutes an alleged violation of the collective agreement, and falls squarely within the [arbitrator's] jurisdiction", despite the fact that the agreement may be silent with respect to discrimination (at p. 282).

While the Supreme Court's decision appears to put to rest the "nexus" theory, it should be noted that the collective agreement in issue *did* contain an express provision dealing with the discharge of probationary employees — albeit one intended by the parties to restrict access to arbitration. What the Court did was to "read down" the restrictive provision, recasting it to state, as the Court put it: "A probationary employee may be discharged at the sole *lawful* discretion of and for any *lawful* reason satisfactory to the Employer" (at p. 275; emphasis in original).

Subsequently, in an important clarification of the scope of the decision in *Parry Sound*, the Supreme Court of Canada held that only statutory provisions which are "compatible" with the labour relations scheme are incorporated in collective agreements: *Isidore Garon Ltée v. Syndicat du Bois Ouvré de la Région de Québec Inc.* (2006), 262 D.L.R. (4th) 385. In that case, the Court ruled, unionized employees of companies that go out of business are not entitled to claim pay in lieu of reasonable notice of termination, as provided for by the Quebec *Civil Code*, S.Q. 1991, c. 64, because the rule providing for the termination of employees by way of notice is not compatible with the labour relations scheme, and is not a "supplementary or mandatory norm". As the rule remained outside the ambit of the collective agreement, it was not enforceable at arbitration.

In *B.C.T.F. v. British Columbia Employers' Ass'n* (2005), 251 D.L.R. (4th) 497 (B.C.C.A.), an arbitrator had concluded that class size limits prescribed by the provincial *School Act* could not be enforced through the grievance and arbitration procedures under the collective agreement, notwithstanding the *Parry Sound* decision, because the legislation expressly prohibited the inclusion of provisions on class size in a collective agreement. The award was reversed by the British Columbia Court of Appeal, which found that *Parry Sound* did in fact confer jurisdiction on the arbitrator to enforce the rights and obligations contained in the Act. In so ruling, the Court observed that the determination of class size represented a significant part of the employment relationship, and was an important exercise of the management rights clause in the collective agreement. There was, therefore, in the Court's words, "a real contextual connection between the statute and the collective agreement such that a violation of the statute gives rise . . . to a violation of the provisions of the collective agreement" (at para. 38).

In *Calgary (City) and A.T.U., Local 583* (2004), 133 L.A.C. (4th) 114 (Ivankovich), the union had filed a discharge grievance, while the grievor, acting on her own, had filed a human rights complaint arising from essentially the same facts. The union opposed an employer request that the human rights complaint be heard at arbitration, together with the grievance. Relying on *Parry Sound*, Arbitrator Ivankovich ruled in the employer's favour. The arbitration hearing, he found, represented a "better fit", as it would permit all aspects of the dispute to be addressed in one proceeding. Similarly, in *Serca Foodservice Inc. and Teamsters, Local 987*, [2004] A.G.A.A. No. 2 (QL), Arbitrator Tom Jolliffe applied the longer time limit set out in employment standards legislation, as opposed to the shorter time limit imposed by the collective agreement, in providing a remedy for a continuing breach of the negotiated vacation pay provisions.

Additional Reading

S.R. Luciw, *"Parry Sound* and Its Successors in the Supreme Court of Canada: Implications for the Scope of Arbitral Authority" (2004), 11 Canadian Labour and Employment Law Journal, p. 365.

J.B. Hall, "Employment Standards and the Collective Agreement: A Neutral's Perspective" in K. Whitaker, J. Sack, M. Gunderson & R. Filion, eds., *Labour Arbitration Yearbook 2001-2002*, vol. II, p. 317; and companion articles by D.M. Sartison and S.A. Temple.

D.D. Carter, "The Arbitrator as Human Rights Adjudicator: The Lessons of *Orillia Soldiers Memorial Hospital"* in K. Whitaker, J. Sack, M. Gunderson & R. Filion, eds., *Labour Arbitration Yearbook 1999-2000*, vol. I, p. 55.

1.2.4 *Charter of Rights and Freedoms*

Section 32(1) of the *Canadian Charter of Rights and Freedoms* states:

This *Charter* applies

(a) to the Parliament and government of Canada in respect of all matters within the authority of Parliament including all matters relating to the Yukon Territory and Northwest Territories; and

(b) to the legislature and government of each province in respect of all matters within the authority of the legislature of each province.

As the courts have put it, the *Charter* by its strict terms applies only to "government" and "government action". In *McKinney v. University of Guelph* (1990), 76 D.L.R. (4th) 545, the Supreme Court of Canada held that, if an employer is an arm or agency of government, any collective agreement that it negotiates amounts to "law" for the purposes of the *Charter* and compliance with its values. In the *McKinney* case, the Court found that, notwithstanding the provision of public funding and extensive regulatory intervention, there was insufficient legal or *de facto* control by the government to render Canadian universities subject to the *Charter.*

In *Douglas College v. Douglas/Kwantlen Faculty Ass'n* (1990), 77 D.L.R. (4th) 94, released at the same time as *McKinney*, the Supreme Court of Canada adopted the same principles, but on the facts, which related to provincial community colleges, arrived at the opposite conclusion. See also *Lavigne v. O.P.S.E.U.* (1991), 81 D.L.R. (4th) 545 (S.C.C.), in which the *Charter* was applied to collective agreements with community colleges, as an arm of government, and *Godbout v. Longueuil (City)* (1997), 152 D.L.R. (4th) 577 (S.C.C.), in which a municipality was held to be simply an extension or delegate of the provincial government.

The breadth of the definition of "government" for *Charter* purposes is illustrated in *Eldridge v. British Columbia (Attorney General)* (1997), 151 D.L.R. (4th) 577 (S.C.C.). In that case, the Court ruled that government actors include not only entities which in themselves constitute "government", or are controlled by government, but also non-governmental agencies, to the extent that they are charged with implementing a specific government program. The Court summarized the law as follows, at pp. 607-608:

> As the caselaw discussed above makes clear, the *Charter* may be found to apply to an entity on one of two bases. First, it may be determined that the entity is itself "government" for the purposes of s. 32. This involves an inquiry into whether the entity whose actions have given rise to the alleged *Charter* breach can, either by its very nature or in virtue of the degree of government control exercised over it, properly be characterized as "government" within the meaning of s. 32(1). In such cases, all of the activities of the entity will be subject to the *Charter*, regardless of whether the activity in which it is engaged could, if performed by a non-governmental actor, correctly be described as "private". Second, an entity may be found to attract *Charter* scrutiny with respect to a particular activity that can be ascribed to government. This demands an investigation not into the nature of the entity whose activity is impugned, but rather into the nature of the activity itself. In such cases, in other words, one must scrutinize the quality of the act at issue, rather than the quality of the actor. If the act is truly "governmental" in nature — for example, the implementation of a specific statutory scheme or a government program — the entity performing it will be subject to review under the *Charter* only in respect of that act, and not its other, private activities.

Applying *Eldridge*, Arbitrator Herman has held that a non-share capital corporation set up by the Ontario government for the purpose of implementing and administering its energy policy was an agency of the government, and therefore subject to the *Charter*. In the arbitrator's view, it was not determinative that the corporation's founding statute included a provision expressly stating that the entity was not "an agency of Her Majesty for any purpose": see *Independent Electricity Market Operator and Society of Energy Professionals* (2003), 118 L.A.C. (4th) 385. In *Toronto Transit Commission and A.T.U., Local 113* (2004), 126 L.A.C. (4th) 353, Arbitrator Shime found that security officers employed by a municipal transit system were engaged in governmental activity because they had been appointed "special constables" by the Police Services Board, and therefore had authority to enforce a number of provincial and federal statutes, including the *Criminal Code*.

Even where the *Charter* does not apply directly to the dispute between the parties, the Supreme Court of Canada has asserted that, insofar as it reflects the current state of Canada's social values, it forms a relevant background to interpreting and developing the common law between private parties. First propounded in *R.W.D.S.U. v. Dolphin Delivery Ltd.* (1986), 33 D.L.R. (4th) 174 (S.C.C.), this amplification of the *Charter*'s impact was discussed further in *Hill v. Church of Scientology* (1995), 126 D.L.R. (4th) 129 (S.C.C.), where the Court stated, at p. 156: "The *Charter* represents a restatement of the fundamental values which guide and shape our democratic society and our legal system. It follows that it is appropriate for the courts to make such incremental revisions to the common law as may be necessary to have it comply with the values enunciated in the *Charter*". For an example of arbitral use of the *Charter* as a source of prevailing values, see *Doman Forest Products Ltd. and I.W.A., Local 1-357* (1990), 13 L.A.C. (4th) 275 (Vickers), discussed in Chapter 6.8.

Apart from the general question of what constitute *Charter* "values", it is clear that arbitrators must interpret and apply the *Charter* in any case in which the constitutional validity of a statute relevant to the dispute is being challenged. If a legislative provision is found to violate the *Charter*, the arbitrator is bound to treat the provision as having no force or effect. While early decisions left open the question of whether an administrative tribunal could properly be characterized as a "court of competent jurisdiction" within the meaning of s. 24(1) of the *Charter*, for the purpose of granting a *Charter* remedy, the Supreme Court of Canada affirmed that there are practical advantages in having such a tribunal consider a provision's constitutionality in the first instance (*Douglas College, supra*). Subsequently, in *Weber v. Ontario Hydro* (1995), 125 D.L.R. (4th) 583, the Supreme Court definitively held that, in appropriate circumstances, a board of arbitration can be regarded as a "court of competent jurisdiction" having the power to grant a *Charter* remedy: see Chapter 1.3. This conclusion has been reinforced by the Court's decision in *Nova Scotia (Workers' Compensation Board) v. Martin and Laseur* that administrative tribunals which have, either expressly or impliedly, statutory authority to determine questions of law are presumed to have concomitant authority to decide the constitutional validity of legislation: see (2003), 231 D.L.R. (4th) 385 (S.C.C.).

The ruling in *Weber* was applied in *Mount Sinai Hospital and O.N.A. (Tilley)* (2000), 91 L.A.C. (4th) 215, where Arbitrator Devlin held that the statutory obligation to provide a final and binding settlement of all matters in dispute requires an arbitrator to determine whether a statutory provision, relevant to interpreting the collective agreement, offends the *Charter*. The arbitration board's subsequent decision in *Mount Sinai Hospital*, dismissing the *Charter* claim on its merits, has been overturned by the Ontario Court of Appeal: see (2005), 255 D.L.R. (4th) 185.

Additional Reading

J. Fichaud, "The Labour Arbitrator's Jurisdiction Under the *Charter*" in W. Kaplan,
    J. Sack & M. Gunderson, eds., *Labour Arbitration Yearbook 1992*, p. 3.

1.3   *WEBER*: WHAT IS THE PROPER FORUM?

Of all the Supreme Court of Canada's decisions, it is *Weber v. Ontario
Hydro* (1995), 125 D.L.R. (4th) 583, together with the companion judgment in
New Brunswick v. O'Leary (1995), 125 D.L.R. (4th) 609, which is likely to
have the most far-reaching impact on the kinds of claims that come before arbitrators.

In *Weber*, which contains most of the Supreme Court's commentary, the
employer engaged private investigators to gain entry to an employee's resi-
dence in the course of investigating his sick leave claim under the collective
agreement. The employee then sued the employer in the courts for trespass,
nuisance, deceit and invasion of privacy, as well as for breaching his *Charter*
rights. Basing its decision on the conventional statutory scheme in which arbitration is identified as the sole forum for resolving collective agreement disputes, the Court dismissed the actions, holding that all matters arising expressly
or inferentially from the agreement are *exclusively* within an arbitrator's jurisdiction. The collective agreements in both *Weber* and *O'Leary* included
unusual provisions, which, in the opinion of some commentators, are capable
of explaining the result; nevertheless, the Court expressed itself in surprisingly
broad terms. Writing for the majority, Justice McLachlin made it clear that the
determination of whether a dispute falls within arbitral jurisdiction does not
depend on the ability of creative counsel to cast the matter as a tort or other
common law cause of action. Rather, the "essential character of the dispute"
must be ascertained, having regard to both the nature of the dispute and the
ambit of the collective agreement. Furthermore, in a passage which clearly
expands the jurisdiction of arbitrators, Justice McLachlin ruled that in "fashioning an appropriate remedy, the arbitrator will have regard to whether the
breach of the collective agreement also constitutes a breach of a common law
duty, or of the *Charter*" (at p. 603). This direction to consider a comprehensive remedy, once the dispute has properly been placed before an arbitrator,
indicates with particular clarity the Court's policy of consolidating in a single
forum the hearing of all issues arising from or related to a claim.

Since *Weber*, arbitrators and the courts have struggled to define the limits
of the Supreme Court's landmark pronouncement. The earlier cases were cat-
alogued in *Air Canada and Air Canada Pilots' Ass'n* (unreported, June 1, 1998
(Mitchnick)). The courts, especially, tended to embrace with alacrity the sup-
posed spirit of *Weber*, generally refusing to hear any dispute originating in a
unionized workplace. As the arbitrator notes, these decisions have focused on

the nature of the dispute at the expense of the ambit of the collective agreement, overlooking the fact that *Weber* establishes a two-part test.

More recently, though, the courts have become more circumspect in their response to *Weber*. In *Piko v. Hudson's Bay Company* (1998), 167 D.L.R. (4th) 479, for example, the Ontario Court of Appeal ruled that a former employee was entitled to bring a court action for malicious prosecution and mental distress, notwithstanding the overlap with a potential grievance for unjust dismissal, because the employer's added step in invoking criminal proceedings was distinct from the act of discharge, and took the matter outside the sphere of labour relations. In delivering the judgment of the Court, Justice John Laskin stated, at pp. 486-87:

> Neither consideration emphasized by McLachlin J. in *Weber* applies in the present appeal. The language of the collective agreement for the Bay's employees is not nearly as broad as the language in the Hydro agreement. And the Bay's actions in instigating criminal proceedings are not directly related to the dispute over whether Piko was unjustly dismissed. The Bay's actions are neither a prerequisite to nor a necessary consequence of its dismissal of Piko. In short, the collective agreement does not regulate the Bay's conduct in invoking the criminal process, which is the conduct at the heart of the present dispute. The dispute, therefore, does not arise under the collective agreement.

As well, at p. 485:

> The difference between this case and cases such as *Ruscetta* and *Dwyer* is that although the dispute between the Bay and Piko arises out of the employment relationship, it does not arise under the collective agreement. A dispute centred on an employer's instigation of criminal proceedings against an employee, even for a workplace wrong, is not a dispute which in its essential character arises from the interpretation, application, administration or violation of the collective agreement.

(Leave to appeal to S.C.C. refused September 16, 1999.)

Similar circumspection is evident in the British Columbia Court of Appeal's decision in *Fording Coal Ltd. v. U.S.W.A., Local 7884* (1999), 169 D.L.R. (4th) 468. There, the only issue in dispute was the veracity of a union official's published statements that the employer's production practices compromised safety. The employer launched a defamation suit in the courts, but also filed a grievance as a precautionary measure. The maintenance of safe work practices was not a matter covered by the collective agreement, and the Court of Appeal found that the essence of the dispute was not, in any respect, one which arose out of the collective agreement. The defamation action was, accordingly, held to be the proper vehicle for the claim.

The important point, as the Ontario Court of Appeal observed in *Piko*, and one initially overlooked by some of the lower courts, is that not every dispute relating to an employment relationship in a unionized workplace can be said to have a nexus to, or to arise from, the collective agreement. The demarcation line can be particularly difficult to draw in cases involving allegedly defamatory statements about an employee by a member of management. Where the impugned statement is part of some other inherently grievable *action* by the employer, the entire "factual matrix" will likely be found within the sphere of an arbitrator's authority. The Court in *Fording Coal*, for example, commented that its opinion might have been different had the union official in question been discharged for his allegedly defamatory statements. This was precisely the conclusion arrived at by the Ontario Court of Appeal in *Bhaduria v. Toronto Board of Education* (1999), 173 D.L.R. (4th) 382, where the plaintiff's defamation suit arose out of the very minutes setting out the employer's grounds for discharge. Similarly, see *Giorno v. Pappas* (1999), 42 O.R. (3d) 626 (C.A.); and *Sloan v. York Region District School Board*, [2000] O.J. No. 2754 (QL) (C.A.), leave to appeal to S.C.C. refused March 22, 2001.

In the absence of a link to an otherwise grievable employer action, however, the question is more difficult. Subsequent to its decision in *Fording Coal*, the British Columbia Court of Appeal, in *Haight-Smith v. Neden* (2002), 211 D.L.R. (4th) 370, set out guidelines for determining when statements by an employer about an employee engage the collective agreement so as to make the dispute arbitrable. The Court adopted a three-fold test:

(1) the comments concern the employee's character, history, or capacity as an employee;

(2) the comments were made by someone whose job it was to communicate a workplace problem; and

(3) the comments were made to persons who would be expected to be informed of workplace problems.

The approach adopted by the Supreme Court in *Weber*, giving arbitrators exclusive jurisdiction over all aspects of a dispute arising from the collective agreement, also has ramifications for an arbitrator's remedial authority. The Court indicated that, once an arbitrator is properly seized of jurisdiction over the particular "factual matrix", *all* elements of the parties' dispute can and ought to be resolved by the arbitrator. While this may cause the scope of the proceedings to expand to other causes of action that might not, standing alone, have been arbitrable, so too, the Court emphasized, the arbitrator's remedial response may expand to meet the requirements of the case. For the most part, this expansion of remedial jurisdiction has manifested itself in the area of damages: see the discussion of "*Weber* damages" in Chapter 7.4.2. However, as Arbitrator Newman commented in *Tenaquip Ltd. and Teamsters, Local 419* (2002), 112 L.A.C. (4th) 60, once jurisdiction over the subject-matter of a grievance has been established, "there is an obligation upon a board of arbitration to deal with all disputes or differences between the parties arising expressly or inferentially from the collective agreement, and to grant the labour remedies which will give complete and final effect to the resolution of those disputes and differences" (at p. 71). Thus, in the context of an employee's discipline grievance, Arbitrator Newman was prepared to consider a claim against the employer not only for damages arising out of alleged harassment and assault by a supervisor, but also a request that the supervisor be removed from the workplace on the ground that he constituted an "unsafe condition".

In Ontario, the Grievance Settlement Board has taken an even more assertive view of an arbitrator's powers following *Weber.* That tribunal has held that, if no other suitable remedy can be found, it has jurisdiction to order the employer to discharge a managerial employee. See *Ontario (Ministry of Community Safety & Correctional Services) and O.P.S.E.U. (Pinazza)* (2004), 131 L.A.C. (4th) 132 (Ont. G.S.B.). Conversely, in *School District No. 42 (Maple Ridge – Pitt Meadows) and C.U.P.E., Local 703* (1999), 81 L.A.C. (4th) 92, Arbitrator Munroe permitted, as an add-on to the grievor's unjust discharge grievance, a claim for restitution by the employer involving alleged "kickbacks" illicitly diverted by the grievor.

In *Jadwani v. Canada (Attorney General)* (2001), 52 O.R. (3d) 660 (C.A.) (leave to appeal to S.C.C. denied September 13, 2001), the plaintiff sought, by launching a court action, to reopen issues which had already been made the subject of numerous grievances and been submitted to arbitration. The Ontario Court of Appeal made it clear that deference to arbitration extends to all claims which, on the facts, *could* have been asserted in an earlier arbitral proceeding. It made no difference that a number of individuals were named in the action as defendants, in addition to the employer, since relief based on the employer's vicarious liability for torts committed by its employees was equally available in both forums.

The Supreme Court of Canada provided a strong affirmation of *Weber* in *Allen v. Alberta* (2002), 223 D.L.R. (4th) 385. The plaintiff employees asserted entitlement to severance pay under the collective agreement, claiming that they had been pressured into resigning. In holding that the proper forum for the dispute was arbitration, the Court observed that "[a]bsent this provision [in the collective agreement], the respondents' right to the severance pay they claim does not exist" (at p. 394). Of particular significance is the fact that the claim had been brought in the courts because a provision in the side-letter under which the plaintiffs resigned precluded resort to arbitration. In the Alberta Court of Appeal, this provision was found to reinstate the jurisdiction of the courts. Reversing the Court of Appeal's ruling, the Supreme Court of Canada held that *Weber* applied, notwithstanding the express exclusion of arbitration, and that the question of arbitrability was also one which fell to be decided by the arbitrator. In *Vaughan v. Canada* (2005), 250 D.L.R. (4th) 385, the Supreme Court took this reasoning one step further, ruling that foreclosure of access to independent adjudication of a claim, pursuant to the provisions of the federal *Public Service Staff Relations Act*, R.S.C. 1985, c. P-35, is not a sufficient reason to override the *Weber* principle of deference to the statutory scheme of dispute resolution. Thus, while the employee was entitled to grieve the government's denial of early retirement benefits, he was precluded from advancing a claim in the courts, and had no right to pursue the matter to arbitration.

In *Goudie v. Ottawa (City)* (2003), 223 D.L.R. (4th) 395, by contrast, the Supreme Court concluded that claims based on an alleged pre-employment agreement belong in the courts, not at arbitration.

The courts have also resisted the assertion of exclusive arbitral jurisdiction where what is involved is the vindication of express employee rights granted by another statute. *Weber* itself is founded on the recognition that the legislature intended grievance arbitration as the forum for pursuing collective agreement rights regulated, ultimately, by the applicable labour relations legislation. Similarly, where the legislature has established a specialized mechanism for enforcing other kinds of rights relating to the employment relationship, the courts have affirmed that *Weber* does not oust a unionized employee's access to that mechanism. As the Saskatchewan Court of Appeal pointed out in the so-called "Saskatchewan Trilogy", an allegation that a statutory right has been violated is not, in essence, a difference between the parties to a collective agreement. To accord exclusive jurisdiction to an arbitrator, then, would amount to an impermissible attempt to contract out of the legislative scheme. Moreover, the Court suggested, while *Weber* may have rejected a concurrent jurisdiction model with respect to the enforcement of common law rights, it did not do so with respect to statutory rights: see *Prince Albert (District Health Board) v. Saskatchewan (Occupational Health & Safety)* (1999), 173 D.L.R. (4th) 588; *Dominion Bridge v. Routledge* (1999), 173 D.L.R. (4th) 624, leave to appeal to S.C.C. denied March 30, 2000; and *Saskatchewan (Human Rights Commission) v. Cadillac Fairview Corp.* (1999), 173 D.L.R. (4th) 609, leave to appeal to S.C.C. denied March 30, 2000.

The concurrent jurisdiction model, however, leaves open the question of which of two competing fora in a given case should be given primacy. This question is particularly likely to arise at grievance arbitration as a result of the Supreme Court of Canada's decision in *Parry Sound (District) Social Services Administration Board v. O.P.S.E.U., Local 324* (2003), 230 D.L.R. (4th) 257, holding that the provisions of all employment-related statutes are implicit in each collective agreement over which an arbitrator has jurisdiction: see Chapter 1.2.3. Where concurrent jurisdiction does exist between a board of arbitration and a statutory tribunal, the Supreme Court, applying the *Weber* analysis, has indicated that close regard must, once again, be had to the "essential nature" of a dispute in order to determine which forum is the "better fit": *Quebec (Commission des droits de la personne et des droits de la jeunesse) v. Quebec (Attorney General) (Morin)* (2004), 240 D.L.R. (4th) 577. In *Morin*, the Court rejected the proposition that an arbitrator had exclusive authority over a dispute involving an alleged violation of human rights legislation, ruling that primacy lay with the statutory tribunal.

In the opposite direction, the Supreme Court of Canada has held that the establishment of a specialized statutory tribunal to hear discharge or discipline grievances filed by police officers inferentially deprived a collective agreement arbitrator of jurisdiction to consider the matter: see *Regina Police Ass'n Inc. v. Regina (City) Board of Police Commissioners* (2000), 183 D.L.R. (4th) 14 (S.C.C.). Applying the two-part test in *Weber*, the Court concluded that the dispute did not arise either expressly or inferentially from the collective agreement, adding that the agreement must be interpreted consistently with the legislative scheme. In *Quebec (Attorney General) v. Quebec (Human Rights Tribunal) (Charette)* (2004), 240 D.L.R. (4th) 609 (S.C.C.), the legislation was specific in making all questions of entitlement exclusively a matter for the statutory tribunal to decide, and this consideration was, for a majority of the Supreme Court, determinative.

Additional Reading

A.K. Lokan & M. Yachnin, "From *Weber* to *Parry Sound*: The Expanded Scope of Arbitration" (2004), 11 Canadian Labour and Employment Law Journal, p. 1.

J.P. Alexandrowicz, "Restoring the Role of Grievance Arbitration: A New Approach to *Weber*" (2003), 10 Canadian Labour and Employment Journal, p. 269.

I. Johnstone, "Police, Discipline Forums and the Application of *Weber*: *Regina Police Association v. Regina (City) Board of Police Commissioners*" (2002), 9 Canadian Labour and Employment Journal, p. 169.

B. Adell, "Jurisdictional Overlap Between Arbitration and Other Forums: An Update" (2000), 8 Canadian Labour and Employment Journal, p. 179.

D.D. Carter, "Looking at *Weber* Five Years Later: Is it Time for a New Approach?" (2002), 8 Canadian Labour and Employment Journal, p. 231.

M.G. Picher, "Defining the Scope of Arbitration: An Arbitrator's Perspective" in K. Whitaker, J. Sack, M. Gunderson & R. Filion, eds., *Labour Arbitration Yearbook 1999-2000*, vol. I, p. 99; and companion articles by E. Durnford and L.N. Gottheil.

G.T. Surdykowski, "The Limits of Grievance Arbitration: *Weber* and *Pilon* in Perspective" in K. Whitaker, J. Sack, M. Gunderson & R. Filion, eds., *Labour Arbitration Yearbook 1999-2000*, vol. I, p. 67.

CHAPTER 2

PROCEDURAL OBJECTIONS TO ARBITRABILITY

2.1   GRIEVANCES ARISING UNDER A PRIOR COLLECTIVE AGREEMENT

Where a grievance asserts a claim relating to a prior, expired collective agreement, or seeks damages that flow back to a period of time covered by a predecessor agreement, two issues arise. The first, as discussed in Chapter 2.6, is the *timeliness* of the grievance. Based on the time limits fixed by the collective agreement for processing the claim through the grievance procedure and making a referral to arbitration, or on the principle of "laches" or unreasonable delay, the grievance may be barred as untimely. The second issue, considered here, is the arbitrator's *jurisdiction* to deal with a grievance arising under a collective agreement which is no longer in force. It is important to keep this distinction in mind when considering arbitral responses to what is, in all cases, the underlying question: should a party be entitled to relief in respect of an alleged violation of the collective agreement about which it had no knowledge — and could not, with reasonable diligence, have had any knowledge — before the agreement expired?

One of the first cases to address the problem of jurisdiction was *Canadian General Electric Co. Ltd. and U.E., Local 524* (1951), 2 L.A.C. 710. There, Arbitrator Lang held that a valid claim, properly arising under an earlier collective agreement, was not automatically terminated by the mere passage of time or the consummation of a new collective agreement. In *Red River Division*

Ass'n No. 17, M.T.S. v. Red River School Division No. 17 (1972), 25 D.L.R. (3d) 106, the Manitoba Court of Queen's Bench expressed the same view. The expiry of a collective agreement does not, without more, put an end to the right of either party to call for adjudication of a dispute, as long as the dispute concerns a benefit allegedly vested during the term of the agreement in question and is within the terms of reference of its arbitration clause.

In *Dayco (Canada) Ltd. v. C.A.W.* (1993), 102 D.L.R. (4th) 609, the Supreme Court of Canada affirmed that rights which have vested during the currency of a collective agreement are capable of being enforced following its expiry. The Court indicated that, while collective agreements are said to expire as of a certain date, they are not thereby rendered a nullity. Although the agreement ceases to have *prospective* application to the parties' relationship, the Court reasoned, the rights that have accrued under it continue to subsist. That being the case, those rights continue to be enforceable through the grievance and arbitration machinery of the collective agreement. Although the *Dayco* case dealt with retiree benefits, the Court clearly stated that there was nothing to differentiate a promise to pay such benefits from a promise to pay regular wages or vacation pay. As the Court put it, "[a]ny other conclusion would render meaningless a wide range of promises to employees that might extend beyond the expiration of a collective agreement" (at p. 636).

The issue in a given case, therefore, will be whether the rights being asserted have accrued or "vested" during the period of the collective agreement that established those rights. In *Columbia Forest Products and I.W.A. – Canada, Local 2995* (2003), 119 L.A.C. (4th) 214, Arbitrator Haefling ruled that employees who had qualified for and commenced drawing weekly indemnity payments prior to the expiry of the "statutory freeze" period and an ensuing strike were entitled to continue receiving those payments. By contrast, in *Royal Diamond Casino Inc. and C.A.W., Local 3000* (2003), 118 L.A.C. (4th) 371, Arbitrator Dorsey held that an employee to whom the pay-out of accrued vacation pay was not owing as of the commencement of a lockout was not entitled to insist on such payment during the lockout.

While *Dayco* thus put to rest the enforceability of rights that have crystallized or vested under a prior collective agreement, the question of the precise arbitral mechanism available to pursue those grievances may still be open to debate (at least in the absence of an agreement between the parties specifying a method of recourse). In *Goodyear Canada Inc. and U.R.W., Local 232* (1980), 28 L.A.C. (2d) 196, Arbitrator Michel Picher questioned whether an arbitration board appointed under one collective agreement could order a remedy in respect of a period covered by a previous collective agreement. While suggesting that relief might be available from a board *specifically constituted* under the previous agreement, subject to considerations of timeliness, he held that the board of which he was then Chair was not entitled to assume that jurisdiction. More recently, though, Arbitrator O'Neil has held that an arbitration board can effectively be constituted under more than one collective agreement at a time: *Air Canada and I.A.M. (Graham)* (1999), 80 L.A.C. (4th) 224. So long as there is nothing in the predecessor collective agreement(s) that would limit retroactive recovery, it would, in Arbitrator O'Neil's view, unnecessarily frustrate the expectations of the parties to require that a series of separate boards of arbitration be constituted in order to provide a remedy with full retroactive effect.

In *Advanced Metal Products Ltd. and C.A.W., Local 636* (2000), 93 L.A.C. (4th) 170, Arbitrator Luborsky determined that termination of the collective agreement by an assignment in bankruptcy does not preclude the appointment of an arbitrator under a statutory expedited arbitration scheme, provided that the alleged breach of the agreement occurred prior to its termination.

Issues with respect to enforcement of a collective agreement can also arise in cases involving a new or "successor" employer or union. In *Miramar Giant Mine Ltd. and C.A.W., Local 2304* (2001), 94 L.A.C. (4th) 388, Arbitrator Ready applied the successor employer provisions of the *Canada Labour Code*, R.S.C. 1985, c. L-2, to hold that the purchaser of a business stood in the shoes of the vendor with respect to unresolved grievances.

A similar issue concerning the rights of successor unions was considered in *Kensington Village and S.E.I.U., Local 220* (2002), 106 L.A.C. (4th) 14 (Rayner). Pursuant to the Ontario *Labour Relations Act*, S.O. 1995, c. 1, Sch. A, certification of a new bargaining agent terminates the bargaining rights of the predecessor union, as well as any collective agreement which is in effect. Arbitrator Rayner held that, despite the termination of its bargaining rights, the predecessor union continues to have the right to advance outstanding grievances to arbitration, and is therefore entitled to authorize the successor union as its agent for the purpose of prosecuting such grievances. Alternatively, a predecessor union has the right to continue carriage of such grievances on its own: *Coca-Cola Bottling Co. and U.F.C.W., Local 175/633* (2004), 127 L.A.C. (4th) 218 (Beck).

In *Middlesex (County) and C.A.W.* (2001), 96 L.A.C. (4th) 197, Arbitrator Lynk concluded that this principle does not, at least under Ontario's legislation, make arbitrable an alleged violation of the predecessor collective agreement if the claim arises in the period following the agreement's termination by operation of the Act. The arbitrator also noted, however, that the statutory freeze provisions in effect during the period leading to the new union's certification may entitle that union to seek relief from the Ontario Labour Relations Board.

2.2 DEFECTS IN FORM

The labour relations legislation of a number of Canadian jurisdictions specifically grants arbitrators the authority to identify and deal with the "true substance" of the matters in dispute. Both arbitrators and the courts, however, have long espoused this principle, even in the absence of statutory authorization. As stated by the Ontario Court of Appeal in *Blouin Drywall Contractors Ltd. v. C.J.A., Local 2486* (1975), 57 D.L.R. (3d) 199, at p. 204: "These cases should not be won or lost on the technicality of form, rather on the merits and as provided in the contract and so the dispute may be finally and fairly resolved with simplicity and dispatch". Similarly, in *Communications Union Canada v. Bell Canada* (1976), 71 D.L.R. (3d) 632, at p. 639, the Ontario Divisional Court commented:

> Nothing can be more calculated to exacerbate relations between employers and employees, than to be told that their differences, plainly designed to be finally settled by arbitration, as the statute requires, cannot be examined because of a defect in form.

The Supreme Court of Canada, in *Parry Sound (District) Social Services Administration Board v. O.P.S.E.U., Local 324* (2003), 230 D.L.R. (4th) 257 (S.C.C.), noted that the failure to specify even a *statutory* provision alleged to have been violated will not necessarily invalidate the claim. However, arbitrators have observed that this flexible approach should not be taken so far as to allow parties to raise what is, in substance, a new matter at the hearing, as this would defeat the purpose of the grievance procedure as an opportunity to discuss and resolve the issues in dispute. These two competing themes were canvassed in *Electrohome Ltd. and I.B.E.W., Local 2345* (1984), 16 L.A.C. (3d) 78 (Rayner), and were applied in *Cold Springs Farms and Cold Springs Farms Employees' Ass'n, Local 100* (2000), 88 L.A.C. (4th) 213 (Goodfellow). The award affirms that a party will not be permitted to expand a grievance to include matters which the parties have not had an opportunity to consider during the grievance procedure. In order to determine whether this principle applies, Arbitrator Goodfellow noted, it may be necessary to hear evidence relating to the parties' discussions during the grievance procedure for the limited purpose of ascertaining how the issues in contention were framed. The caselaw was again reviewed and affirmed by Arbitrator Dissanayake in *Greater Sudbury Hydro Plus Inc. and C.U.P.E., Local 4705* (2003), 121 L.A.C. (4th) 193.

In *Timberjack Inc. and Glass, Molders, Pottery, Plastics & Allied Workers Union, Local 446* (1996), 62 L.A.C. (4th) 438, Arbitrator Brandt addressed the issue of form from a different perspective, as the employer in its grievance had named the union improperly. To consider the grievance inarbitrable because of a minor defect such as this, the arbitrator held, "would represent a triumph of form over substance" and run counter to the prevailing trends in the caselaw.

2.3 FAILURE TO FOLLOW GRIEVANCE PROCEDURE

Arbitrators have held that, in order to be arbitrable, a matter must have been properly processed through all the steps of the agreed-upon grievance procedure.

Failure to advance the grievance through each step normally voids a referral to arbitration. In *Horizon Operations (Canada) Ltd. and C.E.P., Local 2000* (2000), 93 L.A.C. (4th) 47, however, Arbitrator Coleman affirmed that such will not be the case where an attempt to advance the grievance was frustrated by the opposing party.

2.4 LACK OF EMPLOYEE SIGNATURE

Does the absence of the employee's signature on an individual grievance form render the grievance inarbitrable? At least where the collective agreement expressly requires that the grievance be signed by the employee, Arbitrator Ellis has concluded that the employer is entitled to be satisfied that the grievance represents a *"bona fide,* individual, personal, complaint": *Royalcrest/ Yorkview Lifecare and S.E.I.U., Local 204*, [2000] O.L.A.A. No. 752 (QL). The arbitrator rejected the notion, espoused in some decisions, that such a requirement is directory only and not enforceable, as well as the argument that the union should be presumed to have signing authority unless the grievance is specifically renounced by the employee. Rather, a grievance not signed by the employee, is, as a matter of substance, invalid on its face. This presumption, Arbitrator Ellis added, can be rebutted by evidence that the employee, at the time of the grievance, authorized the union to sign on his or her behalf.

2.5 INDIVIDUAL, GROUP AND POLICY GRIEVANCES

A common objection to the arbitrability of a grievance is that it has been filed as a union "policy" grievance when its subject-matter demands that it be filed as an individual grievance, that is, by or on behalf of a specific employee. Typically, the basis for the objection is that the union, through the format of a policy grievance, is seeking relief for an individual employee. Debate over this issue had already polarized the labour relations community when, in *Weston Bakeries Ltd. and Milk & Bread Drivers, Dairy Employees, Caterers & Allied Employees, Local 647* (1970), 21 L.A.C. 308, Paul Weiler, Chair of a board of arbitration, reviewed the competing positions and outlined a number of principles:

(1) Under the arbitration provisions of the Ontario *Labour Relations Act*, a union has the right to grieve any violation of the collective agreement, even without the consent of an individual employee who may be directly affected

(2) The general principle that certain kinds of individual claims are inherently or presumptively unsuited for policy grievances is no longer accepted.

(3) The *Labour Relations Act* does not prevent the parties in their collective agreement from restricting the type of grievance that can be used in particular circumstances to access the arbitration process.

(4) Such restrictions on the use of policy grievances should be upheld only when the explicit language of the collective agreement, interpreted without any assumptions, leads to that conclusion.

Weiler observed as well that the caselaw permits a substantial degree of overlap between union and individual grievances. Whenever a claim advanced by an individual employee raises a problem of general interest to other members of the bargaining unit, either because it involves an issue of interpretation or because it addresses a recurring point of contention, a policy grievance is valid.

In *Weston Bakeries*, Weiler did not specifically address what, if any, limitations there may be on the type of remedy to which a union is entitled in an otherwise valid policy grievance. Such limitations may flow either explicitly or implicitly from the language of the collective agreement. In *Canada Post Corp. and C.U.P.W.* (1993), 35 L.A.C. (4th) 300, Arbitrator Christie held that the union was entitled to bring the matter forward by way of a policy grievance if it chose, but indicated that, if the union was successful, he would award a declaration only, and not damages.

In British Columbia arbitrators possess express statutory authority to relieve against breaches of any "procedural requirements": see s. 89(e) of the *Labour Relations Code*, R.S.B.C. 1996, c. 244. In *Fraser Valley Child Development Centre and H.S.A.B.C.* (1996), 54 L.A.C. (4th) 111, Arbitrator Munroe held that s. 89(e) allowed him to determine a policy grievance on its merits, whether or not it should have been filed as an individual grievance.

See also *St. Joseph's Hospital and S.E.I.U.* (1997), 65 L.A.C. (4th) 160 (Solomatenko), in which the union brought a policy grievance to forestall a loss of jobs through the proposed purchase of pre-prepared food from an outside supplier. The employer objected to the form in which the grievance had been filed, but Arbitrator Solomatenko held that, since no employee had yet been affected by the alleged breach, it was "a textbook case for the subject-matter of a policy grievance".

It may be added that, even without express recognition in the collective agreement, arbitrators have accepted group grievances on the basis that a group grievance is "really an accumulation of individual grievances": see *Canadian Broadcasting Corp. and N.A.B.E.T.* (1973), 4 L.A.C. (2d) 263 (Shime). Thus, group grievances are to be distinguished from policy grievances in the same way as individual grievances.

Nonetheless, the filing of a group grievance may raise discrete issues. In *British Columbia and B.C.G.E.U. (Maddocks)* (1988), 35 L.A.C. (3d) 114 (Ladner), only one of 30 grievors signed the grievance, which concerned entitlement to a car allowance. When the grievance was allowed, the employer paid the grievor whose name had appeared on the form as of the date of the grievance, but paid the others only as of the date of the award. In a supplementary ruling, Arbitrator Ladner held that the grievance had been properly brought on behalf of the whole group. As long as it is clear on whose behalf a grievance is brought, the absence of signatures makes no difference. In *Southern Railway of British Columbia Ltd. and C.U.P.E., Local 7000* (2001), 99 L.A.C. (4th) 138 (Larson), on the other hand, the union filed a single grievance on behalf of four named employees who had incurred varying levels of discipline as a result of their involvement in the same incident. The arbitrator had been appointed to hear the grievance of only one of the employees, and the employer insisted that each matter be dealt with separately. On the basis that the collective agreement contained no express recognition of group grievances, Arbitrator Larson ruled that the status of the grievances was tantamount to that of a series of individual grievances. Additionally, while it might be open to the union, in an appropriate case, to request an order for consolidation, an arbitrator cannot make such an order unless he or she otherwise has jurisdiction over all the grievances in question. For further discussion of the circumstances in which a consolidation order may be made, see Chapter 5.7.

The interrelationship of individual, policy and group grievances, in the context of a collective agreement which provides for all three, was discussed in *University of Western Ontario and Staff Ass'n* (2002), 108 L.A.C. (4th) 139. Arbitrator Davie affirmed the conclusion reached by Arbitrator Weiler in *Weston Bakeries, supra,* that the inclusion of provisions for both *individual* and *policy* grievances does not necessarily mean that they should be treated as being mutually exclusive, at least in the absence of express language in the agreement making them so. The presence of the two forms of grievance, each governed by a different procedure, may simply reflect an intention by the parties to create a "hierarchy" of grievances. On the other hand, Arbitrator Davie observed, where the collective agreement explicitly entitles the union to file a *group* grievance, and the signatures of affected employees are *not* required on the grievance form, this militates against permitting a broader use of policy grievances.

2.6   TIME LIMITS

2.6.1   Is the Language Mandatory or Directory?

Historically, arbitrators have categorized collective agreement time limits for the bringing or processing of a grievance as being either "mandatory" or "directory". If the language is directory, arbitrators will generally entertain the grievance provided the other party has not been prejudiced by delay. Only where the time limits are mandatory is an arbitrator bound to apply the strict terms of the collective agreement and refuse to proceed further with a grievance which has been shown to be untimely. In such a case, absent specific *statutory* discretion, an arbitrator has no latitude to alleviate against the deadline: *Union Carbide Canada Ltd. v. Weiler* (1968), 70 D.L.R. (2d) 333 (S.C.C.).

In order to determine whether the time limits established by a collective agreement are mandatory or directory, it is necessary to analyze the precise wording of the collective agreement. Usually, an express stipulation of the consequences of non-compliance with the time limits indicates that the parties intended them to be mandatory. As the Ontario Divisional Court stated in *Dominion Consolidated Truck Lines Ltd. v. Teamsters, Local 141* (1975), 60 D.L.R. (3d) 37, however, one cannot go so far as to say that mere failure to spell out the consequences of non-compliance renders the language directory only. Nor does casting the language in imperative terms necessarily make it mandatory. In each case, the parties' intentions must be gleaned from a review of the collective agreement as a whole.

In a recent case, the collective agreement provided for a three-step grievance procedure, and included the following admonition: "If advantage of the grievance procedure has not been taken within the time limits specified in this agreement, the alleged grievance shall be deemed to have been abandoned and cannot be re-opened". When an arbitrator found that referral to arbitration was a step in the arbitration procedure, not the grievance procedure, and that in any event the time limits were directory only, the P.E.I. Court of Appeal held that, in light of the structure and language of the agreement, the arbitrator was wrong on both counts. That holding was fatal to the union's discharge grievance, as the Prince Edward Island *Labour Act*, R.S.P.E.I. 1988, c. L-1, does not contain a provision empowering arbitrators to relieve against mandatory time limits: *C.U.P.E., Local 3373 v. Queen's County Residential Services Inc.* (2004), 236 D.L.R. (4th) 133 (P.E.I.C.A.), leave to appeal to S.C.C. denied September 2, 2004.

For a review of other cases on the mandatory/directory distinction, see the summary set out in *School District No. 39 (Vancouver) and Vancouver Teachers' Federation* (1995), 48 L.A.C. (4th) 108 (Hope).

2.6.2   Waiver

Even where the language prescribing the stages of the grievance and arbitration procedure is found to be mandatory, an arbitrator may decide that the right to object to a missed time limit has been waived. Failure to object promptly to a party's failure to adhere to time limits, or acquiescence in the carriage of the grievance to a fresh step in the procedure, has often been held to give rise to a waiver of rights or to an estoppel. The case cited most frequently in this regard is *Regency Towers Hotel Ltd. and Hotel & Club Employees' Union, Local 299* (1973), 4 L.A.C. (2d) 440 (Schiff).

However, as seen, for example, in *Canada Post Corp. and C.U.P.W. (McGrogan)* (1991), 22 L.A.C. (4th) 430 (Jolliffe), arbitrators have repeatedly held that only a "procedural" right, as opposed to a "substantive" one, is capable of being waived. The distinction between the substantive and procedural provisions of a collective agreement may therefore become critical in determining whether a matter is arbitrable.

Where the parties have engaged in a joint effort to settle or investigate a grievance, without reservation of their formal position, it has been held that the employer is not permitted to invoke a time limit defence at the conclusion of that process: *National Gallery of Canada and P.S.A.C. (Jolicoeur)*, [2004] C.L.A.D. No. 426 (QL) (Bastien).

2.6.3   Continuing Breach

A grievance may be arbitrable notwithstanding a breach of mandatory time limits where the matter complained of constitutes a "continuing breach" of the collective agreement. In the case of a continuing breach, a grievance will be timely if the most recent recurrence of the alleged violation took place within the time limits fixed by the collective agreement for bringing a grievance. The remedy to which the grieving party is entitled, however, is normally limited to damages that have accrued within the time limit. That approach was initially developed in such cases as *Automatic Screw Machine Products Ltd. and U.S.W.A., Local 7105* (1972), 23 L.A.C. 396 (Johnston). More recently, it was affirmed in *California Marble & Tile Ltd. and Tilesetters Int'l Union, Local 3* (1995), 49 L.A.C. (4th) 174 (Glass).

As the arbitral jurisprudence demonstrates, the most difficult problem lies not in calculating the damages, but in determining when a breach is properly characterized as a continuing one. The applicable principles and caselaw are discussed in *Religious Hospitallers of St. Joseph of Hotel Dieu of Kingston and O.P.S.E.U., Local 452* (1992), 29 L.A.C. (4th) 326 (Stewart). To apply the doctrine of continuing breach, Arbitrator Stewart explained, it is necessary to differentiate between what are really a series of discrete breaches committed on a continuing basis — for example, failure to pay a specified amount due at repeated intervals — and ongoing damages *suffered* by a party as a result of a single breach. The existence of recurring damages will not in itself be adequate to transform a party's violation of the collective agreement into a continuing breach.

2.6.4   Laches – Excessive Delay

Even where the time limits in a collective agreement are directory rather than mandatory, arbitrators have a discretion to refuse to proceed with a grievance on the basis of unreasonable delay, in accordance with the equitable doctrine of laches. As Arbitrator Laskin put it in *Canadian Westinghouse Co. Ltd. and U.E., Local 504* (1963), 14 L.A.C. 139, at p. 142, where the procedure is directory only, the parties "must accept reasonableness as a touchstone of the time limit for arbitration". That arbitrator-created limit on excessive delay was discussed more recently in *School District No. 39 (Vancouver) and Vancouver Teachers' Federation* (1995), 48 L.A.C. (4th) 108, where Arbitrator Hope emphasized the importance of preserving the parties' entitlement to a fair hearing.

Another way in which arbitrators have responded to unreasonable delay, where at least some element of the claim remains timely, has been to limit the extent of retroactive recovery. This was the solution fashioned by Arbitrator Bendel in *FPC Flexible Packaging Corp. and G.C.I.U., Local 500-M* (1998), 77 L.A.C. (4th) 198.

Despite the arbitral emphasis on timely prosecution of grievances, *U.F.C.W., Local 280P v. Pride of Alberta Meat Processors* (1998), 159 D.L.R. (4th) 35 (Alta. C.A.) stands as a reminder that the equitable doctrine of laches should not be applied too strictly. In that case, the employer, without objection from the union, had for years overcharged employees for health care premiums. The Alberta Court of Appeal quashed an arbitrator's decision not to inquire into the matter on the basis of undue delay, as there was no indication of prejudice or detrimental reliance on the part of the employer.

2.6.5   Statutory Discretion to Extend Time Limits

In British Columbia, New Brunswick, Ontario and Saskatchewan, the applicable labour relations statute grants arbitrators a discretion to relieve against breaches of mandatory time limits. Section 48(16) of the Ontario *Labour Relations Act*, S.O. 1995, c. 1, Sch. A, reads:

> Except where a collective agreement states that this subsection does not apply, an arbitrator or arbitration board may extend the time for the taking of any step in the grievance procedure under a collective agreement, despite the expiration of the time, where the arbitrator or arbitration board is satisfied that there are reasonable grounds for the extension and that the opposite party will not be substantially prejudiced by the extension.

The provisions which apply in other jurisdictions may be less specific. For example, s. 89 of the British Columbia *Labour Relations Code*, R.S.B.C. 1996, c. 244, provides that an arbitrator "may relieve, on just and equitable terms, against breaches of time limits or other procedural requirements in the collective agreement".

In exercising his or her judgment, the arbitrator must weigh all of the pertinent facts, and particularly whether the opposite party has suffered prejudice from the delay. In the often-cited case of *Greater Niagara General Hospital and O.N.A.* (1981), 1 L.A.C. (3d) 1, Arbitrator Schiff described a number of inter-related factors that ought to be taken into account, emphasizing that no single factor will be paramount:

(1) the nature of the grievance;

(2) whether the delay occurred initially, in launching the grievance, or at some later stage;

(3) whether the grievor was responsible for the delay;

(4) the reasons for the delay;

(5) the length of the delay; and

(6) whether the employer could reasonably have assumed that the grievance had been abandoned.

A similar analysis, drawn from the decisions of British Columbia arbitrators, can be found in *Nelson & District Credit Union and I.W.A., Local 1-405* (1998), 71 L.A.C. (4th) 333 (Greyell). In Arbitrator Greyell's view, whether or not the arbitral discretion to extend time limits should be exercised depends on the proper balancing of a variety of considerations, including the language of the collective agreement, the reasons for the delay, the length of the delay and the overall equities. At the same time, he cautions against an excessively permissive approach.

When considering requests for an extension of time limits, arbitrators are not necessarily limited to the traditional criteria. Dismissing the employer's application for review, the Nova Scotia Court of Appeal has ruled that it was not patently unreasonable for an arbitrator to take into account the strength of a case on its merits in deciding whether to grant relief against mandatory deadlines for presenting a grievance. In the Court's view, the "arbitrator was not obliged to follow 'the relevant case law' developed by other arbitrators or to limit himself to 'recognized criteria' ": *Halifax Employers Ass'n v. I.L.A., Local 269* (2004), 243 D.L.R. (4th) 101 (N.S.C.A.), at p. 126.

It has been held that, in the absence of a credible explanation for the delay, the fact that a claim directly affects the rights of other employees in the bargaining unit (for example, job posting or work assignment cases) militates against granting an extension: *Cominco Ltd. and U.S.W.A., Local 480* (2000), 87 L.A.C. (4th) 380 (Ready).

Where the language of a statutory provision authorizes arbitrators to relieve against breaches of time limits in the "grievance procedure", rather than the "grievance and arbitration procedure", a question arises as to whether such language applies to an untimely referral to arbitration. Arbitrations conducted in Ontario are now specifically subject to the courts' interpretation of the legislative history of the *Labour Relations Act*. In 1992, the Ontario *Labour Relations Act*, which previously used "grievance procedure" language, was amended to make explicit the authority of arbitrators to extend the time for taking "any step in the grievance procedure *or arbitration procedure* under a collective agreement" (emphasis added): see S.O. 1992, c. 21, s. 23(3). The effect of the amendment was to codify the jurisdiction which arbitrators had for some years asserted to extend the time for referring a grievance to arbitration. The succeeding government deleted the additional phrase from what is now s. 48(16) of the Act leaving the provision in substantially the same form as before the amendment. In *S.E.I.U., Local 204 v. Leisureworld Nursing Homes Ltd.* (1997), 99 O.A.C. 196, the Ontario Divisional Court held that the intention of the legislature was to restrict the arbitral discretion to the grievance procedure itself. Where a party's referral to arbitration was untimely, therefore, the arbitrator no longer had power to relieve against the consequences. The Ontario Court of Appeal has since affirmed the decision: see [1997] O.J. No. 4815 (QL).

The New Brunswick Court of Appeal has declined to follow *Leisureworld*, upholding an arbitrator's ruling that the referral of a grievance to arbitration was properly characterized as part of the grievance procedure: see *Pepsi-Cola Canada Beverages v. Dollar* (1999), 221 N.B.R. (2d) 124 (C.A.). A similar conclusion was reached by the Ontario Divisional Court in *James Bay General Hospital v. P.S.A.C.* (2004), 238 D.L.R. (4th) 730, on the ground that the grievance and arbitration procedures under the collective agreement in question were "inextricably intertwined".

In *Hotel-Dieu Grace Hospital and C.A.W., Local 2458* (2002), 106 L.A.C. (4th) 1 (Knopf), where the grievances alleged a violation of the *Human Rights Code*, R.S.O. 1990, c. H.19, the union admitted that the mandatory time limits under the collective agreement had not been met. It contended, however, that because the grievances raised human rights issues, the applicable time limit was that prescribed by the *Code*, which imposes a six-month deadline for filing a complaint. Arbitrator Knopf dismissed the grievances as untimely. In her view, the decision in *Leisureworld* precluded an arbitrator from assuming jurisdiction to "interpret and apply" an external statute unless the grievance had been the subject of a timely referral to arbitration: "[T]he fact that the substance of the grievance concerns human rights matters does not vest an arbitrator with jurisdiction unless and until the arbitrator is properly appointed under the collective agreement" (at p. 13).

In Ontario it appears to be settled law that the system of statutory expedited arbitration is subject to its own specified time limit, and stands apart from the general statutory discretion to modify time limits stipulated by a collective agreement. Thus, even where the time limits under the collective agreement can be said to be directory, an arbitrator has no discretion to modify the time limit specified by statute for requesting the appointment of an arbitrator on an expedited basis: see *Hamilton (City) and C.U.P.E., Local 5* (2000), 88 L.A.C. (4th) 86 (Dissanayake).

CHAPTER 3

FUNDAMENTAL OBJECTIONS TO ARBITRABILITY

3.1 MATTERS NOT COVERED BY THE COLLECTIVE AGREEMENT

3.1.1 General

The classic objection to the "arbitrability" of a dispute is that the collective agreement does not cover the matter. However, it may not be strictly accurate to cast the issue as one of arbitrability. If there are provisions in the collective agreement dealing with the subject-matter of the dispute, the question might better be cast as whether these provisions go far enough to create the specific right or obligation asserted in the grievance. As Arbitrator Veniot observed in *Resi-Cure Cape Breton Ass'n and C.U.P.E., Local 3008* (1996), 58 L.A.C. (4th) 46, the underlying point of contention in such cases is the proper construction to be given to the collective agreement, not the arbitrator's jurisdiction to decide the matter. In the case in question, Arbitrator Veniot agreed with the employer that the provisions of the collective agreement did not establish the right asserted by the union.

In *Weber v. Ontario Hydro* (1995), 125 D.L.R. (4th) 583, the Supreme Court of Canada held that arbitrators have exclusive jurisdiction over all claims arising either "expressly or inferentially" out of the collective agreement: see Chapter 1.3. However, as Vice-Chair Richard Brown emphasized in *Ontario (Ministry of Correctional Services) and O.P.S.E.U.* (2002), 113 L.A.C. (4th)

49 (Ont. G.S.B.), the scope of arbitral jurisdiction has long been defined by reference to the express and implied provisions of the collective agreement; to say
that arbitral authority encompasses disputes that arise "expressly or inferentially" from the collective agreement is simply to assert that the matter must
be governed by an express or implied provision of that agreement. Thus, Vice-
Chair Brown concluded, the judgment in *Weber* did not broaden the range of
disputes which may be submitted to arbitration. In particular, he noted, the
Supreme Court did not empower arbitrators to hear "separate 'cases' of tort,
contract or *Charter*". Rather, once a violation of the collective agreement has
been established, arbitrators are mandated, in fashioning a remedy, to consider
whether such violation "also constitutes a breach of a common law duty, or of
the *Charter*".

It remains to be seen to what extent, in cases where the matter in dispute is
governed by a statute, the Supreme Court of Canada's decision in *Parry Sound
(District) Social Services Administration Board v. O.P.S.E.U., Local 324*
(2003), 230 D.L.R. (4th) 257 will modify the fundamental principle that an
arbitrator's jurisdiction must be grounded in the collective agreement: see the
discussion in Chapter 1.2.3.

On the question of "implied rights" as a rule of collective agreement interpretation, see Chapter 16.3. The issue of whether, in the exercise of its management rights, the employer is subject to a general duty of fairness is
considered in Chapter 16.2.2. A related question is whether management rules,
the breach of which may result in discipline, can be challenged on the basis
that they are unreasonable: see Chapter 13.2.7. With respect to a dismissed
employee's entitlement to grieve "just cause" in the absence of a specific provision in the collective agreement permitting this, see Chapter 10.1.1.

3.1.2   Pre-Employment Matters

In order for a grievance to be advanced under the collective agreement, the
claim must pertain to individuals who were covered by the agreement at the
time the matter is said to have arisen. Or, to put it another way, the act of hiring employees into the bargaining unit does not fall within the purview of an
arbitrator unless the collective agreement expressly deals with the issue (for
example, by way of a "hiring hall" provision). Thus, in *Trimac Transportation
Services and T.C.U.* (1998), 74 L.A.C. (4th) 444, Arbitrator Burkett concluded
that he had no jurisdiction to inquire into or rule upon the application of the
employer's drug-testing policy at the pre-employment or hiring stage. The arbitrator's reasoning is consistent with the judgment in *Goudie v. Ottawa (City)*
(2003), 223 D.L.R. (4th) 395, where the Supreme Court of Canada held that
the question of whether there had been a pre-employment agreement regarding the transfer of employees from one bargaining unit to another was properly one for the courts, rather than an arbitrator, to determine.

On the other hand, a distinction must be drawn where a condition sought to be imposed on a job applicant continues to have an effect beyond the decision to hire, and impinges on a matter that is specifically addressed by the collective agreement. Thus, in *Loyalist College of Applied Arts and Technology v. O.P.S.E.U.* (2003), 225 D.L.R. (4th) 123, leave to appeal to S.C.C. denied November 20, 2003, the Ontario Court of Appeal upheld an arbitration board's ruling that the employer violated the collective agreement by requiring, as a condition of employment, that an applicant upgrade her credentials after hiring. In the Court's opinion, the condition imposed by the employer did not involve a matter which lay outside the scope of the collective agreement; rather, the disputed term went to the core of the employee's continued employment, and as such could not be made the subject of individual bargaining.

It has also been held that, where an employer makes pre-employment representations to its employees that they will receive a benefit not included in the collective agreement, and the employees rely on those representations to their detriment, the union may invoke the doctrine of estoppel to require that the employer provide the promised benefits: *C.H. Heist Ltd. and C.E.P., Local 866-0*, [2003] O.L.A.A. No. 459 (QL) (Springate).

3.2 COLLECTIVE AGREEMENT NOT IN EFFECT

In order for a matter to be considered arbitrable, the collective agreement (and its relevant provisions) must have been in effect during the period to which the grievance relates. It may become critical, therefore, to determine the exact date on which the agreement was actually consummated. In doing this, arbitrators have had to consider the ramifications of the formal requirements found in labour relations legislation as to what constitutes a "collective agreement". Even though a collective agreement is generally required by statute to be "in writing", arbitrators have held that the agreement need not be contained in a single document. What adjudicators *have* looked for is evidence that bargaining between the parties has come to an end, as well as documentation of the settlement sufficient to enable its terms to be clearly identified. If, on the other hand, the statutory definition requires that the collective agreement be "signed", the evidentiary standard may be somewhat more exacting. Even then, however, arbitrators have made it clear that unsigned documents, setting out the agreed-upon terms, may be incorporated by reference into a document (such as a ratification letter) that does bear a signature: *Cape Breton Healthcare Complex and C.A.W., Locals 4600 & 4603* (1999), 83 L.A.C. (4th) 289 (Outhouse).

Another problem that arises from the emergence of a gap during which no collective agreement is in force is the extent to which the rights that it ultimately contains are retroactive. Where the parties are bargaining for a renewal agreement, it is common to include a duration clause that is nominally retroactive to the expiry date of the predecessor agreement. However, in the interval in which there was *in fact* no collective agreement, events giving rise to a grievance may already have occurred. As a consequence, arbitrators have had to grapple with the question of which of the provisions of the new collective agreement were intended to be given full retroactive effect. In the seminal case on this point, *Penick Canada Ltd. and Int'l Chemical Workers, Local 412* (1966), 17 L.A.C. 296, Arbitrator Weatherill observed that the practice of backdating collective agreements had generally been adopted with the monetary provisions in mind. To extend the principle of retroactivity further, as, for example, to the seniority provisions of the new collective agreement, would, in his opinion, require the "clearest language".

The requirement to stipulate, in express terms, the retroactive effect of particular provisions when renewing a collective agreement was affirmed in *Ass'n of Community Living and U.F.C.W., Local 832*, [2004] M.G.A.D. No. 24 (QL) (Teskey).

In *Penticton & District Retirement Service and H.E.U., Local 180* (1977), 16 L.A.C. (2d) 97, Paul Weiler, Chair of the British Columbia Labour Relations Board, reviewed the authorities. Restating the test somewhat, Weiler concluded that *all* the terms of the new collective agreement are deemed to be retroactive, except where the operation of retroactivity "would appear to lead to quite impractical and unintended results". *Penticton* itself involved a claim for the retroactive application of a wage increase that had been agreed upon in negotiations — the typical function of a retroactive duration clause, even on Arbitrator Weatherill's view. Chair Weiler stressed that unions have a legitimate twofold interest in securing retroactive wage increases: to assure its members that prolonged negotiations will not enure to their detriment, and to discourage employers from believing that procrastination will reward them with a financial windfall.

However, a union may negotiate a clause in the collective agreement expressly restricting the right to retroactive pay increases to persons with employee status on the date the agreement was signed, without violating the duty of fair representation or prohibitions against discrimination: *Tremblay v. S.I.E.P.B., section locale 57* (2002), 212 D.L.R. (4th) 212.

A more recent summation of the caselaw can be found in *Bearskin Lake Air Services Ltd. and U.F.C.W., Local 175* (1997), 69 L.A.C. (4th) 421 (Bendel). *Canteen of Canada Ltd. and R.W.D.S.U., Local 414* (1984), 15 L.A.C. (3d) 305 (Mitchnick), one of the decisions to which Arbitrator Bendel referred, involved the arbitrability of a discharge that took place at a time when the parties had still not consummated their renewal collective agreement. There were particular facts which led the arbitrator to conclude that it was the mutual understanding of the parties that, during these bargaining intervals, provisions such as "just cause" protection would continue to govern the parties' relationship. However, in *Commemorative Services of Ontario and S.E.I.U., Local 204*

(1997), 69 L.A.C. (4th) 11, Arbitrator Brandt denied access to the grievance procedure in respect of a discharge which occurred before the signing of a *first* collective agreement, ruling that different principles applied.

Clearly, the suspension of just cause protection in the interval between successive collective agreements poses a problem. In a number of jurisdictions, labour relations legislation specifically affords the right to arbitrate disciplinary matters during the so-called "freeze period", when the statute prohibits the employer from unilaterally altering terms and conditions of employment while negotiations for a new collective agreement are taking place. The legislation thus assures the right of employees to have any alleged misconduct for which discipline was imposed judged against the standard of just cause, regardless of the parties' understanding with respect to retroactivity. See, for example, the *Canada Labour Code*, R.S.C. 1985, c. L-2, s. 67; Manitoba's *Labour Relations Act*, R.S.M. 1987, c. L10, s. 78(5); New Brunswick's *Industrial Relations Act*, R.S.N.B. 1973, c. I-4, s. 55(8); and Nova Scotia's *Trade Union Act*, R.S.N.S. 1989, c. 475, s. 44.

Another issue connected to the operation of the "statutory freeze" is the effect of limiting words in a contract clause which expressly state that the provision applies only during the term of the collective agreement. In *Port of Saint John Employers' Ass'n and I.L.A., Local 273* (2003), 116 L.A.C. (4th) 385, where the dispute arose during the freeze period under the *Canada Labour Code*, Arbitrator Kuttner concluded that such language amounted to nothing more than a reiteration of the collective agreement's duration clause. Accordingly, the arbitrator held, the clause remained in effect beyond the expiry date of the collective agreement by virtue of the statutory freeze mandated by the *Code*.

For further discussion of problems relating to retroactivity, see Chapter 22.8.

3.3　SETTLEMENT OF THE GRIEVANCE

It is well established as a matter of law and of policy that, where a grievance has been settled, an arbitrator's jurisdiction is normally limited to determining whether or not the terms of the settlement have been complied with. The case which has been cited most frequently in support of this proposition is *Zehrs Markets and Retail Clerks Union, Local 1977* (1984), 14 L.A.C. (3d) 379 (Barton).

Expanding upon this viewpoint in *Canada Post Corp. and C.U.P.W. (Winlaw)* (1993), 36 L.A.C. (4th) 216, Arbitrator Tom Jolliffe affirmed the following principles:

(1) Where a settlement has clearly been reached, that is the end of the matter; neither party may back away from it at a later date.

(2) As long as the settlement is reached by persons with actual or apparent authority, it binds both the employer and the union.

(3) It is immaterial that the settlement might not have been entered into if one of the parties possessed more information at the time the settlement was reached.

(4) Failure by a party to include all items that could have been included is not a "mutual mistake" going to the root of the settlement.

(5) The settlement need not have been arrived at during a formal meeting pursuant to the grievance procedure.

In the case before Arbitrator Jolliffe, the union sought to reopen the terms of a settlement to which it had agreed. There was no allegation that the employer had engaged in misrepresentation. As for the union's argument that the parties made a mutual mistake invalidating the settlement, the arbitrator held that that doctrine applied only where there had been a fundamental misunderstanding; the mere fact that the union overlooked certain aspects of the compensation owing to the grievor did not suffice.

It has also been held that a letter from the union to the employer setting out the details of an oral agreement constituted a "written settlement" within the meaning of Ontario's *Labour Relations Act*, S.O. 1995, c. 1, Sch. A, such that an arbitrator had authority to enforce the agreement. As there had been a "meeting of the minds", a joint memorandum of settlement was not necessary, and the employer was not permitted to resile from its offer: *Ralston (Canada) Inc. and C.E.P., Local 819* (2000), 90 L.A.C. (4th) 47 (Shime), affirmed [2001] O.J. No. 2195 (QL) (Div. Ct.).

A.G. Simpson Co. and C.A.W., Local 222 (1996), 58 L.A.C. (4th) 411 (Kennedy) is authority for the proposition that, where the union settles a claim in favour of a particular grievor, the settlement bars the potential claims of other grievors with respect to a closely-related matter. In that case, the parties settled a number of grievances alleging discrimination by the employer on the basis of sex by conferring retroactive seniority on a number of the grievors, contrary to the collective agreement. A group of employees whose seniority ranking had, as a consequence, been diminished filed grievances of their own. In the settlement agreement, the union accepted that "all grievances on this subject (whether or not they have actually been commenced) will be withdrawn and deemed to be fully resolved". This agreement did not make explicit that any grievances with respect to seniority rights — as opposed to further grievances with respect to discrimination — would be barred. Arbitrator Kennedy nonetheless held that, subject to the grievors' right to file an unfair representation complaint, the union had the authority to foreclose their right of grievance in the course of settling the discrimination complaint.

Arbitrators have repeatedly emphasized the importance of holding parties to their settlements. In *Alcan Smelters & Chemicals Ltd. and C.A.W., Local*

2301 (1994), 46 L.A.C. (4th) 388 (Hope), the employer agreed to reinstate an employee who suffered from alcoholism, provided certain conditions were met (abstention from alcohol and completion of a treatment program). When the grievor failed to remain abstinent, he was refused admittance to the program, leading the employer to terminate his employment. The arbitrator rejected the union's argument that the settlement had been frustrated and was unenforceable, holding that the doctrine did not apply in circumstances where the source of the alleged frustration was, in effect, the grievor's own non-compliance with the reinstatement agreement.

In *Alberta (Department of Transportation) and A.U.P.E. (Hodge)* (2004), 135 L.A.C. (4th) 15, the settlement agreement did not contain a "confidentiality clause", and Arbitrator Francis Price rejected the employer's contention that the grievor's mocking and misleading characterization of the agreement over the workplace e-mail system undermined the integrity of the settlement. On the other hand, where the settlement agreement did contain a confidentiality clause, and the grievor was found to have violated the clause, the Ontario Grievance Settlement Board ruled that the only effective remedy was to order repayment of the settlement monies: *Ontario (Ministry of the Attorney General) and O.P.S.E.U.* (2004), 124 L.A.C. (4th) 382 (for further discussion, see Chapter 7.9).

A final consideration in the enforceability of settlements is the overriding effect of public statutes: see the discussion in Chapter 14.5 regarding the validity of last-chance agreements, in light of human rights legislation prohibiting discrimination based on disability.

3.4 WITHDRAWAL OF A PRIOR GRIEVANCE

The strict approach taken by arbitrators in favour of enforcing settlement agreements relates to "true" settlements between the parties, that is, agreed-upon resolutions of disputes in which each party receives some consideration or benefit. Where what is involved is simply a unilateral withdrawal or abandonment of the grievance, however, there is no blanket rule that a subsequent grievance raising the same issue is necessarily barred from proceeding. As Arbitrator Burkett explained in *Saint-Gobain Abrasives and C.E.P., Local 12* (2003), 120 L.A.C. (4th) 73, a grievance may be withdrawn for reasons other than acceptance of the other side's interpretation of the collective agreement. The question for the arbitrator in each case, therefore, is whether in all the circumstances the withdrawal or abandonment of the grievance could fairly have been relied upon by the other party as indicating acceptance of its position. Arbitrator Burkett added that the most common way for a grieving party to protect itself from such an inference is to withdraw the grievance on a "without prejudice" basis.

Where nothing has been given in exchange for the withdrawal, arbitrators have required evidence of prejudice or detrimental reliance before declining to deal with a subsequent grievance on its merits. In *Commercial Bakeries Corp. and C.A.W., Local 462* (2004), 126 L.A.C. (4th) 298 (Brunner), the union had withdrawn an earlier grievance similar to the one at hand, and founded on the same contracting out provisions. The arbitrator was satisfied that, on the previous occasion, the union had reviewed the facts put forward by the employer and concluded that management had acted within the parameters of the agreement. In the arbitrator's view, this did not preclude the union from bringing a fresh grievance at a different point in time, based on different facts.

Hyatt Regency Vancouver Hotel and Hotel, Restaurant & Culinary Employees & Bartenders Union, Local 40, [2004] B.C.C.A.A.A. No. 57 (QL) (Lanyon) represents a further extension of this principle of arbitral flexibility where a grievance has been withdrawn unilaterally. The union's business agent had decided to withdraw a discharge grievance. However, on hearing from the grievor's lawyer and obtaining legal advice of his own, the union's director of legal services reinstated the grievance. Arbitrator Lanyon ruled that the grievance had been withdrawn by mistake, and that s. 89(e) of the British Columbia *Labour Relations Code*, R.S.B.C. 1996, c. 244, empowering arbitrators to "relieve, on just and reasonable terms, against breaches of time limits *or other procedural requirements* set out in the collective agreement", allowed him to deal with the case on its merits. The alternative, Arbitrator Lanyon pointed out, was to bring the matter before the Labour Relations Board on the basis of an alleged breach of the duty of fair representation, a course of action which would likely result in the dispute being referred to arbitration in any event.

3.5 MOOTNESS

In many cases, an employer will take steps to provide the relief claimed in a grievance without actually admitting that the grievance has any merit. Where the employer's concession of the relief is unilateral and not part of an agreed settlement of the grievance, the union will sometimes press for an arbitral ruling on the merits, at which point the arbitrator must assess the issue of mootness, *i.e.* whether there is any practical importance in making a determination. In an early case, *Int'l Nickel Co. of Canada Ltd. and U.S.W.A.* (1972), 24 L.A.C. 51, a board of arbitration chaired by Paul Weiler ruled that the employer cannot necessarily, by granting the relief sought, avoid adjudication of an issue raised by the grievance which may be significant in the ongoing administration of the collective agreement.

On the facts in *Welland County Roman Catholic Separate School Board and O.E.C.T.A.* (1992), 30 L.A.C. (4th) 353, on the other hand, Arbitrator Brunner found that a declaration would serve no useful or practical purpose, "other than perhaps to score a debating point" for one side or the other in the forth-coming round of negotiations. The issue being moot, the grievance was ruled inarbitrable.

Adopting a test used by the courts, arbitrators have generally inquired whether a "live controversy" continues to exist. In *Toronto Star Newspapers Ltd. and C.E.P., Local 87-M* (2001), 98 L.A.C. (4th) 428 (Goodfellow), the employer offered "retention bonuses" to employees without first consulting with the union. When the union grieved, the employer withdrew its offer. Arbitrator Goodfellow concluded that the alleged violation occurred not just in the payment of the bonus, but in the offering of it. The union was entitled, therefore, to a determination as to whether what had taken place constituted improper interference with its status as exclusive bargaining agent.

Similarly, in *Securicor Canada Ltd. and C.A.W., Local 114*, [2004] C.L.A.D. No. 377 (QL) (Dorsey), the employer introduced a policy reducing staffing levels on armoured vehicles, then withdrew it in the face of the union's grievance and announced that implementation would be postponed until the next round of collective bargaining. The union sought a determination that the change would be unsafe, and Arbitrator James Dorsey ruled that, since the employer's intention to proceed was clear, the issue of safety was not moot.

In general terms, the granting of relief by the employer is less likely to lead to a finding of mootness where the grievance raises an underlying issue of contract interpretation that remains unresolved (unless the employer is prepared to concede that point as well: see *Atlantic Pilotage Authority and C.M.S.G.* (2004), 130 L.A.C. (4th) 204 (Christie)). In *Fraser Health Authority and B.C.N.U.* (2004), 134 L.A.C. (4th) 120 (Kinzie), for example, two nurses claimed overtime payment when their scheduled union leave was cancelled without the notice required by the collective agreement. The employer conceded the payment, but insisted that its decision did not set a precedent. The arbitrator distinguished the situation before him from a discharge case, in which reinstatement of the employee generally disposes of the substantive issue, and ruled that the union was entitled to a determination of the contract interpretation question.

3.6   MATTERS PREVIOUSLY DECIDED

3.6.1   *Res Judicata* and Issue Estoppel

Since the decision of the Ontario Court of Appeal in *Rasanen v. Rosemount Instruments Ltd.* (1994), 112 D.L.R. (4th) 683, the issues of "*res judicata*" and "issue estoppel" have received considerable attention from the courts and arbitrators. These doctrines were developed at common law in order to protect the integrity and finality of judicial decision-making (which includes administrative decision-making that is required to be made in a "judicial" manner), and to avoid duplicative litigation. In both cases, the basic principle is that an issue, once decided, should not be relitigated to the benefit of the losing party or to the harassment of the winning one. It may involve "claim" or "cause of action" estoppel, whereby an entire claim is found to be barred because it was disposed of in an earlier proceeding (*res judicata*); or it may be limited to certain constituent issues or material facts embraced by a previous decision (issue estoppel). The established requirements for the application of both *res judicata* and issue estoppel are:

(1) the same question was decided in a prior proceeding that had the authority to decide it;

(2) the decision which is said to create the estoppel was judicial in nature; and

(3) the parties to the decision, or their privies, were the same as those in the subsequent proceeding.

Another statement of the same principle is the rule against "collateral" (or "back-door") attack: that is, a judicial decision pronounced by a tribunal of competent jurisdiction ought not to be brought into question other than through an avenue of appeal or review expressly provided for that purpose.

The claimant in *Rasanen* was a senior executive whose position had been eliminated in the course of a corporate downsizing. The employer offered Rasanen two alternative managerial positions at the same rate of pay. The claimant, however, declined both offers, asserting that he had been constructively dismissed. Rasanen filed a claim under Ontario's employment standards legislation for termination pay and, as well, launched a civil action in court seeking damages for wrongful dismissal. After a full hearing, in which the claimant was represented against the employer by the Employment Standards Branch, a referee appointed pursuant to the legislation held that no termination pay was owing, since cause for discharge had been established. When Rasanen sought to pursue his wrongful dismissal action in the courts, the trial judge held that the claim, although without merit in any event, was barred on the basis of issue estoppel, *i.e.* the issue of cause for discharge had been decided, and Rasanen could not relitigate it. A majority of the Court of Appeal agreed, ruling that the three elements of the test had been met: the issue to be decided was essentially the same; Rasanen, through his privies, was represented in the earlier proceeding; and the decision was final, since Rasanen had not exercised his right to seek judicial review of the referee's decision.

In response to the submission that the proceedings before the referee could not be equated to those of the courts, and the referee's ruling was thus not a "judicial" decision, Justice Abella stated in very strong terms (at pp. 704-705):

> This is an argument, in my opinion, which seriously misperceives the role and function of administrative tribunals. They were expressly created as independent bodies for the purpose of being an alternative to the judicial process,

including its procedural panoplies. Designed to be less cumbersome, less expensive, less formal and less delayed, these impartial decision-making bodies were to resolve disputes in their area of specialization more expeditiously and more accessibly, but no less effectively or credibly . . .

. . .

As long as the hearing process in the tribunal provides parties with an opportunity to know and meet the case against them, and so long as the decision is within the tribunal's jurisdiction, then regardless of how closely the process mirrors a trial or its procedural antecedents, I can see no principled basis for exempting issues adjudicated by tribunals from the operation of issue estoppel in a subsequent action.

The *proviso* that the procedure adopted in the earlier proceeding meet the requirements of natural justice, *i.e.* due process, was echoed in the concurring reasons of Justice Morden.

In *Rasanen*, therefore, the Ontario Court of Appeal clearly recognized that *res judicata* or issue estoppel can apply to decisions by administrative tribunals. However, subsequent courts have since emphasized that the application of these doctrines is governed by an overriding consideration of fairness; moreover, they have held, there are other considerations which must be weighed, including the desirability of preserving the accessibility of administrative processes: see the remarks of Justice John Laskin in *Minott v. O'Shanter Development Co.* (1999), 42 O.R. (3d) 321 (C.A.).

These competing considerations have now been elaborated by the Supreme Court of Canada in *Danyluk v. Ainsworth Technologies Inc.* (2001), 201 D.L.R. (4th) 193. There, an employment standards officer (not an adjudicative "referee") had determined that the claimant was not entitled to $300,000 in commissions. As the officer's process was essentially "investigative", the claimant was not provided with information submitted to the officer by the employer. Despite these procedural flaws, the Ontario Court of Appeal was of the view that the requirements of issue estoppel had been satisfied. In particular, since the claimant had not exercised her statutory right to apply for an internal review, the officer's ruling was deemed to be final. Accordingly, the claimant's entitlement to commissions was not open to relitigation (or "collateral attack").

The Supreme Court of Canada disagreed. Despite the fact that the threefold test for issue estoppel had been satisfied, the Court declined to apply the doctrine to bar the claimant from proceeding with her action, since the proceeding before the employment standards officer had not conformed with the rules of natural justice. While affirming the importance of finality and avoidance of duplicative litigation, the Court emphasized the comments of the Ontario Court of Appeal in *Minott*, and indeed in *Rasanen*, that the application of so harsh a doctrine to the decisions of administrative tribunals is discretionary; that is, the outcome must rest on a determination of whether, in all the circumstances, it would be fair to hold a party to the decision in the earlier

proceeding. Without attempting to be exhaustive, the Court listed seven factors
which may be relevant in making this determination:

(1) whether the initial tribunal's governing statute contemplates parallel
    proceedings;

(2) whothor tho purpooo or foouo of tho two ooto of proooodingo io oimilor;

(3) whether the earlier process included a right of appeal that was not taken
    advantage of;

(4) whether the procedural safeguards in the earlier proceeding were ade-
    quate to ensure natural justice;

(5) whether the specialization or expertise of the first decision-maker is
    suited to making the determination called for in the subsequent inquiry;

(6) whether the earlier proceedings by their nature occurred at a time when
    the claimant was particularly vulnerable; and

(7) whether, having regard to all the circumstances, the strict application
    of the doctrine of estoppel would work an injustice.

Arbitrators, particularly in Ontario, have taken a similar approach: see, for
example, *Toronto Police Services Board and Toronto Police Ass'n* (1998), 71
L.A.C. (4th) 289 (Herman), decided before *Danyluk*, and *Metropolitan Hotel
and H.E.R.E., Local 75* (2002), 112 L.A.C. (4th) 252 (Springate), decided after.
Indeed, the current state of the law may be as expressed by the Ontario Superior Court in *D'Aoust v. 1374202 Ontario Inc.*, [2003] O.J. No. 2642 (QL). In
the Court's view, in order for issue estoppel to apply without working an unfairness, the prior administrative decision must have been based on "real evidence
heard under oath and subject to cross-examination" (at para. 53). A contrary
award, it might be noted, can be found in *Quinsam Coal Corp. and U.S.W.A.,
Local 9347* (2002), 111 L.A.C. (4th) 237 (Larson). In that case, after investigating a work refusal in a mine, an official representing British Columbia's
Chief Inspector of Mines determined that the work to which the grievor
objected was in fact safe. Arbitrator Larson ruled that he had no jurisdiction to
inquire into the validity of the work refusal, despite allegations by the union
that the inspector had violated the rules of natural justice and had failed to can-
vass all the issues. Adopting, in essence, the approach of the Ontario Court of
Appeal in *Danyluk*, the arbitrator concluded that the question raised by the
grievance had been substantially answered by the inspector, and that there was,
accordingly, "nothing left for [him] to decide" (p. 251).

Where a claim involves an alleged breach of a statute, concurrent proceedings are often instituted before an arbitrator and a specialized statutory tribunal.
Consequently, it is important to ascertain when an arbitration award can be
relied upon to establish a foundation for issue estoppel in a subsequent proceeding. The situation appears to arise most commonly in the case of alleged
violations of human rights legislation. Apart from arguments based on the fact

that the parties in each proceeding are differently constituted (the "mutuality" requirement), the applicability of issue estoppel is largely a function of whether the "same question" now before the human rights tribunal was previously determined by an arbitrator. In *Ford Motor Co. of Canada Ltd. v. Ontario (Human Rights Commission)* (2001), 209 D.L.R. (4th) 465, the Ontario Court of Appeal rejected the contention that issue estoppel should be applied to invalidate a decision by a human rights board of inquiry arising from the same factual matrix as that involved in a prior arbitration proceeding, since the arbitration award (which had been issued ten years earlier) did not on its face consider the allegation that the grievor's discharge was discriminatory. The Alberta Court of Appeal reached a similar conclusion in *Saggers v. Alberta (Human Rights Commission)* (2000), 193 D.L.R. (4th) 120, on the basis that the arbitration award dealt only with the employee's discrimination claim regarding physical disability, and did not appear to consider his claim of mental disability.

According to the Supreme Court in *Danyluk*, issue estoppel, when applicable, encompasses not only the precise issue before the tribunal in the prior proceeding, but also "the issues of fact, law, and mixed fact and law that are necessarily bound up with the determination of that 'issue' " (at p. 216). This principle was applied in *Canada Customs & Revenue Agency and Sherman* (2004), 132 L.A.C. (4th) 142 (P.S.S.R.B.), where the government had instructed a disabled employee not to report for work and eventually discharged her for non-disciplinary reasons. An "independent third-party reviewer" appointed by the government held a hearing into the matter, and overturned the discharge. In the opinion of the Public Service Staff Relations Board, hearing a grievance against the employee's removal from the workplace, it would be inappropriate to permit relitigation not only of the discharge, but of any of the essential facts which the union had been required to establish in the earlier proceeding.

It is doubtful, though, that a court ruling with respect to the admissibility of evidence creates an issue estoppel by which a subsequent board of arbitration will be bound. In *Greater Niagara Transit Commission v. A.T.U., Local 1582* (1987), 43 D.L.R. (4th) 71, where the board considered itself bound by a ruling in parallel criminal proceedings excluding certain evidence because the grievor's *Charter* rights had been infringed, and refused to admit the evidence, the Ontario Divisional Court, on review, quashed the award. Arbitrators, the Court held, enjoy an express statutory discretion to accept evidence whether or not it is admissible in a court of law, and it was a reviewable error for the board to have treated the earlier criminal court ruling as dispositive of the issue before it. In a similar vein, see *British Columbia (Attorney General) and B.C.G.E.U. (Fotheringham)* (1995), 51 L.A.C. (4th) 225 (Bruce).

One situation which is now subject to a quite different set of considerations is the arbitration of a discharge grievance involving alleged criminal misconduct, where a full criminal trial has taken place and a verdict of "guilty" has been rendered. In Ontario, the evidentiary effect of a criminal conviction on a subsequent civil proceeding is governed by the *Evidence Act*, R.S.O. 1990, c. E.23. Section 22.1 states that, "in the absence of evidence to the contrary", and provided no appeal is being pursued, a prior conviction is proof that the person committed the crime. The practice of arbitrators has thus been generally to treat a conviction as affording *prima facie* evidence that the offence was committed, while permitting the union to challenge the factual foundation of the conviction by adducing other evidence.

In *Toronto (City) v. C.U.P.E., Local 79* (2003), 232 D.L.R. (4th) 385 (S.C.C.), however, the Supreme Court of Canada severely restricted the circumstances in which a union is entitled, at arbitration, to relitigate the grievor's culpability. In the Court's view, even where the requirements of issue estoppel or *res judicata* have not been satisfied, the union should be precluded from disputing the facts underlying a criminal conviction if to permit relitigation of the issue would constitute an abuse of process. Only in three circumstances, the Court found, would an arbitrator be justified in declining to treat the conviction as conclusive proof of guilt:

(1) the first proceeding was tainted by fraud or dishonesty;

(2) fresh evidence that was previously unavailable conclusively impeaches the result of the original proceeding; or

(3) fairness dictates that the original result should not be binding in the subsequent proceeding.

It should be noted that, because of the higher standard of proof required in a criminal proceeding, a similar conclusion does not flow in the case of an acquittal; that is, acquittal on a criminal charge cannot be relied upon as a finding of innocence binding on the employer in a civil proceeding such as grievance arbitration: *Toronto (City) and Toronto Civic Employees Union, Local 416* (2004), 131 L.A.C. (4th) 188 (Randall). Nor can the dismissal of criminal charges for lack of evidence at a preliminary inquiry be taken as a finding of innocence binding in a subsequent civil proceeding: *Alberta and A.U.P.E. (Crepeau)* (2003), 124 L.A.C. (4th) 176 (Jolliffe).

The rationale for the Supreme Court of Canada's ruling in *Toronto (City)*, as Arbitrator Oakley pointed out in *Newfoundland & Labrador Housing Corp. and C.U.P.E., Local 1860* (2004), 127 L.A.C. (4th) 353, is to avoid bringing the administration of justice into disrepute as a result of inconsistent decisions. However, this rationale does not necessarily preclude the employer from revisiting the facts underlying a criminal conviction. The *Newfoundland & Labrador Housing Corp.* case involved four separate criminal charges, only one of which (common assault) led to a finding of guilt. The arbitrator ruled that it was open to the employer not only to call evidence relating to the offences of which the grievor was acquitted, but also evidence indicating that the assault was more serious than the trial judge had found.

Additional Reading

T. Archibald, *"Toronto (City) v. C.U.P.E., Local 79*: The End of Relitigation?" (2005), 12 Canadian Labour and Employment Law Journal, p. 65.

S.C. Doyle, "The Discretionary Aspect of Issue Estoppel: What Does *Danyluk* Add?" (2002), 9 Canadian Labour and Employment Journal, p. 295.

C. Flood, "Efficiency v. Fairness: Multiple Litigation and Adjudication in Labour & Employment Law" (2000), 8 Canadian Labour and Employment Journal, p. 383.

J.E. Goodman, "Approach with Caution: Issue Estoppel and Employment Insurance Adjudications" (2000), 8 Canadian Labour and Employment Journal, p. 461.

3.6.2 Arbitral Deference to Prior Awards

While there is no doctrine of precedent, or *stare decisis*, obliging one arbitrator to follow the decision of another, arbitrators are of the view that, for the sake of consistency and predictability, an award involving the same parties should be followed, even if the same grievor is not involved, unless the second arbitrator has a "clear conviction that it is wrong". This principle, which was first advanced by Arbitrator Bora Laskin in *Brewers' Warehousing Co. Ltd. and Int'l Union of Brewery, Flour, Cereal, Malt, Yeast, Soft Drink & Distillery Workers of America, Local 278C* (1954), 5 L.A.C. 1797, has been repeatedly adopted and applied, although the words used to articulate the test have, without any discernible difference in meaning, undergone some variation over the years.

The precise difference between *res judicata* or issue estoppel and the arbitral principle of deference was explained by Arbitrator Liang in *Stelco Inc. and U.S.W.A., Local 1005* (1999), 82 L.A.C. (4th) 120, as follows: "while arbitrators appear prepared to use the language of *res judicata* when a grievance is an attempt to reopen or reprocess an earlier grievance which has already been decided, in most cases, they prefer to see the matter as grounded in their *discretion* rather than the application of a mandatory bar" (at p. 125; emphasis in original). In this case, since the facts could not be meaningfully distinguished from those giving rise to the earlier grievance, and the issue in dispute had already been determined at arbitration, Arbitrator Liang concluded that the usual rule of deference applied. She therefore declined to inquire into the matter, and denied the grievance.

Arbitrator Keller, in *Canada Safeway Ltd. and U.F.C.W., Local 175/633* (2004), 128 L.A.C. (4th) 175, emphasized the policy reasons for according deference to prior arbitration awards involving the same parties, particularly the importance of providing finality to disputes.

3.7   *FUNCTUS OFFICIO* – MANDATE SPENT

According to the doctrine of *functus officio*, once an arbitrator has issued a final award, his or her jurisdiction is exhausted and the award cannot be altered, except to correct a clerical error. The arbitrator cannot subsequently clarify a finding already made or interpret the award for the parties. The leading case in this area is *Consumer's Gas and Int'l Chemical Workers' Union, Local 161* (1974), 6 L.A.C. (2d) 61 (Weatherill), which affirms that the doctrine of *functus officio* applies to labour arbitrators. At the same time, however, Arbitrator Weatherill noted that, before an award can be considered final, it must contain "unambiguous and enforceable language". A simple direction, for example, that a grievor "is to be reinstated and compensated" would not meet that test; in such circumstances, an arbitrator would retain jurisdiction to provide more particulars if required, even without an express reservation to that effect.

A similar view was expressed by the British Columbia Labour Relations Board in *Gearmatic Co. and U.S.W.A., Local 6613*, [1978] 1 Can. L.R.B.R. 502. In the Board's view, consistent with the authority of arbitrators under the *Labour Relations Code*, now R.S.B.C. 1996, c. 244, to provide a final and conclusive settlement of a dispute, according to its real substance, it was appropriate to accord to arbitrators some flexibility in "completing" the original award. At the same time, the Board cautioned, there was a need for and a belief in the finality of a decision, once rendered. Accordingly, it was inappropriate and contrary to the provisions of the *Code* for an arbitrator, having made an award, to issue another decision "representing a wholesale change of mind". The Board also noted that, in accordance with cases decided by the courts, a decision is deemed to have been issued "when the arbitrator has done all that he can do, namely, reduce[d] it to writing, and published it as his award" (at p. 509).

It is, therefore, open to an arbitrator to address an issue that has not been dealt with, or to complete an award that is not final. In this regard, the prevailing view is that no explicit reservation of jurisdiction is necessary to enable an arbitration board to complete its award, and to rule on any unresolved issues fairly raised by the grievance. In *Inmet Mining Corp. and U.S.W.A., Local 4464* (1998), 78 L.A.C. (4th) 175, for instance, Arbitrator Harris ruled that this principle extends to the granting of a monetary remedy following the conclusion of the initial hearing on the merits of a grievance. As noted by the arbitrator, it is the practice in labour relations to sever consideration of compensatory issues from the merits.

In *Toronto (City) and C.U.P.E., Local 416* (2002), 113 L.A.C. (4th) 282, upon concluding that the grievor's claim for long-term disability benefits was meritorious, Arbitrator Starkman remained seized of the matter in order to address any difficulties in "implementation". While a claim for interest was set out in the grievance, and adverted to at the hearing, the award did not mention interest. Dismissing the employer's objection that he was *functus officio*, and thus without authority to determine the union's request for payment of interest, the arbitrator ruled that he had retained jurisdiction to "complete" his award with respect to all issues in dispute.

Kingston (City) and O.N.A. (1996), 55 L.A.C. (4th) 148 (H.D. Brown), on the other hand, makes it clear that, once a board has dealt with the factual situation encompassed in a grievance, the jurisdiction of the board is exhausted, and does not extend to providing a remedy in respect of subsequent breaches of the collective agreement, even if they are identical to the one prompting the original grievance. Nor does an arbitrator retain jurisdiction to reconsider an award on the basis that new developments in the caselaw may render it unlawful or unenforceable: *Maple Leaf Meats and U.F.C.W., Local 832* (1997), 68 L.A.C. (4th) 95 (Teskey).

Finally, it should be noted that interest arbitrators, whose role it is to fashion the terms of a collective agreement, have more flexibility, and interest arbitration legislation in Ontario now generally provides that they retain jurisdiction until a collective agreement is signed: see, for example, the *Hospital Labour Disputes Arbitration Act*, R.S.O. 1990, c. H.14, s. 9(2).

3.8　DISCHARGE OF PROBATIONARY EMPLOYEES

Recognizing the fundamental purpose of a probation period, collective agreements often include a provision denying probationary employees who are dismissed the benefit of full just cause protection and access to the grievance and arbitration procedures. Whether, and the extent to which, such provisions may be given effect has been the subject of much debate. The decisions of the courts have been particularly influential in this area. The problem, however, has been that the courts' interpretations of the applicable labour relations statute have not always been consistent. The New Brunswick *Public Service Labour Relations Act*, R.S.N.B. 1973, c. P-25, the governing statute in *New Brunswick v. Leeming* (1981), 118 D.L.R. (3d) 202 (S.C.C.), effectively provided that *every* employee had the right to refer to adjudication a grievance against disciplinary action or discharge. However, when an adjudicator held that he had jurisdiction to hear the grievance of a probationary employee who had been dismissed, the Supreme Court of Canada disagreed, ruling that the provisions of the Act "do not purport to confer substantive rights upon employees in addition to their rights as defined in the collective agreement" (at p. 206). Reading the collective agreement as a whole, the Court held that it granted the employer the right to dismiss a probationary employee without having to show just cause.

Since that time, however, the courts, especially in Ontario, have tended to focus on the usual statutory mandate for "the final and binding settlement by arbitration . . . of all differences" between the parties. Such provisions have been read as limiting the application of the Supreme Court's ruling in *Leeming* to strictly substantive rights, as distinct from procedural ones. See *Toronto Hydro-Electric System v. C.U.P.E., Local 1* (1980), 111 D.L.R. (3d) 693 (Ont. Div. Ct.), affirmed (1980), 113 D.L.R. (3d) 512n. (Ont. C.A.); and *Ontario Hydro v. Ontario Hydro Employees' Union, Local 1000* (1983), 147 D.L.R. (3d) 210 (Ont. C.A.). Therefore, where on a reading of the collective agreement as a whole, it is found that a probationary employee enjoys substantive rights in regard to dismissal, but is barred from asserting those rights through the grievance procedure, the procedural bar is deemed to be void as contrary to the governing statute. It may be noted that the courts in Nova Scotia go even further, having taken the view that *any* attempt to limit the rights of probationers in a discharge situation is contrary to the statute (although it is not clear how such a view can be reconciled with the decision of the Supreme Court in *Leeming*). See *Halifax (City) v. I.A.F.F., Local 268* (1982), 131 D.L.R. (3d) 426 (N.S.C.A.). Appellate courts in Newfoundland and New Brunswick take opposite positions: compare *N.A.P.E. v. Newfoundland (Treasury Board)* (2003), 227 Nfld. & P.E.I.R. 37 (Nfld. and Labrador C.A.), following *Ontario Hydro*, and *Noranda Mining and Exploration Inc. v. U.S.W.A., Local 5385* (2003), 258 N.B.R. (2d) 324 (C.A.), holding that the probationers in that case were not entitled to any level of substantive "just cause" protection.

The development of the law was traced in *Abitibi Consolidated Ltd. and C.E.P., Local 92* (1998), 75 L.A.C. (4th) 414 (Mitchnick). While determining that he could give effect to the clear intent of the parties that the release of a probationary employee not be subject in every case to the full just cause standard, Arbitrator Mitchnick concluded that management nonetheless bears a duty to exercise its discretion in a manner that is not arbitrary, discriminatory, or in bad faith. However, unlike cases involving the discharge of an employee who has completed his or her probation, it is the union which bears the onus of proving that management's exercise of its discretion was improper. This was the essence of the judgment of the Ontario Divisional Court in *Brampton Hydro Electric Commission v. C.A.W., Local 1285* (1993), 108 D.L.R. (4th) 168 (although, in a recent judgment, the New Brunswick Court of Appeal appeared to disagree that there exists such a lesser, implied limitation on the employer: see *Noranda Mining and Exploration, supra*). Furthermore, an apparently unrestricted management right to discharge probationary employees may be subject to arbitral review on the ground that the employer has infringed protections accorded to employees under a statute: see *Parry Sound (District) Social Services Administration Board v. O.P.S.E.U., Local 324* (2003), 230 D.L.R. (4th) 257 (S.C.C.), discussed in Chapter 1.2.3. In addition, the Ontario Court of Appeal has ruled, in *Loyalist College of Applied Arts and Technology v. O.P.S.E.U.* (2003), 225 D.L.R. (4th) 123, that an employer cannot dismiss a probationary employee in reliance on a pre-employment hiring condition that is illegal or in conflict with the collective agreement: see Chapter 3.1.2.

The difference between the normal just cause test and the more limited scope of review to be applied to probationary employees was extensively considered in *McRae Waste Management and I.U.O.E., Local 115* (1998), 71 L.A.C. (4th) 197 (Sanderson). The arbitrator noted that, where the collective agreement specifically confers on the employer a discretion to dismiss an employee during his or her probationary period, management is free to determine what standards or qualifications are required for the job. If management determines in a manner that is not arbitrary, discriminatory or in bad faith, or based on a misapprehension of the facts, that the employee is unsuitable when measured against those standards, it is not the role of an arbitrator to substitute his or her judgment as to whether discharge was justified.

A similar statement of the applicable standard of arbitral review can be found in the Ontario case of *Thunder Bay (City) and I.B.E.W., Local 339*, [2004] O.L.A.A. No. 412 (QL) (Brandt).

On the other hand, even where the just cause standard is found not to apply, it is well established that the employer is required to set out clearly the expectations which employees on probation must meet, to provide them with a fair opportunity to satisfy those expectations, and to assess work performance in a fair and objective manner. Failure to do so may result in the reversal of a termination decision on the ground that the employer has acted arbitrarily or in bad faith: see *Jeanne Sauvé Family Services and O.P.S.E.U. (Bouvier)*, [2004] O.L.A.A. No. 8 (QL) (Samuels); and *Venice Bakery Ltd. and U.F.C.W., Local 1518*, [1995] B.C.C.A.A.A. No. 137 (QL) (Kinzie).

3.9 INSURED BENEFIT PLANS

The widespread involvement of insurance companies in the administration of employee benefit programs has been the source of considerable controversy relating to the employer's liability for a disputed claim as well as the availability of arbitration as a forum for adjudicating the dispute. Without the consent of all interested parties, an arbitrator's jurisdiction is invariably limited by statute to disputes which arise from the interpretation, application, administration or alleged violation of the collective agreement. The intermediacy of an insurance carrier in the processing of claims for sick leave payments, health and welfare benefits, or short-term or long-term disability support may put the dispute beyond an arbitrator's jurisdiction for two interrelated reasons. First, whereas the employer is a party to the collective agreement, against whom the arbitrator has authority to make a remedial order, the insurer is not. Second, the dispute as to an employee's entitlement may derive from the proper

application of an insurance policy. Unless the policy bears a sufficiently prox-
imate relationship to the collective agreement, the employer bears no contractual responsibility for denial of the claim. Again, the authority of the arbitrator
is restricted to enforcing a bargain struck by the employer and the union, the
parties that are signatories to the agreement.

Where an arbitrator concludes that the collective agreement does not furnish a sufficient foundation to justify inquiring into an employee's claim, and
that any liability which may exist is solely that of the insurer, the employee's
only recourse is to sue the insurer in the courts. In light of the cost and inconvenience of this mode of enforcement, unions have, as a rule, sought to maximize the range of disputes which can be brought to arbitration. Employers,
conversely, have normally resisted what they perceive as an attempt to expand
the scope of their negotiated obligations.

As a guideline to assist in resolving challenges to their jurisdiction, arbitrators had by the 1980s widely accepted the so-called Brown and Beatty "four
categories" approach. Derived from the text by D.J.M. Brown and D.M. Beatty,
Canadian Labour Arbitration, the "four categories" approach attempts to
schematize the various situations in which a grievance can or cannot be brought
directly against the employer for payment of a benefit. The categories are:

(1) A benefit plan or policy exists, but it is not mentioned in the collective
    agreement.

(2) The collective agreement specifically provides for the payment of a
    benefit in certain circumstances.

(3) The collective agreement stipulates that the employer must provide a
    particular type of benefit plan, and that the employer will pay the req-
    uisite premiums.

(4) An insurance policy or benefit plan is incorporated by reference into
    the collective agreement.

In the first category, there is no basis for employer liability under the agreement and the matter is inarbitrable. In category two, a grievance can be brought
against the employer for failing to provide the benefit, whether or not the
employer has taken out an insurance policy to cover the cost of the benefit. Similarly, under the fourth category, because the terms of the plan form part of the
collective agreement, a dispute concerning an employee's entitlement can be
heard at arbitration, and the employer is liable for any breaches of the plan. A
conclusion that the policy falls within the third category, however, has the
effect of limiting arbitrable claims to those in which it is alleged that the
employer has failed to provide the specific insurance policy or plan contemplated by the agreement. In such cases, it has been held that the employer did
not intend to assume the obligations of an insurer, and therefore that a grievance does not lie against the employer for a denial of benefits under the policy.

The "four categories" and the underlying principles are set out in the frequently cited case of *Andres Wines (B.C.) Ltd. and United Brewery Workers, Local 300* (1981), 30 L.A.C. (2d) 259 (Christie).

The "four categories" are, however, only a guideline, and it is not always easy to fit the dispute into one of them. In the leading case of *Coca-Cola Bottling Ltd. and U.F.C.W. (Boud)* (1994), 44 L.A.C. (4th) 151 (Swan), the arbitrator emphasized that, while the categories may be of assistance, the fundamental task is to determine what the parties actually intended. Was it within their contemplation that the employer would bear primary liability for the payment of benefits, whether or not it chose to reduce its risk by taking out a policy of insurance, or did they intend that the employer could fully meet its obligation by purchasing a specified type of plan, which would be administered by an outside carrier?

The validity of the traditional "four categories" as an index to issues of arbitrability and employer liability has recently been affirmed by the courts, following a period of confusion sparked by the decision of the Ontario Court of Appeal in *Pilon v. Int'l Minerals and Chemical Corp. (Canada) Ltd.* (1996), 141 D.L.R. (4th) 72. In *Pilon*, an employee brought an action in the courts challenging the decision of an insurance carrier to deny his claim for long-term disability benefits. While, under the "four categories" approach, a claim against the employer may or may not have been arbitrable, the employee's suit in any event was directed solely against the insurer (as expressly permitted by the Ontario *Insurance Act*, R.S.O. 1990, c. I.8). Notwithstanding that fact, the Court struck out the action, purporting to apply the Supreme Court of Canada's ruling in *Weber v. Ontario Hydro* (1995), 125 D.L.R. (4th) 583 (see Chapter 1.3) that arbitrators have exclusive jurisdiction to consider any claim which arises expressly or inferentially out of the collective agreement. In the Court's view, because the employee would have had no claim for the disputed benefit but for the collective agreement, an arbitrator — and not the courts — had exclusive jurisdiction over the dispute.

Some arbitrators, taking *Pilon* at face value, followed the Court of Appeal's decision and ruled that, if the benefit in dispute would not have existed but for the provisions of the collective agreement, an employee was entitled to make a claim directly against the insurer through the grievance and arbitration procedures. This was the holding, in particular, in *Honeywell Ltd. and C.A.W.* (1997), 65 L.A.C. (4th) 37 (Mitchnick), and *Dubreuil Forest Products Ltd. and I.W.A., Local 2693*, unreported, June 12, 1998 (Bendel).

In a pair of companion decisions, however, the reasons for which are set out in *London Life Insurance Co. v. I.W.A., Local 2693* (2000), 190 D.L.R. (4th) 428, the Ontario Court of Appeal upheld judgments of the Divisional Court quashing the *Honeywell* and *Dubreuil Forest Products* awards. The Court asserted that its earlier decision in *Pilon* should not be read as intended in any way to change the law relating to the arbitrability of benefit claims. Rather, the

Court explained, its earlier decision was to be read simply as a finding that the facts in that case gave rise to a "category four" situation, effecting an incorporation by reference. Accordingly, where, as in *Honeywell* and *Dubreuil Forest Products*, the collective agreement merely obligated the employer to purchase a policy of insurance administered by an outside carrier, an arbitrator has no jurisdiction to hear disputes respecting an individual employee's entitlement. Nor, it followed, did an arbitrator have authority to add the insurer as a third-party "defendant" to the arbitration proceedings.

As noted by Arbitrator Christie in *Pepsi Bottling Group and C.A.W., Local 1015* (2001), 102 L.A.C. (4th) 118, the decision of the Court of Appeal in *Pilon* to deny the plaintiff access to the courts was probably incorrect. However, by choosing in *London Life Insurance* to uphold *Pilon* on the basis that the facts in that case indicated a "category four" arrangement, the Court has stimulated a reconsideration of the language required in a collective agreement to effect an incorporation by reference, and thus to render the employer liable for the denial of a benefit by the insurer. Reflecting a perhaps more conservative approach than he took previously in *Coca-Cola Bottling Ltd. and R.W.D.S.U., Local 1065* (1998), 76 L.A.C. (4th) 104, Arbitrator Christie pointed out in *Pepsi Bottling Group* that the mere acknowledgment in a collective agreement that another document exists or may come into existence does not amount to an incorporation by reference.

The British Columbia Court of Appeal, in *Elkview Coal Corp. v. U.S.W.A., Local 9346* (2001), 205 D.L.R. (4th) 80, approached the matter somewhat differently. The dispute in that case arose when the insurer denied an employee's request that coverage be extended to her same-sex partner as a dependant, and the union grieved that the definition of "common law spouse" in the plan violated human rights legislation. The Court held that the dispute did not, in its essential character, arise from the collective agreement, and was inarbitrable. The employer's only obligation under the collective agreement, the Court found, was to pay the necessary premiums for an insurance policy that would provide the negotiated benefits, the nature and extent of which had been agreed to by the union. Moreover, the union had the policy in its possession before the collective agreement was signed, and made no objection to either the plan or the language used by the insurer to describe the benefit. Therefore, the Court ruled, there was no issue as between the union and the employer that was properly referable to arbitration, and any dispute over the legality of the plan was exclusively between the union and the insurer.

It may be that the *Elkview Coal* decision reflects the view articulated by Arbitrator Swan in *Coca-Cola Bottling*, *supra*, that "it is unlikely that the employer would willingly place itself in a position of both paying premiums to an insurer to have these benefits provided, while taking on primary liability for the payment of the benefits in any case" (at p. 157). That is, where the parties have clearly contemplated the provision of benefits by way of an insurance policy, the focus of arbitration will be limited to an examination of the policy obtained by the employer, to ensure that it meets the requirements of the collective agreement as to coverage.

Whether or not the Ontario Court of Appeal's decision in *Pilon*, *supra*, was correct, it had the benefit of fixing liability for a claim ultimately found valid at arbitration where the parties had intended it: on the insurer. See *Clarington (Municipality) and C.U.P.E., Local 74* (1999), 83 L.A.C. (4th) 27 (Mitchnick). In view of the same Court's subsequent decision in *London Life Insurance*, the only recourse left to the union, if it wishes to be able to arbitrate the denial of an insured benefit claim, is to negotiate a provision in the collective agreement expressly making the denial of an insured benefit claim subject to arbitration.

However, as the award in *Hôtel-Dieu Grace Hospital and O.N.A. (Beaudet)*, [2004] O.L.A.A. No. 458 (QL) (Hunter) emphasizes, referring the matter to an arbitration proceeding in which the insurance carrier is not a party may produce a perverse result. In that case, although decisions regarding eligibility for long-term disability benefits were made by the insurance company, the collective agreement expressly provided that disputes over entitlement could be dealt with through the grievance and arbitration procedures. Arbitrator Hunter allowed a grievance seeking payment of benefits, holding that the grievor was "totally disabled" within the meaning of the policy, and further that the insurer's refusal of the claim was unreasonable, high-handed and arbitrary. In the result, the employer was ordered to pay the monies owing to the grievor, plus interest, pursuant to its obligations under the collective agreement. However, despite the fact that the insurance company was found to have acted in bad faith, a claim for punitive damages was denied. The arbitrator reluctantly concluded that he had no jurisdiction to award such damages against the insurer because it was not a party to the collective agreement, and that the hospital — which had itself acted properly in processing the claim — should not be deemed the guarantor of good-faith conduct by its insurance carrier.

Thus, the employer, if it is the responsible party under the collective agreement, may have had no role in the insurer's decision to deny the claim, but nevertheless assumes potential liability for the full cost of the benefits, over and above the premiums it has paid. At the same time, an employee with a meritorious claim for punitive damages may be left with no recourse against the offending party.

The situation may be different in cases where the insurance policy has been found to be incorporated in the collective agreement (a "category four" arrangement). In *Rivtow Marine Inc. and I.U.O.E., Local 115*, [2005] C.L.A.D. No. 17 (QL), Arbitrator Glass, citing *Pilon* as authority, asserted jurisdiction to join the insurance company and its benefits administrator as parties to the arbitration proceedings.

Additional Reading

S. Tacon, "Arbitrating Insured Benefit Disputes: An Arbitrator's Perspective" in K. Whitaker, J. Sack, M. Gunderson & R. Filion, eds., *Labour Arbitration Yearbook 1999-2000*, vol. II, p. 251; and companion articles by M.A. Brunsdon and D. Wright.

CHAPTER 4

PRE-HEARING PROCEDURE

4.1 ENTITLEMENT TO NOTICE/STATUS

Under the labour relations legislation of all Canadian jurisdictions, it is the union and the employer who are parties to a collective agreement, and with few exceptions only they may refer a grievance to arbitration. Unless the collective agreement specifically provides otherwise, an individual employee cannot file a grievance independently of the union, and a grievor cannot claim status as a party to the proceedings independently of the union. For an analysis of a union's duty to fairly represent bargaining unit members in the grievance and arbitration process, see Chapter 9.

There may be circumstances, however, where employees other than the grievor could be affected by an arbitration award and whose legitimate interests the union has chosen not to represent. Two early appellate court decisions, *Hoogendoorn v. Greening Metal Products & Screening Equipment Co.* (1967), 65 D.L.R. (2d) 641 (S.C.C.), and *Bradley v. Ottawa Professional Fire Fighters Ass'n* (1967), 63 D.L.R. (2d) 376 (Ont. C.A.), are generally considered to have established the guidelines for determining when individual employees in the bargaining unit are entitled to receive notice of an arbitration proceeding that may directly affect them, and to fully participate as a party should they so choose. In *Hoogendoorn*, the arbitrator upheld a policy grievance in which the union demanded the dismissal of an employee who, contrary to the collective agreement, refused to authorize the deduction of union dues. *Bradley* involved the grievances of a group of employees who had been passed over in a job competition. Allowing the grievances, the arbitrator ordered the employer to promote the grievors to the positions awarded to the successful applicants, thus displacing them from their jobs. In neither case had the employee(s) whose interest was in jeopardy been afforded notice of the arbitration hearing. The awards were quashed, the Court in both instances ruling that the individual employees were entitled to notice and the right to participate as parties. Of particular importance, in the view of the Court, was the fact that the statutory bargaining agent was taking a position contrary to the employees' interests (as was the employer, in the case of *Hoogendoorn*), and that those interests were directly the subject-matter of the proceedings.

In *Orillia Soldiers' Memorial Hospital and O.N.A.* (1993), 34 L.A.C. (4th) 315, a layoff case, Arbitrator Swan considered the rights of junior employees into whose positions the grievors wanted to bump. Whereas the job competition in *Bradley* was governed by a so-called "competition clause", in accordance with which each applicant had the right to have his relative ability evaluated in relation to other applicants, bumping rights in *Orillia Soldiers' Memorial Hospital* were governed by a "threshold clause". The clause provided that, if the senior employee was capable of doing the work, she was entitled to the job. Notwithstanding this difference in the weight accorded to seniority, Arbitrator Swan followed the general arbitral practice of giving notice, at the employer's request, to any employee who might be affected by the successful exercise of bumping rights. Employees, he held, were entitled "to participate in the hearing to the extent that such participation is consistent with the nature of the rights which they are entitled to protect" (at p. 332). The arbitrator's conclusion leaves the ultimate question of the extent of participation somewhat unresolved, but the Ontario Divisional Court has upheld the award: see [1997] O.J. No. 825 (QL).

However, other arbitrators have had difficulty reconciling *Hoogendoorn* and *Bradley* with the ruling in *Syndicat Catholique des Employés de Magasins de Québec Inc. v. Cie Paquet Ltée* (1959), 18 D.L.R. (2d) 346 (S.C.C.), as adopted by Chief Justice Laskin in *McGavin Toastmaster Ltd. v. Ainscough* (1975), 54 D.L.R. (3d) 1 (S.C.C.). The latter cases emphasize that the introduction of collective bargaining, which elevated trade unions to the status of exclusive bargaining agent, has effectively supplanted individual employment contracts. Because the extension of party status to individual employees could have a serious impact on grievance arbitration, prolonging proceedings and increasing costs, some arbitrators have limited the application of *Hoogendoorn* and *Bradley* to cases that are precisely identical to them on the facts. This line of awards was reviewed in *John Noble Home and O.N.A., Local 102* (1994), 39 L.A.C. (4th) 324, also a case involving bumping rights, where Arbitrator Mitchnick rejected the employer's assertion that the right to notice and standing should be extended to any nurse who could be affected by the ruling. With respect, for example, to seniority-based issues such as promotion, the board drew a distinction between the effect of a "competition" clause (which permits the successful applicant for a job posting to intervene and contest the grievor's claim) and a "threshold" provision (which does not). In this instance, since bumping rights were based entirely on seniority, and the applicable clause made no reference to minimum qualifications, the rights of junior nurses were purely "contingent" in nature. The board held, accordingly, that any requests for standing would be considered only on a case-by-case basis.

In a decision dated January 29, 2002, *Ontario and A.M.A.P.C.E.O.*, where the provision in question was, again, a threshold clause, Arbitrator Mitchnick noted that the number of employees whose job ranking stood to be affected by the employer's decision could be substantial. However, none of the other employees in the "daisy chain", the arbitrator held, possessed an independent right capable of being asserted: the union alone had the right to participate in the hearing, as well as the duty to decide which of the employees' claims were paramount.

In *Regina Qu'Appelle Health Region and C.U.P.E., Local 3967* (2004), 127 L.A.C. (4th) 325 (Pelton), the dispute did not involve conflicting claims under a seniority clause, but a claim by one employee to revert to her job following a trial period in another position, and a competing claim by the new incumbent, who had been transferred into the job in order to accommodate her disability. The arbitrator ruled that, given the distinct nature of the claims, and the fact that one of them raised a human rights issue, both employees ought to have standing to present their cases. In *Thunder Bay Regional Hospital and O.N.A.* (2004), 129 L.A.C. (4th) 106, by contrast, the issue was whether a position was included in the scope of the bargaining unit. Arbitrator Davie rejected the incumbent's request for intervenor status, ruling that the employee had nothing to add which could not be presented by the union and the employer.

In an increasing number of cases, such as those involving allegations of sexual harassment, it is a member of management who claims the right to independent representation. Where the allegations are serious, and the interests of the individual may not necessarily be aligned with those of the employer, arbitrators have been inclined to grant full party status: *Andromeda Productions Ltd. and I.A.T.S.E., Local 891* (2001), 94 L.A.C. (4th) 405 (McPhillips). Arbitrator McPhillips, having decided that the granting of party status was appropriate, stated that the apportionment of costs was best left for assessment after the proceedings had been completed. (Section 90(1)(c) of the British Columbia *Labour Relations Code*, R.S.B.C. 1996, c. 244, specifically authorizes arbitrators to order a third party to pay a portion of the costs of the hearing.)

Where the union alleges that the employer has assigned work in a manner that contravenes the collective agreement, the purported intervenor is likely to be another trade union, asserting its competing rights in what is essentially a jurisdictional dispute. The participation of a union as a third party has raised several additional problems which arbitrators have had to address. For example, an arbitrator's remedial jurisdiction is normally limited to the parties under whose collective agreement he or she has been appointed. Similarly, the union requesting intervenor status may wish to hold in reserve the right to file a parallel grievance under its own collective agreement, and accordingly be unwilling to agree that the first arbitrator's decision will be determinative. Arbitrators have thus been required to focus on the *effect* of a third-party's participation in the proceedings, while trying to accomplish what the courts have described as "a practical, common-sense compulsion to put all these parties in one room, before one tribunal, to obtain one ruling on their differences": *C.U.P.E. v. Canadian Broadcasting Corp.* (1990), 70 D.L.R. (4th) 175 (Ont. C.A.), at p. 177.

In *Weston Bakeries Ltd. and Milk & Bread Drivers, Dairy Employees, Caterers & Allied Employees, Local 647* (1999), 79 L.A.C. (4th) 189, Arbitrator Gray concluded that nothing in the rules of natural justice permitted an intervenor to claim the advantages of party status without accepting the corresponding burdens. In the result, he made the intervenor's right to participate conditional on its undertaking:

(a) to be bound by the award in the same manner and to the same extent as any other party would be bound; and

(b) to reimburse the parties such portion of the arbitrator's fees and disbursements as, at the end of the hearing, would be found just.

In *Toronto (City) and Toronto Civic Employees Union, Local 416* (2001), 100 L.A.C. (4th) 200, another carefully considered analysis of the issue, Arbitrator Janice Johnston concurred with the conclusions of Arbitrator Gray, save to note that, in a subsequent proceeding, being "bound" by the decision might have a somewhat different meaning when applied to an intervenor rather than the parties to the agreement. Nevertheless, the question of what conditions can or should be placed on a third-party union seeking to intervene continues to be the subject of debate. In *Toronto (City) and C.U.P.E., Local 416* (2003), 117 L.A.C. (4th) 193, Arbitrator Davie expressed doubt as to whether arbitrators have the authority to require, as a condition of granting participation rights, that the intervenor agree to be bound by the award.

The analysis of Vice-Chair Richard Brown in *Ontario (Ministry of Health & Long-Term Care) and O.P.S.E.U.* (2001), 110 L.A.C. (4th) 80 (Ont. G.S.B.) may be helpful in resolving this apparent divergence of viewpoints. In *C.U.P.E. v. Canadian Broadcasting Corp.* (1992), 91 D.L.R. (4th) 767 (S.C.C.), discussed at length by Vice-Chair Brown, the Supreme Court of Canada upheld a decision of the Ontario Court of Appeal that an arbitrator in a work jurisdiction dispute had erred by failing to provide notice of the hearing to two third-party unions asserting a claim to the work. As the Supreme Court pointed out, a right to notice is valuable even without an accompanying right to standing, since notice provides a third party with an opportunity to refer a jurisdictional dispute to the labour relations board, or to decide whether it wishes to submit to the arbitrator's determination. The Supreme Court disapproved of the proposition, which it attributed to the Court of Appeal, that a third party can be bound without its consent. However, as Vice-Chair Brown demonstrated in

Ontario (Ministry of Health & Long-Term Care), the Court of Appeal did not in fact suggest otherwise. The point made by Vice-Chair Brown is that nowhere has it been established that a stranger to the collective agreement can insist on participating as an "affected party" without agreeing to be bound by the arbitrator's ruling.

On the basis of this analysis, Vice-Chair Brown went on to decide the issue before him, which was whether a third party whose commercial interests may be affected by the outcome of an arbitration proceeding is entitled to participate. In his view, the rights of a party whose interest in the matter is merely commercial are more limited than the rights of an employee for whom the union holds exclusive bargaining rights, or those of a third-party union in a work assignment dispute.

Additional Reading

B.R. Bluman, "Due Process at Arbitration: Who Has the Right to Participate?" in W. Kaplan, J. Sack, M. Gunderson & R. Filion, eds., *Labour Arbitration Yearbook 1996-97*, p. 119.

4.2 PARTICULARS

One feature which distinguishes labour arbitration from the litigation procedure of the courts is that it lacks any formal process for advance discovery or disclosure of the other party's case. In its place, one of the expected functions of the grievance procedure is to provide, prior to the hearing, reasonable disclosure of the case to be met. Where, however, the grievance procedure fails to do that, arbitrators have been prepared to order a party to particularize its position in order to ensure the fairness and efficiency of the hearing. The jurisdiction of arbitrators to order particulars was set out in *Devonian Electrical Services Ltd. and I.B.E.W., Local 424* (1971), 23 L.A.C. 358 (Lucas).

The particulars to which a party is entitled include the time at which and place where the alleged breach of the collective agreement took place, the identity of the individuals involved, and the nature of the underlying facts. Arbitrators have made clear, however, that a party is not obligated to provide a statement of the evidence by which it intends to prove its case: *Consumers Distributing Co. Ltd. and Teamsters, Local 419* (1985), 20 L.A.C. (3d) 223 (O'Shea).

In the Quebec case of *Brasserie Molson O'Keefe and T.U.A.C.* (1996), 59 L.A.C. (4th) 221 (Frumkin), the union argued that, given the magnitude of the consequences for the grievor, the time had come to require complete pre-hearing disclosure from the employer in all discharge cases, as is the rule in criminal prosecutions. That position was rejected by Arbitrator Frumkin, who held that it was important to maintain the informality of the grievance and arbitration procedures, and that specific requests for disclosure should be dealt with on an item-by-item basis.

In some jurisdictions, the labour relations legislation expressly confers on arbitrators the power to order the furnishing of particulars prior to a hearing. See, for example, s. 120(1)(e) of the Manitoba *Labour Relations Act*, R.S.M. 1987, c. L10, and s. 48(12)(a) of the Ontario *Labour Relations Act*, S.O. 1995, c. 1, Sch. A. Under s. 60(1)(a) of the *Canada Labour Code*, R.S.C. 1985, c. L-2, an arbitrator has the same power as the Canada Industrial Relations Board to order "any person to provide information".

4.3 PRODUCTION OF DOCUMENTS

4.3.1 Arbitral Jurisdiction

Since arbitrators are generally not considered to be clothed with inherent powers to determine procedure, at least beyond the conduct of the hearing itself, the question of an arbitrator's jurisdiction to order pre-hearing production is primarily decided on the basis of the enabling statute. In *Halifax (City) and Halifax Civic Workers' Union, Local 108* (1986), 28 L.A.C. (3d) 384, for example, Arbitrator Cotter analyzed the provisions of the Nova Scotia *Trade Union Act*, now R.S.N.S. 1989, c. 475, and concluded that they grant arbitrators only the power to enforce the attendance of a witness by way of summons. The arbitrator did, however, find that the Nova Scotia *Arbitration Act*, now R.S.N.S. 1989, c. 19, which, unlike comparable legislation in other provinces, covers grievance arbitrations, confers a more expansive jurisdiction, including the power to order a party to disclose documents prior to the hearing.

The power to enforce the attendance of witnesses, discussed in Chapter 4.4, is technically distinct from the power to make an order for production. However, pursuant to the arbitrator's power to issue a summons (or subpoena) *duces tecum*, the witness may be required, not only to give testimony at the hearing, but to bring all relevant documents or other materials in his or her possession. The issuance of a subpoena *duces tecum* can therefore operate as a form of "production" order. Confronted with a subpoena *duces tecum*, a third party will often choose to tender the documents rather than attend at the hearing: see *Share Family & Community Services Society and H.S.A.B.C.* (2002), 109 L.A.C. (4th) 289, at p. 311 (Lanyon). Furthermore, while the practice is by no means universal, some adjudicators have drawn a distinction between the two aspects of the summons *duces tecum*, namely the *ad testificandum* (order to testify) and the *duces tecum* (order to produce). The effect of the latter is to require a witness to produce documents for the opposing party's inspection without actually compelling the witness to testify. That is, the witness must attend at the hearing with the requisite documents, and, without taking the witness-stand, turn the documents over to the summonsing party. The summonsing party can thus avoid having to call the custodian of the document as its own witness and losing the right to cross-examine him or her. It seems clear, though, that in the absence of express statutory authorization an arbitrator has no power to compel production before the start of the hearing, when the witness will attend with the document. The development of this jurisprudence prior to amendments to Ontario's statutory regime was canvassed in *Winchester District Memorial Hospital and O.N.A.* (1989), 8 L.A.C. (4th) 342 (Bendel).

The Ontario *Labour Relations Act* has now been amended to grant arbitrators the express power to order pre-hearing production of documents: S.O. 1995, c. 1, Sch. A, s. 48(12)(b). Similar provisions are found in the Manitoba *Labour Relations Act*, R.S.M. 1987, c. L10 (s. 120(e)), and the *Canada Labour Code*, R.S.C. 1985, c. L-2 (ss. 60(1)(a), 16(f.1)). As discussed in *Nova Pole Int'l Inc. and Marine Workers' & Boilermakers' Industrial Union, Local 1* (2001), 100 L.A.C. (4th) 289 (Blasina), some arbitrators in British Columbia have inferred a power to order pre-hearing disclosure from the statutory requirement to "have regard to the real substance of the matters in dispute": *Labour Relations Code*, R.S.B.C. 1996, c. 244, s. 82(2). Arbitrator Blasina declined, however, to extend the inference to authorize an order for the production of documents in the possession or control of a third party (in this instance, the grievor's doctors).

The same point has been made by the Supreme Court of Nova Scotia in *Halifax Shipyard Ltd. v. Marine, Office & Technical Employees Union, Local 28* (1996), 155 N.S.R. (2d) 357 (T.D.), affirmed (1997), 160 N.S.R. (2d) 15 (C.A.). The Court ruled that the authority of arbitrators in that province to order production is limited to parties to the proceedings, and that a sister company of the employer, though owned by the same corporate parent, could not be compelled to produce documents in its control and possession.

4.3.2 Scope of Production

With respect to the exercise of the power to order production, in *Belleville (City) Children's Aid Society and C.U.P.E., Local 2197* (1994), 42 L.A.C. (4th) 259, Arbitrator Briggs expressed the same kind of concerns about "fishing expeditions" as have been enunciated in cases dealing with requests for a summons *duces tecum* (see Chapter 4.4). However, the arbitrator firmly rejected the suggestion found in some awards that documents, in order to be producible, must not only be relevant, but intended to be relied upon by the opposing side. In many circumstances, she noted, a party requesting production of a document may not be in a position to ascertain its relevance until after it has had an opportunity to examine it. The arbitrator concluded that even highly sensitive and confidential information must be produced for inspection where it is essential to the other party's ability to properly put forward its case.

In *Toronto District School Board and C.U.P.E., Local 4400* (2002), 109

L.A.C. (4th) 20, Arbitrator Shime strongly endorsed the "liberal" approach to production adopted in *Belleville (City) Children's Aid Society*. Indeed, in Arbitrator Shime's view, the rules of the courts in both civil and criminal matters have much to commend themselves in defining the issues, promoting full disclosure, and avoiding trial by ambush. Thus, at the pre-hearing stage, *all* documents in the possession of a party which have a "semblance of relevance" ought to be disclosed or, where privilege is claimed, at least identified. Moreover, since a party may have limited knowledge of the opposing party's internal affairs, a production request is not required to be specific; in the opinion of Arbitrator Shime, a general request for any documents which have a bearing on the matter is sufficient. Similarly, Arbitrator Etherington has held that, in accordance with its right to pre-hearing disclosure of "arguably relevant" documents, the union was entitled to production of investigative reports, including notes of interviews with witnesses, prepared by management prior to the issuance of discipline against the grievor: *Central Park Lodges and S.E.I.U., Local 210* (2001), 95 L.A.C. (4th) 192.

For a discussion of privilege based on an employee's confidentiality or right to privacy, see Chapter 6.7.5. On the issue of whether government documents may be shielded from disclosure because of "public interest immunity", see Chapter 6.7.4.

4.3.3   Remedy for Non-Compliance

Where the union or the employer refuses to comply with an arbitral order for production, what remedies are available to the party to whom the production is owed? In the unusual circumstances which gave rise to the award in *National-Standard Co. of Canada Ltd. and C.A.W., Local 1917* (1994), 39 L.A.C. (4th) 228, Arbitrator Palmer ruled that he had jurisdiction to dismiss the grievance on the basis of an "abuse of process".

The award in *National-Standard* was based on explicit statutory authority "to prevent the abuse of the arbitration process". In *Budget Car Rentals Toronto Ltd. and U.F.C.W., Local 175* (2000), 87 L.A.C. (4th) 154, Arbitrator Davie concluded that, if arbitrators have the power to make production orders, it logically follows that they have the power to enforce them, even in the absence of an express statutory provision to that effect.

4.4   SUMMONS TO A WITNESS

Labour arbitrators are typically clothed with statutory authority to compel the attendance of witnesses by way of the issuance of a summons. Citing the early English case of *R. v. Baines*, [1909] 1 K.B. 258, an arbitration award from Alberta makes it clear that no individual, including a cabinet minister of the provincial government, stands outside the ambit of this summonsing power, as long as it can be shown that there are reasonable grounds to believe that he or she may have relevant evidence to give: *Alberta and A.U.P.E. (Smith)* (1995), 53 L.A.C. (4th) 184 (Moreau).

Collateral to the general summonsing power is the arbitral power to issue a subpoena *duces tecum*, which orders a witness to attend at the hearing and to bring all relevant documents or other material, as specified in the subpoena. Frequently, the issue in dispute between the parties is the appropriate scope of the order to disclose documents. In the oft-cited case of *Bell Canada and C.W.C.* (1980), 25 L.A.C. (2d) 200, Arbitrator Pamela Picher made it clear that a summons *duces tecum* should not be viewed as a "licence to engage in a fishing expedition". Neither is it intended "to enable a party . . . to determine at the hearing whether it has any case at all". Rather, there must be some reasonable and specific basis on which to conclude that the requested document may be material to the proceeding.

The more recent case of *Winchester District Memorial Hospital and O.N.A.* (1989), 8 L.A.C. (4th) 342 (Bendel) examines the use of the summons *duces tecum* power as a tool for ordering pre-hearing production (see Chapter 4.3.1). As to the proper scope of the order, the arbitrator reiterated that there must be a "rational link between the [document] request and the issue". Significantly, however, Arbitrator Bendel goes on to express the view that this link is capable of being established through counsel's definition of the issues and his or her theory of the case, and not only, as some arbitrators have suggested, through the laying of an "evidentiary foundation" at the hearing.

Where necessary, arbitrators also have the power to enforce a summons through the issuance of a warrant for the arrest of the witness: *Acme Strapping Inc. and U.S.W.A., Local 6572* (1992), 26 L.A.C. (4th) 255 (Satterfield).

Additional Reading

M.R. Gorsky, "Discovery at Arbitration: The Subpoena *Duces Tecum* and Proposals for Reform" in W. Kaplan, J. Sack & M. Gunderson, eds., *Labour Arbitration Yearbook 1993*, p. 57.

4.5   MEDICAL EXAMINATION OF EMPLOYEE

In general terms, given the recognition of employees' privacy rights, the right of an employer to insist on having an employee examined by a doctor of its choosing is severely limited. Reference in this regard is typically made to *Thompson v. Oakville (Town)* (1963), 41 D.L.R. (2d) 294 (Ont. H.C.). Notwithstanding the respective rights of employers and employees in the context of their working relationship, however, the arbitral caselaw indicates that, in the context of the litigation of a grievance, different considerations may apply. This line of awards begins with the decision of Arbitrator McColl in

University of British Columbia and A.U.C.E., Local 1 (1984), 15 L.A.C. (3d) 151. Noting the power of courts in British Columbia to direct a medical examination by a party adverse in interest "where the physical or mental condition of a person is in issue in a proceeding", he ruled that a similar power was implicit in the authority of arbitrators to provide a final and conclusive settlement of the parties' dispute. The arbitrator was careful, however, to limit his ruling to the specific situation before him, where the conflicting and indeterminate nature of the medical reports submitted by the union raised a substantive issue as to their reliability. Contrary to the employer's request, Arbitrator McColl directed the employer and the union to jointly select the examining physician, adding that, if the grievor elected not to submit to an examination, the grievance was to be stayed.

Arbitrator McColl's decision has since been adopted and applied in a number of other cases ordering the referral of a grievor to a psychiatrist retained by the employer. As explained by Arbitrator Burkett in *Canada Post Corp. and C.U.P.W.* (1998), 69 L.A.C. (4th) 393, the purpose of doing so is to allow for a full and fair hearing, and thus to "level the playing field". As noted in *Oliver Paipoonge (Municipality) and L.I.U.N.A., Local 607* (1999), 79 L.A.C. (4th) 241 (Whitaker), however, such examinations are, by their nature, highly intrusive, and ought not to be ordered until such time as the union has clearly put the grievor's mental health in issue.

Arbitrator Brandt, in an unreported award dated October 30, 2002, reasoned that the authority of arbitrators to order an employee to undergo a medical examination is implicit in their power to ensure a fair and just hearing: *Kodak Canada Inc. and Employees' Ass'n of Kodak*. The arbitrator also noted that a physical examination (in this case, an examination of the grievor's knees and shoulders) is less intrusive than a psychiatric examination, and therefore does not engage the employee's privacy interest to the same extent.

Some arbitrators have also invoked their statutory power to control procedure at the hearing as a basis for ordering a medical examination. In *Hastings & Prince Edward Counties Health Unit and C.U.P.E., Local 3314* (2004), 125 L.A.C. (4th) 272, Arbitrator Starkman relied upon s. 48(12)(i) of the Ontario *Labour Relations Act* (S.O. 1995, c. 1, Sch. A), which provides arbitrators with authority "to make interim orders concerning procedural matters", to conclude that he had jurisdiction to require the grievor to undergo psychiatric testing. The arbitrator pointed out, however, that this remedy is of an exceptional nature, because it requires a party to "create" evidence that does not already exist, and because it constitutes an infringement of privacy. Consistent with the cautionary comments of Arbitrator McColl in *University of British Columbia, supra*, Arbitrator Starkman emphasized that a medical examination should not automatically be granted every time the status of an employee's health is in issue: in every case, the employer must demonstrate a *need* for such an extraordinary step, and that need must be balanced against the right of an employee not to be subjected to intrusive medical examinations or procedures.

The British Columbia *School Act*, R.S.B.C. 1996, c. 412, permits school boards to require employees, on the advice of a school medical officer, to undergo a medical examination arranged by the board. In a split decision, the province's Court of Appeal has upheld an arbitrator's ruling that this requirement does not infringe the guarantee of life, liberty and security under s. 7 of the *Charter of Rights and Freedoms*: *School District No. 39 (Vancouver) v. B.C.T.F.* (2003), 224 D.L.R. (4th) 63 (B.C.C.A.).

Given the privacy considerations that may attach to medical information, arbitrators have in appropriate circumstances imposed limitations on disclosure of reports that are ordered to be produced: see Chapter 6.7.5, "Privilege Based on Personal Privacy".

Additional Reading

P.A. Chapman, "Mental Disability and the Arbitration Process: An Emerging Concern" in K. Whitaker, J. Sack, M. Gunderson & R. Filion, eds., *Labour Arbitration Yearbook 1999-2000*, vol. II, p. 189; and companion articles by R.W. Little and T. Hadwen.

D.L. Larson, "The Use of Medical Evidence at Arbitration: An Arbitrator's Perspective" in K. Whitaker, J. Sack, M. Gunderson & R. Filion, eds., *Labour Arbitration Yearbook 1999-2000*, vol. II, p. 137; and companion articles by R.A. Macpherson, D.G. Pulayew & H.C. Devine, and V.M. Lemieux.

CHAPTER 5

PROCEDURE AND PROOF AT THE HEARING

5.1 ADJOURNMENT

In the absence of provisions in the collective agreement to the contrary, an arbitrator has the discretion to grant an adjournment at any stage of the arbitration hearing, a power which is generally held to flow from his or her authority over procedure. In ruling on a request for an adjournment, arbitrators will ordinarily take into account whether there is a valid reason for the request, whether the other party was advised in advance so that witnesses are not needlessly inconvenienced, and whether adjourning the hearing would prejudice the other party. In *Tank Truck Transports Inc. and Teamsters, Locals 938, 91, 106, 141 & 880* (1998), 75 L.A.C. (4th) 296, Arbitrator Rayner affirmed the power of arbitrators, as a matter of controlling procedure at the hearing, to attach conditions to the granting of an adjournment request, including an order for costs and the posting of security.

5.1.1 Concurrent Proceedings

A request for an adjournment may arise in a variety of circumstances. One of the more frequent (and problematic) contexts in which the request tends to occur is the existence of concurrent proceedings involving the same or a related factual matrix. Most typically, a criminal matter is scheduled to be heard concurrently with the grievance arbitration, and a party alleges that evidence given in one proceeding will prejudice its interests in the other.

As Arbitrator Archibald stated in *Nova Scotia Liquor Commission and N.S.G.E.U. (Donovan)* (1997), 63 L.A.C. (4th) 430, though, there is "an established framework for the use of evidence" by courts and tribunals with jurisdiction over different aspects of a dispute. Thus, in most jurisdictions, the provisions of the applicable *Evidence Act* offer protection against the risk of "self-incrimination" by witnesses. In the result, Arbitrator Archibald concluded that, where an employee has been charged with a criminal offence relating to the grounds for his or her discharge, an employer is entitled to a reasonably prompt resolution of the grievance, independent of "the vagaries of the criminal court dockets and the schedules of police, Crown attorneys and defence counsel" (at pp. 438-39).

A similar viewpoint was expressed by Arbitrator Lucas in *O.J. Pipelines Corp. and U.A., Local 488* (2001), 96 L.A.C. (4th) 388, with respect to parallel proceedings which had been initiated before a human rights commission. On the other hand, where the essence of the dispute falls within the primary, specialized jurisdiction of another tribunal, proceedings there are well under way, and a decision by that tribunal may effectively end the dispute through some form of *res judicata*, a strong case exists for the arbitrator's deciding to defer: *Blue Line Taxi Co. Ltd. and R.W.D.S.U., Local 1688* (1995), 51 L.A.C. (4th) 49 (Lavery).

Arbitrators have made it clear, however, that where overlapping or parallel jurisdiction does exist, there is no presumption of institutional primacy in favour of the statutory tribunal: *Switching Services Ltd. and Teamsters, Local 938* (2003), 117 L.A.C. (4th) 163 (Liang). Rather, arbitrators will weigh all of the competing considerations in deciding, in a given case, whether to defer to the parallel proceedings: *Autoland Chrysler (1981) Ltd. and Teamsters, Local 879* (2003), 119 L.A.C. (4th) 309 (Bendel). In *Switching Services*, the delay incurred by the union before referring the matter to the Canada Industrial Relations Board was a critical factor in the arbitrator's decision to proceed with the arbitration hearing. In *Autoland*, it was the relevance of the issue to the labour relations community in general that persuaded the arbitrator to defer to the Ontario Labour Relations Board.

The fact that some labour relations statutes grant arbitrators an express power to "interpret and apply" employment-related legislation makes it more likely that an issue submitted to a statutory tribunal will also fall within the competence of an arbitrator. The same is true as a result of the Supreme Court of Canada's judgment in *Parry Sound (District) Social Services Administration Board v. O.P.S.E.U., Local 324* (2003), 230 D.L.R. (4th) 257, holding that the rights and obligations contained in employment-related statutes are implicit in every collective agreement over which an arbitrator has jurisdiction (although, in *Isidore Garon Ltée v. Syndicat du Bois Ouvré de la Région de Québec Inc.* (2006), 262 D.L.R. (4th) 385, the Supreme Court added the proviso that a statutory rule which is found to be "incompatible" with the labour relations scheme is not incorporated into the collective agreement): see Chapter 1.2.3. Moreover, in the area of human rights, where the problem of competing forums arises most frequently, the legislation itself may permit the human rights commission to defer to arbitration if, in all the circumstances, the arbitral forum is more appropriate: see *Young v. Coast Mountain Bus Co. Ltd.* (2003), 47 C.H.R.R. D/1 (B.C.H.R. Trib.); *Gurofsky v. Ontario Human Rights Commission* (2004), 70 O.R. (3d) 25 (Div. Ct.).

Another common issue is whether an arbitrator ought to proceed with a discharge grievance when related criminal charges are pending before the courts. The Supreme Court of Canada has ruled that, in most cases, a finding of guilt in a criminal trial must be taken as conclusive proof of the accused's culpability for the purpose of all other proceedings: see *Toronto (City) v. C.U.P.E., Local 79* (2003), 232 D.L.R. (4th) 385, discussed in Chapter 3.6.1. In *Maple Villa Long Term Care Centre and S.E.I.U., Local 532* (2004), 123 L.A.C. (4th) 377, however, Arbitrator Davie concluded that the decision in *Toronto (City)* is only one of a number of considerations which must be weighed in the context of a request for an adjournment. Given that no date had been set for the criminal trial or was imminent, the arbitrator ultimately ruled that the requirement for an expeditious resolution of the grievance militated against awaiting the outcome of the criminal proceedings. Given the possibility of a lengthy delay before the commencement of the criminal process, the arbitrator found, the reasons for postponing the arbitration hearing were less compelling.

Additional Reading

R.H. Abramsky, "The Problem of Multiple Proceedings: An Arbitrator's Perspective" in W. Kaplan, J. Sack, M. Gunderson & R. Filion, eds., *Labour Arbitration Yearbook 1996-97*, p. 45; and companion articles by D.R. Franklin and B. Chivers.

5.2   PUBLIC ACCESS TO HEARINGS

In accordance with the principle that the functioning of legal institutions should be transparent, there is a presumption that court proceedings are normally open to the public. Legislation often extends this presumption to the deliberations of various statutory or "quasi-judicial" tribunals. Section 9(1) of

the Ontario *Statutory Powers Procedure Act*, R.S.O. 1990, c. S.22, for example, limits the situations in which tribunals subject to the legislation are free to
depart from the norm of open hearings:

> A hearing shall be open to the public except where the tribunal is of the opin-
> ion that,
>
> (a) matters involving public security may be disclosed; or
>
> (b) intimate financial or personal matters or other matters may be disclosed
>   at the hearing of such a nature, having regard to the circumstances, that
>   the desirability of avoiding disclosure thereof in the interests of any per-
>   son affected or in the public interest outweighs the desirability of adher-
>   ing to the principle that hearings be open to the public,
>
> in which case the tribunal may hold the hearing in the absence of the public.

Like the legislation in every Canadian jurisdiction, the Ontario *Labour
Relations Act*, S.O. 1995, c. 1, Sch. A, stipulates that all differences between
the parties to a collective agreement must be settled by final and binding arbi-
tration. The courts have held that the compulsory nature of arbitration is sufficient to constitute arbitrators or boards of arbitration as "statutory tribunals"
(*Int'l Nickel Co. of Canada Ltd. v. Rivando*, [1956] 2 D.L.R. (2d) 700 (Ont.
C.A.)). The *Statutory Powers Procedure Act* itself, however, expressly excludes
arbitrations conducted under the *Labour Relations Act*. In *Toronto Star Ltd. and
Toronto Newspaper Guild, Local 87* (1975), 9 L.A.C. (2d) 193, Arbitrator
Adams considered this exclusion a clear legislative affirmation of what he
called "the essentially private nature of labour arbitration", and held that, in the
absence of the parties' consent, he had no discretion to admit the public to the
hearing.

On judicial review, however, Arbitrator Adams' award in *Toronto Star* was
quashed: see (1976), 73 D.L.R. (3d) 370 (Ont. Div. Ct.). In the opinion of the
Ontario Divisional Court, which noted that "the public has an interest in the
functioning of statutory arbitration tribunals", the arbitrator erred in concluding that one party's objection to the presence of the public effectively ousted
his jurisdiction to decide the matter: "[T]here is a discretion to determine
whether the public should be admitted to the proceedings of the board. That
discretion is, however, the board's and not that of this Court on judicial review"
(at p. 376). Notwithstanding this emphatic recognition of an arbitral discretion,
subsequent to the Court's decision arbitrators appear to have read the admonition as establishing a presumption, rebuttable only in exceptional circumstances, that hearings should be open to the public. That was true, for example,
of the follow-up decision by Arbitrator Adams in *Toronto Star Ltd. and Toronto
Newspaper Guild, Local 87* (1977) 14 L.A.C. (2d) 155.

More recently, arbitrators have come to express the view that there is in
reality no presumption favouring either the inclusion or the exclusion of the
public; in each case, it is simply an issue for the arbitrator to decide by weighing the competing interests. The rationale for this view was set out by Arbitrator

Baxter in *Ottawa Public Library and Ottawa-Carleton Public Employees Union, Local 503* (2003), 117 L.A.C. (4th) 435. The arbitrator was persuaded that, in order to preserve the efficacy of a witness exclusion order he had granted, the press should be excluded as well.

In *Dough Delight Ltd. and B.C.T., Local 181* (1998), 72 L.A.C. (4th) 34, Arbitrator Elaine Newman extended the concept of a "private proceeding" to rule that the two parties to the process had the right to insist that the grievor not have his own lawyer present as a personal advisor.

In assessing whether or not the public should be permitted to attend, it is necessary to be mindful of the terms of governing legislation. In Manitoba, for example, the *Labour Relations Act*, R.S.M. 1987, c. L10, expressly provides that all arbitration hearings are open to the public, except where "intimate financial or personal matters may be disclosed". See *Winnipeg Free Press v. Winnipeg (City)* (2004), 188 Man. R. (2d) 119 (Q.B.).

5.3 DISQUALIFICATION OF COUNSEL

In *Construction Industry Affiliated Trades Unions and Office & Technical Employees' Union, Local 15* (2000), 91 L.A.C. (4th) 47 (Moore), the dispute centred on whether an arbitrator has jurisdiction to disqualify counsel appointed by one of the parties on the basis of conflict of interest. Arbitrator Moore concluded that an arbitrator's broad power to determine procedure in the interests of ensuring a fair hearing, and thus an effective resolution of the dispute, necessarily includes such authority.

5.4 TAPE-RECORDING OF PROCEEDINGS

A party appearing before an adjudicative tribunal unquestionably has the right to make notes of the proceedings for its own use. Yet the use of a tape-recorder in the hearing room to capture the proceedings verbatim has on occasion generated opposition from both the other party and the tribunal itself. What had been the practice of the Canada Labour Relations Board (now the Canada Industrial Relations Board) to prohibit the creation of such "transcripts" came under judicial scrutiny in *Eastern Provincial Airways Ltd. v. Canada Labour Relations Board* (1983), 2 D.L.R. (4th) 597 (F.C.A.). While expressing some concern that the Board's motivation was, in part, to make access to judicial review more difficult, the Federal Court of Appeal viewed the practice as falling within a tribunal's broad latitude over its own procedure.

Where, however, a tribunal enjoys a less explicit statutory mandate to control its own procedure, the situation may be different, and a more cautious approach may be called for at arbitration. One possible model is the policy of the Ontario Labour Relations Board, as articulated in *John Kohut and C.A.W.* (1990), 9 Can. L.R.B.R. (2d) 58 (Ont. L.R.B.). Although it enjoys the same procedural authority as the Canada Industrial Relations Board, the Ontario Board permitted a party who insisted on tape-recording the proceedings to do so on the understanding that it would tolerate no interference whatsoever with the conduct of the hearing, and that the resulting "transcript" would have no official status. In the Board's view, tape-recording simply constituted an alternative form of "note-taking" for the party's own use.

For authority to the contrary, see *Clarke Institute of Psychiatry and O.N.A.* (1995), 45 L.A.C. (4th) 284, where Arbitrator Knopf considered it an appropriate exercise of her jurisdiction to deny the grievors' request to record the proceedings.

5.5 EXCLUSION OF WITNESSES

Like the courts, arbitrators will typically grant an order for the exclusion of witnesses at the request of either party. The purpose of an exclusion order is to ensure that a witness' testimony is not tainted or influenced by hearing the evidence of prior witnesses. Whether or not such an order at an arbitration hearing may be extended to the grievor is a difficult issue. In *C.J.A., Local 1525 v. Norfab Homes Ltd.* (1975), 62 D.L.R. (3d) 516, a decision to exclude the grievor came under review by the Alberta Supreme Court, Trial Division. Finding that the grievor was not an actual party to the proceeding, the Court ruled that it was within the arbitration board's discretion to determine its own procedure, and that the procedure adopted in this case did not contravene the principles of fairness or natural justice.

However, it should be noted that the collective agreement in *Norfab Homes* expressly provided that the union had carriage of grievances at arbitration. Regardless of whether *Norfab Homes* is distinguishable on the facts, arbitrators have since relied on the judgment to exclude the grievor where his or her credibility is deemed to be a critical issue. However, in *Toronto Transit Commission and A.T.U., Local 113* (1997), 65 L.A.C. (4th) 78, Arbitrator Thorne made the point that grievors, though technically not parties, stand in a special position because they are the persons who are most directly affected by the outcome, and should not be excluded without an exceptional justification. Even then, he found, in view of the special status of grievors, an order excluding them should interfere with their attendance at the hearing as little as possible. Thus, each of the grievors was excluded only while another grievor was testifying. An arbitrator may therefore be reluctant to exclude a grievor on the basis that he or she is tantamount to a party. In such circumstances, of course, an arbitrator has a discretion to deny the request for an exclusion order altogether, if he or she is of the view that the order would have an uneven impact on the participants.

Courts, it might be noted, may have less discretion, based on their own rules of practice. Rule 52.06(2) of the Ontario *Rules of Civil Procedure*, R.R.O.

1990, Reg. 194, for example, specifies that an order for the exclusion of witnesses "may not be made in respect of a party". The Ontario Court of Appeal recently admonished a trial judge because he had applied an exclusion order to two spouses, both of whom were parties to the action: *Liu Estate v. Chau* (2004), 236 D.L.R. (4th) 711. In the Court of Appeal's view, even if the judge had authority to exclude a "party" in exceptional circumstances, the possibility that the evidence could be "tailored" was not a sufficient ground on which to override a party's fundamental right to attend at the hearing. The Court added, however, that the presence of one member of a common-interest group during the testimony of another member can be taken into account in assessing the weight to be accorded to the evidence.

5.6 INTERPRETERS

Where necessary, a court or administrative agency of government usually provides translation services at a hearing. In the context of an arbitration funded privately by the parties, however, the answer to the question of who should bear the costs of translation is not readily apparent. In *Supply & Services Union and O.P.E.I.U., Local 225* (1997), 60 L.A.C. (4th) 423, Arbitrator Lavery held that, even though it was understood that part of the hearing would be in French, a party was entitled to attend with a unilingual advisor and to have the costs of translation borne equally by both parties. In so ruling, Arbitrator Lavery held that affording simultaneous translation was a fundamental part of the right to a fair hearing.

In contrast to *Supply and Services Union* is the award in *Canadian National Railway Co. and C.A.W.*, [1999] C.L.A.D. No. 104 (QL) (M.G. Picher), decided under the *Canada Labour Code*, R.S.C. 1985, c. L-2. In Arbitrator Picher's view, it is the party who needs the translation or interpretation services which must bear the cost. He did not, however, rule out the possibility that the demands of natural justice may sometimes require the allocation of the cost equally between the parties.

The view of Arbitrator Picher was adopted in preference to that of Arbitrator Lavery in *Hurley Corp. and U.F.C.W.* (2002), 111 L.A.C. (4th) 378 (Bendel). In the opinion of Arbitrator Bendel, a party which produces a witness to testify in a language other than that in which the hearing is conducted bears the responsibility of arranging for competent translation and paying for it.

Similar issues arise where sign-language interpreters are required to assist deaf individuals to participate in the proceedings. It has been held that, while the cost of interpreters to enable the grievor and other deaf witnesses to testify should be treated as an arbitrator expense, and be shared equally by the parties, the cost of interpretation during the remainder of the hearing, while other individuals testified, was to be borne by the union: *Insurance Corp. of British Columbia and C.O.P.E., Local 387* (2005), 140 L.A.C. (4th) 302 (Dorsey).

5.7 CONSOLIDATION OF GRIEVANCES

In *Maple Leaf Pork and U.F.C.W., Local 1227* (1999), 84 L.A.C. (4th) 62, Arbitrator Armstrong rejected the argument that an arbitrator has no power to consolidate grievances unless both parties consent. In his opinion, the issue was an entirely procedural one, and therefore within an arbitrator's power "to make interim orders respecting procedural matters" under s. 48(12)(i) of the Ontario *Labour Relations Act*, S.O. 1995, c. 1, Sch. A. The arbitrator indicated as well that it was appropriate to look for guidance to the *Rules of Civil Procedure*, which govern the disposition of consolidation requests in the courts. Given that the parties were, in each case, identical, that the grievances gave rise to common questions of fact and law, and that the relief claimed arose out of the same transaction or occurrence, Arbitrator Armstrong concluded that a consolidation order was appropriate, and directed that the grievances be heard together.

In *Toronto District School Board and C.U.P.E., Local 4400* (2002), 109 L.A.C. (4th) 20, where the purpose clause of the collective agreement expressed the parties' commitment "to provide a prompt and equitable disposition of grievances", Arbitrator Shime went still further, finding that both parties were obligated to consent to the consolidation of grievances if it was reasonable to do so.

However, arbitrators acting pursuant to a ministerial appointment, as provided for by the expedited arbitration procedure under Ontario's *Labour Relations Act*, have dismissed applications for consolidation where the other grievances in question had already been referred to a different arbitrator: see *Ottawa Hospital and C.U.P.E., Local 4000* (2004), 131 L.A.C. (4th) 151 (Hornung); and *1048271 Ontario Inc. and U.F.C.W., Local 1000A* (2004), 124 L.A.C. (4th) 216 (Roach). In those decisions, it was held that an arbitrator's jurisdiction is restricted to the matter referred to him or her by the Minister, even though other grievances have been filed which may raise an identical issue or arise out of the same occurrence.

5.8 ONUS AND STANDARD OF PROOF, ORDER OF PROCEEDING

In considering the question of which party must establish its case in order to succeed, it is important to distinguish between the "legal onus" and the "evidentiary onus". Whereas the legal onus, which except in discipline or discharge grievances usually rests on the grieving party, never shifts in a case, the evidentiary burden may shift back and forth between the union and the employer as the hearing progresses. In *Central Park Lodges and S.E.I.U., Local 210* (2000), 88 L.A.C. (4th) 188 (Etherington), the union argued that, since the facts on their face showed a violation of the collective agreement, the onus was on the employer to proceed first to explain its "defence". Arbitrator Etherington rejected this submission. In his view, the fact that it might be relatively easy to establish a *prima facie* case did not change the normal rules: if the union is the grieving party, it bears the legal onus of proving a violation of the collective agreement, and thus the burden of proceeding first in the matter.

Generally, the party bearing the legal onus to make out its case — ordinarily the party bringing the grievance — proceeds first. However, this is not always so; thus, it has long been recognized that, in cases in which an employee grieves his or her dismissal or the imposition of discipline, the legal onus rests on the employer to establish just cause, since the grounds for discharge are within the employer's knowledge, and the employer is, accordingly, called upon to proceed first. In *Spar Aerospace Ltd. and Spar Professional & Allied Technical Employees Ass'n* (1994), 40 L.A.C. (4th) 215 (H.D. Brown), where the union grieved the employer's exclusion of a classification of employees from the bargaining unit, Arbitrator Howard Brown ruled that the employer bore the onus of establishing that the employees did in fact fall within an exclusionary category, and directed it to proceed first. In reasoning similar to that found in discipline and discharge cases, the arbitrator noted that the basis on which the exclusion allegedly rested lay entirely within the employer's knowledge.

There is, however, authority for the proposition that, where no factual dispute exists between the parties, and the only outstanding issue involves the interpretation of the collective agreement, which is a matter of law, it is inappropriate to speak of a burden of proof resting on *either* party (although presumably the party bringing the grievance would still be required to proceed with its case first): *School District No. 39 (Vancouver) and Vancouver Teachers' Federation* (1996), 53 L.A.C. (4th) 33 (Hope).

In assessing the sufficiency of the evidence adduced in support of a claim, the standard of proof applied at arbitration is the civil standard of a "balance of probabilities", *i.e.* the party bearing the burden of proof on an issue must establish that its version of the facts is more likely to be true. The same standard is applied in discipline cases, and arbitrators have rejected arguments that the employer must prove the alleged offence in accordance with the standard used in criminal proceedings, *i.e.* "beyond a reasonable doubt". It is well established, however, that "the standard of probability applied in arbitration proceedings may increase with the gravity of the consequences that will flow from an affirmative finding": *Indusmin Ltd. and United Cement, Lime & Gypsum Workers Int'l Union, Local 488* (1978), 20 L.A.C. (2d) 87 (M.G. Picher), at p. 89. Thus, where serious misconduct is involved, such as criminal or quasi-criminal behaviour, arbitrators have required "clear and cogent" evidence of the facts alleged. For further discussion, see Chapters 10.4 and 11.6.3.

5.9 TESTIFYING BY TELECONFERENCE

Arbitrators are on occasion faced with a request to hear the evidence of a witness by teleconference. This procedure may be problematic because, while it enables the parties to conduct a full examination and cross-examination, it deprives the adjudicator of the opportunity to view the witness while he or she testifies. Nonetheless, arbitrators have ruled that the reception of testimony by teleconference lies within their power, given their broad statutory latitude to admit evidence, whether admissible in a court or not, and to control their own procedure. It thus becomes a question of when it would be appropriate to make an exception to the normal rule of *viva voce* testimony.

In *Canadian Broadcasting Corp. and A.C.T.R.A.* (1993), 33 L.A.C. (4th) 250, Arbitrator Palmer considered it appropriate to resort to this procedure, since a key witness for the employer resided overseas, and could not be served with a subpoena. In an unjust dismissal adjudication under the *Canada Labour Code*, R.S.C. 1985, c. L-2, Adjudicator Wakeling permitted the complainant to testify by way of teleconference solely on the basis of travel time and cost (the complainant lived 1,600 miles north of the designated hearing location): *McDonald and Reimer Express World Corp.*, [1997] C.L.A.D. No. 609 (QL).

5.10 MOTION FOR NON-SUIT

After the party bearing the legal onus has led off and presented its evidence, the opposing party may bring a "non-suit" motion to have the grievance dismissed on the basis that a *prima facie* case has not been made out. In such circumstances, the arbitrator is asked to rule whether the evidence adduced, taken as a whole, is incapable of sustaining the party's case, even in the absence of contradictory evidence. However, whether the moving party, as a condition of being permitted to proceed with its motion, must first elect not to call any evidence of its own is an issue on which there is a divergence among arbitrators in different jurisdictions.

BRITISH COLUMBIA, ALBERTA, NOVA SCOTIA

Modelling themselves on provincial rules of court, arbitrators in British Columbia generally distinguish between non-suit motions alleging *no evidence* and those alleging *insufficient evidence*. Where the argument is that the party with the legal onus has presented no evidence to make out one or more crucial elements in a case, the arbitral practice is to entertain the motion without first putting the moving party to its election. Thus, if the motion is unsuccessful, the moving party retains the right to call evidence. Where, on the other hand, the submission is that the evidence is merely insufficient, the moving party is required to close its case and undertake not to adduce any further evidence. The rationale developed by the British Columbia courts is that an "insufficient evidence" motion necessarily assumes the existence of *some* evidence on point, the assessment of which, on a balance of probabilities, is not possible until all the evidence is in: see *Surfwood Supply Ltd. v. General Alarms Ltd.* (1975),

[1976] 3 W.W.R. 93 (B.C.S.C.). On the view that grievance arbitration should not follow a more technical procedure than the courts, arbitrators in Alberta and British Columbia have adopted a similar practice: *Canada Post Corp. and C.U.P.W. (Musson)* (1993), 34 L.A.C. (4th) 36 (Jones).

In Nova Scotia and the Northwest Territories, similarly, arbitrators have favoured a more relaxed approach to the traditional requirement for an election, after the pattern of the rules of practice in their court system: see, for example, *Seagull Pewter & Silversmiths Ltd. and U.S.W.A., Local 9331* (1998), 76 L.A.C. (4th) 224 (Kydd); and *Northwest Territories and Union of Northern Workers* (1998), 75 L.A.C. (4th) 150 (Jolliffe).

ONTARIO

The approach taken by Ontario arbitrators has generally been different. Here, although court procedure in non-suit motions is not governed by statute, the courts have themselves institutionalized the practice of requiring the moving party to make its election. In *Ontario v. O.P.S.E.U.* (1990), 37 O.A.C. 218 (Div. Ct.), Justice Reid affirmed that this was the practice of the Ontario courts, adding that, in his view, administrative tribunals should follow the same procedure. The task of a court, Justice Reid stated, is to determine whether there is any case at all to meet, not to weigh the evidence: "A *prima facie* case is no more than a case for the defendant to answer . . . If there is some evidence, a motion for non-suit must be dismissed. If there is none, it must be granted" (at p. 226). Arbitrators in Ontario have generally adhered to these principles, as reflected, for example, in *Canadian Airlines Int'l Ltd. and C.U.P.E.* (1993), 38 L.A.C. (4th) 160, where Arbitrator Burkett specifically rejected the distinction between non-suit motions based on "no evidence" and those based on "insufficient evidence".

However, the practice of requiring the non-suiting party to make its election is not without exceptions in Ontario. In *Toronto (City) and Toronto Civic Employees' Union, Local 416* (2000), 93 L.A.C. (4th) 372, taking into account the evolving practice of the Ontario Labour Relations Board, Arbitrator Surdykowski concluded that it was proper to entertain a non-suit motion without calling for an election if it appeared to the adjudicator that the party bearing the onus of proof was "going nowhere" with its case. A similar practice has developed at the Ontario Grievance Settlement Board as a means of promoting efficiency and the expeditious resolution of disputes: *Ontario (Ministry of the Solicitor General & Correctional Services) and O.P.S.E.U. (Ross)* (2003), 120 L.A.C. (4th) 171 (Ont. G.S.B.).

Nevertheless, in *Hamilton Health Sciences Corp. and C.U.P.E., Local 4800* (2003), 117 L.A.C. (4th) 119, Arbitrator Herman noted that *Toronto (City)* was a case in which the arbitrator himself sought to encourage a non-suit motion on the basis of his own assessment of the evidence adduced by the party bearing the onus of proof. Apart from such instances, Arbitrator Herman stated, Ontario arbitrators generally follow the practice of the province's courts in requiring that the moving party be put to its election.

NEWFOUNDLAND AND LABRADOR

In Newfoundland and Labrador, in *Canada Games Park 1995 Inc. and C.U.P.E., Local 3336* (1997), 63 L.A.C. (4th) 423, Arbitrator Oakley considered the competing arguments as to the necessity of putting a party to its election. Based on considerations of fairness, expedition and cost, he adopted, as a matter of arbitral discretion, the prevailing Ontario approach, even though Newfoundland and Labrador's rules of court are more similar to those of Alberta and British Columbia.

5.11   REPLY EVIDENCE

Once the responding party has closed its case, the party that proceeded first is entitled to call reply evidence. However, the party leading reply evidence is not permitted to split its case. The responding party is entitled to know the case it has to meet, and the party which proceeded first will not be allowed to bolster in reply the case that it should have made out in the first instance. Thus, a party may exercise its right of reply for the purpose of addressing new matters raised by the responding party or of explaining inconsistencies, but it cannot attempt to introduce evidence which should have been introduced during the presentation of its case-in-chief, or evidence on a new subject matter unrelated to what has gone before. As stated by Arbitrator Mikus in *Canadian Pacific Forest Products Ltd. and I.W.A., Local 2693* (1993), 32 L.A.C. (4th) 18, where the employer seeks to introduce reply evidence in a discipline case, the "test to be applied . . . is whether the evidence . . . arises from something newly raised in the grievor's defence" (at p. 23). Because the evidence was tendered to contradict the grievor on a central fact which was known from the outset to be in dispute, the arbitrator ruled that the evidence should have been part of the employer's case-in-chief, and was now inadmissible. Nonetheless, Arbitrator Weatherill has articulated a more informal approach that is frequently followed, namely, that "[i]n labour arbitrations, the right to present evidence in reply ought not to be narrowly construed": *Canada Post Corp. and L.C.U.C.* (1988), 1 L.A.C. (4th) 447.

Considerations of fairness to the party against whom the reply evidence is sought to be adduced may, in some cases, dictate the opposite result. In *School District No. 39 (Vancouver) and Vancouver Teachers' Federation* (1996), 56 L.A.C. (4th) 8 (Taylor), a dispute over the interpretation of the collective agreement, the union claimed that, since the contract language was clear, past practice was irrelevant, and it elected not to call any witnesses. When, however, the employer built its case entirely on the basis of extrinsic evidence, to which the union sought to respond by way of reply (proposing to call a witness who had been present throughout the proceedings), Arbitrator Taylor ruled that the union should have called its evidence on past practice and negotiating history in chief. The arbitrator reasoned that the union had, from the outset, been aware of the employer's theory of the case. Although the arbitrator could have adopted a middle ground, allowing the union to call its evidence and giving the employer a right of *surrebuttal*, he appears to have been persuaded to take a stricter view by the fact that the union not only had advance notice of the employer's position, but had been given various particulars as well. In circumstances where it is not clear what evidence should be called in-chief and what evidence should be called in reply, therefore, it may be wise for the parties to clarify at the outset of the hearing the issues in dispute, the order in which they will be addressed, and the nature of the evidence that will be adduced.

5.12   THE RULE IN *BROWNE V. DUNN*

According to the rule in *Browne v. Dunn* (1893), 6 R. 67 (H.L.), where a party intends to call evidence to contradict a witness on a particular point, the contradiction must first be put to the witness during cross-examination so that he or she has the opportunity to offer an explanation. If the party fails to do this, an arbitrator has the discretion to refuse to admit the contradictory evidence. However, it should be borne in mind that arbitrators equally have a discretion to admit evidence that would not be accepted by a court, and may decide to hear potentially material evidence, notwithstanding the rule, particularly where there is still an opportunity for the offended party to call reply evidence. In *R. v. Nissan (A.)* (1996), 89 O.A.C. 389 (C.A.), an appeal from a conviction on sexual assault charges, the Court suggested that the trial judge should not have considered himself strictly bound by the rule:

> Had the trial judge considered the issue from the perspective of *Browne v. Dunn* he might well have permitted the defence to lead the evidence of what the complainant said at the meeting. He could have insisted that the complainant first be recalled and questioned on her alleged statements, or he could have permitted the Crown to question her in reply. As Father Bouza's evidence may have been helpful to the appellant, it would have been preferable had the trial judge obtained an outline of this evidence before making his ruling.
>
> The truth of what occurred between the complainant and the appellant may have emerged at this meeting. On the new trial this evidence should be before the trier of fact, after the required foundation for it is laid. (at pp. 393-94)

Nonetheless, it is clear that some arbitrators choose to apply the rule in *Browne v. Dunn*, and refuse to admit evidence where the rule has not been complied with. In *Laidlaw Waste Systems Ltd. and C.U.P.E., Local 1045* (1993), 37 L.A.C. (4th) 146, Arbitrator Whitehead characterized the rule as "a fundamental principle of fairness and not a mere legal technicality". Since relaxing the rule would have been unfair to the employer, he rejected the evidence proffered by the union, notwithstanding his broad discretion as to the admission of evidence and the statutory mandate to address the "real substance" of a dispute.

A comparably strict approach was taken in *Delta Catalytic Industrial Services and I.B.E.W., Local 105* (2002), 112 L.A.C. (4th) 72, where Arbitrator Surdykowski refused to admit contradictory evidence tendered by the employer which was not identified either during the grievor's cross-examination or at any point earlier in the hearing. The employer's argument that its failure to put the contradictory evidence to the grievor in cross-examination could be cured by permitting the union to lead reply evidence was rejected. In the arbitrator's view, "the reply evidence window is a small one", and should not be used to excuse a party's failure to conduct its case fairly.

The situations in which a more flexible practice might be called for were canvassed by Arbitrator Armstrong in *Grand River Hospital Corp. and C.A.W., Local 302* (2002), 114 L.A.C. (4th) 278, where the grievor had been dismissed for alleged patient abuse. There were, the arbitrator found, several reasons in this case why the rule in *Browne v. Dunn* should not be followed. The witness whose evidence was sought to be impugned was not a party to the proceeding, and the union's rejection of the witness' version of events was manifest from the outset. Moreover, in light of the witness' frail health, it was professionally appropriate to exercise restraint in cross-examination.

The rule in *Browne v. Dunn* applies to the impeachment of a witness' credibility through the calling of contradictory evidence. There is, however, no requirement that a witness be cross-examined as a precondition to counsel's right to impugn the witness' credibility in final argument. The extent to which cross-examination is appropriate will depend on the circumstances. As Lord Morris, one of the concurring judges in *Browne v. Dunn* remarked, "a story told by a witness may have been of so incredible and romancing a character that the most effective cross-examination would be to ask him to leave the box". This point was affirmed by the Ontario Court of Appeal in *Hurd v. Hewitt* (1994), 120 D.L.R. (4th) 105, as follows (at p. 117):

> My analysis . . . leads to the conclusion that there are no absolute rules in Canada as to the questioning of witnesses at hearings or trials adjudicating between parties. The argument that a party puts after failing to ask obvious questions of a witness may be so severely impaired as to be characterized as incredible. Yet the evidence of a witness may be so obviously flawed that a party's best interest lies in leaving that evidence to stand naked. In either event, the tribunal must assess the evidence and adjudicate upon the rights of the parties as those rights appear from that evidence, and not the evidence minus that which appears unfair to third parties.

5.13   MEDICAL REPORTS

Fundamental to the issue of the admissibility of medical reports is a recognition that, in the absence of the *viva voce* testimony of the physician who prepared them, they are hearsay evidence and ordinarily inadmissible. However, in most jurisdictions, the applicable *Evidence Act* creates an exception to the rule against hearsay, making medical records admissible at the court's discretion, and thus sparing parties the cost and inconvenience of having the author attend the hearing in order to present evidence. The legislation typically provides that a medical report is admissible without the attendance of the author, as long as the opposing party has been given a copy of the report in advance of the hearing.

However, there may be circumstances in which the opposing party wishes to challenge the validity of the report by cross-examining its author. In *Miracle Food Mart of Canada and U.F.C.W., Local 175/633* (1996), 58 L.A.C. (4th) 232, Arbitrator Mitchnick suggested that the most sensible way for arbitrators to deal with this issue is to be mindful of the guidelines provided by the applicable *Evidence Act* itself. Where a medical report is sought to be adduced in evidence, these statutory guidelines entrench the opposing party's right to insist that the physician be made available at the hearing for cross-examination. Furthermore, the courts have now clarified that the cost and responsibility of ensuring the physician's attendance rests with the party seeking to introduce the report (as they did prior to the enactment of the *Evidence Act* procedure). Equally, however, where it is found that a party was unjustified in insisting on the physician's attendance, the legislation empowers the trial judge to shift costs to that party. In Arbitrator Mitchnick's opinion, arbitrators have jurisdiction to make a similar order as a condition of directing that the physician attend the hearing.

5.14 BUSINESS RECORDS

Like medical records, business records are hearsay documents, often many times removed from the individual who had direct knowledge of the matters set out in the document. As a practical reality, however, both the courts and the legislatures have recognized the need to admit business documents without the necessity of calling the author to give *viva voce* evidence. Thus, it is generally accepted that a business record may be admitted without the author's attendance where the record was made in the usual and ordinary course of business, and within a reasonable time after the incident or occurrence that has been recorded. Any frailties in the evidence that arise from the circumstances in which the record was created may diminish the weight to be accorded to the document, but they do not affect its admissibility. This is the regime codified, for instance, by the Ontario *Evidence Act*, R.S.O. 1990, c. E.23:

> 35(1) In this section,
>
> "business" includes every kind of business, profession, occupation, calling, operation or activity, whether carried on for profit or otherwise;
>
> "record" includes any information that is recorded or stored by means of any device.

(2) Any writing or record made of any act, transaction, occurrence or event is admissible as evidence of such act, transaction, occurrence or event if made in the usual and ordinary course of any business and if it was in the usual and ordinary course of such business to make such writing or record at the time of such act, transaction, occurrence or event or within a reasonable time thereafter.

(3) Subsection (2) does not apply unless the party tendering the writing or record has given at least seven days notice of the party's intention to all other parties in the action, and any party to the action is entitled to obtain from the person who has possession thereof production for inspection of the writing or record within five days after giving notice to produce the same.

(4) The circumstances of the making of such a writing or record, including lack of personal knowledge by the maker, may be shown to affect its weight, but such circumstances do not affect its admissibility.

(5) Nothing in this section affects the admissibility of any evidence that would be admissible apart from this section or makes admissible any writing or record that is privileged.

As an example of the way in which the Act has been applied by the courts, see *Tecoglas Inc. v. Domglas Inc.* (1985), 19 D.L.R. (4th) 738 (Ont. H.C.J.). At arbitration, while following the exact procedure set out in the legislation is perhaps the safest course for a party, the early case of *Libby, McNeill & Libby of Canada Ltd. and C.U.O.E., Local 107* (1976), 14 L.A.C. (2d) 402 (O'Shea) established that arbitrators have a general discretion that the courts do not, and can admit business documents even in the absence of full compliance with the notice requirements of the *Evidence Act*.

In contrast to Arbitrator O'Shea's flexible views on the question of notice, in *Ottawa-Carleton Children's Aid Society and O.P.S.E.U., Local 454* (1997), 63 L.A.C. (4th) 439, Arbitrator Richard Brown adhered strictly to the courts' approach to the reception of "opinion evidence". In accordance with the practice of the courts, where the business record sought to be introduced contains elements of opinion evidence, it is not admissible through the procedure established by the *Evidence Act*.

5.15 CREDIBILITY

Often, an arbitrator's findings will turn on his or her assessment of the credibility of witnesses who gave evidence at the hearing. There can be no exhaustive list of the factors an adjudicator may take into account in making this assessment. The important point is that the courts have repeatedly emphasized the danger of relying on an "impressionistic" approach based solely on considerations such as demeanour and the witness' apparent conviction. Rather, as Justice McIntyre stated for the Supreme Court of Canada in *R. v. Béland* (1987), 43 D.L.R. (4th) 641, at p. 656:

I would seek to preserve the principle that in the resolution of disputes in litigation, issues of credibility will be decided by human triers of fact, using their experience of human affairs and basing judgment upon their assessment of the witness and on consideration of how an individual's evidence fits into the general picture revealed on a consideration of the whole of the case.

That is, in addition to evaluating how clearly and convincingly a witness appears to give testimony, the adjudicator must also weigh the witness' evidence in terms of its internal consistency, consistency with other established facts, and overall probability as a matter of common sense or experience. These principles were set out in *Faryna v. Chorney*, [1952] 2 D.L.R. 354 (B.C.C.A.), at p. 357, in an oft-quoted passage by Justice O'Halloran:

> The credibility of interested witnesses, particularly in cases of conflict of evidence, cannot be gauged solely by the test of whether the personal demeanour of the particular witness carried conviction of the truth. The test must reasonably subject his story to an examination of its consistency with the probabilities that surround the currently existing conditions. In short, the real test of the truth of the story of a witness in such a case must be its harmony with the preponderance of the probabilities which a practical and informed person would readily recognize as reasonable in that place and in those conditions.

Arbitrator Roberts' reliance on this judgment in *McMaster University and S.E.I.U., Local 532* (1972), 24 L.A.C. 265 entrenched it in the subsequent development of arbitral jurisprudence.

5.16   FAILURE TO CALL A WITNESS

In arbitration proceedings, the failure of a party to call a witness who may have material evidence to give, including the grievor, can lead to an adverse inference being drawn against that party. In such circumstances, an arbitrator may draw the inference that the witness was not called because he or she would have disclosed facts unfavourable to the party. The inference only arises, however, where the party who does not call the witness can fairly be seen as having been in a position to do so. Where the evidence of the witness in question is material, and the witness is available to testify, if no reasonable explanation is provided for the failure to call the witness, the uncontradicted evidence presented by the opposing party will generally be accepted: see *Alberta and A.U.P.E.* (1994), 51 L.A.C. (4th) 397 (McFetridge).

5.17   WITHDRAWAL OF GRIEVANCE

In *Burnaby (City) and C.U.P.E. (Rossner)* (2000), 91 L.A.C. (4th) 40, Arbitrator Sanderson considered the right of a party to withdraw its grievance midway through the proceedings, in the face of an objection by the opposing party. While the caselaw suggests that an arbitrator may have authority to deny the request, in practical terms, the question is the one posed by Arbitrator Sanderson at the conclusion of his analysis: given the stage at which the request is made, should the party with carriage of the grievance be entitled to withdraw it on a "without prejudice" basis? The arbitrator noted that the party withdrawing the grievance should not be permitted to "insulate" itself from the potential consequences of its decision by seeking an order imposing such terms as "without prejudice or precedent". In the absence of special circumstances, the arbitrator pointed out, nothing in the decision granting the withdrawal should preclude the other party from making submissions to another tribunal regarding the effect of the withdrawal from arbitration on the deliberations of that tribunal. It will then be up to the other tribunal to decide whether the matter ought to proceed.

For a discussion of the impact of a settlement agreement on a party's right to advance similar grievances in the future, see Chapter 3.3.

CHAPTER 6

ADMISSIBILITY OF EVIDENCE

6.1   STATUTORY DISCRETION

The labour relations legislation of every jurisdiction in Canada includes a provision conferring broad discretion on arbitrators as to the admission of evidence in arbitration proceedings. Usually, the provision makes expressly clear that arbitrators need not follow the practice of the courts in making evidentiary rulings. Section 16(c) of the *Canada Labour Code*, R.S.C. 1985, c. L-2, which is representative of the statutory regime in force in other jurisdictions, enables an arbitration board "to receive and accept such evidence and information on oath, affidavit or otherwise as the Board in its discretion sees fit, *whether admissible in a court of law or not* " (emphasis added). Keying in on those words, the courts have repeatedly affirmed that arbitrators who consider themselves bound by a common law rule or decision commit a reviewable error of law. This principle was emphatically expressed in *Toronto (City) v. C.U.P.E., Local 79* (1982), 133 D.L.R. (3d) 94, in which the Ontario Court of Appeal ruled that an arbitrator may *exclude* evidence which is *admissible* in a court of law, and *admit* evidence which is *inadmissible* in a court of law. (In that case, though, the arbitrator's decision not to admit an investigative report tendered by the employer was overturned on the ground that he had failed to give *any* consideration to whether it should be admitted, contrary to the rules of natural justice.) The same principle was affirmed in *Greater Niagara Transit Commission v. A.T.U., Local 1582* (1987), 43 D.L.R. (4th) 71 (Ont. Div. Ct.).

The principle of arbitral discretion has also been affirmed by the Supreme Court of Canada. In *C.J.A., Local 579 v. Bradco Construction Ltd.* (1993), 102 D.L.R. (4th) 402, the Court upheld an award in which the arbitrator had admitted and relied on extrinsic evidence (a conciliator's report). Since arbitrators are often laypersons, without formal legal training, the Court observed that the express statutory latitude permits an arbitrator to relax the rules of evidence, and to apply them "in the same way as would be done by reasonable persons in the conduct of their business". In this case, the arbitrator was not required to apply strictly the concept of ambiguity as a precondition of admitting extrinsic evidence in order to elucidate the parties' intentions; it was sufficient that he determine, on a reasonable basis, that the collective agreement was unclear.

The tendency on the part of most arbitrators today, where a dispute arises, is to hear evidence that is arguably relevant, without ruling on admissibility, and to decide at the conclusion of the hearing how much weight to place upon the evidence. This approach was fortified by the Supreme Court of Canada's ruling in *Syndicat des Employés Professionels de l'Université du Québec à Trois-Rivières v. Université du Québec*, quashing an arbitration award where crucial evidence on an important point was disallowed; see (1993), 101 D.L.R. (4th) 494.

At the same time, however, the courts have indicated that arbitrators, who exercise a quasi-judicial function, must act only on evidence having "cogency in law" (*R. v. Barber* (1968), 68 D.L.R. (2d) 682 (Ont. C.A.)), and that an award in which an evidentiary ruling has the effect of denying a party's right to a fair hearing will be overturned (*Girvin v. Consumers' Gas Co.* (1973), 40 D.L.R. (3d) 509 (Ont. Div. Ct.)). There is thus a tension between the broad legislative discretion conferred on arbitrators in the interests of efficiency and informality, and the requirement to render a fair decision based on reliable evidence. A useful commentary on the balance that arbitrators are called upon to strike is found in *Kingsway Transports Ltd. and Teamsters, Local 938* (1983), 10 L.A.C. (3d) 440 (Brandt).

There is one respect, however, in which arbitral autonomy in the admission of evidence has apparently been curtailed. In *Toronto (City) v. C.U.P.E., Local 79* (2003), 232 D.L.R. (4th) 385 (S.C.C.), the grievor had been tried and found guilty of criminal offences in a court proceeding. The arbitrator in parallel discharge proceedings, though accepting the conviction as *prima facie* proof of guilt, considered himself obligated to try the underlying allegations anew, and came to the opposite conclusion as to the grievor's culpability. The Supreme

Court of Canada upheld a decision quashing the award, ruling that, in the absence of compelling circumstances, it constituted an abuse of process for the union to relitigate the issue. Accordingly, the arbitrator was required to accept evidence of a conviction as conclusive proof of the grievor's guilt: see further discussion in Chapter 3.6.1.

Additional Reading

B. Adell, "Arbitral Discretion in the Admission of Evidence: What Limits Should There Be?" in K. Whitaker, J. Sack, M. Gunderson & R. Filion, eds., *Labour Arbitration Yearbook 1999-2000*, vol. II, p. 1.

6.2 Best Evidence Rule

The "best evidence" rule states that a party must produce the best or strongest evidence available. With respect to documents, for example, the rule requires a party to produce the original rather than a photocopy, unless it can be shown that the original is not available. In accordance with their statutory discretion, however, arbitrators are not bound by the best evidence rule in the same way that a court might be. As Arbitrator Swan held in *Canada Post Corp. and C.U.P.W. (Varma)* (1985), 19 L.A.C. (3d) 361, the rule has been largely supplanted by more specific rules of evidence. In the arbitral context, while evidence which falls short of the best possible evidence may be given less weight, it is not for this reason alone inadmissible.

6.3 *Charter* Evidentiary Issues

In *Weber v. Ontario Hydro* (1995), 125 D.L.R. (4th) 583, the Supreme Court of Canada affirmed that an arbitration board is a "court of competent jurisdiction" within the meaning of s. 24(1) of the *Charter of Rights and Freedoms*, which provides:

> Anyone whose rights or freedoms, as guaranteed by this *Charter*, have been infringed or denied may apply to a court of competent jurisdiction to obtain such remedy as the court considers appropriate and just in the circumstances.

The ruling in *Weber* empowers arbitrators to determine whether a party's *Charter* rights have been violated, and, if so, to grant an appropriate *Charter* remedy for the violation. Section 24(2) of the *Charter* specifies that one of the available remedies is the exclusion of evidence that has been obtained in a manner which, in the court's view, offends the rights guaranteed by the *Charter*:

> Where in proceedings under subsection (1), a court concludes that evidence was obtained in a manner that infringed or denied any rights or freedoms guaranteed by this *Charter*, the evidence shall be excluded if it is established that, having regard to all the circumstances, the admission of it in the proceedings would bring the administration of justice into disrepute.

In *British Columbia (Attorney General) and B.C.G.E.U. (Fotheringham)* (1995), 51 L.A.C. (4th) 225 (Bruce), the grievor was discharged for off-duty misconduct alleged to be incompatible with the performance of his duties. Criminal charges were laid against the grievor, but they were dismissed when the evidence adduced against him was found to have been acquired in a way which violated the *Charter.* The union argued that the arbitrator should adopt the Court's conclusion that a *Charter* breach had occurred, as well as its remedial decision to exclude the tainted evidence pursuant to s. 24(2). Arbitrator Bruce, however, ruled that the recognition of arbitration boards as courts of competent jurisdiction for *Charter* purposes did not render a s. 24(2) admissibility ruling in related criminal proceedings binding upon her. An arbitrator is required to make an independent determination as to the admissibility of the evidence, since the issues, the parties, the onus and standard of proof, and the relevant policy considerations are all different, and the exclusion of the evidence in a prior proceeding does not give rise to issue estoppel.

In *Toronto Transit Commission and A.T.U., Local 113* (2004), 126 L.A.C. (4th) 353, Arbitrator Shime considered union allegations that evidence arising from the employer's investigation and a search warrant carried out by police violated the *Charter* rights of the grievor, and that the violation justified exclusion of the evidence pursuant to s. 24(2). A key issue in that case was whether the search warrant had been properly obtained. The arbitrator inquired into the adequacy of documentation submitted to the court in support of the application for a warrant and determined, ultimately, that there existed a "credibly-based probability" that a search was justified. Moreover, he found, even if the investigation and search had been implemented in a manner that violated the *Charter*, there was no basis on which to hold that the admission of the evidence would bring the administration of justice into disrepute, so as to justify its exclusion.

Additional Reading

J. Fichaud, "The Labour Arbitrator's Jurisdiction under the *Charter*" in W. Kaplan, J. Sack & M. Gunderson, eds., *Labour Arbitration Yearbook 1992*, p. 3.

6.4   THE RULE AGAINST HEARSAY

As a general rule, witnesses are permitted to give evidence only on matters about which they have direct knowledge. Evidence relating to what another person told the witness — "hearsay" evidence — is normally not admissible in a court of law because, in the absence of the original declarant, the opposing party is deprived of an opportunity to test the veracity or accuracy of the person's recollection of events through cross-examination. While arbitrators have a discretion to admit evidence, whether or not admissible in a court of law,

they almost invariably give hearsay evidence little weight or exclude it altogether. This concern about the inherent unfairness of admitting hearsay is well
set out in the seminal case of *Northern Electric Co. Ltd. and U.A.W., Local 27*
(1971), 22 L.A.C. 163 (Weatherill). It is echoed in the more recent case of
Brewster Transport Co. Ltd. and A.T.U., Local 1374 (1992), 26 L.A.C. (4th)
240. While Arbitrator Tettensor recognized the discomfort which the employer
would feel in requiring one of its customers to attend at the hearing and testify
about his dissatisfaction with the grievor, nonetheless, as a matter of fairness,
he ruled that hearsay evidence of the complaint presented through the
employer's managerial staff could not be relied on to establish just cause for
discipline.

6.5   EXCEPTIONS

6.5.1   Necessity and Reliability

Until recently, hearsay evidence was not admissible in the courts, and generally not in arbitration proceedings, unless it fell within one of the exceptions
recognized at common law. Rejecting this often inflexible and artificial
approach to the issue, however, the Supreme Court of Canada has articulated
a "principled" basis for the recognition of new exceptions where the evidence
sought to be adduced satisfies the twin criteria of "necessity" and "reliability":
R. v. Khan, [1990] 2 S.C.R. 531; *R. v. Smith* (1992), 94 D.L.R. (4th) 590.

According to the Court, the requirement of necessity means that there is
some compelling reason why the person who made the statement cannot be
called to testify directly as, for example, when he or she is too young to testify, vulnerable to trauma, mentally incompetent or deceased. The criterion of
necessity was also found to have been met where it was impossible to identify
which nurse had made key notations on a patient chart (see *Ares v. Venner*
(1970), 14 D.L.R. (3d) 4 (S.C.C.)). In accordance with the second requirement,
that of reliability, the statement must have been made "under circumstances
which substantially negate the possibility that the declarant was untruthful or
mistaken". The judgments of the Supreme Court of Canada were reviewed and
applied in *Unionville Home Society and C.U.P.E., Local 3744* (2000), 90
L.A.C. (4th) 299 (Davie). Arbitrator Davie noted that the weight to be accorded
such statements, once admitted, falls to be determined in the context of all of
the evidence in the case.

Nevertheless, in *R. v. O'Connor* (2002), 62 O.R. (3d) 263, the Ontario Court
of Appeal held that hearsay evidence on a critical issue should be admitted only
as a last resort, and that establishing "necessity" requires more than proof that
a witness is out of the jurisdiction and cannot be compelled to testify.

Moreover, where hearsay evidence *is* admitted, Arbitrator Munroe noted in
British Columbia Maritime Employers Ass'n and I.L.W.U., Local 500 (2001),

100 L.A.C. (4th) 318, it will, as a matter of weight, almost invariably be over-ridden by direct oral evidence that has some credibility. This was amply demonstrated in *Les Suites Hotel and Hospitality & Services Trade Union, Local 261* (2003), 119 L.A.C. (4th) 122 (Dumoulin), where the grievor had been dismissed on the basis of allegations in a letter of complaint. Counsel for the employer decided not to call the complainant to give evidence at the arbitration hearing because she had once testified at an inquest, and had been traumatized by the experience. Arbitrator Dumoulin admitted the letter on the ground of necessity, since it was the only evidence left to the employer to support its case. However, on the merits, the arbitrator found against the employer, primarily for the reason that he had not had the benefit of *viva voce* evidence to offset the testimony given by the grievor.

Additional Reading

D. Paciocco, "The Supreme Court of Canada and Hearsay: The Relevance for Arbitration" in W. Kaplan, J. Sack & M. Gunderson, eds., *Labour Arbitration Yearbook 1994-95*, p. 123.

6.5.2 *Res Gestae* – "In the Course of the Act"

The modern approach to the recognition of exceptions to the prohibition against hearsay evidence has not, however, entirely supplanted the common law categories, which have on occasion been considered in the context of grievance arbitration. One of the traditional exceptions is that which relates to *res gestae* statements, that is, statements forming part of the event itself. The key element in establishing the exception, as noted by the English Privy Council in *Ratten v. R.*, [1971] 3 All E.R. 801, at p. 807, is that the statement was made "in circumstances of spontaneity or involvement in the event [such] that the possibility of concoction can be disregarded". There must also be some compelling reason why the person who made the statement cannot be called to give the evidence at the hearing (the exception, in its origins, arose in situations where the original declarant had died). While this latter requirement is not considered in any detail, Arbitrator Marcotte's award in *Metropolitan Toronto (Municipality) and C.U.P.E., Local 79* (1989), 9 L.A.C. (4th) 178, provides a classic example of the doctrine. In the arbitrator's opinion, although the hearsay statement sought to be adduced was not part of the occurrence itself, the statement followed the occurrence so quickly that it could properly be admitted under the *res gestae* exception.

6.5.3 Admission by a Party

There exists a further exception to the rule against hearsay evidence, often mistakenly referred to as "admissions against interest". Admissions by their very nature are usually to the detriment of the speaker's interest. The basis on which this type of evidence is received, even though hearsay, is that it is an admission by a *party*. To qualify under this exception, the statement must be made by an official or representative of the party, acting within the scope of his or her authority. The rule is well set out in *Fuller Austin Insulation Ltd. and C.J.A., Local 2103* (2002), 107 L.A.C. (4th) 421 (Casey).

Additional Reading

W.K. Winkler & A. Rae, "Admissions and Confessions: A Management Perspective" in W. Kaplan, J. Sack & M. Gunderson, eds., *Labour Arbitration Yearbook 1991*, vol. II, p. 123.

J. Sack, "Admissions and Confessions: The Employee's Perspective" in W. Kaplan, J. Sack & M. Gunderson, eds., *Labour Arbitration Yearbook 1991*, vol. II, p. 133.

6.6 SIMILAR FACT EVIDENCE

In the context of a criminal trial, it is generally held that evidence of the accused's bad character or prior misconduct is not admissible on the basis that it would be prejudicial and unfair to consider such evidence in determining whether the accused committed the offence now being alleged. This stance reflects the courts' concern that the accused may be convicted solely because he or she is deemed to have a predisposition toward criminal or disreputable behaviour. Similarly, although arbitrators enjoy a broad statutory discretion to admit evidence that would be inadmissible in a court of law, "similar fact" evidence is generally excluded if its purpose is simply to show that the grievor is an individual of bad character, and ought not to be believed: *Fraser Health Authority and H.E.U. (D'Emilio)*, [2004] B.C.C.A.A.A. No. 84 (QL) (Dorsey).

In *R. v. B. (C.R.)*, [1990] 1 S.C.R. 717, Justice McLachlin, writing for the Supreme Court of Canada, traced the evolution of the law on bad character evidence. She noted that, historically, evidence of prior misconduct relevant only to an individual's propensity to commit unlawful or immoral acts was inadmissible. An exception developed in respect of evidence of prior acts that were strikingly similar to the conduct in question, provided the evidence was relevant to some issue other than propensity, such as to prove identity or intent, or to rebut a defence of mistake or accident. However, Justice McLachlin rejected this "pigeon-holing" approach to similar fact evidence. Rather, the Court ruled, evidence of prior misconduct may be admissible if the probative value of the evidence outweighs its prejudicial effect. In making this determination, the judge must consider the degree of distinctiveness or uniqueness shared by the similar fact evidence and the offence alleged, as well as the connection, if any, of the evidence to issues other than propensity or predisposition. Applying these principles in *Vancouver (City) and C.U.P.E., Local 15* (1996), 53 L.A.C.

(4th) 137, Arbitrator Bluman emphasized that, where the prejudicial effect of
the evidence sought to be introduced is great, there must be a correspondingly
high degree of similarity between the respective fact situations.

6.7   PRIVILEGE

Evidence which is otherwise relevant and admissible may be excluded on
the ground that it is "privileged". Some of the assertions of privilege which frequently lead to disputes over the admissibility of evidence before the courts,
such as solicitor-client privilege, rarely arise in the arbitral forum. Other forms
of privilege recognized at common law, such as litigation privilege, play a
more prominent part in evidentiary disputes at arbitration and in this connection arbitrators have adopted the principles articulated by the courts. Still other
kinds of privilege are unique to the institution of labour arbitration. The emergence of a "labour relations privilege", for instance, discussed in Chapter 6.7.3,
represents an arbitral adaptation of the common law rules which protect from
disclosure communications which, as a matter of policy, are entitled to remain
confidential.

6.7.1   Statements in the Grievance Procedure

The grievance procedure under a collective agreement is designed to give
the parties an opportunity to address and resolve disputes at an early stage. In
order to foster a full and frank exchange between the parties and to encourage
settlement, arbitrators have generally recognized that discussions entered into
pursuant to the grievance procedure are protected by the common law privilege attaching to settlement discussions. Evidence of such discussions is therefore generally inadmissible at an arbitration hearing. In this regard, reference
is typically made to the comments of Arbitrator Shime in *Scarborough (Borough) and I.A.F.F., Local 626* (1972), 24 L.A.C. 78. The arbitral concern for
fostering settlement discussions can also be seen in *York (City) Board of Education and C.U.P.E., Local 1749-B* (1989), 9 L.A.C. (4th) 282 (H.D. Brown).

The privilege should not, however, be taken to preclude the admission of
evidence relating to grievance procedure discussions in every instance. As discussed in Chapter 2.2, for example, such evidence may be necessary to determine whether a party is improperly attempting to expand the scope of a
grievance. In *Maple Lodge Farms Ltd. and U.F.C.W.* (1985), 21 L.A.C. (3d)
321, Arbitrator Swan noted that an employee's threatening conduct towards his
supervisor during a grievance procedure meeting could not be characterized as
an attempt to settle the dispute, and was therefore admissible in evidence for
the purpose of justifying the imposition of further discipline.

Another context in which evidence of what occurred during the grievance
procedure is admissible arises from a party's allegation or denial that a

settlement was in fact reached at that stage. In *Canada Post Corp. and C.U.P.W.* (1993), 38 L.A.C. (4th) 443, where such evidence was admitted, Arbitrator Wakeling noted the incongruity of encouraging the parties to settle their differences through a prescribed grievance procedure while effectively rendering unenforceable any resulting agreement by precluding it from being proven. The arbitrator stated as well that the evidence proving the settlement can be in either oral or written form.

In keeping with the privileged nature of grievance procedure discussions, a party is normally entitled to insist that its "reply" to a grievance not be admitted in evidence, at least where the reply contains anything of a sensitive or prejudicial nature: *Pirelli Cables & Systems Ltd. and U.S.W.A., Local 2952* (2001), 101 L.A.C. (4th) 270 (Somjen). There have, however, been instances in which, notwithstanding a party's objection on the ground of privilege, the arbitrator ruled that the reply must be admitted "as part of the formal grievance record". See, for example, *Laurentian Hospital and O.N.A.* (1997), 67 L.A.C. (4th) 289 (Pineau).

6.7.2   Documents Prepared in Contemplation of Litigation

Litigation privilege is an outgrowth of the privilege historically accorded by the courts to communications between a solicitor and his or her client. Whereas the purpose of solicitor-client privilege is to protect the confidentiality of communications made in the context of a professional relationship, however, litigation privilege extends to documents provided to counsel to assist in the conduct of litigation, even though not initially part of a solicitor-client communication. Such documents typically include notes or statements by witnesses, or investigative reports prepared by a third party. The original rationale for the privilege was that the opposing party should not have the benefit of counsel's work product, which reflects his or her skill and industry, and which may disclose counsel's theory of the case.

The seminal statement of this principle is found in *Lyell v. Kennedy (No. 3)*, [1881-5] All E.R. Rep. 814 (C.A.), where Lord Justice Cotton held, at p. 825:

> In my opinion, it is contrary to the principle on which the court acts with regard to protection on the ground of professional privilege, that we should make an order for their production: they were got for the purpose of his defence, and it would be to deprive a solicitor of the means afforded for enabling him fully to investigate a case for the purpose of instructing counsel if we required documents, although perhaps *publici juris* in themselves, to be produced; because the very fact of the solicitor having got copies of certain burial certificates and other records, and having made copies of the inscriptions on certain tombstones, and obtained photographs of certain houses, might show what his view was as to the case of his client as regards the claim made against him.

In the words of Lord Justice Bowen, at p. 827:

A collection of records may be the result of professional knowledge, research, and skill, just as a collection of curiosities is the result of the skill and knowledge of the antiquarian or virtuoso; and even if the solicitor has employed others to obtain them, it is his own knowledge and judgment which have probably indicated the source from which they could be obtained. It is his mind, if that be so, which has selected the materials, and those materials, when chosen, seem to me to represent the result of his professional care and skill, and you cannot have disclosure of them without asking for the key which will unlock the treasure of labour which the solicitor has bestowed in obtaining them.

A related rationale for the privilege, articulated in later decisions, is the encouragement of careful preparation of cases, which in turn promotes the possibility of settlement by identifying the strengths and weaknesses of a party's position.

A modern statement of the principle, along with a discussion of other types of privilege with which litigation privilege is frequently confused, is contained in *Canada Post Corp. and C.U.P.W. (McNeil)* (1999), 81 L.A.C. (4th) 213 (Blasina). As Arbitrator Blasina noted, the report or other document for which privilege is claimed need not have been created while litigation was actually under way or in preparation, as long as it can be shown that legal proceedings were pending, threatened or reasonably anticipated.

An issue that continues to be debated is whether potential litigation must have been the "dominant purpose" for the preparation of the document or merely a "substantial purpose" in order for privilege to attach. Following the position adopted in *Hall v. Co-operators General Insurance Co.* (1992), 5 C.L.R. (2d) 318 (Ont. Gen. Div.), the Ontario Grievance Settlement Board ruled in *Ontario (Ministry of Correctional Services) and O.P.S.E.U. (Knight)* (1994), 39 L.A.C. (4th) 205 that the appropriate test to apply was the "dominant purpose" test. In the Board's view, such a conclusion was consistent with its policy of facilitating broad disclosure, thus restricting parties' ability to assert privilege.

The dominant purpose test now appears to have been generally adopted across Canada. In applying this test, a question has arisen as to whether a claim for privilege can be sustained with respect to documents created prior to the time at which the issues giving rise to the litigation have "crystallized". Typically, in the context of grievance arbitration, crystallization takes the form of a decision to impose discipline; thus, it was held in *Ontario (Ministry of Correctional Services), supra*, that documents which are merely fact-finding or investigatory in nature will not attract the privilege. A similar approach was taken in *Central Park Lodges and S.E.I.U., Local 210* (2001), 95 L.A.C. (4th) 192 (Etherington). In *Canad Inns – Polo Park Ltd. and B.C.T., Local 389* (2003), 119 L.A.C. (4th) 302, Arbitrator Peltz drew an analogy to the courts' treatment of incident reports prepared in connection with accidents on the premises of a grocery store ("slip and fall" cases). In some instances, the store's standard form was held not to be privileged, as litigation at that stage was no more than a possibility. In others, the same form was granted privilege on the basis that the store could reasonably have anticipated litigation at the time of the incident, in view of the frequency of claims by customers.

In *W. Ralston (Canada) Inc. and C.E.P., Local 819* (2002), 103 L.A.C. (4th) 279 (Swan), an ergonomics study relating to the grievor's capacity to perform a job, requested and paid for by the union, clearly met the test for litigation privilege. Arbitrator Swan was not persuaded that the desirability of cooperation between the parties in a disability accommodation case justified a departure from the rule. Furthermore, he noted, since the employer was free to commission another report at its own expense, it could not be said that there was a substantial need for the evidence or that the employer was unable to obtain it without undue hardship.

A document that was not prepared in contemplation of litigation does not become privileged merely because it is given to a lawyer. Conversely, even where the original is not privileged, a copy prepared for the dominant purpose of litigation, together with any notes or alterations made by counsel, is protected from disclosure: see *Ottawa-Carleton (Regional Municipality) v. Consumers' Gas Co.* (1990), 74 D.L.R. (4th) 742 (Ont. Div. Ct.).

As Arbitrator Blasina pointed out in *Canada Post Corp.*, *supra*, a document that fails to qualify for litigation privilege may nonetheless be protected from disclosure under the more recently developed "labour relations privilege", discussed in Chapter 6.7.3.

6.7.3 Labour Relations Privilege

The common law does not recognize a privilege shielding the disclosure of relevant information based on labour relations considerations. Arbitrators, however, have adapted the so-called "Wigmore conditions", laid down by the eminent American authority on the law of evidence, as the basis for articulating such a privilege in circumstances where disclosure would have a deleterious impact on the parties' labour relations. The Wigmore conditions, approved by the Supreme Court of Canada in *Slavutych v. Baker* (1975), 55 D.L.R. (3d) 224, posit a discretion in the court or tribunal to exclude evidence of private communications, provided the following conditions are satisfied:

(1) the communication must originate in a confidence that it will not be disclosed;

(2) the element of confidentiality must be essential to the full and satisfactory maintenance of the relation between the parties;

(3) the relation must be one which, in the opinion of the community, ought to be sedulously fostered; and

(4) the injury that would inure to the relationship by the disclosure of the communication must be greater than the benefit thereby gained for the correct disposal of the litigation.

The concept of a labour relations privilege based on the Wigmore criteria has been developed most extensively in British Columbia. In *British Columbia (Ministry of Transportation) and B.C.G.E.U., Local 1103* (1990), 13 L.A.C. (4th) 190, for example, Arbitrator Larson concluded that confidential memoranda prepared by the employer with respect to a disputed promotion were not subject to production at the instance of the union. In the arbitrator's opinion, the recognition of a "shop steward privilege" protecting discussions between a union official and an employee should logically extend to the confidential labour relations information of the employer as well.

The mere fact that a document is "internal" to the union or management, however, does not necessarily lead to the conclusion that its disclosure would have a harmful impact on the parties' labour relations. In *School District No. 59 and Peace River South Teachers' Ass'n* (1996), 57 L.A.C. (4th) 273, at p. 282, for example, Arbitrator Hope emphasized that "[a]rbitrators can be expected to be slow to exclude documents that may be relevant to issues in dispute [based] on an assertion of privilege that falls outside the narrow parameters defined in the Wigmore criteria". Similarly, in *School District No. 65 (Cowichan) and Cowichan District Teachers' Ass'n* (1996), 54 L.A.C. (4th) 378 (Dorsey), which involved a disputed claim for paid union leave, the employer sought an order requiring that the union disclose documents shedding light on the grievor's activities at a conference. The employer made clear, however, that the terms of the order sought did not include information about the union's "collective bargaining strategies, position and proposals". Arbitrator Dorsey granted the request, holding that routine documents relevant to an issue in the proceeding were subject to the normal rule of disclosure, even if they incidentally revealed some information about a party's internal affairs. Furthermore, distinguishing the ruling in *British Columbia (Ministry of Transportation)*, *supra*, Arbitrator Etherington has applied the Wigmore conditions to hold that investigative reports prepared by management prior to its decision to impose discipline were not protected from disclosure: *Central Park Lodges and S.E.I.U., Local 210* (2001), 95 L.A.C. (4th) 192.

The same analysis has been applied by the courts to employment relationships not covered by a collective agreement. In *Straka v. Humber River Regional Hospital* (2000), 193 D.L.R. (4th) 680 (Ont. C.A.), a doctor applying for a staff position at a hospital was turned down on the basis of reference letters supplied by doctors with whom he had previously worked. The Court, in a notable affirmation of the Wigmore principles, denied the doctor access to the letters on the ground that they had been submitted in confidence.

Another aspect of labour relations privilege relates to information disclosed in the context of a dispute resolution process. It was held in *Air Canada and*

Air Canada Pilots' Ass'n (2002), 113 L.A.C. (4th) 372 (Keller) that it is not in the best interests of the parties' long-term bargaining relationship to compel witnesses to testify about discussions held before a conciliator or mediator. In *Essex County Board of Education and O.P.S.T.F. (Grainger)* (2003), 124 L.A.C. (4th) 430, Arbitrator Tom Jolliffe applied the "deliberative secrecy rule" to prohibit the calling of a party's nominee in a previous arbitration to testify from his notes with respect to an alleged inconsistent statement by the grievor.

6.7.4   Public Interest Immunity

At common law the inner workings of government were protected from public scrutiny by the development of a branch of privilege known as "public immunity privilege" or "Crown privilege", which shielded confidential documents from disclosure in the course of legal proceedings. Over time, however, the approach of the courts evolved from almost unquestioning acceptance of claims for executive privilege to an attempt to balance the requirement for confidentiality in the formulation of public policy against the requirement for transparency and fairness in the administration of justice. As held by the British Columbia Supreme Court in *Health Services and Support-Facilities Subsector Bargaining Ass'n v. British Columbia* (2002), 8 B.C.L.R. (4th) 281, claims of privilege in respect of documents which reveal the substance of Cabinet deliberations will prevail only where it is in the public interest that the information remain undisclosed.

Section 39 of the *Canada Evidence Act*, R.S.C. 1985, c. C-5, on its face gives the federal government virtually unlimited discretion to certify a document as privileged on the basis that it is "a confidence of the Queen's Privy Council". However, in *Babcock v. Canada (Attorney General)* (2002), 214 D.L.R. (4th) 193, the Supreme Court of Canada ruled that a certificate must identify the date, title, author and recipient of each document for which privilege is asserted, in order to permit an assessment of whether the document is in fact shielded from disclosure by s. 39. The Federal Court recently rejected a claim for privilege on the basis that the certificate failed to meet these requirements. An appeal was dismissed, but the Federal Court of Appeal permitted the government to file a revised certificate: *Pelletier v. Canada (Attorney General)* (2005), 253 D.L.R. (4th) 435.

6.7.5   Privilege Based on Personal Privacy

The development of much of the law in this area has centred on the right of a person accused of a criminal offence to make full answer and defence. Thus, an accused person has long been considered to have a constitutional right to the disclosure of any available evidence which may assist him or her in making that full answer and defence. Where the accused has been charged with a sexual offence, this right has, until recently, extended to the disclosure of the complainant's medical, therapeutic and other confidential records, both those in the possession of the Crown and those in the possession of a third party, typically a professional counsellor such as a psychiatrist or psychologist. In the ground-breaking case of *R. v. O'Connor* (1995), 130 D.L.R. (4th) 235, the Supreme Court of Canada held that the complainants in a sexual assault trial had a *Charter*-based privacy right in the information contained in records in the hands of a third-party custodian, and that in determining the appropriate scope of disclosure this right must be balanced against the accused's right to raise a defence. The potential breadth of the information covered by a complainant's privacy interest is described in the following passage from the judgment of Justice L'Heureux-Dubé, at p. 283:

> The question of production of private records not in the possession of the Crown arises in a wide variety of contexts. Although many of these contexts involve medical and therapeutic records of complainants to sexual assault, it will become apparent that the principles and guidelines outlined herein are equally applicable to *any* record, in the hands of a third party, in which a reasonable expectation of privacy lies. Although the determination of when a reasonable expectation of privacy actually exists in a particular record (and, if so, to what extent it exists) is inherently fact- and context-sensitive, this may include records that are medical or therapeutic in nature, school records, private diaries, and activity logs prepared by social workers, to name just a few.

In striking an appropriate balance between the competing interests at stake, the Court enunciated a two-step process. Initially, the party seeking production of a private record is required to file an application with the trial judge, supported by affidavit evidence stating the grounds for the request. If the judge is satisfied that the document is "likely relevant" to an issue in the proceedings, it is produced for his or her inspection. The trial judge must then decide whether to release the document, in whole or in part, to the parties. In making this determination, the judge is obligated to assess whether "the salutary effects of [production] outweigh the damage done thereby", *i.e.* whether maintaining the confidentiality of the record would constitute a reasonable limit on the accused's right to make full answer and defence. Factors to be considered at this second stage of the analysis include (1) the extent to which the document is necessary for the accused to make full answer and defence; (2) the probative value of the document; (3) the nature and extent of the reasonable expectation of privacy in the document; (4) whether production would be premised on any discriminatory belief or bias about the victims of sexual assault; and (5) the potential prejudice to the complainant's dignity, privacy or security of the person.

In the aftermath of the considerable public debate generated by the Supreme Court's decision in *O'Connor*, Parliament amended the federal *Criminal Code* in order to deal specifically with the production of records in proceedings involving alleged sexual offences: S.C. 1997, c. 30 ("Bill C-46").

A concern had arisen that records were routinely being produced to the court at the first step, leading to a recurring violation of the privacy interests of complainants and other witnesses. To rectify this, Bill C-46 added to the "likely relevant" standard set out in *O'Connor* the further requirement that production be "necessary in the interests of justice". The legislation also created safeguards to prevent courts from accepting evidence based upon myths or stereotypes about the victims of sexual offences (typically women and children) in assessing whether a document is likely relevant, and set out a number of factors which courts are to take into account in determining whether production is in the interests of justice. In *R. v. Mills* (1999), 180 D.L.R. (4th) 1 (S.C.C.), the amendments withstood a *Charter* challenge by an accused. Both the legislation and the judgment in *Mills* were discussed and applied by Arbitrator Lanyon in *Share Family & Community Services Society and H.S.A.B.C.* (2002), 109 L.A.C. (4th) 289.

In *Mills, supra,* the Supreme Court of Canada emphasized that one of the primary factors to be taken into account in carrying out the balancing analysis mandated by Bill C-46 is the effect of non-disclosure on the accused's right to make full answer and defence. On the other hand, in *M. (A.) v. Ryan* (1997), 143 D.L.R. (4th) 1 (S.C.C.), the Court commented that a complainant's privacy rights may be more compelling in a civil than in a criminal matter, where the liberty of the accused is not at stake. In both civil and criminal proceedings, it has been clear since *O'Connor, supra,* that the requirement in each case is to strike a balance between a litigant's right to disclosure of potentially relevant evidence, and an individual's need for and expectation of privacy. Arbitrator Dissanayake observed in *Stelco Inc. and U.S.W.A., Local 1005* (1994), 42 L.A.C. (4th) 270 that policy considerations weigh more heavily in favour of disclosure where the medical evidence is of a less personal nature, and is clearly probative. Furthermore, as noted by Justice L'Heureux-Dubé in *O'Connor, supra,* the range of documents requiring a balancing of rights is not limited to medical records. In *Overwaitea Food Group and C.L.A.C., Local 66,* [2004] B.C.C.A.A.A. No. 162 (QL) (McPhillips), the union requested disclosure of sealed commercial tenders which, though clearly relevant, contained sensitive and confidential trade information. Applying elements of both *O'Connor* and *Ryan,* Arbitrator McPhillips ordered that the disputed documents initially be disclosed only to counsel for the union, in order to ascertain whether broader disclosure might be necessary.

The British Columbia Court of Appeal, in *British Columbia v. B.C.G.E.U.* (2005), 248 D.L.R. (4th) 462, provided an overview of the caselaw in which *O'Connor* has been applied. The Court noted that, where disclosure is sought of private (usually medical) information, three types of orders are available, providing for progressively more stringent restrictions on disclosure: (1) a "*Jones* order", stipulating that the documents in question are to be disclosed only for the purposes of the litigation; (2) a "*Halliday* order", which permits the objecting party to review the documents prior to disclosure, and to remove irrelevant material; and (3) a " *Ryan* order", which provides that only specified individuals may view the documents. In this case, faced with an employer request for disclosure of the grievor's medical records to its "management team", Arbitrator Lanyon issued a *Ryan* order limiting disclosure to the employer's legal counsel and medical advisors: see (2004), 127 L.A.C. (4th) 419. In a split decision, the Court of Appeal allowed the employer's appeal, holding that the restrictions on disclosure imposed by the arbitrator went too far. In so ruling, the Court allowed the employer to "clarify" that disclosure would be limited to two or three senior management officials, and would not in fact extend to its entire "management team" (the position taken by the employer at the arbitration hearing). Thus, the arbitrator's order was amended by the Court to permit representatives of the employer to view the records to the extent necessary to instruct counsel.

For a discussion of the circumstances in which the arbitrator may require that an employee submit to a medical examination, see Chapter 4.5.

6.8   VIDEOTAPE SURVEILLANCE EVIDENCE

In support of the imposition of discipline for falsifying a claim for sick leave or workers' compensation benefits, or misrepresenting one's ability to attend at work due to disability, the employer may seek to introduce surreptitious videotape surveillance evidence revealing an employee's off-site activities. Frequently, the union objects to the admission of such evidence on the basis that it was acquired in a manner that violated the employee's right to privacy. Although an analogy is often drawn to cases dealing with the right of the employer to conduct employee searches, or to require various medical examinations such as a drug test (see Chapter 13), the question of the admissibility of covert videotape surveillance evidence has given rise to a separate line of caselaw.

A seminal award in this area is *Doman Forest Products Ltd. and I.W.A., Local 1-357* (1990), 13 L.A.C. (4th) 275 (Vickers). Because the case was decided in British Columbia, which has specifically enacted a *Privacy Act* conferring an actionable right of privacy (R.S.B.C. 1996, c. 373), arbitrators in other jurisdictions have tended to distinguish *Doman Forest Products* on that basis. In fact, Arbitrator Vickers appeared to be more influenced by what he described as the "fundamental *Charter* values" expressed in *R. v. Duarte* (1990), 65 D.L.R. (4th) 240 (S.C.C.), a criminal case dealing with the telephone-tapping of a citizen by the state. In determining the admissibility of videotape surveillance evidence at an arbitration hearing, the arbitrator formulated a three-part test:

(1) Was it reasonable, in all the circumstances, to initiate surveillance?

(2) Was the surveillance conducted in a reasonable manner?

(3) Were other, less intrusive alternatives open to the employer to obtain the same evidence?

While the presence of a specific right to privacy under British Columbia legislation is often noted, it would now seem that there is no substantive difference in the approach taken by arbitrators in British Columbia and arbitrators elsewhere. In *Canadian Pacific Ltd. and B.M.W.E. (Chahul)* (1996), 59 L.A.C. (4th) 111, having reviewed *Doman Forest Products*, Arbitrator Michel Picher proposed a two-part test that is not significantly different from that suggested by Arbitrator Vickers:

(1) Was it reasonable, in all the circumstances, to undertake surveillance of the employee's off-duty activity?

(2) Was the surveillance conducted in a reasonable way, which is not unduly intrusive and which corresponds fairly with acquiring information pertinent to the employer's legitimate interests?

This two-part test clearly represents the way in which arbitrators most commonly articulate the applicable approach today. While the test would, in appropriate cases, allow for consideration of what other, less intrusive methods were available, there appears to be a general consensus that requiring the employer to show that it has exhausted all other alternatives in dealing with potential fraud sets the bar too high. That, however, may be the extent of the consensus, as arbitrators continue to grapple with this issue in an increasing number of cases.

There are dissenting views. Thus, in *Kimberly-Clark and I.W.A., Local 1-92-4* (1998), 66 L.A.C. (4th) 266, Arbitrator Bendel, moving the pendulum in the opposite direction, questioned why arbitrators should take a more exclusionary approach to relevant evidence than courts, and why videotape evidence should be treated differently from other forms of surveillance evidence (such as the arguably less reliable or informative oral testimony of an investigator as to what he or she observed), particularly where the surveillance is being conducted in a public place. And, more recently, Arbitrator Snow, in *Hôtel-Dieu Grace Hospital and C.A.W., Local 2458* (2004), 134 L.A.C. (4th) 246, rejected the proposition that the reasonableness of the employer's decision to initiate surveillance was a factor to consider in determining the admissibility of the videotapes. Citing *Greater Niagara Transit Commission v. A.T.U., Local 1582* (1987), 43 D.L.R. (4th) 71, where the Ontario Divisional Court commented that it is "prudent and proper" for an arbitrator to admit evidence that would be admitted by a court, Arbitrator Snow concluded that the *only* test is relevance.

However, the majority view would appear to be that, whether based on a right to privacy or a balancing of employer and employee interests, "the exercise of management's rights to undertake inquiries that intrude into the sphere of what would in the normal course be considered to be an employee's private affairs [is] constrained to only those inquiries which are reasonable": see

Securicor Cash Services and Teamsters, Local 419 (2004), 125 L.A.C. (4th) 129 (Whitaker), at p. 139.

The direction of arbitration caselaw will no doubt be affected by the passage of the federal *Personal Information Protection and Electronic Documents Act, S.C. 2000, c. 5* ("PIPEDA") and its provincial counterparts. In *Ross and Rosedale Transport Ltd.*, [2003] C.L.A.D. No. 237 (QL), an unjust dismissal adjudication under the *Canada Labour Code*, R.S.C. 1985, c. L-2, the complainant was alleged to have malingered following a work-related back injury. Adjudicator Brunner found that private activities of the complainant surreptitiously recorded on a surveillance videotape clearly constituted "personal information" to which the Act applied. Furthermore, he ruled, the principles of "reasonableness" established in arbitral jurisprudence with respect to the admissibility of videotape surveillance evidence were relevant in interpreting PIPEDA, as s. 7(b) of the Act created an exception to the prohibition against the unauthorized collection of personal information where

> . . . it is reasonable to expect that the collection with the knowledge or consent of the individual would compromise the availability or accuracy of the information and the collection is reasonable for purposes related to investigating a breach of an agreement.

Similarly, in another case under federal jurisdiction, *Securicor Cash Services*, *supra*, accepting that "some form of a right to privacy exists at common law", the arbitrator found clear statutory support for a "reasonableness" standard in the provisions of PIPEDA.

In *Ebco Metal Finishing Ltd. and B.S.O.I.W., Local 712* (2004), 134 L.A.C. (4th) 372, Arbitrator Blasina analyzed the caselaw and the provisions of the British Columbia *Personal Information Protection Act*, S.B.C. 2003, c. 63, and arrived at the same conclusion: any surreptitious surveillance of employees by the employer is subject to "the balancing of competing interests and the reasonableness assessments expressed in the authorities, and in legislation" (at p. 392). Additionally, the arbitrator questioned the common arbitral practice of viewing the videotapes before ruling on their admissibility (the "look-and-decide-later" approach). In this case, having found the employer in violation of the Act, Arbitrator Blasina rejected the argument that the videotapes should nevertheless be received. Arbitrators should be vigilant in giving effect to privacy legislation, he stated, and admitting evidence obtained in breach of its provisions would amount to an "error of law and abdication of jurisdiction" (at p. 402). For a contrary view on the appropriateness of viewing the videotapes before determining whether they are admissible, see *Telus Corp. and T.W.U. (Fenske)*, [2004] C.L.A.D. No. 508 (QL) (Tettensor).

One of the points made in *Kimberly-Clark*, *supra*, was that there is no basis for drawing a distinction between videotape surveillance and other forms of surveillance evidence, such as the oral testimony of the investigator regarding his or her observations. Arbitrator Brandt, in *Enwin Utilities Ltd. and I.B.E.W.,*

Local 636 (2003), 114 L.A.C. (4th) 421, effectively agreed, but then concluded that the admissibility of an investigator's first-hand evidence is subject to the same criteria as the videotape itself. As the videotape surveillance evidence in this case had previously been ruled inadmissible (the employer having failed to establish reasonable grounds for initiating surveillance in the first place), so too, the arbitrator held, should the investigator's oral evidence be excluded.

Finally, the question has been raised whether employees have a lesser expectation of privacy if they are on the employer's premises, or off-site but on public property. In this respect, in *Toronto Transit Commission and A.T.U., Local 113 (Russell)* (1999), 88 L.A.C. (4th) 109, Arbitrator Owen Shime characterized the privacy interest of an employee who is in a public location as one of a very low order. Moreover, he indicated, arbitrators should be reluctant to take a more exclusionary view of relevant and probative evidence than would the courts. However, in *Toronto Transit Commission and A.T.U., Local 113 (Belsito)* (1999), 95 L.A.C. (4th) 402, Arbitrator Pamela Chapman expressed the view that there may be a difference between the creation of a videotape record and other forms of surveillance evidence, and that even in public places there may be a reasonable expectation of privacy in some circumstances. In that vein, it might be observed, the Supreme Court of Canada has ruled that the right to privacy under Quebec's *Charter of Human Rights and Freedoms*, R.S.Q., c. C-12, includes the right not to have one's photograph published without consent, even if the photograph was taken in a public place, and that breach of this right will in appropriate circumstances support an action for damages: *Aubry v. Éditions Vice-Versa Inc.* (1998), 157 D.L.R. (4th) 577 (S.C.C.).

For further discussion, see Chapter 13.4.3.

Additional Reading

T.A.B. Jolliffe, "Privacy and Surveillance: An Arbitrator's Perspective" in K. Whitaker, J. Sack, M. Gunderson & R. Filion, eds., *Labour Arbitration Yearbook 1999-2000*, vol. II, p. 91; and companion articles by G.R. Meurin and J.R. Carpenter.

M.G. Picher, "Truth, Lies and Videotape: Employee Surveillance at Arbitration" (1998), 6 Canadian Labour and Employment Journal, p. 345.

6.9 TAPE-RECORDED CONVERSATIONS

The surreptitious tape-recording of telephone and other conversations raises labour relations issues which are perhaps even more acute than those surrounding the use of videotape surveillance evidence. Indeed, where the employer is deemed a government actor for the purposes of the *Charter of Rights and Freedoms*, the reception of covertly tape-recorded evidence is subject to attack on the ground that an employee's *Charter* right to freedom from unreasonable search and seizure has been infringed: see *R. v. Duarte* (1990),

65 D.L.R. (4th) 240 (S.C.C.). Much of the relevant jurisprudence in this area has emanated from the federal and provincial labour boards. The Canada Industrial Relations Board, in particular, has long espoused a policy that such evidence is normally inadmissible because of the paramount importance of maintaining trust and informality in the parties' ongoing relations. The Board affirmed this stance in *D.H.L. Int'l Express Ltd. and Teamsters, Local 31* (1995), 28 Can. L.R.B.R. (2d) 297 (C.L.R.B.), where Vice-Chair Hornung held that a party seeking to adduce in evidence a secretly tape-recorded conversation must meet strict conditions before it will be permitted to do so. In particular, he ruled, a party seeking to introduce such evidence must disclose the existence and contents of the tape to the opposing party and the Board as soon as practicably possible; demonstrate that the same evidence cannot be obtained by other means; and satisfy the Board that the probative value of the tape outweighs any negative consequences or prejudicial effect on the hearing, collective bargaining or the parties' labour relations.

The opposite conclusion was reached, however, in *Canada Post Corp. and C.U.P.W. (Nelson)* (1997), 62 L.A.C. (4th) 201 (Ready). While accepting the policy reasons which normally lead to the exclusion of surreptitiously tape-recorded discussions, Arbitrator Ready ruled that in this case the proposed evidence was highly probative of a critical fact in issue. To preclude the grievor from introducing the tape-recording, he held, would be to unfairly hamper her defence against the employer's allegations.

In *Canadian Transit Co. and Teamsters, Local 880* (1998), 78 L.A.C. (4th) 155, Arbitrator Springate held that the interception of telephone conversations between an employee and a shop steward did not violate the prohibition against interference with a trade union found in s. 94(1)(a) of the *Canada Labour Code*, R.S.C. 1985, c. L-2, because none of the conversations in question could be considered privileged. Nor did the employer's disclosure of the content of these conversations at the arbitration hearing contravene the *Criminal Code*, R.S.C. 1985, c. C-46, or the federal *Radiocommunication Act*, R.S.C. 1985, c. R-2, which prohibit interception of a telephone transmission by a third party, because both statutes authorize the disclosure of a private communication in the context of a civil or criminal proceeding at which a person may be required to testify under oath.

6.10 POLYGRAPH TESTING

The issue of whether the results of a polygraph or lie detector test are admissible in a court of law appears to have been settled by the decision of the Supreme Court of Canada in *R. v. Béland* (1987), 43 D.L.R. (4th) 641. There, the Court firmly rejected the use of such evidence, expressing the view that problems of credibility should be resolved by the trier of fact, not an electronic device. While arbitrators retain their statutory discretion to accept evidence which would not be admissible in the courts, Arbitrator Oakley has noted that the arbitration awards in which the introduction of polygraph evidence was permitted generally pre-date the ruling in *Béland*. In *Canada Games Park 1995 Inc. and C.U.P.E., Local 3336* (1996), 59 L.A.C. (4th) 312, he explored the various arguments for and against polygraph evidence, concluding that its use was normally incompatible with sound labour relations policy.

However, a different conclusion was reached in *Northumberland Children's Aid Society and O.P.S.E.U., Local 344* (1996), 61 L.A.C. (4th) 123 (H.D. Brown). While confirming that polygraph evidence should ordinarily be excluded, the board held that there were unusual extenuating circumstances in the case before it. The grievor, a child services worker, had been discharged for allegedly sexually abusing his four-year-old son. As the boy was not competent to testify at the hearing, the board was prepared to permit the use of any means available that could assist in shedding light on the crucial issue of credibility.

See also Chapter 13.4.4 on the validity of employer rules requiring polygraph testing.

Additional Reading

R.B. Bird, "Polygraph Testing: An Arbitrator's Viewpoint" in W. Kaplan, J. Sack & M. Gunderson, eds., *Labour Arbitration Yearbook 1992*, p. 81; and companion articles by A. Wills and D. Blair.

6.11   Expert Evidence

Generally, witnesses in a judicial or quasi-judicial proceeding are entitled to testify only about facts which they have observed, not about their personal opinions or conclusions. An exception is made, however, in the case of witnesses who are qualified as experts in a particular field. The requirements for the admission of expert evidence, as set out by Justice Sopinka in *R. v. Mohan* (1994), 114 D.L.R. (4th) 419 (S.C.C.), are as follows:

(1) relevance;

(2) necessity in assisting the trier of fact;

(3) the absence of any exclusionary rule; and

(4) a properly qualified expert.

The *necessity* of the evidence in assisting the trier of fact may be the most difficult hurdle for a party to overcome, as the courts strictly enforce the rule that only areas beyond the common knowledge (or common sense) of the trier of fact may properly be the subject of expert evidence. As Justice Sopinka explained in *Mohan, supra*, at p. 428:

There is a danger that expert evidence will be misused and will distort the fact-finding process. Dressed up in scientific language which the jury does not easily understand and submitted through a witness of impressive antecedents, this evidence is apt to be accepted by the jury as being virtually infallible and as having more weight than it deserves.

It was to the criterion of necessity that Arbitrator Greyell turned his attention in *British Columbia (Attorney General) and B.C.G.E.U.* (1996), 57 L.A.C. (4th) 391, finding that the opinion evidence offered did not lie outside the experience and knowledge of an arbitrator to assess. In fact, the arbitrator held that the evidence under challenge violated the so-called ultimate issue rule, because it purported to decide the very question that it was the mandate of the arbitrator to decide.

The same caution against "usurping" the function of the judge was voiced by Arbitrator Larson in *Bullmoose Operating Corp. and C.E.P., Local 443* (2000), 88 L.A.C. (4th) 317. Similarly, in *Sobey's Inc. and C.A.W., Local 1090* (2004), 131 L.A.C. (4th) 166, Arbitrator Luborsky refused to admit "expert" testimony as to what a videotape showed, holding that he was equally capable of viewing the tape and making the assessment on his own.

In some provinces, including Ontario and British Columbia, the rules of court require that expert testimony be reduced to writing, and submitted to the other party in advance (in an attempt to remove the necessity for *viva voce* evidence at trial). In *Hamilton-Wentworth District School Board and O.S.S.T.F. (Chaikoff)* (1998), 75 L.A.C. (4th) 289, Arbitrator Springate noted that such rules are not binding at arbitration, and that arbitrators will not generally require a party to provide to the other side a report which is not yet in existence.

Additional Reading

T. Sheppard, "The Role of Expert Evidence at Arbitration" in K. Whitaker, J. Sack, M. Gunderson & R. Filion, eds., *Labour Arbitration Yearbook 2001-2002*, vol. II, p. 265; and companion articles by T. Sigurdson and T. Arsenault.

CHAPTER 7

REMEDIAL POWERS OF THE ARBITRATOR

7.1 MODIFICATION OF THE PENALTY

7.1.1 Post-Discharge Evidence: *Québec Cartier*

Despite the fact that arbitrators had for years exercised a broad discretion to substitute their own judgment as to the appropriate penalty, even where just cause for discipline was established, in *Port Arthur Shipbuilding Co. v. Arthurs* (1968), 70 D.L.R. (2d) 693, the Supreme Court of Canada ruled that a finding of just cause put an end to the matter and exhausted the arbitrator's jurisdiction. Legislatures across Canada responded by enacting provisions that specifically affirmed the power of an arbitrator to substitute a lesser penalty, notwithstanding a finding of just cause for the discipline. Pursuant to the Court's latest pronouncement in *Cie minière Québec Cartier v. U.S.W.A., Local 6869* (1995), 125 D.L.R. (4th) 577 (S.C.C.), however, the way in which the legislative provision is worded may affect the precise scope of arbitral authority in this regard.

It is important to note that, even before *Québec Cartier*, arbitrators disagreed as to the point in time at which the appropriateness of a penalty ought to be judged, at least in cases involving discharge for excessive absenteeism: as of the time when the employer made the decision that is under review? or, as of the time of the hearing? The latter approach allowed an arbitrator to take into account changes in circumstances that might lend support to a more favourable prognosis respecting the employee's ability to attend at work regularly. The most frequently cited example of the "date of discharge school" is *Sudbury (City) and C.U.P.E., Local 207* (1981), 2 L.A.C. (3d) 161 (P.C. Picher). For a different opinion, one which is representative of the "date of hearing school", see *Canada Post Corp. and C.U.P.W.* (1982), 6 L.A.C. (3d) 385, in which Arbitrator Burkett expressly rejected the approach taken in *Sudbury (City)*.

The issue of the appropriate time-frame for assessing the evidence crystallized in *Québec Cartier*, where an employee who suffered from alcoholism was discharged for excessive absenteeism. An arbitrator appointed to hear the employee's grievance ruled that his conduct had afforded the employer just cause, stating: "At the time the company dismissed [the grievor], I am of the view that it could have seemed justified in doing so". However, in light of the fact that the grievor subsequently entered a rehabilitation program, which he successfully completed, the arbitrator decided that the case was an appropriate one in which to reduce the penalty. In his words, the change in the grievor's circumstances was such as would "allow [him] to intervene to alter the dismissal". The arbitrator's reasons thus displayed a stark juxtaposition of a finding of just cause and a remedial order for reinstatement based on developments following the discharge. Although the Quebec Court of Appeal ruled that any evidence tending to shed light on an employee's prognosis for recovery should be considered, the Supreme Court of Canada strongly disagreed. In its view, the relevant time for assessing the prognosis was the time at which the employer made its decision, that is, "*as at the time when the employee was actually dismissed*" (at p. 581; emphasis in original). Equally, though, the Court held that post-discharge evidence is admissible "if it helps to shed light on the reasonableness and appropriateness of the dismissal under review at the time that it was made".

7.1.2   Arbitral Responses to *Québec Cartier*

ALBERTA AND BRITISH COLUMBIA

In Alberta and British Columbia, it appears to be settled law that the effect of *Québec Cartier* is to limit the use of post-discharge evidence. Several decisions have pointed out that the statutory provision empowering arbitrators to modify a discharge or other penalty is, in both provinces, cast in language very similar to that of the Quebec *Labour Code*, R.S.Q. c. C-27, the legislation under which *Québec Cartier* was decided. Others have gone further and indicated that, given the unequivocal nature of the Supreme Court's ruling, it applies to arbitrations generally, unless there is a clear statutory basis for arriving at a contrary conclusion. This latter interpretation of the scope of *Québec Cartier*'s application was adopted by the Alberta Court of Queen's Bench in *U.N.A., Local 2 v. Red Deer Regional Hospital* (1998), 59 Alta. L.R. (3d) 112.

Similarly, in *Westmin Resources Ltd. and C.A.W., Local 3019* (1998), 45 Can. L.R.B.R. (2d) 54, the British Columbia Labour Relations Board considered *Québec Cartier* in the context of its earlier jurisprudence on mitigation of penalties, as set out in *Wm. Scott & Co. and Canadian Food & Allied Workers, Local P-162*, [1977] 1 Can. L.R.B.R. 1 (B.C.L.R.B.) (see Chapter 10.9.1), and arrived at the same conclusion on the application of *Québec Cartier* as did the Alberta Court of Queen's Bench.

However, in a decision dealing with the issue of whether an employee had voluntarily resigned his employment, Arbitrator Dorsey expressed criticism of the British Columbia Labour Relations Board for directing arbitrators in that province to apply *Québec Cartier* strictly, without sufficient regard for countervailing labour relations principles. In the case at hand, the union sought to introduce evidence from an anger management counsellor who treated the grievor after his employment had ended. The arbitrator was not persuaded that, in these circumstances, *Québec Cartier* had any application. Even if it did apply, he ruled, the disputed evidence should be received because it was "potentially relevant" to the grievor's state of mind, *i.e.* in showing whether he intended to quit: *Titan Steel & Wire Co. and Teamsters, Local 213* (2003), 116 L.A.C. (4th) 300.

ONTARIO AND THE FEDERAL JURISDICTION

In Ontario, arbitrators have reached varying conclusions as to whether *Québec Cartier* ends the debate respecting the proper point in time at which an arbitrator ought to review an employer's decision to discharge. However, the most common approach is to distinguish *Québec Cartier* on the basis of differences in the applicable statute. Though likely a matter of legislative happenstance, the post-*Port Arthur Shipbuilding* provisions in both the Ontario *Labour Relations Act*, S.O. 1995, c. 1, Sch. A, and the *Canada Labour Code*, R.S.C. 1985, c. L-2, expressly state that, once an arbitrator has determined that an employee *has* been discharged for cause, the arbitrator may, notwithstanding, go on to substitute "such other penalty as to the arbitrator . . . seems just and reasonable in the circumstances". This variation in the wording of the legislation formed the basis of the award in *Bell Canada and C.E.P.*, an unreported decision of Arbitrator Devlin dated September 22, 1995.

It has, however, been suggested that, where the employer's decision to discharge was based solely on an employee's innocent absenteeism, any distinctions in the statutory language will not soften the application of *Québec Cartier.* The rationale for this view is that, under the Ontario legislation, an arbitrator has jurisdiction to modify only a "penalty" imposed by the employer, whereas a discharge for non-culpable reasons cannot be characterized as a punitive measure. An illustration of such reasoning can be found in *Case Corp. and U.S.W.A., Local 2868*, an unreported award of Arbitrator Howard Brown dated January 8, 1996. This distinction may be of considerable importance where, as in *Case Corp.*, the innocent absenteeism is the result of an addiction for which post-discharge treatment has been sought.

RELEVANCE OF POST-DISCHARGE EVIDENCE

Since *Québec Cartier*, both the courts and arbitrators have pointed out that the Supreme Court of Canada left the door open to post-discharge evidence which may "shed light" on the reasonableness of the employer's decision at the time it was made. Indeed, in decisions which pre-date *Québec Cartier*, some arbitrators in both British Columbia and Ontario had adopted a compromise position which can readily be harmonized with the rules subsequently laid down by the Supreme Court. In *Raven Lumber Ltd. and I.W.A., Local 1-363* (1986), 23 L.A.C. (3d) 357, a leading British Columbia award, Arbitrator Munroe ruled that an employee seeking reinstatement should be given the benefit of hindsight where the employer itself had failed to recognize alcoholism or drug abuse as a disability, or to afford the employee a reasonable opportunity to seek treatment. To put it in *Québec Cartier* terms, post-discharge evidence of successful efforts by the grievor at rehabilitation is relevant to the reasonableness of the employer's decision if an opportunity for rehabilitation was not offered before the discharge. In *Brewers Distributor Ltd. and Brewery, Winery & Distillery Workers Union, Local 300* (1998), 76 L.A.C. (4th) 1, Arbitrator Munroe revisited his award in *Raven Lumber* and concluded that *Québec Cartier* had not undermined the legitimacy of such an approach.

The award in *Fraser Lake Sawmills and I.W.A., Local 1-424* (2000), 90 L.A.C. (4th) 177 (Burke) provides useful clarification of the difference between subsequent-event evidence, proscribed by *Québec Cartier*, and subsequently available evidence which "helps to shed light" on matters as they existed at the time of the discharge. Critical to the arbitrator's decision to allow evidence of post-discharge diagnosis and treatment was the fact that the grievor had disclosed his addiction to his supervisor immediately upon being apprehended smoking marijuana on company premises; that is, "signals", as Arbitrator Burke put it, were arguably available to management at the time, which might reasonably have suggested a need for closer investigation by the employer prior to making the decision to discharge. The ruling by Arbitrator Burke was upheld on review by the British Columbia Labour Relations Board. Subsequently, the Board denied the employer's application for reconsideration of the review panel's decision: *Fraser Lake Sawmills Ltd. and I.W.A., Local 1-424*, [2000] B.C.L.R.B.D. No. 405 (QL).

Similarly, in *Calgary (City) and A.T.U., Local 583*, [2004] A.G.A.A. No. 75 (QL), Arbitrator Elliott admitted a post-discharge medical report in circumstances where the employer had, at the time of the discharge, "every indication that the grievor's behaviour could, at least in part, have been caused by his mental condition" (at para. 272). Whether a causal link is ultimately established by a report prepared after the date of discharge, as the British Columbia Labour Relations Board emphasized in *Fraser Lake Sawmills*, *supra*, is a question to be decided on the evidence.

Arbitrator Craven, in *Petro-Canada and C.E.P., Local 593* (2004), 129 L.A.C. (4th) 353, suggested that the relevance of post-discharge evidence depends on whether it is advanced for a "diagnostic" use or a "prognostic" use. Where a medical report is tendered to challenge the accuracy of the diagnosis on which the employer relied at the time of discharge, it "helps to shed light on the reasonableness and appropriateness" of the decision (to use the words of *Québec Cartier*), and is therefore admissible. By contrast, where the report is sought to be introduced merely to show that the grievor's prognosis for recovery has improved following the discharge, it constitutes evidence of subsequent events and, in the absence of statutory or contractual authority, is inadmissible. Having regard to s. 48(17) of Ontario's *Labour Relations Act*, which permits an arbitrator to substitute a lesser "penalty" where an employee has been discharged or "otherwise disciplined", Arbitrator Craven found that subsequent-event evidence may be received in Ontario, pursuant to statutory authority, but only in disciplinary cases. Thus, the arbitrator concluded that, in Ontario, post-discharge evidence which speaks to the validity of the prognosis at the time of discharge is admissible in cases of disciplinary termination (to mitigate the penalty), but inadmissible in cases of non-disciplinary termination (most typically for innocent absenteeism). However, post-discharge evidence which speaks to the validity of the diagnosis at the time of discharge may be relevant and admissible in both disciplinary and non-disciplinary cases.

Post-discharge evidence can also "shed light" on the dismissal by affirming the legitimacy of the employer's decision. In *Toronto (City) Board of Education v. O.S.S.T.F., District 15* (1997), 144 D.L.R. (4th) 385, the Supreme Court of Canada quashed the award of an arbitration board on the ground that it had improperly refused to admit subsequent-event evidence which tended to support the concerns of the employer at the time of the discharge, and to refute the defence advanced by the union, namely, that the grievor's misconduct was aberrant or temporary. A further example of relevant post-discharge evidence, mirroring the kind of conduct that led the employer to discharge in the first place, can be found in *University of Manitoba and C.A.W., Local 3007* (2003), 124 L.A.C. (4th) 208 (Wood).

Additional Reading

R. Germaine, "Post-Discharge Evidence: The Varied Response to *Québec Cartier*" in K. Whitaker, J. Sack, M. Gunderson & R. Filion, eds., *Labour Arbitration Yearbook 1999-2000*, vol. I, p. 39; and companion articles by J.B. West & K. Watson, and G. Fiorillo & J. Parmar.

J.E. Dorsey, "Remedial Role of Arbitrators" in W. Kaplan, J. Sack & M. Gunderson, eds., *Labour Arbitration Yearbook 1998*, p. 29.

M.C. Cooper & A.A. Luchak, "Post-Discharge Evidence of Rehabilitation: Can It Be Used at Arbitration?" in W. Kaplan, J. Sack, M. Gunderson & R. Filion, eds., *Labour Arbitration Yearbook 1996-97*, p. 13.

7.2   REINSTATEMENT

At common law, with limited exceptions, where an employee has been wrongfully dismissed, his or her only remedy lies in damages. Based on the view that the remedy of specific performance is not available in the context of a contract for personal services, the courts will not order the employer to reinstate the employee. In contrast, where a collective agreement is in effect, and a discharge is found to have been without just cause, there is a presumption that the appropriate remedy is reinstatement, subject perhaps to a lesser penalty if there is cause for some discipline. The basis for that practice, which has been followed in the overwhelming majority of cases, was extensively canvassed by Arbitrator MacDowell in *Tenant Hotline and Peters and Gittens* (1983), 10 L.A.C. (3d) 130.

The general rule that an employee who has been improperly dismissed should be reinstated, as well as the existence of an arbitral discretion to depart from this rule in exceptional cases, was affirmed by the Ontario Divisional Court in *U.S.W.A., Local 12998 v. Liquid Carbonic Inc.* (1996), 135 D.L.R. (4th) 493, discussed in Chapter 10.9.4. A similar view was expressed by the Alberta Court of Appeal, which stated that "where an employee is dismissed without just cause, the appropriate arbitral response is usually reinstatement". The Court went on to note that "only in very exceptional circumstances" should the goal of maintaining industrial harmony lead an arbitrator to depart from this principle: *A.U.P.E. v. Lethbridge Community College* (2002), 215 D.L.R. (4th) 176 (Alta. C.A.), at p. 191. The *Lethbridge Community College* case involved *non*-culpable conduct (unsatisfactory work performance), and the Court of Appeal quashed the award of an arbitration board which had determined that reinstatement would be inappropriate. On appeal to the Supreme Court of Canada, the award was restored on the basis of deference to the arbitral process: (2004), 238 D.L.R. (4th) 385 (S.C.C.). The Court held that the decision reasonably fell within the board's authority to fashion a "lasting and final solution" for the workplace. Justice Iacobucci did, however, affirm the "general rule" that "where a grievor's collective agreement rights have been violated, reinstatement of the grievor to [his or her] previous position will normally be ordered" (at p. 409). Referring to that statement, the Alberta Court of Queen's Bench has quashed the award of an arbitrator who found no basis for the ground of termination originally put forward by the employer, but declined to reinstate the grievor because of her "medical condition and possible inability to perform her duties": *A.U.P.E. v. Calgary Health Region*, [2004] A.J. No. 1400 (QL).

As noted in the award of Arbitrator Rayner in *DeHavilland Inc. and C.A.W., Local 112* (1999), 83 L.A.C. (4th) 157, the denial of reinstatement generally results from difficult or belligerent conduct on the grievor's part. The arbitrator points out, however, that a history of inappropriate conduct should play no part in calculating compensation when it is awarded in place of the usual order for reinstatement. Furthermore, in the arbitrator's opinion, an employee's entitlement to termination pay under employment standards legislation is not a suitable benchmark for the calculation, as it ignores "the economic value of being a member of a bargaining unit and the recipient of all the benefits and protection that a collective agreement brings" (at p. 162). In the result, Arbitrator Rayner ordered the employer to pay the grievor one month's salary for each year of seniority (a total of 12 months), plus an additional sum of 15 percent to compensate for the loss of fringe benefits. The arbitrator made it clear that this award was over and above the grievor's entitlement to termination and severance pay under employment standards legislation.

In *Alberta and Alberta Union of Provincial Authorities* (1999), 83 L.A.C. (4th) 436, by contrast, Arbitrator Moreau expressed the view that an employee who is denied the customary remedy of reinstatement should simply be compensated in accordance with the standards of "reasonable notice" at common law. Arbitrator Graham, in *Health Sciences Centre and C.U.P.E., Local 1550* (2001), 96 L.A.C. (4th) 404, accepted the period of reasonable notice as a starting-point but, like Arbitrator Rayner, he was of the view that an additional sum should be awarded as compensation for the loss of a position covered by a collective agreement.

Thus, in fashioning an award of damages, the current approach of arbitrators is based on a formula tied to years of service, with an adjustment to take into account the loss of protections and rights that would otherwise have continued under the collective agreement. A percentage in lieu of fringe benefits is generally awarded as well. In *Canadian Blood Services and H.E.U. (Bagley)*, [2004] B.C.C.A.A.A. No. 308 (QL), Arbitrator Jackson discussed the principles underlying this approach, and in addition considered the circumstances in which "*Wallace*" damages and "exemplary" damages may be awarded (for further discussion, see Chapter 7.4.2). The arbitrator also indicated that an award of interest is usually appropriate.

As discussed in Chapter 10.1.2, a non-unionized employee has the right under the *Canada Labour Code*, R.S.C. 1985, c. L-2, to file a complaint alleging that his or her dismissal was without just cause. Adjudicators under s. 240 have the power to order reinstatement, and indeed must consider it as an option, but the courts will not interfere with their exercise of discretion in this regard: *Chalifoux v. Driftpile First Nation* (2002), 299 N.R. 259 (F.C.A.), leave to appeal to S.C.C. denied July 17, 2003.

Section 242(4)(a) expressly empowers an adjudicator who has been appointed to hear such a complaint to order the employer to "pay the person compensation not exceeding the amount of money that is equivalent to the remuneration that would, but for the dismissal, have been paid by the employer to the person". This provision was invoked in *Mathur and Bank of Nova Scotia*, [2002] C.L.A.D. No. 189 (QL), where Adjudicator Armstrong declined to reinstate the complainant, and instead ordered the employer to pay indemnification for lost compensation, subject to the duty to mitigate, from the date of the award to the complainant's 65th birthday — a period of some 14 months.

Additional Reading

T.H. Wagar, "How Effective is Reinstatement?" in W. Kaplan, J. Sack & M. Gunderson, eds., *Labour Arbitration Yearbook 1998*, p. 19.

7.3 DECLARATIONS

The minimum relief that a grieving party can seek is a declaration that the conduct of the respondent violates the collective agreement. Where the impugned conduct has come to an end, and only a declaration is sought, the responding party may argue that no useful purpose would be served by granting it. In *Halton Board of Education and O.S.S.T.F., District 9* (1978), 17 L.A.C. (2d) 279, Arbitrator Swan noted that the Ontario Labour Relations Board typically refuses to grant a declaration once an unlawful strike has ended on the basis that, at that point, it would serve no collective bargaining purpose. In his opinion, however, the Board's practice does not apply to rights arbitration. In fact, the arbitrator considered that a declaration respecting the meaning of a collective agreement provision could serve the useful purpose of guiding the parties' future conduct.

Equally, where the responding party concedes that it has violated the collective agreement, but provides no relief, an arbitrator retains jurisdiction to grant a declaration in order to remedy the harm done. This point was established by Arbitrator Lavery in *Colonial Furniture (Ottawa) Ltd. and R.W.D.S.U., Local 414* (1995), 47 L.A.C. (4th) 165.

On the question of mootness generally, see Chapter 3.5.

7.4   DAMAGES

7.4.1   The "Make-Whole" Principle

The seminal case on the inherent authority of an arbitrator to award damages for any loss suffered as a result of the breach of a collective agreement is *Polymer Corp. Ltd. and Oil, Chemical & Atomic Workers* (1959), 10 L.A.C. 51 (Laskin), affirmed (1962), 33 D.L.R. (2d) 124 (S.C.C.). The arbitrator roundly rejected the notion that the lack of express authorization in the collective agreement curtailed his power to assess damages against the offending party.

In *Firestone Steel Products of Canada and U.A.W., Local 27* (1974), 6 L.A.C. (2d) 18, Arbitrator Weatherill elaborated on the basic principles which guide the awarding of damages. He reiterated that the purpose of damages is to place the aggrieved person as nearly as possible in the position that he or she would have been in had the collective agreement not been breached. Compensation should therefore cover any loss of opportunity to earn incentive or overtime pay. At the same time, however, Arbitrator Weatherill noted that a "make-whole" remedy is subject to the normal duty to mitigate (see Chapter 7.5), and applies only to *actual* loss, not notional loss.

See *Thermal Ceramics and U.S.W.A.* (1993), 34 L.A.C. (4th) 23 (Gray) for an extension of these principles to the loss of pension contributions.

Cheni Gold Mines Inc. and Tunnel & Rock Workers, Local 168 (1991), 22 L.A.C. (4th) 1 (Ladner) affirms that, where necessary, it is permissible to construct a hypothetical set of circumstances in estimating losses such as incentive earnings or opportunities for overtime. Losses that are contingent in nature, such as loss of opportunity to exercise rights as a result of the other party's breach of the collective agreement, are also clearly compensable. In *Ontario (Minister of Community and Social Services) v. Ontario (Grievance Settlement Board)* (2005), 195 O.A.C. 288, the union challenged the government's failure to ensure that seniority rights would be protected following the privatization of correctional facilities for young offenders. The Ontario Divisional Court ruled that difficulty in precise quantification should not deter adjudicators from making a "blanket" award of damages for a clear loss of opportunity arising from the breach. In the words of the Court:

> When a collective agreement is breached by the employer, as has happened here, in a manner affecting the collectivity, or a significant portion of it, collective or blanket remedies are often more appropriate than individual ones. It is incongruous for this defaulting employer to insist on individual remedies for what is a breach of the rights given collectively to the employees. It is all the more incongruous when such an insistence would lead to interminable individual hearings as to the possible decisions and future prospects of employees whose loss is one of opportunity: the chance to have had a different choice to make in the past. (at p. 295)

Arbitrator Hope's award in *Hertz Canada Ltd. and Office & Technical Employees' Union, Local 378* (1994), 46 L.A.C. (4th) 416 is particularly significant on the question of the damages that may be payable where an insurance policy has improperly been allowed to lapse. In this case, the employer discontinued its insurance coverage without properly notifying the employee after it had discharged him, even though the union's discharge grievance remained outstanding. The grievor died prior to the hearing. When the grievance was upheld, the employer was held liable for the full death benefit payable under the lapsed life insurance policy. The test applied by arbitrators is that of "reasonable foreseeability": see the discussion of principles in *British Columbia (Public Service Employee Relations Commission) and B.C.G.E.U. (Provost)* (2000), 92 L.A.C. (4th) 216 (Burke), reviewed in Chapter 7.4.5.

7.4.2 *Weber* Damages

In *Weber v. Ontario Hydro* (1995), 125 D.L.R. (4th) 583 (see Chapter 1.3), the Supreme Court of Canada held that an arbitrator, once properly seized of a matter arising under the collective agreement, can and should award tort or *Charter* relief as required, in order to avoid a "real deprivation of ultimate remedy", and to enable all aspects of a dispute to be dealt with in one proceeding. The enhanced jurisdiction of arbitrators, encompassing the authority to award heads of damages not previously considered within their domain, is particularly evident in the awards of British Columbia arbitrators. In *Pacific Press and C.E.P., Local 115-M* (1998), 73 L.A.C. (4th) 35 (Bruce), for example, the grievance involved a challenge to the employer's denial of an application for sick leave benefits. The employer conceded that the arbitrator also had jurisdiction over the grievor's claim in tort for the intentional infliction of mental suffering, which was based on the employer's repeated calls to the grievor at home exhorting her to return to work. Finding the elements of the tort to have been established, Arbitrator Bruce examined the range of damages being awarded by courts, and decided on an amount in the "mid-range" ($8,000).

Similarly, in allowing a discharge grievance, Arbitrator Suzan Beattie awarded the grievor $20,000 for the tort of intentional infliction of mental distress, and $20,000 for the tort of defamation: *Surrey (City) and C.U.P.E., Local 402*, [2003] B.C.C.A.A.A. No. 243 (QL). The union's claim for aggravated and punitive damages was, however, denied, as there was no evidence that the employer had been motivated by malice, and its conduct was not sufficiently harsh or vindictive to warrant such damages. On appeal, the British Columbia Labour Relations Board declined jurisdiction over the tort issues, but affirmed the award in all other respects: [2004] B.C.L.R.B.D. No. 155 (QL).

In *Transit Windsor and A.T.U., Local 616* (2003), 114 L.A.C. (4th) 385, Arbitrator Brandt found that the grievor's defamation claim arose inferentially from a stipulation in the collective agreement that the employer would exercise its management rights "fairly" and in a "fair and reasonable manner". By contrast, in *Seneca College and O.P.S.E.U. (Olivo)* (2001), 102 L.A.C. (4th) 298, Arbitrator Pamela Picher found nothing in the collective agreement that contemplated the adjudication of tort claims by a labour arbitrator, and declined jurisdiction to do so in this case. The Ontario Divisional Court quashed the decision, based on its reading of the broad directives in *Weber*. On appeal, the province's Court of Appeal was persuaded that the issue before Arbitrator Picher was fundamentally one of interpreting the provisions of the collective agreement, and restored the award on the basis that it was not patently unreasonable: [2006] O.J. No. 1756 (QL).

The arbitral approach to quantification of damages in cases involving assaults at the workplace is reflected in two recent decisions. In *Canada Post Corp. and C.U.P.W. (Fletcher)*, [2004] C.L.A.D. No. 187 (QL), Arbitrator Ponak awarded the grievor $500 in damages for a relatively minor assault (touching) by her supervisor, while in *Toronto Transit Commission and A.T.U. (Stina)* (2004), 132 L.A.C. (4th) 225, Arbitrator Shime awarded $25,000 in general damages for a prolonged pattern of harassment by the grievor's supervisor (together with a direction that the supervisor be removed from any area in which the grievor chose to work): for further discussion, see Chapter 16.3.

The Supreme Court of Canada, in its landmark judgment in *Wallace v. United Grain Growers* (1997), 152 D.L.R. (4th) 1, held that employers are under an obligation of good faith and fair dealing in the manner in which they dismiss employees. Accordingly, the plaintiff in a wrongful dismissal action is entitled to assert a claim for aggravated damages if the dismissal demonstrates bad faith or particular unfairness on the employer's part. So-called "*Wallace* damages" take the form of an "extension" of the period of reasonable notice to which a successful plaintiff is otherwise entitled. In unionized workplaces, though, the remedial practice of arbitrators in discharge cases is different. Where the union establishes that an employee was discharged without just cause, the arbitrator typically awards a remedy by way of reinstatement and back pay rather than forward-looking damages in lieu of reasonable notice. In *Seneca College, supra*, Arbitrator Pamela Picher therefore expressed doubt that *Wallace* applies in the collective agreement context. Compare, however, the decision in *Sunset Lodge and B.C.N.U. (Tataryn)*, [2003] B.C.C.A.A.A. No. 299 (QL), where Arbitrator Hope did rely upon *Wallace* in making an award of compensation which extended beyond the date of the grievor's reinstatement.

7.4.3 Non-Monetary Losses

Section 89(a) of the British Columbia *Labour Relations Code*, R.S.B.C. 1996, c. 244, confers express authority on an arbitrator to award monetary damages for a non-monetary loss. A good example of an award of compensation for non-monetary loss is Arbitrator Dorsey's decision in *B.C. Public School Employers' Ass'n and B.C.T.F.*, [1998] B.C.C.A.A.A. No. 88 (QL), where the employer was found to have violated a provision in the collective agreement limiting class sizes. In his reasons, the arbitrator arrives at a "rough" formula for calculating the damages claimed by the union (each affected teacher was to receive two days' pay for every month the collective agreement was violated). In *School District No. 75 (Mission) and Mission Teachers' Union* (1997), 61 L.A.C. (4th) 8, by contrast, Arbitrator Larson was reluctant to award any monetary compensation for the loss of stipulated preparation time, on the basis that no actual or quantifiable loss had been incurred.

The absence of an explicit provision such as that contained in the British Columbia *Labour Relations Code* does not necessarily preclude an award of damages in respect of non-monetary losses. Ontario arbitrator Stanley Beck, for example, has concluded, as did Arbitrator Dorsey, that if increased workload is the result of a "direct breach of the contract . . . compensation is an appropriate remedy": *Durham District School Board and Elementary Teachers' Federation of Ontario* (2003), 119 L.A.C. (4th) 417, at pp. 425-26.

The decisions cited above attempt to quantify, in monetary terms, compensation for a collective agreement violation that generates unpaid work time. In *Canadian Airlines Int'l Ltd. and I.A.M.* (1999), 82 L.A.C. (4th) 81, Arbitrator Ready extended this principle further, granting a notional amount of damages strictly as a "deterrent" against further breaches of the collective agreement.

In *West Park Healthcare Centre and S.E.I.U., Local 1.ON* (2005), 138 L.A.C. (4th) 213, an arbitration board chaired by Gerald Charney found the employer's disregard for the consultation rights provided under the collective agreement so blatant that he awarded the union and each of 16 employees general damages. The employer had unilaterally reassigned the employees during a reorganization. Despite finding that this was a "first offence", and no one had been laid off or incurred actual wage loss, the arbitrator was of the view that a declaration would not be a sufficient remedy, and that damages were payable for infringement of the union's inherent rights under the collective agreement. This decision applies the principles established in *Canada Safeway Ltd. v. U.F.C.W., Locals 312A, 373A and 401* (2001), 283 A.R. 32 (Q.B.). In that case, an Alberta judge upheld an arbitration award ordering the employer to pay more than $2 million ($300 per employee) to 8,000 striking employees who suffered discrimination, in breach of the collective agreement, when the employer extended more favourable treatment to employees who worked during the strike than to those who did not. Although neither the union nor the striking employees had sustained any actual monetary loss, the grievors were held entitled to general damages "as compensation for the intrinsic value of . . . the right not to be discriminated against" (at p. 37).

7.4.4 Damages to the Union At Large

In *Blouin Drywall Contractors Ltd. v. C.J.A., Local 2486* (1975), 57 D.L.R. (3d) 199 (Ont. C.A.), in circumstances in which a number of union members were out of work, the employer was held to have breached the hiring hall provisions under the collective agreement. The Ontario Court of Appeal affirmed the right of the union to claim damages on behalf of its unemployed members, even though they were not employees of the company at the time. As in *Polymer Corp. Ltd. and Oil, Chemical & Atomic Workers* (1959), 10 L.A.C. 51 (Laskin), affirmed (1962), 33 D.L.R. (2d) 124 (S.C.C.) (see Chapter 7.4.1), the Court held that the statutory scheme of mandatory arbitration conferred on arbitrators the jurisdiction to award a remedy that would effectively enforce rights and obligations under the collective agreement.

Arbitrator Clarke's award in *Milley's Contracting and B.A.C., Local 1* (1999), 81 L.A.C. (4th) 443 has since clarified the manner in which damages are to be apportioned. If the records of the union make it possible to determine with some degree of certainty which union members would have been assigned to the project, they are the ones to whom the distribution should be made, net of applicable deductions. In the event that it is unclear to whom such payments are to be made, the union should distribute the net amount to those of its members who were unemployed and available at the time non-union workers were hired in contravention of the collective agreement.

7.4.5   Compensation for Tax Consequences

Arbitrators have recognized that, in order to put a grievor in the same position which he or she would have been in had the collective agreement not been breached, account must be taken of income tax consequences. In *Ontario (Ministry of Citizenship) and O.P.S.E.U. (Grinius)* (1995), 48 L.A.C. (4th) 345 (Ont. G.S.B.), for example, the Grievance Settlement Board acknowledged the detrimental tax effect of a lump sum award for damages covering four years of income, and ordered the "grossing-up" of the amount payable to compensate for the extra tax burden.

The right to reimbursement for the adverse income tax consequences of a lump-sum award, however, remains subject to the test of reasonable foreseeability. In *British Columbia (Public Service Employee Relations Commission) and B.C.G.E.U. (Provost)* (2000), 92 L.A.C. (4th) 216 (Burke), the union sought reimbursement for the additional tax liability incurred by an employee who, following his improper dismissal, had withdrawn funds from an RRSP account in order to meet expenses. Arbitrator Burke concluded that the liability incurred upon withdrawal of the funds was something that the employee knew he would have to face some day, and that quantification of the loss against a possibly lower tax bracket was too remote and speculative a basis on which to award damages.

7.4.6   Interest

In what is usually considered the seminal case, *Air Canada and Canadian Air Line Employees' Ass'n* (1981), 29 L.A.C. (2d) 142, Arbitrator Pamela

Picher ruled that arbitrators have the clear authority to make an injured party whole by awarding interest. An overview of the arbitral practice since that time is provided in *Fort James Canada Inc. and G.C.I.U., Local 100-M* (2002), 103 L.A.C. (4th) 425, where Arbitrator Elaine Newman concluded that an award of interest normally follows an award of damages as a matter of course. Only where the aggrieved party wrongfully delayed the process, thereby extending the interest claim, is there an exception to this principle. Furthermore, while the parties are free in their collective agreement to relieve against liability for interest in the event of a breach, clear language must be used to accomplish this result.

In *Canadian Broadcasting Corp. and N.R.P.A.* (1995), 45 L.A.C. (4th) 444, Arbitrator Burkett ruled that the principle of compensating an individual for his or her actual loss called for awarding *compound* interest, unless there was some compelling circumstance warranting the denial of such relief. However, rejecting the conclusion in *Canadian Broadcasting Corp.*, Arbitrator Thorne ruled in *Ottawa (City) and Ottawa-Carleton Public Employees Union, Local 503* (1997), 65 L.A.C. (4th) 299 that an award of interest is designed to compensate an individual for the loss of purchasing power, not the loss of notional investment value. Since the agreed-upon interest rate was substantially higher than the current rate of inflation, he ruled that a *simple interest* award was wholly adequate.

7.5   THE DUTY TO MITIGATE

As affirmed by the Supreme Court of Canada in *Red Deer College v. Michaels* (1975), 57 D.L.R. (3d) 386, the responsibility of a defendant to make a wronged plaintiff whole does not extend to compensating him or her for what the Court termed avoidable losses. This principle is the basis for imposing on the aggrieved party a duty to "mitigate" or reduce his or her losses. Although the duty to mitigate was articulated by the courts in the context of wrongful dismissal actions at common law, there has never been any question among arbitrators that it applies in the unionized workplace as well. Generally speaking, the duty requires an employee who has been discharged to make reasonable efforts to find alternative employment. That said, the Court in *Red Deer College* went on to observe that, "[i]f it is the defendant's position that the plaintiff could reasonably have avoided some part of the loss claimed, it is for the defendant to carry the burden of that issue" (at p. 390). Thus, while the employee is subject to a duty to mitigate, the burden of showing that the duty has been breached rests upon the employer.

The way in which arbitrators have applied this onus was reviewed in *Dengarry Professional Services Ltd. and B.C.G.E.U. (Castonguay)* (2001), 94 L.A.C. (4th) 138, where Arbitrator Keras concluded that it is not sufficient for the employer to show a lack of effort on the employee's part. Rather, the evidence must demonstrate that work opportunities were available such that greater effort by the employee would likely have made a difference. In other words, the onus is on the employer to prove that the loss was avoidable. The arbitrator also noted that an employee who is the subject of an unadjudicated discharge grievance may well be expected to have difficulty finding work.

The decision of Arbitrator Michel Picher in *Canada Post Corp. and C.U.P.W. (Crowe)* (1991), 21 L.A.C. (4th) 400 is commonly cited for the proposition that, at some point after attempts to find comparable employment have proven unsuccessful, a discharged employee must "lower her sights" in order to retain the right to claim damages. Notwithstanding the *Canada Post Corp.* case, arbitrators have recognized that finding comparable work on a temporary basis may be difficult, and that employees awaiting arbitration of their claim should therefore be held to a lower standard of effort. This was the view expressed in *Sprayaway Enterprises Ltd. and Teamsters, Local 213* (1997), 62 L.A.C. (4th) 345 (Bruce).

Finding another job is not the only way in which an employee can legitimately attempt to mitigate his or her losses. In *IPSCO Saskatchewan Inc. and U.S.W.A., Local 5890* (1999), 83 L.A.C. (4th) 396 (Stevenson), the arbitrator held that it was a reasonable step on the grievor's part to invest all of his time in a business which he owned. The award also illustrates the principle that the duty of mitigation falls on the union as well as on the individual grievor. Where the union has been dilatory in processing the grievance or referring it to arbitration, the employer is entitled to a reduction in the amount of damages otherwise owing.

Another important issue relating to mitigation arose in the case of *Hertz Canada Ltd. and Office & Technical Employees' Union, Local 378* (1994), 46 L.A.C. (4th) 416 (Hope). The employer provided a policy of group life insurance to its employees. An employee who had been discharged failed to take advantage of the policy's individual conversion feature pending the arbitration hearing. As a result, the employee's participation in the plan lapsed. When, in the interim, he was killed, a dispute arose as to his entitlement to death benefits under the policy. Arbitrator Hope ruled that the employee had not been under any onus to convert the policy, with the result that the employer was held liable for the full amount of the benefit. In a decision dated March 13, 1995, the British Columbia Labour Relations Board upheld Arbitrator Hope's award, highlighting his finding that "the only communication to the grievor concerning [the conversion of] his insurance was contained in a benefit booklet sent to the grievor approximately a year prior to the termination". The opposite conclusion was reached in *A. Estate v. B.C. Rail Ltd.*, where the need to convert *was* explicitly communicated: (1999), 72 B.C.L.R. 227 (C.A.).

With respect to a claim for set-off, it has been held that the duty to mitigate damages is not restricted to cases in which an employee claims to have been dismissed or disciplined without proper cause. In *Ottawa-Carleton (Regional*

Municipality) and C.U.P.E., Local 503 (1997), 63 L.A.C. (4th) 112, Arbitrator
Dissanayake concluded that the duty arises in *any* situation in which an alleged
violation of the collective agreement triggers a loss of earnings, as, for example, in a promotion case. The arbitrator went on to hold that the employer is
therefore entitled to set off amounts found to have been earned "through reasonable efforts from a reasonable employee". Conversely, the employer is not
entitled to set off the accumulated damages by amounts earned as a result of
"extra effort . . . that goes beyond what is reasonably expected". On the facts
before him, Arbitrator Dissanayake concluded that the employer was in fact
entitled to the benefit of the grievor's very substantial overtime earnings,
although solely, it would appear, on the basis that overtime was compulsory in
the grievor's new job, and thus represented nothing more than the "normal performance" of that job.

Furthermore, the employer is entitled to deduct workers' compensation benefits from damages otherwise payable to an employee for lost income resulting from a discharge found to be in violation of the collective agreement:
Enwin Utilities and I.B.E.W., Local 636 (2004), 130 L.A.C. (4th) 179 (Brandt).
At the same time, the arbitrator found, reasonable legal expenses incurred by
the grievor in pursuing his application for benefits should be offset against the
deduction in compensation.

For further discussion of the principles relating to set-off and restitution,
see Chapter 7.9.

7.6   RECTIFICATION

Rectification is a remedy that enables an arbitrator to correct a mutual mistake in the language of a collective agreement. Where it can be established that
the terms of the written agreement do not reflect the parties' real agreement
(because, for example, certain language was incorrectly typed or inadvertently
omitted from the final draft), arbitrators have long claimed the power to bring
the written agreement into line with the true bargain.

However, *Metropolitan Toronto Police Ass'n v. Metropolitan Toronto Board
of Commissioners of Police*, a 1971 decision of the Ontario High Court, upheld
on appeal by both the Ontario Court of Appeal and the Supreme Court of
Canada, appeared to deny arbitrators this authority. The Court held that the
exercise of a power of rectification would conflict with the standard collective
agreement provision prohibiting an arbitrator from adding to, subtracting from,
altering or modifying the agreement. For a period of time, therefore, arbitrators doubted whether they could apply the doctrine. In 1982, however, Arbitrator Arthurs resurrected the doctrine by pointing out that the Court's ruling
may well have been *obiter*; in his view, the collective agreement provision in
question could not have been intended to prevent an arbitrator from enforcing
the parties' "real" agreement. *Alcan Canada Products Ltd. and Metal Foil*

Workers' Union, Local 1663 (1982), 5 L.A.C. (3d) 1 (Arthurs) remains the seminal award on the arbitral power of rectification.

In other jurisdictions, arbitrators have differed as to whether the viewpoint adopted by Arbitrator Arthurs in *Alcan Products* is correct: see the review of cases in *Seminole Management and Engineering Co. and C.A.W., Local 195* (1989), 4 L.A.C. (4th) 380 (Watters). The debate, at least in Ontario, however, appears to have been put to rest by *P.S.A.C. v. NAV Canada* (2002), 212 D.L.R. (4th) 68 (Ont. C.A.). In that case, the Ontario Court of Appeal held that its earlier ruling in *Metropolitan Toronto Police Commissioners, supra*, had been overtaken by subsequent developments in the jurisprudence, most notably the expanded view of arbitral powers espoused by the Supreme Court of Canada in *Weber v. Ontario Hydro* (1995), 125 D.L.R. (4th) 583 (discussed in Chapter 1.3). Thus, the Court held, the power to rectify a collective agreement in appropriate cases must be viewed as flowing from the exclusive jurisdiction of arbitrators to resolve disputes arising under the agreement. However, in order to obtain an order for rectification, a party must meet a four-fold test, which involves:

(1) showing the existence and content of the inconsistent prior oral agreement;

(2) showing that the written document does not correspond with the prior oral agreement, and that permitting the other party to take advantage of the mistake in the written document would be fraud or equivalent to fraud;

(3) showing the precise form in which the written instrument can be made to express the prior agreed-upon intention; and

(4) establishing all of these requirements on a standard of convincing proof.

The Court stated as well that the equitable jurisdiction to rectify does not permit an arbitrator to speculate about the parties' unexpressed intentions, but is limited to putting into words that which the parties can be shown to have agreed to.

The fourth requirement set out by the Court of Appeal, in determining whether a remedy by way of rectification would be appropriate, is that the party seeking rectification must establish its case "on a standard of convincing proof". In *Potash Corp. of Saskatchewan Inc. and C.E.P., Local 922* (2003), 117 L.A.C. (4th) 112, Arbitrator Norman concluded that this threshold had been met, as there was "cogent evidence 'predicated with certainty' about actual agreed terms", not just one party's subjective intentions or assumptions.

In British Columbia, the law from the outset developed with greater certainty than in Ontario. Taking their lead from the decision of the British Columbia Labour Relations Board in *Vernon Fruit Union and B.C. Interior Fruit & Vegetable Workers Union, Local 1572*, [1977] 1 Can. L.R.B.R. 21, arbitrators

in that province have ruled that their authority to apply the doctrine of rectification is rooted in the statutory grant of powers "necessary to provide a final
and conclusive settlement of a dispute" (s. 89 of the *Labour Relations Code*,
R.S.B.C. 1996, c. 244). The most recent award summarizing this view, *B.C.
Hydro & Power Authority and O.P.E.I.U., Local 378* (1997), 63 L.A.C. (4th)
86 (Germaine), emphasizes the necessity, as does the Ontario jurisprudence,
of being able to clearly identify the terms of the actual agreement, typically on
the basis of other documents, and not just the parties' intentions. Arbitrator
Germaine also concluded that subsequent renewals of an agreement do not necessarily prevent the application of the doctrine, if it is demonstrated that the
original mistake has simply been continued.

7.7   INTERIM/INJUNCTIVE RELIEF

It has occasionally been asserted that arbitrators have an implied power to
restrain a party to an arbitration proceeding from taking any action until the
case can be heard: see *NorthwesTel Inc. and I.B.E.W., Local 1574* (1996), 55
L.A.C. (4th) 57 (Kelleher), and *Iron Ore Co. of Canada v. U.S.W.A., Local 5795*
(1984), 5 D.L.R. (4th) 24 (Nfld. C.A.). The explanation that such interim relief
powers flow from the statutory mandate of arbitrators to provide a final disposition of disputes may be problematic in itself. More importantly, however, in
Canadian Pacific Ltd. v. B.M.W.E. (1996), 136 D.L.R. (4th) 289, the Supreme
Court of Canada stated that, where neither the collective agreement nor the relevant labour legislation invests arbitrators with the power to issue an interim
injunction, the courts may do so in the exercise of their residual jurisdiction.

The impact of *Canadian Pacific* on the question of whether arbitrators have
an inherent jurisdiction to issue interim relief was discussed in a subsequent
Ontario award, *Brewers' Retail Inc. and U.B.W.W.* (1998), 74 L.A.C. (4th) 113
(Carrier). Noting a 1995 amendment to s. 48(12)(i) of Ontario's *Labour Rela-
tions Act*, S.O. 1995, c. 1, Sch. A, which expressly limited the power of arbi-
trators to make interim orders to those concerning "procedural matters",
Arbitrator Carrier concluded that the interim power accorded to arbitrators in
Ontario does not extend to granting interim forms of remedy. While the Ontario
Grievance Settlement Board continues to interpret s. 48(12)(i) more broadly
(see *Ontario (Ministry of Community Safety & Correctional Services) and
O.P.S.E.U. (Ranger)* (2004), 134 L.A.C. (4th) 347), the accepted view outside
the public service appears to be that of Arbitrator Carrier in *Brewers' Retail*.
See, for example, *Sudbury & Manitoulin Children's Aid Society and
O.P.S.E.U., Local 668* (2003), 123 L.A.C. (4th) 90 (H.D. Brown). Adherence
to the narrower view, however, has the effect of enabling the courts to exercise
their jurisdiction to entertain an application for interim relief on the basis that
"no adequate alternative remedy exists" (as the Supreme Court put it in
Canadian Pacific, supra). That was precisely the determination of the Ontario

Superior Court in *Aranas v. Toronto East General & Orthopaedic Hospital Inc.*, 2005 C.L.L.C. ¶220-025.

Other than the Ontario legislation, only the *Canada Labour Code*, R.S.C. 1985, c. L-2, and the British Columbia *Labour Relations Code*, R.S.B.C. 1996, c. 244, expressly authorize arbitrators to make interim orders. The grant of power in those jurisdictions is not limited to "procedural matters", and arbitrators have not interpreted it in that manner. In *Luscar Ltd. and I.U.O.E., Local 115* (2001), 95 L.A.C. (4th) 283, a British Columbia case, Arbitrator Kinzie identified the criteria typically used in balancing the interests of the parties and deciding whether to grant pre-hearing relief:

(1) An adequate remedy would not be available to the applicant upon conclusion of the hearing into the merits of the case without an interim order.

(2) The claim must not be frivolous or vexatious and must usually be based on a *prima facie* case.

(3) An interim order must not penalize the respondent in a manner which will prevent redress if the application fails on the merits.

(4) An interim order must be consistent with the purposes and objects of the *Labour Relations Code*.

In *United Parcel Service and Teamsters, Local 938* (2002), 109 L.A.C. (4th) 312, Arbitrator Knopf considered the corresponding provision under the *Canada Labour Code*, and articulated the factors which should be taken into account in weighing a request for interim relief. The issue for the arbitrator was whether that provision extended to the granting of interim "remedial" relief and, comparing the more restrictive language of the Ontario legislation, she concluded that it did. The considerations noted by Arbitrator Knopf include the following:

(1) Interim orders may only be appropriate to "maintain" or "reinstate the status quo".

(2) An interim order may not be appropriate if it would essentially result in or become effectively a final determination of the issues involved in the dispute.

(3) Interim orders may not be appropriate if the harm can be "effectively remedied" by compensation granted after a consideration of the merits of the case.

(4) Financial harm alone may be insufficient to make it appropriate to grant interim relief.

(5) If financial harm escalates to the extent that it becomes irreparable harm, this may be a factor to consider in the balancing of employer and employee interests.

Another critical factor, the arbitrator pointed out, is the promptness with which the requesting party brought forward its application for interim relief.

Additional Reading

R. Ellis & S. Welchner, "Interim Injunctions Pending Arbitration" in W. Kaplan, J. Sack & M. Gunderson, eds., *Labour Arbitration Yearbook 1998*, p. 51.

7.8   *QUIA TIMET* – COMPLIANCE ORDER

Quia timet is a Latin phrase meaning "because he fears" or "because he apprehends". A *quia timet* or compliance order is a form of equitable relief requiring a party to adhere to the terms of the contract in the future. A compliance order may go beyond a mere declaration of rights to include a specific order that certain action be taken or that certain conduct cease. As explained in *Polax Tailoring Ltd. and Amalgamated Clothing Workers of America* (1972), 24 L.A.C. 201 (Arthurs), the advantage of such an order is that it can be enforced in the courts through contempt proceedings; a separate process to establish a breach of the collective agreement is not necessary.

The jurisdiction of Ontario arbitrators to grant compliance orders was confirmed by the Divisional Court in *Samuel Cooper and Co. Ltd. v. I.L.G.W.U.* (1973), 35 D.L.R. (3d) 501. In reasons that would seem to apply equally to other jurisdictions, the Court held that the statutory provision requiring the final and binding settlement of collective agreement disputes by arbitration gives arbitrators the power to grant such a remedy. The *Samuel Cooper* judgment was followed in *Famous Players Ltd. and I.A.T.S.E., Local 348* (1987), 31 L.A.C. (3d) 97 (Bird), the leading award in British Columbia. In that case, Arbitrator Bird enjoined the operation of projection equipment by persons who had obtained their qualifications in contravention of the collective agreement. He did note, however, that his power to issue a continuing order was limited to the term of the existing collective agreement.

Though an extraordinary form of relief, arbitrators continue to show their willingness to grant a compliance order where the record of the respondent indicates that further breaches of the collective agreement are likely to occur in the future. This was demonstrated in *Royal Crest Life Care Group Inc. and C.U.P.E., Local 1712* (1993), 38 L.A.C. (4th) 250 (Carrier).

7.9   RESTITUTION AND SET-OFF

Arbitrators have long exercised a jurisdiction to require employees to repay monies received as a result of clerical error. One of the leading early cases was *Standard Coil Products (Canada) Ltd. and U.E., Local 512* (1971), 22 L.A.C. 377 (P.C. Weiler), where the board observed that "there is a well-established principle of the law of restitution that money paid as a result of a mistake of fact is recoverable in the absence of injurious reliance by the employees" (at p. 382). More recently, in *Electrical Power Systems Construction Ass'n v. Ontario Allied Construction Trades Council* (1993), 101 D.L.R. (4th) 739, the Ontario Divisional Court held that the provincial Labour Relations Board had improperly fettered its jurisdiction by ruling that it did not have power to make a restitution order against an employee who improperly claimed and received a benefit under the collective agreement. In *Belleville (City) and C.U.P.E., Local 907* (1994), 42 L.A.C. (4th) 224, Arbitrator Allison applied the principle of restitution articulated in *Electrical Power Systems Construction Ass'n*, ordering the return of overpayments made to an employee in respect of sick leave benefits.

Other cases in which a restitution order has been made are canvassed more fully by Arbitrator Burke in *U.A., Local 170 and O.P.E.I.U., Local 15* (2004), 134 L.A.C. (4th) 64. It was well established, she found, that arbitrators have jurisdiction to deal with a claim for recovery of overpayment by applying the equitable principles of "unjust enrichment". In this case, Arbitrator Burke held, the doctrine did not apply, since the collective agreement required the payments in question, however implausible the result now seemed. The arbitrator also noted that, where the claimant seeks an equitable remedy, it must "come with clean hands", and this condition had not been met.

The employment standards legislation of most jurisdictions prohibits the employer from making a deduction from wages by way of set-off or otherwise unless the employee consents or the deduction has been authorized by statute. The decision in *Capital Health Authority and U.N.A., Local 85* (2002), 108 L.A.C. (4th) 97 (Sims) confirms that it is improper for an employer of its own accord to recover overpayments by deduction from wages owing, and that in the absence of consent by the employee, the appropriate procedure is to file a grievance under the collective agreement requesting an order authorizing the deduction. In *New Flyer Industries Ltd. and C.A.W., Local 3003* (2004), 132 L.A.C. (4th) 1, where the grievor had been dismissed for carelessly causing damage to the employer's property, Arbitrator Hamilton made restitution for the cost of repairs a condition of reinstatement.

Another situation in which a right to restitution may arise is the breach of a settlement agreement. In *Ontario (Ministry of the Attorney General) and O.P.S.E.U.* (2004), 124 L.A.C. (4th) 382, the province's Grievance Settlement Board was called upon to determine the appropriate remedy flowing from the grievor's violation of the "confidentiality clause" in a settlement agreement, requiring that she not divulge its terms. The Board ruled that a declaration alone would not have a sufficient deterrent effect and, in the interest of promoting the integrity of such agreements, ordered the grievor to return the settlement funds.

7.10   COSTS

It has been recognized that, in the absence of express statutory or contractual authority, arbitrators have no jurisdiction to order one party to pay the other party's costs or the costs of the arbitrator. The primary obstacle to the recognition of any *implied* power to award costs is the stipulation typically found in a collective agreement that the costs of arbitration will be borne equally by both parties. The leading case on this issue is *O.P.S.E.U. and Ontario Public Service Staff Union* (1984), 16 L.A.C. (3d) 278 (Swan). Arbitrator Swan's comments on costs are *obiter*, and in the end he simply describes the existence of a power to award costs as "doubtful". The *O.P.S.E.U.* decision does, however, note the arbitral practice of requiring an undertaking from one party to pay the other party's costs as a condition of granting an adjournment.

In Nova Scotia, one arbitration board has held that the combined effect of the *Trade Union Act*, R.S.N.S. 1989, c. 475, and the provincial *Arbitration Act*, R.S.N.S. 1989, c. 19, is to authorize arbitrators to award costs: *Pictou District School Board and C.U.P.E., Local 867* (1987), 34 L.A.C. (3d) 307 (Veniot). However, in a subsequent decision, Arbitrator Veniot referred to *Pictou District School Board* as an unusual case of "repeated, egregious failure to comply with direct orders" issued by the board of arbitration, and stated that "[c]ost consequences are a very isolated and exceptional occurrence in labour arbitration": see *Scott Maritime Ltd. and C.E.P., Local 440* (1995), 52 L.A.C. (4th) 316, at pp. 330-31.

In British Columbia, the sharing of costs is prescribed by statute, and Arbitrator Moore has observed that it would require "extraordinary circumstances" to persuade an arbitrator to depart from this legislative policy: *Vibrant Health Products Inc. and B.S.O.I.W., Local D400*, [2004] B.C.C.A.A.A. No. 127 (QL).

CHAPTER 8

ENFORCEMENT AND REVIEW OF AWARDS

8.1 ENFORCEMENT OF ARBITRATION AWARDS

In most Canadian jurisdictions, two methods are available for the enforcement of arbitration awards. The first and more frequently used method is to file the award in the superior court. Statutory provisions in each province and the federal jurisdiction generally provide that, once an award has been filed with the appropriate court, the award becomes enforceable as a judgment or order of that court. Under this type of provision, all the enforcement measures provided under the rules of practice for the court become applicable to the enforcement of the arbitration award. In most cases, this means that attachment, sequestration, committal and contempt proceedings can be pursued against a party that does not comply with the award. Although some legislative provisions, such as s. 66 of the *Canada Labour Code*, R.S.C. 1985, c. L-2, require that the applicant observe a minimum waiting period of 14 days or more, s. 48(19) of the Ontario *Labour Relations Act*, S.O. 1995, c. 1, Sch. A, is fairly typical:

> Where a party, employer, trade union or employee has failed to comply with any of the terms of the decision of an arbitrator or arbitration board, any party, employer, trade union or employee affected by the decision may file in the Superior Court of Justice a copy of the decision, exclusive of the reasons

therefor, in the prescribed form, whereupon the decision shall be entered in the same way as a judgment or order of that court and is enforceable as such.

The other method of enforcement is prosecution in the criminal courts. Labour legislation in most provinces makes it an offence to contravene any order or decision made by the labour board or an arbitrator. However, the requirement that the labour board or labour ministry give written consent to the commencement of a prosecution severely limits access to this means of enforcement.

The decision in *North-East Steel Ltd. v. L.I.U.N.A.*, [2003] N.B.J. No. 447 (QL) (Q.B.) points to a third method of enforcing arbitration awards, albeit an indirect one. In that case, as a consequence of the employer's refusal to recognize the union or to comply with the provincial collective agreement, the union obtained a sizeable award of damages at arbitration to compensate for its members' loss of work opportunities resulting from the breach. After the business was sold in a transparent effort to circumvent the employer's contractual obligations, the New Brunswick Labour and Employment Board granted the union's application for a successor employer declaration, found both the original owner and the purchaser to have engaged in unfair labour practices, and ordered the payment of damages in an amount which matched exactly the arbitrator's prior award. The Board's decision was upheld on judicial review. The Court rejected the employer's argument that the decision of the Board constituted an attempt to enforce the arbitration award, and was thus beyond the Board's remedial jurisdiction under the *Industrial Relations Act*, R.S.N.B. 1973, c. I-4. In the Court's opinion, the order represented a remedy for unfair labour practices, and as such, was within the powers of the Board to counteract conduct prohibited by the legislation.

8.1.1   Enforcement by Filing in Court

Some have speculated that an arbitration award may be enforced by a mandatory injunction obtained from the court. However, in several cases an application for an injunction was dismissed on the basis that the statutory filing process provides a more appropriate mechanism. The seminal case on this point is *Tyrrell v. Consumers' Gas Co.* (1963), 41 D.L.R. (2d) 119 (Ont. H.C.J.). The Court dismissed an application for an injunction on the ground that the applicant had an equally effective remedy, namely, the filing and enforcement procedure provided in labour relations legislation. However, the Court also stated that an injunction might have been available had it been necessary to prevent irreparable harm during the first 14 days after the award was issued, since the legislation at that time imposed a two-week waiting period before an award could be filed. Perhaps in response to this concern, the Ontario legislation has since been changed to remove the waiting period. The decision in *Tyrrell* was extensively reviewed and applied in *Kolompar v. Canada Post*

Corp., a judgment of the Ontario Court (General Division): see [1990] O.J. No. 2125 (QL).

In many cases, an arbitrator will render a decision on the merits but retain jurisdiction to supervise the implementation of the award or determine the calculation of compensation, should the parties be unable to arrive at a resolution themselves. Attempts to file an award in respect of which the arbitrator remains seised have usually met with failure because the award is not considered a "final" order and is thus not capable of enforcement under the court's procedures: see *Canadian Broadcasting Corp. v. Canadian Wire Service Guild* (1992), 58 F.T.R. 5. In such cases, the courts have generally held that the more appropriate course of action is for the complaining party to request that the arbitrator deal with any outstanding implementation or non-compliance issues.

8.1.2 Stay of Proceedings

Although the filing procedure under the applicable labour relations legislation makes an arbitration award enforceable in the same manner as an order of the court, it does not render the award subject to appeal like an ordinary court order. Nor does an application for judicial review of the award result in an automatic stay of proceedings or preclude immediate enforcement. As a result, a party seeking a stay of the award must apply to the court for an interim order to this effect, in conjunction with an application for judicial review. These principles are clearly affirmed in *I.W.A. v. Patchogue Plymouth, Hawkesbury Mills* (1976), 14 O.R. (2d) 118 (H.C.J.).

The arbitral jurisprudence has also maintained that, in the absence of an order staying the proceedings, an application for judicial review is not sufficient cause to adjourn a hearing convoked for the purposes of enforcement. In *Canada Post Corp. and C.U.P.W.* (1991), 22 L.A.C. (4th) 214, Arbitrator Burkett stressed the importance of ensuring a timely and effective remedy to the aggrieved party, ruling that the filing of an application for judicial review is not in itself grounds for the adjournment of enforcement proceedings.

Generally, the test for whether a stay of proceedings should be granted by the courts is the same as that relating to interlocutory injunctions, *i.e.* injunctions until trial. The applicant must establish that there is an arguable case to be tried, that irreparable harm would be suffered if the order or award is enforced, and that the balance of convenience favours a stay of proceedings. The cases on this issue are summarized in *Canadian Broadcasting Corp. v. Canadian Wire Service Guild* (1992), 58 F.T.R. 5.

8.1.3 Contempt of Court

Once an arbitration award has been registered with the appropriate court, a party that fails to comply with the award is liable to be found in contempt of court, at least in the absence of a formal order staying the proceedings. In the leading case of *Ajax and Pickering General Hospital v. C.U.P.E.* (1981), 132 D.L.R. (3d) 270, the Ontario Court of Appeal held that disobedience of labour board orders may be punished in the same manner as orders of the court. Belated compliance with a board order prior to the hearing of a contempt application, moreover, does not have the effect of rendering moot prior acts of non-compliance. While this case dealt with orders of the Ontario Labour Relations Board, the Court of Appeal noted that the arbitration provisions of the *Labour Relations Act*, now S.O. 1995, c. 1, Sch. A, are worded in an identical fashion to the labour board provisions. Thus, the principle established in *Ajax and Pickering General Hospital* may well apply in proceedings to enforce an arbitration award.

Because a contempt proceeding is quasi-criminal in nature, the applicant bears the onus of proving its case beyond a reasonable doubt. In *U.E. v. Milltronics Ltd.* (1981), 34 O.R. (2d) 95 (H.C.J.), for example, the Court declined to hold the employer in contempt for allegedly disobeying an arbitration award. The award merely stated that employees must pay union dues, failing which they would be discharged from employment. In the Court's opinion, in the context of a proceeding with such severe potential consequences, the order lacked sufficient specificity. To be enforceable, the Court commented, the order would have to include a clause explicitly directing the employer to dismiss the employees for non-payment of dues.

More recently, the necessity of proving non-compliance with an arbitration award beyond a reasonable doubt was emphasized in *C.U.P.E., Local 4004 v. Air Canada* (1998), 157 F.T.R. 186. In that decision, the Court held that judicial enforcement of purely declaratory awards is not available under the enforcement provisions of the *Canada Labour Code*, R.S.C. 1985, c. L-2.

8.1.4   Enforcement by Prosecution

The labour relations legislation of most jurisdictions in Canada provides that contravention of or failure to obey an order of the labour board or an arbitrator can be prosecuted as a quasi-criminal offence. Sections 104 to 109 of the Ontario *Labour Relations Act*, S.O. 1995, c. 1, Sch. A, are a typical example of statutory provisions imposing liability for the payment of fines on conviction of an offence. However, many jurisdictions make access to this method of enforcement very difficult by requiring that the labour board or Minister of Labour give written consent to commence such a prosecution. Consent to prosecute the employer for failure to implement an arbitration award was in fact granted in the early case of *U.A.W. and Canadian Acme Screw & Gear Ltd.* (1954), 54 C.L.L.C. ¶17,083 (Ont. L.R.B.). However, as commentators have noted, the 1975 amendments giving the Labour Relations Board greater remedial powers in respect of unfair labour practices have made recourse to this mode of enforcement a rarity.

8.2   JUDICIAL REVIEW OF ARBITRATION AWARDS

8.2.1   Contract Interpretation

At the outset, it is important to note that cases concerning the scope of judicial review of arbitration awards decided before the Supreme Court of Canada's watershed judgment in *C.U.P.E., Local 963 v. New Brunswick Liquor Corp.* (1979), 97 D.L.R. (3d) 417 must be read with great caution. In that judgment, the Court explicitly adopted a far more deferential approach to the judicial review of specialized administrative tribunals in general, and specialized labour tribunals in particular. Prior to *New Brunswick Liquor Corp.*, arbitration awards which were not protected by a strong privative clause were generally subject to judicial review for jurisdictional errors, errors of law on the face of the record, and breaches of the rules of natural justice. Arbitrators who were protected by a privative clause, by contrast, could be reviewed only for errors of jurisdiction and breaches of natural justice.

In one of the Supreme Court's first decisions after *New Brunswick Liquor Corp., Douglas Aircraft Co. of Canada Ltd. v. McConnell* (1979), 99 D.L.R. (3d) 385, Justice Estey wrote a summary of the law of judicial review of arbitration awards which has frequently been cited in subsequent cases. In his view, even though the awards of an arbitrator unprotected by a strong privative clause could be reviewed for errors of law on the face of the record, the modern trend was to restrict review to errors which are so serious that they take on a jurisdictional hue. The purpose of statutory arbitration — the speedy, inexpensive and final settlement of differences without interruption of production — would be undermined if the scope of review was not limited to errors of law which assumed jurisdictional proportions. Hence, because the interpretation of the collective agreement is at the heart of an arbitrator's expertise, errors in contract interpretation are reviewable only if the arbitrator has given the language a meaning it cannot reasonably bear. Likewise, an arbitrator's findings of fact are beyond judicial reach, and his or her rulings on evidence and procedure should not be interfered with unless they amount to a denial of natural justice. However, when interpreting general statute law, an arbitrator will be held to a standard of correctness, since the application of external legislation lies outside the area of arbitral expertise.

After *Douglas Aircraft*, a number of lower court decisions, including *Metropolitan Toronto (Municipality) v. C.U.P.E., Local 43* (1990), 69 D.L.R. (4th) 268 (Ont. C.A.), held that a statutory provision making arbitration awards "final and binding on the parties" constitutes a privative clause and therefore limits judicial review to jurisdictional errors and breaches of natural justice. However, in *Dayco (Canada) Ltd. v. C.A.W.* (1993), 102 D.L.R. (4th) 609, the Supreme Court of Canada held that such provisions have little or no privative effect and do not protect arbitration awards from review for errors of law on the face of the record. The majority went further and suggested that, in each case where an arbitration award is being judicially reviewed, the "pragmatic and functional approach" approved in *U.I.E.S., Local 298 v. Bibeault*, [1988] 2 S.C.R. 1048 should be applied to determine the appropriate standard of review. This test requires the reviewing court to ask whether the legislature intended a particular issue to be within the jurisdiction conferred on the arbitrator. If this was in fact the legislature's intention, the matter is *within jurisdiction* and the arbitrator is entitled to some deference. If not, then the matter is characterized as one *of jurisdiction* or one over which the arbitrator is *without jurisdiction*, and the applicable standard of review is correctness. To determine the intention of the legislature with respect to the issue in question, the reviewing court should consider a number of factors: the wording of the statute under which the tribunal is constituted; the purpose of the statute; the reason for the tribunal's existence; the expertise of the members of the tribunal; and the nature of the problem before the tribunal.

It should be noted that the majority in *Dayco* held that, for the purpose of determining what degree of deference is appropriate, labour arbitrators fall toward the lower end of the spectrum of administrative tribunals charged with policy deliberations. In short, they are not worthy of much deference when it comes to policy deliberations which go beyond the mere interpretation of the collective agreement. The majority also suggested, albeit in *obiter dicta*, that even on questions clearly within the jurisdiction of the arbitrator, deference should not be accorded automatically in the absence of a privative clause, and the reviewing court may well have to examine the five *Bibeault* factors to determine whether deference is due.

Quite subtle distinctions in the wording of legislation which purports to make arbitration the final forum for resolving workplace disputes can have a major impact on the legislation's privative effect. A good example is provided by juxtaposing the decision of the Supreme Court of Canada in *Dayco* and its more recent decision in *Canada Safeway Ltd. v. R.W.D.S.U., Local 454* (1998), 160 D.L.R. (4th) 1. In the former case, the words "final and binding on the parties" were held to be insufficient to impose a significant limit on the scope of judicial review of arbitration awards under Ontario's labour legislation. However, in *Canada Safeway*, s. 25(1.2) of the Saskatchewan *Trade Union Act*, R.S.S. 1978, c. T-17, providing that decisions of arbitration boards are "final and conclusive" and "binding upon the parties", was held to be very close to a "true privative clause". Thus, the Supreme Court ruled, where a labour relations tribunal interprets or applies a collective agreement under the umbrella of a privative clause, a reviewing court can intervene only if the tribunal has committed a patently unreasonable error. The judgment also provides some insight into the meaning of the term "patently unreasonable", equating it with a finding that is clearly irrational, where the defect is apparent on the face of the tribunal's reasons.

A graphic demonstration of the difference between correctness and patent unreasonableness as standards of review is offered by *Essex County Roman Catholic School Board v. O.E.C.T.A.* (2001), 205 D.L.R. (4th) 700 (Ont. C.A.). In that case the Ontario Court of Appeal held that it was not patently unreasonable for an arbitrator to interpret a collective agreement provision in a manner that was inconsistent with an interpretation of identical language which had been held to be "entirely reasonable" in a recent decision of the same Court. However, the Court noted, if a different interpretation had been previously upheld on a standard of correctness, any attempt by an arbitrator to depart from the judicially approved interpretation would give rise to a reviewable error.

The application of the standard of patent unreasonableness to arbitral interpretation of collective agreement provisions has been brought into serious question by the Supreme Court of Canada's decision in *Voice Construction Ltd. v. Construction & General Workers' Union, Local 92* (2004), 238 D.L.R. (4th) 217. In that case, the Court applied the "pragmatic and functional approach" set out in *Bibeault, supra,* and other cases in reviewing an arbitrator's interpretation of union hiring hall clauses under a provincial construction industry collective agreement. Despite finding that the arbitrator's decision was protected by a partial privative clause, and the task of the arbitrator was to interpret collective agreement language, a matter on which arbitrators are likely to have greater experience and expertise than judges, the Court held that the appropriate standard of review was reasonableness — *not* the more deferential standard of patent unreasonableness. Defining the "reasonableness *simpliciter*" standard, the Court stated that if any of the reasons given for the decision are tenable, in the sense they can stand up to a "somewhat probing examination", the decision will not be held unreasonable and should not be disturbed. Subsequently, the Supreme Court of Canada applied *Voice Construction* to hold that an Alberta arbitrator's interpretation of the province's labour relations legislation was similarly reviewable on a standard of reasonableness. *A.U.P.E. v. Lethbridge Community College* (2004), 238 D.L.R. (4th) 385 (S.C.C.). See further discussion in Chapter 8.2.2.

Decisions issued after *Voice Construction* have indicated the importance of the content of the applicable privative clause in determining the effect of the Supreme Court's ruling in a given case. For example, in *New Brunswick (Board of Management) v. Doucet-Jones* (2004), 243 D.L.R. (4th) 652 (N.B.C.A.), the Court of Appeal relied on the presence of a "full" privative clause in the province's *Public Service Labour Relations Act,* R.S.N.B. 1973, c. P-25, to distinguish that case from *Voice Construction,* and to find that the proper standard of review was patent unreasonableness. However, in Saskatchewan, where the legislation provides only a "partial" privative clause (stating that an arbitrator's finding is "final and conclusive", and "binding on the parties"), the courts have interpreted *Voice Construction* as mandating the less deferential standard of reasonableness, despite the Supreme Court of Canada's earlier decision in *Canada Safeway*, *supra*, holding that a standard of patent unreasonableness was appropriate under the Saskatchewan *Trade Union Act*. See, for example, *Saskatoon (City) v. C.U.P.E., Local 59* (2004), 255 Sask. R. 77 (Q.B.), and *Canada Safeway Ltd. v. U.F.C.W., Local 1400* (2004), 255 Sask. R. 239 (Q.B.). On the other hand, the same judge who decided the latter case held in *U.F.C.W., Local 1400 v. Westfair Foods Ltd.*, [2004] S.J. No. 634 (QL) (Q.B.) that an arbitrator's application of the just cause provision under the collective agreement was reviewable only on a standard of patent unreasonableness. In so ruling, the judge noted that the issues required the arbitrator to focus on fact-finding and on drawing conclusions from the facts.

In a recent decision, the Ontario Court of Appeal expressed the opinion that the rulings in *Voice Construction* and *Lethbridge Community College* can be "largely explained by the relatively weak privative clause in the Alberta [*Labour Relations Code*]". Comparing the somewhat stronger provision in s. 48(1) of the Ontario *Labour Relations Act*, S.O. 1995, c. 1, Sch. A, the Court concluded that arbitrators in Ontario, when dealing with the interpretation and application of the collective agreement (a matter "at the heart of an arbitrator's expertise"), are subject to review on the standard of patent unreasonableness: *Lakeport Beverages v. Teamsters, Local 938* (2005), 258 D.L.R. (4th) 10 (Ont. C.A.), at pp. 19-20.

Additional Reading

D.J. Mullan, "*Voice Construction* – One Swallow Does Not a Summer Make?" (2004), 11 Canadian Labour and Employment Law Journal, p. 303.

D. Pothier, "Judicial Review of Arbitrators" in W. Kaplan, J. Sack & M. Gunderson, eds., *Labour Arbitration Yearbook 1991*, vol. II, p. 55.

8.2.2 Interpretation of Legislation or Common Law Rules

In *N.A.P.E. v. Newfoundland (Green Bay Health Care Centre)* (1996), 134 D.L.R. (4th) 1, the Supreme Court of Canada dealt with the standard of judicial review to be applied to an arbitral award in which the board interpreted both a no-discrimination clause in the collective agreement and applicable human rights legislation. The Court held that the board's interpretation of the collective agreement should not be interfered with unless it was patently unreasonable, that is, there was no rational basis for the interpretation. However, the portions of the award which interpreted and applied the general law of human rights were reviewable on a standard of correctness.

Where the legislation in question relates to the core area of an arbitrator's expertise, greater deference may be afforded, as shown by the Supreme Court of Canada's decision in *A.U.P.E. v. Lethbridge Community College* (2004), 238

D.L.R. (4th) 385. Applying the "pragmatic and functional approach" now required to be used in determining the standard of review of administrative tribunal decisions (see discussion in Chapter 8.2.1), the Court considered a challenge to an arbitration board's interpretation of s. 142 of the Alberta *Labour Relations Code*, R.S.A. 2000, c. L-1, a provision which empowers arbitrators to substitute a lesser penalty where an employee has been disciplined or discharged for cause. The Court concluded that, although interpretation of the statute raised a question of law and the legislative provision was jurisdictional in nature — factors indicating that less deference was called for — the existence of a partial privative clause, the greater expertise of arbitrators in relation to such issues, and the remedial nature of the legislation all militated in favour of greater deference. In the result, the Court held, the board's interpretation of s. 142 was reviewable against a standard of reasonableness.

Following the Supreme Court's decision in *Lethbridge Community College*, it would appear that most judges have concluded that the appropriate standard of review of arbitral decisions concerning the interpretation and application of employment-related legislation is reasonableness, even where the provisions at issue are at the heart of an arbitrator's authority to apply employment-related statutes. See, for example, *U.N.A., Local 33 v. Capital Health Authority* (2004), [2005] 1 W.W.R. 595 (Alta. C.A.) (dealing with the duty to accommodate under human rights legislation), and *Elementary Teachers' Federation of Ontario v. Toronto District School Board*, 2004 C.L.L.C. ¶220-064 (Ont. Div. Ct.) (dealing with pregnancy leave provisions under employment standards legislation). Nevertheless, in *I.L.A., Local 269 v. Halifax Employers Ass'n* (2004), 243 D.L.R. (4th) 101, a case which involved an arbitrator's decision to extend time limits in the grievance procedure, pursuant to s. 60(1.1) of the *Canada Labour Code*, R.S.C. 1985, c. L-2, the Nova Scotia Court of Appeal held that the applicable standard of review was patent unreasonableness. In arriving at this conclusion, the Court relied on what it viewed as the *Code*'s stronger privative clause.

In both *Dayco (Canada) Ltd. v. C.A.W.* (1993), 102 D.L.R. (4th) 609, discussed in Chapter 8.2.1, and *C.J.A., Local 579 v. Bradco Construction Ltd.* (1993), 102 D.L.R. (4th) 402, the Supreme Court of Canada held that arbitrators were not entitled to deference when deciding questions of law which required the interpretation and application of common law rules that were outside their normal area of expertise. As the Court pointed out in *Bradco Construction*, the policy considerations which justify a deferential stance in matters involving collective agreement interpretation do not apply to general questions of law.

8.2.3   Findings of Fact

Douglas Aircraft Co. of Canada Ltd. v. McConnell (1979), 99 D.L.R. (3d) 385 (S.C.C.), discussed in Chapter 8.2.1, reflected the widely held view that an arbitrator's findings of fact were not reviewable by the courts on the basis of mere insufficiency of evidence. Only where the reviewing court decided that there was "no evidence" for a particular finding of fact could it quash the arbitrator's decision as being patently unreasonable. However, in *Toronto (City) Board of Education v. O.S.S.T.F., District 15* (1997), 144 D.L.R. (4th) 385, the Supreme Court of Canada departed from this very narrow scope of review of factual errors. Despite a strong privative clause under the applicable legislation, it was held that a court can intervene where the evidence, viewed reasonably, is incapable of supporting the tribunal's findings of fact or inferences from the evidence. Thus, the Court has broadened the scope of review from cases in which there is "no evidence" to cases in which the evidence cannot "reasonably" support a particular factual finding by the arbitration board.

8.2.4   Procedural and Evidentiary Rulings

The courts have ruled that arbitrators are generally entitled to deference in defining the scope of the issues raised by the grievance. This principle has shaped consideration of the degree of deference that is due to an arbitrator's rulings on questions of procedure and the admissibility of evidence. In *Syndicat des Employés Professionels de l'Université du Québec à Trois-Rivières v. Université du Québec* (1993), 101 D.L.R. (4th) 494, the Supreme Court of Canada held that an arbitrator has exclusive jurisdiction to define the issues in dispute, and to conduct the proceedings accordingly and admit only the evidence that he or she considers relevant. Arbitral rulings on the scope of the issues and the admissibility of evidence are reviewable only if they are patently unreasonable or constitute a denial of natural justice. Where, for example, an arbitrator decides to exclude relevant evidence which is crucial to a proper resolution of the issues, the decision may constitute a violation of the principle of natural justice known as *audi alteram partem* — that is, every person affected by the decision of a tribunal has the right to be heard (see also Chapter 1.1.2.).

8.2.5   Access to Judicial Review by the Grievor

Traditionally, the courts have been reluctant to recognize grievors as having a right to bring an application for judicial review to challenge an arbitration award. The fact that the grievor is not a party to the collective agreement or, in most cases, the arbitration proceeding, has generally been held to preclude the grievor from obtaining standing for the purposes of judicial review. In *Noël v. Société d'énergie de la Baie James* (2001), 202 D.L.R. (4th) 1, the Supreme Court of Canada affirmed this position, ruling that it would be inconsistent with the basic policy and institutions of collective bargaining to permit the grievor to challenge in the courts an arbitration award upholding his discharge, when the union had chosen not to seek judicial review. However, the

Court went on to note that, under Quebec legislation, an individual grievor may be able to gain access to judicial review by way of an action in nullity if he or she can establish collusion between the employer and the union, fraud or bad faith, that the arbitration board had not been constituted according to law, or that serious breaches of natural justice had occurred. See the discussion in Chapter 9.2.

8.3 THE ROLE OF LABOUR BOARDS

8.3.1 Appellate or Review Role

Canadian legislation generally does not provide for the review of arbitration awards by labour relations boards. Since 1975, however, the British Columbia *Labour Relations Code*, R.S.B.C. 1996, c. 244, has divided the jurisdiction to review arbitration awards between the Labour Relations Board and the courts. Section 99(1) enables a party to appeal the award of an arbitration board to the Labour Relations Board on the ground that the party did not receive a fair hearing or that the award "is inconsistent with the principles expressed or implied in this Act, or any other Act dealing with labour relations". Section 100 provides that the Court of Appeal may review an arbitration award which is based on "a matter or issue of the general law not included in section 99(1)". Section 101 of the Act contains a standard privative clause.

Recently, in *Castlegar & District Hospital v. B.C.N.U.* (2003), 234 D.L.R. (4th) 148, the British Columbia Court of Appeal revisited its earlier decisions concerning the division of appellate jurisdiction under ss. 99 and 100 of the *Code*. Overruling some of its own precedents, the Court held that the province's Labour Relations Board has exclusive jurisdiction under s. 99 to consider an appeal from an arbitral decision on whether an employee has been dismissed for just cause. It makes no difference that the arbitrator was required, in determining this issue, to consider whether the employer had met its duty to accommodate the employee's disability under human rights legislation, as this was a question of fact, not of general law.

The leading decision on the role played by the British Columbia Labour Relations Board on appeal from an arbitration award is *Andres Wines (B.C.) Ltd. and United Brewery & Distillery Workers, Local 300* (1977), 16 L.A.C. (2d) 422 (B.C.L.R.B.). In that decision, the Board rejected the notion that its powers of review should be construed as a full-fledged avenue of appeal by which the Board could freely overturn an arbitrator's decision on the merits, findings of fact, interpretation of the collective agreement or determination of arbitral principle. Instead, it ruled, review should be restricted to the grounds specified in the legislation, namely, denial of a fair hearing or inconsistency with the principles created by provincial labour relations legislation.

In *Canada Bread Co. Ltd. and U.F.C.W., Local 1518*, [2003] B.C.L.R.B.D.

No. 411 (QL), the British Columbia Labour Relations Board held that a party
to an arbitration proceeding is not entitled to introduce new arguments concerning alleged violations of the *Code* on a s. 99 review, where those arguments
had not been raised before the arbitrator, unless they can be said to arise from
the arbitrator's reasons in an unanticipated manner. The Board rejected the
argument that its mandate under s. 99 to ensure consistency with the principles
of the *Code* requires it to consider new arguments, noting that this would undermine the fundamental statutory purpose of arbitration in providing for the
orderly, constructive and expeditious resolution of disputes.

8.3.2   Overlapping Jurisdiction with Labour Board

In every jurisdiction, there are significant areas of overlapping authority
between arbitrators and the labour relations board. Where, for example, an
employee alleges that he or she was discharged wholly or in part because of
participation in union activities, such a discharge could be held to violate a no-
discrimination or just cause clause in the collective agreement, but it could also
be held to contravene the prohibition against unfair labour practices under the
labour relations statute. What, then, should the labour board do if the employee
brings an unfair labour practice complaint without having invoked the grievance procedure, or only after the discharge has been upheld by an arbitrator?
In some jurisdictions, the statute expressly grants the board discretion to defer
to arbitration. For example, s. 16(4) of Alberta's *Labour Relations Code*,
R.S.A. 2000, c. L-1, confers upon the Labour Relations Board the discretion
to decline to proceed, on terms which it considers just, as long as the subject-
matter of the complaint is properly before a grievance arbitrator or some other
statutory mechanism.

In the majority of jurisdictions, however, the statute is silent on the question of deferral. Most labour boards have nevertheless adopted a policy of discretionary deferral to arbitration in cases of overlapping jurisdiction, provided
it is appropriate in the circumstances and the public policy objectives of the
labour relations statute would not thereby be undermined. In the leading decision of *Valdi Inc. and U.F.C.W., Local 175*, [1980] 3 Can. L.R.B.R. 299, the
Ontario Labour Relations Board stressed that in order to avoid duplicative litigation and forum shopping, it would defer to arbitration where there was con-
gruence between the contractual issues and any allegations of unfair labour
practices. But it also noted that it would *not* defer where the respondent's conduct amounted to a total repudiation of collective bargaining, where the issues
required authoritative elaboration or application of key provisions of the labour
relations statute, where arbitration might not be available to the complainant,
or where arbitration might be remedially inadequate to uphold the policy
reflected in the statute. Even if it initially decides to defer to arbitration, a
labour board will ordinarily retain jurisdiction over the complaint to ensure that

the arbitration is conducted in a fair and timely manner, and that the outcome is not remedially inadequate or contrary to policy objectives. And the board may exercise this jurisdiction once an award has been rendered if it feels that the arbitration hearing did not deal directly or explicitly with the unfair labour practice issues. Thus, in areas of overlapping jurisdiction, the labour board may end up assuming what resembles a review role in respect of arbitration awards.

Some labour relations statutes also provide for the referral to the labour board, by an arbitration board or the Minister or a party, of specific questions which might arise in an arbitration proceeding. For example, s. 65 of the *Canada Labour Code*, R.S.C. 1985, c. L-2, permits the referral of questions relating to the existence of a collective agreement, or the identification of the parties or employees who are bound by a collective agreement, to the Canada Industrial Relations Board.

CHAPTER 9

DUTY OF FAIR REPRESENTATION

9.1   SCOPE OF THE DUTY: GENERAL

In Canada, the union's right to represent employees in the bargaining unit is "exclusive", which means that all the rights pertaining to the carriage of a grievance rest with the union, unless they have been specifically delegated to the employee by the union's constitution, the collective agreement, or the governing labour relations statute. Thus, a union has the right to refuse to file, to withdraw, or to settle any grievance advanced by a member. In light of the exclusivity of the union's mandate to protect employee rights, at any rate those arising from collective bargaining, the courts and legislatures have imposed on unions a duty of fair representation of all employees. The leading exposition of the origins, nature and extent of this duty is found in *C.M.S.G. v. Gagnon* (1984), 9 D.L.R. (4th) 641, where the Supreme Court of Canada summarized the applicable principles as follows:

(1) The exclusive power conferred on a union to act as spokesperson for the employees in a bargaining unit entails a corresponding obligation to represent all of them fairly.

(2) When, as is generally the case, the right to take a grievance to arbitration has been reserved to the union, the employee does not have an absolute right to have his or her grievance arbitrated, and the union enjoys considerable discretion over the matter.

(3) This discretion, however, must be exercised in good faith, objectively and honestly, after a thorough study of the grievance and the case, taking into account the significance of the grievance and its consequences for the employee on the one hand and the legitimate interests of the union on the other.

(4) The union's decision must not be arbitrary, capricious, discriminatory or wrongful.

(5) The representation provided by the union must be fair and genuine, and not merely apparent, and must be undertaken with integrity and competence, without serious or major negligence, and without hostility towards the employee.

Similar statements of principle can be found in numerous decisions of the federal and provincial labour relations boards, which in most (though not all) jurisdictions are charged with the administration of the duty of fair representation, as provided for in the applicable legislation. In *Mirza Alam and C.U.P.E., Local 1000*, [1994] O.L.R.B. Rep. 627, for example, the Ontario Labour Relations Board outlined the considerations which the union may validly take into account in deciding whether to proceed with an employee grievance. The Board particularly emphasized the ongoing economic "partnership" between the parties, the cost and uncertainty of litigation, the interests of the bargaining unit as a whole, and the difficulty of allocating scarce union resources. Moreover, the Board pointed out, the union was not required to analyze the merits of the case with the same refinement or sophistication as might be expected of trained legal counsel. In the result, as the prospects for success at arbitration were slight, and the potential benefit to the bargaining unit questionable, the union was held to have discharged its statutory obligation.

As noted by the Newfoundland and Labrador Court of Appeal in *Butt v. U.S.W.A.* (2002), 220 Nfld. & P.E.I.R. 181, there is a general presumption that legislatures, in creating a statutory duty of fair representation, intended to incorporate the whole of the duty as it had been defined at common law, regardless of the precise words used. The Court also held that "simple" negligence did not engage the common law duty of fair representation: only "serious" or "major" negligence gave rise to a breach of the union's obligations. Thus, even where the language of a labour relations statute codifying the duty (and assigning its enforcement to the labour relations board) appears to exclude simple negligence, no action against the union for simple negligence can be brought in the courts, since such negligence was not actionable at common law in any event.

It is similarly well established that the duty of fair representation does not preclude the union from electing to advance the interests of one employee (or group of employees) at the expense of another. As recognized by the Supreme Court of Canada in *Gendron v. Supply & Services Union, Local 50057*, [1990] 1 S.C.R. 1298, unions are routinely required to assess which of two or more competing claims best represents the correct interpretation of the collective agreement, and the choice of one claim over another is not in itself objectionable. Rather, the Court held, the union is entitled to pursue one set of interests to the detriment of others as long as its decision to do so is not actuated by any improper motives, and it has turned its mind to all of the relevant considerations.

These principles were affirmed by the British Columbia Labour Relations Board in *Thomas and I.U.O.E., Local 882*, [2002] B.C.L.R.B.D. No. 21 (QL). While recommending that the union maintain contact with an employee or employees to whose interest it had taken an opposing position, in order to minimize the possibility of a complaint being filed, the Board made it clear that the only obligation of the union was to take reasonable steps to inform itself of the merits of each member's claim, and to deal with the matter in an open and honest fashion.

Where the grievance does have the effect of bringing an employee into conflict with other members of the bargaining unit, the conflict can be addressed through the granting of third-party or intervenor status at the hearing: see Chapter 4.1. In *Kenny v. N.B.T.F.* (1998), 198 N.B.R. (2d) 140 (Q.B.), there was a long-standing animosity between the grievor, a teacher, and her school principal, who also belonged to the bargaining unit. When the employer transferred the grievor to another school, she disputed the propriety of the decision. An arbitration award denying her grievance was quashed on judicial review, and the New Brunswick Court of Appeal dismissed the employer's appeal. From the outset, on the basis of a perceived conflict of interest arising from the school principal's membership in the bargaining unit, the grievor requested the union to provide her with independent legal representation at its own expense. The union permitted the grievor to retain her own counsel, but refused to pay the costs. Furthermore, following the initial dismissal of the grievance, the union declined to seek judicial review of the award. The grievor brought an action against the union for allegedly breaching its duty of fair representation. The New Brunswick Court of Queen's Bench held that, in the unusual circumstances of this case, the union was in fact obligated to pay the grievor's legal costs. In the Court's view, the union had not given due consideration to the invidious position in which it could find itself by subjecting the school principal to cross-examination, potentially compromising his professional reputation and exposing him to discipline. An appeal by the employer was dismissed: see (1999), 208 N.B.R. (2d) 98 (C.A.). It was subsequently held, in *Woodside and Regina Police Ass'n* (2001), 67 Can. L.R.B.R. (2d) 112 (Sask. L.R.B.), that the appropriate measure of legal costs in such circumstances is the amount of time which a "reasonably experienced labour lawyer" would spend on the matter.

The decision in *Kenny* can be contrasted to the award in *3M Canada Inc. and C.A.W., Local 27* (1997), 64 L.A.C. (4th) 213, where Arbitrator Knopf denied the grievor's request for representation by independent counsel. The only alleged "conflict" was with respect to the union's strategy in presenting the case, as the grievor wished to put forward a more expansive version than the union thought necessary. In the arbitrator's view, this was not a suitable basis on which to exercise her discretion to permit third-party standing. Moreover, as the grievor's request was founded on an allegation that the union had violated its duty of fair representation, the appropriate forum was the Ontario Labour Relations Board, which enjoys exclusive jurisdiction over such questions.

If the union *is* found to have acted on the basis of a discriminatory motive, it may be held jointly liable with the employer for financial losses to employees.

This was the result in *Via Rail Canada Inc. v. Cairns* (2004), 241 D.L.R. (4th) 700 (F.C.A.), where the union was held to have violated its duty toward a group of employees formerly represented by a different bargaining agent when it negotiated a new collective agreement without adequately taking their interests into account. Moreover, upholding a decision of the Canada Industrial Relations Board, the Federal Court of Appeal concluded that, "in very unusual circumstances", where "no other reasonably practicable alternative is available", the Board has authority to impose terms and conditions of employment in order to remedy the breach.

Another facet of the union's right to differentiate among employee interests is the practice of "swapping" grievances, in which the disposition of outstanding claims is made the subject of a wider process of bargaining between the parties. Concessions in one grievance might be exchanged for a more favourable settlement of another, or for the betterment of terms and conditions of work as a whole. In *Centre Hospitalier Régina Ltée v. Labour Court* (1990), 69 D.L.R. (4th) 609, the Supreme Court of Canada gave qualified support for the union's right to engage in swapping, particularly in the context of negotiations for a renewal collective agreement. However, the Court specifically precluded resort to such an approach if the union had given no consideration to the merits of a grievance, above all in matters involving discipline or discharge.

In *Massicotte and Teamsters, Local 938*, [1980] 1 Can. L.R.B.R. 427, the union had negotiated a reduction in the wage rates of part-time employees, as well as a requirement for the check-off of dues. Having done so, the Canada Labour Relations Board ruled, it was not open to the union to argue that a part-time employee who had been discharged did not belong to the bargaining unit and therefore had no grievance rights. On application for judicial review, the courts upheld the Board's conclusion that the union was in violation of its duty of fair representation: (1980), 119 D.L.R. (3d) 193 (F.C.A.), affirmed (1982), 134 D.L.R. (3d) 385 (S.C.C.).

Nevertheless, the decision in *Adams and U.S.W.A., Local 13571-34*, [2003] O.L.R.D. No. 72 (QL) confirms that the duty of fair representation applies only to the extent that the union has the exclusive right to represent employees in the unit. The employer in *Adams* had entered into a policy with an insurance company to provide for benefits required to be paid under the collective agreement. When the complainant grieved the carrier's decision to discontinue her disability benefits, an arbitrator determined that the only obligation of the employer under the agreement was to pay the plan premiums. Accordingly, in dismissing the complaint, the Board held that there was no duty resting on the union to provide the complainant with counsel in a court action against the insurance company. This is true even where the union may have provided assistance on a voluntary basis at an earlier stage: *Smith and U.F.C.W., Local 1518* (2004), 104 Can. L.R.B.R. (2d) 109 (B.C.L.R.B.).

Additional Reading

D.H. Howes, "Recent Developments in the Duty of Fair Representation: Current Practice in Alberta" in W. Kaplan, J. Sack, M. Gunderson & R. Filion, *Labour Arbitration Yearbook 1996-97*, p. 133.

T.R. Knight, "Recent Developments in the Duty of Fair Representation: Curtailing Abuse in British Columbia" in W. Kaplan, J. Sack, M. Gunderson & R. Filion, *Labour Arbitration Yearbook 1996-97*, p. 151.

T.J. Christian, "The Developing Duty of Fair Representation" in W. Kaplan, J. Sack & M. Gunderson, *Labour Arbitration Yearbook 1991*, vol. II, p. 3.

9.2   APPLICATION FOR JUDICIAL REVIEW

While most cases end with the issuance of an arbitration award, the courts have made it clear that the duty of fair representation extends to a consideration of whether an application for judicial review or appeal is warranted. At this juncture, a primary element in satisfying the duty is engaging in a careful assessment of the grounds for review. However, the same type of analysis that is required when filing a grievance or making a referral to arbitration, such as evaluating the interests of the bargaining unit as a whole and the relative importance of the matter to the employee, must also be carried out. These principles were set out by the Supreme Court of Canada in *Noël v. Société d'énergie de la Baie James* (2001), 202 D.L.R. (4th) 1.

9.3   THE IMPACT OF HUMAN RIGHTS LEGISLATION

The statutory duty of fair representation typically prohibits the union from engaging in conduct that is arbitrary, in bad faith or discriminatory. Recently, in *K.H. and C.E.P., Local 1-S* (1997), 98 C.L.L.C. ¶220-020, the Saskatchewan Labour Relations Board held that the term "discriminatory" must be interpreted in a manner which is consistent with human rights legislation, and specifically with the union's duty to accommodate disabled employees. In withdrawing the discharge grievance of an employee who suffered from a known mental disability, the Board stated, the union failed to make the required adjustments to its usual policies and procedures so as to take into account the employee's mental condition.

Additional Reading

B. Adell, "The Union's Duty of Fair Representation in Discrimination Cases: The New Obligation to Be Proactive" in K. Whitaker, J. Sack, M. Gunderson & R. Filion, eds., *Labour Arbitration Yearbook 2001-2002*, vol. I, p. 263.

M.K. Joachim, "The Meaning of 'Discrimination' in the Duty of Fair Representation" (1999), 7 Canadian Labour and Employment Journal, p. 91.

PART 2
DISCHARGE AND DISCIPLINE

CHAPTER 10

DISCHARGE AND DISCIPLINE: GENERAL PRINCIPLES

10.1 THE JUST CAUSE STANDARD

Prior to the introduction of collective bargaining and grievance arbitration, the employer's authority to discipline or to discharge employees was regulated by the terms of the common law contract of employment. Under the individual employment contract, the employer was generally limited to two possible responses to misconduct on the part of the employee. If the employee's misconduct was serious enough to amount to a fundamental repudiatory breach of the contract, the employer could assert just cause for dismissal. The employer's other remedy was to sue the employee for damages for breach of contract. In the absence of express language in the contract, however, employers were not normally allowed to suspend an employee, impose a fine or withhold wages as a means of discipline. At common law the employer was also permitted to terminate its employment relationship with an employee even in the absence of just cause. Unless the employment contract included an express term prescribing the period of notice to which an employee was entitled prior to being dismissed, the common law implied a term allowing for termination of the relationship by either party upon reasonable notice. See generally G. England, I. Christie & M. Christie, *Employment Law in Canada*, 3d ed. (Butterworths, 1998).

Collective bargaining brought several important changes to the authority of employers to discipline or dismiss employees. First, most collective agreements expressly require the employer to prove just or reasonable cause for any disciplinary measure. This effectively deprives the employer of its common law authority to discharge simply by giving reasonable notice. These principles are concisely summarized in the often-cited decision of *St. Anne-Nackawic Pulp & Paper Co. Ltd. and U.P.I.U., Local 219* (1974), 5 L.A.C. (2d) 397 (Stanley). The terms "just cause" or "reasonable cause" are seldom defined in the collective agreement. It appears that parties to a collective bargaining relationship have preferred to leave it to arbitrators to give "cause" a content which is appropriate in the context of the particular workplace. The courts have affirmed that, where the collective agreement is silent on the issue, an arbitrator has broad jurisdiction to assess whether just cause for discipline or discharge has been established: see *Cie minière Québec Cartier v. U.S.W.A., Local 6869* (1995), 125 D.L.R. (4th) 577 (S.C.C.).

Although just cause has been left to be defined by arbitral resolution in individual cases, there is a high degree of consensus among arbitrators. This consensus arises from widespread acceptance that the definition of misconduct should be directed at behaviour which is inconsistent with the legitimate business interests of the employer, and not merely conduct which the employer happens to dislike. However, the development of an arbitral consensus has not precluded occasional disagreement, especially in cases where the norms of just cause have been affected by the forces of social change. Arbitrator George Adams has described this process in the following terms:

> [The] substantive elaboration of what is acceptable conduct has achieved a high degree of arbitral consensus. As with the judicial elaboration of the substantive common law, this is probably because many of the norms of behaviour necessary for the efficient and orderly operation of an enterprise are identifiable and not very controversial . . .

> But this is not to say that there has been an absence of either controversy or arbitral disagreement on the content of this substantive "law". While there is increasing acceptance that a "management right" to discipline is rooted in the efficient operation of a business and not in the simple prerogatives of legal

ownership and control, individual arbitrators often disagree over the exact accommodation of competing interests in any particular situation. The cases illustrate that the precise accommodation in recurring factual situations has slowly and unevenly evolved with the passage of time, and in response to social change.

See *Grievance Arbitration of Discharge Cases: A Study of the Concepts of Industrial Discipline and Their Results* (Industrial Relations Centre, Queen's University, 1978), at p. 16.

Another major change brought about by collective bargaining is recognition of the employer's right to use measures short of dismissal to discipline employees with a view to inducing them to conform to workplace norms in the future. Even in cases where the collective agreement does not expressly refer to such measures, arbitrators have generally held that the authority to use lesser sanctions such as suspension without pay is inherent in the power to discharge. Arbitrator Brandt affirmed this principle in *London (City) Board of Education and O.S.S.T.F., District 4* (1984), 14 L.A.C. (3d) 17.

10.1.1   Collective Agreement Silent on Just Cause

Most, but not all, collective agreements explicitly provide for just cause protection in cases of discipline or discharge. In his seminal decision in *A.C. Horn Co. Ltd. and Int'l Chemical Workers Union, Local 424* (1953), 4 L.A.C. 1524, Professor Bora Laskin held that, because just cause clauses are so common, arbitrators should be reluctant to imply a just cause standard where the agreement does not expressly impose one. The rationale articulated by Professor Laskin was applied more recently in *Spantec Constructors Ltd. and I.U.O.E., Local 955* (1994), 51 L.A.C. (4th) 267 (McFetridge).

Despite the warning sounded in *A.C. Horn Co.*, though, it has become common for arbitrators to imply a just cause requirement from the inclusion of other typical collective agreement clauses such as those providing for the accumulation and exercise of seniority rights; empowering an arbitrator to confirm, modify or set aside a disciplinary measure; establishing a probationary period during which an employee may be dismissed for any reason, without access to the grievance procedure; and according a measure of protection from layoff in order of seniority. The reasoning commonly adopted by arbitrators is that such provisions would be rendered ineffective or meaningless if the employer retained the right to dismiss at will or after merely providing reasonable notice. A summary of the principles that have evolved to govern the implication of a just cause requirement is found in *Mississauga Hydro-Electric Commission and I.B.E.W., Local 636* (1990), 13 L.A.C. (4th) 103 (Springate).

There is also some authority for the proposition that arbitrators have jurisdiction to consider a grievance against a disciplinary penalty in the absence of a just cause provision by reason of their statutory authority to substitute a lesser penalty where it is just and reasonable to do so, notwithstanding the existence of cause for discipline. Such statutory provisions are common in labour legislation across Canada. See s. 136(j) of the Alberta *Labour Relations Code*, R.S.A. 2000, c. L-1; s. 88(2) of the Newfoundland and Labrador *Labour Relations Act*, R.S.N.L. 1990, c. L-1; and s. 48(17) of the Ontario *Labour Relations Act*, S.O. 1995, c. 1, Sch. A. This was the approach taken in *National Arts Centre Corp. and P.S.A.C.* (1980), 28 L.A.C. (2d) 79 (Weatherill), where the arbitrator relied on a similar provision in the *Canada Labour Code*, R.S.C. 1985, c. L-2.

10.1.2   Statutory Just Cause Standard

Section 84(1) of the British Columbia *Labour Relations Code*, R.S.B.C. 1996, c. 244, provides that every collective agreement must contain a provision requiring that "the employer have a just and reasonable cause for dismissal or discipline of an employee". In Manitoba, similarly, s. 79(1) of the *Labour Relations Act*, R.S.M. 1987, c. L10, requires that collective agreements in that province prohibit the discipline or dismissal of employees, unless the employer has just cause. Between 1993 and 1995, the Ontario *Labour Relations Act*, R.S.O. 1990, c. L.2, as amended by S.O. 1992, c. 21, also contained a provision stating that every collective agreement was deemed to include a clause prohibiting discipline or discharge without just cause. However, this provision was repealed with the enactment of the current *Labour Relations Act*, S.O. 1995, c. 1, Sch. A.

Furthermore, employment standards legislation in several Canadian jurisdictions extends just cause protection against dismissal to non-unionized employees. Sections 240 to 246 of the *Canada Labour Code*, R.S.C. 1985, c. L-2, for example, provide protection against unjust dismissal for employees within federal jurisdiction who are not covered by a collective agreement and who have at least 12 months of continuous employment with their employer. This statutory scheme also enables an employee to have his or her complaint heard by an *ad hoc* adjudicator appointed by the Minister of Labour. In his seminal decision in *Roberts and Bank of Nova Scotia* (1979), 1 L.A.C. (3d) 259, Adjudicator Adams ruled that, in making the unjustness of a dismissal subject to review, Parliament intended to provide unorganized employees with just cause protection similar to that enjoyed by organized workers under collective agreements. It followed, therefore, that the justness of a dismissal should be determined by applying standards of just cause comparable to those developed by arbitrators.

Additional Reading

G. Simmons, "Unjust Dismissal under Federal Jurisdiction" in W. Kaplan, J. Sack & M. Gunderson, eds., *Labour Arbitration Yearbook 1991*, vol. II, p. 41.

10.2 CULMINATING INCIDENT AND PRIOR RECORD

Where an employee with a poor work record commits a further offence meriting discipline, the doctrine of culminating incident allows the employer to take the overall record into account in assessing the appropriate penalty. Although the employee's final act of misconduct may not, viewed in isolation, warrant the penalty imposed, his or her weak record as a whole may justify the employer in increasing the severity of its disciplinary response. The doctrine is accepted by most arbitrators as a necessary corollary to the corrective approach to discipline; it allows the employer to discharge an employee who could otherwise repeatedly engage in minor forms of misconduct without risk of discharge. The basic elements of the doctrine are described in *Livingston Industries Ltd. and I.W.A.* (1982), 6 L.A.C. (3d) 4 (Adams).

As Arbitrator Adams indicated, the fact that an employee has reached the end of the employer's progressive discipline scheme is an important but not determinative consideration in deciding whether to uphold discharge on the basis of a culminating incident. This admonition was recently applied in *Hershey Canada Inc. and Retail Wholesale Canada, Local 462*, [2005] O.L.A.A. No. 93 (QL). In that case, Arbitrator Roberts, after referring to *Livingston Industries*, *supra*, reinstated the grievor with conditions, even though he had reached the final stage of the progressive discipline scheme in a relatively brief period (28 months). In the arbitrator's view, the fact that the misconduct constituting the culminating incident (falling asleep on the job) had been inadvertent rather than deliberate, and the grievor's 15 years of seniority and service, were important mitigating factors.

10.2.1 What Constitutes a Culminating Incident?

There is general agreement among arbitrators that there must be some final act of misconduct which itself merits discipline before the employer can, under the doctrine of culminating incident, rely on the employee's prior disciplinary record to justify a more serious penalty. *Sauder Industries Ltd. and I.W.A., Local 1-217* (1998), 70 L.A.C. (4th) 316 (McKee) demonstrates that failure on the part of the employer to prove that the alleged final act provides just cause for some form of discipline will preclude it from relying on the culminating incident doctrine.

Although some cases have suggested that a trivial form of misconduct will not suffice as the final incident, others have suggested that even a minor disciplinary incident which, by itself, would warrant no more than a written reprimand may constitute a culminating incident justifying discharge if the prior disciplinary record is sufficiently unfavourable. The decision of Arbitrator Brent in *Cambridge Memorial Hospital and S.E.I.U., Local 204* (1996), 59 L.A.C. (4th) 195 summarizes the arbitral jurisprudence on this issue, and concludes that the key question is whether the employment relationship has been irreparably harmed.

The views expressed in *Cambridge Memorial Hospital* are consistent with those of Arbitrator Shime in *SKF Manufacturing of Canada Ltd. and I.A.M., Local 901* (1975), 9 L.A.C. (2d) 139, to the effect that even a relatively serious offence may not give rise to a culminating incident if the employee's previous record is reasonably good. To determine whether the employer is entitled to rely on the theory of culminating incident, one must examine both the prior record, including the offence and the discipline meted out, and the nature of the final incident. For example, in *Courtesy Dodge Chrysler (1998) Inc. and C.A.W., Local 195*, [2001] O.L.A.A. No. 387 (QL) (Watters), the prior record during the six months preceding the culminating incident consisted of two warnings, a one-day suspension and a two-day suspension. The arbitrator held that the record did not furnish a sufficient basis on which to apply the doctrine of culminating incident.

In applying the requirement that the infraction which is relied on as a culminating incident must itself be proven to be misconduct warranting some form of discipline, arbitrators must be careful not to rely on the earlier incidents that form part of the disciplinary record. This proposition was affirmed in *Canada Safeway Ltd. and U.F.C.W., Local 1518*, [2005] B.C.C.A.A.A. No. 24 (QL) (Kinzie). However, while the prior record cannot be permitted to colour the characterization of the grievor's most recent misconduct, Arbitrator Kinzie accepted that the grievor's denial of responsibility for previous offences could be used to impugn the credibility of his testimony regarding the final incident.

10.2.2   What Forms Part of the Prior Record?

All prior incidents of discipline can be considered part of an employee's record, provided they are not subject to a sunset clause in the collective agreement which requires them to be expunged after a specified period of time. While some of the early cases suggested that previous incidents are relevant for the purpose of applying the culminating incident doctrine only if they involved the same type of misconduct, most arbitrators have come to accept that prior acts of unrelated misconduct which resulted in some form of discipline can be taken into account in assessing the penalty for a culminating incident. The awards on this subject are summarized in *Calgary (City) and A.T.U., Local 583* (1997), 61 L.A.C. (4th) 317 (Lucas).

However, arbitrators in several cases have concluded that whether significant weight is to be given to discipline for prior unrelated misconduct depends on whether the overall record supports a finding that the grievor has not learned from the discipline, and is therefore not likely to meet acceptable norms of conduct in the future. This inference may arise if the grievor has engaged in a pattern of continuing offences, undeterred by escalating penalties. By contrast, a prior record of unrelated acts of misconduct will be given less weight if there is no pattern to support such an inference. For an example of this approach, see *Northwestel Inc. and I.B.E.W., Local 1574*, [2003] B.C.C.A.A.A. No. 369 (QL) (Hope). In a related development, Arbitrator Glass, in *Emergency Health Services Commission and C.U.P.E., Local 873*, [2003] B.C.C.A.A.A. No. 365 (QL), held that discipline previously imposed on the grievor for failing to respond when paged by the employer could not be invoked to trigger the doctrine of culminating incident following an unrelated act of misconduct, since the grievor had corrected the problem which led to the prior discipline.

Reliance on alleged misconduct which was not made part of the grievor's formal disciplinary record is more controversial. In the frequently cited award of *SKF Manufacturing of Canada Ltd. and I.A.M., Local 901* (1975), 9 L.A.C. (2d) 139, Arbitrator Shime ruled that such incidents should not be considered in evaluating whether the penalty imposed for an alleged culminating incident is appropriate. It would, in his view, be unfair to consider evidence of non-disciplined incidents because the employee in question may not have been made aware of his or her shortcomings or the need to correct them in order to avoid incurring discipline in the future. Arbitrator Shime also noted that the employer's failure to act upon incidents later claimed to be disciplinary deprives the employee of an opportunity to file a grievance challenging the allegations against him or her at the time they are made.

Several years later, however, in *Air Canada and Canadian Air Line Employees' Ass'n* (1981), 4 L.A.C. (3d) 68, Arbitrator Shime acknowledged the existence of an exception to the general rule that an employer is barred from raising past non-disciplined conduct to support a disciplinary response. In cases involving poor work performance as the basis for discipline, he ruled, an arbitrator may properly consider a record of prior misconduct which was not originally made the subject of discipline. An employee may make mistakes which, though initially seen as non-disciplinary, are justifiably viewed as disciplinary in light of subsequent misconduct. In these circumstances, the past mistakes indicate a pattern of conduct in the performance of duties which justifies the imposition of discipline, provided the incidents are not too stale (stale being defined, for the purposes of that case, as more than one year old). However, where the grievor works in a high-pressure situation in which customers are likely to be irate, complaints about the grievor's performance must be brought to his or her attention promptly if the employer intends at any time to rely on them as a basis for discipline: see *Greyhound Lines of Canada Ltd. and A.T.U., Local 1374* (1991), 22 L.A.C. (4th) 291 (McFetridge).

Since *Air Canada*, many arbitrators have recognized a further ground for the consideration of prior non-disciplined conduct. In their view, while such alleged misconduct cannot be considered in the initial determination of whether the culminating incident warranted discharge, it can be considered in determining whether there are mitigating circumstances in support of a lesser penalty. This is particularly the case where the union advances the grievor's good record as a mitigating factor. In *Newfoundland Light & Power Co. Ltd. and I.B.E.W., Local 1620* (1990), 13 L.A.C. (4th) 341, Arbitrator Thistle summarizes the arbitral development of this approach to earlier non-disciplined conduct.

Metropol Security and U.S.W.A. (1994), 44 L.A.C. (4th) 378 (Mitchnick) affirms that, in applying the doctrine of culminating incident, employers may also look to disciplinary episodes predating the parties' first collective agreement. However, where the employer seeks to rely on a pre-collective agreement record of discipline, it must be prepared to prove each part of that record because normal grievance arbitration rights were not then available to the employee.

There is some disagreement among arbitrators concerning the extent to which details of an employee's disciplinary history can be admitted as part of the formal record. What is perhaps the dominant position is presented by Arbitrator Howard Brown in *Sunnybrook Hospital and Sunnybrook Hospital Employees' Union, Local 777* (1987), 32 L.A.C. (3d) 381. In that case, he held that where a past disciplinary record is introduced for the purpose of separating the appropriateness of discipline for a subsequent offence, the arbitrator should be provided with a statement of the general character of the incident, the date on which discipline was imposed and the specific penalty. Other details, the arbitrator ruled, are not required and should not be admitted, because to do so would mean that the opposing party must be given an opportunity to call evidence in response. This would be contrary to the general principle that employees are not entitled to explain the factual background of disciplinary action which they elected not to challenge through the grievance procedure.

However, in *Cambridge Memorial Hospital and S.E.I.U., Local 204* (1996), 59 L.A.C. (4th) 195 (Brent), the board ruled that detailed letters prepared by the employer setting out the basis for prior suspensions were admissible in their entirety, despite the fact that the grievor disagreed with the employer's version of events. In the board's view, the fact that the grievor did not challenge the discipline at the time was tantamount to an admission of the alleged misconduct and acceptance of the penalty imposed by the employer.

The principle that the union is not allowed to present evidence to explain or dispute ungrieved incidents of discipline is firmly entrenched, and rests in part on the concern that allowing the grievor to dispute prior discipline would amount to an adjudication of grievances which are manifestly and grossly untimely. The rationale is explained in *Greyhound Lines of Canada, supra*.

Conversely, evidence of prior disciplinary measures which have been grieved and which remain unresolved at the time of the hearing may not be admitted as part of the employee's record. Evidence of disputed notices of discipline is felt to present a risk of prejudice which far outweighs any benefit that might be derived from having them before the arbitrator. This principle is set out in *Mental Health Hospital Board, Edmonton and Health Care Employees Union of Alberta, Local 1* (1990), 12 L.A.C. (4th) 301 (Price).

The jurisprudence reveals a division of opinion as to whether a prior award upholding discipline against the grievor forms part of his or her discipline record in the context of an arbitration hearing dealing with a subsequent disciplinary measure. Some arbitrators have taken the view that only a description of the prior offence, the penalty and the fact that the penalty was confirmed or modified at an arbitration hearing is admissible, while the arbitrator's comments or reasons are to be excluded. The decision of Arbitrator Shime in *Canada Post Corp. and C.U.P.W. (Dwyer)* (1992), 24 L.A.C. (4th) 436 is often cited as an example of this approach. However, in *Toronto (City) and Toronto Civic Employees Union, Local 416* (2003), 121 L.A.C. (4th) 127, Arbitrator Tacon held that a prior award should be considered part of the grievor's record, provided that it is not barred by a sunset clause and the arbitrator gives due consideration to the potential prejudicial impact of the reasoning in the prior award.

In *Marriot Corp. of Canada Ltd. and C.U.P.E., Local 229* (1998), 75 L.A.C. (4th) 1, Arbitrator Brandt recognized a growing trend among arbitrators to permit the employer to adduce evidence of prior discipline, despite the presence of a sunset clause, for the limited purpose of refuting a claim by the union that the employee in question has a clear record and is thus a good candidate for rehabilitation. However, if the union does not advance such a claim, the sunset clause will be effective to bar any reference to prior discipline covered by the clause.

Additional Reading

T. Cromwell, "Prior Misconduct and the Determination of Penalty" in W. Kaplan, J. Sack & M. Gunderson, eds., *Labour Arbitration Yearbook 1992*, p. 127.

10.3 ONUS OF PROOF AND ORDER OF PROCEEDING

Unless the employer disputes the employment status of the grievor, the applicability of the collective agreement, or whether the employee has been disciplined, it is universally accepted that the employer bears the burden of proving just cause for discipline on a balance of probabilities and should proceed to present its case first at the arbitration hearing. The employer will also have a right to enter reply evidence after the union has finished presenting its case. These basic principles concerning burden of proof and order of proceeding are set out in the oft-cited decision of *Canadian Broadcasting Corp. and Ass'n of Radio & Television Employees* (1968), 19 L.A.C. 295 (Christie).

If preliminary issues such as employment status or whether discipline has taken place are in dispute, the union may be required to proceed first and to prove a *prima facie* case in order to put the grievance properly before the arbitrator. Even where this is done, though, the employer continues to bear the onus of proof on just cause, and the order of proceeding on this issue remains as was described in *Canadian Broadcasting Corp., supra.* This was established in *Brown Brothers Ltd. and Graphic Arts Int'l Union, Local 28B* (1973), 2 L.A.C. (2d) 347 (Weatherill).

In *United Parcel Service of Canada Ltd. and Teamsters, Local 91* (2002), 112 L.A.C. (4th) 427, a discharge case, Arbitrator Palmer denied a preliminary motion by the employer for permission to call the grievor as its first witness. The arbitrator held that the employer did not have an unfettered right to call the grievor as a witness, although it may be entitled to do so in some circumstances. Some of the factors to be considered include the right of both parties to a fair hearing, the adequacy of the notice given to the grievor, the extent of the grievor's knowledge of the case against him or her, and the employer's purpose in making the request — was it to assist in proving its case, or solely to discredit the witness?

Note that, while the grievor has a duty to take reasonable steps to mitigate damages by seeking alternative employment following discharge, the employer bears the onus of proof if it alleges that the grievor failed to satisfy this duty: see the discussion in Chapter 7.5.

Additional Reading

M.B. Keller, "The Employer's Right to Call the Grievor as Its Witness: An Arbitrator's Perspective" in W. Kaplan, J. Sack & M. Gunderson, eds., *Labour Arbitration Yearbook 1994-95*, p. 155; and companion articles by L.H. Harnden and N. Roland.

10.3.1   Employee's Failure to Provide an Explanation

It has been suggested in several decisions that the refusal of an employee to provide an explanation for apparent misconduct in itself furnishes a ground for discipline. Much of this line of reasoning derives from the award in *Toronto East General Hospital Inc. and S.E.I.U.* (1975), 9 L.A.C. (2d) 311, where Arbitrator David Beatty stated that "arbitrators have in fact recognized that in certain circumstances an employee may be disciplined for failing to provide an adequate explanation for certain facts or circumstances when requested to do so by his employer" (at p. 314). Subsequently, however, arbitrators have made clear that the basis for discipline is not the employee's silence in the face of incriminating circumstances, but the presumption of wrongdoing created by *other* evidence which the employee has not rebutted. As Arbitrator Larson put it in *Coquitlam (District) and C.U.P.E., Local 386* (1977), 14 L.A.C. (2d) 263, at p. 267: "The duty is therefore in the nature of a shifting burden of proof. Suspicious circumstances require an explanation". While an employee may have a "right" to remain silent, particularly if other proceedings are pending, the decision to forgo an opportunity to explain can, as a practical matter, have negative consequences: first, the employer is more likely to form a conclusion that discipline is warranted; second, the grievor may well be prejudiced in his or her attempts later to defend the case at arbitration, either by risking the loss of credibility respecting the substance of the allegations, or by jeopardizing entitlement to a particular remedy. For example, the arbitrator may decline to award compensation or, if the misconduct is proven, conclude that the grievor's silence indicates a lack of remorse, such that an order for reinstatement would be inappropriate.

This characterization of the matter as one of "opportunity" rather than "duty" was discussed and adopted in *Tober Enterprises Ltd. and U.F.C.W., Local 1581* (1990), 7 Can. L.R.B.R. (2d) 148, where the British Columbia Labour Relations Board held that the grievor's failure to explain alleged misconduct did not constitute an independent ground for discipline. Nevertheless, the Board observed, an employee's silence in the face of suspicious circumstances may lead an arbitrator to draw an adverse inference and to uphold the discipline. Moreover, noting the authority of arbitrators to provide a remedy that is just and equitable in all the circumstances, the Board pointed out that the lack of a timely explanation may be held to justify a reduction in the compensation owing or a refusal to order reinstatement.

10.4 STANDARD OF PROOF

In all cases of discipline or discharge, the employer must prove just cause on the civil standard of a balance of probabilities. Thus, it is quite possible for an employer to defeat a grievance against discipline based on allegations of illegal or criminal conduct, despite the fact that the Crown failed in a criminal prosecution against the same employee for the same offence. This is so because, in a criminal proceeding, the Crown must meet the more onerous standard of proving the accused's guilt beyond a reasonable doubt.

Nevertheless, there is a long-standing consensus among arbitrators that, where allegations of misconduct involve criminal, illegal or morally reprehensible behaviour, or behaviour which might seriously harm an employee's professional reputation, the employer must prove its case through evidence which is "clear, cogent and convincing". This does *not* represent the creation of a third standard of proof lying between the criminal and civil standards. Rather, as arbitrators have explained, while there is but one civil burden of proof, *i.e.* a balance of probabilities, the degree of probability required is commensurate with the seriousness of the alleged offence and the consequences which may follow. This concept was set out in a seminal decision of Arbitrator Michel

Picher, *Indusmin Ltd. and United Cement, Lime & Gypsum Workers Int'l Union, Local 488* (1978), 20 L.A.C. (2d) 87.

See also the discussion of standard of proof in Chapter 11.

Additional Reading

H.A. Hope, "Criminal and Immoral Acts: Evidence, Proof and Penalty Assessment" in W. Kaplan, J. Sack & M. Gunderson, eds., *Labour Arbitration Yearbook 1991*, vol. II, p. 111.

10.5   DOUBLE DISCIPLINE PROHIBITED

It is well established that, once a member of management with the requisite authority to discipline has assigned a penalty for a disciplinary offence, the incident is closed, and neither the same management representative nor anyone else in management who feels that a more severe penalty is called for may issue additional disciplinary measures. In the leading case of *A.H. Tallman Bronze Co. Ltd. and U.E., Local 520* (1957), 7 L.A.C. 253, Professor Bora Laskin held that, after a first-level foreman had given a final warning and accepted the grievor's apology, senior management could not discharge the grievor upon learning the details of his misconduct.

In *Calgary Co-Operative Ass'n Ltd. and Calco Club* (1991), 23 L.A.C. (4th) 142, Arbitrator McFetridge applied the rule against double discipline to prevent the employer from discharging the grievor for her alleged bad attitude and refusal to admit wrongdoing at a meeting following her return from a one-day suspension. The arbitrator also held that allowing the employer to increase a penalty because of the employee's disagreement with the initial disciplinary decision would be inconsistent with the right to grieve discipline and with the prohibition against discrimination on the basis of union activity.

Notwithstanding the prohibition against double discipline, the employer is entitled to impose separate penalties in respect of the same event if they relate to different acts of misconduct that are qualitatively distinct from each other. However, the evidence must clearly indicate the existence of separate acts of misconduct, rather than simply the use of different disciplinary headings to justify multiple penalties for what is really the same offence. These principles are illustrated in *Zehrs Markets Inc. and U.F.C.W., Local 1977*, [2000] O.L.A.A. No. 503 (QL) (Lynk).

In considering the prohibition against double discipline, it is important to distinguish between a single disciplinary decision taken at one time to issue a multi-faceted penalty (such as a 12-shift unpaid suspension combined with an 18-month demotion) and two decisions taken by management imposing two separate penalties (such as a written reprimand, followed weeks later by a separate notice imposing a one-day unpaid suspension). The former is permissible, as held in *Vancouver (City) and Vancouver Firefighters' Union, Local 18*, [2004] B.C.C.A.A.A. No. 309 (QL) (Devine), while the latter is clearly a violation of the arbitral principle, as held in *Treasury Board (Correctional Service of Canada) and Babineau*, [2004] C.P.S.S.R.B. No. 132 (QL).

10.6 NON-COMPLIANCE WITH DISCIPLINARY PROCEDURE

Many arbitration awards deal with employer breaches of collective agreement procedures relating to the investigation of misconduct or the implementation of disciplinary measures. It is very common for collective agreements to contain provisions requiring employers to provide notice of discipline or intention to discipline, to hold disciplinary meetings, and to adhere to specific time limits from the date of misconduct to the issuance of discipline. Most common of all, perhaps, are provisions stipulating that employees are entitled to union representation at disciplinary meetings or at the time of notification of discipline. The consequences of a failure to adhere to specified procedures of this kind may be spelled out in the collective agreement, but in most cases they are not. To fill the void, arbitrators have devised a number of general principles that are consistent with the purpose of including procedural protections in connection with the imposition of discipline.

A number of these general principles are set out in the leading case of *Hickeson-Langs Supply Co. and Teamsters, Local 419* (1985), 19 L.A.C. (3d) 379 (Burkett), which deals with the breach of a union representation clause. The arbitrator must first decide if the procedural requirement confers a substantive right of a mandatory nature. If it does, arbitrators will generally rule that the discipline was void *ab initio* — that is, void from the outset — and provide the grievor with full compensation, unless the union has waived the right in question. Breach of a provision which is regarded merely as procedural only will normally have much less severe consequences for the employer. *Hickeson-Langs Supply Co.* is also frequently cited for the proposition that clauses providing for union representation at the time discipline is imposed are generally seen as conferring a mandatory substantive right, such that failure to comply with them renders the discipline null and void. The rationale for this view is that, had the employee been accorded union representation in accordance with the collective agreement, the employer may have been persuaded not to levy discipline or to impose lesser discipline, whereas management was now committed to a particular disciplinary response. Moreover, if the employee made inculpatory admissions, such statements might not have been made had a union representative been present. Moreover, Arbitrator Burkett held that, in the absence of an express provision in the collective agreement requiring that an employee request union representation, there is an implied obligation on the employer to advise the employee of his or her right to union representation when calling a disciplinary meeting.

These principles were strongly affirmed in *Toronto (City) and C.U.P.E., Local 79* (1995), 47 L.A.C. (4th) 197 (Charney), upheld on judicial review (1997), 147 D.L.R. (4th) 548 (Ont. Div. Ct.). On the question, however, of the employer's obligation to inform the grievor of his or her right to union representation, the view is not unanimous. In *Metropolitan Toronto (Municipality) and C.U.P.E., Local 43* (1995), 49 L.A.C. (4th) 289 (Tacon), for example, the employer failed to advise the grievor of his right under the collective agreement to have a union official present at a disciplinary meeting. Arbitrator Tacon decided that, as the employer was not expressly obligated to do so, there had not been a violation of the grievor's representational rights. On the other hand, in *N.A.P.E. v. Newfoundland (Treasury Board)* (2003), 231 Nfld. & P.E.I.R. 333, the Newfoundland and Labrador Court of Appeal concluded that it was not patently unreasonable for an arbitrator to hold that the employer was under an implied duty to advise employees of their right to union representation, even though the collective agreement in that case expressly provided that such representation was to be provided "at [the employee's] request".

Most arbitrators appear to consider a breach of a union representation clause more serious than a breach of other procedural requirements. In *Network North Community Mental Health Group and O.P.S.E.U., Local 666* (1998), 72 L.A.C. (4th) 61, Arbitrator Burkett stressed that union representation provisions have to be interpreted against the backdrop of labour board rulings stating that the right to union representation is protected from employer interference by the prohibition against unfair labour practices. Nevertheless, in ruling on union objections to the sufficiency of an employee's opportunity to secure union representation, some arbitrators have distinguished between the substantive content of the right and ancillary procedural aspects. In their opinion, where the purpose or object of the representation clause has been met, but technically the employer has contravened some procedural requirement related to the right to representation, the discipline can stand. An example of this approach is found in *Toronto Hospital (General Division) and O.N.A.* (1996), 52 L.A.C. (4th) 1 (H.D. Brown), in which the grievor was not told beforehand that the meeting would be disciplinary, but nonetheless knew that her union representative would be in attendance. In these circumstances, the arbitrator reasoned, while the employer's procedure was deficient in that management failed to provide proper notice, the grievor had received the benefit of the substantive right to representation.

10.6.1   When Is Union Representation Required?

Many cases focus on what constitutes an event which triggers the entitlement to union representation. Frequently, the collective agreement requires the employer to observe union representation rights in any disciplinary meeting or disciplinary discussion. Confronted by the allegation that these rights were breached, the employer typically responds that the impugned meeting was merely investigatory in nature, and that it had no intention of imposing discipline. How an arbitrator will ultimately characterize the meeting depends on the specific language in the collective agreement and the evidence concerning what occurred before and during the meeting. In *Hickeson-Langs Supply Co. and Teamsters, Local 419* (1985), 19 L.A.C. (3d) 379 (see Chapter 10.6), Arbitrator Burkett spoke of the difficulty of distinguishing between an investigatory interview and a disciplinary one. A disciplinary interview was said to occur where, in the course of conducting its investigation, the employer approached an employee with the intention of securing an admission of culpability or an exculpatory statement, which would then be considered in deciding whether to take disciplinary action against the employee. The difference between an investigation and a disciplinary meeting therefore was held to hinge on whether the employer had resolved to "confront" the employee.

A very similar approach was adopted in *Brink's Canada Ltd. and I.C.T.U., Local 1* (1997), 69 L.A.C. (4th) 199. Arbitrator Jamieson held that a supervisor's telephone call to the grievor at his home constituted a disciplinary meeting for the purposes of the union representation provisions, because the call was made for the purpose of confronting the grievor with incriminating evidence in the employer's possession.

In cases arising in the retail food industry, by comparison, a number of arbitrators have held that the employer's request to see receipts for goods in an employee's possession does not constitute an accusation of wrongdoing sufficient to trigger the right to union representation. The same holds true for spotchecks which are not based on a specific suspicion of wrongdoing. *Loblaws Supermarkets Ltd. and U.F.C.W., Local 175* (1994), 45 L.A.C. (4th) 120 (R.M. Brown) provides a summary of the caselaw relating to the distinction between investigative and disciplinary meetings in the retail food industry.

More recently, a number of arbitrators have held that the determination of whether a union representation clause applies should not rest on the distinction between meetings which are disciplinary in nature and those which are merely investigatory, but on an analysis of whether the employee's rights could be materially affected to his or her detriment by the actions of the employer. The decision of Arbitrator Kirkwood in *Medis Health & Pharmaceutical Services and Teamsters, Local 424* (2001), 100 L.A.C. (4th) 178 provides a summary of this line of cases.

In *J.H. McNairn Ltd. and U.F.C.W., Local 175*, [2003] O.L.A.A. No. 424 (QL) (Solomatenko), the grievor attended an investigatory interview with management and his union steward three days after an alleged incident in the workplace. A few hours later, after he had gone home, the grievor received a telephone call from a supervisor, who instructed him not to report for work until further notice and to consult with a steward. No one other than the supervisor and the grievor took part in the phone call. The employer subsequently summoned the grievor to a meeting and, in the presence of a steward, issued a disciplinary notice imposing a three-day suspension. Arbitrator Solomatenko held that the supervisor's telephone call to the grievor was covered by a clause in the collective agreement requiring management to "ensure that a representative (*i.e.* steward) of the union is in attendance when employees are being disciplined". As a result, he ruled, the disciplinary notice was null and void. The arbitrator rejected employer arguments that the requirements of the clause had been met by the presence of the union steward at the meeting where formal notice of discipline was issued. In the arbitrator's opinion, the defect in observing the grievor's representation rights at the time of initial imposition of discipline could not be cured by representation at a subsequent meeting.

In *CHBC TV Kelowna and C.E.P., Local 823-M*, [2005] C.L.A.D. No. 23 (QL), Arbitrator Burke noted a divergence of opinion in arbitral caselaw as to whether union representation rights stem solely from the collective agreement, or whether such rights arise independently from labour relations legislation providing for the union's exclusive bargaining agency. Arbitrator Burke concluded that, while labour relations legislation is a source of the right to union representation, this does not prevent the parties from negotiating the specific way in which representational rights are to be exercised. At the same time, she held, collective agreement provisions regarding the scope of union representation rights should be interpreted broadly, in a manner that takes into account the statutory framework.

Additional Reading

G.J. Brandt, "Remedial Guidelines in Representational Rights Cases" in W. Kaplan, J. Sack, M. Gunderson & R. Filion, eds., *Labour Arbitration Yearbook 1998*, p. 169.

M.I. Chertkow, "Mandatory Union Representation at Discipline: An Arbitrator's Perspective" in W. Kaplan, J. Sack & M. Gunderson, eds., *Labour Arbitration Yearbook 1993*, p. 137; and companion articles by K. Lercher and G. Caroline.

10.6.2   Other Procedural Defects

Grievances alleging a breach of other procedural requirements such as notice of disciplinary meetings or the provision of reasons for discipline are treated in a similar fashion. The key issue is whether the provision in question creates a mandatory substantive right, in which case the discipline is generally held to be void *ab initio* in the event of non-compliance. A summary of the arbitral jurisprudence on breach of notice requirements in the discipline process is found in *Northwestern General Hospital and O.N.A.* (1992), 30 L.A.C. (4th) 95 (Starkman). The award shows that, in some instances, a provision which merely requires that notification of the reasons for discipline be provided within a specified time may be held to create a mandatory substantive right.

The principle that a breach of notice provisions in a collective agreement which are held to create substantive rights invalidates the discipline is forcefully demonstrated in *Canada Post Corp. and C.U.P.W.* (2000), 89 L.A.C. (4th) 265 (Burkett). In that case, following a lengthy investigation in which the workplace was placed under surreptitious video surveillance, the employer discharged 29 employees for theft. After the investigation was under way, the employer invited the police to initiate an independent criminal investigation, but the police declined. Nevertheless, based on the results of the employer's investigation, the police laid criminal charges. Contrary to the strict time limits prescribed by the collective agreement, which required the employer to notify an employee within ten days of alleged misconduct having come to its attention, none of the employees were advised of the allegations until the criminal charges were laid. Arbitrator Burkett held that, while the employer would be exempted from compliance with the notice requirements in circumstances where a covert police investigation was in progress, in this case the investigation had been conducted by the employer itself. Since the employer had knowledge of the alleged criminal misconduct, there was no reason to defer providing the employees with notice. In the result, the employer was precluded from relying on the thefts as a basis for discharge, and the employees were ordered reinstated with full compensation. The arbitrator's decision was upheld on judicial review: see (2000), 50 O.R. (3d) 448 (Div. Ct.), affirmed (2001), 56 O.R. (3d) 457 (C.A.).

10.6.3   Waiver

In cases in which a breach of procedural provisions concerning discipline is alleged, it is frequently argued that the claim should be denied because the grievor's conduct made it impossible for the employer to comply with the agreement, or because the grievor and the union either waived their rights or should be estopped from enforcing them. The leading decision of Arbitrator Burkett in *Canada Post Corp. and C.U.P.W. (Gibson)* (1992), 29 L.A.C. (4th) 7 deals with all three types of arguments. Although it recognizes that, where an employee's conduct prevents the employer from complying with notice requirements (as, for example, where the employee "disappears"), the union may be precluded from relying on the employer's subsequent breach of procedural requirements, the case appears to set a fairly high threshold for misconduct that will be sufficient to relieve the employer of its collective agreement obligations. Serious misconduct on the part of the employee constituting a repudiation of all obligations under the agreement may be required.

Arbitrator Burkett also sets stringent standards for a finding of waiver. He reiterates his observation in *Hickeson-Langs Supply Co. and Teamsters, Local 419* (1985), 19 L.A.C. (3d) 379 (see Chapter 10.6) that arbitrators should be reluctant to find that a substantive right has been waived. He goes on to hold that, while waiver may be implied from a party's conduct, the waiver must be intentional and voluntary, and the other party must have altered its position in reliance on it. The union must clearly and unequivocally waive the procedural safeguard, and the waiver must occur with full knowledge of the rights that the procedure was intended to protect and of the effect that waiver will have on the process. Moreover, the arbitrator ruled, there must be direct evidence that the union put its mind to the question and purposely waived the employee's right. In the absence of such evidence, an arbitrator should be reluctant to infer waiver from the mere failure of the union to raise the procedural breach during the grievance procedure. Estoppel arguments were rejected on the basis of similar reasoning.

10.6.4   Reimposition of Discipline

There is some divergence of opinion as to whether, on the basis of the same misconduct, an employer can successfully reinstitute an invalid penalty by rerunning the discipline procedures in accordance with the collective agreement requirements. The prevalent view appears to be that, where there is a breach of the right to union representation, a vital opportunity to make representations to the employer has forever been lost, with the consequence that the prejudice to the employee's substantive rights cannot be cured. Thus, the justification for ruling that discipline imposed in violation of the collective agreement is void *ab initio* is also invoked in support of the view that discipline cannot be reinstituted for the same offence. A good example of the prevailing approach is found in *J & A Building Services Ltd. and U.F.C.W., Local 175/633* (1997), 63 L.A.C. (4th) 49 (Sarra). Other arbitrators, however, perhaps uncomfortable with the prospect of reinstating with full compensation an employee who may be guilty of misconduct, have held that an employer can reimpose discipline where the prior procedural defect is capable of being corrected and the grievor put in the position he or she would have been in had the prior procedural defect not occurred. In their opinion, an arbitrator should consider whether the grievor has suffered real prejudice as a result of the prior procedural defect. The jurisprudence reflecting these contrasting approaches is canvassed in *Sunnybrook Hospital and Sunnybrook Hospital Employees' Union, Local 777* (1993), 36 L.A.C. (4th) 129 (Langille).

In contrast to the case-by-case inquiry into the existence of actual prejudice advocated by Arbitrator Langille, Arbitrator Burkett, in *Ontario Hydro and Power Workers' Union (McNally)*, [1998] O.L.A.A. No. 230 (QL), held that the breach of a collective agreement requirement for union representation prior to any disciplinary decision being made gives rise, in the event of noncompliance, to a presumption of prejudice sufficient to prevent the reimposition of discipline. In order to rebut the presumption, the employer must establish beyond a reasonable doubt that it would have taken the same course of action, regardless of the intervention of a union representative. As the arbitrator suggests, this is a very high threshold, which may be met only in cases involving gross misconduct on the grievor's part. If the employer fails to rebut the presumption, it cannot seek to reinstitute the discipline. However, in cases in which the requirement of union representation rights in the agreement applies only after the disciplinary decision has been made, a presumption of prejudice does not arise, and the employer may be entitled to reinstitute the discipline following reinstatement, subject of course to compliance with the representation requirements of the collective agreement.

10.6.5 Remedial Discretion

An issue which has arisen in several recent cases is whether an arbitrator has jurisdiction, in a discharge case, to award a remedy that does not include reinstatement, despite finding that the discharge was invalid because of the employer's violation of a right to union representation or another substantive right under the collective agreement. In *Bombardier Aerospace and C.A.W., Local 673*, [2003] O.L.A.A. No. 628 (QL), Arbitrator Howard Brown rejected union arguments that, because the dismissal had been declared void *ab initio*, his remedial authority was restricted to an order reinstating the grievor. According to the arbitrator, the employer was precluded, as a result of its breach of mandatory discipline procedures (in this instance, the provision of union representation) from proceeding with the discharge case on its merits. However, he reasoned, this did not automatically lead to reinstatement. In the arbitrator's view, the circumstances of the grievor's discharge involved the imposition of a "penalty" within the meaning of s. 48(17) of the Ontario *Labour Relations Act*, S.O. 1995, c. 1, Sch. A, and this penalty had been the subject of a grievance under the collective agreement. This, the arbitrator held, gave him authority to exercise his remedial discretion under the Act and the collective agreement, which included making an order for damages in lieu of reinstatement.

10.7 DELAY IN IMPOSING DISCIPLINE

It is a widely accepted arbitral principle that, once the employer has learned of employee misconduct, or ought to have known of it, any delay in imposing discipline may render the penalty void. In *University of Ottawa and I.U.O.E., Local 796-B* (1994), 42 L.A.C. (4th) 300 (Bendel), the arbitrator identified several possible rationales for the rule against delay in issuing discipline: unreasonable delay indicates employer condonation; the employee's right to procedural fairness must be preserved; delay effectively denies the grievor the opportunity to defend the allegations because it compromises his or her recollection of the alleged incident. Arbitrator Bendel also pointed out that the requirement for reasonably expeditious discipline has been held to be a general arbitral principle that applies even in the absence of evidence of actual prejudice or unfairness to the employee.

The principles underlying the arbitral rule against delay in imposing discipline are conveniently summarized in *AFG Industries Ltd. and Aluminum, Brick & Glass Workers Int'l Union* (1998), 75 L.A.C. (4th) 336 (Herlich). In determining whether there has been unreasonable delay which invalidates the discipline, Arbitrator Herlich suggested, arbitrators should examine three criteria: the length of the delay, the reasons for the delay and the impact or prejudicial effect of the delay. *AFG Industries* also held that the nature of the alleged misconduct may be a major factor in deciding whether prejudice can be inferred or presumed: some events, the arbitrator noted, are inherently memorable, but delay in bringing an allegation concerning functions which the employee performs on a daily or regular basis clearly prejudices his or her ability to recall what happened on the occasion in question.

In *Winnipeg (City) and C.U.P.E., Local 500*, [2003] M.G.A.D. No. 8 (QL), Arbitrator Graham provided a comprehensive summary of the arbitral caselaw on the effects of delay. He noted that arbitrators are split on the issue of whether evidence of actual prejudice to the grievor is a prerequisite to a decision voiding the discipline on the ground of excessive delay.

10.8 ALTERATION OF GROUNDS PROHIBITED

Since the seminal decision of Arbitrator Laskin in *Aerocide Dispensers Ltd. and U.S.W.A.* (1965), 15 L.A.C. 416, it has been widely accepted that an employer is not allowed to change or add to the grounds for discipline which were given at the time the penalty was imposed. The rationale on which the rule rests is that allowing an employer to rely at arbitration on grounds that were not raised or discussed in the grievance process would undermine the grievor's right to fair treatment.

10.8.1 Exceptions

Arbitrators have recognized numerous exceptions to the general principle stated in *Aerocide Dispensers Ltd. and U.S.W.A.* (1965), 15 L.A.C. 416 (Laskin). Among the most commonly invoked exceptions are cases where the alternative grounds raised by the employer were unknown to it at the time it took disciplinary action, or where the nature of the grievor's misconduct was surreptitious, making detection difficult. In such instances, arbitrators are more willing to admit evidence to support the altered grounds as long as the union and the employee have had adequate notice to enable them to prepare properly for the hearing. A discussion of the exceptions to the rule against alteration of grounds is contained in the frequently cited case of *Ontario Hydro and C.U.P.E., Local 1000* (1988), 3 L.A.C. (4th) 112 (Brent).

Some arbitrators have gone slightly further than Arbitrator Brent, and suggested that evidence relating to new or altered grounds for discipline may be admitted as long as the union has had sufficient notice in advance of the arbitration hearing to ensure that the requirements of natural justice are met. This position is put forward in the leading decision of *York (City) Board of Education and C.U.P.E., Local 994* (1993), 37 L.A.C. (4th) 257 (Burkett).

In addition to the exceptions recognized in the above-mentioned cases, arbitrators have frequently held that the bar to altering grounds does not apply to new evidence relating to old grounds or to additional examples of wrongdoing which are demonstrative of the grounds initially advanced by the employer. These exceptions to the rule in *Aerocide Dispensers*, as well as the difficulty of categorizing certain facts as evidence of new grounds or as new evidence of old grounds, are discussed in *Pictou District School Board and N.S.T.U.* (1997), 63 L.A.C. (4th) 14 (Christie).

10.9 ASSESSMENT OF DISCIPLINE

Arbitrators have long adhered to the view that they possess an implied or inherent authority to substitute a lesser penalty, notwithstanding that cause for some form of discipline has been shown. In *Port Arthur Shipbuilding Co. v. Arthurs* (1968), 70 D.L.R. (2d) 693, however, the Supreme Court of Canada arrived at a different conclusion, holding that arbitrators lacked jurisdiction to reduce the penalty once they found just cause for discipline. Within several years of that decision, all jurisdictions in Canada enacted statutory provisions expressly giving arbitrators the authority to substitute a lesser penalty where it seems just and reasonable in all the circumstances, despite a finding that the employer has established cause for discipline or discharge. In some jurisdictions, the legislation limits the exercise of this arbitral discretion to cases where the collective agreement does not contain a specific penalty for the infraction that is the subject-matter of the arbitration. See, for example, s. 76(4) of the New Brunswick *Industrial Relations Act*, R.S.N.B. 1973, c. I-4; and s. 48(17) of the Ontario *Labour Relations Act*, S.O. 1995, c. 1, Sch. A. In other jurisdictions, the arbitral jurisdiction to substitute a lesser penalty is not limited in this fashion. See s. 89(d) of the British Columbia *Labour Relations Code*, R.S.B.C. 1996, c. 244.

Nevertheless, there was initially some disagreement among arbitrators as to the scope of their discretion to review a disciplinary penalty. Some felt that they should be deferential to the decisions of management regarding the appropriate penalty. However, following the seminal decision of Arbitrator Adams in *Phillips Cables Ltd. and U.E., Local 510* (1974), 6 L.A.C. (2d) 35, most arbitrators came to accept that they should apply a broad standard of review to determine if it would be just and reasonable to substitute a lesser penalty, and that deference to management's views is unnecessary. Indeed, in the years since *Port Arthur Shipbuilding* was decided, the Supreme Court of Canada has regarded the existence of just cause as a matter within the purview of an arbitrator, and will defer to the arbitral determination, unless a jurisdictional error is made: *Blanchard v. Control Data Canada Ltd.* (1984), 14 D.L.R. (4th) 289 (S.C.C.).

Generally speaking, collective agreement provisions which are alleged to oust the remedial discretion of arbitrators by prescribing a specific penalty for an offence are construed strictly. In *General Drivers, Warehousemen & Helpers Union, Local 979 v. Brink's Canada Ltd.* (1983), 145 D.L.R. (3d) 761, a discharge case, the Supreme Court of Canada upheld this stringent approach to provisions which purportedly limit the arbitral power to substitute a lesser penalty. For a more recent example of this reasoning, see *Deep Sea Trawlers and U.F.C.W., Local 864*, [2000] N.S.L.A.A. No. 1 (QL) (Veniot).

10.9.1   Factors Affecting Penalty

Over the years, arbitrators have identified a variety of factors — some related to the conduct of the employer, others to the conduct or circumstances of the grievor — which should be considered in deciding if the penalty imposed by the employer is just and reasonable. Some factors are of an aggravating nature, others mitigating. The case most frequently cited in this regard is *Steel Equipment Co. Ltd. and U.S.W.A., Local 3257* (1964), 14 L.A.C. 356 (Reville), which enumerated ten key factors for consideration:

(1) The previous good record of the grievor.

(2) The long service of the grievor.

(3) Whether or not the offence was an isolated incident in the employment history of the grievor.

(4) Provocation.

(5) Whether the offence was committed on the spur of the moment as a result of a momentary aberration, due to strong emotional impulses, or whether the offence was premeditated.

(6) Whether the penalty imposed has created a special economic hardship for the grievor in the light of his or her particular circumstances.

(7) Evidence that the company rules of conduct, either unwritten or posted, have not been uniformly enforced, thus constituting a form of discrimination.

(8) Circumstances negativing intent, *e.g.*, likelihood that the grievor misunderstood the nature or intent of an order given to him or her, and as a result disobeyed it.

(9) The seriousness of the offence in terms of company policy and company obligations.

(10) Any other circumstances which the board should properly take into consideration.

The other decision most frequently cited on the assessment of discipline is *Wm. Scott & Co. Ltd. and Canadian Food & Allied Workers Union, Local P-162* (1976), [1977] 1 Can. L.R.B.R. 1 (B.C.L.R.B.). In that case, Chair Paul Weiler contrasted the rigid approach to wrongful dismissal under the common law of master and servant with the much more flexible approach to disciplinary penalties under arbitral jurisprudence. Indeed, *Wm. Scott* stressed the importance of an individualized and corrective approach to discipline, a concept that gained prominence among arbitrators in the 1970s, holding that arbitrators should no longer consider serious forms of misconduct such as theft or assault as automatically giving rise to cause for discharge. After referring to the *Steel Equipment* criteria, Weiler named what in his view are the five most important factors in determining the appropriateness of the penalty:

(1) How serious is the immediate offence which precipitated the discharge?

(2) Was the grievor's conduct premeditated or repetitive, as opposed to a momentary aberration, or was it provoked by someone else?

(3) Does the grievor have a record of long service with relatively little discipline?

(4) Have there been earlier attempts at corrective discipline that were unsuccessful?

(5) Does the penalty given the grievor appear to be consistent with the employer's prior practice, or does it single out the grievor for arbitrary and harsh treatment?

Some arbitrators have slightly modified the list of factors in order to adapt them to particular types of misconduct. One of the most frequently cited lists, in cases involving breach of trust or theft, is that established in *Canadian Broadcasting Corp. and C.U.P.E.* (1979), 23 L.A.C. (2d) 227 (Arthurs) (see Chapter 12.1). The factors identified there are as follows:

(1) Was the grievor genuinely confused or mistaken as to his or her right to do the act complained of?

(2) Was the grievor unable to appreciate the wrongfulness of his or her conduct due to drunkenness or emotional problems?

(3) Was the act impulsive or was it premeditated?

(4) How serious was the harm done?

(5) Did the grievor make a frank acknowledgment of misconduct?

(6) Did the grievor have a sympathetic personal motive for being dishonest, such as family need, as opposed to hardened criminality?

(7) What is the grievor's past record?

(8) What are the grievor's rehabilitative prospects?

(9) What economic impact would discharge have on the grievor in light of his or her personal circumstances?

The award in *Dominion Glass Co. and United Glass & Ceramic Workers, Local 203* (1975), 11 L.A.C. (2d) 84 (Linden) (see Chapter 13.5) has long been cited in cases of assault in the workplace for its list of relevant factors. More recently, the considerations outlined in that decision were expanded somewhat in *SRI Homes Inc. and I.W.A., Local 1-184* (1996), 58 L.A.C. (4th) 385 (Hood):

(1) Did the employer have a clear policy against fighting in the workplace?

(2) How serious was the assault?

(3) Was the assault premeditated, or was it a momentary flare-up?

(4) Was the grievor provoked?

(5) What is the likelihood of recurrence?

(6) What is the grievor's length of service and work record?

(7) Can the grievor be reintegrated into the workforce?

(8) Is discharge of the grievor necessary to deter other employees?

(9) Has the employer maintained a consistent policy and practice in respect of similar incidents?

(10) What economic impact would discharge have on the grievor?

(11) Did the grievor cooperate in the employer's investigation?

(12) Did the grievor show remorse or apologize to the victim?

Noting that none of these factors is in itself determinative, Arbitrator Hood ruled that the grievor's failure to show due remorse and to provide an unconditional apology did not, in the circumstances, disentitle him to reinstatement.

However, in the more recent decision of *Cariboo-Chilcotin School District No. 27 and I.U.O.E., Local 859*, [2004] B.C.C.A.A.A. No. 317 (QL), Arbitrator Hope noted that for many arbitrators the failure to openly acknowledge misconduct and apologize is a significant aggravating factor that inclines them against exercising their discretionary power to modify the discipline. In the opinion of these arbitrators, the failure to admit wrongdoing and apologize invites the conclusion that the conduct might well be repeated and the rehabilitative goals of progressive discipline are unlikely to be achieved by substitution of a lesser penalty.

It also appears that, in the face of dishonesty by the grievor during an investigation or in testimony at the arbitration hearing, arbitrators will often decline to substitute a lesser penalty for discharge, particularly in cases of theft or other forms of dishonest conduct. In *Shell Canada Ltd. and C.E.P., Local 835*, [2003] A.G.A.A. No. 65 (QL), where the grievor had been dismissed for theft, a board chaired by Arbitrator Sims held that the grievor's dishonesty in the course of the employer's investigation made him a poor candidate for reinstatement, despite 17 years of good service. Similarly, in *Peace Regional Emergency Medical Services Society and H.S.A.A. (Wilson)*, [2003] A.G.A.A. No. 67

(QL), a case involving discharge for sexual harassment, Arbitrator Moreau concluded that the grievor's failure to tell the truth at the hearing closed any window of opportunity for rebuilding the employment relationship.

However, as Arbitrator Veniot opined in *Farmers Co-operative Dairy Ltd. and C.E.P., Local 40N*, [2003] N.S.L.A.A No. 24 (QL), while an early admission of wrongdoing is a mitigating factor, "the reverse will rarely be true", and the fact that an employee who is found to have committed theft did not admit the offence at the hearing should not be considered an aggravating factor, except in "rare and exceptional" cases. This was so, the arbitrator found, because "no grievor should ever feel that he or she should admit to an act which he or she says was not committed, to seek mitigation, and avoid a possible condemnation that might come with adverse findings of fact" (at paras. 154-56).

10.9.2 Illness or Disorder as a Mitigating Factor

In discipline cases, the union sometimes asserts that the grievor's breach of trust or other misconduct can be explained as a consequence of an illness or disease, such as drug or alcohol addiction or bipolar mental disorder, and that reinstatement would be appropriate because the grievor is undergoing treatment for the condition which caused the misconduct. In *Canada Post Corp. and C.P.A.A. (MacMillan)* (2001), 102 L.A.C. (4th) 97, Arbitrator Christie held that the existence of an illness or disorder should result in reinstatement only if the following criteria are satisfied:

(1) The grievor was experiencing an illness or condition at the time of the misconduct.

(2) A causal linkage or nexus between the illness or condition and the aberrant conduct has been established.

(3) If a causal linkage is found, the arbitrator must be persuaded that there was a sufficient displacement of responsibility from the grievor to render the conduct less culpable. In other words, even if it is found that the misconduct would not have occurred but for the illness or condition, the arbitrator may nevertheless conclude that the grievor was sufficiently responsible for his or her actions to make modification of the penalty inappropriate.

(4) Even where the above criteria are met, the arbitrator must be satisfied that the grievor has been rehabilitated, and that the risk of a recurrence of the aberrant behaviour is minimal.

Finally, Arbitrator Christie noted, even in cases where it is established that the grievor was suffering from a disability within the meaning of human rights legislation, and the disability was causally connected to the misconduct, it may amount to undue hardship to require that the employer reinstate the grievor. In such instances, he observed, evidence of rehabilitation and the risk of recurrence will be of great importance.

Additional Reading

P.A. Chapman, "Mental Disability and the Arbitration Process: An Emerging Concern" in K. Whitaker, J. Sack, M. Gunderson & R. Filion, eds., *Labour Arbitration Yearbook 1999-2000*, vol. II, p. 189; and companion articles by R.W. Little and T. Hadwen.

10.9.3 Progressive Discipline

Most arbitrators accept that implicit in the concept of just cause for discharge is a requirement to take a progressive or corrective approach to discipline before resorting to the ultimate penalty of discharge. The principle of progressive discipline is based, generally, on the notion that it would be unjust to discharge an employee if the employer has not first attempted to correct the misconduct with a lesser penalty or penalties. It is also premised on the belief that discipline will better achieve its corrective purpose if penalties are imposed on a progressive basis, from less severe ones for the first offence to more severe ones for repeated and serious infractions. Adherence to progressive discipline should also avoid claims that the employee was surprised or lacked warning of the seriousness with which the employer regarded the misconduct. These principles and their rationale are explained in *Ocean Paving Ltd. and I.U.O.E., Local 721* (1997), 64 L.A.C. (4th) 82 (Cromwell).

Prior to the 1970s, arbitrators usually took the view that the rationale for applying a corrective or progressive approach to discipline did not apply to the most egregious forms of misconduct, such as theft or assault, and that summary discharge was in all such cases an appropriate disciplinary response. However, beginning with a number of ground-breaking awards in the mid-1970s, many arbitrators adopted the view that the norms of progressive discipline that focus on the grievor's rehabilitative potential should be also applied to very serious misconduct. *Galco Food Products Ltd. and Amalgamated Meat Cutters & Butchers Workmen of North America, Local P-1105* (1974), 7 L.A.C. (2d) 350 (D.M. Beatty) is one of the seminal decisions urging arbitrators to apply a corrective approach to discipline wherever possible.

New Dominion Stores and R.W.D.S.U., Local 414 (1997), 60 L.A.C. (4th) 308 (Beck) provides a more recent example of the application of progressive discipline to theft in the retail food industry. Despite a traditional presumption in favour of upholding discharge for theft in this sector, Arbitrator Beck adopted a corrective approach, reinstating the grievor with a lengthy suspension notwithstanding her failure to admit to stealing and to express remorse. On the other hand, the award of Arbitrator McPhillips in *Sarowa Investments*

Inc. and C.A.W., Local 3000 (2001), 94 L.A.C. (4th) 238 suggests that the presumption, which reflects the view that the employer's deterrence interest in such cases is preeminent, is not easily overcome.

In *Grand & Toy Ltd. and U.S.W.A., Local 9197*, [2001] O.L.A.A. No. 242 (QL), Arbitrator Craven applied the principles of progressive discipline to a case in which four employees were alleged to have committed time theft. In his opinion, employer policies dictating "zero tolerance" for certain forms of misconduct were inconsistent with the requirement for a progressive approach to discipline, and therefore with the just cause standard under the collective agreement.

The importance of applying a corrective approach to discipline has long been recognized by arbitrators when inadequate work performance is alleged as the basis for just cause for dismissal. In *North York General Hospital and Canadian Union of General Employees* (1973), 5 L.A.C. (2d) 45, Arbitrator Shime set out the reasons for this arbitral attitude. Arbitrator MacDowell's award in *Invista Canada and Kingston Independent Nylon Workers Union (Wollerman)*, [2004] O.L.A.A. No. 813 (QL) also addresses the application of progressive discipline to the discharge of a long-service employee for deteriorating work performance.

10.9.4   Compensation in Lieu of Reinstatement

Where an employee is found to have engaged in misconduct meriting discipline but not discharge, the normal arbitral response is reinstatement with a lesser penalty. Nonetheless, the arbitrator has jurisdiction to deny the customary remedy of reinstatement, awarding instead compensatory damages. In *U.S.W.A., Local 12998 v. Liquid Carbonic Inc.* (1996), 135 D.L.R. (4th) 493 (Ont. Div. Ct.), the Court affirmed the authority of arbitrators to make this disposition, noting, however, that it was appropriate only in exceptional circumstances.

The Supreme Court of Canada has recently affirmed that an arbitrator has authority, in "exceptional" cases in which "the employment relationship is no longer viable", to deny reinstatement, and to award damages instead: *A.U.P.E. v. Lethbridge Community College* (2004), 238 D.L.R. (4th) 385. For a discussion of recent cases that illustrate the circumstances in which compensation has been ordered in lieu of reinstatement, see Chapter 7.2.

Additional Reading

A. Ponak, "Discharge Arbitration and Reinstatement: An Industrial Relations Perspective" in W. Kaplan, J. Sack & M. Gunderson, eds., *Labour Arbitration Yearbook 1991*, vol. II, p. 31.

CHAPTER 11

DISHONEST AND ILLEGAL CONDUCT

11.1 DISHONESTY

Arbitrators and judges have long viewed honesty and trust as the cornerstones of a viable and productive employment relationship. As a result, dishonesty and breach of trust by employees are considered very serious forms of misconduct warranting discipline. Perhaps the leading case on the arbitral approach to dishonest behaviour is *Phillips Cables Ltd. and U.E., Local 510* (1974), 6 L.A.C. (2d) 35 (Adams) (see also Chapter 11.2.2):

> Moreover, in a very general sense, honesty is a touchstone to viable employer-employee relationships. If employees must be constantly watched to ensure that they honestly report their comings and goings, or to ensure that valuable tools, material and equipment are not stolen, the industrial enterprise will soon be operated on the model of a penal institution. In other words, employee good faith and honesty is one important ingredient to both industrial democracy and the fostering of a more co-operative labour relations climate.
>
> The board feels that these are the sentiments underlying the arbitral castigation of dishonest conduct. Arbitrators are not equating the role of a plant to that of a church. Rather, they are ensuring that the role of the plant will not evolve into a role resembling that of a penal institution . . .

However, whether dishonesty warrants discharge or a lesser penalty depends on a variety of factors, including the nature of the offence, the effect on the employer's operations, the values of deterrence on the one hand and correction on the other, and the circumstances of the grievor, including aggravating and mitigating factors.

It is interesting to note that in *McKinley v. BC Tel* (2001), 200 D.L.R. (4th) 385, the Supreme Court of Canada adopted a similar "contextual" approach in addressing alleged dishonesty or breach of trust as a ground for summary dismissal at common law. "More specifically", the Court stated, "the test is whether the employee's dishonesty gave rise to a breakdown in the employment relationship" (at p. 404). The Court rejected a long-standing line of common law authority holding that proof of dishonesty should in itself be regarded as just cause for discharge in favour of an approach which recognized and applied the principle of proportionality in determining whether particular acts justify termination of employment. Under the proportionality approach, courts are required to seek an effective balance between the nature and severity of an employee's misconduct and the disciplinary sanction imposed. This requires adherence to a contextual, two-step framework of analysis. The first step is to determine whether dishonesty or breach of trust has been proven. If so, the court must go on to inquire whether, having regard to the particular facts of the case, the nature and seriousness of the dishonesty can be reconciled with the continuance of the employment relationship.

Additional Reading

J.M. Fantini, *"McKinley v. BC Tel*: The Supreme Court Considers Dishonesty as a Ground for Summary Dismissal" (2002), 9 Canadian Labour and Employment Journal, p. 283.

11.2   FALSIFICATION OF RECORDS

11.2.1   Application Forms

During the 1970s, arbitrators were divided in their response to the problem of employees who provided false information on employment application forms. Under the approach proposed by Professor Simmons in *Douglas Aircraft Co. of Canada Ltd. and U.A.W., Local 1967* (1973), 2 L.A.C. (2d) 147, all cases were classified into four rigid categories, each having its own prescribed outcome. Many arbitrators criticized this scheme as focusing solely on the employer's interests. The other approach, developed by Arbitrator Shime in *Gould Manufacturing of Canada Ltd. and U.S.W.A.* (1972), 1 L.A.C. (2d) 314, affirmed on judicial review (1973), 33 D.L.R. (3d) 527 (Ont. Div. Ct.), identified eleven relevant factors to consider in determining whether falsification of an application document presents just cause for discharge:

(1) The nature and character of the falsification and the matter or offence concealed.

(2) The number of matters concealed.

(3) The date when the falsified or concealed matter occurred in relation to the signing of the employment application.

(4) Any warning contained on the employment application.

(5) Whether the revelation of the matter or offence concealed would have resulted in the employer not hiring the individual.

(6) The time that has elapsed between the signing of the false application form and the date of discovery.

(7) Whether the employer acted promptly upon learning of the falsification of the employment record.

(8) The seniority of the grievor.

(9) Whether the grievor was in fact discharged for the falsification.

(10) The materiality of that falsification or matter or offence concealed to the work performed.

(11) Special considerations such as a sensitive employment position.

The result is a more flexible analysis that allows for consideration of both employer and employee interests. The two approaches and the modern arbitral consensus in favour of *Gould Manufacturing* are set out in *Ralston Purina of Canada Inc. and E.C.W.U., Local 4* (1982), 7 L.A.C. (3d) 45 (Prichard). The principles canvassed in *Ralston Purina* were applied in a comprehensive manner in *C & C Lath Ltd. and I.W.A., Local 1-80* (1992), 28 L.A.C. (4th) 111 (Vickers).

In *Ontario (Ministry of Community Safety and Correctional Services) and O.P.S.E.U. (Seguin)* (2005), 136 L.A.C. (4th) 339, the Ontario Grievance Settlement Board dealt with the issue of whether an employee is under a duty to disclose to the prospective employer that he or she had been discharged for cause by a former employer. After reviewing the limited caselaw on this question, Vice-Chair Richard Brown concluded that an employee is not under any such obligation, unless specifically asked during the hiring process about the way in which the previous employment ended. However, in this case, because the grievor had suggested in his application letter that he continued to work for his former employer, he was found to have actively engaged in misrepresentation, and this was held to merit discipline. Accordingly, the grievor was reinstated, but without compensation.

Additional Reading

G. Davenport, "Applications for Employment and the Failure to Disclose: A Critical Perspective" in K. Whitaker, J. Sack, M. Gunderson & R. Filion, eds., *Labour Arbitration Yearbook 2001-2002*, vol. II, p. 207; and companion articles by S.M. Kearney & A. Davies, and K. Young.

11.2.2   Attendance and Production Records

Phillips Cables Ltd. and U.E., Local 510 (1974), 6 L.A.C. (2d) 35 (Adams) is the seminal decision on the falsification of production records. It identified the harmful impact of this type of misconduct on the workplace and the employment relationship, and established the modern approach to determining an appropriate penalty in such cases. According to the board, "honesty is a touchstone to viable employer-employee relationships . . . employee good faith and honesty is one important ingredient to both industrial democracy and the fostering of a more co-operative labour relations climate" (at p. 37). However, the board wrote, while the need for deterrence was an extremely important factor, it was also necessary to consider whether it would be just and reasonable to substitute a lesser penalty than discharge, especially if there were substantial mitigating circumstances.

It has been held that, in determining whether it would be appropriate to substitute a penalty short of discharge, a significant consideration is whether or not the grievor obtained a direct monetary benefit from the falsification of production records: *Accucaps Industries Ltd. and C.A.W., Local 195*, [2004] O.L.A.A. No. 21 (QL) (Watters).

One of the most common examples of falsification of production documents involves wilful tampering with attendance records or timecards. Because arbitrators treat such conduct as a form of fraud or theft, they frequently uphold the imposition of severe penalties, including discharge. However, discharge is not the inevitable result. In *Canada Bread and U.F.C.W., Local 1518* (2001), 100 L.A.C. (4th) 244 (MacIntyre), which reviews extensively the recent arbitral jurisprudence on falsification of time cards, the arbitrator followed the trend identified in *Stelco Inc. (Hilton Works) and U.S.W.A.* (1994), 40 L.A.C. (4th) 229 (Tacon), by substituting a substantial suspension for discharge where the employee made a full admission of misconduct and did not attempt to mislead the arbitrator at the hearing.

This emphasis on admission of guilt is also evident in two recent decisions arising in the retail food industry, which indicate that even long-term employees with clear records are subject to discharge if they fail to acknowledge wrongdoing at any stage of the investigation process or the arbitration hearing. In *Canada Safeway Ltd. and U.F.C.W., Local 401*, [2003] A.G.A.A. No. 95 (QL) (Moreau), the arbitrator refused to reinstate employees with 39 and 33 years' seniority, respectively, because he felt that their deceit in claiming pay for hours not worked, combined with their dishonesty at the hearing, had destroyed the bond of trust on which the employment relationship was based. Similarly, in *Canada Safeway Ltd. and U.F.C.W., Local 401*, [2003] A.G.A.A. No. 77 (QL), Arbitrator Ponak upheld the discharge of a 24-year employee who had falsely claimed six hours' pay. The arbitrator noted that a common element of cases in which employees found to have engaged in time theft were reinstated was full acknowledgment of wrongdoing by the grievor. By contrast, he observed, where the grievor has failed to admit his or her offence, despite opportunities to do so, arbitrators have rarely modified the penalty of discharge.

On the other hand, the employer has the onus of establishing by clear, cogent and convincing evidence that the grievor intentionally or deliberately committed fraud or theft of time, and it has been held that "theft" in this context must be given a meaning consistent with the definition of theft in the *Criminal Code*, R.S.C. 1985, c. C-46. In *Tantalum Mining Corp. of Canada Ltd. and U.S.W.A., Local 7499*, [2004] M.G.A.D. No. 39 (QL), for example, Arbitrator Hamilton found that the grievor's carelessness and negligence in completing his time card warranted discipline. However, he ruled, as the employer had failed to prove an intention on the grievor's part to commit theft in accordance with the *Criminal Code* definition, discharge was excessive.

11.2.3 Medical Certificates

In a number of cases, arbitrators have considered the disciplinary consequences of the submission by an employee of forged or altered medical records. Because this type of misconduct can be difficult to detect, and strikes at the heart of the trust that is necessary in an employment relationship, arbitrators have generally viewed the falsification of medical records as a serious offence which merits a harsh penalty. Nevertheless, in the leading case of *TDS Automotive and C.A.W., Local 222*, [2002] C.L.A.D. No. 384 (QL), Arbitrator Tom Jolliffe concluded that discharge was not invariably the appropriate response; rather, the penalty should be assessed on an individualized basis, taking into account all the circumstances surrounding the offence.

11.3 ABUSE OF SICK LEAVE

Abuse of sick leave is considered a serious form of fraudulent misconduct, similar to theft in its impact on the employment relationship. Many arbitrators have stated that, because this type of fraud is easy to commit but difficult to detect, there is a special need to deter employees by enforcing rigorous standards of discipline. In the absence of compelling mitigating factors, as outlined in *Canadian Broadcasting Corp. and C.U.P.E.* (1979), 23 L.A.C. (2d) 227 (Arthurs) (see Chapter 10.9.1), therefore, the employer's deterrence interest will ordinarily justify discharge. The application of these principles is demonstrated in *Canada Post Corp. and A.P.O.C. (Gilbert)* (1990), 12 L.A.C. (4th) 210 (H.D. Brown).

In most cases, the employer will be required to prove abuse of sick leave by presenting direct evidence that an employee took time off for reasons other than illness. Some arbitrators, though, have held that circumstantial evidence demonstrating "pattern absenteeism" may also establish the employee's liability to discipline. In *Canada Post Corp. and C.U.P.W. (Sigaty)* (1992), 26 L.A.C. (4th) 180, Arbitrator Tom Jolliffe decided that, in the absence of evidence to the contrary, a sufficiently strong pattern of sick leave taken in conjunction with regular days off or holiday time can support an inference of abuse of sick leave.

However, in assessing the appropriate quantum of discipline for abuse of sick leave, it is important to distinguish between wilful fraud, which requires an intent to deceive the employer in order to obtain benefits, and less serious acts of dishonesty. In *Laurentian University and Laurentian University Staff Union (Groulx)*, [2003] O.L.A.A. No. 477 (QL) (H.D. Brown), the grievor had been off work for almost three months on the basis of medical evidence that she was unable to perform her regular duties. Despite this, she was observed working at a gift shop which she ran with other members of her family. The evidence ultimately supported a finding that the grievor's duties at the shop were not inconsistent with the physical limitations which prevented her from attending at work. However, she had been less than truthful during the employer's investigation, maintaining that she had not worked anywhere else while on sick leave. In these circumstances, Arbitrator Brown concluded that the employer had failed to establish fraudulent conduct on the grievor's part, since she had no intention of obtaining benefits to which she was not entitled. However, he found that, in responding to management's inquiries about her activities, the grievor had violated her obligation of good faith and fidelity to the employer. In the result, the arbitrator overturned the grievor's discharge and substituted a two-month suspension.

11.4   THEFT

Historically, arbitrators have viewed theft as being among the most egregious forms of misconduct, one which justifies discharge because it destroys the trust which is fundamental to the employment relationship. The actual value of the stolen property, accordingly, was often considered to be of little significance in the determination of whether just cause exists or in the choice of penalty. However, many recent decisions suggest that, while theft continues to be considered a very serious offence, dismissal does not automatically follow. In deciding whether to uphold a discharge, the arbitrator should inquire whether the trust relationship between the employer and the employee has been irremediably destroyed. The particular facts of each case — including the nature of the business, the level of employee supervision, the seriousness of the offence, the admission or non-admission of wrongdoing, the existence of genuine remorse, and the credibility of the grievor — will all affect the outcome of the inquiry. An example of the modern approach is *Livingston Distribution Centres Inc. and Teamsters, Local 419* (1996), 58 L.A.C. (4th) 129 (MacDowell).

Some arbitrators, taking this modern approach still further, suggest that in deciding whether discharge is appropriate, the interest of the employer in deterring acts of theft should be balanced against the entitlement of individual employees to have their conduct assessed on the basis of whether the employment relationship is capable of being restored. In this analysis, the nature of the employer's business, including its vulnerability to theft, is a major factor. A leading example of such an approach is *MacMillan Bloedel Ltd. and I.W.A., Local 1-85* (1993), 33 L.A.C. (4th) 288 (Hope).

The decision in *Richardson Terminals Ltd. and T.C.U., Lodge 650* (1998), 85 L.A.C. (4th) 104 (Shime) provides a comprehensive summary of the arbitral treatment of theft in recent cases. The arbitrator concluded that the trend is to reinstate an employee found to have committed theft if the offence was an isolated incident, the employee promptly admitted his or her misconduct when confronted by the employer, and upholding the discharge would result in "grave and serious economic hardships". Moreover, while acknowledging that a number of arbitrators are of the view that the value of the items stolen is irrelevant, Arbitrator Shime concluded that the tendency in recent cases has been to reinstate the grievor, subject to an unpaid suspension, if the goods are of "minimal or inconsequential value". "These acts", he opined, "unlike acts where items of substantial value are taken, are not considered by arbitrators to be so harmful to the employment relationship that discharge is the inevitable result, particularly where there is some indication that corrective action may resolve the problem" (at p. 118).

Some arbitrators have extended this individualized approach to the retail food industry, which has historically maintained a policy of zero-tolerance for theft by employees. For example, in *New Dominion Stores and C.A.W., Local 414* (2002), 111 L.A.C. (4th) 265, Arbitrator Herlich rejected the argument that the "automatic arbitral penalty" for theft in the industry is discharge, holding that the employer's legitimate interest in deterrence "must be balanced against what is otherwise just and reasonable in relation to particular employees" (at p. 274). At the same time, the decision of Arbitrator Chertkow in *Canada Safeway Ltd. and U.F.C.W., Local 2000* (2002), 108 L.A.C. (4th) 161 indicates that the traditional approach to theft in a retail food setting continues to be influential.

In *1293446 Ontario o/a Comfort Suites and U.F.C.W., Local 206* (2004), 127 L.A.C. (4th) 436, Arbitrator Trachuk accepted the proposition that the doctrine of "recent possession of stolen goods" can be applied by arbitrators to assist in determining whether an employee has committed theft. This common law doctrine, which is frequently applied in criminal theft cases, permits an adjudicator to draw the common-sense inference that a person found in possession of recently stolen goods is the person who stole them, or at least is a party to the theft. The doctrine is subject to the qualification that it may not be reasonable to draw such an inference where the person in possession of the goods provides another plausible explanation.

11.4.1 Definition of Theft

In many cases, the applicable definition of theft is a critical issue. Some jurisdictions, including Alberta, New Brunswick and Ontario, permit the parties to a collective agreement to curtail an arbitrator's remedial discretion in disciplinary matters by fixing the penalty for a particular offence. In industries prone to theft by employees, it is fairly common to provide in the collective agreement that the penalty for theft shall be discharge, thereby preventing the arbitrator from exercising his or her jurisdiction to substitute a lesser penalty. The determination of whether the grievor's conduct constitutes "theft" thus becomes the basis on which the arbitrator's authority to order reinstatement depends.

However, while arbitrators are in general agreement that the parties can define theft in any manner they choose, there is considerable disagreement concerning the definition to be applied if they do not. For one group of arbitrators, if the parties fail to incorporate their own definition of theft in the collective agreement, they must be taken to have intended it to have the meaning given in the Canadian *Criminal Code*, R.S.C. 1985, c. C-46. However, another group takes the position that the term "theft" should be given its "ordinary meaning", according to definitions found in respected dictionaries such as the *Concise Oxford English Dictionary* or *Black's Law Dictionary*. Clearly, theft according to its "ordinary meaning" is less onerous for the employer to prove. This divergence of opinion is summarized in *Toronto Transit Commission and A.T.U., Local 113* (1997), 62 L.A.C. (4th) 30, in which Arbitrator Brunner adopts the *Criminal Code* approach.

11.5 VANDALISM OR SABOTAGE

The deliberate destruction of employer property, product or production facilities is an extremely serious form of misconduct. Like theft, it has the potential to irreparably destroy the trust necessary for continuation of the employment relationship. The arbitral attitude toward sabotage is revealed in the following oft-quoted passage from *Redirack Ltd./Ltée and U.S.W.A., Local 9088* (1988), 33 L.A.C. (3d) 226, at p. 242 (Haefling):

> Acts of industrial sabotage, and specifically in this instance where the grievor's action constitutes wilful destruction of the employer's property, are among the most invidious forms of misconduct which may be engaged in by an employee, and such behaviour is among the most difficult for an employer to prevent or keep under control. As is so in a case of theft, in a situation involving acts of sabotage and wanton destruction of property, an issue arises as to whether or not the underlying employment relationship, based as it is upon maintaining a level of mutual respect and trust, has been irremediably breached. An employer must be able to expect that it can manage and operate its business affairs and production processes without risk or fear of an employee's undertaking any

self-motivated actions which are obviously intended to undermine such processes and to serve as a challenge to the authority of management.

Equally, however, arbitrators have ruled that motive and intention are critical elements in proving sabotage or vandalism. Thus, for the purpose of assessing the appropriate measure of discipline, cases involving damage to employer property or product must be divided into three different categories, depending on whether the damage was caused by (1) pure accident; (2) lack of care or negligence; or (3) deliberate and wilful destruction. The distinction between deliberate sabotage and carelessness or negligence is illustrated in *Burns Meats and U.F.C.W., Local 832* (1993), 38 L.A.C. (4th) 172 (Hamilton).

The importance of motive is seen also in *Inco Ltd. and U.S.W.A., Local 6500* (1991), 20 L.A.C. (4th) 386 (Simmons). In this case, Arbitrator Simmons applied the three-category approach outlined above to distinguish between damage resulting from employees' "horseplay" and sabotage arising from outright hostility or malice toward the employer. The significance of the distinction between damage caused by horseplay and deliberate sabotage was affirmed more recently in *New Flyer Industries Ltd. and C.A.W., Local 3003* (2004), 132 L.A.C. (4th) 1 (Hamilton). Ruling that it was a case of horseplay, not sabotage, the arbitrator overturned the discharge and substituted a four-month suspension, together with an order that the grievor pay for the damage.

11.6 OFF-DUTY CONDUCT

The seminal decision on the extent to which an employee's off-duty conduct may present just cause for discipline is *Millhaven Fibres Ltd. and Oil, Chemical & Atomic Workers Int'l Union, Local 9-670* (1967), 1(A) U.M.A.C. 328 (Anderson). For the employer to discipline an employee for off-duty conduct, it must prove that the conduct is work-related in the sense of having a detrimental impact on its business. Arbitrator Anderson concluded that the employer can prove this by establishing one or more of the following:

(1) The conduct of the grievor harms the company's reputation or product;

(2) the grievor's behaviour renders the employee unable to perform his or her duties satisfactorily;

(3) the grievor's behaviour leads to refusal, reluctance or inability of the other employees to work with him or her;

(4) the grievor has been guilty of a serious breach of the *Criminal Code*, and thus rendering his or her conduct injurious to the general reputation of the company and its employees;

(5) the conduct of the grievor places difficulty in the way of the company properly carrying out its function of efficiently managing its works and efficiently directing its working forces.

In *Edmonton (City) and Civil Service Union, Local 52*, [2000] A.G.A.A. No. 77 (QL) (Jolliffe), where a civilian employee of the municipal police force had been discharged for possession and distribution of child pornography, Arbitrator Jolliffe provides a useful summary of the arbitral jurisprudence concerning dismissal for off-duty conduct. The decision also demonstrates that, where the employer can establish just cause, it need not await the outcome of a criminal trial before resorting to dismissal.

11.6.1   Criminal Convictions

When applying the *Millhaven Fibres* criteria (see above, Chapter 11.6) to determine the effect of an employee's criminal conviction on the business interests of the employer, arbitrators consider the nature of the business, the character of the criminal activity, and the job duties of the employee. The decision in *Emergency Health Services Commission and C.U.P.E., Local 873* (1987), 28 L.A.C. (3d) 77, in which Arbitrator McColl upheld the discharge of an ambulance attendant who had misappropriated valium in connection with a drug-trafficking scheme orchestrated by his brother, demonstrates the industry-sensitive nature of these criteria. The arbitrator observed that an employer is not permitted to take action against an employee solely on the basis of an "excessive concern" with its public reputation. At the same time, he concluded, where the criminal conduct of an employee is directly related to the nature of the business, an employer has "a right and a duty" to dissociate itself from the employee's illegal off-duty activities.

A more recent exploration of these principles is found in *Port Moody (City) and C.U.P.E., Local 825* (1997), 63 L.A.C. (4th) 203 (Laing). Emphasizing the need for a real connection between the criminal activity and the grievor's job duties, the arbitrator held that reluctance on the part of fellow employees to work with the grievor because of personal dislike or repugnance for his or her offences does not justify dismissal. Rather, there must be reliable evidence that the refusal of others to continue working with the grievor is based on a legitimate fear of injury or harm.

Arbitrator Steeves has noted, in a recent award, that the criterion of harm to the general reputation of the employer requires the arbitrator to use her or his judgment in assessing how a fair-minded and well-informed member of the public or relevant constituency would respond to the grievor's off-duty behaviour: *Money's Mushrooms Ltd. and Retail Wholesale Union, Local 580*, [2003] B.C.C.A.A.A. No. 314 (QL) (Steeves). Adopting the traditional arbitral approach, the arbitrator ruled that this determination does not depend on whether the employer has actually suffered damage to its reputation because of adverse publicity. Rather, he noted, an arbitrator is required to use reasonable conjecture as to the consequences of allowing the grievor to remain in his or her position in the event the public became aware of the off-duty conduct in question. Thus, while the presence or absence of publicity may be relevant to the issue of harm to reputation, a finding of potential injury or harm can be made even in the absence of publicity.

In *Alberta and A.U.P.E. (Khan)* (2002), 112 L.A.C. (4th) 289 (Elliott), an arbitration board held that a correctional officer's conviction on sexual assault charges in respect of an incident that took place off-duty would in itself have given rise to just cause for dismissal, had he not appealed the conviction and notified the employer of his appeal. However, once the grievor had put management on notice that an appeal was pending, the employer was limited in its response to two courses of action: (1) maintaining the grievor's suspension from duty until the disposition of the appeal; or (2) conducting an independent investigation by reviewing the transcripts from the criminal trial and discussing the incident with the grievor, in order to determine whether there was just cause for discharge.

11.6.2   Criminal Charges

Upon learning that an employee has been charged with the commission of a serious criminal offence, employers frequently choose to suspend the employee without pay pending trial of the charges. *Phillips Cables Ltd. and U.S.W.A., Local 7276* (1974), 5 L.A.C. (2d) 274 (Adams) is the pre-eminent statement on the right of an employer to suspend an employee who faces criminal charges.

Unlike many earlier awards, this decision attempted to balance the employee's interest in maintaining his or her livelihood with the interest of the employer in protecting its business, employees, property and reputation. Although the presumption of innocence in criminal matters cannot be transplanted wholesale to the arbitral context, the fact that the charges have not been proved means that they cannot by themselves justify discharge, however work-related they may be. Arbitrator Adams ruled that the employer must therefore prove that the continued presence of the accused in the workplace would present a substantial and immediate hardship to its business or other workers that could not be alleviated by less drastic measures, such as reassignment or closer supervision. Furthermore, to establish this kind of genuine business detriment, the employer must show that it conducted a reasonable investigation into the risk created by the employee's conviction and the dangers of retaining him or her in the workplace. Finally, the arbitrator expressed reluctance to uphold a suspension where the employer played a substantial role in the original investigation which led to the laying of criminal charges. In such circumstances, he noted, the employer can be presumed to possess sufficient evidence to decide on immediate discharge, without the need to await the outcome of the criminal process.

A frequently-cited restatement of the principles to be applied in such cases is found in *Ontario Jockey Club and S.E.I.U., Local 528* (1977), 17 L.A.C. (2d)

176 (Kennedy). A further application of the rationale expressed in *Phillips Cables* and *Ontario Jockey Club* is contained in *Langley (Township) and C.U.P.E., Local 404* (1995), 46 L.A.C. (4th) 30 (Greyell).

The decision in *School District No. 91 (Nechako Lakes) and C.U.P.E., Local 4177* (2004), 134 L.A.C. (4th) 100 (Ready) provides an illustration of the importance of assessing the degree of risk to the employer's business interests in relation to the seriousness of the charge and the nature of the employer's operation. In that case, an employee faced charges of murdering a school principal, and Arbitrator Ready held that it was reasonable to suspend the employee without pay, given the role of the school board and its staff in the community. In the circumstances, he reasoned, the risk that the grievor would be found guilty of the charges was potentially harmful to the employer's reputation and business interests. Assessing the potential damage to the employer's reputation, Arbitrator Ready followed the general consensus that it is not necessary for the employer to provide testimony from a parade of witnesses in an effort to establish actual public outcry. Rather, it is up to the arbitrator to draw reasonable inferences from the nature of the charges, the circumstances giving rise to the charges, and the structure and organization of the workforce (*i.e.* in determining whether retention of the employee would have a harmful impact on other workers).

Despite the line of authority represented by *Tober Enterprises Ltd. and U.F.C.W., Local 1581* (1990), 7 Can. L.R.B.R. (2d) 148 (B.C.I.R.C.) (discussed in Chapter 10.3.1) holding that an employee cannot be disciplined for remaining silent when asked to explain potentially incriminating circumstances, some arbitrators have upheld discipline against employees for failing to cooperate with the employer's investigation into criminal charges arising from off-duty behaviour. In *Nova Scotia (Department of Justice) and N.S.G.E.U. (MacAskill)*, [2003] N.S.L.A.A. No. 18 (QL), Arbitrator Ashley upheld a two-day suspension levied against the grievor because of his refusal to answer questions by the employer as to whether he had been charged criminally in respect of a violent off-duty incident. The arbitrator noted that, in such circumstances, employers have a "right and obligation" to conduct an investigation in order to determine whether disciplinary action is warranted. In that context, she held, the employer had a right to know whether charges had been laid and, if so, what they were.

The issue of whether an employee who is eventually acquitted of criminal charges is entitled to back pay, where suspension pending trial was held to be justified, has been the subject of several arbitral awards. In *Humber River Regional Hospital and O.P.S.E.U., Local 577*, [2003] O.L.A.A. No. 247 (QL), Arbitrator Springate indicated that the employer may be liable for back pay if it played a substantial role in the investigation or the laying of charges against the employee. Another relevant consideration, in the arbitrator's view, was whether the employee was subject to bail conditions which would have precluded him or her from working for the employer in any event, at least where the employer had not played a part in setting those conditions. In *Humber River Regional Hospital*, the grievor's claim for compensation was denied, largely on the basis that the charges arose from an incident at a different facility, and the employer had not participated in the investigation or instigated police involvement.

11.6.3 Onus and Standard of Proof

As in all cases of discipline or discharge, where the allegations against an employee involve illegal or criminal conduct, the employer bears the burden of proving them on the civil standard of a balance of probabilities. Nevertheless, there is a long-standing consensus among arbitrators that, where allegations of misconduct involve criminal, illegal or morally reprehensible behaviour, or behaviour which might seriously harm an employee's professional reputation, the employer must prove its case through evidence which is "clear, cogent and convincing". In *British Columbia Telephone Co. and T.W.U.* (1978), 18 L.A.C. (2d) 225, one of the main authorities on the issue, Arbitrator Joseph Weiler expressed the rationale for this requirement as follows, at p. 229:

> [A] discharge or discipline for "criminal cause" carries with it connotations of corruption, illegality, or moral turpitude not apparent in other cases of industrial discipline. "Criminal cause" involves a significant loss of reputation and the social effects and stigma of such a sanction places a permanent blot on the employee's record that is qualitatively different than in the context of a non-criminal discharge or discipline.

This does *not*, however, represent the creation of a third standard of proof lying between the criminal and civil standards, as some arbitrators have speculated. Rather, the vast majority of arbitrators have explained that, while there is but one civil burden of proof, *i.e.* a balance of probabilities, the degree of probability required is commensurate with the seriousness of the alleged offence and the consequences which may follow. In this regard, see the discussion by Arbitrator Michel Picher in *Indusmin Ltd. and United Cement, Lime & Gypsum Workers Int'l Union, Local 488* (1978), 20 L.A.C. (2d) 87, referred to in Chapter 10.4.

Another leading case which reflects the arbitral consensus on the necessity for clear, cogent and convincing evidence is *Normandy Hospital Ltd. and H.E.U., Local 180* (1987), 32 L.A.C. (3d) 397 (Greyell). For the contrary, albeit minority, view that the standard of proof is no different where criminal conduct is alleged, see *McMaster University and S.E.I.U., Local 532* (2000), 86 L.A.C. (4th) 129 (Surdykowski).

In meeting its burden of proof, where the employee has been convicted by a criminal court, the employer is normally entitled to rely on a conviction in order to establish that the employee committed the misconduct underlying the conviction. In *Toronto (City) v. C.U.P.E., Local 79* (2003), 232 D.L.R. (4th) 385, the Supreme Court of Canada held that, save in very limited circumstances, an arbitrator is required to accept evidence of a criminal conviction as conclusive proof of the misconduct, and that it would constitute an abuse of process to permit the union to relitigate the issue of the grievor's culpability. As a rule, the Court stated, relitigation should not be sanctioned unless it is necessary to preserve the integrity of the judicial system, such as where the first proceeding was tainted by fraud or dishonesty; new evidence, previously unavailable, conclusively impeaches the result of the criminal proceedings; or fairness dictates that the original decision should not be binding in the context of the subsequent proceedings. It is clear from the Court's emphasis on the need to ensure finality in the judicial system and the harmful effects of relitigation that the union will be precluded from challenging a conviction in all but a few cases. See Chapter 3.6.1 for further discussion.

However, it is quite possible for an employer to defeat a grievance against discipline based on allegations of illegal or criminal conduct, despite the fact that the Crown failed in a criminal prosecution against the same employee for the same offence. This is so because, in the criminal proceeding, the Crown must meet the more onerous standard of proving the accused's guilt beyond a reasonable doubt. This long-standing arbitral approach to an acquittal or the dismissal of criminal charges against an employee was recently affirmed in *Alberta and A.U.P.E. (Crepeau)* (2003), 124 L.A.C. (4th) 176 (Jolliffe). In that case, a judge had determined at a preliminary hearing that there was insufficient evidence to proceed with criminal charges against the grievor for allegedly trafficking in cocaine. Arbitrator Tom Jolliffe held that, in such circumstances, the Supreme Court of Canada's ruling in *Toronto (City)*, *supra*, did not preclude an arbitration board from permitting the employer to lead evidence in an effort to establish, on a balance of probabilities, that the grievor had committed the offence which formed the subject of the charges.

Additional Reading

H.A. Hope, "Criminal and Immoral Acts: Evidence, Proof and Penalty Assessment" in W. Kaplan, J. Sack & M. Gunderson, eds., *Labour Arbitration Yearbook 1991*, vol. II, p. 111.

CHAPTER 12

DISLOYALTY AND BREACH OF TRUST

12.1 BREACH OF TRUST

The leading case on breach of trust or breach of fiduciary duty is *Canadian Broadcasting Corp. and C.U.P.E.* (1979), 23 L.A.C. (2d) 227 (Arthurs). This case is also frequently cited for the criteria to be used in determining whether an employee who has been dismissed for theft or dishonesty should be reinstated: see Chapter 10.9.1.

A comprehensive summary of arbitration decisions concerning the imposition of discipline for accessing, taking or disclosing confidential employer information is found in *Samuel-Acme Strapping Systems and U.S.W.A., Local 6572*, [2001] O.L.A.A. No. 579 (QL) (Ellis).

12.2 CONFLICT OF INTEREST

Arbitral norms allowing the imposition of discipline for conflict of interest have evolved from the fundamental common law principle that employees owe a duty of fidelity and loyalty to their employer, and must not participate in activities which conflict, or appear to conflict, with the employer's interests. Thus, arbitrators have generally held that, even in the absence of collective agreement provisions or company rules, an employee has a duty to avoid conflicts of interest.

12.2.1 Public Sector

In many workplaces, definitions of conflict of interest are found in employer policies or the collective agreement. In the absence of an express definition, however, defining conflict of interest in a particular case can be difficult, as a number of arbitrators have commented. The definition formulated in *McKendry and Treasury Board* (unreported, May 31, 1973 (E.B. Jolliffe)) has been widely adopted in cases involving employees in the public service. While he disavowed the possibility of creating a comprehensive code of conduct, Adjudicator Edward Jolliffe established the following principles to identify conflicts of interest:

(1) Public servants must not seek, for private gain, to make use of information not available to the general public to which they have access by reason of their official duties.

(2) A conflict of interest occurs when the public interest in proper administration of a government office and a government official's interest in his private economic affairs clash or appear to clash; and a finding of conflict of interest does not depend on wilful wrongdoing by the official or on the issue of whether the official's judgment has in fact been affected.

(3) A government official should not put himself in a position where his judgment could, even unconsciously, be affected by friendship.

. . .

The essential requirements are that the public servant should serve only one master and should never place himself in a position where he could be even tempted to prefer his own interests or the interests of another over the interests of the public he is employed to serve. Those requirements constitute the rationale of the doctrine that he should avoid a position of apparent bias as well as actual bias, and that he should never place himself in a position where . . . "two interests clash, or appear to clash".

The decision of Arbitrator Kennedy in *Hamilton-Wentworth (Regional Municipality) and C.U.P.E., Local 167* (1978), 18 L.A.C. (2d) 46, in which the *McKendry* award is extensively quoted, demonstrates the application of these principles in a municipal government context. The case also confirms that a conflict of interest warranting discipline may arise even in the absence of proof that the employee's judgment was actually affected by outside involvements; all that is required is the appearance of a conflict which could prejudice public faith in the integrity of the government agency. Finally, this award indicates that the grievor's intent or awareness of the potential for conflict may be a significant factor in determining the appropriate penalty.

In several cases, the principles articulated in *McKendry* and *Hamilton Wentworth (Regional Municipality)* have been applied to situations in which an employee's obligations to the employer have come into conflict with an intimate personal relationship. A good example is found in *Northwest Territories (Minister Responsible for the Public Service) and Union of Northern Workers (B.M.)*, [2004] C.L.A.D. No. 349 (QL), where Arbitrator Tom Jolliffe upheld the discharge of an employee who had had an extramarital affair with the account manager of an outside company providing information technology services to her department under an outsourcing agreement. Although most of the decided cases dealt with an employee's use of his or her position to promote private economic interests, the arbitrator observed, the principles set out in those cases were not limited to situations involving financial gain. Rather, he stated, "[i]t is always a matter of considering whether the employee is reasonably perceived as 'serving only one master'. . . and if not what are the possible detrimental consequences, all things considered, for the public sector employer" (at para. 61). In this case, Arbitrator Jolliffe held that, as an IT manager, the grievor owed the employer a fiduciary duty in administering the outsourcing contract, and her failure to recognize the risk to the employer's interests rendered the employment relationship irreparable.

However, in *Treasury Board (Human Resources Development Canada) and Douglas*, [2004] C.P.S.S.R.B. No. 56 (QL), which concerned a similar conflict of interest, the Public Service Staff Relations Board reinstated the grievor without compensation. The grievor, a program administrator, had approved government grants for an individual with whom she had been cohabiting. The Board was of the view that, as the grievor's bipolar disorder may have been a contributing cause of the misconduct, discharge was excessive.

12.2.2   Private Sector

In the private sector, the prohibition against conflict of interest comes into play most frequently where an employee has entered into business in competition with the employer or is working for a competing business. The decision in *Woodward Stores Ltd. and U.F.C.W., Local 2000* (1987), 28 L.A.C. (3d) 59 (Fraser) demonstrates that the applicable analysis focuses on whether there is direct competition which could reasonably cause harm to the employment relationship. If this is established, the extent or scale of the competition is not significant.

In *Northwestel Inc. and I.B.E.W., Local 1574*, [2003] B.C.C.A.A.A. No. 369 (QL), Arbitrator Hope held that just cause for discipline may arise from the violation of an employee's "intrinsic" duty to avoid conflicts of interest with his or her employer, even where the conduct in question does not fall within the specific prohibitions of an express conflict of interest policy. The grievor, who together with his spouse owned a motel, wrote a letter to the Canadian Radio-Television and Telecommunications Commission criticizing a decision, made by a subsidiary of his employer, to discontinue cable television services in the area in which the motel was situated. The letter included a request that the Commission compel the subsidiary company to continue offering cable services until a new provider could be found. Arbitrator Hope ruled that this conduct amounted to a conflict of interest because the grievor was in fact asking that the subsidiary provide services at a loss which, in turn, would have a detrimental impact on the employer. However, the arbitrator ruled, in determining the appropriate penalty, it was a mitigating factor that the grievor was not aware that the letter would constitute a conflict of interest.

In a number of cases in which the conflict of interest was found sufficiently serious to justify a disciplinary response, the arbitrator has gone on to consider whether, in place of discharge, the employee should have been given an opportunity to resign the other position, or to discontinue the competing business, as a condition of retaining his or her job with the original employer. Where the arbitrator has determined that the latter option would have been appropriate, rather than discharge, the employee has generally been reinstated, subject to meeting the prescribed conditions. In *Schneider Foods and U.F.C.W., Local 709-3* (2004), 128 L.A.C. (4th) 381, Arbitrator Randy Levinson reviewed the jurisprudence and concluded that conditional reinstatement has been ordered in those cases where it was possible to restore a viable employment relationship. This, he found, depended on an evaluation of the employee's trustworthiness, which in turn depended on the nature of the conflict of interest, and in particular on whether the employee had a *bona fide* (though mistaken) belief that the competing employment or business did not harm the employer's interests. In contrast, an employee who has been less than forthright about his or her outside activities, or has attempted to mislead the employer, will not normally be provided with the option of reinstatement with conditions.

12.3   PUBLIC CRITICISM OF EMPLOYER POLICIES

The guidelines set out by the Supreme Court of Canada in *Fraser v. Public Service Staff Relations Board* (1985), 23 D.L.R. (4th) 122 continue to be extremely important in determining when a government employer is justified in disciplining an employee for public criticism of its policies, despite the fact that the events at issue in that case arose prior to the enactment of the *Canadian Charter of Rights and Freedoms*. In *Fraser*, a federal public servant had been discharged for engaging in sustained, vicious criticism of government policy. While upholding the discharge, the Court recognized that it was necessary to balance society's interest in maintaining the loyalty of public employees against the employees' legitimate interest in freedom of expression. According to the Court, public criticism was justified where the government had engaged in illegal acts or had pursued policies which endangered health or safety, or where the expression of criticism would have no impact on the public servant's ability to perform effectively his or her duties, or the public's perception of that ability. However, the Court ruled, by engaging in a series of highly visible attacks on major government policies, the employee in this case had displayed a lack of loyalty that was inconsistent with his duties.

The Supreme Court's analysis in *Fraser* was recently applied by the Federal Court of Canada in *Haydon v. Canada*, [2001] 2 F.C. 82 (T.D.). In *Haydon*, the Court held that the common law duty of loyalty and fidelity represented a reasonable limit on a public servant's right to freedom of expression under the *Charter*, provided that the duty was applied in a manner which recognized exceptions similar to those identified in *Fraser*. In cases that fell within the *Fraser* exceptions, the Court held, the public interest in disclosure outweighed the objective of promoting an impartial and effective public service. The Court also indicated that the exceptions set out in *Fraser* may be expanded to cover any issue of "legitimate public concern requiring a public debate".

A similar analysis has been recently adopted by the Public Service Staff Relations Board. In *Treasury Board (Health Canada) and Chopra* (2001), 96 L.A.C. (4th) 367, where a public servant had made public criticisms of the employer for allegedly failing to take adequate measures to combat racism in the workplace, the Board ruled that there was no just cause for discipline. However, in a later case involving the same employee, the Board applied the approach set out in *Fraser* and *Haydon* to uphold a five-day suspension. In that case, in comments reported by the national media, the grievor had criticized the government's policy of stockpiling anthrax antibiotics and smallpox vaccine in the weeks following the terrorist attacks of 9/11. The Board noted that the issues raised by the grievor were clearly important to public safety. However, it ruled, the grievor had failed to satisfy the requirement that public employees who wish to criticize their employer's policies should first make reasonable attempts to resolve the matter internally, unless the situation is urgent and makes it impossible or inappropriate to use internal mechanisms: *Treasury Board (Health Canada) and Chopra*, (2003), 124 L.A.C. (4th) 149 (P.S.S.R.B.).

The decision of Arbitrator Hope in *Nanaimo (City) and I.A.F.F., Local 905* (2002), 109 L.A.C. (4th) 408 affirms that union officials cannot be disciplined for publicly criticizing the employer in relation to collective bargaining matters, unless the statements were made maliciously, or were knowingly or recklessly false. For further discussion of the ambit, and limits, of union criticism of employer conduct, see Chapter 24.2.2.

CHAPTER 13

INSUBORDINATE AND ABUSIVE CONDUCT

13.1 INSUBORDINATION – THE "WORK NOW, GRIEVE LATER" RULE

Insubordination poses a threat to the employer's ability to manage its operations without costly interruptions to production. For this reason, arbitrators have ruled that in appropriate cases insubordination justifies the imposition of discipline. It has also been held that, where an employee's insubordinate behaviour challenges the symbolic authority of the employer, discipline may be warranted even in the absence of any apparent disruption to productive processes. This emphasis on the protection of the employer's productivity interests and symbolic authority has resulted in the arbitral adoption of the "work now, grieve later" rule. Under this principle, employees have an obligation to comply with all management orders and policies, even those that are alleged to be inconsistent with the collective agreement. If an employee disagrees with a management directive, or believes that it is contrary to the collective agreement, he or she should nevertheless obey the order, and only *then* seek redress through the grievance procedure. The most frequently cited rationale for the "work now, grieve later" rule is that articulated by Professor Harry Shulman in *Ford Motor Co.* (1944), 3 L.A. 779:

> Some men apparently think that, when a violation of contract seems clear, the employee may refuse to obey and thus resort to self-help rather than the grievance procedure. That is an erroneous point of view. In the first place, what appears to be a clear violation may not seem so at all to the other party. Neither party can be the final judge as to whether the contract has been violated. The determination of that issue rests in collective negotiation through the grievance procedure. But, in the second place, and more important, the grievance procedure is prescribed in the contract precisely because the parties anticipated that there would be claims of violations which would require adjustment. That procedure is prescribed for all grievances, not merely for doubtful ones . . .
>
> [A]n industrial plant is not a debating society. Its object is production. When a controversy arises, production cannot wait for exhaustion of the grievance procedure. While that procedure is being pursued, production must go on. And some one must have the authority to direct the manner in which it is to go on until the controversy is settled. That authority is vested in supervision. It must be vested there because the responsibility for production is also vested there; and responsibility must be accompanied by authority. It is fairly vested there because the grievance procedure is capable of adequately recompensing employees for abuse of authority by supervision.

While this principle may appear to be unduly protective of management rights, it reflects the conviction that employee interests will not be prejudiced, as long as the grievance procedure is capable of providing adequate relief for any harm suffered as a result of compliance with an improper order. Furthermore, from the very outset, arbitrators began to carve out specific exceptions in cases where compliance with a directive would result in harm to the employee which could *not* be adequately redressed through the grievance procedure. (These exceptions are explored more fully below.) The seminal Canadian arbitration decision on insubordination and the "work now, grieve later" rule is *Lake Ontario Steel Co. Ltd. and U.S.W.A.* (1968), 19 L.A.C 103 (P.C. Weiler), in which the rationale stated by Professor Shulman was adopted. A more recent restatement of the rule is found in *Squamish Terminals Ltd. and I.L.W.U., Local 514* (1997), 68 L.A.C. (4th) 165 (McPhillips).

Additional Reading

J.M. Chapman, "The Employee's Duty to 'Work Now, Grieve Later': An Arbitrator's Viewpoint" in W. Kaplan, J. Sack & M. Gunderson, eds., *Labour Arbitration Yearbook 1991*, vol. I, p. 187; and companion articles by E. Durnford and J. Sack.

13.1.1   Definition of Insubordination

Generally, to establish that an employee has been insubordinate, the employer must prove three elements: (1) there was a clear order which the grievor understood; (2) the order was given by a person in authority; and, (3) the grievor disobeyed the order. In some cases, arbitrators have also ruled that the definition of insubordination extends beyond outright disobedience, and also includes insolent or uncooperative behaviour which could reasonably be said to challenge the employer's authority in a meaningful way. Conduct that merely expresses disagreement with the employer's policy or decision without meaningfully defying managerial authority, however, does not constitute insubordination. A leading modern authority on the gradations of conduct which may or may not be insubordinate is *Southern Railway of British Columbia and I.C.T.U., Local 7* (1996), 60 L.A.C. (4th) 11 (Moore).

In *Upper Grand District School Board and C.U.P.E., Local 256*, [2004] C.L.A.D. No. 282 (QL), Arbitrator Tom Jolliffe provides a helpful discussion of arbitral decisions on the issue of when an employee's use of harsh, profane or abusive language rises to the level of a "challenge to the authority of a supervisor", such that it constitutes insubordination warranting the imposition of discipline. In making that determination, the arbitrator pointed out, it is important to take into account contextual factors, including the extent of permissible "shop talk", or profanity, in the particular workplace.

In *IPEX Inc. and C.E.P., Local 777*, [2004] A.G.A.A. No. 15 (QL), Arbitrator Warren provides a comprehensive review of the arbitral authorities concerning discipline for insubordination based on an employee's refusal to work compulsory overtime. In that case, while finding that the employer had given a clear direction to work overtime, that the grievor understood the task assigned to him, and that he wilfully chose to disobey the order, the arbitrator concluded that the penalty of discharge was excessive, and substituted a six-month suspension. Key to this ruling was the fact that the employer had not fully investigated the incident in order to determine the reasonableness of the grievor's actions, and that the employer (contrary to its discipline policy) had not previously warned the grievor that his employment was at risk.

13.2   EXCEPTIONS

There are a number of well-recognized exceptions to the "work now, grieve later" rule. Once a *prima facie* case of insubordination has been made out, the burden rests on the employee to prove that the alleged incident falls within one of the exceptions. Underlying all the exceptions is the rationale that the grievance procedure would not be capable of providing the employee with adequate redress for management's abuse of its authority. In *Stancor Central Ltd. and I.W.A., Local 2-500* (1970), 22 L.A.C. 184, Arbitrator Paul Weiler, who wrote many of the seminal awards on the doctrine, invoked this rationale in explaining why the list of exceptions was not closed.

13.2.1   Health and Safety

The pre-eminent decision in which the health and safety exception to the "work now, grieve later" rule was developed is *Steel Co. of Canada Ltd. and U.S.W.A., Local 1005* (1973), 4 L.A.C. (2d) 315 (Johnston). An employee who argues that he or she refused to carry out a management order on the basis that it was unsafe must satisfy the arbitrator on four points:

(1)   Did the grievor honestly believe that his or her health or well-being was endangered?

(2)   Did the grievor communicate this belief to his or her supervisor in a reasonable and adequate manner?

(3)   Was the belief reasonable in the circumstances?

(4)   Was the danger sufficiently serious to justify the particular action that the grievor took?

Although an employee who invokes this exception must meet all four criteria, many of the cases tend to focus on the reasonableness of the grievor's belief that his or her well-being was endangered. This is an objective standard requiring the arbitrator to inquire whether a reasonable employee in the grievor's position would believe that performing the work constituted a risk to health or safety. In making this determination, arbitrators often consider the willingness of other employees in the workplace to perform the same work. Equally, however, they will take into account any circumstances peculiar to the grievor which may have reasonably justified an apprehension of danger, including his or her medical condition, and level of training or experience. It should be noted that the existence of specific provisions in the collective agreement may affect the application of these general principles. An example of the application of these principles in a modern context is found in *H.M. Trimble & Sons (1983) Ltd. and I.U.O.E., Local 115* (1994), 42 L.A.C. (4th) 313 (Kinzie).

Although the arbitral tests respecting the right to refuse unsafe work are generally consistent with the occupational health and safety legislation of most jurisdictions, an employee will be entitled to rely on the statute if it affords a greater measure of protection, and the employee is able to satisfy the specified criteria. The decision of Arbitrator Knopf in *Lennox Industries (Canada) Ltd. and U.S.W.A., Local 7235*, [1999] O.L.A.A. No. 158 (QL), demonstrates the application of the Ontario legislation in the arbitration context. Relying on s. 43(3)(b) of the *Occupational Health and Safety Act*, R.S.O. 1990, c. O.1, which permits an employee to refuse to perform work "where he or she has reason to believe that . . . the physical condition of the workplace . . . is likely to endanger himself or herself", the arbitrator concluded that the legislation requires only a *subjective* belief that the work assignment in question is hazardous.

13.2.2 Illegality

Among the most commonly invoked exceptions to the "work now, grieve later" rule are orders that are contrary to law. Arbitrators have recognized that employees should not be required to place themselves in jeopardy of prosecution by performing an illegal act. Note that "illegality" in the sense of conduct which would violate the collective agreement or a workplace policy does not suffice. Furthermore, conduct which might result in a violation of legislative standards or prohibitions on the employer's part does not qualify for the exception unless the employee may be personally subject to legal liability as well. The evolution of these principles is explained in the seminal decision of *York Farms Ltd., Sardis and Canadian Food & Allied Workers, Local P430* (1981), 2 L.A.C. (3d) 112 (Christie).

As shown in *Thibodeau-Finch Express Inc. and Union des Chauffeurs de Camions, Local 106* (1987), 30 L.A.C. (3d) 58 (Frumkin), an employee is also excused from compliance with a management directive if he or she has a reasonable apprehension of exposure to prosecution. The illegality exception applies even where the employer undertakes to indemnify and compensate the employee for the consequences of prosecution, since it may well be impossible to follow up on such assurances.

13.2.3 Union Officials

In general, a different standard of conduct is applied in assessing the behaviour of union officials in their dealings with management. The cases suggest that the nature of their duties often requires union officials to operate, in effect, on the borderline of insubordination. For this reason, union officials are granted immunity for actions taken in the legitimate discharge of their union function. The seminal decision on this issue is *Firestone Steel Products of Canada and U.A.W., Local 27* (1975), 8 L.A.C. (2d) 164. Arbitrator Brandt held that, while a union official does not have *carte blanche* to ignore management's instructions, or to direct others to disobey them, acts or omissions committed in the legitimate exercise of union duties are not subject to discipline on the ground of insubordination. These principles were recently affirmed in *National Steel Car Ltd. and U.S.W.A., Local 7135* (2001), 101 L.A.C. (4th) 316 (Shime).

Whether or not an employee will be entitled, in a given case, to protection against discipline because of his or her status as a union official depends to a large degree on the facts. In *Ivaco Rolling Mills and U.S.W.A., Local 7940*, [2003] O.L.A.A. No. 611 (QL) (R.M. Brown), for example, the grievor did not indicate that he was carrying out his duties as a union steward, and there was nothing in the context of his confrontation with supervisors to suggest that he was acting in a representational capacity rather than simply trying to advance personal interests. Accordingly, Arbitrator Richard Brown upheld the discipline, and dismissed the grievance. However, the opposite result prevailed in *Cancoil Thermal Corp. and U.F.C.W., Local 175*, [2004] O.L.A.A. No. 149 (QL) (Starkman), even though the employee whom the grievor (a union steward) was assisting did not, in the circumstances, have a right to union representation under the collective agreement. At a meeting called to investigate a workplace injury, the grievor told the company's president that he was harassing the employee, and advised the employee to stop answering the employer's questions. Arbitrator Starkman concluded that the grievor was entitled to immunity from discipline for insubordination because the employee had requested union representation, and the employer had agreed to permit the grievor to attend the meeting as an observer.

Occasionally, a union official will refuse to comply with a directive to continue working or to return to work because the official considers it necessary to conduct union business. The parties to a collective agreement frequently negotiate specific language to deal with such situations. In the absence of explicit provisions in the agreement, arbitrators have generally held that a union official is not obligated to "work now, grieve later", as long as the official has a reasonable belief that attending to his or her union duties is necessary to prevent irreparable harm to the rights of other employees. One of the early awards on this issue was *Gulf Canada Ltd. and E.C.W.U., Local 593* (1982), 3 L.A.C. (3d) 348 (Palmer), in which a union official refused to stay at his work station. As the official had reason to believe that his presence was necessary at a union-management meeting to stop a wildcat strike from breaking out, his conduct was held to fall within the exception. Similarly, in *Stancor Central Ltd. and I.W.A., Local 2-500* (1970), 22 L.A.C. 184, Arbitrator Paul Weiler overturned the dismissal of an employee (the vice-president of the local union) who had absented himself from work in order to attend an urgent union meeting, contrary to an express direction not to do so. The arbitrator determined that, in light of the necessity of immediate action, the grievor could reasonably conclude that attendance at the meeting was more important than preservation of management's "symbolic authority".

The decision in *Pacific Press and C.E.P., Local 115M* (1997), 69 L.A.C. (4th) 214 (Bruce) summarizes recent developments in this area and demonstrates the importance of establishing the inadequacy of the grievance procedure to deal with the aftermath of adherence to a management directive.

13.2.4 Personal Appearance

In order to be enforceable, employer rules that prescribe norms for the personal appearance of employees must be reasonable and have a legitimate business purpose: see the discussion in Chapter 13.9. While the "work now, grieve later" rule means that employees who violate a personal appearance policy are liable to discipline for insubordination, even if the policy is later held to be invalid, an exception is made where compliance with the policy would cause harm to the employee which could not be adequately compensated through the grievance procedure. In applying these principles, most arbitrators have drawn a distinction between management directives which affect employees' freedom with respect to personal appearance during off-duty hours, such as a restriction on beard or hair length, and directives which merely affect employees' appearance while on duty, such as the wearing of a particular uniform. In the former instance, it has frequently been held that the employee could not be adequately recompensed through the grievance procedure. On the other hand, in cases addressing the propriety of a rule prescribing attire at work, it has usually been held that the employee should in fact have "worked now, grieved later". These principles are explained in *York Farms Ltd., Sardis and Canadian Food & Allied Workers, Local P430* (1981), 2 L.A.C. (3d) 112 (Christie). A more recent application of the same principles is found in *Thrifty Canada Ltd. and O.P.E.I.U., Local 378* (2002), 106 L.A.C. (4th) 420 (Larson).

Additional Reading

E. Bosveld, "Loopholes and the Law: Facial Jewelry, Personal Expression, and the Regulation of the Workplace" (2004), 11 Canadian Labour and Employment Law Journal, p. 351.

13.2.5 Medical Examinations and Disclosure of Medical Information

It is now well accepted that an employee who refuses to comply with an order to undergo a medical examination by a doctor chosen by the employer, or to supply or consent to the release of confidential medical information, cannot be disciplined for insubordination. Often-cited as a seminal award in this area is *Monarch Fine Foods Co. Ltd. and Milk & Bread Drivers, Dairy Employees, Caterers & Allied Employees, Local 647* (1978), 20 L.A.C. (2d) 419 (M.G. Picher). Recognizing the importance of the employee's interest in privacy and personal integrity, Arbitrator Picher affirmed that, in the absence of specific authority under statute or the collective agreement, the employer has no power to demand that an employee submit to a medical examination unless the purpose is to ensure that the employee is physically fit to perform his or her work safely and efficiently, and there are reasonable and probable grounds for questioning the employee's capacity. Most typically, this occurs in the context of an employee's return to work following illness or injury: see the discussion in Chapter 14.4.

If the employee produces a medical report that is inadequate, a further report may be required, containing a statement as to fitness, restrictions, and date of return to work, though not a diagnosis of the employee's specific condition or a description of prescribed treatment, unless this is necessary to achieve a requested accommodation (to satisfy the employer's duty to accommodate). In *Shell Canada Products Ltd. and C.A.I.M.A.W., Local 12* (1990), 14 L.A.C. (4th) 75, Arbitrator Larson held that, where the employer has reasonable cause to believe that an employee is unfit to return to work, or that a medical certificate tendered by the employee is insufficient or lacking in particulars, it can refuse to permit the employee to work until the situation is corrected, but cannot resort to a disciplinary discharge, which requires proof of culpable conduct. The arbitrator reasoned that orders to submit to a physical examination or to disclose confidential medical information are not subject to the "work now, grieve later" rule because the grievance procedure would be incapable of redressing the invasion of privacy suffered by the employee. Finally, he noted, the employer cannot override this arbitral bar against resort to discipline simply by promulgating unilateral rules. For further affirmation of these principles, even in the safety-sensitive context of air traffic control, see *NAV Canada and C.A.T.C.A.* (1998), 74 L.A.C. (4th) 163 (Swan).

Similarly, in *St. Peter's Health System and C.U.P.E., Local 778* (2002), 106 L.A.C. (4th) 170 (Charney), an arbitration board held that the employer was not entitled to rely on its management right to promulgate workplace rules to justify a policy requiring nurses in a chronic care hospital to either take flu vaccinations or stay at home without pay during flu outbreaks. In the board's view, in the absence of consent or legislative authority, the administration of a flu shot would amount to an assault on the employee, and it was therefore inappropriate to assess the validity of the policy by engaging in a "balancing of interests" analysis. However, other arbitrators have disagreed, taking the position that it is necessary to weigh the invasion of an employee's bodily integrity against the employer's legitimate business interests. In *Chinook Health Region and U.N.A., Local 120*, [2002] A.G.A.A. No. 88 (QL), Arbitrator Tom Jolliffe applied a balancing of interests analysis, and dismissed a union challenge to a policy requiring caregivers in a nursing home either to submit to influenza vaccination or to stay off work during an outbreak. Furthermore, in *School District No. 39 (Vancouver) and B.C.T.F.* (2001), 98 L.A.C. (4th) 385, a case in which the requisite statutory authority did exist, Arbitrator Dorsey rejected the union's argument that requiring employees to undergo a medical examination on the advice of a medical officer violated the *Charter* right to "life, liberty and security of the person".

Note that the issue of an employer's right to compel submission to a medical examination or disclosure of medical records by employees must be distinguished from the issue of arbitrators' well-recognized authority to order an employee to undergo a medical examination, by a physician selected by the employer, where the employee's medical condition is in question, and such an examination is necessary in order to ensure a fair hearing: see *Canada Post Corp. and C.U.P.W.* (1998), 69 L.A.C. (4th) 393 (Burkett), discussed in Chapter 4.5.

Additional Reading

F. Work, "Freedom of Information and Protection of Privacy" in K. Whitaker, J. Sack, M. Gunderson & R. Filion, eds., *Labour Arbitration Yearbook 2001-2002*, vol. II, p. 61.

D.L. Larson, "The Use of Medical Evidence at Arbitration: An Arbitrator's Perspective" in K. Whitaker, J. Sack, M. Gunderson & R. Filion, eds., *Labour Arbitration Yearbook 1999-2000*, vol. II, p. 137; and companion articles by R.A. Macpherson, D.G. Palayew & H.C. Devine, and V.M. Lemieux.

13.2.6   Grievance Procedure Would Not Provide Adequate Remedy

As outlined in Chapter 13.2, all of the recognized exceptions to the "work now, grieve later" rule rest on the rationale that recourse to the grievance procedure would be ineffectual in remedying the harm caused by compliance with an improper order. Several arbitrators have therefore ruled that, in addition to the recognized exceptions, an employee need not obey an order in *any* case in which the grievance procedure would be ineffective to protect the employee's interests, and the potential harm of compliance outweighed the importance of maintaining workplace discipline. The seminal decision on this "general" exception is *British Columbia Telephone Co. Ltd. and Federation of Telephone Workers of British Columbia* (1976), 13 L.A.C. (2d) 312 (MacIntyre). Because the employer persistently flouted the collective agreement provisions facilitating a system of expedited arbitration of contracting-out disputes, a refusal by workers to perform contested work was held not to constitute insubordination.

The same rationale was applied in *Meat Connection Inc. and U.F.C.W., Local 1105P* (1985), 23 L.A.C. (3d) 159 (Solomatenko). The grievor, who had informed a supervisor that he was leaving early to see a doctor about nagging back pain, disobeyed an order to stay on the job on light duties until the end of his shift. When the grievor was disciplined for insubordination, Arbitrator

Solomatenko allowed the union's grievance, ruling that the "work now, grieve later" rule did not apply in these circumstances.

13.2.7   Grievance in Anticipation of Discipline

Prior to the decision of the Ontario Court of Appeal in *Metropolitan Toronto (Municipality) v. C.U.P.E., Local 43* (1990), 69 D.L.R. (4th) 268, some arbitrators were of the view that they lacked jurisdiction to consider a grievance against the introduction of a workplace rule or policy unless it violated a specific term of the collective agreement or an employee had been disciplined for breaching it. The Court, however, held that, even in the absence of any breach or the issuance of discipline, the operation of the "work now, grieve later" principle practically required arbitrators to adjudicate a grievance if a breach of the rule or policy would be likely to constitute insubordination and result in disciplinary action. Endorsing the views of an arbitrator who had decided to accept jurisdiction over a grievance against the imposition of discipline "in the abstract", the Court agreed that it would be "hypocritical, and transparently so, to deny employees the promise of the rule, having exposed them to its command" (at p. 281). In other words, because employees had chosen to obey the rule and continue working, the union's right to grieve a rule the violation of which would lead to discipline could not be denied. For a more recent application of the Court of Appeal's ruling in *Metropolitan Toronto (Municipality)*, see *Auto Haulaway Inc. and Teamsters, Local 880* (1997), 69 L.A.C. (4th) 275 (Rayner).

However, in a decision that limits the reach of *Metropolitan Toronto (Municipality)*, the Manitoba Court of Appeal has held that a disciplinary consequence, whether actual or apprehended, is an essential factor in a determination that the reasonableness of a management rule or policy is arbitrable: *St. James-Assiniboia Teachers' Ass'n No. 2 v. St. James-Assiniboia School Division No. 2* (2002), 222 D.L.R. (4th) 636. In the absence of a disciplinary consequence, the Court found, a challenge to the rule is outside an arbitrator's jurisdiction. Moreover, in *N.A.P.E. v. Western Avalon Roman Catholic School Board* (2000), 190 D.L.R. (4th) 146, the Newfoundland Court of Appeal held that the principle set out in *Metropolitan Toronto (Municipality)* applies only to rules for the breach of which an employee may be disciplined; it does not give rise to an implied requirement that all managerial rules be reasonable.

13.3   FAILURE TO COMPLY WITH EMPLOYER RULES

The seminal decision on the imposition of discipline for failure to comply with employer rules is *KVP Co. Ltd. and Lumber & Sawmill Workers' Union, Local 2537* (1965), 16 L.A.C. 73 (Robinson) (hereinafter "*KVP*"). According to the ruling in *KVP*, the breach of a rule introduced unilaterally by the employer, without the union's assent, will give rise to just cause for discipline only if the rule meets the following criteria:

(1) it is consistent with the collective agreement;

(2) it is reasonable;

(3) it is clear and unequivocal;

(4) it was brought to the attention of the employee(s) affected before the employer attempts to act on it;

(5) where the rule is invoked to justify discharge, the employee was notified that a breach of the rule could result in discharge; and

(6) the employer has enforced the rule consistently since its introduction.

Although the employer must satisfy all of these requirements, many awards turn on the arbitrator's assessment of the reasonableness of the rule in question. Whether or not a rule is found to be reasonable generally depends on whether the employer is able to establish that it promotes health and safety in the workplace or advances legitimate business interests. As discussed in Chapter 13.2.7, most arbitrators take the view that they have jurisdiction to review a unilaterally-imposed rule in accordance with the *KVP* criteria, as long as the evidence suggests that breach of the rule would probably result in discipline.

13.4 EMPLOYER RULES AFFECTING PRIVACY

13.4.1 Searches

In applying the *KVP* criteria (reviewed in Chapter 13.3) to rules which subject employees to searches, arbitrators have for many years recognized the need to balance an individual employee's interest in privacy against the employer's interest in safeguarding its premises and preventing theft. In a large number of cases dating back to the 1960s, however, arbitrators have held that a policy of random searches of workers' lunch boxes, lockers or other personal effects does not meet the reasonableness requirement. Generally, the employer may search an employee's personal effects only if there is an express or implied term of the agreement to that effect, or there is a real and substantial suspicion that the employee has committed theft. An example of an implied term of the collective agreement would be the existence of a long-standing practice in which the union has acquiesced. The jurisprudence in which these principles have been developed is summarized in the leading decision of *Lornex Mining Corp. Ltd. and U.S.W.A., Local 7619* (1983), 14 L.A.C. (3d) 169 (Chertkow). The arbitrator struck down a policy providing for security checks of employees' lunch boxes, holding that the random selection of employees to be searched, without any objective criteria, was inherently unreasonable. Furthermore, the arbitrator ruled, the imposition of an automatic suspension against employees who refused to undergo a search was arbitrary and unreasonable.

A few arbitrators, however, have held that a random search policy of employees' personal effects may be justified if there is evidence of an increase in theft of employer property, provided the policy is explained and implemented in a reasonable manner. Reasonableness in this context has been taken to mean that the search procedure does not intimidate employees or appear to implicate them as suspects in a theft investigation. Even so, the result in *Royal Oak Mines Inc. and C.A.S.A.W., Local 4* (1992), 25 L.A.C (4th) 26 (Bird) — the leading decision espousing this view — indicates that it may be difficult for employers to implement random search policies that will withstand arbitral scrutiny.

The decision of Arbitrator Margo Newman in *Progistix-Solutions Inc. and C.E.P., Local 26* (2000), 89 L.A.C. (4th) 1 offers a summary of the law relating to employer search policies. Initially, in the aftermath of the discovery of a major theft ring, the employer imposed a policy under which employees, but not other users of the facility, were required to undergo a clothing search upon leaving the warehouse. The arbitrator held that, as the employer had not first exhausted less intrusive alternative measures to address its security problems, the policy constituted an unjustifiable violation of privacy rights. Subsequently, however, the employer implemented an overall security plan, extended the policy to non-employees, and introduced a system for randomly selecting individuals to be searched. In light of these revisions, the arbitrator upheld the policy, subject to the clarification that only outer clothing could be searched, and only after it had been removed from the body. Resort to body searching or a requirement that an employee's inner clothing be raised to permit visual inspection were deemed impermissible. Arbitrator Newman pointed out that, where the employer has reasonable grounds to suspect that an employee has concealed items underneath his or her inner clothing, only the police have authority to carry out a search.

Additional Reading

B. Bilson, "Search and Surveillance in the Workplace: An Arbitrator's Perspective" in W. Kaplan, J. Sack & M. Gunderson, eds., *Labour Arbitration Yearbook 1992*, p. 143; and companion articles by L. Bevan & A. Staniusz, and A. Barss.

13.4.2   Drug and Alcohol Testing

Arbitrators have generally held that the arbitral approach to employer rules concerning searches of employees should be applied by analogy to drug and alcohol testing. In short, when assessing whether the *KVP* criteria have been met (see Chapter 13.3), the arbitrator must determine the reasonableness of the rule or policy by weighing the interference with employees' privacy against the legitimate business interests of the employer. In his seminal decision in *Canadian Pacific Ltd. and U.T.U.* (1987), 31 L.A.C. (3d) 179, Arbitrator Michel Picher ruled that even safety-sensitive employers such as railroads could not encroach on the privacy and dignity of employees by subjecting them to random and speculative drug testing. The employer's legitimate business interests will justify testing only where there are reasonable grounds to believe that an employee may be impaired by drugs or alcohol while on duty. Where good and sufficient grounds do exist, the employee may be subject to discipline for refusing to comply with a directive that he or she undergo testing.

The decision of Arbitrator Brent in *Provincial-American Truck Transporters and Teamsters, Local 880* (1991), 18 L.A.C. (4th) 412 applies the principles developed in *Canadian Pacific*. In this case, the employer attempted to extend the medical examinations broadly authorized by the collective agreement to include mandatory random drug and alcohol testing of employees. The arbitrator ruled that the employer did not have the right to compel an employee's submission to such a test unless it had reasonable grounds for believing that his or her fitness to perform job duties safely was impaired by drugs or alcohol. Furthermore, she held, in the absence of specific authorization in the collective agreement, mandatory random testing is permissible only where the employer proves that it has a drug or alcohol problem in the workplace which cannot be combated using less invasive means.

In *Entrop v. Imperial Oil Ltd.* (2000), 189 D.L.R. (4th) 14, the Ontario Court of Appeal confirmed that mandatory drug and alcohol testing, including testing in pre-employment situations, is *prima facie* discriminatory on the prohibited ground of handicap or disability, and must satisfy the criteria for a *bona fide* occupational qualification (BFOQ) in order to survive a challenge under human rights legislation. The same was held to be true of a requirement for disclosure of any past or present substance abuse problems. Applying the unified three-part test for establishing a BFOQ in *British Columbia (Public Service Employee Relations Commission) v. B.C.G.E.U. (Meiorin)* (1999), 176 D.L.R. (4th) 1 (S.C.C.), the Court held that the drug testing provisions of the employer's policy were not reasonably necessary to ensure that employees are free from impairment on the job. This was so because, in the Court's view, urinalysis is not capable of demonstrating actual impairment, as opposed to the mere presence of drugs in an employee's system. The requirement for random drug testing was also held to go beyond what was reasonably necessary insofar as the consequence of a single positive test result was automatic discharge, thus infringing the employee's right to individual evaluation and accommodation. By contrast, random alcohol testing through the administration of a breathalyzer was found to be capable of measuring current impairment. The Court held, consequently, that such testing can be justified as long as the employer meets its duty to accommodate the needs of employees who test positive. To meet this obligation of individual accommodation, the employer must consider sanctions less severe than automatic dismissal if an employee tests positive, and where appropriate enable the employee to seek treatment and rehabilitation.

The decision of Arbitrator Michel Picher in *Canadian National Railway and C.A.W.* (2000), 95 L.A.C. (4th) 341 provides an exhaustive summary and analysis of the arbitral jurisprudence respecting drug and alcohol testing. In assessing the reasonableness of the policy in question, the arbitrator purported to balance the privacy interest of employees against the employer's interest in maintaining safety. He stated, however, that certain industries are inherently safety-sensitive, and in such circumstances the need to introduce a drug and alcohol testing policy should not be subject to stringent scrutiny in the form of an inquiry as to whether alternative means for addressing substance abuse in the workplace have been exhausted. Consistent with many prior awards, including *Canadian Pacific, supra*, Arbitrator Picher held that, subject to the requirement to establish just cause for discipline, the employer was entitled to compel employees in safety-sensitive positions to undergo drug and alcohol testing where there existed reasonable grounds for suspecting impairment, as, for example, where an accident had occurred, and that such testing did not violate human rights legislation. He further ruled that the employer's interest in risk avoidance justified testing as a pre-condition to promotion or transfer of an employee to a safety-sensitive position. As the arbitrator noted, this appears to be the first award in which a requirement for drug and alcohol testing in order to determine an employee's fitness prior to commencing work in a safety-sensitive position was held to comply with human rights legislation and the *KVP* criteria. At the same time, he affirmed that "[f]or reasons well elaborated in prior jurisprudence, random drug testing has not been found to be a permissible exercise of management's rights in Canada" (at p. 394).

A decision which cuts against the grain of Canadian jurisprudence is *Milazzo v. Autocar Connaisseur Inc. (No. 2)* (2003), 47 C.H.R.R. D/468. In that case, the Canadian Human Rights Tribunal, in addition to recognizing the legality of pre-employment drug testing in the transportation industry, held that the employer was entitled to require employees in safety-sensitive jobs to undergo random drug tests. However, the decision in *Milazzo*, insofar as it permits such tests, may be confined to situations in which employees must, as part of their jobs, work in the U.S. (where testing is required by regulations).

The question of what constitutes a "safety-sensitive position" was considered by an arbitration board chaired by Arbitrator M.G. Picher in *J.D. Irving Ltd. and C.E.P., Local 104/1309* (2002), 111 L.A.C. (4th) 328. Adopting a flexible and expansive approach, the board held that a safety-sensitive position is one in which impairment by drugs or alcohol puts at risk the safety of the employee, or other employees or persons generally, or the safety of property or equipment. Relevant considerations include the work performed by the employee, as well as the nature of the equipment and materials. The union's argument that the definition should be restricted to jobs with little or no direct supervision was rejected.

In *Weyerhaeuser Co. and I.W.A.* (2004), 127 L.A.C. (4th) 73, Arbitrator Taylor considered a union policy grievance against the employer's national drug and alcohol testing policy. The union contended that the policy, which was limited to post-incident, for-cause, and safety-sensitive entry-level testing, and did not provide for random testing, violated the collective agreement because it was discriminatory and unreasonable. Adopting the approach set out by Arbitrator Michel Picher in *Canadian National Railway* and *J.D. Irving, supra*, the arbitrator upheld the policy. Notably, he rejected the union's argument that the employer was not entitled to impose a drug and alcohol testing policy unless it first established an extensive history of substance abuse in the workplace. In the arbitrator's view, the employer is permitted to take preventative measures in an inherently safety-sensitive industry without first proving a history of problems in the workplace due to substance abuse.

Arbitrator Taylor further ruled, based on a task force report issued in 2004, that forestry constituted an inherently safety-sensitive industry. The industries which have attracted this designation are growing in number, and now include airlines, railways, nuclear generating plants, open-pit mines (see *Fording Coal Ltd. and U.S.W.A., Local 7884*, [2002] B.C.C.A.A.A. No. 9 (QL) (Hope)), and a nylon plant (see *Dupont Canada Inc. and C.E.P., Local 28-0* (2002), 105 L.A.C. (4th) 399 (P.C. Picher)). Arbitrator Taylor stressed the need to distinguish between the designations "inherently safety-sensitive", which applies to an industry, and "safety-sensitive position", which refers to specific jobs within an industry. While the former designation relieves the employer from the requirement to establish the existence of a substance abuse problem in its workplace, it remains critical to determine which positions can be designated as safety-sensitive, and hence governed by the policy.

Similarly, in *ADM Agri-Industries Ltd. and C.A.W., Local 195*, [2004] O.L.A.A. No. 405 (QL), Arbitrator Springate concluded that an agricultural products processing plant (producing edible oils, margarine and animal feed) was an "inherently" dangerous or safety-sensitive industrial operation. It followed from this designation that the employer's policy, which provided for reasonable cause and post-incident testing, was upheld, even though there was no evidence of a drug or alcohol abuse problem at the plant, or of prior drug- or alcohol-related accidents.

Additional Reading

J.D.R. Craig, *"Entrop v. Imperial Oil Ltd.*: Employment Drug and Alcohol Testing Is Put to the Test" (2002), 9 Canadian Labour and Employment Journal, p. 147.

H.A. Hope, "Drug/Alcohol Testing and Workplace Privacy: An Arbitrator's Perspective" in K. Whitaker, J. Sack, M. Gunderson & R. Filion, eds., *Labour*

Arbitration Yearbook 2001-2001, vol. II, p. 85; and companion articles by W.J. Armstrong and J.M. Andrew.

13.4.3   Video Surveillance

In the past decade, a large number of arbitral awards have addressed the use of video surveillance of employees, both inside and outside the workplace. Two primary issues arise in this context. The first is the admissibility in arbitration proceedings of evidence acquired from surreptitious video surveillance, a topic which is discussed more fully in Chapter 6.8. The second is whether employer rules or policies instituting video surveillance of employees can stand up to arbitral review in accordance with the *KVP* criteria (see Chapter 13.3). The leading case in this area is *St. Mary's Hospital (New Westminster) and H.E.U.* (1997), 64 L.A.C. (4th) 382 (Larson). Following an exhaustive review of the jurisprudence, Arbitrator Larson held that the right to implement video surveillance is analogous to the right to search an employee's personal effects, in that both involve a conflict between individual privacy interests and management's interest in maintaining the security of its business. The arbitrator noted that, while most arbitrators have recognized a right to workplace privacy which should be preserved, this right is not absolute and its scope will depend on what is reasonable in the circumstances. Borrowing from the criteria established in *Doman Forest Products Ltd. and I.W.A., Local 1-357* (1990), 13 L.A.C. (4th) 275 (Vickers), an important decision on the admissibility of videotape surveillance evidence, Arbitrator Larson concluded that resort to videotape surveillance will be upheld only where three conditions have been met: (1) there are reasonable grounds for the surveillance; (2) the surveillance is carried out in a reasonable and non-discriminatory manner; and (3) no other, less intrusive alternatives were open to the employer to protect its legitimate business interests. The type, purpose, place and frequency of the surveillance are all factors that will be weighed in applying these criteria. For example, surreptitious video surveillance, which is considered more intrusive than overt video surveillance, may require more convincing justification by the employer.

In one of the most frequently cited decisions concerning the installation of non-surreptitious video surveillance in the workplace, *Lenworth Metal Products Ltd. and U.S.W.A., Local 3950* (1999), 80 L.A.C. (4th) 426, Arbitrator Armstrong observed that there were three bases on which he could assert jurisdiction under the collective agreement to hear a union policy grievance challenging video surveillance by the employer: a provision in the agreement stipulating that workplace rules must be reasonable; the requirement that rules or policies which are likely to become the basis of discipline, if they are not complied with, must be reasonable; and the arbitral principle that an employer's actions are subject to challenge on the basis that they are not motivated by a legitimate business interest. The arbitrator rejected the proposition that the authority to entertain the union's grievance could be founded only on an alleged breach of a legal right to privacy. The Ontario Divisional Court has upheld the arbitrator's ruling: *Lenworth Metal Products Ltd. v. U.S.W.A., Local 3950*, [2000] O.J. No. 4352 (QL). In his decision on the merits, Arbitrator Armstrong, while holding that there was no legal "right" to privacy in Ontario, concluded that it was unreasonable to conduct ongoing electronic surveillance of employees during working hours in the absence of "clear and convincing" evidence of security problems which cannot be addressed by other means: see (1999), 84 L.A.C. (4th) 77.

In several subsequent cases, following the approach adopted in *Lenworth Metal Products*, arbitrators have inquired whether the decision to institute surveillance is reasonable because, unless the employer's policy meets this requirement, it will be treated as inconsistent with the just cause provisions of the collective agreement. An example of this line of reasoning is found in *The Calgary Herald and G.C.I.U., Local 34M*, [2004] A.G.A.A. No. 23 (QL) (Tettensor). The arbitrator concluded that, while it was reasonable for the employer to operate a video surveillance system in order to address security and safety issues, it was not reasonable to conduct such surveillance or to monitor production for disciplinary purposes (except to the extent necessary to achieve the employer's legitimate objectives relating to security and safety). Thus, in the arbitrator's view, videotapes could be utilized for disciplinary purposes only in respect of matters involving the safety and security of equipment.

It should be noted that cases decided in British Columbia, and in particular *Doman Forest Products*, have adopted an analysis which gives some recognition to the statutory guarantee of a right to privacy found in s. 1 of the provincial *Privacy Act*, R.S.B.C. 1996, c. 373. *Doman Forest Products* and certain other British Columbia decisions also take the view that analysis of the appropriate balance between employee interests and management interests should be informed by the right to privacy enshrined in s. 8 of the *Canadian Charter of Rights and Freedoms*, even though the *Charter* does not directly apply to private employment relationships. For the most part, arbitrators in the rest of Canada have held that, in the absence of similar privacy legislation in their jurisdictions, they should approach the British Columbia precedents with caution, and furthermore that the *Charter* has no application to disputes regarding video surveillance in a private-sector workplace.

In *Securicor Cash Services and Teamsters, Local 419* (2004), 125 L.A.C. (4th) 129, Arbitrator Whitaker provides a concise but comprehensive summary of the ongoing debate among arbitrators as to whether there is a statutory or common law right to privacy which should be recognized at arbitration and, if so, whether arbitrators have authority to exclude videotape surveillance evidence obtained as a result of an infringement of employee privacy rights. This decision is one of the first to consider the application of the federal *Personal Information Protection and Electronic Documents Act* (PIPEDA), S.C. 2000,

c. 5, to a federal employer's use of videotape surveillance in a collective bargaining setting.

As framed by Arbitrator Whitaker (and other adjudicators), the test to be applied in assessing the admissibility of video surveillance evidence is twofold: (1) were the employer's reasons for initiating covert surveillance reasonable? and (2) were the methods used to conduct the surveillance reasonable? Although the requirement for reasonableness set out in *Securicor Cash Services* appears to be the position taken by a majority of arbitrators in Ontario, there continues to be a relatively small group of Ontario arbitrators who are of the view that the only limitation on the admissibility of such evidence is relevance. These arbitrators have maintained that there is no statutory or common law right to privacy in Ontario, and thus no basis for imposing a requirement that the surveillance be reasonable, either in terms of the decision to undertake surveillance or the methods used to carry it out. A recent example of this minority position is found in *Hôtel-Dieu Grace Hospital and C.A.W., Local 2458* (2004), 134 L.A.C. (4th) 246, where Arbitrator Snow identified Arbitrators Bendel, Solomatenko and Welling as other Ontario arbitrators who have confined their inquiry to the question of whether the proffered video surveillance evidence was relevant to the issues at hand.

However, the continued prevalence of the reasonableness approach, requiring a balancing of employee privacy interests against the legitimate interests of the employer, is indicated by several recent Ontario decisions, including *Centre for Addiction & Mental Health and O.P.S.E.U. (Cann)* (2004), 131 L.A.C. (4th) 97 (Nairn), and *Toronto (City) and C.U.P.E., Local 79* (2004), 128 L.A.C. (4th) 217 (Kirkwood). Perhaps the strongest affirmation that unionized employees in Ontario have a common law right to privacy is the award of Arbitrator Lynk in *Prestressed Systems Inc. and L.I.U.N.A., Local 625* (2005), 137 L.A.C. (4th) 193. In that decision, instead of the more common two-part test adopted in *Securicor Cash Services, supra*, Arbitrator Lynk formulated a new, more stringent four-part test that places a significant onus on the employer to explain why other, less intrusive alternatives to covert video surveillance were not used to investigate management's concerns. The application of this more restrictive approach led, in that case, to the rejection of surveillance evidence that showed the grievor playing recreational hockey in a public municipal arena while on sick leave, even though similar evidence, also obtained in a public hockey arena, had been admitted only months earlier by another arbitrator using the traditional two-part analysis: see *Johnson Matthey Ltd. and U.S.W.A., Local 9046* (2004), 131 L.A.C. (4th) 249 (Slotnick). On this point, a number of arbitrators have suggested that employees have a lower expectation of privacy when in a public place: see, for example, *Transit Windsor and A.T.U., Local 616* (2001), 99 L.A.C. (4th) 295 (Brandt). Other arbitrators disagree, maintaining that an employee who puts himself or herself in public view does not thereby abandon the right to be free from surveillance: see *Toronto Transit*

Commission and A.T.U., Local 113 (Belsito) (1999), 95 L.A.C. (4th) 402 (Chapman). For further discussion, see Chapter 6.8.

Additional Reading

G. Radwanski, "Workplace Privacy: A New Act, A New Era" in K. Whitaker, J. Sack, M. Gunderson & R. Filion, eds., *Labour Arbitration Yearbook 2001-2002*, vol. II, p. 1.

T.A.B. Jolliffe, "Privacy and Surveillance: An Arbitrator's Perspective" in K. Whitaker, J. Sack, M. Gunderson & R. Filion, eds., *Labour Arbitration Yearbook 1999-2000*, vol. II, p. 91; and companion articles by G.R. Meurin and J.R. Carpenter.

13.4.4 Polygraph Testing

Very few cases have dealt with the right of an employer to issue rules requiring employees to submit to a polygraph or lie-detector test. Some jurisdictions, such as Ontario, have prohibited employers from compelling or even influencing employees to take a polygraph test (see ss. 69 and 70 of the *Employment Standards Act*, S.O. 2000, c. 41). Most other jurisdictions, however, have not created a comparable prohibition, and in the absence of statutory regulation, arbitrators have proposed conflicting resolutions of the issue. Indeed, two of the reported awards — one from the federal jurisdiction, the other from British Columbia — involve the same employer and the same workplace policy. In the first decision, *Loomis Armored Car Service Ltd. and C.A.W., Local 4266A (No. 1)* (1996), 57 L.A.C. (4th) 305 (Young), the arbitrator adopted the prevailing approach to mandatory drug testing and employee search policies, holding that the privacy interest of an employee must be balanced against the property and business interests of the employer. In addition to finding that the company's policy was reasonable, Arbitrator Young ruled that where an employee was under suspicion of theft, the requirement for polygraph testing was an express, or at least implied, term of the collective agreement.

However, in the subsequent case of *Loomis Armored Car Service Ltd. and I.C.T.U., Local 1 (No. 2)* (1997), 70 L.A.C. (4th) 400, Arbitrator Kelleher decided that, because lie detector tests involve a greater invasion of privacy and bodily integrity than do employee searches, a balancing-of-interests approach is not appropriate. Instead, arbitrators should protect an employee's right to be free from compulsory polygraph testing unless there is clear statutory authority or an unequivocal provision in the collective agreement on which the employer can rely. In other words, if an express right to conduct polygraph tests cannot be found in the collective agreement, the employer cannot assert that right merely by virtue of its residual management prerogatives.

For further discussion, see Chapter 6.10.

Additional Reading

R.B. Bird, "Polygraph Testing: An Arbitrator's Viewpoint" in W. Kaplan, J. Sack & M. Gunderson, eds., *Labour arbitration Yearbook 1992*, p. 81; and companion articles by A. Wills and D. Blair.

13.5   FIGHTING, ASSAULTS AND THREATS

Arbitrators have repeatedly emphasized that violent behaviour by employees in the workplace is a serious form of misconduct which is inconsistent with the effective functioning of the enterprise and warrants severe discipline. In many of the earliest awards, violence was recognized as one of the "capital offences" which merited immediate discharge, especially if it was directed against a supervisor. However, in more recent times, arbitrators have recognized that there are many factors which may mitigate the severity of the offence and which must be considered in determining whether discharge is in fact an appropriate penalty.

Dominion Glass Co. and United Glass & Ceramic Workers, Local 203 (1975), 11 L.A.C. (2d) 84 (Linden), in which the grievor assaulted a fellow employee, contains a frequently-cited statement of principle on the employer's right and duty to keep peace in its operation. In that case, the board stressed that discharge should be upheld only where the circumstances in which the violence occurred make it unlikely that the employee will be able to function effectively in the workplace again. The board set out the following factors to be considered in making this determination:

(1) Who was attacked? (*i.e.* a supervisor or fellow employee, or someone with whom the grievor will have to work in the future?)

(2) Was it a momentary flare-up or a premeditated attack?

(3) How serious was the attack?

(4) Was there any provocation?

(5) What is the grievor's employment and discipline record?

(6) What is the grievor's length of service?

(7) What are the grievor's economic prospects?

(8) Has the grievor apologized or expressed a willingness to apologize?

In *Toronto Police Services Board and Toronto Police Ass'n (De Sa)* (2002), 110 L.A.C. (4th) 232, Arbitrator Swan rejected the union's contention that the disciplinary penalty imposed on two officers who took part in a fight while at work should be reduced because the altercation had originated in consensual horseplay. According to the arbitrator, what separates assault from horseplay is the intention to inflict harm: as soon as the altercation escalates to the point where a participant intends to do harm, a defence of horseplay evaporates.

Just as self-defence can negate criminal responsibility for assault under the *Criminal Code*, R.S.C. 1985, c. C-46, so too can it negate a finding of assault and thereby just cause for discipline in an arbitration proceeding. In *Sealy Canada Ltd. and U.S.W.A., Local 8300*, [2004] O.L.A.A. No. 391 (QL), Arbitrator Haefling relied on the *Criminal Code* definitions of assault and self-defence in finding that a fight between the grievor and a co-worker did not give rise to just cause. According to the arbitrator, the grievor had been acting in self-defence, and the employer had not established that the grievor had provoked the co-worker.

Arbitrators generally have also held that uttering threats or engaging in threatening behaviour warrants the imposition of a severe penalty. In *McCain Foods (Canada) and U.F.C.W., Local 114P3* (2002), 107 L.A.C. (4th) 193, Arbitrator Simmons noted that, in the aftermath of certain highly-publicized incidents of workplace violence, it was not possible to take as tolerant an approach to threats today as in the past. In the words of the arbitrator, at p. 210:

> . . . death threats made in the workplace have no place in today's society, whether made in jest or seriously made. Indeed, society has become acutely aware that there is a zero tolerance relating to such threats being uttered in certain places . . . "Shop talk", as that term has come to be defined, bears no relation to utterances of death threats in the workplace, especially in today's society.

The award in *Ajax Pickering Transit Authority and C.U.P.E., Local 129-01*, [2003] O.L.A.A. No. 511 (QL) (Craven) involved a comparable set of facts. In that case, the grievor had been dismissed for uttering the words, "What do I have to do to be heard around here, come in and shoot someone?" Although the arbitrator ordered that the grievor be reinstated, his return to active duty was made conditional on receipt of a medical clearance following examination by a medical specialist familiar with issues of occupational stress and workplace violence.

In many cases, often relying on the provisions of applicable human rights legislation, the union asserts that the grievor was suffering from a medical disability at the time of the incident, and that his or her assaultive or threatening behaviour should therefore not be treated as culpable misconduct warranting discipline. Arbitrators have uniformly held that, although the employer bears the burden of proof in a discipline case, the union bears the onus of establishing with credible evidence, first, that the grievor was disabled at the relevant time and, second, that there was a causal connection between the alleged disability and the conduct giving rise to the discipline. In this regard, as Arbitrator Tims has observed, such evidence must "clearly [address] the question of causation, establishing that a medical condition is 'intimately connected' with the misconduct in issue, thereby diminishing an individual's responsibility for his actions, in such a way that a disciplinary response is simply not appropriate": see *Domtar Inc. and I.W.A., Local 2995*, [2003] O.L.A.A. No. 569 (QL), at para. 150.

Additional Reading

M.A. Nairn, "Violence in the Workplace: An Arbitrator's Perspective" in K. Whitaker, J. Sack, M. Gunderson & R. Filion, eds., *Labour Arbitration Yearbook 2001-2002*, vol. I, p. 193; and companion articles by P. Sirota; L.F. Molnar, L.D. Mayzes & J. Schlotter; and D. Wright.

13.5.1   Assault on a Supervisor

The decision in *Howe Sound Forest Products Ltd. and I.W.A., Local 1-71* (1996), 57 L.A.C. (4th) 100 (Fuller) demonstrates the arbitral view that attacks on supervisors are considered more seriously than attacks on fellow employees due to their harmful impact on order in the workplace. The arbitrator suggests that, where an employee has assaulted a supervisor, there is a presumption that discharge is appropriate unless there are significant mitigating factors. He also states that the presence of provocation is perhaps the most crucial of these mitigating factors.

13.5.2   Penalty

Some arbitrators have determined that the viability of reinstating an employee who has engaged in workplace violence depends on whether the offence involved only threatening words or minor physical contact, or a serious assault. However, in *Toronto Western Hospital and C.U.P.E., Local 1744* (1989), 6 L.A.C. (4th) 150, Arbitrator Mitchnick observed from a review of awards that such a categorization has not been consistently applied. Instead, he concluded, the most influential factor in the determination of penalty has been "an over-all assessment of the type of employee the individual has shown him or herself to be", with particular emphasis on the possibility of a recurrence of violent behaviour. It should also be noted that, where reinstatement is ordered, the order is almost always made conditional on the grievor not engaging in similar behaviour over the course of a fairly lengthy period.

For a more recent application of the factors to be considered in determining the appropriate penalty in a case of assault on a supervisor, see *Accuride Canada Inc. and C.A.W., Local 27*, [2004] O.L.A.A. No. 133 (QL) (Etherington).

13.6   SEXUAL HARASSMENT/MISCONDUCT

The arbitral recognition of sexual harassment as serious misconduct meriting discipline has occurred relatively recently. Much of the arbitral jurisprudence on sexual harassment stems from *Bell v. Ladas*, a decision of a human rights board of inquiry chaired by Owen Shime (*sub nom. Bell and Korczak*

(1980), 27 L.A.C. (2d) 227 (Ont. Bd. of Inquiry)). Shime held that sexual harassment in the workplace constitutes employment discrimination on the basis of sex, contrary to the Ontario *Human Rights Code* (now R.S.O. 1990, c. H.19). The following passage sets out the rationale for this landmark decision (at p. 229):

> The forms of prohibited conduct that, in my view, are discriminatory run the gamut from overt gender-based activity, such as coerced intercourse to unsolicited physical contact to persistent propositions to more subtle conduct such as gender-based insults and taunting, which may reasonably be perceived to create a negative psychological and emotional work environment. There is no reason why the law, which reaches into the workplace so as to protect the work environment from physical or chemical pollution or extremes of temperature, ought not to protect employees as well from negative psychological and mental effects where adverse and gender-directed conduct emanating from a management hierarchy may reasonably be construed to be a condition of employment.

While the framework of arbitral analysis has its origins in human rights legislation, in the years since *Bell v. Ladas* arbitrators have made it clear that their authority to discipline employees who engage in sexual harassment exists independently of any statutory human rights provisions. *Canadian National Railway Co. and C.B.R.T. & G.W.* (1988), 1 L.A.C. (4th) 183 (M.G. Picher), a leading authority outlining the evolution of arbitral norms, is frequently relied upon by arbitrators for its approach to the mitigation of penalty in the context of this serious offence. Arbitrator Picher observed that the seriousness of sexual harassment, and in particular of unwanted sexual touching, could scarcely be understated, especially where the employer has undertaken measures designed to correct a gender imbalance in the workplace. Nevertheless, he ruled, sexual harassment does not automatically justify discharge, and like any other disciplinary offence, must be assessed with due regard to mitigating factors, including the general standards of conduct in the workplace, the grievor's length of service, and his or her prior record.

In a number of recent decisions involving wrongful dismissal actions launched by employees who have been accused of sexually harassing coworkers, courts have drawn a distinction between different types of harassment-related misconduct. According to these decisions, if the sexual harassment at issue falls in the "middle of the spectrum" or lower (in terms of the degree and nature of the harassment), just cause for dismissal will not be found unless the employee has been warned that such conduct is inappropriate, and that a recurrence could lead to dismissal. This approach was applied in *Brazeau v. I.B.E.W.*, 2004 C.L.L.C. ¶210-032 (B.C.S.C.).

In more serious cases, though, a single incident is enough to warrant discharge, particularly where the grievor does not have long service: *Siemens VDO Automotive Inc. and C.A.W., Local 1841*, [2005] O.L.A.A. No. 630 (QL) (Watters).

Additional Reading

D. McPhillips, "Workplace Harassment: An Arbitrator's Perspective" in K. Whitaker, J. Sack, M. Gunderson & R. Filion, eds., *Labour Arbitration Yearbook 1999-2000*, p. 255; and companion articles by B. Smeenk & D.G. Palayew, and M. Rans.

E. McIntyre, P. Pasieka, W. Kaplan *et al.*, "Employer Liability for Workplace Harassment" (1998), 6 Canadian Labour and Employment Journal, p. 219.

G. Eden, "Sexual Harassment at Arbitration" in W. Kaplan, J. Sack & M. Gunderson, eds., *Labour Arbitration Yearbook 1993*, p. 117.

13.6.1   Definition of Sexual Harassment

In *Janzen v. Platy Enterprises Ltd.* (1989), 59 D.L.R. (4th) 352, the Supreme Court of Canada adopted the *Bell v. Ladas* rationale (see Chapter 13.6), holding that sexual harassment was a form of sex discrimination under Manitoba's human rights legislation. Although there are many statutory definitions of sexual harassment in the human rights and employment standards legislation of various jurisdictions, *Janzen v. Platy Enterprises* has become the leading case on the definition of sexual harassment and on the scope of employer responsibility for sexual harassment in the workplace. Chief Justice Dickson stated, at p. 375:

> Without seeking to provide an exhaustive definition of the term, I am of the view that sexual harassment in the workplace may be broadly defined as unwelcome conduct of a sexual nature that detrimentally affects the work environment or leads to adverse job-related consequences for the victims of the harassment. It is, as Adjudicator Shime observed in *Bell v. Ladas* . . . and as has been widely accepted by other adjudicators and academic commentators, an abuse of power. When sexual harassment occurs in the workplace, it is an abuse of both economic and sexual power. Sexual harassment is a demeaning practice, one that constitutes a profound affront to the dignity of the employees forced to endure it. By requiring an employee to contend with unwelcome sexual actions or explicit sexual demands, sexual harassment in the workplace attacks the dignity and self-respect of the victim both as an employee and as a human being.

Human rights tribunals and arbitrators have distinguished between "*quid pro quo*" sexual harassment (for example, discharge or demotion of an employee as a reprisal for refusing to engage in sexual activity) and "abusive environment" sexual harassment, which is generally characterized by multiple incidents of offensive conduct. In *Toronto Board of Education and C.U.P.E., Local 63* (1997), 65 L.A.C. (4th) 174, Arbitrator Howe discusses the arbitral evolution of the definition of sexual harassment following *Bell v. Ladas*, with particular emphasis on gender-based insults and taunting which may create a negative psychological work environment.

When considering the validity of discipline based on allegations of "abusive environment" sexual harassment, many arbitrators have required proof of a pattern or repetition of the conduct in question. Thus, unless it is extremely serious, a single incident will not normally support a ruling that the work environment has been poisoned so as to justify discipline. See, for example, *Western Star Trucks and I.A.M., Lodge 2710* (1997), 69 L.A.C. (4th) 250, where Arbitrator Bruce noted, at p. 268: "In a case involving a hostile work environment, where the conduct alleged to be harassment does not deprive the complainant of an employment benefit, human rights tribunals have generally required proof that the impugned actions are persistent or sufficiently severe to effectively alter the employee's conditions of employment".

However, in *Prestressed Systems Inc. and L.I.U.N.A., Local 625* (2005), 143 L.A.C. (4th) 340, Arbitrator Snow ordered a manager to apologize for a single comment that was held to violate the prohibition against discrimination in Ontario's *Human Rights Code*, R.S.O. 1990, c. H.19, even though that legislation defines "harassment" as a "course of vexatious comment or conduct that is known or ought reasonably to be known to be unwelcome".

In *Simpson v. Consumers' Ass'n of Canada* (2001), 209 D.L.R. (4th) 214, the Ontario Court of Appeal provided an important clarification of the definition of sexual harassment. Allowing an action for wrongful dismissal, the trial judge discounted most of the incidents on which the employer relied as constituting a course of harassment meriting discharge, on the basis that they took place at social events after working hours. The Court of Appeal rejected this approach and overturned the judgment, ruling:

> It would be artificial and contrary to the purpose of controlling sexual harassment in the workplace to say that after-work interaction between a supervisor and other employees cannot constitute the workplace for the purpose of the application of the law regarding employment-related sexual harassment. The determination of whether, in any particular case, activity that occurs after hours or outside the confines of the business establishment can be the subject of complaint will be a question of fact. In this case, the trial judge erred by making an overall finding without considering the individual circumstances of each incident. (at p. 234)

Several provinces have introduced legislation targeting workplace violence, bullying and harassment as occupational hazards. Amendments to Quebec's *Labour Standards Act* place an onus on employers to make reasonable efforts to prevent "psychological harassment" in the workplace and, "whenever they become aware of such behaviour, to put a stop to it". The Act states that the psychological harassment rules are "deemed to be an integral part of every collective agreement". Under the legislation, Quebec employers face liability to victims of workplace harassment for lost wages, punitive damages, compensation for loss of employment, and the cost of psychological support: see R.S.Q., c. N-1.1, Division V.2.

Other legislative initiatives include the harassment provisions of Saskatchewan's *Occupational Health and Safety Act*, which impose a duty on employers to "ensure, insofar as is reasonably practicable, that the employer's workers are not exposed to harassment at the place of employment". Harassment is defined in the Act as "any objectionable conduct, comment or display" that is based on a prohibited ground of discrimination, and that "constitutes a threat to the health or safety of the worker": see R.S.S., c. O-1.1, ss. 2(1), 3 and 4.

13.6.2   Consensual Sex in the Workplace

Consenting adults who engage in sexual intimacy in the workplace or during working hours may not be guilty of sexual harassment, but they may nevertheless be subject to discipline. The leading decision concerning the harmful impact of such activity on the employer's interests and on the workplace environment is *Indusmin Ltd. and United Cement, Lime & Gypsum Workers Int'l Union, Local 488* (1978), 20 L.A.C. (2d) 87 (M.G. Picher).

13.7   PATIENT/RESIDENT ABUSE

When considering the imposition of discipline for abusive treatment of patients or residents in a health care setting, arbitrators have recognized the need to weigh the public interest together with the interests of the employer and employees. In their view, individual employees as well as the institutional employer are charged with a public trust in providing for the physical and emotional well-being of persons who are unable to care for themselves. There has, accordingly, been widespread consensus that a high standard of conduct is expected from employees in the health care and elder care fields, which in turn has led to a broad definition of the kinds of conduct that may constitute abuse.

Prior to the early 1980s, however, there was a divergence of opinion about the role of the arbitrator where rigorous industry standards, in effect, called for "zero tolerance". For some arbitrators, the public trust was so important that, if a case of patient abuse was made out, discharge of the offending employee should follow automatically. However, following the decision in *Baptist Housing Society and H.E.U., Local 180* (1982), 6 L.A.C. (3d) 430 (Greyell), there has been fairly broad agreement that, once an incident of abuse has been established, the arbitrator should go on to consider the appropriateness of the penalty in light of the nature of the abuse and the circumstances in which it occurred, the importance of the competing interests at stake, and the mitigating factors that are normally considered in discipline cases.

The approach in *Baptist Housing Society* was adopted in *Simon Fraser Lodge Inc. and H.E.U.* (1992), 27 L.A.C. (4th) 300 (McPhillips). This decision also emphasizes that, because allegations of patient abuse threaten an employee's professional reputation, there is a heavy burden on the employer to present clear, cogent and convincing evidence in support of its case. In that case, the employer was held to have met its burden, and the arbitrator denied the grievance and sustained the discharge. The grievor was only in her third week of employment, had committed repeated offences, and failed to acknowledge the seriousness of her misconduct.

In *Northern Health Authority (North Peace Care Centre) and B.C.N.U. (Pringle)* (2004), 131 L.A.C. (4th) 370, Arbitrator Dorsey pointed to the distinction between inadvertence or negligence and intentional or reckless conduct that results in harm to a patient or resident. As the arbitrator explained, while the careless or negligent performance of duties may well warrant a disciplinary response, it is in cases of wilful abuse that more severe penalties are normally justified.

Like health care workers, teachers accused of abuse of students will be held to a high standard of conduct. Arbitrator Taylor, upholding the discharge of a 20-year teacher who was found to have sexually assaulted a student, pointed out that teachers are required to act as role models, both on- and off-duty:

> Teachers occupy a special role in society, and society expects and is entitled to demand a certain standard of behavior in the relationship of teachers with students. It is a position of trust. It is a fiduciary relationship. A fiduciary stands in a position of trust and confidence toward another and has a duty to act only in that person's best interests.

See *British Columbia Public School Employers' Ass'n und B.C.T.F. (Samson)*, [2000] B.C.C.A.A.A. No. 264 (QL) (Taylor), at para. 265 and ff. Nevertheless, as in health care cases, discharge is not automatic, and arbitrators will take into account any mitigating circumstances that may justify modifying the penalty.

13.8 LATENESS

In the absence of a reasonable explanation or excuse, lateness by itself is viewed by arbitrators as just cause for discipline. Usually, however, it is not an adequate basis for imposing a serious penalty unless there is a persistent pattern of lateness which the employer has previously attempted to curb by imposing disciplinary measures. Lateness also frequently appears as part of a disciplinary record consisting of various forms of misconduct, and thus plays a role in the employer's decision to discharge an employee under the "culminating incident" doctrine. The question of whether lateness warrants discipline or merits a more severe penalty depends heavily on the extent to which the causes for it are found to be within the control of the employee and therefore preventable. A useful statement of the arbitral approach to these issues is found in *Canada Safeway Ltd. and U.F.C.W., Local 1518*, [2002] B.C.C.A.A.A. No. 330 (QL) (Nordlinger).

Evidence indicating that the employer has failed in the past to take lateness seriously may lead to the vitiation of a disciplinary penalty at arbitration. As indicated by the decision in *Okanagan Beverages Ltd. and Teamsters, Local 213* (1975), 8 L.A.C. (2d) 105 (Monroe), this is especially so where the employer has introduced a strict regime of punctuality without giving the union proper notification.

Similarly, in *Shoppers Drug Mart Inc. No. 297 and U.F.C.W., Local 1518*, [2004] B.C.C.A.A.A. No. 242 (QL) (Steeves), the arbitrator indicated that the employer must consistently maintain a formal disciplinary response to repeated lateness in order to justify dismissal for this infraction, in keeping with a progressive approach to discipline. In that case, the informality of the discussions, the absence of clear disciplinary warnings, and the employer's failure to inform the grievor of the likely consequences if her lateness persisted were important considerations in the arbitrator's decision to rescind the discharge and substitute a lesser penalty.

13.9   RULES RELATING TO PERSONAL APPEARANCE

In order to form the basis for imposing discipline, employer rules governing personal appearance and dress codes must satisfy the *KVP* criteria (see Chapter 13.3), including reasonableness. *Scarborough (Borough) and I.A.F.F., Local 626* (1972), 24 L.A.C. 78, a seminal decision by Arbitrator Shime, reveals the dominant arbitral approach to the employer's ability to make personal appearance rules. In determining whether a personal appearance rule is reasonable, arbitrators have attempted to balance the personal rights of employees against the legitimate business interests of the employer.

Because the determination of whether a personal appearance rule is justified requires a balancing of competing considerations, the nature of the potential interference with an employee's freedom and personal rights will be a significant factor. Rules which limit hair length or prohibit facial hair, for example, affect employees' appearance during off-duty hours, and therefore require a stronger business justification than rules which prescribe the clothing to be worn on duty. On the other side of the equation, the nature and severity of the threat to the employer's business interests, and the cogency of the evidence indicating such a threat, will also receive close scrutiny. Arbitrators frequently emphasize the need for some objective evidence to substantiate claims that an employee's personal appearance jeopardizes the business interests of the employer (such as financial records indicating a loss of business, or surveys of customer attitudes). The necessity of balancing these considerations is described in the brief but important decision of *Dominion Stores Ltd. and U.S.W.A.* (1976), 11 L.A.C. (2d) 401 (Shime).

As Arbitrator Shime explains, when attempting to measure the tolerance of customers or clients towards the expression of personal taste in employees' appearance, and the potential impact on an employer's business, arbitrators must be cognizant of changing social standards. A large number of cases in the 1970s arose from grievances against rules restricting hair length or facial hair. Similarly, the advent of the mini-skirt and blue jeans as part of the mainstream wardrobe generated challenges to the enforcement of restrictive dress codes. In the 1980s, there were several cases on the wearing of earrings or ear-studs by male employees, while in the 1990s the focus was on facial jewellery, such as nose or lip studs.

The award of Arbitrator Larson in *Thrifty (Canada) Ltd. and O.P.E.I.U., Local 378* (2001), 100 L.A.C. (4th) 162 makes it clear that, even where the scope of the dress code is confined to apparel or removable jewelry, the employer will be required to establish four elements in order to justify its policy: (1) the policy has a legitimate business purpose; (2) it is rationally connected to that purpose; (3) it is likely to be effective in achieving its purpose; and (4) the employer's interest in obtaining compliance with the policy is more important than the interest of employees in choosing their personal appearance.

In *United Parcel Service Canada and Employés du transport local et industries diverses, local 931*, [2003] D.A.T.C. No. 582 (QL), Arbitrator Foisy held that an employer dress code which prohibited certain hair and beard styles offended the grievor's privacy rights under s. 7 of the *Canadian Charter of Rights and Freedoms*. In that case, the grievor had been denied a promotion to a position in which compliance with the company's dress code was mandatory. To comply with the dress code, which required male employees to be clean-shaven and have neatly cut hair, would be inconsistent with the grievor's beliefs as a follower of the Rastafarian religion. While the employer was entitled under the collective agreement to impose a dress code, the agreement incorporated the provisions of the *Charter* by reference. As a consequence, the scope of management's rights pursuant to the collective agreement was required to be interpreted and applied in accordance with the *Charter.* In light of his conclusion that personal appearance involved a fundamentally private and personal choice, and was thus protected by the *Charter*, the arbitrator upheld the grievance, finding it unnecessary to deal with the grievor's allegation that he had been discriminated against because of his religion. In the result, the matter was referred back to the employer for a determination on the grievor's qualifications for the posted position.

For a discussion of whether the employer can impose discipline for breach of personal appearance rules, on the ground that the grievor's failure to comply constitutes insubordination, see Chapter 13.2.4.

Additional Reading

E. Bosveld, "Loopholes and the Law: Facial Jewelry, Personal Expression, and the Regulation of the Workplace" (2004), 11 Canadian Labour and Employment Law Journal, p. 351.

13.10   ILLEGAL STRIKES/STRIKE-RELATED MISCONDUCT

Arbitrators have long accepted that participation in an unlawful strike merits serious discipline. However, in more recent years, arbitrators have been less likely to regard discharge as the automatic penalty for such misconduct. Instead, they have tended to reason that the severity of the penalty should vary according to the grievor's culpability. Aggravating factors, such as active participation in the organization or promotion of the work stoppage, often lead to the imposition of a lengthy suspension or to discharge. At the same time, arbitrators give close scrutiny to the issue of whether the employer has applied discipline fairly and even-handedly in accordance with the degree of involvement of the individual employee. These general principles were summed up in *Camco Inc. and U.E., Local 550* (1988), 34 L.A.C. (3d) 12 (Barton).

The appropriateness of this approach was confirmed in *Abitibi Consolidated Inc. and C.E.P., Local 161* (1998), 72 L.A.C. (4th) 422 (Oakley). In that case, the arbitrator also rejected the union's claim that there was an exception to the "work now, grieve later" principle in respect of work stoppages provoked by conduct that amounted to an obvious and unambiguous violation of the collective agreement by the employer.

The issue of whether the employer can issue a blanket disciplinary penalty, without conducting individual disciplinary interviews or taking into account individual disciplinary records, against a large number of employees who have engaged in an unlawful work stoppage has arisen in a number of cases. Unions have frequently argued that such penalties are inconsistent with the individualized approach to discipline that is contemplated by just cause provisions in collective agreements and labour relations statutes providing for an arbitral discretion to substitute a lesser penalty that is just and reasonable in all the circumstances. The decision of Arbitrator Hickling in *British Columbia Hydro & Power Authority and C.O.P.E., Local 378*, [2004] B.C.C.A.A. No. 199 (QL) provides a thorough analysis of the caselaw on this issue, and sets out the circumstances in which the imposition of a blanket penalty for unlawful strike activity will be found consistent with the requirement for an individual approach to the application of the just cause standard. In particular, the arbitrator wrote, an employer is required to exempt from discipline employees with a legitimate excuse for not reporting to work, and to justify any decision to single out employees for more severe discipline. Such justification may exist where the employee took an active role in promoting the work stoppage and was not merely a passive participant, or had previously incurred discipline for taking part in an illegal strike.

13.10.1   Definition of Illegal Strike

The labour relations legislation of most jurisdictions in Canada provides that every collective agreement is deemed to include a no-strike/lockout clause (see, for example, s. 99(1) of the Newfoundland and Labrador *Labour Relations Act*, R.S.N.L. 1990, c. L-1, and s. 44 of the Saskatchewan *Trade Union Act*, R.S.S. 1978, c. T-17, as amended). Usually, the legislation also contains a broad definition of the kinds of activity which constitute a "strike". Section 1 of the Ontario *Labour Relations Act*, S.O. 1995, c. 1, Sch. A, is fairly representative:

> "strike" includes a cessation of work, a refusal to work or to continue to work by employees in combination or in concert or in accordance with a common understanding, or a slow-down or other concerted activity on the part of employees designed to restrict or limit output.

Where the employer alleges that an employee or group of employees has violated the collective agreement by engaging in an illegal strike or work stoppage, arbitrators have applied the statutory definition in effect in the particular jurisdiction in determining whether the conduct at issue warrants discipline.

Notwithstanding the statutory prohibition on strikes and lockouts during the term of a collective agreement, the parties to a number of agreements have negotiated clauses which purport to give employees the right to refuse to cross picket-lines or to handle struck work ("hot cargo clauses"). On the basis that the parties cannot contract out of a clear and unequivocal statutory obligation, labour boards and the courts have stated on numerous occasions that the union is not entitled to rely on such clauses as a defence to what would otherwise be unlawful strike activity. See, for example, *Empress Graphics Inc. (Council of Printing Industries of Canada) and G.C.I.U., Local 500M* (1989), 3 Can. L.R.B.R. (2d) 141, where the Ontario Labour Relations Board decided that a hot cargo clause was of no avail to the union in defending the employer's application for an unlawful strike declaration and a cease-and-desist order.

Until recently, however, many arbitrators were willing to accept that a hot cargo clause at least provided a shield against the imposition of discipline for engaging in an illegal work stoppage. See, for instance, *McCormick's Ltd. and Milk & Bread Drivers, Dairy Employees, Caterers & Allied Employees, Local 647* (1974), 7 L.A.C. (2d) 334 (O'Shea). A more recent decision by a well-known arbitrator brings into question whether this line of authority will continue to be followed. In *Kingston Whig-Standard and C.W.A., Local 204* (1995), 51 L.A.C. (4th) 137, a board of arbitration chaired by Howard Brown refused to give effect to a hot cargo clause, holding that it was void *ab initio* as an attempt to contract out of public and legislative policy. In the board's opinion, the clause "cannot be used for any purpose by either party".

Ultimately, whether a hot cargo or struck work clause violates the "no strike" provisions of a particular labour relations statute will depend on the definition of "strike", the language of the statute in question, and its interpretation by the appropriate labour relations board. Section 58 of the British Columbia *Labour Relations Code*, R.S.B.C. 1996, c. 244, like the legislation of other provinces, incorporates in all collective agreements a no strike/lockout clause, but is silent on the issue of whether this prevents the parties from agreeing to a hot cargo clause. This provision has been interpreted as allowing the inclusion of hot cargo clauses in British Columbia, provided the refusal to handle such goods is clearly authorized by the collective agreement: see *Pacific Press and C.E.P., Local 2000* (2000), 86 L.A.C. (4th) 1 (Dorsey).

Manitoba is currently the only province with legislation that specifically permits employees to refuse to take delivery or assist in the handling of struck goods: *Labour Relations Act*, R.S.M. 1987, c. L10, s. 15(1).

It is now clear that "secondary picketing" of the suppliers or customers of a struck employer is lawful unless it involves wrongful or criminal conduct: *R.W.D.S.U., Local 558 v. Pepsi-Cola Canada Beverages (West) Ltd.* (2002), 208 D.L.R. (4th) 385 (S.C.C.). This decision rests on the foundation that picketing is a form of expression protected by the *Charter of Rights and Freedoms*, and therefore cannot be restricted without justification. However, while the ruling in *Pepsi-Cola* has clarified the status of secondary picketing at common law, such activity may also be subject to legislative limits under the applicable labour relations code.

The *Charter* guarantee of freedom of expression has also been held to apply to peaceful or "informational" leafleting. In the absence of otherwise illegal conduct, leafleting at an employer's place of business does not constitute picketing, and is therefore not caught by any legislative restrictions: *Sobeys Capital Inc. and U.F.C.W., Local 401* (2003), 98 Can. L.R.B.R. (2d) 1 (Alta. L.R.B.), citing the Supreme Court of Canada's decision in *U.F.C.W., Local 1518 v. KMart Canada Ltd.* (1999), 176 D.L.R. (4th) 607. In British Columbia, the Labour Relations Board has adopted a "bright-line" test to distinguish between constitutionally protected consumer leafleting and conventional primary or secondary picketing, which is subject to regulation under the province's *Labour Relations Code*. Thus, "if some individuals at secondary sites are handing out leaflets while others at the same location are wearing placards, those wearing placards will be engaged in conventional picketing, not leafleting, and the placards will be enjoined. Individuals will continue to be free to leaflet within the guidelines set out in *KMart*": *Overwaitea Food Group and U.F.C.W., Local 1518* (2003), 102 Can. L.R.B.R. (2d) 211 (B.C.L.R.B.), at p. 225.

The Ontario Labour Relations Board has upheld mid-contract restrictions on the right to engage in "political protest strikes", despite the *Charter* right to freedom of expression, concluding that a blanket prohibition on such strikes is justified as a reasonable limit under s. 1 of the *Charter*. In the Board's opinion, it would not be possible to adopt a less restrictive approach permitting some forms of political protest strike action without undermining the objective of the "no strike" provision in the *Labour Relations Act*: see *Ontario Hospital Ass'n and O.P.S.E.U.*, [2003] O.L.R.B. Rep. 622. Similarly, the British Columbia Labour Relations Board, while accepting that political strikes may constitute expressive activity for *Charter* purposes, and that the prohibition against work stoppages undertaken for a political rather than a collective bargaining purpose ran afoul of s. 2(b) of the *Charter*, has held that the ban on such stoppages is justified under s. 1, with few exceptions: *Health Employers' Ass'n of British Columbia and H.E.U.* (2004), 108 Can. L.R.B.R. 1.

Additional Reading

B. Adell, "Secondary Picketing after *Pepsi-Cola*: What's Clear, and What Isn't?" (2003), 10 Canadian Labour and Employment Law Journal, p. 135.

P. Macklem, "Secondary Picketing, Consumer Boycotts and the *Charter*" (2000), 8 Canadian Labour and Employment Journal, p. 1.

13.10.2   Discipline of Union Officials

The issue of whether union officials expose themselves to more severe discipline than other employees for participating in an unlawful strike has been the subject of some controversy. Prior to the decision of the Supreme Court of Canada in *Douglas Aircraft Co. of Canada Ltd. v. McConnell* (1979), 99 D.L.R. (3d) 385, many arbitrators took the view not only that union officials were liable to greater discipline, but also that they were under a positive obligation to help prevent or bring an end to an improper work stoppage. However, in *Douglas Aircraft*, the Court made it clear that, for the purposes of assessing discipline, union officials owe no special duty to the employer to ensure that the terms of the collective agreement are enforced.

Some arbitrators extended this ruling to mean that union officials who actively participate in an unlawful strike cannot be disciplined more severely than other employees, even if their participation appears to indicate union support for the stoppage. While there continues to be an element of uncertainty, the prevalent view is that of Arbitrator Burkett in *Port Hope & District Hospital and C.U.P.E., Local 1653* (1982), 6 L.A.C. (3d) 173. He suggests that, in assessing a suitable penalty, arbitrators should distinguish among three levels of participation by union officials: *active leadership*, *active involvement*, and *passive participation*. A union official whose misconduct falls into the first or second categories is subject to more serious discipline than a rank-and-file employee; a union official whose misconduct falls into the third category, however, is disciplinable only to the same extent as other passive participants.

The views articulated in *Port Hope & District Hospital* were adopted in *Mill & Timber Products Ltd. and I.W.A., Local 1-3567* (1996), 61 L.A.C. (4th) 52 (Munroe). In this case, the arbitrator made it clear that, before a union official can be held liable to a greater degree of discipline, there must be evidence either that the official intended to exert a leadership role or that other employees were consciously following his or her example.

The issue of discipline against union officials, however, must be distinguished from the question of the union's liability for damages in respect of an unlawful strike. On the latter point, it is well established that a union is obligated to repudiate and take reasonable steps to prevent or end an illegal work stoppage, and that its failure to do so may result in liability for damages suffered by the employer as a result of the strike. For further discussion, see Chapter 25.3.

13.10.3   Onus of Proof

In *Alberta and A.U.P.E. (Banack)* (1992), 26 L.A.C. (4th) 327 (Koshman), the arbitration board concluded that, where an employee has been disciplined for involvement in an unlawful strike, the onus of proof rests initially on the employer to establish that a work stoppage did in fact take place. The onus then shifts to the employee to justify his or her absence from work with a valid explanation. This approach is consistent with the ruling in *Strasser v. Roberge* (1979), 103 D.L.R. (3d) 193, in which the Supreme Court of Canada considered the location of the onus in labour board proceedings arising from an illegal strike, and held as follows, at p. 223: "If the prohibition [against mid-term strikes] is to be effective — and it must be assumed that the Act intends it to be — the only method is to reverse the burden of proof and impose on the accused the obligation of showing that he did not have the required intent and took reasonable steps to avoid committing the offence".

CHAPTER 14

NON-DISCIPLINARY DISCHARGE

14.1 INNOCENT ABSENTEEISM

If the employer can establish that an employee has been absent without medical or other justification, the employer is free to treat the employee's conduct as culpable and to impose discipline. More typically, however, the absence is due to factors beyond the employee's control, such as illness or injury, and a disciplinary response is inappropriate. Nonetheless, arbitrators have long recognized that even absenteeism which is "innocent" may entitle the employer to bring the employment relationship to an end. The rationale for this approach is not that an employee's non-culpable absence becomes culpable after a certain point, but that the employer is entitled to expect a reasonable level of attendance on the part of its employees. The right to regular attendance is usually said to be implicit in the employment contract itself.

In his oft-quoted ruling in *Massey-Ferguson Industries Ltd. and U.A.W., Local 458* (1972), 24 L.A.C. 344, Arbitrator Shime reviewed and synopsized the early cases in which these propositions were established. The arbitrator identified two criteria that the employer must meet in order to justify dismissal based on an employee's innocent absenteeism:

(1) the employee's past record of absenteeism is undue or excessive; and

(2) there is no reasonable prospect for improvement in the foreseeable future.

In other words, the record is poor, and the prognosis is no better. Furthermore, arbitrators have long recognized that the employer should have greater latitude in dismissing an employee whose absences are sporadic and unpredictable, since this causes increased difficulty in scheduling work: *Massey-Ferguson Ltd. and U.A.W.* (1969), 20 L.A.C. 370 (P.C. Weiler).

In *Niagara Structural Steel Ltd. and U.S.W.A., Local 7012* (1978), 18 L.A.C. (2d) 385 (O'Shea), it was held that the assessment of an employee's future prognosis may be based on an inference drawn from his or her past record alone, without the necessity for additional evidence. However, as Arbitrator Gordon ruled in *Coast Mountain Bus Co. and C.A.W., Local 111*, [2004] B.C.C.A.A.A. No. 325 (QL), the onus of establishing an unfavourable prognosis ultimately rests with the employer, and it is difficult to see how an employer could support a termination decision without the benefit of a current medical assessment. The arbitrator noted, however, that the evidentiary burden may shift to the union and the employee, depending on what the medical evidence appears to indicate.

As discussed in Chapter 14.3, the established arbitral principles relating to innocent absenteeism must now be read in the light of federal and provincial human rights legislation which prohibits discrimination on the basis of an employee's disability or handicap. Where an employee's failure to attend work is attributable to a specific, identifiable mental or physical disability within the meaning of the legislation, the employer has no right to dismiss the employee unless it has met its statutory duty of accommodation to the point of undue hardship: see *Alcan Smelters & Chemicals Ltd. and C.A.W., Local 2301* (1996), 55 L.A.C. (4th) 261 (Hope). However, where an employee's disability cannot be accommodated by the employer without undue hardship, arbitrators have made it clear that the principles of innocent absenteeism continue to apply. As long as the employer has satisfied its duty of accommodation, evidence of excessive absenteeism in the past, unameliorated by any prospect for improvement in the foreseeable future, will justify the dismissal of an employee, regardless of the existence of a recognized disability. This residual right of the employer to terminate a worker's employment because of innocent absenteeism is discussed in the oft-quoted case of *AirBC Ltd. and C.A.L.D.A.* (1995), 50 L.A.C. (4th) 93 (McPhillips).

The principles underlying the employer's right to terminate the employment of an employee whose absenteeism is excessive though innocent was affirmed in *Ottawa (City) v. Canadian Human Rights Commission* (2004), 267 F.T.R. The Canadian Human Rights Tribunal had found that the employer should have done more to accommodate an employee with a poor attendance record, since at least some of the employee's absenteeism was related to a disability. The Federal Court quashed the decision. Notwithstanding the duty to accommodate, the Court indicated, there comes a point when it becomes clear that the employee is not able to maintain his or her end of the employment bargain.

Additional Reading

I. Christie, "The Right to Dismiss for Innocent Absenteeism: An Arbitrator's Perspective" in W. Kaplan, J. Sack & M. Gunderson, eds., *Labour Arbitration Yearbook 1993*, p. 201; and companion articles by J.G. Petrie and P. Turtle.

14.2   EFFECT OF BENEFIT PLANS

Virtually all employer benefit plans require, as a condition of eligibility, that a claimant have the status of an "employee". An issue has therefore arisen as to whether the employer's normal right to discharge an employee for innocent absenteeism is affected by the availability of a benefit under the collective agreement. In this regard, the current state of arbitral law was captured in *Maple Leaf Meats and U.F.C.W., Local 175/633* (2001), 98 L.A.C. (4th) 40 (Whitaker). Following a review of previous awards, Arbitrator Whitaker concluded that a distinction has been drawn between benefits the very purpose of which is to assist an employee who is unable to attend at work, and benefits which are intended to apply more generally. In the former situation, the employer is precluded from terminating the employment of a disabled worker who has not yet had an opportunity to take advantage of the benefit (typically, long-term disability benefits). Once application for the benefit has been made, however, the employer's right to terminate revives, since termination can have no subsequent effect on the employee's entitlement to receive or continue receiving the benefit — that entitlement, in the language of the caselaw, having already "vested". In the *Maple Leaf Meats* case, seven disabled employees were discharged for innocent absenteeism. Although the discharges did not affect the grievors' entitlement to long-term disability benefits, they were no longer eligible for other insured benefits under the collective agreement (such as dental, vision and semi-private hospital coverage) because of their loss of employee status. Arbitrator Whitaker dismissed the grievances, ruling that, unlike LTD benefits, for which all the grievors had already applied, the benefits in question were not specifically designed for employees who were unable to work.

Another element in this line of cases is exemplified by *Money's Mushrooms Ltd. and R.W.D.S.U., Local 580*, [2000] B.C.C.A.A.A. No. 83 (QL) (Germaine). In that case, as a result of the employer's decision to close one of its facilities, employees at the plant were entitled to severance pay under the collective agreement. In order to reduce its potential liability, the employer purported to dismiss a group of long-absent employees in accordance with the doctrine of innocent absenteeism. Arbitrator Germaine held that, notwithstanding the employer's right to dismiss employees whose disability cannot be accommodated, the fact that the decision was motivated by an improper purpose — to disentitle employees from a collective agreement benefit — gave rise to a violation of the British Columbia *Human Rights Code*, R.S.B.C. 1996, c. 210.

In *NAV Canada and C.A.W., Local 5454*, [2004] C.L.A.D. No. 266 (QL), Arbitrator Swan held that a disabled employee's release was barred by the *Canadian Human Rights Act*, R.S.C. 1985, c. H-6, where termination of employment resulted in an end of the employee's membership in the pension plan, and hence the loss of credit for pensionable service while on disability leave.

14.3   EMPLOYEE DISABILITY AND THE DUTY TO ACCOMMODATE

14.3.1   Prohibition Against Disability-Based Discrimination

Human rights legislation across Canada prohibits discrimination in employment on a number of grounds, including disability. Ordinarily, it is a defence to a charge of disability-based discrimination that the employee cannot perform the essential duties of the job or that a job requirement (such as regular attendance at work) is a *bona fide* occupational qualification. However, this defence is normally available only where the employer can establish that it has attempted to accommodate the employee, short of undue hardship to the employer or other employees.

The Supreme Court of Canada has affirmed that collective agreements are deemed to incorporate the terms of human rights and other employment-related legislation: see *Parry Sound (District) Social Services Administration Board and O.P.S.E.U., Local 324* (2003), 230 D.L.R. (4th) 257 (S.C.C.), and the discussion in Chapter 1.2.3. Additionally, the labour relations legislation of a number of jurisdictions specifically empowers arbitrators to interpret and apply employment-related legislation, including human rights legislation. See s. 89(g) of the British Columbia *Labour Relations Code*, R.S.B.C. 1996, c. 244; s. 48(12)(j) of the Ontario *Labour Relations Act*, S.O. 1995, c. 1, Sch. A; and s. 43(1)(e) of the Nova Scotia *Trade Union Act*, R.S.N.S. 1989, c. 475.

Human rights legislation, as legislation of a quasi-constitutional order, is deemed to override collective agreement provisions to the contrary, and cannot be waived by an agreement of the parties to contract out of the statute. The jurisprudence on the validity of "deemed termination clauses" provides a good example of the paramountcy of human rights norms over the parties' negotiated agreement. The effect of such clauses is generally to extinguish an employee's seniority and to deem his or her employment automatically terminated after a specified period of absence from work. It is now clear that the application of a deemed termination clause to an employee whose absence is due to a "disability" as defined by human rights legislation is discriminatory and unenforceable: see *Syndicat des employés de l'Hôpital général de Montréal v. Centre universitaire de santé McGill, Hôpital général de Montréal*, in which the Quebec Court of Appeal held that the employer's failure to apply an individualized approach to the grievor's disability-related absenteeism was not consistent with the duty to accommodate: [2005] J.Q. No. 1724 (QL). In *Glengarry Industries/Chromalox Components and U.S.W.A., Local 6976* (1989), 3 L.A.C. (4th) 326, Arbitrator Hinnegan held that legislation prohibiting discrimination in employment based on disability protects an employee's right to challenge the legitimacy of his or her discharge in accordance with the just cause standard, notwithstanding an agreed-upon deemed discharge provision. The arbitrator's analysis and conclusions were subsequently affirmed by the Ontario Divisional Court in *O.N.A. v. Etobicoke General Hospital* (1993), 104 D.L.R. (4th) 379.

In *Maple Leaf Meats Inc. v. U.F.C.W., Local 175/633*, [2001] O.J. No. 2739 (QL), the Ontario Divisional Court made it clear that post-discharge evidence that an employee could *not* have been accommodated will not save a discharge if the employer at the time acted solely on the basis of a deemed termination provision. Conversely, if the evidence demonstrates that the employer fully assessed the possibility of accommodation prior to its resort to discharge, reference to the deemed termination provision will not be fatal to the discharge: *C.E.P., Local 212 v. Domtar Fine Papers Inc.*, [2000] O.J. No. 2018 (Div. Ct.). See also the discussion of "last chance agreements" in Chapter 14.5.

Another important aspect of the paramountcy of human rights legislation relates to the choice of remedy. In *Ontario Power Generation Inc. and Society of Energy Professionals* (2000), 92 L.A.C. (4th) 240, Arbitrator Michel Picher noted that the courts have not in every instance ordered that a discriminatory benefit provision be "read up" so as to apply to everyone equally, as the resulting cost may be so inconsistent with the scope of the parties' original bargain as to render such a remedy inappropriate. In that case, the arbitrator struck down a collective agreement clause providing that supplementary unemployment benefits (SUB) were payable to adoptive parents, but not to birth parents. However, he rejected the union's request that the employer be required to make SUB payments equally available to adoptive parents and biological parents, since this would expose the employer to substantial costs which neither party anticipated when they concluded the collective agreement. In the result, Arbitrator Picher ordered the parties to renegotiate the terms of the agreement so as to make it consistent with the applicable human rights legislation. (See also the cases referred to in Chapter 23.3.2.)

Arbitrator Veniot, in *Izaak Walton Killam Health Centre and N.S.N.U. (Bennett)* (2003), 120 L.A.C. (4th) 353, similarly took into account the relative disparity in size between the group initially bargained for and the group now sought to be included, and rejected the union's request for a "read-in" remedy. Instead, he ordered a remedy virtually identical to that fashioned by Arbitrator Picher in *Ontario Power Generation, supra*. At the same time, he commented that a "nullification" remedy, *i.e.* striking down the discriminatory benefit in its entirety — otherwise referred to as "equality with a vengeance" — was hardly in keeping with the advancement of the protections provided by human rights legislation and the *Charter.*

14.3.2   Definition of "Disability"

As the human rights legislation of most jurisdictions in Canada explicitly prohibits discrimination based on the mere perception of disability or handicap, an employee is not required to show an actual functional inability to perform the work as a precondition of invoking the legislation. The definition of "disability" found in s. 10(1) of the Ontario *Human Rights Code*, R.S.O. 1990, c. H.19, for example, enumerates a series of injuries, disabilities and disorders, while s. 10(3) prohibits discrimination against an individual who "has or has had, or is believed to have or have had" a disability, thus making explicit that disability has a subjective component rooted in the attitudes or preconceptions of others as well as an objective component based on empirical medical evidence. Where, however, the applicable legislation does not contain an express stipulation to this effect, the existence of a right to be free from discrimination because of a subjective perception of disability has been less clear. In fact, a number of decisions in the United States hold that a claimant who cannot demonstrate actual physical or mental impairment does not attract the protection of human rights enactments: see *Sutton v. United Air Lines Inc.*, 527 U.S. 471 (1999).

In Canada, this issue has been definitively resolved by the Supreme Court in *Québec (Commission des droits de la personne et des droits de la jeunesse) v. Montreal (City)* (2000), 185 D.L.R. (4th) 385 (S.C.C.). The City of Montreal refused to hire M as a gardener-horticulturalist because the pre-employment medical exam revealed an anomaly in her spinal column. The City of Boisbriand dismissed T from his position as a police officer because he suffered from Crohn's disease. The medical evidence in each case indicated that the individual could perform the normal duties of the position in question, and had no functional limitations. Finding that the employer's misconceptions were based on precisely the kind of prejudice and stereotyping that human rights codes were designed to eliminate, the Court affirmed the judgment of the Quebec Court of Appeal, remitting the complaints to the province's Human Rights Tribunal for reconsideration.

The Supreme Court of Canada's broad approach to the definition of disability or handicap is meant to ensure that the fundamental objectives of human rights legislation are met. At the same time, however, the Supreme Court in *Montreal (City)* pointed out that such legislation was never intended to include protection for what it described as mere "personal characteristics or 'normal' ailments". As an Ontario board of inquiry stated in *Ouimette v. Lily Cups Ltd.* (1990), 12 C.H.R.R. D/19, the result of adopting too low a threshold, whereby the definition of disability would extend to common, everyday illnesses, would be to detract from the "high purpose" which the legislation was designed to serve (at para. 67).

This point was explored in greater detail by Justice Cameron of the Newfoundland and Labrador Court of Appeal in *Evans v. Health Care Corp. of St. John's* (2003), 223 Nfld. & P.E.I.R. 1. The central issue in *Evans* was whether "disparate, unrelated and temporary episodes of injury or illness", resulting in a poor attendance record, constituted a "physical disability" within the meaning of the province's *Human Rights Code*, R.S.N.L. 1990, c. H-14. The Court held that, on the face of the record alone, such transient illnesses did not establish the existence of a disability. While the complainant had from time to time been incapable of working due to sickness, there was no evidence of a pattern of illness or injury which would indicate the degree of permanence and impairment necessary to prove a disability. However, the Court noted, "it may be possible that use of sick leave demonstrates a frailty of health which may result in [a finding of] a disability" (at p. 10).

The latter decision may be at odds with the Supreme Court of Canada's holding in *Montreal (City)*, *supra*, that the absence of functional limitations in employment is not determinative. Moreover, the Supreme Court stated, human rights legislation "prohibits discrimination based on the actual or perceived possibility that an individual may develop a handicap in the future" (at p. 415). In addition, while courts and tribunals have posited that the term "disability" should not be interpreted so broadly as to trivialize the purpose of the legislation, the fact that an impairment is temporary in nature has not in every case been held to bar a claim: see, for example, *Shirley v. Eecol Electric (Sask.) Ltd.* (2001), 39 C.H.R.R. D/168 (Sask. H.R. Bd. of Inquiry).

14.3.3 *Bona Fide* Occupational Requirements: The Effect of *Meiorin*

In applying human rights legislation to workplace rules and employer decisions, the courts until recently maintained a distinction between "direct" and "indirect" (or "constructive" or "adverse-effect") discrimination. "Direct" discrimination denoted discrimination that was open and intentional. If a court or tribunal upheld the complaint, the normal remedy was that the discriminatory qualification, requirement or rule was struck down. Confronted with an allegation of direct discrimination, the defence open to the employer was that the impugned standard constituted a *bona fide* occupational requirement. In the case of disabled employees who brought a complaint of work-related discrimination, the job requirements most often advanced by the employer as being *bona fide* occupational qualifications have been regular attendance at work and the performance of heavy duties alleged to be essential to the position. "Indirect" discrimination, by contrast, referred to a workplace rule or qualification which on its face was seemingly "neutral" (that is, non-discriminatory), but which had the effect of excluding or putting at a disadvantage employees identified by a prohibited ground of discrimination (for example, sanctions under attendance rules that did not take into account absences caused by disability, or a requirement to work rotating weekend shifts where this affected employees for whom Saturday was a day of religious observance). In this situation, the courts held that the requirement remained valid, provided the employer discharged its duty of offering reasonable accommodation to individual employees on whom the requirement had a discriminatory impact.

In *British Columbia (Public Service Employee Relations Commission) v. B.C.G.E.U. (Meiorin)* (1999), 176 D.L.R. (4th) 1, however, a case which involved the exclusion of a female firefighter because, even though she could perform the job adequately, she failed an aerobic test that was based on standards set by male firefighters, the Supreme Court of Canada rejected the dichotomy between direct and indirect discrimination as the basis for interpreting human rights legislation, and in its place adopted a unified three-part test. In *any* case in which the complainant establishes that a workplace rule is *prima facie* discriminatory, the onus shifts to the employer to justify it as a *bona fide* occupational requirement, and to demonstrate on a balance of probabilities that:

(1) The impugned standard was adopted for a purpose rationally connected to the performance of the job. The focus at the first step is not on the validity of the particular standard, but rather on the validity of its more general purpose.

(2) The standard was adopted in an honest and good-faith belief that it was necessary to the fulfilment of that legitimate work-related purpose.

(3) The standard is reasonably necessary to the accomplishment of the purpose. To show that the standard is reasonably necessary, the employer must prove that it is impossible to accommodate individual employees sharing the characteristics of the complainant without undue hardship.

Thus, the concept of a *bona fide* occupational qualification now applies to all instances in which discrimination is alleged, while the duty to accommodate individual employees has been incorporated into the criteria by which the validity of the rule or standard is assessed.

To satisfy the third step of the three-part test, which relates to the reasonable necessity of the impugned rule or standard, the Court in *Meiorin* held that "it must be demonstrated that it is *impossible* to accommodate individual employees sharing the characteristics of the plaintiff" (at p. 25; emphasis added). In *Community Lifecare Inc. and O.N.A. (Clark)* (2001), 101 L.A.C. (4th) 87, Arbitrator Howe noted that in using the term "impossible" the Court meant to say no more than that the employee "cannot" be accommodated without undue hardship.

In its subsequent decision in *British Columbia (Superintendent of Motor Vehicles) v. British Columbia (Council of Human Rights) (Grismer)* (1999), 181 D.L.R. (4th) 385, the Supreme Court of Canada applied *Meiorin* to strike down a blanket rule denying a driver's licence to anyone who suffered from a particular eye condition which restricted visual acuity. Henceforth, the Court ruled, the provincial Superintendent of Motor Vehicles was required to test each applicant having this disability on an individual basis in order to determine whether he or she was able to meet highway safety standards.

In the arbitral forum, the principles set out in *Meiorin* were applied in *Toronto District School Board and C.U.P.E., Local 4400* (2003), 120 L.A.C. (4th) 395 (Howe), which dealt with an employer requirement that all employees classified as part-time cleaners be able to lift a 50-pound weight from floor to shoulder height. Expert evidence adduced at the hearing established that, because an average adult female can generate not more than 50-55 percent of the upper body strength of an average adult male, the requirement in question had the effect of disproportionately excluding female applicants. Arbitrator Howe held that the employer was under an onus to demonstrate that it could not adapt the job or otherwise accommodate individual employees without undue hardship. In this case, the arbitrator concluded that the evidence fell "far short" of meeting that onus, and directed the employer to cease applying the impugned lifting condition to employees and applicants.

In *Ronald C. MacGillivray Guest Home Corp. and C.U.P.E., Local 1562* (2004), 128 L.A.C. (4th) 225 (Veniot), the employer restricted an orderly position to male applicants only, in order to provide care to elderly residents (including retired priests) who were male, despite a provision in the collective agreement prohibiting discrimination. Arbitrator Veniot dismissed the grievance on the ground that gender was a *bona fide* occupational requirement, given the considerations of physical intimacy and personal dignity. Unless the collective agreement provides to the contrary, the arbitrator ruled, a standard "no discrimination" clause must be read as importing the same "*bona fide* occupational requirement*" exception as the *Human Rights Act*, R.S.N.S. 1989, c. 214.

Additional Reading

D.D. Carter, "The Arbitrator as Human Rights Adjudicator: Has *Meiorin* Made a Difference?" in K. Whitaker, J. Sack, M. Gunderson & R. Filion, eds., *Labour Arbitration Yearbook 2001-2002*, vol. I, p. 1; and companion articles by P. Meier; and E.J. McIntyre, K. Schucher & F. Faraday.

14.3.4 Order of Proceeding

In a case in which accommodation is sought, it is the individual, or his or her union, who must "make the first moves", as Arbitrator Barrett put it in *Brampton (City) and A.T.U., Local 1573* (1998), 75 L.A.C. (4th) 163 (see the discussion in Chapter 14.3.5). In *Brampton (City)*, this principle was applied to the procedural issue of which party ought to proceed first at the hearing of a grievance in which the employer was alleged to have discriminated against an employee on the ground of handicap. Relying on *Ontario (Human Rights Commission) v. Simpsons-Sears Ltd. (O'Malley)* (1985), 23 D.L.R. (4th) 321, a case in which the Supreme Court of Canada pointed out that the plaintiff in a civil proceeding is normally required to state a case for the defence to meet, the arbitrator held that it is incumbent upon the union to lead its evidence first. More specifically, the union bears the onus of establishing a *prima facie* case of discrimination — that the grievor has a disability (of which the employer was aware) and that it is the disability which prevents the grievor from performing his or her job — and also of identifying what abilities the grievor retains to perform other duties which the employer may reasonably have available.

While the onus of proceeding first in a discrimination case rests with the union, the facts pertaining to the employee's disability and consequent medical restrictions are often not in dispute. The only issue is the extent of the employer's obligation to accommodate those restrictions, and whether the employer has satisfied its obligation. In such cases, arbitrators have held, it makes more sense to require the employer to proceed first, as the party possessing the most knowledge with respect to current vacancies or the existence of jobs that could be performed by the employee with reasonable adjustment. This approach, where a *prima facie* case has been agreed to or otherwise established, was applied in *Unilever and Teamsters, Local 132* (2002), 106 L.A.C. (4th) 360 (Springate).

The question, therefore, will be whether on the undisputed facts the requisite elements of a *prima facie* case of discrimination have been established. In *Grand Erie School Board and O.S.S.T.F. (Stewart)*, [2004] O.L.A.A. No. 661 (QL) (Devlin), for example, the extent to which the grievor was disabled was very much in issue, and the union was directed to proceed first.

14.3.5   The Employee's Duty

Under federal and provincial human rights legislation, the employer is not permitted to dismiss a disabled employee for reasons related to disability unless it can show that accommodating the employee would cause undue hardship: *Central Alberta Dairy Pool v. Alberta (Human Rights Commission)* (1990), 72 D.L.R. (4th) 417 (S.C.C.). Although the focus of much of the caselaw has been the nature and extent of the employer's duty of accommodation (see Chapter 14.3.6), the legislation imposes duties on the union and the complainant as well, a subject on which the Supreme Court of Canada has commented extensively. In *Central Okanagan School District No. 23 v. Renaud* (1992), 95 D.L.R. (4th) 577, for example, the Court ruled that the union may be obligated to accept some modification of other employees' rights under the collective agreement if this is necessary to implement a reasonable accommodation proposal (see Chapter 14.3.7). Similarly, it has been held that an employee bears the onus of coming forward and identifying the nature of his or her handicap and any resulting medical restrictions, so as to facilitate a proper assessment of what accommodation is required. As the Supreme Court pointed out in *Renaud*, "the search for accommodation is a multi-party inquiry", in which the complainant has a duty "to assist in securing an appropriate accommodation".

Belleville General Hospital and S.E.I.U., Local 183 (1993), 37 L.A.C. (4th) 375 (Thorne) was a case in which a disabled employee had not met the duty to come forward and identify her needs, with particularly harsh consequences. Over the course of some nine years of poor attendance, the grievor consistently denied that she suffered from an ongoing medical problem which would impede regular attendance in the future. When the employer finally dismissed her, the union argued that the employer had failed to meet its duty to accommodate. The arbitrator held that, before the employer's duty of accommodation can arise, it is incumbent on the employee to identify his or her medical problems, and to indicate to the employer the nature of the accommodation which may be required. The grievor not having done that, the employer was not obligated to extend accommodation at the point of discharge.

The employee's failure to make appropriate medical disclosure had a similar consequence in *Jones v. Companion* (2002), 214 Nfld. & P.E.I.R. 183 (Nfld. and Labrador C.A.). Although the employee had provided a note from her physician confirming that she was absent from work for medical reasons, she refused to divulge the nature of her malady. The Newfoundland and Labrador Court of Appeal affirmed the reversal of an adjudicator's decision that the employee had been discriminated against. In the Court's opinion, "it is difficult to see how the employer can be faulted for failure to accommodate when it does not have sufficient information upon which to conclude that accommodation is necessary" (at p. 196). An employee with a disability may therefore have difficulty asserting both a right to be accommodated and a right to preserve the full privacy of his or her medical records.

The issue of pre-discharge disclosure by the employee has taken on added significance since the decision of the Supreme Court of Canada in *Cie minière Québec Cartier v. U.S.W.A., Local 6869* (1995), 125 D.L.R. (4th) 577 (S.C.C.), discussed in Chapter 7.1. Arbitrators now tend to frame the issue as whether the employee exhibited sufficiently clear symptoms that the employer should have been aware of a possible disability requiring accommodation. Where the employer is fixed with such constructive knowledge, arbitrators have held that the duty to accommodate arises prior to the employee's discharge and, consequently, that the decision in *Québec Cartier* will not be a bar to post-discharge evidence relating to the disability, or steps taken to recover therefrom: see *Brewers Distributor Ltd. and Brewery, Winery & Distillery Workers Union, Local 300* (1998), 76 L.A.C. (4th) 1 (Munroe), and the other cases cited in Chapter 7.1.

Denial of drug or alcohol addiction raises particularly perplexing issues, because denial is often one of the symptoms of the disease. Nonetheless, as Arbitrator Hood concluded in *Weyerhaeuser Saskatchewan Ltd. and I.W.A. – Canada, Local 1-184*, unreported, November 7, 2003, the obligation on an employer has its limits. Where the employer has repeatedly offered accommodation in the form of treatment, but the employee continues to deny the need for medical assistance or the existence of a problem, evidence of rehabilitation efforts after the discharge may be irrelevant. Additionally, as Arbitrator Jones has pointed out, it may be difficult for the employer to assume that an employee's use of alcohol or drugs is based on an addiction unless the employee acknowledges this or there exists other compelling evidence: *Suncor Energy Inc. and C.E.P., Local 707*, [2004] A.G.A.A. No. 35 (QL). The arbitrator upheld the dismissal of a longtime recreational pot smoker who tested positive for marijuana metabolites after being involved in a minor accident while driving a company truck. Because the grievor had always maintained that his off-duty drug use was not pathological, Arbitrator Jones ruled, he was unable to establish a *prima facie* case that the employer had discriminated against him on the basis of an actual or perceived disability.

As a further element of an employee's duty "to assist in securing an appropriate accommodation", the Supreme Court in *Renaud, supra*, noted that the search for accommodation does not require a "perfect" solution from the employee's point of view, and that an employee who has declined a reasonable offer may be barred from pressing a complaint. This principle was discussed and applied by Arbitrator Michel Picher in *CANPAR and U.S.W.A., Local 1976* (2000), 93 L.A.C. (4th) 208.

A similar point was made by the British Columbia Human Rights Tribunal in *Quackenbush v. Purves Ritchie Equipment Ltd.*, [2004] B.C.H.R.T.D. No. 10 (QL). An employee cannot insist on an "ideal" position when it is not reasonably available. A judge of the Alberta Court of Queen's Bench has gone even further, holding that once the employer had put forward a job that reasonably accommodated the employee's disability, the employee was under an obligation to accept it, whether it was a job that she liked or not. In the judge's view, the employer (the Alberta Department of the Solicitor General) was not required to search "every nook and cranny" of the public service in an effort to find a job that the employee liked better: *Anderson v. Alberta*, [2004] A.J. No. 1216 (QL).

Additional Reading

M. Lynk, "Disability and the Duty to Accommodate: An Arbitrator's Perspective" in K. Whitaker, J. Sack, M. Gunderson & R. Filion, eds., *Labour Arbitration Yearbook 2001-2002*, vol. I, p. 51; and companion articles by C.L. Peters and W.J. Johnson.

K. Swinton, "Disability and the Duty to Accommodate: An Academic Perspective" in W. Kaplan, J. Sack, M. Gunderson & R. Filion, eds., *Labour Arbitration Yearbook 1998*, p. 93; and companion articles by N.A. Eber, L. Marvy, G. Hopkinson and R. Murdock.

M.G. Picher, "The Duty to Accommodate at Arbitration: An Arbitrator's Perspective" in W. Kaplan, J. Sack, M. Gunderson & R. Filion, eds., *Labour Arbitration Yearbook 1996-97*, p. 211; and companion articles by K.W. Kort and E. McIntyre.

14.3.6   The Employer's Duty

Under Canadian human rights legislation, the obligation of the employer and the union to accommodate a disabled employee extends to the point of "undue hardship". The Supreme Court of Canada has emphasized that this is a rigorous standard, going significantly beyond the *de minimis* test adopted by the United States Supreme Court in *Trans World Airlines Inc. v. Hardison*, 432 U.S. 63 (1977). As Justice Sopinka set out in *Central Okanagan School District No. 23 v. Renaud* (1992), 95 D.L.R. (4th) 577, at p. 585 (S.C.C.):

> The *Hardison de minimis* test virtually removes the duty to accommodate and seems particularly inappropriate in the Canadian context. More than mere negligible effort is required to satisfy the duty to accommodate. The use of the term "undue" infers that some hardship is acceptable; it is only "undue" hardship that satisfies this test. The extent to which the discriminator must go to accommodate is limited by the words "reasonable" and "short of undue hardship". These are not independent criteria but are alternate ways of expressing the same concept. What constitutes reasonable measures is a question of fact and will vary with the circumstances of the case. Wilson J., in [*Central Alberta Dairy Pool v. Alberta (Human Rights Commission)* (1990), 72 D.L.R. (4th) 417 (S.C.C.)], listed factors that could be relevant to an appraisal of what amount of hardship was undue as:
>
> > . . . financial cost, disruption of a collective agreement, problems of morale of other employees, interchangeability of workforce and facilities. The size of the employer's operation may influence the assessment of whether a given financial cost is undue or the ease with which the workforce and facilities can be adapted to the circumstances. Where safety is at issue both the magnitude of the risk and the identity of those who bear it are relevant considerations.
>
> She went on to explain that: "This list is not intended to be exhaustive and the results which will obtain from a balancing of these factors against the right of the employee to be free from discrimination will necessarily vary from case to case".

How the duty to accommodate defines the scope of the inquiry that the employer must undertake has been the subject of numerous arbitration awards. Arbitrators have held that the employer is required to do more than simply satisfy itself that the employee cannot perform the essential duties of any of the jobs in the workplace as they are constituted *currently*. Rather, as indicated by Arbitrator Ponak in *Calgary District Hospital Group and U.N.A., Local 121-R* (1994), 41 L.A.C. (4th) 319, the employer is obliged to consider whether there are existing jobs whose essential duties could be "adjusted, modified or adapted" to enable the employee to continue his or her participation in the workplace.

In *United Air Lines and I.A.M.* (1993), 33 L.A.C. (4th) 89 (MacIntyre), the employer carried out a full survey of the workplace, but concluded unilaterally that the employee would not be able to cope for any substantial period of time. Allowing the employee's grievance, the arbitrator held that he should have been given a reasonable chance to demonstrate his ability. For a contrasting decision, see *U.N.A., Local 33 v. Capital Health Authority*, where the Alberta Court of Appeal held that the duty to accommodate did not require a hospital to train a disabled nurse to do a job for which she was not suited. In the Court's opinion, the arbitration board had sufficient evidence before it to conclude that the grievor had no reasonable chance of success in the position, even with training, and therefore the award denying the grievance was not unreasonable: [2005] 1 W.W.R. 595, leave to appeal to S.C.C. denied May 19, 2005.

Arbitrators have also held that the duty to accommodate represents a permanent obligation of the parties, and may well require more extensive measures than those provided under a temporary "work-hardening" program administered by the employer (although the same measures which, considered on a short-term basis, do not give rise to undue hardship, may do so in the context of a proposed permanent arrangement). Furthermore, a growing number of arbitrators have ruled that the employer is required to consider "bundling" discrete duties from different jobs so as to create a new permanent position which is within the employee's medical restrictions. Early awards seemed to speak against this approach: see *Hamilton Civic Hospitals and C.U.P.E., Local 794* (1994), 44 L.A.C. (4th) 31 (Kennedy), and *Better Beef Ltd. and U.F.C.W., Region 18* (1994), 42 L.A.C. (4th) 244 (Welling). In *Mount Sinai Hospital and O.N.A.* (1996), 54 L.A.C. (4th) 261, however, Arbitrator Richard Brown ruled that where no other accommodation is available, the employer must consider whether assigning the grievor to perform a bundle of duties which did not constitute an existing job would give rise to undue hardship. Both of the above propositions, regarding the ongoing nature of the duty to accommodate and the obligation to consider "bundling", were approved by Arbitrator Howe in *Community Lifecare Inc. and O.N.A. (Clark)* (2001), 101 L.A.C. (4th) 87.

In Alberta, Arbitrator Sims has also held that it is incumbent on the employer to consider "bundling" otherwise discrete duties into a new job: *Canada Safeway and U.F.C.W., Local 401* (2000), 89 L.A.C. (4th) 312. The arbitrator emphasized, however, that the proposed position must consist of duties that are "productive" within the employer's enterprise, to use the words of Arbitrator Kennedy in *Hamilton Civic Hospitals*, *supra*, and not merely "make-work". Arbitrator Sims commented as well that, depending on the size and nature of the workplace, there may be a limit, in practical terms, on the number of such reconstructed jobs which the employer can be expected to absorb. A proposed arrangement which is possible in theory may nonetheless give rise to undue hardship because the accommodative measures previously offered to other employees render further accommodation impossible.

For a discussion of the emerging arbitral consensus on the requirement, in appropriate cases, to consider the "bundling" of duties, see *Vancouver Shipyards Co. and Marine Shipbuilders, Local 506*, [2004] B.C.C.A.A.A. No. 151 (QL). Arbitrator Taylor concluded that, while the duty to accommodate may require the creation of a new position, the employer was not obligated to assign a disabled employee supernumerary or non-productive duties on a permanent basis. In that case, having accommodated the grievor in a "make-work job" for two years, the employer was held to have discharged its duty, and the grievance was dismissed. On the other hand, in *O.P.S.E.U. v. Ontario (Ministry of Public Safety and Security)*, [2004] O.J. No. 5481 (QL), the Ontario Divisional Court held that as long as an employee was doing modified work that clearly fell within his or her normal classification (albeit comprising only a portion of that classification), the employer was not entitled to create a new classification as a means of justifying a reduction in the employee's rate of pay. Such a course of action, in the Court's view, would not be an accommodation of the grievor's disability, but merely a "cost-reducing measure".

As the courts have recognized, the relative size of the employer is an important factor in determining the scope of accommodation that is considered reasonable. Where the employer is a small organization, its limited financial resources, as well as the lesser number of employees who must shoulder the burden of accommodation, may well result in a finding that the requested accommodation would create undue hardship. See *Community Unemployed Help Centre and C.U.P.E., Local 2348* (1997), 67 L.A.C. (4th) 33 (Freedman), and *Edgell v. Board of School Trustees, District No. 11* (1996), 97 C.L.L.C. ¶230-009 (B.C.C.H.R.). Similarly, in *Winpack Portion Packaging Ltd. and U.S.W.A. (Bai)*, [2003] O.L.A.A. No. 416 (QL), Arbitrator Pamela Picher dismissed a discrimination grievance asserting that the employer should have bundled light duties into a single, permanent job for the grievor. Under the Ontario *Human Rights Code*, R.S.O. 1990, c. H.19, the arbitrator noted, health and safety requirements (along with cost and outside sources of funding, if any) must be taken into account in assessing whether a proposed accommodation would give rise to undue hardship. In this case, she found, acceding to the union's request would preclude the employer from temporarily assigning light duties to other injured employees, thereby posing a risk to *their* health and safety.

It should be noted that, in assessing undue hardship, arbitrators disagree as to whether they are restricted to the factors set out in the applicable human rights legislation. In *Ingersoll (Town) and London Civic Employees, Local 107* (2003), 122 L.A.C. (4th) 402, for example, Arbitrator Williamson concluded that the factors enumerated by the Ontario *Human Rights Code* were exhaustive. However, in *Bowater Canadian Forest Products Inc. and I.W.A., Local 2693*, [2003] O.L.A.A. No. 597 (QL), Arbitrator Surdykowski expressed the opposite view. He also noted that the "Policy and Guidelines on Disability and the Duty to Accommodate", issued by Ontario's Human Rights Commission, did not limit arbitrators either.

In any event, the caselaw in this area is evolving, and adjudicators have shown an increasing inclination to afford protection to disabled employees, whether at the expense of the employer (within the limits of undue hardship), or of other, non-disabled employees in the workplace. Arbitrator Pamela Chapman provides a detailed overview of this evolution in *Mohawk Council of Akwesasne and Ahkwesahsne Police Ass'n (White)* (2003), 122 L.A.C. (4th) 161, where a preliminary issue arose as to whether there existed a legal obligation on the employer to consider creating a vacancy for a disabled employee by transferring an incumbent employee from his or her position. In the arbitrator's opinion, it could no longer be said that there is a "rule" which relieves the employer from the requirement to undertake such an inquiry; rather, each case must be examined on its own facts. However, it should be noted that no evidence had yet been heard as to the availability of alternative methods of accommodation, and arbitrators are likely to take the view that displacing an incumbent employee should be considered only as a last resort.

Mental disabilities often raise more difficult problems for employers than physical disabilities. The nature and extent of the employer's duty to accommodate mentally disabled employees was thoroughly canvassed in *Shuswap Lake General Hospital and B.C.N.U. (Lockie)*, [2002] B.C.C.A.A.A. No. 21 (QL) (Gordon). Applying the Supreme Court of Canada's judgment in *Meiorin* (see Chapter 14.3.3), the arbitrator concluded that the employer had failed to consider all the steps that were reasonably available to permit the grievor to continue functioning as a nurse without creating undue risk to patients or other staff. The grievor was therefore ordered reinstated, subject to strict conditions designed to ensure compliance with her treatment regimen, and to provide an opportunity for early detection of any signs of relapse.

The *Oak Bay Marina* case, discussed by Arbitrator Gordon in *Shuswap Lake General Hospital*, dealt with the extent of an employer's obligation to conduct an accommodation inquiry in the face of strong evidence of mental illness. The complainant in that case was a seasonal fishing guide whose work regularly took him into dangerous waters, with sole responsibility for the safety of his party. After the complainant had been diagnosed with bipolar disorder, he exhibited erratic behaviour, and the employer, acting on the basis of its own observations, declined to rehire him. The British Columbia Human Rights

Tribunal upheld the complaint, finding that the employer did not have "any accurate information about bipolar disorder or the likelihood of a relapse". On judicial review, the courts ruled that the province's *Human Rights Code*, R.S.B.C. 1996, c. 210, did not require an "already informed" employer to undertake a process of further investigation, and referred the case back to the Tribunal for rehearing on the issue of accommodation: *Oak Bay Marina Ltd. v. British Columbia (Human Rights Commission)* (2002), 217 D.L.R. (4th) 747 (B.C.C.A.). In the result, however, the Tribunal found that the employer was not, in fact, "already informed", as it had failed to educate itself about the risk resulting from the complainant's bipolar disorder, or to consider alternative positions in which he could be accommodated: *Gordy v. Oak Bay Marine Management Ltd.*, [2004] B.C.H.R.T.D. No. 180 (QL).

In *Canada Post Corp. and C.U.P.W. (Racky)*, [2003] C.L.A.D. No. 624 (QL), Arbitrator Pamela Picher focused on the depressive effects of a continuous pattern of sexual harassment by the grievor's supervisor and held that, quite apart from the appropriate remedies flowing from the sexual harassment itself, the employer was required by its duty of accommodation to offer the grievor a transfer to another facility.

The principles relating to workplace accommodation are developing with respect to the protected ground of family status as well. In *H.S.A.B.C. v. Campbell River & North Island Transition Society* (2004), 240 D.L.R. (4th) 479, the British Columbia Court of Appeal rejected the proposition that the mere fact of a conflict between family responsibilities and work-related requirements is sufficient to establish discrimination on the basis of family status. On the other hand, the Court held, quashing the decision of an arbitrator, where there is a "serious interference with a substantial parental or other family duty or obligation", an employee is entitled to the protection of human rights legislation. For further discussion, see Chapter 21.4.

Additional Reading

M. Lynk, "Disability and the Duty to Accommodate: An Arbitrator's Perspective" in K. Whitaker, J. Sack, M. Gunderson & R. Filion, eds., *Labour Arbitration Yearbook 2001-2002*, vol. I, p. 51; and companion articles by C.L. Peters and W.J. Johnson.

K. Swinton, "Disability and the Duty to Accommodate: An Academic Perspective" in W. Kaplan, J. Sack, M. Gunderson & R. Filion, eds., *Labour Arbitration Yearbook 1998*, p. 93; and companion articles by N.A. Eber, L. Marvy, G. Hopkinson and R. Murdock.

M.G. Picher, "The Duty to Accommodate at Arbitration: An Arbitrator's Perspective" in W. Kaplan, J. Sack, M. Gunderson & R. Filion, eds., *Labour Arbitration Yearbook 1996-97*, p. 211; and companion articles by K.W. Kort and E. McIntyre.

14.3.7 The Union's Duty

In *Central Okanagan School District No. 23 v. Renaud* (1992), 95 D.L.R. (4th) 577, the Supreme Court of Canada made it clear that a union has an obligation to assist in the search for appropriate accommodation, and this may in some instances require the union to waive its rights under the collective agreement. In the words of the Ontario Divisional Court in *O.P.E.I.U., Local 267 v. Domtar Inc.* (1992), 8 O.R. (3d) 65: "Discrimination in the workplace is everybody's business. There can be no hierarchy of responsibility" (at p. 72). In that case, the union was held jointly liable in damages with the employer for its failure to waive certain provisions in the collective agreement, thereby erecting a bar to the complainant's continued employment.

Similarly, in a recent case involving a complaint brought by a disabled employee, the Saskatchewan Human Rights Tribunal ordered both the union and the employer to "amend [their] seniority standards and division boundary standards to respond to the needs of people with disabilities", and apportioned damages for loss of dignity and hurt feelings: *Kivela v. C.U.P.E., Local 21 (No. 1)* (2003), 47 C.H.R.R. D/442, at para. 125. In *Bubb-Clarke v. Toronto Transit Commission (No. 3)* (2002), 42 C.H.R.R. D/326 (Ont. Bd. of Inquiry), it was only the union that stood in the way of allowing a disabled employee to transfer his seniority to a department in which he could have been accommodated. As a result, the full measure of $22,000 in damages was awarded against the union. For further discussion of the union's duty to accommodate in the context of seniority rights, see Chapter 18.3.

These principles have been extended to contract negotiations as well. In *Canada Safeway Ltd. v. Alberta (Human Rights and Citizenship Commission)* (2003), 231 D.L.R. (4th) 285 (Alta. C.A.), leave to appeal to S.C.C. denied May 6, 2004, the union was held jointly liable with the employer for negotiating a buyout program that discriminated on the ground of disability. Under the terms of the program, employees were eligible for a lump-sum payment, provided they had worked some hours during the preceding 52 weeks. A number of employees were excluded from the program because they had been absent from work for at least 52 weeks due to illness or injury. In the Alberta Court of Appeal's view, the union had participated in the creation of the buyout program, and was equally responsible for its discriminatory impact. In any event, the Court held, the union had not made reasonable efforts "to remove or prevent the discriminatory effects of the buyout on the complainants" (at p. 300).

In a case in which the union had agreed with the employer to limit preferential hiring of students to those aged 24 or under, a human rights board of inquiry concluded that the union was jointly liable for engaging in age discrimination: *Mayo v. Iron Ore Co. of Canada* (2002), 43 C.H.R.R. D/65 (Nfld. and Labrador Bd. of Inquiry).

Additional Reading

M. Lynk, "Disability and the Duty to Accommodate: An Arbitrator's Perspective" in K. Whitaker, J. Sack, M. Gunderson & R. Filion, eds., *Labour Arbitration Yearbook 2001-2002*, vol. I, p. 51; and companion articles by C.L. Peters and W.J. Johnson.

K. Swinton, "Disability and the Duty to Accommodate: An Academic Perspective" in W. Kaplan, J. Sack, M. Gunderson & R. Filion, eds., *Labour Arbitration Yearbook 1998*, p. 93; and companion articles by N.A. Eber, L. Marvy, G. Hopkinson and R. Murdock.

M.G. Picher, "The Duty to Accommodate at Arbitration: An Arbitrator's Perspective" in W. Kaplan, J. Sack, M. Gunderson & R. Filion, eds., *Labour Arbitration Yearbook 1996-97*, p. 211; and companion articles by K.W. Kort and E. McIntyre.

14.3.8   Accommodation outside the Bargaining Unit

Because of the benefits which attend membership in the bargaining unit, arbitrators have ruled that the employer must first exhaust its duty of reasonable accommodation within the bargaining unit before contemplating the possibilities for accommodation outside the bargaining unit: see *Mount Sinai Hospital and O.N.A. (Natividad)* (1997), 66 L.A.C. (4th) 221 (Emrich). Arbitrators, however, have been cautious about assuming the jurisdiction to require employers to explore opportunities for accommodation outside the bargaining unit in circumstances where none of the positions inside the unit is suitable. Nonetheless, there have been decisions providing explicit support for the existence of such jurisdiction: see the references in *Dearness Home (City of London) and C.L.C., Local 102*, unreported, September 17, 2001 (Mitchnick).

Where the search does lead to a position that is outside the bargaining unit, the secondary question becomes whether, as part of the accommodation, the employer is required to extend the terms and conditions of the collective agreement to the non-bargaining unit position. Arbitrators who have considered this issue have generally indicated that employees accommodated in an excluded position are not entitled to retain their status as members of the bargaining unit: see *West Park Hospital and O.N.A.* (1996), 55 L.A.C. (4th) 78 (Emrich); and *Interlink Freight Services and T.C.U.* (1996), 55 L.A.C. (4th) 289 (M.G. Picher).

These issues were considered in *Kelowna (City) and C.U.P.E., Local 338*, [2003] B.C.C.A.A.A. No. 272 (QL), where Arbitrator Lanyon ruled that the "scope clause" of a collective agreement cannot be used to circumscribe the employer's obligations under the British Columbia *Human Rights Code*, R.S.B.C. 1996, c. 210. On the other hand, the arbitrator pointed out, the *Code* did not provide disabled employees with a "guarantee [of] full indemnification"; if, as in this case, the only suitable position is one outside the bargaining unit, the employee seeking accommodation must accept that position based on its existing terms and conditions. Accordingly, Arbitrator Lanyon denied the union's demand that the position be included in the bargaining unit. At the same time, the arbitrator expressed the view that it would be discriminatory to deprive the grievor of his accumulated seniority pursuant to the "loss of seniority" provisions in the collective agreement.

In *Insurance Corp. of British Columbia and O.P.E.I.U., Local 378* (2003), 123 L.A.C. (4th) 422, Arbitrator Germaine held that it was discriminatory for the employer to refuse to allow a disabled employee who was able to work only four days a week to continue accruing seniority as a full-time rather than a part-time employee (whether having to continue providing full-time *benefits* would result in undue hardship to the employer was left to be determined later). A contrary view was taken by the Saskatchewan Court of Appeal in *Canada Safeway Ltd. v. R.W.D.S.U., Local 454* (2005), 257 Sask. R. 199, where the Court rejected as patently unreasonable the decision of an arbitrator who had come to a similar conclusion to that of Arbitrator Germaine. According to the Court of Appeal, the employer's decision to reclassify the worker as a part-time employee was not discriminatory because, in matters of compensation, "to distinguish among employees on the basis of whether and to what extent work has been performed does not contravene . . . equality principles" (at p. 202).

In *Queen's Regional Authority and I.U.O.E., Local 942* (1999), 78 L.A.C. (4th) 269 (Christie), the issue of the reasonableness of accommodation outside the bargaining unit was even more sharply defined, as the accommodation proposed by the employer involved placing a handicapped employee in another bargaining unit represented by a different union. Allowing a grievance filed by the competing union, Arbitrator Christie held that the duty of accommodation extends across bargaining unit lines only in strictly limited circumstances, given the potential disruption to the other unit. Furthermore, the Ontario Divisional Court has quashed an arbitrator's award holding that a police board was entitled to place disabled police officers into vacant positions in the force's civilian bargaining unit, in violation of the posting provisions under the collective agreement. The Court ruled that the arbitrator erred in law by not first examining each disabled officer's individual circumstances to determine whether the officer could be accommodated in the "uniform" (*i.e.* officers') bargaining unit without undue hardship: *Hamilton Police Ass'n v. Hamilton Police Services Board* (2005), 200 O.A.C. 7 (Div. Ct.). In another case, Arbitrator Barton concluded that the duty of accommodation did not go so far as to require the employer to offer a disabled employee a management position: *Canadian Waste Services and U.F.C.W., Local 175*, [2004] O.L.A.A. No. 383 (QL).

The relationship between the parties' duty to accommodate a disabled employee and the collective agreement rights of other employees, especially those connected with seniority, is further explored in Chapter 18.3.

14.3.9   Drug and Alcohol Addiction

Although the courts' recognition of substance abuse as a "disability" or "handicap" for the purposes of human rights legislation is relatively recent, arbitrators have long treated alcohol and drug addiction as diseases, in both legal and practical terms. In *British Columbia Telephone Co. and T.W.U.* (1978), 19 L.A.C. (2d) 98, Arbitrator Gall observed that a disciplinary approach based on the notion of fault was inappropriate, because substance abusers have very little control over their behaviour. Rather, misconduct related to alcoholism or drug addiction was more properly dealt with on the basis of the same principles underlying the arbitral approach to innocent absenteeism, with particular emphasis on the prognosis for change. Because of this stress on the employee's rehabilitative potential, the arbitrator ruled that the point at which the prognosis should be assessed is not limited to the date of the employer's decision to dismiss, but extends to the date of the hearing. The latter point is now subject to the application of *Cie minière Québec Cartier v. U.S.W.A., Local 6869* (1995), 125 D.L.R. (4th) 577 (S.C.C.), discussed in Chapter 7.1.

Where an employee's substance abuse can be said to be at the level of an addiction, the employee is now entitled to invoke the protection of human rights legislation. As discussed in Chapter 14.3.5, the courts have held that the employee in question is under an onus to identify the need for accommodation and to cooperate in the implementation of a reasonable accommodation arrangement. Meeting these obligations may create significant difficulties for an addicted employee, given the denial and lack of self-control which typically accompany alcoholism or drug abuse: see *Mitchell Island Forest Products Ltd. and I.W.A., Local 1-217* (1996), 60 L.A.C. (4th) 73. In that case, Arbitrator Blasina decided that the judgment of the Supreme Court of Canada in *Québec Cartier* did not preclude the reception of post-discharge evidence as to the employee's rehabilitation efforts, insofar as such evidence could be said to "shed light" on the reasonableness of the dismissal.

The characterization of drug or alcohol addiction as a disability or handicap, requiring accommodation to the point of undue hardship, is thus beyond dispute. A difficulty may nonetheless arise in assessing the extent to which the addiction is causally related to the misconduct in question, in the sense that it impaired the employee's judgment, or undermined his or her freedom of choice. This assessment, in turn, will determine whether the employee's behaviour should be viewed as "culpable" or "non-culpable". An important element in some adjudicators' reasoning has been to view alcoholism and drug dependency as treatable illnesses "which can be controlled through the effort and commitment of the victim": see the decision of the British Columbia Council of Human Rights in *Handfield v. North Thompson School District No. 26* (1995), 25 C.H.R.R. D/452, at para. 137. It is not in an employee's long-term interest, the Council noted in that case, to adopt an approach which allows him or her to evade responsibility for taking available measures to overcome the addiction.

In *Fraser Lake Sawmills Ltd. and I.W.A., Local 1-424* (2002), 2003 C.L.L.C. ¶220-041, a reconsideration panel of the British Columbia Labour Relations Board set aside an earlier Board decision holding that arbitrators, in deciding the extent to which a disabled employee should be held accountable for misconduct, were now required to apply the so-called "significant impairment" test. In accordance with this test, the arbitrator was called upon to make an initial determination as to whether the employee's judgment had been "significantly impaired" as a result of drug or alcohol addiction. If the answer to this threshold inquiry was "yes", the use of a non-culpable approach was mandatory. In the view of the reconsideration panel, the new test would create confusion, and unduly fetter the scope of the arbitrator's remedial discretion. Instead, the panel ruled, given the hybrid nature of the disease (*i.e.* it has both culpable and non-culpable elements), arbitrators should make a determination of the degree of culpability based on the circumstances of each case.

An issue that frequently arises in addiction cases is whether a "last-chance agreement" which the grievor entered into as a result of previous drug- or alcohol-related infractions is consistent with human rights legislation. In such cases, the arbitrator is generally required to assess whether the employer's actions, including the opportunity afforded the grievor in the last-chance agreement itself, constituted accommodation to the point of undue hardship. In *Slocan Group and Pulp, Paper & Woodworkers of Canada, Local 18* (2001), 97 L.A.C. (4th) 387, Arbitrator Taylor canvassed this issue at length, identifying the high potential for relapse inherent in the course of rehabilitation, and balancing it against the importance of enforcing parties' agreements. Although allowing the grievance on the particular facts of that case, the arbitrator affirmed that "compelling reasons" must exist to justify varying the consequences which would otherwise flow from a breach of a last-chance agreement.

For discussion of last chance-agreements generally, see Chapter 14.5.

Additional Reading

H.C. Jain & S. Muthuchidambaram, "Alcohol and Drugs in the Workplace: Problems and Responses" in W. Kaplan, J. Sack & M. Gunderson, eds., *Labour Arbitration Yearbook 1994-95*, p. 267.

J.E. Dorsey & S.D. Charlton, "Alcoholism, Drug Dependency and the Workplace" in W. Kaplan, J. Sack & M. Gunderson, eds., *Labour Arbitration Yearbook 1991*, vol. I, p. 69.

14.3.10   Human Rights Remedies

The Supreme Court of Canada, in *Weber v. Ontario Hydro* (1995), 125 D.L.R. (4th) 583, expressed the view that arbitrators, once properly seized of a matter, must have a broad range of remedial powers in order to avoid "a real deprivation of ultimate remedy", and to enable all aspects of a dispute to be dealt with in one proceeding. Thus, in addition to the remedies traditionally available at arbitration, arbitrators have begun in some instances to award damages in cases involving tort claims such as defamation and intentional infliction of mental harm. See Chapter 7.4.2, "*Weber* Damages", and Chapter 1.3 on *Weber* generally. Moreover, the labour relations legislation of several provinces and the federal jurisdiction was amended in the 1990s to give arbitrators express authority to interpret and apply human rights and other employment-related statutes: see, for example, s. 60(1)(a.1) of the *Canada Labour Code*, R.S.C. 1985, c. L-2, and s. 48(12)(j) of the Ontario *Labour Relations Act*, S.O. 1995, c. 1, Sch. A. As Arbitrator Joachim observed in *Waterloo Furniture Components and U.S.W.A., Local 7155*, [1999] O.L.A.A. No. 962 (QL), at para. 82, "it would make little sense to empower arbitrators to determine infringements under the *Human Rights Code*, but to deprive them of adequate power to remedy the effects of the discrimination".

The authority of arbitrators to apply statutes relating to employment has been further strengthened by the decision in *Parry Sound (District) Social Services Administration Board v. O.P.S.E.U., Local 324* (2003), 230 D.L.R. (4th) 257, where the Supreme Court of Canada held that the rights and obligations under such statutes are deemed to form part of every collective agreement. This wide-ranging mandate is subject only to the qualification that statutory provisions which are deemed "incompatible" with the statutory labour relations scheme are not incorporated in the collective agreement: *Isidore Garon Ltée v. Syndicat du Bois Ouvré de la Région de Québec Inc.* (2006), 262 D.L.R. (4th) 385. See Chapter 1.2.3. If arbitrators are to carry out the functions of the specialized tribunals which ordinarily administer human rights and other employment-related legislation, it can be expected that the claims heard at arbitration, as well as the resulting awards, may come to more closely reflect the provisions of the applicable statute and the statutory tribunal's caselaw.

As a consequence, it is important to note with care the variations that exist from jurisdiction to jurisdiction in the way in which the tribunal's remedial powers are articulated. With respect to "general damages", for example, the *Canadian Human Rights Act*, R.S.C. 1985, c. H-6, provides for a maximum award of $20,000 for "any pain and suffering that the victim experienced as a result of the discriminatory practice", plus additional damages to a maximum of $20,000 if the discriminator engaged in the practice "wilfully or recklessly". By contrast, under s. 41(1)(b) of the Ontario *Human Rights Code*, R.S.O. 1990, c. H.19, the maximum amount which can be awarded in cases involving wilful or reckless infliction of "mental anguish" is $10,000. Importantly, however, the Ontario provision also permits "compensation . . . for loss arising out of the infringement". In *Waterloo Furniture Components*, *supra*, Arbitrator Joachim noted that the term "loss" in s. 41(1)(b) has consistently been interpreted to include damages for loss of the right to be free from discrimination, and that this right has "intrinsic value". Furthermore, as the Ontario Divisional Court concluded in *Human Rights Commission (Ontario) v. Shelter Corp.* (2001), 143 O.A.C. 54, there is "no ceiling on the amount of general damages" available under the *Code* (at para. 43). Thus, in *Toronto (City) Board of Education v. Quereshi (No. 5)* (2003), 46 C.H.R.R. D/352, for example, the Ontario Human Rights Tribunal awarded $25,000 in general damages by way of compensation for infringement of the *Code*. Notably, the Tribunal also awarded general damages in the amount of $10,000 in recognition of the "personal expenses" incurred by the complainant, which included legal costs and disbursements.

Commenting on the widening gap in the awards for general damages between British Columbia and Ontario, the British Columbia Human Rights Tribunal noted in *Fenton v. Rona Revy Inc. (No. 2)*, 2004 50 C.H.R.R. D/419 that damages granted in the enforcement of human rights legislation must be sufficiently large to be effective. This approach to the calculation of damages, the Tribunal observed, was consistent with the "almost constitutional" nature of human rights.

Clearly, what the Tribunal in *Quereshi, supra*, has done is find a way, through an interpretation of the terms "loss" and "personal expenses", to provide an element of relief to a complainant in the nature of costs. Where no direct authority to award costs is contained in the statute, there has been some debate, particularly at the federal level, as to whether jurisdiction to do so derives from the general power to order compensation. The Canadian Human Rights Tribunal, however, now appears to have adopted a view similar to that of the Ontario Tribunal: see *Milano v. Triple K Transport Ltd.*, [2003] C.H.R.D. No. 23 (QL). On the reverse side of the coin, the British Columbia Human Rights Tribunal, which has been given express authority to award costs to *either* party, has ordered that a complainant pay a portion of the employer's costs after finding that she gave false testimony: see *Bains v. Metro College Inc. (No. 2)* (2004), 48 C.H.R.R. D/432. Similarly, in *Jeffrey v. Dofasco Inc. (No. 5)* (2004), 51 C.H.R.R. D/287, the Ontario Human Rights Tribunal ordered the province's Human Rights Commission to pay costs to the employer because the Commission had proceeded with a complaint ultimately found to be frivolous.

With respect to the specific monetary ceiling set out, for example, in the *Canadian Human Rights Act* ($20,000), the Canadian Human Rights Tribunal has stated that this upper limit is reserved "for the very worst of cases": see *Desormeaux v. Ottawa-Carleton Regional Transit Commission (No. 2)* (2003), 46 C.H.R.R. D/1, at para. 128. Adopting that approach, the Saskatchewan Court of Queen's Bench in *Country Leathers Manufacturing Ltd. v. Graham*, [2003] S.J. No. 610 (QL) ruled that the amount of the award must be based on an objective assessment of the employer's conduct, not simply on the complainant's reaction to it. An award at the high end ($3,500) was held, in that case, to be "wholly disproportionate to the error in the employer's conduct", and was reduced to $750.

At the same time, the expansion in the remedial powers of an arbitrator may provide some benefit to employers by reducing the number of duplicate proceedings in the arbitral and human rights fora. In *Young v. Coast Mountain Bus Co.* (2003), 47 C.H.R.R. D/1, for example, the British Columbia Human Rights Tribunal found that the more ample remedial authority now accorded to arbitrators was a relevant consideration in determining whether it was appropriate, in a given case, to exercise its statutory discretion to defer consideration of a complaint pending the outcome of another proceeding. Similarly, the expanding jurisdiction of arbitrators to grant human rights remedies may promote the policy objective of finality in litigation. Where an arbitrator has already considered and decided a matter, including the issue of appropriate remedy, statutory tribunals may be more inclined to treat the arbitrator's disposition of the case as *res judicata*, and therefore final. This would be in sharp contrast to the ruling in *Parisien v. Ottawa-Carleton Regional Transit Commission (No. 1)* (2002), 44 C.H.R.R. D/94, where the Canadian Human Rights Tribunal decided to hear a complaint of discrimination on the ground of disability, despite an arbitrator's ruling that the employer had just cause to terminate the complainant's employment because of innocent absenteeism (decision affirmed on this point: see *Desormeaux v. Ottawa-Carleton Regional Transit Commission*, [2005] F.C.J. No. 1647 (QL) (C.A.).

Additional Reading

M. Lynk & L. Slotnick, "Labour Arbitrators and Human Rights Remedies: The Final Frontier" in K. Whitaker, J. Sack, M. Gunderson & R. Filion, eds., *Labour Arbitration Yearbook 1999-2000*, vol. I, p. 23.

14.4   CERTIFICATION OF FITNESS

In a number of situations, most typically an employee's return to work after an incapacitating illness, there may be legitimate grounds for questioning the ability of the employee to perform his or her prior job. In his oft-cited decision in *Firestone Tire & Rubber Co. of Canada Ltd. and U.R.W., Local 113* (1973), 3 L.A.C. (2d) 12, at p. 13, Arbitrator Weatherill held that the employer "has both the entitlement and the obligation to satisfy itself as to the fitness of its employees to carry out the tasks to which they will be assigned". This award, however, also established the proposition that a demand for medical certification of fitness, or better certification than that tendered by the employee, is improper unless the employer has reasonable and probable grounds for questioning the employee's capacity to do the work.

The same requirement to show reasonable and probable grounds applies where the employer demands certification of mental fitness before permitting an employee to continue working or to return to work. See, for example, *British Columbia (Public Service Employee Relations Commission) and B.C.G.E.U. (Teixeira)* (1998), 72 L.A.C. (4th) 309 (Jackson).

In *Air Canada and I.A.M.*, unreported, October 5, 1998, Arbitrator Beck clarified the magnitude of the risk which the employer must prove in order to justify its refusal to permit an employee to return to work following illness or injury. The risk must be above average and immediate, and must relate to the employee's ability to perform his or her job effectively and safely. It is not for the employer to assert that the job will be detrimental to the employee's long-term health, as the assumption of risk in such circumstances is a choice for the *employee* to make.

Even where the employer is found to have reasonable grounds for questioning the medical certification provided by an employee, management is not entitled to require the employee to undergo examination by a physician of its own choosing, or even an independently-appointed physician, as a condition of being permitted to return to work, as to do so would infringe the employee's privacy rights. Rather, the employer's remedy is to continue to hold the employee off work until satisfactory medical evidence has been provided: *Masterfeeds and U.F.C.W., Local 1518* (2000), 92 L.A.C. (4th) 341 (Kinzie).

As with established arbitral principles respecting dismissal for innocent absenteeism, the earlier cases on the employer's right to require certification of "full" fitness from an employee must now be read in light of human rights legislation and the prohibition against discrimination on the basis of disability. In *Thermal Ceramics and U.S.W.A.* (1992), 30 L.A.C. (4th) 314 (Gray), for example, although the grievor's medical clearance was subject to certain restrictions, the employer was obligated to allow the grievor to return to work, since these restrictions could easily be accommodated in his old job.

In *Greater Toronto Airport Authority and P.S.A.C. (Tremblay)*, [2004] C.L.A.D. No. 50 (QL), Arbitrator Simmons recognized that the grievor's reluctance to divulge medical information was founded on privacy concerns. However, rejecting a claim that the employer had delayed the grievor's return to work by seeking unrestricted access to medical information, the arbitrator observed that there is a "price" to be paid for asserting a right to privacy in such circumstances. An employer, he ruled, is entitled to information from the treating physician in order to satisfy its legitimate interest in ensuring the employee's fitness to perform the assigned work.

Where a government employer is involved, a requirement that an employee undergo a medical examination by a practitioner not of his or her own choosing may also raise *Charter* issues. Addressing the constitutionality of mandatory referral for examination under the *School Act*, R.S.B.C. 1996, c. 412, the British Columbia Court of Appeal in a split decision issued on February 19,

2003 ruled that such form of intrusion, affecting only "economic" or employment rights, was not encompassed by the protections in s. 7 (the right to "life, liberty and security") or s. 8 (the right to be free from "unreasonable search or seizure") of the *Charter of Rights and Freedoms*: *School District No. 39 (Vancouver) v. B.C.T.F.* (2003), 224 D.L.R. (4th) 63 (B.C.C.A.).

Additional Reading

D.L. Larson, "The Use of Medical Evidence at Arbitration: An Arbitrator's Perspective" in K. Whitaker, J. Sack, M. Gunderson & R. Filion, eds., *Labour Arbitration Yearbook 1999-2000*, vol. II, p. 137; and companion articles by R.A. Macpherson, D.G. Palayew & H.C. Devine; and V.M. Lemieux.

14.5   LAST-CHANCE AGREEMENTS

Where an employee has been discharged for culpable or non-culpable reasons, including poor attendance, the parties often agree to settle the ensuing grievance by entering into what is known as a "last-chance agreement". Typically, the agreement makes the employee's reinstatement conditional on his or her meeting a number of conditions, such as maintaining specified levels of attendance in the future or refraining from the behaviour which led to the discharge. The parties may also stipulate that failure to adhere to any of the prescribed conditions will result in the employee's automatic termination, without recourse to the grievance procedure. Where, however, an employee's difficulty with attendance is due to a disability within the meaning of human rights legislation, the lawfulness or enforceability of the conditions must be assessed against the obligation of the employer not to discriminate.

The development of the law on this issue begins with the decision of the Ontario Divisional Court in *Ontario (Human Rights Commission) v. Gaines Pet Foods Corp.* (1993), 16 O.R. (3d) 290. In that case, the Court found that it was only because of an employee's prior absences, which had been caused by cancer, that the employer had imposed an attendance standard on her in the first place. The Court concluded that the condition was discriminatory and in violation of the Ontario *Human Rights Code*, R.S.O. 1990, c. H.19. Subsequently, in *O.P.S.E.U. v. Ontario (Minister of Community and Social Services) (Blackhall)* (1996), 89 O.A.C. 161 (Div. Ct.), an employee's discharge grievance was settled by a last-chance reinstatement agreement that required him to equal or to surpass the departmental attendance average. Both before and after his reinstatement, the employee's absences were due to a mental disorder, a handicap within the meaning of the *Code*. When the employer sought to enforce the terms of the agreement, the union challenged them on the basis that they were discriminatory. Following the reasoning in *Gaines*, the Court struck down the condition as unlawful and rescinded the employee's discharge.

These principles were reviewed and applied in *Fantom Technologies Inc. and U.S.W.A., Local 6444* (1998), 70 L.A.C. (4th) 241 (Beck), and *Ottawa-Carleton (Regional Municipality) and Ottawa-Carleton Public Employees Union, Local 503* (2000), 89 L.A.C. (4th) 412 (Mitchnick). Any adverse employer action linked to a disability, even where ostensibly founded on the employee's agreement, must meet the standard of lawfulness prescribed by the applicable human rights legislation. However, as noted in *Ottawa-Carleton*, the fact that a last-chance agreement imposes conditions connected directly to an employee's disability does not end the inquiry. Before such conditions will be held to violate the legislation, it must be established that the employer failed to accommodate the employee's disability to the point of undue hardship. In that regard, arbitrators have ruled, the terms of a last-chance agreement, together with the employer's past efforts to assist the employee in dealing with the disability, may themselves amount to reasonable accommodation. See *Toronto District School Board and C.U.P.E. (G. (P.))* (1999), 79 L.A.C. (4th) 365 (Knopf). Furthermore, to the extent that the employee retains an element of control in managing the disability — such as in cases involving drug or alcohol dependency — it has been emphasized that the employee is under a corresponding duty to take available steps towards rehabilitation. This obligation on the employee's part to uphold his or her "part of the bargain" was the focal point of the award in *Alcan Rolled Products Co. and U.S.W.A., Local 343* (1996), 56 L.A.C. (4th) 187 (Gray), and is discussed more fully in Chapter 14.3.9 (Alcohol and Drug Addiction).

In most cases involving a union challenge to the validity of a last-chance agreement, there is a tension between arbitrators' desire to respect settlements that the parties themselves have made and the statutory threshold imposed by human rights legislation. On the one hand, arbitrators are reluctant to interfere with such agreements because to do so would inhibit parties from fashioning their own resolution, and discourage employers from providing employees with a "last chance" at all. On the other hand, as the Supreme Court of Canada stated in *N.A.P.E. v. Newfoundland (Green Bay Health Care Centre)* (1996), 134 D.L.R. (4th) 1, at p. 9, "[h]uman rights legislation sets out a floor beneath which the parties cannot contract out". These competing considerations were discussed by Arbitrator Randy Levinson in *Kimberly-Clark Forest Products Inc. and P.A.C.E., Local 7-0665* (2003), 115 L.A.C. (4th) 344. In that case, applying the three-fold test set out by the Supreme Court of Canada in *British Columbia (Public Service Employee Relations Commission) v. B.C.G.E.U. (Meiorin)* (1999), 176 D.L.R. (4th) 1 (see Chapter 14.3.3), the arbitrator framed the issue as whether the conditions imposed by the last-chance agreement were "*bona fide* occupational requirements", *i.e.* whether they were proportional to the grievor's needs. On this basis, the arbitrator upheld requirements for:

(1) total abstinence from marijuana for a prescribed period;

(2) random drug testing without notice; and

(3) automatic termination of employment for use of non-prescription drugs.

As Arbitrator Craven observed in *York Region District School Board and C.U.P.E., Local 1196* (2004), 128 L.A.C. (4th) 317, a voluntary agreement entered into by the parties, recognizing termination of employment as the appropriate consequence of a further breach, constitutes a "high hurdle" for the union to surmount in convincing an arbitrator to grant relief. Nonetheless, the parties' stipulations as to the appropriate penalty, or as to whether the agreement itself represents "reasonable accommodation", cannot override the requirements of the legislation. In the words of the Canadian Human Rights Tribunal in *Milazzo v. Autocar Connaisseur Inc. (No. 3)* (2005), 52 C.H.R.R. D/15, at para. 33:

> The fact that the parties have agreed to a "last-chance agreement" which states that they have decided that it would be unreasonable for the employer to further accommodate the employee beyond the first accommodation and that any further accommodation by the employer would be undue hardship under the *Canadian Human Rights Act*, "does not, of itself, confirm whether there has been sufficient compliance with the duty of accommodation established under human rights legislation of general application, legislation which the parties cannot contract out of": *Canadian Pacific Railway Co. and Canadian Council of Railway Operating Unions (U.T.U.)* (2002), C.R.O.A. No. 3269 (M.G. Picher).

Thus, the key inquiry is whether, taking into account *all* of the employer's efforts, the employer can be said, upon entering the last-chance agreement, to have met its duty of accommodation.

The decision in *Brewery, Beverage and Soft Drink Workers, Local 250 v. Labatt's Alberta Brewery* (1996), 96 C.L.L.C. ¶210-035 (Alta. C.A.), which appeared to recognize the primacy of private agreements over legislation, even in the area of human rights, has led some to argue that the law of Alberta may be different from that of Ontario and other jurisdictions. Arbitrator Ponak refuted this suggestion in *Edmonton (City) and A.T.U., Local 569* (2003), 121 L.A.C. (4th) 289, noting that the issue in *Labatt's Alberta Brewery* was put to the Court on narrow jurisdictional grounds. In his opinion, an arbitrator's right and duty to apply the mandatory requirements of human rights legislation can no longer be in question after the Supreme Court of Canada's decisions in *N.A.P.E. v. Newfoundland, supra,* and *Parry Sound (District) Social Services Administration Board v. O.P.S.E.U., Local 324* (2003), 230 D.L.R. (4th) 257 (see Chapter 1.2.3). The arbitrator found that there has in fact been no difference in the approach taken by arbitrators. In each case, regardless of the jurisdiction in which the case arose, the evidence must establish that the terms of a last-chance agreement providing for the automatic termination of employment are consistent with the employer's duty to accommodate the employee's disability to the point of undue hardship.

The British Columbia Court of Appeal, in *C.U.P.W. v. Canada Post Corp.*, [2001] B.C.J. No. 680 (QL), has similarly ruled that conditions imposed by an arbitrator providing for an employee's reinstatement on a "last chance" basis must satisfy the test for a *bona fide* occupational requirement.

Finally, it should be noted that, where the performance issues dealt with in a last-chance agreement do not relate to a disability or other protected ground, no conflict with human rights legislation arises in giving effect to the parties' agreement: see, for example, *Westfair Foods Ltd. and U.F.C.W., Local 247*, [2004] B.C.C.A.A.A. No. 273 (QL) (Hickling).

Additional Reading

O.V. Gray, "Attendance Management and 'Last Chance' Agreements: An Arbitrator's Perspective" in K. Whitaker, J. Sack, M. Gunderson & R. Filion, eds., *Labour Arbitration Yearbook 1999-2000*, vol. I, p. 181; and companion articles by E.L. Stringer & R. Anstruther, and R.A. Pink & L.D. Veinotte.

14.6 ATTENDANCE MANAGEMENT PROGRAMS

An increasingly common employer response to the problem of excessive absenteeism has been the establishment of an attendance or absenteeism management program. Sometimes developed in consultation with the union, such programs set out benchmarks identifying a threshold level of absenteeism which draws employees into the program, as well as a procedure for counselling the employees and discussing any problems, and measures that could be taken to ameliorate the situation. Typically, the program establishes a series of steps, involving meetings with higher levels of management, which reflect the escalating seriousness with which the employer views the problem, and which may result in warnings to the employee that he or she may face dismissal unless there is an improvement in attendance. The establishment of an attendance management program falls within the employer's residual rights to manage the enterprise, in the sense that the employer has the right to dismiss an employee for innocent absenteeism (see Chapter 14.1). Thus, each step of the program is seen as fulfilling the requirement that, even in the case of non-disciplinary discharge, an employee is entitled to notice that his or her absenteeism is unacceptable, and to have the opportunity to effect an improvement. Reflecting the arbitral principles applicable to innocent absenteeism generally, the caselaw on attendance management programs also indicates that employees enjoy less protection from dismissal where their absenteeism is of the short-term, intermittent type, or where there is no single, accommodatable cause for the absenteeism.

In *Scarborough (City) and Scarborough Firefighters'Ass'n, Local 626*, unreported, June 2, 1995, Arbitrator Mitchnick set out the terms of a variety of attendance policies whose validity has been upheld, and distilled from the caselaw a number of principles:

(1) If the policy purports to rely on purely objective or numerical criteria, that is, the number of days or incidents of absence, it must not mix culpable absences with non-culpable absences.

(2) Such objective criteria cannot be arbitrary, and must be defensible as a reasonable indicator of a problem with a particular employee's level of attendance.

(3) The various steps of the monitoring or counselling program must not be applied mechanically, that is, without due consideration of the explanation put forward for the employee's unusually high level of absenteeism.

(4) Notwithstanding the appropriateness of the program and the employer's compliance with its obligations at every step, the employer's right to invoke the final step of dismissal remains subject to the duty to accommodate a recognized disability to the point of undue hardship.

A comprehensive review of the caselaw was undertaken in *Health Employers'Ass'n of British Columbia and H.E.U.*, 2002 C.L.L.C. ¶220-021, in which the British Columbia Labour Relations Board emphasized that an attendance management program that purports to focus on non-culpable absenteeism must not appear in its essence to be punitive or disciplinary. In the Board's view, while the concept of progressive discipline involving the imposition of suspensions has no place in addressing non-culpable absenteeism, the use of "progressively escalating responses" may well be appropriate as a means of bringing home to the employee the seriousness of the employer's concerns and the fact that, following each (unsuccessful) step, the employee moves closer to the "last resort" — the possibility of discharge. The Board also observed that characterizing a series of absences as non-culpable does not necessarily carry the implication that the employee is incapable of correcting the problem through, for example, lifestyle changes or medical treatment.

In an earlier, similarly comprehensive case, *Health Employers' Ass'n of British Columbia and H.E.U.* (1999), 54 Can. L.R.B.R. (2d) 96 (B.C.L.R.B.), the Board observed that the attendance management program in question was "intended to provide employees with an opportunity to make the employer aware of the non-culpable nature of their absences" (at p. 122). This "opportunity", however, can be a two-edged sword; a consistent failure to identify a health problem, or to ask for help with it, may preclude an employee from alleging discrimination after he or she has been dismissed pursuant to the program: see *Grand & Toy Ltd. and U.S.W.A., Local 919*, unreported, November 27, 2002 (Luborsky). The "failure to come forward" issue is discussed more fully in Chapter 14.3.5.

For a review of the distinction between counselling and discipline in the context of an attendance management policy, see *Oshawa (City) and C.U.P.E., Local 250* (1996), 56 L.A.C. (4th) 335. Arbitrator Brandt held that a counselling letter which advises an employee of the employer's concerns as to absenteeism, and indicates that a failure to improve attendance may result in discharge, is not in itself disciplinary, and cannot be the subject of a grievance.

The essential point to be noted is that, notwithstanding arbitrators' broad acceptance of attendance management plans when they are properly designed and administered, such plans do not displace the requirements of human rights legislation. Where an employee suffers from an identifiable disability, any decision to dismiss the employee pursuant to a plan will be struck down unless the employer has satisfied its overarching duty of accommodation to the point of undue hardship. In fact, in *Purolator Courier Ltd. and Teamsters, Local 31* (2000), 89 L.A.C. (4th) 129, one of the few amendments which Arbitrator Greyell insisted be made to the employer's program was the inclusion of an explicit statement that all its terms were subject to the applicable human rights code.

In *Hamilton (City) v. C.U.P.E., Local 5167*, [2003] O.J. No. 657 (QL), the Ontario Divisional Court considered whether it was appropriate to include, for the purposes of an attendance management program, periods of absence resulting from a workplace injury for which workers' compensation benefits were payable. The Court held that, while the employer was not precluded from including such absences in its tabulation of attendance statistics, it could not rely on them to justify discharge in the absence of evidence that the employee had been accommodated to the point of undue hardship. Furthermore, in a recent decision of Arbitrator Swan, it was held that the employer violated Ontario's *Employment Standards Act*, S.O. 2000, c. 41, when it used emergency leave days provided under that legislation to place an employee over an attendance plan threshold: *Natrel Inc. and Teamsters, Local 647*, [2004] O.L.A.A. No. 75 (QL). In *Cadbury-Trebor Allan Inc. and Retail Wholesale Canada, Local 462*, [2004] O.L.A.A. No. 269 (QL), Arbitrator Barton ordered that the attendance management policy be amended to make it clear to employees that the use of such statutory leave days did not constitute an "occurrence" under the policy.

Additional Reading

O.V. Gray, "Attendance Management and 'Last Chance' Agreements: An Arbitrator's Perspective" in K. Whitaker, J. Sack, M. Gunderson & R. Filion, eds., *Labour Arbitration Yearbook 1999-2000*, vol. I, p. 181; and companion articles by E.L. Stringer & R. Anstruther, and R.A. Pink & L.D. Veinotte.

D. Ish, "Absenteeism and Attendance Programs" in W. Kaplan, J. Sack & M. Gunderson, eds., *Labour Arbitration Yearbook 1994-95*, p. 249.

CHAPTER 15

OTHER FORMS OF SEPARATION

15.1   QUIT

The employer may challenge an employee's right to grieve the termination of his or her employment on the basis that the employee has voluntarily resigned. An employee who quits or resigns invokes a unilateral right to end the employment relationship, and for this reason foregoes the possibility of regaining his or her position through the application of the just cause standard. Whether or not the employee has in fact quit may therefore become a critical preliminary inquiry. All arbitral jurisprudence on the issue of what constitutes a "quit" devolves from *Anchor Cap & Closure Corp. of Canada Ltd. and U.E., Local 512* (1949), 1 L.A.C. 222, in which Arbitrator Finkelman held that the act of quitting a job has both a subjective and an objective element. That is, to be characterized as having voluntarily quit, an employee must first have resolved to do so, and then done something to carry this resolution into effect.

A summary of basic principles is set out in the award of Arbitrator Gray in *Wellesley Central Hospital and S.E.I.U., Local 204* (1996), 61 L.A.C. (4th) 433. He notes that the underlying rationale for the two-fold test is that resignations are often offered in the heat of the moment or at times of personal stress, and may not express the employee's true wishes. Arbitrators will therefore look to whether the employee has taken steps to carry the announcement of his or her resignation into effect, and in particular whether there is evidence of a continuing intention to resign following a reasonable cooling-off period. Where there is clear objective evidence of an intention to resign, Arbitrator Gray adds, the subjective element may nevertheless be vitiated by a finding that the employee was unable to form a conscious intent to resign because of duress, or anxiety, depression or other mental disorder. Arbitrator Gray makes the point, however, that proof of a genuine cognitive dysfunction, as opposed to mere poor judgment, is required in order to establish this form of defence.

The requirement for evidence of "significant cognitive impairment" was alleviated somewhat by Arbitrator Goodfellow in *Goodyear Canada Inc. and U.S.W.A., Local 189* (2002), 107 L.A.C. (4th) 289. In the arbitrator's view, while a mere "change of heart" will not suffice, a lack of intent to quit can be established by demonstrating that the resignation was the product of duress or emotional upset. In such cases, a critical circumstance may be the length of time it takes for the employee "to come to his or her senses".

The claim that a resignation was procured under duress was considered in *Save-On Foods and C.L.A.C. (Walker)* (1999), 82 L.A.C. (4th) 172, where Arbitrator Sims conducted a detailed review of the jurisprudence and identified four key questions:

(1) Did the employee have notice of the allegations which led the employer to demand his or her resignation?

(2) Did the employee have the benefit of consultation with a union representative?

(3) Did the employee have enough time to consider his or her options?

(4) Was the resignation proffered in the face of an employer threat to invoke criminal proceedings?

With respect to the latter point, the arbitrator noted that while the threat of criminal prosecution can legitimately be used to prompt a resignation, the employer must identify to the employee a "substantial basis" for the laying of charges before making such a threat.

One point consistently made by arbitrators is that taking a second job is not, *per se*, evidence of an intention to quit. *Prince Rupert Fishermen's Co-Operative Ass'n and U.F.A.W.U.* (1985), 19 L.A.C. (3d) 129 (Larson), however, stands for the proposition that failure to respond to a recall because of the demands of a second job may furnish evidence of a quit. Even where workers can be expected to have more than one job, as in sectors in which irregular or seasonal employment is the norm, an employee is not entitled to undertake responsibilities that are inconsistent with his or her obligations to the employer.

15.2 RETIREMENT

In *Bell Canada v. O.P.E.I.U., Local 131* (1973), 37 D.L.R. (3d) 561, at p. 566, the Supreme Court of Canada ruled that "[d]ismissal . . . and retirement on pension are . . . different and distinct concepts". Since then, it has been accepted that the just cause provisions of a collective agreement do not cover an employee who is subject to mandatory retirement, whether or not the employer provides its own pension plan. However, the right of management to impose a mandatory retirement policy is not unfettered. In *U.S.W.A., Local 6500 and O.P.E.I.U., Local 343* (1982), 8 L.A.C. (3d) 71, Arbitrator Swan set out various restrictions that may bear on management in the implementation of such a policy:

(1) restrictions in the general law, such as human rights legislation, relating to discrimination on the basis of age;

(2) restrictions expressed or implied by the collective agreement;

(3) a retirement policy must be introduced with adequate notice to affected employees; and

(4) the right to retire employees cannot be exercised in a manner that is arbitrary, discriminatory or in bad faith.

One of the key issues in *U.S.W.A., Local 6500* was the effect of the Ontario *Human Rights Code*, R.S.O. 1990, c. H.19, on the interpretation of a provision in the collective agreement prohibiting discrimination on the basis of age. Although s. 5(1) of the *Code* guarantees the right "to equal treatment with respect to employment" without discrimination because of age, the legislation (at that time) adopted a qualified definition of "age". According to s. 10(1), "age" meant "an age that is eighteen years or more and less than sixty-five years". As a result, the *Code* effectively permitted age discrimination in the form of mandatory retirement of employees who reached the age of 65. (See also s. 1 of the British Columbia *Human Rights Code*, R.S.B.C. 1996, c. 210; but compare s. 15(c) of the *Canadian Human Rights Act*, R.S.C. 1985, c. H-6.) The question before Arbitrator Swan was whether the prohibition in the collective agreement should be read as incorporating the limitations found in the *Code*. He held that, in the absence of an express stipulation adopting the statutory definition, the no-discrimination clause was not qualified in that manner. Such a qualification may, however, be imported into the clause when it is read in conjunction with the other provisions of the collective agreement, particularly those incorporating by reference the terms of an existing pension plan.

For a time, it appeared that some arbitrators, particularly in British Columbia, disagreed with Arbitrator Swan's conclusion that the prohibition against age discrimination in a collective agreement was not, without more, limited by the definition of "age" in the applicable human rights legislation. In *North Central Plywoods and Pulp, Paper & Woodworkers of Canada, Local 25* (2000), 88 L.A.C. (4th) 387, however, Arbitrator Kelleher found that this apparent difference in approaches was essentially fact-driven, and he distinguished those cases in which the mandatory retirement policy was already in effect when the no-discrimination clause was included in the collective agreement from those in which it was not. In the former situation, the arbitrator noted, it was reasonable to infer that the parties would not have agreed to a provision the effect of which was to render the policy unlawful; in the latter situation, no similar foundation for implying a limitation existed. This ruling is consistent with the Supreme Court of Canada's decision in *N.A.P.E. v. Newfoundland (Green Bay Health Centre)* (1996), 134 D.L.R. (4th) 1, holding that while human rights legislation sets out "a floor beneath which the parties cannot contract out", the union and the employer are free to negotiate increased protection against discrimination in their collective agreement.

In applying a no-discrimination clause, a question may arise as to whether the provision speaks to retirement as an issue of age discrimination at all. In *Haida Harbourside Inn and B.C.G.E.U.*, [2003] B.C.C.A.A.A. No. 257 (QL) (Kelleher), the provision in question prohibited discrimination "in the matter of . . . discharge or otherwise by reason of age". Arbitrator Kelleher considered two conflicting lines of authority as to whether "discharge or otherwise" should be interpreted to include retirement, finding in the case before him that it should (and that the statutory limitation of age 65 could not be implied into the clause).

Where the collective agreement does not include an express prohibition against discrimination because of age, the validity of a mandatory retirement policy falls to be determined on the basis of the other criteria identified by Arbitrator Swan in *U.S.W.A., Local 6500, supra*. Focusing in particular on the requirement that the policy not be arbitrary, discriminatory or unreasonable, Arbitrator Germaine has noted that it is permissible for an employer to allow discretionary exceptions. However, the application of such a discretion must also meet the test of reasonableness, or objective consistency: *Pacific Newspaper Group Inc. and C.E.P., Local 2000* (2003), 123 L.A.C. (4th) 209.

As the *U.S.W.A., Local 6500* case noted, where the retirement age stipulated by a mandatory retirement policy is under the statutory limit of 65, as often happens in police and fire departments, the policy must also qualify as a *bona fide* occupational requirement (BFOR) under the applicable human rights law. The issue of whether a policy can stand as a BFOR entails applying a subjective test as well as an objective test, both of which were reviewed in *Large v. Stratford (City)* (1995), 128 D.L.R. (4th) 193 (S.C.C.). A board of inquiry appointed under the Ontario *Human Rights Code* struck down a policy of the municipal police force requiring officers to retire at age 60. When the Ontario Divisional Court and the Court of Appeal upheld the board's ruling, the employer appealed to the Supreme Court of Canada. The Supreme Court allowed the appeal. With respect to the subjective test, the Court held, the employer must establish that the rule or policy was adopted in good faith for a valid reason, and without any ulterior purpose that would be contrary to the purposes of the legislation. Commenting on the objective test, the Court emphasized the necessity for satisfactory proof that it would be impractical to identify and exempt from the rule or policy those employees lacking the requisite characteristics. As the employer had met both tests, the Court concluded, the board of inquiry erred in considering whether the normal duties of a police officer could have been modified so as to permit reasonable accommodation on a case-by-case basis.

With respect to employers who are deemed to form part of "government" and are therefore subject to the *Canadian Charter of Rights and Freedoms*, a further issue has arisen as to whether a mandatory retirement policy violates the right to equality without discrimination because of age guaranteed by s. 15.

In a number of decisions, most notably *McKinney v. University of Guelph* (1990), 76 D.L.R. (4th) 545, the Supreme Court of Canada has upheld such policies as a reasonable limit on equality rights. The consistency with which the Court has reached this conclusion led some employers to argue that, provided the impugned policy was permissible under federal or provincial human rights legislation, the legality of the policy under the *Charter* was beyond question. However, in *Greater Vancouver Regional District and G.V.R.D.E.U.* (2000), 90 L.A.C. (4th) 93, Arbitrator Germaine engaged in a careful review of the decisions in *McKinney* and other cases, and held that the constitutionality of any mandatory retirement policy established by a government employer remains an open question, and must be determined on a case-by-case basis. On appeal, a majority of the British Columbia Court of Appeal affirmed the award: (2001), 206 D.L.R. (4th) 220.

The principle expressed in *Greater Vancouver Regional District* was applied in *British Columbia and B.C.G.E.U. (Wybert)* (2002), 113 L.A.C. (4th) 1. Arbitrator Glass affirmed that, where mandatory retirement is alleged to be justified under s. 1 of the *Charter* as a reasonable limit on an employee's right to be free from discrimination, the institutional or societal concerns raised by the employer must, in each case, be weighed against the severity and degree of infringement of s. 15 equality rights. The grievance was, nonetheless, denied.

A number of jurisdictions, including Manitoba, Quebec, Alberta, Ontario and Prince Edward Island, have introduced legislation abolishing mandatory retirement. In those provinces, if an employer wants to impose mandatory retirement at the age of 65, it must establish that the policy is a BFOR.

15.3   LOSS OF SENIORITY

Many collective agreements contain a clause stating that an employee "shall lose all seniority" in a number of specified situations, typically in the event of an unauthorized absence from work or an absence for which a valid explanation is not offered. Sometimes, the clause adds that the employee's "employment shall cease". The extent to which such "deemed termination" clauses, as they are known, are inconsistent with human rights legislation is discussed in Chapter 14.3.1. Where, however, the collective agreement does *not* specify that the penalty for a named offence is the loss of employment, there has been considerable confusion as to the precise meaning and effect of a loss of seniority. Some arbitrators, equating a loss of seniority with the termination of employment, have upheld the discharge of employees who were found to have committed the particular offence. Others, however, have held that without more explicit language, a contractual stipulation for the forfeiture of an employee's seniority is insufficient to bring the employment relationship itself to a close. In *Dwyer v. Chrysler Canada Ltd.* (1978), 87 D.L.R. (3d) 279, the Ontario Divisional Court put an end to the dichotomy in the caselaw, emphatically ruling that a clause providing for the loss of seniority cannot reasonably be interpreted as effecting discharge.

In the subsequent arbitration hearing ordered by the Court, Arbitrator O'Shea took the view that the only question left for him to decide was whether, in the Court's words, the employer had taken any overt steps to "discharge" the grievor or to effect a "termination": see *Chrysler Canada Ltd. and U.A.W., Local 1285* (1978), 20 L.A.C. (2d) 220. In defining the issue so narrowly, the arbitrator read the decision of the Court as reducing the grievor to the unprotected status of a probationary employee, at best. Finding on the evidence that the company *had* in fact advised the grievor that he was being dismissed, he declined jurisdiction to hear the grievance on the basis that the dismissal of a probationary employee was inarbitrable. A second application for judicial review was denied: (1979), 24 L.A.C. (2d) 448n. Nevertheless, in an apparently contradictory judgment issued only two years later, the Ontario Divisional Court rejected the proposition that a loss of seniority has the effect of reverting an employee to probationary status: *United Glass & Ceramic Workers of North America v. Libbey-St. Clair Inc.* (1981), 125 D.L.R. (3d) 702. In the Court's view, this approach to the interpretation of loss-of-seniority clauses rendered the employee's status "somewhat hollow", being tantamount once again to a loss of employment unless the employer in its discretion elected not to end the employment relationship. Rather, the employee, though reduced to zero on the seniority scale, remained a seniority employee with the right to access the just cause provisions of the collective agreement if he or she was dismissed.

With these judicial pronouncements, the law now appears to be clear. In *Cami Automotive Inc. and C.A.W., Local 88* (1994), 45 L.A.C. (4th) 71, for example, Arbitrator Brandt refused to use his powers of rectification to convert a loss-of-seniority clause into a deemed termination clause.

In *MTD Products Ltd. and C.A.W., Local 1532* (2004), 129 L.A.C. (4th) 313 (Schiff), the practice of the parties for at least 15 years had been to treat a clause providing for the loss of seniority as tantamount to an "automatic termination" provision. Arbitrator Schiff held that the parties' practice could not override the clear interpretation that arbitrators and the courts have given to such language, and the union was thus entitled to assert, for the first time, that the provision meant what the jurisprudence says it means: the employee's seniority is reduced to zero, but he or she does not thereby become a probationary employee, subject to discharge at the discretion of the employer.

PART 3
CONTRACT INTERPRETATION

CHAPTER 16

INTERPRETING THE COLLECTIVE AGREEMENT

16.1 THE NATURE OF A COLLECTIVE AGREEMENT

In an early series of cases, the Supreme Court of Canada ruled that interpreting and applying a collective agreement requires a fundamentally different approach than that utilized at common law in respect of individual contracts of employment. These cases, summarized by Chief Justice Laskin in *McGavin Toastmaster Ltd. v. Ainscough* (1975), 54 D.L.R. (3d) 1, emphasize that it is inappropriate to apply ordinary contract doctrines such as repudiation and fundamental breach in a collective bargaining regime, where the relationship between the parties is a continuing one.

In the arbitral context, the principles expressed by the Supreme Court in *McGavin Toastmaster* were applied in *Air Canada and I.A.M., District Lodge 148* (1978), 18 L.A.C. (2d) 400 (Swan). Arbitrator Swan rejected the proposition, axiomatic at common law, that theft inevitably constitutes just cause for dismissal, or that the seriousness of the offence diminished the scope of his discretion to substitute a lesser penalty. In his view, the common law of master and servant had little bearing on the issues before him.

16.2   LIMITATIONS ON MANAGEMENT RIGHTS

16.2.1   Laskin School vs. Residual Rights School

Even accepting the unique features of collective bargaining and its product, the collective agreement, there was initially a sharp debate among arbitrators as to what, if any, presumptions should be brought to the task of interpreting a collective agreement. In *Peterboro Lock Manufacturing Co. Ltd. and U.E., Local 527* (1954), 4 L.A.C. 1499, Arbitrator Bora Laskin, as he then was, articulated an approach based on a "common law" of collective bargaining. Seeing collective bargaining as the start of an entirely new regime of workplace relations, Laskin held that it made no sense to read the agreement as limiting the employer's traditional prerogatives only to the extent expressly stipulated. In the arbitrator's view, the institution of collective bargaining changed all prior assumptions about the employer-employee relationship.

A competing view is represented by the so-called "residual rights theory". Proponents of this view maintain that, notwithstanding the consummation of a collective agreement, the employer is presumed to retain all its customary rights to manage the business, except to the extent of any restrictions specifically negotiated by the union. An early expression of the residual rights theory is found in the frequently quoted case of *Electric Auto-Lite Ltd. and U.A.W., Local 456* (1957), 7 L.A.C. 331 (Thomas).

To a large extent, the debate between the Laskin school and the residual rights school has by now effectively merged into the issue of whether the employer is constrained by a general duty of fairness or reasonableness, which is canvassed in the following section.

16.2.2   General Duty of Fairness

The question of whether, in the absence of express language in the collective agreement, employers are required to act fairly and reasonably in exercising their managerial authority has been addressed by the courts on several occasions. However, the courts' definition of the precise scope of a general duty on the employer to act fairly has developed incrementally. Initially, in *Metropolitan Toronto Board of Commissioners of Police v. Metropolitan Toronto Police Ass'n* (1981), 124 D.L.R. (3d) 684, the Ontario Court of Appeal ruled that it would be inconsistent with the meticulous, clause-by-clause way in which collective agreements are negotiated to impute to the employer a general duty to act fairly. On the other hand, the Court also recognized that all the provisions of a collective agreement must be read together, and that the duty to act fairly may arise by "necessary implication" in order to give effect to other terms in the collective agreement. This key qualification was affirmed and applied in a subsequent decision, *Council of Printing Industries of Canada v. Toronto Printing Pressmen & Assistants' Union No. 10* (1983), 149 D.L.R. (3d) 53 (Ont. C.A.). In that case, three temporary employees who were laid off grieved that the employer had disregarded their seniority in selecting employees for permanent classification. The Ontario Court of Appeal affirmed an arbitration decision holding that, in light of the seniority rights conferred by the collective agreement, the employer was required to make the selection on a reasonable basis, without bad faith, discrimination or arbitrariness.

In *Metropolitan Toronto (Municipality) v. C.U.P.E., Local 43* (1990), 69 D.L.R. (4th) 268, the Ontario Court of Appeal extended this reasoning to encompass management's right to make workplace rules having potential disciplinary consequences. In the Court's view, the arbitrator had not overstepped his authority by requiring the employer to exercise its powers reasonably. To hold otherwise, the Court noted once again, would in effect nullify or circumscribe the effect of other provisions in the collective agreement, in particular the requirement for just cause for discipline.

Arbitrator Bendel summarized these judicial decisions in his frequently-cited award in *Blue Line Taxi Co. and R.W.D.S.U., Local 1688* (1992), 28 L.A.C. (4th) 280. He noted, first, that if a provision of the collective agreement expressly confers a discretion on the employer, it can be presumed that the parties understood that it would be exercised fairly and reasonably. Second, even in the absence of explicit restrictions in the collective agreement, the employer is not entitled to exercise its management rights unreasonably if to do so would negate or undermine some other provision of the agreement.

Conversely, it is an error for an arbitrator to impose on the employer a general requirement to exercise its management rights reasonably, without linking that requirement to an express or implied term in the collective agreement: *Toronto Transit Commission v. A.T.U., Local 113* (2005), 194 O.A.C. 322 (Div. Ct.).

The limitations on the general duty of fairness have been examined in recent times in the context of alleged harassment of employees by members of management. In *Northern Alberta Institute of Technology and Academic Staff Ass'n* (1999), 88 L.A.C. (4th) 358 (Ponak), the union was unable to identify any specific provision in the agreement to which a duty to act fairly or reasonably could attach, and Arbitrator Ponak ruled that he did not have the power to test the allegation of harassment against a general duty of fairness. The arbitrator also considered it a stretch to read into a generic health and safety clause an implied prohibition against employer harassment. A contrasting decision is found in *Toronto Transit Commission and A.T.U. (Stina)* (2004), 132 L.A.C. (4th) 225, where Arbitrator Shime interpreted a health and safety provision as importing a duty on the part of supervisors not to abuse their authority by harassing employees. The arbitrator found that the parties' concern to ensure safety in the workplace, as reflected in the terms of the collective agreement, included psychological as well as physical safety: for further discussion, see Chapter 16.3.

Arbitrator Wakeling, in *L/3 Communications/Spar Aerospace Ltd. and I.A.M., Northgate Lodge 1579* (2004), 127 L.A.C. (4th) 225, noted that the debate on the limits which management must observe when making discretionary decisions had "not run its course". Nevertheless, following a review of arbitral and common law jurisprudence in this area, the arbitrator was firmly of the view that "principled, rational decision-making" must be taken to underlie collective agreement administration in Canada, and that "arbitrary, capricious or discriminatory" decision-making is permissible only where the language of the agreement expressly countenances it.

It will be recalled that, in *Blue Line Taxi, supra*, Arbitrator Bendel observed that, if a provision of the collective agreement expressly confers a discretion on the employer, it was open to an arbitrator to conclude that the discretion was intended to be exercised fairly or reasonably. In *Norampac Inc. v. C.E.P., Local 88* (2003), 7 Admin. L.R. (4th) 162, the New Brunswick Court of Queen's Bench upheld an arbitrator's decision that a collective agreement provision permitting the employer to grant a leave of absence for "legitimate personal reasons" required the company to reasonably balance the needs of the employee against the operational difficulty of accommodating the request. In that case, the employer was found to have unreasonably denied the employee a leave of absence to serve a jail term for armed robbery. However, the result may be different if the decision in dispute clearly engages an inherent management right (such as contracting out) that is not expressly or impliedly circumscribed by the collective agreement.

The recognition of an implied duty to exercise a discretion fairly, it may be added, is consistent with what the courts are doing in the commercial field. In *Marshall v. Bernard Place Corp.* (2002), 58 O.R. (3d) 97 (C.A.), for example, an agreement for the purchase of a residential property provided that the purchase was conditional upon receipt of an inspection report satisfactory to the purchaser "in his sole and absolute discretion". The Court affirmed that even clauses such as this are subject to an implied requirement to act honestly and in good faith.

Additional Reading

A.V.M. Beattie, "Reasonableness in the Administration and Interpretation of Collective Agreements" in W. Kaplan, J. Sack & M. Gunderson, eds., *Labour Arbitration Yearbook 1993*, p. 249.

16.3   IMPLIED TERMS

As seen in the preceding discussion, the courts in the course of considering a general duty of fairness have also made reference to the doctrine of "necessary implication". As Justice Tarnopolsky noted in *Metropolitan Toronto (Municipality) v. C.U.P.E., Local 43* (1990), 69 D.L.R. (4th) 268, discussed in Chapter 16.2.2:

> It is also true that parties intent on reaching a settlement do not always have the time, the incentive, or the resources to consider the full implications of each and every phrase. There is, therefore, a place for some creativity, some recourse to arbitral principles, and some overall notion of reasonableness. See, for example, David M. Beatty, "The Role of the Arbitrator: A Liberal Version" (1984), 34 U.T.L.J. 136. The presence of an implied principle or term of reasonable contract administration was also acknowledged by Craig J. in [*Wardair Canada Inc. v. C.A.L.F.A.A.* (1988), 63 O.R. (2d) 471 (Div. Ct.)], at pp. 476-77.

Arbitrators have long recognized this. In *Andres Wines (B.C.) Ltd. and United Brewery & Distillery Workers, Local 300* (1977), 16 L.A.C. (2d) 422, for example, Paul Weiler, Chair of the British Columbia Labour Relations Board, recognized that it is impossible for the parties to a collective agreement to anticipate and deal with every contingency which might arise in relation to a given provision. It therefore falls to an arbitrator to attempt to reconstruct a "hypothetical intent" of the parties, based on their language and behaviour, as to what the "sensible" resolution of the now-crystallized issue would have been.

The scope for the implication of terms in a collective agreement is, however, a matter of debate. In *McKellar General Hospital and O.N.A.* (1986), 24 L.A.C. (3d) 97, Arbitrator Saltman applied the common law test. In her view, before a term can be implied into the collective agreement, two essential criteria must be met:

(1) the term is necessary to give business or collective agreement efficacy to the contract; or, in other words, to make the collective agreement work; and,

(2) if, having been made aware of the omission of the term, both parties to the agreement would have agreed without hesitation to its insertion.

Since neither test had been satisfied, the arbitrator refused to entertain the union's contention that an absenteeism control program introduced by the employer constituted an unreasonable exercise of management rights. Similarly, in *Kennedy Lodge Nursing Home and S.E.I.U., Local 204* (1980), 28 L.A.C. (2d) 388, an arbitration board chaired by John Brunner refused to imply a term into the collective agreement restricting the employer's right to contract out bargaining unit work, since, in its view, the insertion of such a term was not necessary to give the collective agreement "business efficacy".

For an articulation by the Supreme Court of Canada of the doctrine of necessary implication, see *Canadian Pacific Hotels Ltd. v. Bank of Montreal* (1987), 40 D.L.R. (4th) 385.

In *McKellar General Hospital, supra,* Arbitrator Saltman highlighted the debate over the type of collective agreement provision to which the doctrine of necessary implication may be applied, and in particular whether it can be taken as attaching to a management rights clause or other broad statement of employer rights. In *Brewers' Distributor Ltd. and Brewery, Winery & Distillery Workers Union, Local 300*, [2004] B.C.C.A.A.A. No. 54 (QL), Arbitrator Moore concluded that it could not. Such provisions, he found, referring to the caselaw, were not usually intended to limit management's exercise of its residual powers, but to preserve them.

However, in *Toronto Transit Commission and A.T.U. (Stina)* (2004), 132 L.A.C. (4th) 225, Arbitrator Shime reached a different conclusion, noting that the Supreme Court of Canada's decisions in *Weber v. Ontario Hydro* (1995), 125 D.L.R. (4th) 583, and *New Brunswick v. O'Leary* (1995), 125 D.L.R. (4th) 609 (see Chapter 1.3) specifically directed arbitrators to determine whether a dispute arises under the collective agreement "either expressly or inferentially". Arbitrator Shime reasoned that "[s]ince most of management's functions and responsibilities derive from the management rights clause, any notion of reasonable contract administration would have minimal relevance if it did not apply to the management rights provision" (at p. 239). The arbitrator's ruling is consistent with the view he expressed more than 25 years previously that "implicit" in a collective agreement is the assumption that its provisions "must be construed so as to operate reasonably and with good faith": *Int'l Nickel Co. of Canada Ltd. and U.S.W.A., Local 6500* (1977), 14 L.A.C. (2d) 13 (Shime), at p. 18.

16.4   USE OF EXTRINSIC EVIDENCE TO INTERPRET THE COLLECTIVE AGREEMENT

16.4.1   Parole Evidence Rule

At common law, evidence extrinsic to a written agreement, or "parole evidence", is generally inadmissible to contradict, vary, add to or subtract from the terms of the agreement. Where the terms of the written agreement are ambiguous, however, extrinsic evidence, such as past practice or negotiating history, may be admissible as an aid to interpretation in order to resolve the ambiguity. Save in British Columbia (see below), arbitrators tend to pay heed to these common law principles, even where the applicable labour relations legislation affords a broad discretion to admit evidence which would be inadmissible in a court of law. Indeed, in *R. v. Barber* (1968), 68 D.L.R. (2d) 682, the Ontario Court of Appeal quashed the award of a board of arbitration which made use of extrinsic evidence to interpret a collective agreement whose language was clear and unambiguous. The Court observed that the provision of Ontario's *Labour Relations Act* (now S.O. 1995, c. 1, Sch. A) granting arbitrators latitude with respect to the admissibility of evidence does not relieve them from ultimately acting only upon the basis of evidence having "cogency in law".

The Court's affirmation of the primacy of the written document was echoed more recently by Arbitrator Hamilton in *DHL Express (Canada) Ltd. and C.A.W., Locals 4215, 144 & 4278* (2004), 124 L.A.C. (4th) 271. The arbitrator emphasized that, in accordance with the normal principles of contract interpretation, it is primarily from the written word that the parties' common intention is to be ascertained, and that objective tests must be used — not what one party or the other, "*post contractu*, may wish to say was their intent". Moreover, Arbitrator Hamilton noted, the disputed provision must be read in the context of the collective agreement as a whole, and it must be assumed that the parties did not intend any of the language which they have included in the agreement to be without meaning.

16.4.2   Ambiguity: Patent and Latent

The "parole evidence rule" precludes the admission of extrinsic evidence unless an ambiguity, either "patent" or "latent", can be shown. Language that is patently ambiguous is unclear on its face; language is said to be latently ambiguous when certain facts relating to its negotiation or application reveal a lack of clarity. Consistent with the latter concept, courts have held that, where a party alleges latent ambiguity in the agreement, extrinsic evidence may be admissible not only to resolve the ambiguity, but also to prove the existence of an ambiguity in the first place. In *Leitch Gold Mines Ltd. v. Texas Gulf Sulphur Co. Inc.* (1968), 3 D.L.R. (3d) 161, the Ontario High Court stated, at p. 216:

> Extrinsic evidence may be admitted to disclose a latent ambiguity, in either the language of the instrument or in its application to the facts, and also to resolve it, but it is to be noted that the evidence allowed in to clear up the ambiguity may be more extensive than that which reveals it. Thus, evidence of relevant surrounding circumstances can be accepted to ascertain the meaning of the document and may clarify the meaning by indirectly disclosing the intention of the parties.

This willingness to admit extrinsic evidence in order to ensure that no injustice is being done was affirmed by the Ontario Court of Appeal in *Noranda*

Metal Industries Ltd. v. I.B.E.W., Local 2345 (1983), 44 O.R. (2d) 529 (C.A.). As Arbitrator Richard Brown observed in *Securitas (Canada) Ltd. and U.S.W.A.* (2003), 114 L.A.C. (4th) 259, at p. 263, "[w]hen the language of an agreement is not ambiguous on its face, but a party . . . asserts facts which would reveal an ambiguity lurking beneath the surface, the evidence bearing upon this assertion should be heard".

A related question is whether the inclusion in a collective agreement of an "entire agreement" or "zipper" clause (stating that the written document represents the whole of the agreement) precludes resort to extrinsic evidence where its admission would otherwise be appropriate. In *IPSCO Inc. and B.S.O.I.W., Local 805* (2004), 124 L.A.C. (4th) 403, Arbitrator Warren found that, while the effect of such clauses will depend on their wording, they do not necessarily render inadmissible evidence of negotiating history or past practice.

Arbitrators have noted, however, that extrinsic evidence is not admissible simply because the parties disagree about the meaning of a particular provision. This caveat was perhaps first expressed by Arbitrator Weatherill in the early case of *General Spring Products Ltd. and U.A.W., Local 1524* (1971), 23 L.A.C. 73. In particular, the mere fact that the application of a provision produces a result which is unpalatable to one of the parties does not in itself establish an ambiguity justifying the reception of extrinsic evidence.

Arbitrator Brent emphasized the same point in *Metro Toronto Zoo and C.U.P.E., Local 1600*, [2004] O.L.A.A. No. 217 (QL). To be ambiguous, in the sense that it is necessary to seek clarification by way of extrinsic evidence, a provision must be reasonably susceptible of more than one meaning; and the dispute cannot be satisfactorily resolved by reference to the language itself, read in the context of the collective agreement as a whole.

16.4.3   The British Columbia Approach

In British Columbia, s. 82(2) of the *Labour Relations Code*, R.S.B.C. 1996, c. 244, provides that an arbitrator "must apply principles consistent with the industrial relations policy of this *Code*, and is not bound by a strict legal interpretation of the issue in dispute". This section has been interpreted as freeing arbitrators from the strict application of common law rules of interpretation, including the parole evidence rule. In a seminal case decided in 1976, Chair Paul Weiler of the British Columbia Labour Relations Board articulated what he described as a simpler approach to the admission of extrinsic evidence: in any case where there is a *bona fide* doubt about the proper meaning of the language in a collective agreement, an arbitrator should be able to consider a broad range of evidence about the meaning that was mutually intended by the negotiators: *University of British Columbia and C.U.P.E., Local 116*, [1977] 1 Can. L.R.B.R. 13 (B.C.L.R.B.).

This approach was affirmed in *Nanaimo Times Ltd. and G.C.I.U., Local 525-M*, [1996] B.C.L.R.B.D. No. 40 (QL), where the British Columbia Labour Relations Board upheld an arbitrator's decision to admit extrinsic evidence. Nevertheless, the Board suggested that there is little real difference between the "*bona fide* doubt" test and the traditional common law "ambiguity" test. In either case, all that is necessary is that the arbitrator, before or after receiving the disputed evidence, "find some doubt arising from the language of the collective agreement" (at para. 31). That would appear to be fair comment when one considers, for example, the statements of the Ontario Court of Appeal in *Noranda Metal Industries Ltd. v. I.B.E.W., Local 2345* (1983), 44 O.R. (2d) 529, as discussed by Arbitrator Brown in *Securitas (Canada) Ltd. and U.S.W.A.* (2003), 114 L.A.C. (4th) 259: see Chapter 16.4.2. These varying statements of principle, furthermore, all appear to be in accord with the judgment in *C.J.A., Local 579 v. Bradco Construction Ltd.* (1993), 102 D.L.R. (4th) 402 (S.C.C.), discussed in Chapter 6.1. In this case, the Supreme Court of Canada ruled that an arbitrator was not required to apply the strict common law rules as to what constitutes an ambiguity, including the distinction between patent and latent ambiguity, but only to conclude on a reasonable basis that the collective agreement was unclear.

16.4.4   Negotiating History

One of the most prevalent forms of extrinsic evidence sought to be introduced is the negotiating history which underlies a contentious provision in the collective agreement. Arbitrators have stated, however, that evidence of negotiating history has probative value only to the extent that it demonstrates a true consensus by the parties as to the meaning and application of a provision. Paul Weiler, Chair of the British Columbia Labour Relations Board, made this point in *University of British Columbia and C.U.P.E., Local 116*, [1977] 1 Can. L.R.B.R. 13 (discussed in Chapter 16.4.3), where it was stressed that evidence which merely reveals the objectives or understanding of one side only is unhelpful. That is exactly what Arbitrator Burkett found in, for example, *Hallmark Containers Ltd. and C.P.U., Local 303* (1983), 8 L.A.C. (3d) 117.

Reflecting an appreciation of the complex dynamic of collective agreement negotiations, other arbitrators have expressed similar caution in placing reliance upon the parties' discussions at the bargaining table as an aid to interpretation. The reasons for this reluctance were stated in *The Globe & Mail and Southern Ontario Newspaper Guild, Local 87*, unreported, February 3, 1987, where Arbitrator Joyce commented on "the ease with which negotiators hear what they wish to hear as they wheel and deal". According to the arbitrator, evidence of negotiating history might be of little use in interpreting the collective agreement, since bargaining often results in the adoption of compromise language whose meaning is deliberately left ambiguous. In such cases, the parties may tacitly agree to "leave it to the arbitrator to decide" in the event a dispute arises regarding the provision's interpretation. At the same time, though, the arbitrator acknowledged that a clear commitment made in the course of negotiations may well give rise to an estoppel (see Chapter 16.5).

16.4.5   Past Practice

Another form of extrinsic evidence commonly sought to be introduced is the parties' "past practice" at the workplace. To be admissible or of value as an aid to interpretation, such evidence must meet the following conditions, set out by Arbitrator Weiler in *John Bertram & Sons Co. Ltd. and I.A.M., Local 1740* (1967), 18 L.A.C. 362, at p. 368:

(1) there is no clear preponderance in favour of one meaning stemming from the words and structure of the collective agreement, as seen in their labour relations context;

(2) one party has engaged in conduct which unambiguously is based on one meaning attributed to the relevant provision;

(3) the other party has acquiesced in this conduct, a fact which is either quite clearly expressed or can be inferred from the continuance of the practice for a long period without objection; and

(4) there is evidence that members of the union or management hierarchy who have some real responsibility for the meaning of the agreement have acquiesced in the practice.

While, as with estoppel, a practice or representation can arise through silence or passive condonation, Arbitrator Richard Brown has emphasized that, to support either ground, the pattern of acquiescence must be long-standing and substantial: *Drug Trading Co. Ltd. and U.S.W.A., Local 3313* (1998), 71 L.A.C. (4th) 231.

One element in a prior course of conduct may be the withdrawal of a previous grievance that dealt with the same subject-matter as the current dispute. Apart from the issue of whether the withdrawal of a prior, apparently identical grievance can provide the necessary representation to found an estoppel (see Chapter 16.5), the other party may argue that the withdrawal supports an inference that the employer and the union had a shared understanding as to the meaning of the collective agreement provision in question. In *Saint-Gobain Abrasives and C.E.P., Local 12* (2003), 120 L.A.C. (4th) 73, Arbitrator Burkett held that the withdrawal of such a grievance by a responsible union official, after a discussion of the case on its merits, constitutes extrinsic evidence of a mutual intention and may be relied upon as such, at least in the absence of compelling evidence to the contrary. However, the arbitrator pointed out, a withdrawal will have this effect only if it was not made on a "without prejudice" basis. For further discussion, see Chapter 3.4.

16.5   USE OF EXTRINSIC EVIDENCE TO FOUND AN ESTOPPEL

16.5.1   The Rule in Equity

Apart from clarifying ambiguities in the collective agreement, the other common use of extrinsic evidence in arbitration proceedings is to establish the elements of the doctrine of promissory estoppel. The classic statement of the doctrine is that of Lord Denning in *Combe v. Combe*, [1951] 1 All E.R. 767 (C.A.), at p. 770:

> The principle, as I understand it, is that where one party has, by his words or conduct, made to the other a promise or assurance which was intended to affect the legal relations between them and to be acted on accordingly, then, once the other party has taken him at his word and acted on it, the one who gave the promise or assurance cannot afterwards be allowed to revert to the previous legal relations as if no such promise or assurance had been made by him, but he must accept their legal relations subject to the qualification which he himself has so introduced, even though it is not supported in point of law by any consideration, but only by his word.

In other words, where the employer or the union foregoes a right which it would otherwise enjoy under the collective agreement, the doctrine of estoppel will bar it from enforcing the strict terms of the parties' contractual relations where it would be inequitable to do so.

In *Amalgamated Investment & Property Co. Ltd. v. Texas Commerce Int'l Bank Ltd.*, [1981] 3 All E.R. 577 (C.A.), Lord Denning responded to the controversy generated by his earlier statement of the doctrine, particularly with respect to the scope of its application, by restating the principle in the following terms, at p. 584:

> The doctrine of estoppel is one of the most flexible and useful in the armoury of the law . . . At the same time it has been sought to be limited by a series of maxims: estoppel is only a rule of evidence; estoppel cannot give rise to a cause of action; estoppel cannot do away with the need for consideration, and so forth. All these can now be seen to merge into one general principle shorn of limitations. When the parties to a transaction proceed on the basis of an underlying assumption (either of fact or law, and whether due to misrepresentation or mistake, makes no difference), on which they have conducted the dealings between them, neither of them will be allowed to go back on that assumption when it would be unfair or unjust to allow him to do so. If one of them does seek to go back on it, the courts will give the other such remedy as the equity of the case demands.

16.5.2   Arbitral Jurisdiction and the Elements of Estoppel

In earlier years, there was considerable debate as to whether arbitrators had the power to apply an "equitable" doctrine such as estoppel, to bar a party from relying on what would otherwise be its clear rights under the collective agreement. The authority of arbitrators to apply the doctrine was perhaps most clearly recognized by Paul Weiler, Chair of the British Columbia Labour Relations Board, in *Penticton (City) and C.U.P.E., Local 608* (1978), 18 L.A.C. (2d) 307 (B.C.L.R.B.). However, Chair Weiler noted that the introduction of extrinsic evidence has a more limited effect in the context of estoppel than in the context of determining the correct interpretation of ambiguous contract language. In the latter situation, the meaning ascribed to the language continues to bind the parties until an amendment has been negotiated, whereas estoppel can be brought to an end unilaterally by the presentation of adequate notice to the other party. That said, a party will be precluded from insisting on its strict legal rights under the collective agreement where it is established that:

(1) it made a representation, either by words or conduct, including silence;

(2) the representation was intended to be acted on by the other party, that is, to affect the parties' legal relations; and

(3) the other party did in fact rely on the representation, to its detriment or prejudice.

In Ontario, the power of arbitrators to apply estoppel in appropriate circumstances has been undisputed since the decision of the Divisional Court in *Canadian National Railway Co. v. Beatty* (1981), 128 D.L.R. (3d) 236, upholding the award of Arbitrator Beatty in *CN/CP Telecommunications and Canadian Telecommunications Union* (1981), 4 L.A.C. (3d) 205.

Courts in some other jurisdictions, however, have been considerably less comfortable with the prospect of arbitrators applying equitable principles such as estoppel to a collective agreement. In *Hawker Siddeley Canada Inc. v. U.S.W.A., Local 1237* (1983), 150 D.L.R. (3d) 509, Justice Nathanson of the Nova Scotia Supreme Court, Trial Division, expressed doubt as to whether the doctrine extends to grievance arbitration, and disagreed with the proposition that the law had been settled by the *Canadian National Railway* case. Similarly, the Alberta Court of Queen's Bench has taken issue with *Canadian National Railway*, criticizing arbitrators who "blithely" follow it without adequate consideration. In a case decided in 1984, the Court quashed an arbitration award in which the doctrine of estoppel was applied to compel the payment of overtime in accordance with the employer's long-standing practice, holding that the arbitrator had exceeded his jurisdiction by assuming an authority which is not granted by statute. On appeal, while upholding the result in the Queen's Bench decision, the Alberta Court of Appeal did comment that it had "grave reservations about the proposition that an arbitrator cannot apply so-called equitable principles in carrying out his obligations": see *Smoky River Coal Ltd. v. U.S.W.A., Local 7621* (1985), 18 D.L.R. (4th) 742, at p. 745 (Alta. C.A.), discussed in Chapter 16.5.3. Thus, the real issue of concern to the Alberta and Nova Scotia courts may have been the one examined in the following chapter, *i.e.* whether the right sought to be established through estoppel must relate to a specific provision of the collective agreement.

Additional Reading

C. Albertyn, "Silence and Estoppel: An Arbitrator's Perspective" in K. Whitaker, J. Sack, M. Gunderson & R. Filion, eds., *Labour Arbitration Yearbook 1999-2000*, vol. II, p. 317; and companion articles by L. Harnden & K. Lopes, and C.D. Watson.

16.5.3 Must the Estoppel Relate to an Express Provision of the Collective Agreement?

Even where the authority of arbitrators to apply the doctrine of promissory estoppel appears to be well settled, the precise scope of this jurisdiction continues to be the subject of debate. In his award in *CN/CP Telecommunications and Canadian Telecommunications Union* (1981), 4 L.A.C. (3d) 205, subsequently upheld by the Ontario Divisional Court (1981), 128 D.L.R. (3d) 236, Arbitrator Beatty suggested that estoppel can be invoked in any situation in which a party's conduct or representation has the effect of modifying "some pre-existing legal relationship". Although in the case before him the practice which the employer was precluded from discontinuing clearly related to a specific provision in the collective agreement, the arbitrator's remarks could be taken to open the door to a greatly expanded role for estoppel in the governance of the parties' relations. In particular, the employer could arguably be prevented from changing any workplace practice, whether or not it is addressed by the collective agreement, as long as there is a pre-existing relationship, and the existence of the practice in question is capable of being characterized as a "representation". An example of the application of this approach is *Eastern Bakeries Ltd. and B.C.T., Local 446* (2001), 102 L.A.C. (4th) 430 (MacKeigan).

This more liberal approach to the application of the doctrine of estoppel does not appear to be in the mainstream of arbitral authority, and was in fact strongly rejected in the Alberta Court of Appeal's decision in *Smoky River Coal Ltd. v. U.S.W.A., Local 7621* (1985), 18 D.L.R. (4th) 742. In the Court's view, such reasoning amounts to a "bald attempt to turn a policy or practice into a term of a contract when the parties never bargained that it be such" (at p. 746). While disavowing any intent to revive the discredited axiom that estoppel can be used as a "shield", but not as a "sword", the Court does state unqualifiedly that promissory estoppel cannot be invoked to create a positive obligation (or "cause of action", as it is frequently termed). The presence of a provision in the collective agreement to establish the basis of the right claimed would appear, therefore, in the Alberta Court of Appeal's view, to be a prerequisite. Further restricting what it viewed as the excessively permissive approach taken in *Canadian National Railway*, the Court commented as well that there can be no finding of detrimental reliance (particularly with regard to a loss of opportunity to bargain) without satisfactory evidence of this fact.

The more restrictive approach espoused by the Alberta court appears to mean that a party is under no obligation to wait until the commencement of bargaining to initiate a change in practice, if that practice is not related to the administration of a right referable to the terms of the collective agreement. Arbitrator Moore, in *Simon Fraser University and C.U.P.E., Local 3338*, [2004] B.C.C.A.A.A. No. 63 (QL), provides an overview of British Columbia's arbitral caselaw, and arrives at the same conclusion. Indeed, this point was made by Arbitrator Burkett in his seminal decision in *Hallmark Containers Ltd. and C.P.U., Local 303* (1983), 8 L.A.C. (3d) 117. The one exception noted by Arbitrator Burkett relates to circumstances in which an employer has qualified its management rights by an *express* representation, relied upon by the union, that a specific practice not covered by the collective agreement will be continued.

Thus, some nexus to a collective agreement provision, other than the management rights clause, appears to be a requirement of the estoppel doctrine. An illustration of the kind of collective agreement "hook" upon which estoppel can be based is found in *Tembec Inc. and C.E.P., Local 32* (2002), 111 L.A.C. (4th) 313, where Arbitrator Luborsky found that the employer had by its practice expanded the scope of the existing clause as written.

16.5.4   Negotiating History

It is not uncommon for a party to rely at arbitration on statements made or silence by the other party in the course of negotiations as the basis of an estoppel argument. However, as discussed in Chapter 16.5.3, without an express representation by the employer that a particular practice will continue, the weight of authority suggests that estoppel can arise only in connection with the administration or application of a specific provision in the collective agreement. Moreover, if the position sought to be established through evidence of negotiating history is not consistent with the collective agreement as written, arbitrators have required that the party asserting estoppel prove its case with "clear and cogent" evidence. As Arbitrator Adams held in *Sudbury District Roman Catholic Separate School Board and O.E.C.T.A.* (1984), 15 L.A.C. (3d) 284, evidence that is circumstantial or equivocal will not suffice to vary the effect of the parties' written agreement.

At the same time, however, arbitrators have recognized that collective agreements differ from ordinary commercial contracts because the bargaining relationship between the employer and the union is an ongoing one. As Arbitrator Burkett pointed out in his oft-cited decision in *Hallmark Containers Ltd. and C.P.U., Local 303* (1983), 8 L.A.C. (3d) 117 (Burkett), there is a "special need for trust and openness" in the parties' dealings with each other. Thus, even silence at the bargaining table, where the circumstances give rise to a duty to speak, or to disabuse the other party of its stated understanding of a proposal, the arbitrator concluded, can ground an estoppel. In *Hallmark Containers* itself, the arbitrator found that the employer, by failing to respond to the union's explanation of its proposal during negotiations, had "acted in a manner designed to convey to the union its acceptance of the union's interpretation of the language at issue" (at p. 131). Estoppel was applied.

A "duty to speak" was also found to have arisen in *Health Employers' Ass'n of British Columbia and H.S.A.B.C.* (2004), 123 L.A.C. (4th) 390 (Ready), where the dispute centred on entitlement to compensation under the collective agreement's "on-call" provisions. Prior to the commencement of bargaining, the employers had agreed to "local arrangements" whereby the provisions would be applied to a group of employees even when they were not on call. As the employers had not raised at the bargaining table their intention to discontinue those arrangements, it was held that the renewed collective agreement continued to bear this "special meaning" for the life of that renewed agreement.

Arbitrator Hope, on the other hand, has rejected the argument that the employer, by abandoning a proposal to introduce clarifying language, thereby represented to the union that it would not revert to its strict legal rights in any event. Citing the leading British Columbia court decision on negotiating-history estoppel, *Litwin Construction (1973) Ltd. v. Pan* (1988), 52 D.L.R. (4th) 459 (B.C.C.A.), the arbitrator found nothing in the employer's past practice which indicated an intention to waive its right under the existing collective agreement to make changes as needed. Therefore, he held, there was no detrimental reliance on the part of the union, and no duty to speak on the part of the employer: see *University of British Columbia and Ass'n of Administrative & Professional Staff*, [2004] B.C.C.A.A.A. No. 112 (QL).

On the other hand, while the underlying concern of arbitrators is to maintain a foundation of trust between the parties, Arbitrator Elaine Newman, in *TRW Canada Ltd. and T.P.E.A.* (2001), 95 L.A.C. (4th) 129, noted that intentional deception is not a prerequisite to the application of estoppel. The existence of a clear representation, which the opposing party has accepted and acted upon, is sufficient to trigger the doctrine.

Nor does the representation have to be made at the bargaining table. In *New Brunswick (Department of Natural Resources & Energy) and New Brunswick Government Employees Union*, [2002] N.B.L.A.A. No. 19 (QL) (MacPherson), a union official telephoned a management official prior to the ratification meeting in order to confirm the union's understanding of a clause. The management official (erroneously) did so, and the arbitrator held that the employer was bound by that representation.

The doctrine of equitable estoppel can, of course, also operate to bind the *union* to a waiver of rights, where an express representation has been made at the bargaining table that such rights would not be exercised. See *Zellers Inc. and U.F.C.W., Local 1518* (2000), 94 L.A.C. (4th) 37 (Jackson).

16.5.5 Representations to Individual Employees

Labour relations legislation generally prohibits the employer from circumventing the union's rights as exclusive bargaining agent by entering into arrangements with individual employees that are outside the framework of the collective agreement. In the face of such prohibitions, some doubt had existed as to whether an individual employee is entitled to assert estoppel against the employer in respect of promises or assurances given specifically to the employee. In Ontario, at least, that doubt appears to have been removed by the decision of the Divisional Court in *O.P.S.E.U. v. Ontario (Ministry of Community and Social Services)* (1995), 27 O.R. (3d) 135. The Grievance Settlement Board dismissed a grievance on the basis that estoppel cannot apply at the instance of an individual employee. Justice Adams, writing for the Court, quashed the decision, ruling that the Board had erred in law and had improperly fettered its jurisdiction.

The state of the law, in Ontario at least, was set out by Arbitrator Mac-Dowell in *George Brown College of Applied Arts & Technology and O.P.S.E.U. (Bartley)* (2003), 113 L.A.C. (4th) 208. In the words of the arbitrator, at p. 231: "an individual employee *may* be able to establish and rely upon estoppel in appropriate circumstances. It is not a principle that operates only as between the bargaining parties; and it is for a board of arbitration to determine how the principles of estoppel should be interpreted and applied in the context of the case before it" (italics in original).

The principle set out in Ontario decisions was perhaps taken one step further in *Newtel Communications and C.E.P., Local 410*, unreported, July 3, 2002 (Thistle). The grievor had accepted a job with the employer in Goose Bay rather than another in Toronto on the basis of a manager's repeated assurances that the job would become permanent after three months. The arbitrator held that the employer was bound by its promise on ordinary estoppel principles, notwithstanding an express clause in the collective agreement purporting to invalidate any individual agreements in which the union was not a participant.

16.6 RULES OF CONSTRUCTION

In interpreting the collective agreement, the role of an arbitrator is to ascertain the true intention of the parties, based on the language that they used in the agreement. Arbitrator MacRae made this point in one of the earliest reported cases, *Massey-Harris-Ferguson Ltd. and U.A.W., Local 439* (1955), 5 L.A.C. 2123.

Because the language used by the parties may not readily disclose their intention, arbitrators have from time to time resorted to various rules of construction to assist in construing the collective agreement. Developed at common law, such rules were meant to embody principles "founded in law, reason and common sense", as the Court of King's Bench put it long ago: *Goodtitle v. Bailey* (1777), 98 E.R. 1260. What rule is appropriate in any given case depends largely on the context in which the interpretative dispute arises. Some of the rules commonly applied by arbitrators are identified below.

16.6.1   The Plain Meaning Rule

The primary rule governing the interpretation of written contracts is that the parties' intentions are normally to be found in the "ordinary" or "plain meaning" of the language in which they have expressed themselves. In *PCL Construction Ltd. and Construction & General Workers, Local 1111* (1982), 8 L.A.C. (3d) 49, Arbitrator Sychuk set out the essence of the plain meaning rule as follows:

(1) All contracts must be interpreted according to the primary and natural meaning of the language used by the parties.

(2) If the plain and ordinary meaning is unambiguous, is not excluded by the context and is sensible with reference to the extrinsic circumstances, then such meaning must be taken conclusively as being the intention of the parties.

Similarly, in *Lear Siegler Industries Ltd. and U.A.W., Local 1524* (1977), 17 L.A.C. (2d) 168, Arbitrator Palmer ruled that the common usage of a term is to be preferred over some specialized meaning or "term of art", unless there is evidence that the parties intended the latter to apply. Of course, the collective agreement may itself indicate that the parties intended a phrase to function as a term of art. For example, the agreement may refer to an external plan of insured benefits in which the term is accorded a specialized definition: see *Dufferin Area Hospital and S.E.I.U., Local 204* (1981), 2 L.A.C. (3d) 323 (Rayner).

As held in *Edmonton (City) and C.U.P.E., Local 52* (1972), 1 L.A.C. (2d) 369 (Lefsrud), the corollary of the plain meaning rule is that it may be departed from where it would involve an absurdity or inconsistency with the rest of the collective agreement. Applying this exception, Arbitrator Lefsrud decided the grievance on the basis of his own "corrected" reading of the contested provision. However, the ruling in *Edmonton (City)* should be read in conjunction with the award in *General Spring Products Ltd. and U.A.W., Local 1524* (1971), 23 L.A.C. 73. In the opinion of Arbitrator Weatherill, not every anomaly or ill-considered result justifies departing from the clear language of the collective agreement.

16.6.2   Reading the Collective Agreement as a Whole

The courts have also stressed the importance of reading the agreement as a whole. While like terms are ordinarily interpreted alike, it should not be assumed that a term which appears in different parts of the collective agreement necessarily bears an identical meaning throughout. In such instances, the context in which the term is used may be a better guide to the parties' intent than the meaning that emerges from some unrelated provision. The award of Arbitrator Outhouse in *F.A. Tucker (Atlantic) Ltd. and I.B.E.W., Local 1928* (1985), 20 L.A.C. (3d) 33 is illustrative.

In *Hoover Co. Ltd. and U.E., Local 520* (1981), 29 L.A.C. (2d) 162, Arbitrator McLaren affirmed that, where there are inconsistencies within the collective agreement, a specific provision normally takes precedence over a general provision. Otherwise, it is a normal rule of construction that, if possible, all words in the agreement are to be given meaning; arbitrators are loath to adopt an interpretation that renders a word or clause redundant. In this regard, see *De Havilland Aircraft of Canada Ltd. and U.A.W., Local 112* (1961), 11 L.A.C. 350 (Laskin).

16.6.3   "Inclusion of the One Excludes the Other"

Another commonly argued interpretive maxim is *inclusio unius est exclusio alterius*, which literally means "inclusion of the one excludes the other". In the context of construing a collective agreement, the concept is usually invoked to support the submission that, by making specific reference to a person or thing in one provision, the parties necessarily intended to exclude that person or thing in another provision in which there is no such specific reference. A demonstration of the way in which this principle applies is Arbitrator Kennedy's decision in *Hamilton (City) Board of Education and O.S.S.T.F., District 8* (1983), 10 L.A.C. (3d) 126. The arbitrator held that, by explicitly excluding weekends and statutory holidays from the computation of time limits under the grievance procedure, the parties must be taken to have included off-days in the calculation of paid bereavement leave.

16.6.4   Use of Headings

In *Kenora Roman Catholic Separate School Board and O.E.C.T.A. (Liddle)* (1993), 37 L.A.C. (4th) 28, Arbitrator Brandt held that the headings in a collective agreement, unlike the headings in the published version of a statute, form part of the instrument itself, and can therefore be used as an aid to interpretation. Analogizing from the Supreme Court of Canada's discussion of the significance of the headings found in the *Canadian Charter of Rights and Freedoms*, the arbitrator enumerated the following factors to be taken into account in assessing the relationship between the headings and the main text:

(1) the degree of difficulty in construing the provision by reason of ambiguity or obscurity;

(2) the apparent homogeneity of the provision appearing under the heading;

(3) the use of generic terminology in the heading; and

(4) the relationship of the terminology used in the heading to the substance of the headlined provision.

16.6.5 *Contra Proferentem* – Construing Against the Proposer

A further canon of construction, though invoked relatively infrequently in a collective bargaining context, is the *contra proferentem* rule; that is, the language of a document may be construed against the interest of the party who put it forward. The rationale for this canon is that, in drafting contract language, a party is assumed to have spelled out what was necessary to protect its own interests. In particular, the rule applies where a party has drafted an exception to a benefit which would otherwise be available to the other party. The origins and rationale of this rule are discussed by Arbitrator Armstrong in *Medis Health and Teamsters, Local 424* (2000), 93 L.A.C. (4th) 118.

CHAPTER 17

ASSIGNMENT OF BARGAINING UNIT WORK

17.1   ASSIGNMENT TO NON-BARGAINING UNIT EMPLOYEES

17.1.1   Implied Restrictions

Arbitrators have repeatedly emphasized that certification and the conclusion of a collective agreement do not confer on the union a property interest in the work performed by members of the bargaining unit. In the absence of specific restrictions in the collective agreement, therefore, the employer retains an inherent right to assign or reassign bargaining unit work to employees outside the bargaining unit, including supervisors. Management's right in this regard is not, however, completely unfettered, notwithstanding that the parties have failed to address the matter expressly. In contrast to the development of the caselaw on contracting out (see Chapter 17.2.1), arbitrators have generally been prepared to imply some restriction into the collective agreement in order to ensure that the job classification, seniority, promotion and layoff provisions which *have* been negotiated are not rendered meaningless. Otherwise, arbitrators have held, the employer would be at liberty to undermine the integrity of the bargaining unit by reassigning or transferring its work.

The extent to which bargaining unit work can be delegated to employees outside the bargaining unit without triggering an implied restriction is determined on a case-by-case basis. Broadly speaking, though, the test is whether the individual in question performs bargaining unit work to such an extent as to bring himself or herself within the bargaining unit. Initially articulated by Arbitrator Little in *Fittings Ltd. and U.S.W.A., Local 1817* (1960), 10 L.A.C.

294, this benchmark was adopted in what has since become the seminal case, *Irwin Toy Ltd. and U.S.W.A.* (1982), 6 L.A.C. (3d) 328 (Burkett). In *Irwin Toy*, the arbitrator concluded that the disputed work assignment must be enough quantitatively to fill most if not all of a bargaining unit employee's regular shift on an ongoing basis.

Subsequent decisions have made it clear that the principles summarized by Arbitrator Burkett apply with equal force to rank-and-file employees outside the bargaining unit, and not only to supervisory personnel. In *North West Co. Inc. and R.W.D.S.U., Local 468* (1996), 57 L.A.C. (4th) 158, for example, Arbitrator Freedman adopted an analysis that is applicable to any non-bargaining unit employee, even though the contested work assignment again involved a managerial employee. The arbitrator also suggested that, while attempts to quantify the disputed work may furnish important evidence, in the end a qualitative assessment must be made as to whether the migration of work outside the bargaining unit has had the effect of undermining the integrity of the unit or the collective agreement.

In *Grande Prairie General & Auxiliary Nursing Home, District No. 14 and U.N.A., Local 237* (1996), 57 L.A.C. (4th) 173 (Christian), the arbitrator noted that, where the union invokes the implied restriction, the assumption of bargaining unit work by non-unit employees must be "sustained and substantial". Often, however, the difficulty lies in distinguishing a transfer of bargaining unit work to supervisors that represents a new management initiative from an overlap of duties that has always been in place. The problem, in other words, is to identify the work of the bargaining unit. In *J.S. Jones Timber Ltd. and I.W.A., Local 1-3567* (2000), 93 L.A.C. (4th) 72, when several bargaining unit employees who performed certain supervisory duties joined management, the union grieved that the employer had improperly transferred bargaining unit work to excluded personnel. Arbitrator Ready dismissed the grievance, holding that in the case of duties which by their very nature typically form part of the functions of a supervisor or manager, there must be "a rather favourable evidentiary foundation" to demonstrate that such duties had, over time, been completely and irretrievably abandoned to the bargaining unit. Also relevant, the arbitrator added, is the extent to which the duties in question are "core" bargaining unit functions, as opposed to merely incidental or peripheral functions.

In *Weyerhaeuser Co. and I.W.A., Local 2171*, [2004] B.C.C.A.A.A. No. 152 (QL), Arbitrator Taylor rejected a union argument that, in accordance with the decision in *J.S. Jones Timber*, evidence of damage to the integrity of the bargaining unit was in itself sufficient to trigger the implied restriction against reassignment of bargaining unit work. The arbitrator concluded that, in those cases where it was found that the integrity of the bargaining unit had been undermined, the work transferred to management personnel consisted of "classic bargaining unit functions", to use the words of Arbitrator Ready in *J.S. Jones Timber*. This work is to be distinguished from typically managerial functions, including supervision. Where bargaining unit employees can be said to have performed such functions at all, it would generally not be to the exclusion of members of management. Such "inherently overlapping" duties, Arbitrator Taylor held, do not fall within the scope of the implied restriction.

17.1.2 Express Restrictions: "Work Normally Performed"

The cases discussed in Chapter 17.1.1 address situations in which the union has not seen fit or been able to negotiate express limitations on management's right to reassign bargaining unit work. Where the collective agreement does contain such limitations, arbitrators have generally construed restrictively any stated exceptions, as representing the clear point of demarcation settled upon by the parties. In *New Brunswick (Board of Management) and C.U.P.E., Local 1190* (1997), 63 L.A.C. (4th) 56 (McAllister), for instance, the collective agreement prohibited supervisors from performing bargaining unit work "except in the case of emergencies". On the ground that the parties had negotiated a very narrow and focused qualification, Arbitrator McAllister ruled that there was no justification for "reading down" the provision to give management further latitude beyond the stated exception.

Express limitations on management's right to have bargaining unit work done by employees outside the unit are typically expressed as protecting work that is "normally performed" by or "normally assigned" to members of the bargaining unit. Although the presence of an express restriction may provide substantially more protection than the implied restriction, the factual problem of identifying what is "bargaining unit work" has been a vexing one for arbitrators, particularly where the work in question has historically been shared by employees inside and outside the bargaining unit.

Most graphically, the issue of shared work has arisen in the context of job protection clauses covering, respectively, registered practical nurses (also known as registered nursing assistants) and registered nurses, whose job duties commonly overlap to a regular and significant degree. As Arbitrator Thorne noted in *Fairhaven Home for Senior Citizens and O.N.A.* (1992), 28 L.A.C. (4th) 399, "instances of an overlap in duties have given rise to a number of awards, with results that do not at first blush seem entirely consistent". On the one hand, a number of arbitrators have espoused the view that work which has in the past been shared with employees outside the bargaining unit cannot properly be considered "bargaining unit work", "normally performed" by bargaining unit employees, within the meaning of the work-protection clause. Although the volume or frequency of the work at issue may have changed, the non-bargaining unit employees may also rightly be said to be performing their *own* work. Other arbitrators, however, have held that the phrase "normally performed" cannot be read down to mean "exclusively performed" without doing violence to the parties' intentions. Accordingly, in the face of the words "normally performed", where a specific parcel of work has been assigned to bargaining unit personnel on a consistent basis, this work — or "bundle of duties" — is said to fall within the express parameters of the clause. In other words, the terms "normally assigned" or "normally performed" are said to cover both the *type* and the *volume* of the work customarily given to members of the bargaining unit, thus preserving the status quo in existence when the collective agreement was settled. Of this second line of decisions, the award of Arbitrator Howard Brown in *Rideaucrest Home for the Aged and O.N.A.* (1995), 48 L.A.C. (4th) 1 is generally regarded as seminal.

Rejecting the approach typified by *Rideaucrest Home for the Aged*, other arbitrators, as noted, have required the union to establish that the disputed work has been performed exclusively by bargaining unit employees. Often cited as a prime example of an award adopting a stricter interpretation along these lines is *Fairhaven Home for Senior Citizens, supra*, where Arbitrator Thorne reviewed a number of previous decisions. In his view, in all the awards in which both the type and the volume of work have been held reserved to the union, the evidence clearly showed a long-standing and discrete pattern of work assignment in favour of the complainant union. In the case before him, by contrast, the evidence revealed such fluctuations in this pattern that it would have been difficult to reconstruct the exact "type and volume" of work in any event. Thus, the arbitrator ruled, even if the *Rideaucrest Home for the Aged* approach were followed, the union's grievance would fail.

As Arbitrator Thorne indicated, the apparent divergences in the jurisprudence can often be reconciled by a close examination of the historical evidence in each case; that is, by focusing on the extent to which a discrete allocation of duties as between the two classifications can be clearly identified. In the words of Arbitrator Haefling in *St. Joseph's General Hospital and S.E.I.U., Local 478*, [1999] O.L.A.A. No. 782 (QL), at para. 22, the applicable clause will protect "those work tasks, responsibilities or functions which have some historical precedent or are observable through some time continuum". The award in *St. Joseph's General Hospital* reflects as well the practical approach increasingly being adopted by arbitrators when wrestling with this problem. Where the reassignment of overlapping duties occurs on a fluctuating and day-to-day basis, without any obvious impact on job security, the employer will be able to avoid liability under the collective agreement by invoking the *de minimis* rule. Where, however, the realignment of duties has the effect of undermining the integrity of the bargaining unit, the clause will operate more restrictively. An example of such a realignment can be found in *St. Mary's General Hospital and London & District Service Workers' Union*, [1998] O.L.A.A. No. 578 (QL), in which Arbitrator Kaplan ruled that the elimination of a job classification on a particular shift and the transfer of its work to a position in another bargaining unit violated a clause protecting work "normally assigned" to employees covered by the collective agreement.

The rapid computerization of the workplace has presented arbitrators with a major challenge in formulating a workable approach to bargaining unit work-protection clauses, and particularly in identifying the duties to which the protection attaches. The first award in which these issues were explored at length was *Kamloops (City) and C.U.P.E., Local 900*, [1996] B.C.C.A.A.A. No. 611 (QL), where Arbitrator Germaine examined the alleged breach from the point of view of the express restrictions on the reassignment of bargaining unit work set out in the collective agreement. The arbitrator's extensive analysis focused on whether the growing use of computers and computerized equipment represented simply an enhancement of the way in which the bargaining unit work was done previously, in which case the restrictions applied, or a major alteration, or even elimination, of work that had previously existed, in which case management's right to reorganize work and introduce technological changes prevailed.

Arbitrator Browne, in *Newfoundland (Treasury Board) and N.A.P.E.* (2004), 128 L.A.C. (4th) 389, concluded that the extent of the work reassignment required to trigger a violation is much greater in relation to a clause prohibiting "work on any *jobs*" in the bargaining unit than in relation to a clause prohibiting the transfer of "any *work* normally performed" by bargaining unit employees. Because job classifications should not be viewed as "watertight", and employees cannot assert a property right to the tasks comprising their jobs, the arbitrator reasoned, the parties could not have intended to preclude the transfer of one or more duties previously performed by bargaining unit employees to staff outside the unit.

17.2   CONTRACTING OUT

17.2.1   Necessity for Express Provision

In earlier years, there was considerable arbitral support for the view that the employer did not retain an inherent right to contract out, as this would effectively nullify the bargaining unit rights otherwise entrenched in the collective agreement. This was the response formulated, for example, by Arbitrator Cross in *Studebaker-Packard Ltd. and U.A.W., Local 525* (1957), 7 L.A.C. 310.

Decisions such as that in *Studebaker-Packard* were a manifestation of the "clean slate" approach advocated by Arbitrator Bora Laskin in *Peterboro Lock Manufacturing Co. Ltd. and U.E., Local 527* (1953), 4 L.A.C. 1499. On the specific question of contracting out, however, this framework was overtaken by a line of awards represented by *Electric Auto-Lite Ltd. and U.A.W., Local 456* (1957), 7 L.A.C. 331, in which Arbitrator Thomas held that it would be improper to imply such a fundamental restriction on management's right to govern the enterprise if the collective agreement itself was silent on the issue. (For further discussion of *Peterboro Lock Manufacturing* and *Electric-Auto Lite*, see Chapter 16.2.1.)

Thus, by the time Arbitrator Arthurs rendered his famous award in *Russelsteel Ltd. and U.S.W.A.* (1966), 17 L.A.C. 253, he was able to conclude that, in light of the trend in arbitral law, the union must be assumed to have known of the need to negotiate specific limitations on the right of management to contract out. The award also conclusively resolved the issue of whether a provision prohibiting non-bargaining unit employees from performing bargaining unit work was sufficient to preclude the employer from contracting out such work to a third party. In the arbitrator's view, such a clause did not constitute the kind of explicit restriction that was capable of supporting a union grievance in a contracting out situation.

However, where the collective agreement prohibited any "person" who was not in the bargaining unit from doing bargaining unit work if this would result in layoffs of employees in the unit, it was held that the term "person" included workers engaged by an outside contractor, and thus constituted a restriction on the employer's right to contract out: *Country Place Nursing Home Ltd. and C.U.P.E., Local 1854* (1981), 1 L.A.C. (3d) 341 (Prichard).

17.2.2   Determining the Scope of Management's Right to Contract Out

Arbitral jurisprudence reveals great variety in the form of provision which the parties may adopt as a limitation on the employer's right to contract out bargaining unit work. The union's right to lodge a grievance may be made contingent on satisfactory evidence that the decision to contract out has led to layoffs, a failure to recall employees on layoff, or a reduction in the work hours of regular employees. Alternatively, the employer may retain the right to contract out unless the union establishes that bargaining unit employees possess the requisite skill to perform the work in question, in which case the arbitrator will embark on a factual inquiry similar to that involved in promotion or layoff grievances (see Chapters 19 and 20). Contracting out may be prohibited altogether except in the event of an emergency. Equally, the parties may devise any combination of these or other criteria as a means of balancing the union's interest in job security against the employer's interest in efficiency and cost-effectiveness.

For example, in *Ivaco Rolling Mills and U.S.W.A., Local 8794* (1997), 67 L.A.C. (4th) 66 (Adell), the collective agreement expressly allowed the employer to contract out, subject to the restriction that, "wherever practicable", work would be performed by employees in the bargaining unit. The issue of whether it would be "practicable" to keep a disputed work assignment in-house involves the arbitrator in an open-ended inquiry in which a variety of factors must be considered. In *Ivaco Rolling Mills*, the employer alleged that it was more practicable to contract out an electrical project because assigning the job to bargaining unit employees would have entailed paying excessive amounts of overtime. Rejecting the employer's unsubstantiated statement to this effect, Arbitrator Adell allowed the grievance, noting that the employer should have adduced concrete evidence of the cost differential.

The award in *Ivaco Rolling Mills* also addresses the proper interpretation of an increasingly common form of restriction on management's right to contract out, namely, the obligation to consult with the union before finalizing any decision affecting bargaining unit work. Reiterating a widely accepted view, the arbitrator held that a provision of this kind requires the employer to engage in a meaningful dialogue in which it is open to any alternative proposals put forward by the union.

As in the case of restrictions on the employer's ability to devolve bargaining unit work upon employees outside the unit (see Chapter 17.1), restrictions on the right to contract out are frequently expressed by reference to work "normally performed" by or "normally assigned" to employees in the bargaining unit. All the usual difficulties of delineating what constitutes bargaining unit work are compounded where the contractor to whom the employer proposes to give the work makes use of markedly different technological processes. Does a change in the way in which work is performed because of technological advances give rise to such an alteration in the work itself that it can no longer be considered "work" of the bargaining unit to which the union has a negotiated right? To date, arbitrators have focused on the essential *work* being performed for the employer, as opposed to the individual tasks or duties — the tools or instruments — by which this work is accomplished. In *Weyerhauser Canada Ltd. and C.E.P., Local 1120* (unreported, May 13, 1998), for instance, Arbitrator Hood ruled that the disputed work did not cease to be work "normally done" by members of the bargaining unit, despite the transformation of the job process made possible by the contractor's state-of-the-art computer technology. Similarly, see the award of Arbitrator Germaine in *Kamloops (City) and C.U.P.E., Local 900*, [1996] B.C.C.A.A.A. No. 611 (QL), discussed in Chapter 17.1.2.

Frequently, the collective agreement entitles the employer to contract out bargaining unit work as long as it does not result in layoffs. Where this is the case, the issue of causation is essentially one of fact. In *Saskatoon School Division No. 13 and C.U.P.E., Local 34* (2003), 120 L.A.C. (4th) 150, Arbitrator Hood explores the difference between clauses that prohibit contracting out only if it is the "sole" reason for the layoff, and those that do not have the restriction so narrowed. With respect to the latter, the arbitrator noted, the union need only establish that the decision to contract out was an "effective" cause of the workforce reduction, notwithstanding the presence of other contributing factors.

Additional Reading

M.G. Mitchnick, "Contracting Out: Two Solitudes" in W. Kaplan, J. Sack, M. Gunderson & R. Filion, eds., *Labour Arbitration Yearbook 1998*, p. 79.

R.O. MacDowell, "Contracting Out at Arbitration: An Arbitrator's Perspective" in
W. Kaplan, J. Sack & M. Gunderson, eds., *Labour Arbitration Yearbook 1994-
95*, p. 325; and companion articles by R.A. Macpherson, and J.K.A. Hayes &
M.D. Wright.

17.2.3   Validity of the Contracting Out: Who Is the "True" Employer?

Even where the collective agreement does permit the contracting out of
bargaining unit work, the union may allege that the employer has not effected
a valid or effective contracting out. In other words, it may be argued that, for
the purposes of the collective agreement, the individuals who are now performing the work should be treated as employees of the employer, *not* employees of the third-party contractor. The potential consequences of a ruling to this
effect are twofold. First, the employer will be obligated to extend to the individuals in question the wage structure and ancillary benefits under the collective agreement, and to remit union dues on their behalf. Second, because all
seniority-related rights under the agreement also become applicable, the retention of the individuals supplied by the contractor as employees may give rise
to a violation of any layoff, recall or work protection provisions affecting other
bargaining unit employees.

Historically, three tests have been used at arbitration to determine whether
the "true employer" of individuals whose status is in dispute is in fact the third-
party contractor or the entity which is party to the collective agreement: the common law test derived from the judgment of the English Privy Council in
Montreal Locomotive Works, [1947] 1 D.L.R. 161; the so-called *York Condo-
minium* test developed by the Ontario Labour Relations Board, [1977] O.L.R.B.
Rep. 645; and the "organization test". An exhaustive analysis of these tests and
the elements of which they are composed is set out in the oft-quoted case of *Don
Mills Foundation for Senior Citizens and S.E.I.U., Local 204* (1984), 14 L.A.C.
(3d) 385 (P.C. Picher), and more recently in *Simon Fraser Health Region and
H.E.U.*, [2000] B.C.C.A.A.A. No. 307 (QL). In the latter decision, Arbitrator
Munroe affirmed that, while the inquiry invariably involves identifying the "seat
of fundamental control" over an employee, no single factor is necessarily deci-
sive, and the appropriate weight to be accorded to each factor may vary according to the circumstances of the case. While the employer clearly intended to use
the "contracted services" model, not the "in-house employee" model, Munroe
nonetheless found the employer had in its contract with the supplier retained sufficient elements of control over the guards to create an employment relationship.
Management was not entitled to "have the best of both worlds". This was true,
however, only of the "regular cadre" of security officers. The evidence fell short
of establishing the same kind of relationship in respect of guards who were periodically referred by the agency on an *ad hoc* basis.

The distinction drawn by Arbitrator Munroe between the "regular cadre" of agency guards and those dispatched on an as-needed basis is consistent with the analysis by Arbitrator Pamela Picher in *IKO Industries Ltd. and U.S.W.A.* (2002), 118 L.A.C. (4th) 1. The *IKO Industries* award draws on the decision of the Supreme Court of Canada in *Pointe-Claire (City) v. Quebec (Labour Court)* (1997), 146 D.L.R. (4th) 1 (S.C.C.), where the dispute centred on the use of temporary replacement employees obtained from a personnel agency. The Court emphasized that, in this context, control over an employee's day-to-day work performance and integration into the business must not be used as the exclusive criteria for identifying the true employer. Rather, a more comprehensive and flexible approach should be adopted in order to ensure that the employees are "able to bargain with the party that exercises the greatest control over all aspects of their work" (at pp. 21-22). The confusion or apparent inconsistency in the caselaw, Arbitrator Picher posits, is the result of insufficient attention being paid to the difference between "temporary replacement employees" and "permanent replacement employees". In the latter instance, because the individual works permanently for the client business, the factor of day-to-day control and direction typically plays a pivotal role in the assessment of which entity exercises fundamental control, and other criteria may quite properly be discounted as matters of mere form. In the temporary replacement situation, conversely, greater significance may attach to the relationship between the agency that initially hires the individual and is responsible for his or her work assignments on an ongoing basis. The longer the duration of an on-site assignment, the arbitrator adds, the harder it may be to establish that fundamental control rests with the agency rather than the client business.

The recent jurisprudence thus appears to leave unchanged the proposition, accepted by most arbitrators, that employees furnished by a third-party contractor who are brought in-house to perform bargaining unit work on an ongoing or permanent basis are employees of the employer for the purposes of the collective agreement: see Arbitrator Picher's earlier award in *Don Mills Foundation for Senior Citizens*, *supra*. To support a different conclusion, there must be evidence that the contractor is providing something more than simply the labour component, as was the case, for example, in *Christie Brown and B.C.T., Local 426* (2001), 99 L.A.C. (4th) 147 (Tacon).

Similar issues may arise where the employer is actually part of an interrelated group of companies. In addition to filing a grievance challenging the validity of a contracting-out arrangement, it is open to the union to apply, under the applicable labour relations legislation, for a declaration that the party-employer and another entity constitute "one employer" for the purposes of the collective agreement. For example, s. 1(4) of the Ontario *Labour Relations Act*, S.O. 1995, c. 1, Sch. A, provides:

> Where, in the opinion of the [Labour Relations Board], associated or related activities or businesses are carried on, whether or not simultaneously, by or

through more than one corporation, individual, firm, syndicate or association or any combination thereof, under common control or direction, the Board may, upon the application of any person, trade union or council of trade unions concerned, treat the corporations, individuals, firms, syndicates or associations or any combination thereof as constituting one employer for the purposes of this Act and grant such relief, by way of declaration or otherwise, as it may deem appropriate.

Comparable provisions exist in most other jurisdictions: see, for instance, s. 21 of the Nova Scotia *Trade Union Act*, R.S.N.S. 1989, c. 475, and s. 47 of the Alberta *Labour Relations Code*, R.S.A. 2000, c. L-1. The purpose of these enactments is to prevent an employer from evading its obligations under the collective agreement by redirecting bargaining unit work to a non-unionized entity with which it does not have an arm's-length relationship. However, the power conferred by s. 1(4) of the Ontario legislation to "pierce the corporate veil" and issue a single-employer declaration has been held to vest solely in the Ontario Labour Relations Board: *Remembrance Services Inc. v. U.F.C.W., Local 175* (2001), 147 O.A.C. 297 (Div. Ct.). In the latter decision, the Court emphasized the fact that, under s. 1(4), the question is stated to be one for "the opinion of the Board" — language which also appears in the provisions in effect in other jurisdictions. It would therefore appear that an arbitrator has no authority to apply such provisions, even where the governing legislation expressly grants arbitrators the power to interpret and apply employment-related statutes.

Additional Reading

G. Trudeau, "Temporary Employees Hired Through a Personnel Agency: Who Is the Real Employer?" (1997), 5 Canadian Labour and Employment Law Journal, p. 359.

17.3   JOB CLASSIFICATIONS AND THE ORGANIZATION OF WORK

The purpose of a schedule of job classifications in the collective agreement, arbitrators have consistently maintained, is to ensure that employees are paid at a wage rate appropriate to the work that they perform. At the same time, however, as Arbitrator Adams pointed out in *Windsor Public Utilities Commission and I.B.E.W., Local 911* (1974), 7 L.A.C. (2d) 380, the employer has a presumptive right to reorganize its workforce, provided it does so in good faith, for valid business reasons, and with due regard for the collective agreement. From his extensive review of the caselaw, the arbitrator distilled a number of guiding principles for the adjudication of union grievances relating to changes in job duties or classification structure:

(1) Job classifications are not "completely self-contained water-tight compartments", and some overlap between classifications is unexceptional.

(2) To justify a claim to be paid the rate for a new or different classification, an employee must establish a substantial change in his or her job duties.

(3) Conversely, to justify paying an employee a lower rate than previously, the employer must establish a substantial change in the employee's job duties.

(4) To justify a claim to be paid the rate for an existing, higher-rated classification, an employee must be performing the central or core duties of that job.

(5) At least in the absence of negotiated job descriptions in the collective agreement, the employer has the right to abolish classifications, and to redistribute the duties to employees in the remaining classifications.

The principle that an employee seeking reclassification must demonstrate a "substantial" change in his or her job duties was discussed and applied more recently by Arbitrator Sullivan in *Vancouver (City) and C.U.P.E., Local 15*, [2005] B.C.C.A.A.A. No. 4 (QL). It is not every modification of duties and responsibilities that will justify a change in rate or job classification. The changes must be significant and substantial, Arbitrator Sullivan pointed out, such that the current classification no longer captures the nature and level of work being performed in the position.

More broadly, the principles outlined in *Windsor Public Utilities Commission, supra*, were affirmed by Arbitrator Outhouse in *Auto Haulaway Inc. and Teamsters, Local 927* (1995), 47 L.A.C. (4th) 301. Even though the abolition of the classification in question caused the layoff of bargaining unit employees, and the transfer of core functions to a different classification created scheduling problems, the arbitrator dismissed the union's grievance. In his view, in the absence of any specific restrictions in the collective agreement, the employer was acting within its management right to restructure the workforce, and it was not appropriate for an arbitrator to imply restrictions on that right.

CHAPTER 18

SENIORITY RIGHTS DEFINED

18.1 THE MEANING AND IMPORTANCE OF SENIORITY

The central importance of seniority in a collective bargaining relationship has frequently been recognized by arbitrators and academic observers. Seniority vies with discipline as the most frequently litigated issue in the arbitral forum. Under most collective agreements, seniority plays a critical role in determining employees' rights with respect to promotion, transfer, layoff, recall and entitlement to benefits ranging from vacation pay to pensions. The following statement by two American academics captures the significance of seniority for most workers:

> [S]eniority enables an employee to acquire valuable interests by his work, to capitalize his labor and obtain something more than a day's wages for his continued production. When seniority determines promotion rights, it gives the employee a claim to better jobs when they become available; when seniority determines the order of layoff, it provides the employee a measure of insurance against unemployment. Seniority does not guarantee that vacancies in higher rated jobs will be filled or that any jobs will be available; but by giving the senior employee priority when a choice is made as to who will be promoted or who will remain employed, seniority gives an employee an interest of substantial practical value. As Professor Aaron has pointed out, "[m]ore than any other provision of the collective agreement . . . seniority affects the economic security of the individual covered by its terms", and it has understandably come to be viewed as one of the most highly prized possessions of any employee. Seniority may be the most valuable capital asset of an employee of long service.

See C.W. Summers and M.C. Love, "Work Sharing as an Alternative to Layoffs by Seniority" (1976), 124 U. Pa. L. Rev. 893, at p. 902.

The most frequently cited Canadian arbitration award on the centrality of seniority in the employment setting is *Tung-Sol of Canada Ltd. and U.E., Local 512* (1964), 15 L.A.C. 161 (Reville). This decision established the principle that the provisions of a collective agreement should be construed strictly against authorizing the loss, forfeiture or undermining of seniority, or the rights and privileges which would otherwise attach to seniority.

18.2   THE MEASUREMENT AND DURATION OF SENIORITY

Because seniority is recognized as a collective bargaining concept, it is generally open to the parties to stipulate the terms of its commencement, acquisition and termination, subject to statutory restrictions. The Supreme Court of Canada has declared that seniority rights are ultimately based on the collective agreement and, like other negotiated rights, are subject to modification if the employer and the union so agree: *Hémond v. Coopérative fédére du Québec*, [1989] 2 S.C.R. 962. However, largely because of the sentiments expressed in *Tung-Sol of Canada Ltd. and U.E., Local 512* (1964), 15 L.A.C. 161 (Reville) (discussed in Chapter 18.1), the majority of arbitrators has held that unqualified collective agreement references to "seniority", "continuous service" or "length of continuous service" simply mean continuous employment as measured by time since the date of hire. Thus, absences from the workplace for reasons which do not result in termination of employment will generally not interfere with the accumulation of seniority or entitlement to benefits based on seniority. As the Supreme Court of Canada has stated, "in the absence of a clearly expressed intention to the contrary, the provisions in a collective agreement should not generally be interpreted in a way that undermines acquired seniority rights of employees": *Battlefords and District Co-Operatives Ltd. v. R.W.D.S.U., Local 544* (1998), 160 D.L.R. (4th) 29 (S.C.C.), at p. 35. This principle was applied in *Dufferin-Peel Roman Catholic Separate School Board and Ass'n of Professional Student Services Personnel* (1995), 48 L.A.C. (4th) 316, in which Arbitrator Michel Picher refused to pro-rate the seniority or seniority credits of part-time employees because there was no clear language in the collective agreement importing such a limitation on the acquisition of seniority.

A similar approach was adopted in *Durham District School Board and Elementary Teachers' Federation of Ontario (Cubitt)*, [2004] O.L.A.A. No. 550 (QL), where Arbitrator Pamela Picher held that a teacher who was working only part of the week pursuant to a graduated return to work plan should not suffer any loss of seniority or interruption in service accrual for the purpose of placement on the salary grid. The arbitrator found that there was nothing in the collective agreement to indicate an intention that time taken as unpaid sick leave would not count as "continuous employment". Although there was some evidence of a past practice to the contrary, it was not clear whether this practice had been discussed with or made known to the union.

The question of whether employers have the right to lay off workers who are on maternity leave or leave of absence due to injury was considered by Arbitrator Pekeles in *Brewers Distributor Ltd. and Brewery, Winery &*

Distillery Workers Union, Local 300 (2004), 128 L.A.C. (4th) 34. According to the arbitrator, there is a general consensus in the caselaw that, unless the contract expressly permits it, an employer cannot lay off an employee who is absent on pregnancy or parental leave, medical leave, or workers' compensation leave. This principle may be critical to determining the duration of an employee's seniority, since many collective agreements contain provisions similar to the one in *Brewers Distributor* permitting termination of seniority after a certain number of months on layoff. As Arbitrator Pekeles noted, the arbitral principle applies independently of any protection offered by employment standards or human rights legislation. However, such legislation might be brought into play if the collective agreement does include express provisions allowing for layoff and loss of seniority during such leaves, as discussed in the following chapter.

18.2.1 Statutory Rights to Maintain Seniority

EMPLOYMENT STANDARDS LEGISLATION

Recent amendments to employment standards legislation in several jurisdictions have provided that an employee continues to enjoy entitlement to benefits and participation in benefit programs during maternity, pregnancy or parental leave. Generally speaking, these amendments have also attempted to preserve accumulated seniority and to entrench an employee's right to continue accruing seniority during the period of leave. In the aftermath of the legislative changes, a large number of grievances were filed attacking collective agreement provisions and employer practices that allowed for the prorating of benefits (such as paid vacation or sick leave credits) in respect of time spent on pregnancy or parental leave.

While one or two early decisions held that the pro-rating of benefits did not contravene employment standards legislation, most arbitrators have followed the reasoning of Arbitrator Michel Picher in *Barrie (City) and C.U.P.E., Local 2380* (1994), 40 L.A.C. (4th) 168. At that time, s. 42(4) of Ontario's *Employment Standards Act* simply stated that "[s]eniority continues to accrue during pregnancy leave or parental leave". After reviewing the remedial purpose of the provision — to ensure that employees who take pregnancy or parental leave do not suffer the loss or diminution of any accrued rights, benefits or entitlements — the arbitrator ruled that the term "seniority" must be interpreted liberally as extending protection to service and service-related rights as well as seniority and seniority-related rights. Collective agreement provisions or employer practices which eliminate or reduce the benefits to which an employee on leave is entitled are therefore null and void as being contrary to the Act.

Ontario later amended s. 42(4) to incorporate expressly the Picher approach: see S.O. 1996, c. 23. The current provision is found in s. 52(1) of the Act (S.O. 2000, c. 41), and reads as follows:

52(1)   The period of an employee's leave under this Part shall be included in calculating any of the following for the purpose of determining his or her rights under an employment contract:

1. The length of his or her employment, whether or not it is active employment.
2. The length of the employee's service whether or not that service is active.
3. The employee's seniority.

In *Kenora Ass'n for Community Living and O.P.S.E.U., Local 702* (2004), 124 L.A.C. (4th) 86, Arbitrator Roberts observed that the express provisions in s. 52(1) of the Ontario *Employment Standards Act* entitling employees to continuation of benefit coverage and seniority or service accrual will often provide stronger protection than the equality guarantees under human rights legislation. In that case, because the grievors had taken pregnancy and parental leave, they were ineligible to participate in the employer's group pension plan, which required that employees work not less than 700 hours in a calendar year. The arbitrator held that the impugned eligibility requirements did not violate the province's *Human Rights Code* because, in accordance with the reasoning in *O.N.A. v. Orillia Soldiers Memorial Hospital* (1999), 169 D.L.R. (4th) 489 (Ont. C.A.) (see discussion below), employers are entitled to insist on actual service in exchange for earned benefits or compensation. However, the grievance was allowed on the basis that s. 52(1) of the *Employment Standards Act* expressly requires that the period of an employee's pregnancy or parental leave be included in calculating her rights under a contract of employment. Similarly, in *Dresden Industrial and U.F.C.W., Local 175* (2003), 124 L.A.C. (4th) 55 (Barton), it was held that s. 52(1) required the reinstatement of an employee who had taken alternative employment during parental leave. In the arbitrator's view, s. 52(1) precluded the enforcement of a collective agreement clause that provided for automatic termination of seniority where, without the employer's prior consent, an employee accepted gainful employment while on an authorized leave of absence.

The approach formulated by Arbitrator Picher was also adopted in *Stoney Creek (City) and C.U.P.E., Local 1220* (1998), 71 L.A.C. (4th) 272 (Knopf), and *B.C. Tel and T.W.U.* (1997), 64 L.A.C. (4th) 129 (Kelleher). The latter case applied this analysis to the provisions in the *Canada Labour Code*, R.S.C. 1985, c. L-2, relating to maternity leave.

However, in *Ontario (Management Board Secretariat) and A.M.A.P.C.E.O.*, [2004] O.G.S.B.A. No. 27 (QL), the Ontario Grievance Settlement Board ruled that it was not a contravention of s. 52(1) to pro-rate a pay-for-performance bonus scheme in respect of time spent on pregnancy or parental leave. The terms of the collective agreement made it clear, the Board found, that the bonus was a "work driven", not a "service driven", benefit to which the *Employment Standards Act* did not apply.

HUMAN RIGHTS LEGISLATION

The expansion of protection for the disabled under human rights legislation has led to numerous challenges to collective agreement provisions which limit the service or seniority accrual of an employee who, for any reason, is absent from work beyond a threshold period. The argument is that such provisions, while neutral on their face, nevertheless result in discrimination against persons who suffer from a disability. In the early 1990s, the Ontario courts declared that so-called "automatic termination clauses", which deem employees absent for a specified period (usually 12 to 24 months) to be dismissed, constitute adverse-effect discrimination on the basis of handicap, contrary to s. 11(1) of the *Human Rights Code*, R.S.O. 1990, c. H.19. That provision states as follows:

> 11(1)   A right of a person under Part I is infringed where a requirement, qualification or factor exists that is not discrimination on a prohibited ground but that results in the exclusion, restriction or preference of a group of persons who are identified by a prohibited ground of discrimination and of whom the person is a member, except where,
>
> > (a) the requirement, qualification or factor is reasonable and *bona fide* in the circumstances; or
> >
> > (b) it is declared in this Act, other than in section 17, that to discriminate because of such ground is not an infringement of a right.

The employer, the courts decided, did not have the right to discharge disabled employees without first satisfying its obligation under the *Code* to accommodate their needs to the point of undue hardship.

Initially, there was some inconsistency among arbitrators as to whether this rationale could be extended to contract clauses purporting to pro-rate or to stop the accrual of an employee's seniority based on absence from work. More recently, however, a consensus has emerged around the analysis of Arbitrator Richard Brown, who has held that a distinction should be drawn between "competitive seniority" — which affects the ability of an employee to participate in the workplace in the context of promotion, layoff and recall — and "benefit seniority" — which determines the level of an employee's compensation, including benefits such as employer contributions to a plan of insured benefits. The distinction rests on the premise that, in dealing with disability, the Ontario *Human Rights Code* treats the right to participation and the right to compensation differently. According to Arbitrator Brown, s. 11(1) of the *Code* should be read in light of s. 17 because the latter provision deals specifically with the rights of disabled workers:

> 17(1)   A right of a person under this Act is not infringed for the reason only that the person is incapable of performing or fulfilling the essential duties or requirements attending the exercise of the right because of disability.
>
> (2)   The Commission, the Tribunal or a court shall not find a person incapable unless it is satisfied that the needs of the person cannot be accommodated

without undue hardship on the person responsible for accommodating those
needs, considering the cost, outside sources of funding, if any, and health and
safety requirements, if any.

As the focus of s. 17 is on an individual's capacity to perform duties, not on
compensation, it is only in connection with the performance of duties that the
legislation requires accommodation of a disability. To the extent, therefore, that
the collective agreement has the effect of curtailing or limiting the competitive
seniority of an employee who is unable to attend at work due to disability, it
gives rise to discrimination and is unlawful. However, where the provision in
question involves benefit seniority or eligibility for particular forms of compensation, a disabled employee's only right is to be remunerated in the same
way as an employee without a disability. If employees who are absent from
work for a reason unrelated to disability do not accrue service or seniority, and
as a consequence do not qualify for parts of the compensation package, a disabled employee has no ground for complaint if he or she is treated in an identical fashion. First developed in the seminal decision of *Versa Services Ltd. and
Milk & Bread Drivers, Dairy Employees, Caterers & Allied Employees Union,
Local 647* (1994), 39 L.A.C. (4th) 196 (R.M. Brown), affirmed by the Ontario
Divisional Court, [1995] O.J. No. 4931 (QL), this framework was further elaborated by the same arbitrator in *Porcupine & District Children's Aid Society
and C.U.P.E., Local 2196* (1996), 56 L.A.C. (4th) 116.

A similar conclusion was reached in *Orillia Soldiers Memorial Hospital
and O.N.A.* (1996), 58 L.A.C. (4th) 72, where Arbitrator Mitchnick presents a
comprehensive review of the jurisprudence on the issue of whether clauses
which limit seniority accrual, service accrual or benefit plan participation during a period of absence from work offend the prohibition against discrimination on the ground of disability. The arbitrator ruled that automatically
terminating the accrual of *seniority* after an employee has been absent for a particular length of time constitutes discrimination, contrary to the Ontario *Human
Rights Code.* He also held, however, that clauses which limit *service* accrual
and entitlement to the payment of benefit plan premiums after a prescribed
period of absence from work do not infringe human rights legislation. Noting
that length of service under the collective agreement was tied to the amount of
compensation to which an employee was entitled, he relied on the *Versa Services* principle that differentiating among employees in matters pertaining to
compensation does not violate the *Code.*

On an appeal from the judgment of the Ontario Divisional Court, hearing an
application for judicial review, the arbitrator's award was affirmed by the Court
of Appeal: see *O.N.A. v. Orillia Soldiers Memorial Hospital* (1999), 169 D.L.R.
(4th) 489 (leave to appeal to S.C.C. denied December 9, 1999). However, the
Court disagreed with the *Versa Services* proposition that, in setting out the equality rights of the disabled, the *Human Rights Code* draws a distinction between
issues relating to compensation and issues relating to access or participation.

The suggestion that the broad application of s. 11(1) should be circumscribed by reference to s. 17 was also rejected. In the Court's opinion, s. 11 of the *Code* mandates the same approach to all collective agreement provisions or employer policies which discriminate against disabled employees, regardless of whether the effect is on compensation or on access to the workplace. The extent of the employer's duty of accommodation, and the criteria by which the *bona fides* of an occupational qualification is evaluated, do not vary. In the result, the Court of Appeal upheld the restrictions on service accrual and benefit plan contributions while striking down the restrictions on seniority accrual. While the requirement of work in exchange for compensation was found to be a reasonable and *bona fide* job requirement, the same could not be said of the limitations on seniority accrual, since the right to accumulate seniority was triggered simply by the status of being an employee, and did not require the active provision of labour. In the Court's view, denial to disabled persons of benefits that are designed to provide compensation in exchange for services is not discriminatory because in these circumstances disabled employees are not being denied a benefit because of their disability, but because they are unable to provide the services in question. On the other hand, the denial of seniority accrual to disabled employees is discriminatory because the purpose of seniority does not relate directly to compensation but to "the ability of employees to access, remain in, and thrive in the workplace". Seniority, the Court observed, is therefore a "right that is at the core of human rights legislation as it affects the disabled" (at p. 517). Thus, while the reasoning may differ, the judgment appears to continue the *Versa Services* distinction between seniority provisions affecting access or participation, and those affecting matters of compensation.

Arbitrators in jurisdictions outside Ontario have been divided in their response to the Court of Appeal's ruling in *Orillia Soldiers Memorial Hospital*. In a recent British Columbia case, for example, where the grievor suffered from a permanent disability and could work only four days a week, not five, Arbitrator Germaine endorsed and applied the *Versa Services* distinction between collective agreement provisions regarding compensation or benefits and those relating to status or participation in the workplace: *Insurance Corp. of British Columbia and O.P.E.I.U., Local 378* (2003), 123 L.A.C. (4th) 422. On the basis of this distinction, the arbitrator held that the employer was required, pursuant to its duty of accommodation, to treat the grievor as a full-time employee for the purposes of seniority accrual, even though she no longer worked full-time hours as defined by the collective agreement. However, the arbitrator held, the employer was not obligated to pay the grievor wages for a five-day work week, and would not normally have been required to treat her as a full-time employee for the purposes of benefit plan participation, save for the fact that in this case, the collective agreement specifically required the payment of full-time benefits to regular part-time employees who worked at least 75 percent of the hours worked by full-time employees.

In an important decision, the Ontario Court of Appeal has ruled that the province's former *Employment Standards Act*, R.S.O. 1990, c. E.14, discriminated against persons with severe long-term disabilities by denying them entitlement to severance pay, in contravention of the *Charter of Rights and Freedoms*: *O.N.A. v. Mount Sinai Hospital* (2005), 255 D.L.R. (4th) 195 (Ont. C.A.). Section 58(5)(c) of the Act, which gave Ontario employers the right to refuse severance pay to disabled employees, was unconstitutional and of no force or effect, the Court held, because the provision denied disabled persons equal treatment and equal compensation in employment, thereby affecting a "crucially important" aspect of their dignity. Thus, rather than limiting its inquiry to whether the benefit in dispute was compensation-related or access-related, as in *Orillia Soldiers Memorial Hospital*, *supra*, the Court of Appeal undertook a detailed analysis of the purpose served by the benefit, in order to determine whether its denial to persons with a disability was justified. The province's current *Employment Standards Act*, S.O. 2000, c. 41, has been amended to remove the offending provision.

Additional Reading

D.D. Carter, "The Arbitrator as Human Rights Adjudicator: Has *Meiorin* Made a Difference?" in K. Whitaker, J. Sack, M. Gunderson & R. Filion, eds., *Labour Arbitration Yearbook 2001-2002*, vol. I, p. 1; and companion articles by P. Meier; and E.J. McIntyre, K. Schucher & F. Faraday.

18.3   The Contest Between Seniority and Human Rights

As discussed in Chapter 18.2.1, the effect of applicable human rights legislation may be to preserve a disabled employee's right to continue accumulating seniority while he or she is absent from work for reasons related to the disability. Where, however, the employer attempts to discharge its statutory duty of accommodating an employee's disability in a manner which impinges on the seniority rights of *other* members of the bargaining unit, different considerations apply. The conflict between seniority rights under the collective agreement and a disabled employee's right to be reasonably accommodated has generated considerable controversy in the arbitral forum. In *Bayer Rubber Inc. and C.E.P., Local 914* (1997), 65 L.A.C. (4th) 261, for example, Arbitrator Watters made it clear that an employer is not entitled to *unilaterally* impose an accommodation arrangement that contravenes the seniority provisions of the collective agreement, without having given full consideration to the feasibility of alternative measures.

As the Supreme Court of Canada has repeatedly stated, most notably in *Central Okanagan School District No. 23 v. Renaud* (1992), 95 D.L.R. (4th) 577, the union no less than the employer owes a duty of accommodation, a duty which could include the waiver of normal seniority rights to facilitate an accommodation proposal (provided the proposal does not give rise to "significant interference with the rights of others" in the bargaining unit). In the *Renaud* case, the union, together with the employer, was found liable for violating the complainant's right to freedom from discrimination in employment on the basis of religion, because it had insisted on adherence to the shift schedules prescribed by the collective agreement, which included Friday afternoon shifts; the complainant was unable to work such shifts, since he observed the Sabbath from sundown Friday to sundown Saturday. This is consistent with the judgment in *O.P.E.I.U., Local 267 v. Domtar Inc.* (1992), 8 O.R. (3d) 65 (Div. Ct.), where the union refused to waive the application of collective agreement provisions which discriminated against certain employees on the basis of religion. The Court held the union jointly liable with the employer for the damages flowing from the discriminatory acts.

However, in *Roosma v. Ford Motor Co. of Canada Ltd.*, 2002 C.L.L.C. ¶230-036, the Ontario Divisional Court upheld a human rights tribunal decision dismissing a complaint of discrimination on the basis of religion against both the union and the employer. The shift schedule in effect at the plant regularly required the complainants to work on Friday evenings, which contravened the tenets of their religious faith. When the complainants incurred discipline and, in the end, dismissal for missing Friday evening shifts, the union declined to file grievances on their behalf. It was held, with respect to the union, that the various accommodation proposals advanced by the complainants would all have given rise to an unacceptable degree of disruption to the job rights of other employees under the collective agreement, and seniority rights in particular (whereas in *Renaud, supra*, the union apparently gave no consideration to the possibility of modifying the regular shift schedule). Accordingly, the Court ruled, the union had satisfied its duty to accommodate the complainants to the point of undue hardship.

In *Mohawk Council of Akwesasne and Ahkwesahsne Police Ass'n (White)* (2003), 122 L.A.C. (4th) 161, Arbitrator Pamela Chapman held that the duty to accommodate requires the employer and the union to at least consider displacing an incumbent from his or her position in the bargaining unit. It should, however, be noted that the employee who was at risk of being displaced in that case had less seniority than the grievor, and the collective agreement gave the employer a general discretion to make job assignments to the position in question without regard to seniority. See the discussion in Chapter 14.3.6. The issue of whether the employer is under an obligation to transfer an incumbent out of a position in order to accommodate a disabled employee continues to divide arbitrators, as indicated by the award in *Kelowna (City) and C.U.P.E., Local 338*, [2003] B.C.C.A.A.A. No. 272 (QL) (Lanyon). The arbitrator, in summarizing the principles of accommodation, expressed the view that "a disabled employee is not entitled to displace another employee (bumping)" in order to implement an accommodation proposal (at para. 25).

In *Queen's Regional Authority and I.U.O.E., Local 942* (1999), 78 L.A.C. (4th) 269, Arbitrator Christie was confronted with the issue of whether the Prince Edward Island *Human Rights Act*, R.S.P.E.I. 1988, c. H-12, imposes a duty on employers and unions to accommodate protected employees across bargaining unit lines. He concluded that, when interpreted in accordance with recent Supreme Court of Canada decisions, human rights legislation does impose such a duty in appropriate circumstances. However, because accommodating an employee across bargaining unit lines significantly increases the degree of hardship to employees and unions by interfering with collective agreement rights, the situations in which such accommodation may be appropriate are rare. In the arbitrator's view, the duty to accommodate overrides collective agreement rights of any significance only where (1) the need to accommodate is clear, in that the claim of the employee to be accommodated obviously outweighs the claims of employees whose rights will be displaced; and (2) no other reasonable mode of accommodation is available.

In *Kelowna (City)*, *supra*, Arbitrator Lanyon held that the employer's duty to accommodate may require placement of a disabled employee in a vacant position outside the bargaining unit. Similarly, he found, an employee's duty to act reasonably in cooperating with the employer and the union in achieving a suitable accommodation may require that he or she accept a position outside the bargaining unit if the parties are unable to identify a position within the unit which is substantially similar to the employee's pre-injury job, despite sincere efforts to do so. As noted above, the arbitrator also indicated that other employees should not be displaced from bargaining unit positions as part of an accommodation arrangement for a disabled co-worker. Perhaps even more significantly, it was held that the employer's duty to accommodate does not give rise to an obligation to apply the terms of the collective agreement to an accommodated position outside the bargaining unit. However, Arbitrator Lanyon qualified this conclusion by noting that the grievor would be entitled to retain seniority rights accumulated under the collective agreement, and could use them to claim positions which became available within the unit. In addition, having regard to provisions in the agreement which contemplated the loss of seniority following a period of employment outside the bargaining unit, the arbitrator indicated that such provisions would be inoperative during the period the grievor remained in the accommodated position.

In *Toronto District School Board and C.U.P.E., Local 4400*, [2004] O.L.A.A. No. 355 (QL), Arbitrator Pamela Picher rejected a claim that the employer had failed in its duty to accommodate the grievor to the point of undue hardship by taking too long to arrive at an agreement with the union to transfer her to a position in another bargaining unit. The agreement had ultimately been reached during a lengthy med-arb process before Arbitrator Picher, almost 20 months after the grievor first sought to return to work. The arbitrator ruled that, as long as the employer acts with reasonable diligence in investigating the grievor's functional abilities and exploring opportunities for accommodation both within and outside the bargaining unit, including opportunities proposed by the union, it will not be found in violation of its duty, despite the fact that it may take a considerable amount of time to arrive at a suitable accommodation.

Additional Reading

C. Rootham, S. McGee & B. Cole, "More Reconcilable Differences: Developing a Consistent Approach to Seniority and Human Rights Interests in Accommodation Cases" (2004), 11 Canadian Labour and Employment Law Journal, p. 69.

B. Bilson, "Seniority and the Duty to Accommodate: A Clash of Values" in K. Whitaker, J. Sack, M. Gunderson & R. Filion, eds., *Labour Arbitration Yearbook 1999-2000*, vol. I, p. 73.

M.G. Picher, "The Duty to Accommodate at Arbitration: An Arbitrator's Perspective" in W. Kaplan, J. Sack, M. Gunderson & R. Filion, eds., *Labour Arbitration Yearbook 1996-97*, p. 211; and companion articles by K.W. Kort and E. McIntyre.

18.4 Time Spent Outside the Bargaining Unit

There has been a serious division of opinion among arbitrators as to whether an employee should receive seniority credit for periods spent outside the bargaining unit once he or she returns to the unit. As with most seniority issues, the matter is to be resolved by resort to the language used in the collective agreement. However, difficulties arise where the agreement does not provide a clear answer. One school of opinion, sometimes referred to as the "Laskin school" due to its association with the award of Arbitrator Laskin in *Federal Wire & Cable Co. Ltd. and U.S.W.A.* (1960), 3 U.M.A.C. 276, holds that, because seniority is purely a collective bargaining concept, the accumulation of seniority is generally restricted to time employed within the bargaining unit, unless there is express language to the contrary. However, another group of arbitrators has adopted an opposing view premised on the importance of seniority to the individual employee, drawing an analogy between seniority and property rights. These arbitrators contend that, as long as the language of the collective agreement is broad enough to cover out-of-unit employment, a non-bargaining unit employee may retain, accumulate and exercise seniority. A seminal decision in this line of authority is *Loblaw Groceterias Co. Ltd. and United Brewery Workers, Local 800* (1967), 18 L.A.C. 231 (Christie). A more recent award which describes the development of both schools and discerns a trend in favour of the individual rights approach is *Cape Breton Children's Aid Society and C.U.P.E., Local 3577* (1996), 61 L.A.C. (4th) 70 (La Forest). Another decision which arrives at the same conclusion, and which includes a comprehensive review of the caselaw, is *Zellers Inc. and U.F.C.W., Local 175* (1997), 60 L.A.C. (4th) 336 (Whitehead).

The calculation of seniority in respect of time worked outside the bargaining unit may also be affected by statute. Where the purchaser of a business continues to employ the vendor's employees, s. 13 of the former Ontario *Employment Standards Act*, R.S.O. 1990, c. E.14, deemed the employees' period of employment with the vendor to be employment with the purchaser for the purpose of entitlement to holiday pay, vacation pay, pregnancy and parental leave, and termination pay under the Act. In *Metroland Printing, Publishing & Distributing Ltd. and C.E.P., Local 87-M* (2001), 101 L.A.C. (4th) 365 (Surdykowski), the employer sought to invoke this provision to obtain *full* seniority rights under the collective agreement for employees who entered the bargaining unit following the employer's acquisition of other businesses. The arbitrator rejected the claim, ruling that the effect of s. 13 was merely to require the recognition of service with the predecessor employer for the purpose of the specified entitlements. The provision was held not to affect the calculation of seniority for the purpose of applying the job security provisions of the collective agreement, which explicitly defined seniority as length of service with the employer, and made no reference to service with predecessor employers.

The Ontario *Employment Standards Act* has since been repealed and replaced by new legislation: S.O. 2000, c. 41. Section 9 of the new Act simply provides that employment with the vendor prior to the sale of a business shall be deemed to be continuous employment with the purchaser "for the purposes of the Act". On the basis of the reasoning in *Metroland Printing, Publishing & Distributing*, it appears likely that s. 9 does not affect the calculation of seniority under the collective agreement in respect of rights or benefits which are not governed by the legislation.

18.5   SUPER-SENIORITY

It is common for collective agreements to provide for special or "super" seniority rights for employees who hold union office. The usual rationale for such provisions is that they facilitate the representation of employee interests in a layoff or recall situation by enabling union officials to remain in the plant as long as possible or to return to work at the earliest opportunity. However, as the rights conferred by a super-seniority clause tend to conflict with the "general" seniority rights of other employees, the application of the concept in particular cases can be controversial. Arbitrators will generally enforce the super-seniority provision in a manner which reflects the intention of the parties. The decision in *Formart Graphics Inc. and G.C.I.U., Local 500M* (1994), 45 L.A.C. (4th) 219 (Newman) identifies the rationale for super-seniority and illustrates its impact on other workers in the bargaining unit.

Whether a super-seniority provision enables union officials to "bump up" into a higher job classification has been a contentious issue. Some arbitrators, taking what is perhaps the dominant view, maintain that because bumping up has a disruptive effect on normal job posting and layoff procedures, clear language in the collective agreement to that effect is required. The opposing view (espoused in *Indalex and U.S.W.A., Local 2729* (1977), 15 L.A.C. (2d) 390 (McLaren)) posits that, if the super-seniority clause is silent on the question, it is appropriate for an arbitrator to infer bumping up as well as bumping down and lateral bumping rights. Both positions are summarized in *Miracle Food Mart and U.F.C.W., Local 175/633* (1991), 21 L.A.C. (4th) 433, where Arbitrator Marszewski refused to allow the grievor to bump up into a managerial position.

CHAPTER 19

PROMOTION

19.1 VACANCIES AND JOB POSTING

The job posting provisions of the collective agreement generally prescribe the procedure which the employer must follow in filling vacancies that arise in the workplace. With respect to the employer's selection among the applicants, such provisions also identify the substantive criteria that govern the relationship between seniority on the one hand, and employees' skill, ability and qualifications on the other. Arbitrators have recognized that adherence to the posting procedure is essential for the protection of the seniority rights of employees covered by the agreement. Consequently, failure by the employer to comply with the procedure may result in a ruling that the disputed position must be reposted in a manner which complies with the collective agreement, and that any experience gained by an employee who was appointed to the position as a result of the improper posting must be disregarded in a subsequent competition. As affirmed by Arbitrator Verity in *Sudbury General Hospital and O.P.S.E.U., Local 660* (1996), 58 L.A.C. (4th) 289, arbitrators have gone yet further, maintaining that the employer is under an obligation to apply and administer the posting procedure in a fair and reasonable manner.

It has also been held in a number of cases that, once a vacancy has been posted, the employer is not permitted to cancel the competition in the absence of a sound and practical business reason for doing so. The caselaw was reviewed in *Ontario (Ministry of Community & Social Services) and O.P.S.E.U. (Perez)*, [2002] O.G.S.B.A. No. 52 (QL), where Vice-Chair Abramsky of the Ontario Grievance Settlement Board concluded that an even more stringent standard applies where the competition has been completed and offers of employment made and accepted. Credible allegations of widespread cheating did not justify the employer's decision to cancel the postings. Instead, the Board held, the employer should have postponed implementing the appointments pending the outcome of a complete investigation into the allegations.

However, on the threshold question of whether there exists a vacancy which triggers the posting requirements under the collective agreement, arbitrators have generally held that, in the absence of a specific provision in the agreement to the contrary, the employer retains a discretion to discontinue a job. Thus, even if an employee quits or retires, a vacancy may not arise if the employer decides that the work previously performed by the departing employee should no longer be performed, redistributed to other bargaining unit employees, or carried out by other means that do not violate the collective agreement. In those circumstances, the operation of the posting provisions will not be triggered. These principles were summarized and affirmed in *Dupont Canada Inc. and C.E.P., Local 28-0*, [2003] O.L.A.A. No. 624 (QL) (Simmons).

Consistent with the line of authority represented by *Dupont Canada*, most arbitrators appear to support the view that, at least in bargaining units that combine full-time and part-time employees, an employer does not violate standard job posting procedures by posting and filling two part-time positions to perform the work formerly done by a full-time employee who has left the bargaining unit. At one time, there was some division of opinion on this question, and a few arbitrators suggested that the practice was inconsistent with implied restrictions on management rights arising from seniority provisions under the collective agreement. In recent cases, however, the trend has been to allow the redistribution of formerly full-time duties among part-time employees on the basis of general management rights, unless the practice is precluded by specific restrictions in the job posting provisions. The decision of Arbitrator Goodfellow in *North Wellington Health Care Corp. and O.P.S.E.U., Local 226*, [2004] O.L.A.A. No. 468 (QL) provides a summary of the arbitral jurisprudence on this issue.

19.1.1   Reliance on Criteria Not Included in Posting

Arbitrators have generally held that employer reliance on non-posted qualifications, skills or characteristics constitutes an unfair and unreasonable selection procedure, and may invalidate the results of the competition. The critical concern in such cases is whether the posting gave applicants proper notice of the criteria to be applied in filling the vacancy. To the extent that the employer has applied non-posted criteria, it will be found to have asked itself the "wrong question" in assessing candidates for the position. These principles were followed in *Elgin (County) Roman Catholic Separate School Board and London & District Service Workers' Union, Local 220* (1992), 26 L.A.C. (4th) 204 (Rose).

19.2 PROMOTION CLAUSES

19.2.1 Sufficient Ability and Relative Ability Distinguished

In negotiating the content of a promotion clause, the union normally attempts to maximize the weight of an employee's seniority in the evaluation and selection process. The employer's interest, by contrast, lies in preserving the full range of managerial discretion to hire a candidate who, in its view, possesses the finest skills, ability and qualifications. The relative weight to be given seniority on the one hand, and skill or ability on the other, therefore depends on the particular language agreed upon by the parties. There are two common types of clause. The first kind of provision stipulates that the applicant with the most seniority is entitled to the job, provided he or she has the necessary skill, ability or qualifications. Referred to as a "threshold" or "sufficient ability" or "non-competitive clause", such a provision affords greater weight to seniority because the senior applicant who meets the threshold requirements must be offered the position, even if there is a junior applicant with more attractive credentials. The second type of provision, known as an "equal ability" or "relative ability" or "competitive clause", stipulates that seniority determines the outcome of the competition only where the skill and ability of the various applicants are relatively equal.

The difference between threshold and relative ability clauses was explained by Arbitrator Laskin in *Westeel Products Ltd. and U.A.W.* (1960), 11 L.A.C. 199. In that case, the arbitrator expressed the view that a reference to "equal ability" in a competitive clause should be construed to mean "relatively equal ability", since it is impossible to measure the qualifications and suitability of different candidates with absolute precision. As summarized in *Halifax (City) and I.A.F.F., Local 268* (1991), 19 L.A.C. (4th) 392 (Outhouse), this interpretive approach has become the prevalent position among arbitrators. The award also illustrates the danger which an employer risks in assuming a direct correlation between an employee's skill or ability and the results of a standardized test or interview, topics which are reviewed elsewhere in this chapter.

In *Edmonton (City) and C.U.P.E., Local 30*, [2002] A.G.A.A. No. 12 (QL), an arbitration board chaired by Phyllis Smith concurred with the suggestion by Arbitrator Outhouse in *Halifax (City)* that a ten percent differential in cumulative point scoring represents a realistic guideline in applying the concept of relative equality. However, in *Ottawa Hospital and O.P.S.E.U. (Jamal)* (2002), 109 L.A.C. (4th) 168, Arbitrator Kaplan held that, where the competition involves a complex, responsible and highly skilled position, a narrower differential of as little as six percent may be sufficient to demonstrate that the senior applicant is not relatively equal in qualifications, skill and ability.

For a case in which the grievor was unable to rely on his seniority ranking to obtain a position in the face of a relative ability clause, see *Ivaco Rolling Mills Ltd. and U.S.W.A., Local 7940* (1997), 69 L.A.C. (4th) 1 (Adell), discussed in Chapter 19.5. On the other hand, many promotion decisions have been reversed at arbitration because, in ranking employees according to ability, the employer exceeded its rights as delimited by a sufficient ability clause in the collective agreement. As demonstrated in *Hôpital Général Juif Sir Mortimer B. Davis and S.C.F.P., Local 3113* (1990), 16 L.A.C. (4th) 277 (Frumkin), choosing one type of clause rather than another may have a striking impact on the parties' respective rights in job posting situations.

In promotion disputes, the way in which the burden of proof is allocated varies, depending on whether the situation is governed by a sufficient ability clause or a relative ability clause. Where the parties have opted for a threshold or sufficient ability clause, it is well settled that the grievor bears the initial onus of proving that his or her skills and qualifications are adequate for the job. Once the grievor has established, on the basis of objective evidence, that he or she has the requisite skills, the onus shifts to the employer to justify its choice: see *Maple Ridge (District) and C.U.P.E., Local 622* (1979), 23 L.A.C. (2d) 86 (Hickling), discussed in Chapter 19.3.2. In relative ability cases, however, if the grievor demonstrates skills or qualifications that are approximately equal to those of the successful applicant, the burden falls on the employer to rebut this evidence with proof that the successful applicant's ability is "demonstrably superior" or "substantially superior" to the grievor's: see, for example, *Halifax (City), supra.*

The operation of the onus of proof can be illustrated by reference to two contrasting awards of Arbitrator Mitchnick. In *North York General Hospital and S.E.I.U., Local 204* (1989), 7 L.A.C. (4th) 418, the collective agreement provided for a relative ability or competition clause to determine contests between two or more members of the full-time bargaining unit. However, the clause went on to stipulate that the employer was entitled to look at candidates from outside the bargaining unit only if no one in the full-time unit was qualified to do the work. This meant that the clause required the employer to apply a threshold or sufficient ability approach where a bargaining unit applicant was pitted against a non-unit applicant, which was in fact the situation that gave rise to the grievance. Despite the grievor's seniority-based right to the job (a maintenance position for which he was qualified), the employer chose a non-bargaining unit employee who had been doing the work on a part-time basis. As the evidence of the grievor's significant experience in maintenance went virtually unchallenged, the arbitrator overturned the decision, ruling that the employer had entered into a comparison of the candidates' relative abilities which it was "simply not entitled" to make. In *Ottawa Civic Hospital and O.N.A.* (1989), 9 L.A.C. (4th) 348, by contrast, the collective agreement contained a simple relative ability clause. Like the successful applicant, who had greater seniority, the grievor could do the work of a delivery room nurse. In addition, though, the grievor was a certified midwife, possessed surgical experience, and had acted as nurse-in-charge. The employer made its choice entirely on the basis of seniority. In what he noted was an "unusual 'turning of the tables'", the arbitrator allowed the union's grievance, holding that junior employees had a collective agreement right to have their qualifications measured against those of senior applicants. Because the superiority of her qualifications was "substantial and demonstrable", the grievor was awarded the position.

Arbitrators have held that union by-laws which restrict the way in which seniority may be used in applying for a posted vacancy cannot override collective agreement provisions governing the role of seniority. Arbitrator Larson recently upheld an employer grievance that union directives ordering junior applicants to withdraw from a competition whenever a more senior employee applied were contrary to the collective agreement, which contained a competitive promotion clause: *Island Farms Dairies Co-Operative Ass'n and Teamsters, Local 464* (2002), 107 L.A.C. (4th) 13.

19.2.2   Hybrid Clauses

In addition to sufficient ability clauses and relative ability clauses, arbitral jurisprudence has recognized a third category of job posting provision, somewhat less prevalent than the others. A "hybrid" clause, as it is called, requires the employer to *take into account* the enumerated criteria — which may include any combination of seniority, service, skill, ability, qualifications or other considerations — in determining the successful applicant for promotion. Although, typically, a hybrid clause does not specify the weight to be accorded to a particular criterion, or describe the relationship among the listed criteria, most arbitrators have held that such provisions should be interpreted to make seniority the deciding factor where the other factors are relatively equal among the applicants. Some arbitrators have also suggested that, where the applicants' merit is in fact relatively equal, the employer bears the burden of justifying why skill and ability were given greater weight than seniority in bypassing a more senior employee. These principles were applied and the arbitral jurisprudence on hybrid clauses summarized in *Zellers Inc. and U.S.W.A., Local 1000* (1997), 62 L.A.C. (4th) 76 (Beck).

Some hybrid clauses provide for a two-step analysis and state that, while promotions are to be determined on the basis of skill, ability, qualifications and seniority, seniority will govern if two or more applicants are relatively equal. In *Espanola & District Credit Union Ltd. and C.E.P., Local 74-1*, [2003] O.L.A.A. No. 608 (QL), Arbitrator Springate held that this type of hybrid clause requires the employer to consider seniority in its initial determination of the relative ranking of the candidates; taking seniority into account only during the second step, after the candidates have been found to be relatively equal on the basis of the other criteria set out in the first step, will not suffice.

19.3   Scope of Arbitral Review

19.3.1   Employer's Determination of the Necessary Qualifications

It falls within the ordinary exercise of the employer's management rights to fix the requisite qualifications for a vacant position, as well as the relative weight to be ascribed to the various qualifications in selecting the successful candidate. Accordingly, as stated in the leading case of *Reynolds Aluminum Co. Canada Ltd. and I.M.A.W., Local 28* (1974), 5 L.A.C. (2d) 251 (Schiff), the appropriate standard of arbitral review of management's decisions in this regard is comparatively narrow. Arbitrator Schiff held that the stipulated qualifications should not be interfered with unless the employer has manipulated them in bad faith to subvert the legitimate claims of employees for job advancement, or the qualifications themselves bear no reasonable relation to the work to be done.

More recently, while affirming the principles outlined by Arbitrator Schiff, Arbitrator Laing ruled that the employer violated the collective agreement by establishing qualifications for a labourer position which, although relevant to higher-rated positions, were unreasonable in relation to the basic requirements and duties of the job itself. In the arbitrator's view, the employer cannot artificially "puff up" the minimum qualifications for a job so that employees who, on an objective standard, have the knowledge and ability to perform the job are discouraged from applying or are disqualified altogether: see *School District No. 37 (Delta) and C.U.P.E., Local 1091* (1994), 46 L.A.C. (4th) 216

School District No. 37 (Delta) can be contrasted to the award in *Union Carbide Canada Ltd. and U.E., Local 523* (1967), 18 L.A.C. 109, discussed in Chapter 19.3.2. In *Union Carbide Canada*, Arbitrator Paul Weiler noted that in most cases it would be improper to require as a necessary qualification the ability to be promoted out of the job in question, that is, to define the qualifications for the position by reference to some higher-rated job. The arbitrator held, however, that where the vacant position is essentially an apprenticeship for another position, it is reasonable for the employer to consider criteria which may enable the candidate to assume the responsibilities of the target position. Similar considerations may apply where the vacancy is part of an automatic job progression scheme established pursuant to the collective agreement (as opposed to a promotion system based on competition for posted vacancies).

A notable application of the standard of reasonable relevance to the imposition of higher minimum job qualifications is found in *Victoria General Hospital and Manitoba Nurses' Union, Local 3*, [2004] M.G.A.D. No. 32 (QL) (Peltz). In that case, the union challenged the employer's decision to upgrade an experience requirement for positions in a nursing unit from "one year of current relevant clinical nursing experience" to "one year current post-anaesthesia and surgical nursing experience". One year of post-operative care or recovery room experience had never been required in this particular unit, and most of the nurses in the unit did not have that qualification and thus would have been ineligible for vacancies. The arbitration board, applying the standard of reasonable relevance or relationship to the work, upheld the job posting on the basis that the requirement was reasonably related to the prevention of mistakes in patient care. In the board's view, practices and standards that had been accepted in the past may not be adequate in the future, and the standard of review should allow for the reality of change.

19.3.2 Employer's Assessment of Employee Skill and Ability

The seminal decision on the standard of review to be applied by arbitrators in reviewing the employer's evaluation of employee skill or ability is *Union Carbide Canada Ltd. and U.E., Local 523* (1967), 18 L.A.C. 109 (P.C. Weiler). Weiler, whose reasoning reflects the traditional reluctance on the part of arbitrators to take over the function of management, ruled that the employer's assessment should not be interfered with unless it was dishonest, discriminatory, biased, actuated by ill-will, or unreasonable. The arbitrator must also ensure that, in arriving at its decision, the employer considered all relevant factors, and avoided considering any irrelevant factors.

Although the deferential approach advanced in *Union Carbide Canada* continues to be followed by some arbitrators, most recent awards have concluded that the proper standard of review in such cases is *correctness*, at least in the absence of any provisions in the collective agreement to the contrary. This line of authority stems from the decision of the Ontario Divisional Court in *Great Atlantic & Pacific Co. of Canada Ltd. v. Canadian Food and Allied Workers Union, Local 175* (1976), 76 C.L.L.C. ¶14,056. The Court held that, where the collective agreement provides for the selection of candidates for promotion, arbitrators have an obligation to ensure that the agreement has been complied with, and cannot restrict themselves to deciding whether the employer has acted honestly and reasonably. If the parties desire a more lenient standard of review to apply, they can say so in the agreement. Thus, where the employer has misjudged an employee's skill, ability or qualifications, or otherwise failed to appraise the relative entitlement of applicants in accordance with the collective agreement, an arbitrator has jurisdiction to overturn the results of a job competition.

A summary of the divergence between the standards of review — reasonableness and good faith on the one hand, and correctness on the other — and the rationale for each is found in *Maple Ridge (District) and C.U.P.E., Local 622* (1979), 23 L.A.C. (2d) 86 (Hickling). This decision is frequently cited in support of the application of the correctness standard. Arbitrator Hickling acknowledges, however, that even arbitrators who assert authority to review the correctness of a promotion decision often defer to the employer's opinion on the basis that management is better situated to assess an employee's capability or aptitude for the job.

Similarly, in *Ivaco Rolling Mills Ltd. and U.S.W.A., Local 7940* (1997), 69 L.A.C. (4th) 1, Arbitrator Adell noted that arbitrators, including those who have opted for the correctness standard, are generally reluctant to interfere with management's evaluation of the relative ability of applicants for a posted position.

19.4   VALIDITY OF TEST OR INTERVIEW

In an effort to provide an objective basis for choosing among the candidates for a posted job, the employer often institutes some mechanism for assessing their skill, ability or qualifications, most commonly an interview and/or an examination. Where an employee claims that he or she was wrongly denied a posted position, arbitrators are frequently called upon to review the validity or accuracy of the mechanism in relation to the particular job. The union may attack the way in which the employer administered the evaluation device, or it may take issue with the viability of the device itself. A summary of the arbitral approach to reviewing management's use of tests and interviews is found in *Acadian Platers Co. Ltd. and U.S.W.A., Local 8059* (1997), 68 L.A.C. (4th) 344 (Knopf).

19.4.1   Denial of Interview

In a number of awards, the failure to grant an interview to an applicant with relatively high seniority ranking has led the arbitrator to invalidate the successful candidate's appointment. Generally, no applicant is guaranteed an interview, since the employer clearly has the right to undertake an initial screening or to create a short-list based solely on employees' application forms, résumés or records of employment. However, arbitrators have been quite willing to inquire whether the decision not to interview an employee is reasonable in light of his or her seniority and ability to meet the minimum requirements of the position. This has been the case even where the applicable posting provision is a competitive or relative equality clause. These principles were affirmed in

Alberta Government Telephones and I.B.E.W., Local 348 (1992), 28 L.A.C. (4th) 426 (Ponak).

For a summary of cases in which the employer's refusal to grant an interview was held to be unreasonable, see *Halton Adolescent Support Services and O.P.S.E.U., Local 262* (1994), 44 L.A.C. (4th) 129 (Simmons).

19.4.2 Undue Weight Assigned to Interview

In recent years, many arbitrators have held that undue reliance on an employee's interview performance created a fatal flaw in the selection process. In such cases, excessive emphasis on the interview has often come at the expense of a more balanced consideration of other relevant factors, including work history, past training, performance appraisals, comments of supervisors and co-workers, and test scores. The risk of placing too much reliance on an interview is especially acute where the grievor has had significant work experience in the employer's establishment, since this is likely to offer a more dependable prognosis of future performance than the ability to communicate at an interview. A leading case which demonstrates these concepts is *University of Toronto and C.U.P.E., Local 3261* (1995), 52 L.A.C. (4th) 387 (Burkett).

Another decision in which the grievor, a long-term employee with experience in the posted position, was passed over because of a poor showing at the interview is *Greater Niagara General Hospital and O.N.A. (Robb)* (1997), 60 L.A.C. (4th) 289. In Arbitrator Devlin's view, the employer acted unreasonably by overlooking other pertinent considerations, focusing instead on an interview process which was better suited to test an applicant's ability to recount anecdotal information than her ability to do the job.

Additional Reading

R.D. Hackett, J.B. Rose & J. Pyper, "The Employment Interview: An Analysis of Arbitration Decisions" in K. Whitaker, J. Sack, M. Gunderson & R. Filion, eds., *Labour Arbitration Yearbook 1999-2000*, vol. I, p. 233.

19.4.3 Characteristics of a Valid Test Procedure

In the absence of collective agreement language to the contrary, employers are generally free to require applicants for a posted position to submit to a test designed to assess skill and ability. Such a test may require employees to meet appropriate standards of performance or to demonstrate satisfactory aptitude for the job. However, the extent to which the employer is entitled to rely on the results in making its decision depends on whether the test satisfies the criteria of fairness, reasonableness, relevance to the posted job, reliability and validity. These principles were stated in the seminal decision of Arbitrator Weatherill in *Polymer Corp. Ltd. and Oil, Chemical & Atomic Workers, Local 9-14* (1968), 19 L.A.C. 386.

In a second seminal decision on the employer's right to rely on test results, *Northern Electric Co. Ltd. and C.W.A., Local C-9* (1969), 20 L.A.C. 222, Arbitrator Palmer ruled that the reasonableness of the testing procedures should be considered from five perspectives: the reasons for instituting the test; the adequacy of the opportunities for preparation given to prospective applicants; the way in which the test was administered; the reliability of the marking; and the relevance of the content of the test to the posted position.

The principles established in *Northern Electric* were applied in *Consumers Glass and Aluminum, Brick & Glassworkers Int'l Union, Local 269G* (1997), 61 L.A.C. (4th) 303 (Shime). An applicant with less seniority than the grievor was selected for a job as maintenance helper on the basis of his superior performance on a written examination. The evidence disclosed that the examination, which was intended to gauge mechanical reasoning skills, had been fairly administered and marked, and furthermore that applicants had been apprised of the necessity of undergoing an examination. As, in the arbitrator's opinion, the test was relevant and bore a reasonable relation to the work in question, the employer was entitled to rely on the results in concluding that the grievor was not relatively equal in ability to the successful applicant.

One sign that a test held in connection with a job competition may have been unreasonable or irrelevant is the failure of highly experienced applicants to achieve a passing grade, especially if their experience was obtained by performing the duties of the posted position in an acting or temporary capacity. However, as observed by Arbitrator Springate in *Metropolitan Toronto (Municipality) and C.U.P.E., Local 79* (1994), 45 L.A.C. (4th) 174, a single aberration, not amounting to a clear numerical pattern, will not likely be sufficient to invalidate the outcome of the test.

A test which meets the requirement for relevance may nonetheless be held invalid if it has not been fairly administered. In *Oshawa Transit Commission and C.A.W., Local 222* (2002), 110 L.A.C. (4th) 345 (H.D. Brown), for example, the test administered to applicants was the same one used in a previous competition. Because one of the applicants had taken part in the earlier competition, he had already had an opportunity to write the test, and Arbitrator Howard Brown found that the test could not be relied upon as a fair assessment of the candidates' relative skill and ability. A written test, he pointed out, should be administered in the same manner and under the same conditions, without any appearance of bias, in order to ensure a fair evaluation of each applicant.

Additional Reading

J.C. Koshman, "Employment Testing at Arbitration: An Arbitrator's Perspective" in W. Kaplan, J. Sack, M. Gunderson & R. Filion, eds., *Labour Arbitration Yearbook 1996-97*, p. 359; and companion articles by K.P. Dunn and P. Engelmann.

C.L. Rigg, "Testing at Arbitration: An Arbitrator's Perspective" in W. Kaplan, J. Sack & M. Gunderson, eds., *Labour Arbitration Yearbook 1993*, p. 177; and companion articles by D. Orsborn & L.A. Marshall, and I.A. Mackenzie.

19.4.4   Undue Weight Assigned to Test Results

As in the case of interviews, arbitrators have held that undue reliance on the results of a test, at the expense of a balanced consideration of all relevant factors, may invalidate a promotion decision. This was demonstrated in *Winnipeg (City) and C.U.P.E., Local 500* (1990), 12 L.A.C. (4th) 231 (Freedman).

19.5   TRIAL, TRAINING AND FAMILIARIZATION PERIODS

Arbitrators have long held that, unless the collective agreement expressly provides for it, an applicant for a job vacancy is not entitled to either a trial period (in order to prove that he or she possesses the requisite skill and ability) or a training period (in order to acquire the requisite skill and ability with the employer's instruction and assistance). Rather, in the absence of collective agreement provisions to the contrary, a grievor seeking to establish his or her eligibility for a position must have *immediate* or *present* skill and ability to do the work, regardless of whether the provision in question is a sufficient ability clause or a relative ability clause. However, since the early 1970s, most arbitrators have recognized that strict adherence to this position could seriously undermine employees' seniority rights in the context of promotions, transfers and layoffs. Consequently, it has been held that, although the employer may have a legitimate need for immediate expertise in highly skilled or technical positions, an employee is generally entitled to a brief familiarization period to master the basic routines and details of the job, especially in the case of work that is not considered technically demanding. These principles are set out in a leading decision by Arbitrator Adams in *St. Catharines General Hospital and S.E.I.U., Local 204* (1975), 10 L.A.C. (2d) 258.

The principles articulated in *St. Catharines General Hospital* were applied in *Ivaco Rolling Mills Ltd. and U.S.W.A., Local 7940* (1997), 69 L.A.C. (4th) 1 (Adell). Here, the collective agreement provided for a one-week familiarization period, followed by a 30-day trial period, but it made no reference to a training period. Unlike a training period, which is deemed to impose an obligation on the employer to help the successful applicant raise his or her skill level, the existence of a trial or familiarization period does not by itself entitle an employee to any instruction or teaching. Because the grievor, the senior applicant, would require additional training before being able to do the job, the arbitrator upheld the employer's conclusion that she was not relatively equal to the successful applicant and denied the grievance.

Collective agreements often provide that an employee who has been promoted is subject to being returned or "reverted" to his or her former position during the trial period if, in the employer's opinion, the employee has proven incapable of meeting the normal demands of the job. Arbitrators have emphasized that, before the employer can exercise its right in this regard, the employee must be given an adequate opportunity to perform the duties of the new position, and be afforded a fair and objective assessment. The employee also has the right to notice during the trial period that his or her performance is considered deficient. If the employer does decide to revert the employee to his or her previous position, it will generally bear the burden of proving the validity of its negative assessment, since the initial promotion decision establishes a *prima facie* case of the sufficiency of the employee's skill and ability. Arbitrator Burkett explained these principles in *Brantford (City) and C.U.P.E., Local 181* (1990), 17 L.A.C. (4th) 149.

Where the collective agreement expressly states that job postings are to be awarded solely on the basis of seniority, does not include the usual caveat that the successful applicant must have the ability to perform the duties of the job in question, and provides for a training period of a specified duration, the employer is not entitled to hire from outside the bargaining unit on the view that none of the internal candidates is qualified. In such cases, the senior applicant must be awarded the position and given an opportunity to establish that, with the prescribed training, he or she would have the requisite skill and ability to do the job: see *Dare Foods Ltd. and B.C.T., Local 264* (2004), 128 L.A.C. (4th) 331 (Beck).

19.6 REMEDIES

The most common remedial issue in promotion grievances is whether the arbitrator, having found the employer in violation of the collective agreement, should go on to determine which applicant should be awarded the contested position, as opposed to simply remitting the matter to the employer for a new decision. For some time, where the grievor and the incumbent were not the only applicants for the position, and the collective agreement explicitly reserved to management the right to assess employees' skill and ability, arbitrators considered themselves bound by the decision of the Ontario Court of Appeal in *Falconbridge Nickel Mines Ltd. v. U.S.W.A.* (1972), 30 D.L.R. (3d) 412 to remit the matter to the employer for a fresh determination. In *Falconbridge Nickel Mines*, where there were three applicants for the job, the Court held that the arbitrator had "usurped the function of management" and exceeded his jurisdiction by awarding the job to the grievor, although it suggested that it might have taken a different view had there been only two applicants:

> On the question of whether the board acted without jurisdiction in ordering the company to place Cowen [the grievor] in the vacant position, it is

unnecessary to decide what the powers of the board would be if there had been only two applicants for the vacant position — Simard and Cowen. In such a case the question is academic. In fact, there was a third applicant and in my opinion under arts. 3.01, 12.10 and 12.11 the appellant has a clear management right, if not the duty, to make a choice between Cowen and the third applicant in accordance with the terms of the agreement. By its award, in my opinion, the board usurped the function of management I have mentioned and exercised a power it did not have . . . (at pp. 414-15)

However, subsequent judicial and arbitral authority has significantly undermined the demarcation suggested in *Falconbridge Nickel Mines*. Ten years later, in *R. v. O.P.S.E.U.* (1982), 133 D.L.R. (3d) 596, the Ontario Divisional Court ruled that *Falconbridge Nickel Mines* did not necessarily prohibit an arbitration board from granting the job to the grievor (or one of the grievors) simply because there had been more than two applicants. In the Court's opinion, the choice of a suitable remedy depends on the circumstances of the case, the terms of the collective agreement and the applicable legislation. In appropriate cases, an arbitration board may award the position to one of the unsuccessful candidates pursuant to its general statutory power to resolve grievances, even in the absence of express authority under the collective agreement.

Nevertheless, in the absence of good reason to question the fairness of having a re-run of the competition, the majority of arbitrators prefer to remit the matter for a fresh determination, with or without specific directions to govern the conduct of the re-run. This is so because arbitrators are usually reluctant to preempt management's role, and because they recognize the greater expertise and knowledge of the employer in filling its needs from among the available candidates. The modern approach to the problem of remedy in a successful job posting grievance is perhaps best reflected in *Sudbury General Hospital of Immaculate Heart of Mary and C.U.P.E., Local 1023* (1990), 16 L.A.C. (4th) 172. In that case, Arbitrator Craven suggested that the choice between remittance of the matter to the employer or an arbitral decision on the merits should be made on a case-by-case basis, depending on where the balance falls between the employer's legitimate interest in making the selection itself, and the union's legitimate interest in securing a final and binding settlement of the dispute at arbitration.

An illustration of this approach to determining when it is appropriate to award the position to the grievor rather than ordering a re-run of the competition was provided in the more recent decision of Arbitrator Hope in *Interior Health Authority and B.C.N.U.*, [2004] B.C.C.A.A.A. No. 316 (QL), which concerned a job posting for a nursing position. It was noted that arbitrators normally see themselves as less equipped than the employer to assess the applicants' relative skill and ability in the context of professional positions. The arbitrator further acknowledged that, where the selection process was flawed, general arbitral principles contemplated that the process be repeated, unless there were factors that called into question the objectivity of a re-run. In the case before him, Arbitrator Hope concluded that it would be inappropriate to direct a re-run of the competition, as the selection process was relatively unstructured and was administered by an individual who had demonstrated that she was prone to bias and prejudgment.

In the event the grievor is awarded the position in question, either by the arbitrator or after a re-run of the competition, the grievor is normally entitled to compensatory damages equal to the amount of wages and benefits lost due to the wrongful denial of the position, as of the date of the original decision. This is simply an example of the general principle governing recovery of damages for breach of the collective agreement, namely, that the purpose of damages is to put the grievor in the position he or she would have been in had there been no violation of the agreement. Such damages may be reduced if the grievor was in part responsible for the employer's failure to arrive at the correct decision in the first place, as, for example, where the grievor fails to adequately explain his or her qualifications at the interview. See *Acadian Platers Co. Ltd. and U.S.W.A., Local 8059* (1997), 68 L.A.C. (4th) 344 (Knopf), discussed in Chapter 19.4.1.

CHAPTER 20

LAYOFF AND RECALL

20.1 GENERAL CONSIDERATIONS

It is perhaps in layoff situations that seniority rights, with their impact on job security, are most important to an employee. The layoff and recall provisions of most collective agreements recognize seniority as a significant factor in determining which employees will retain their jobs following a reduction in the workforce, and the order in which employees will be recalled as work again becomes available. Bumping provisions, giving laid-off employees the right to displace or "bump" into a position held by an employee with less seniority, often comprise an important part of the collective agreement. The weight that will be given to seniority in allocating individual employees' entitlement to a share in a diminishing volume of work depends on whether the parties have included a "threshold" or "sufficient ability" clause, a "competitive" clause, or a "hybrid" clause. The way in which these provisions are interpreted and applied by arbitrators is similar in the context of both layoff and recall, and competitions for a posted vacancy: see Chapter 19.

20.2   COMPLIANCE WITH LAYOFF PROCEDURE

20.2.1   Definition of Layoff

An employee cannot exercise his or her seniority rights unless a layoff is in fact found to have taken place. For this reason, many arbitration awards deal with the threshold issue of whether the disruption in the employment relationship which has occasioned the grievance constitutes a layoff for the purposes of the collective agreement. To the extent that the parties have included a definition of layoff in the agreement, the arbitrator is bound to apply it. However, in many cases, the agreement does not include a definition, or includes a definition that does not clearly encompass the situation which confronts the arbitrator. As a consequence, an extensive body of arbitral jurisprudence has arisen which attempts to identify the indicia of a layoff.

The award in *Northern Electric Co. Ltd. and U.A.W., Local 1525* (1971), 23 L.A.C. 104 (Weatherill) contains perhaps the most oft-cited definition of a layoff. Arbitrator Weatherill held that a layoff involves some temporary severance of the employment relationship for the purpose of reducing the workforce to meet the employer's staffing requirements. In holding that a layoff merely requires some form of cessation of work involving a reduction in the workforce, the arbitrator expressed the view that the circumstances precipitating the reduction are of no significance in deciding whether a layoff has occurred. Thus, in the case before him, the fact that the lack of work had been caused by a legal strike in another bargaining unit did not preclude a finding of layoff. The sole exception to the proposition that the cause of the reduction in work is irrelevant occurs where the disruption has been caused by the union or the employee in question.

The Supreme Court of Canada has made several important rulings on the meaning of layoff in the arbitral context. In *Air-Care Ltd. v. U.S.W.A.* (1974), 49 D.L.R. (3d) 467, discussed in Chapter 21.1, the Court approved a dictionary definition of layoff as a period during which a worker is temporarily discharged. In 1998, the Supreme Court returned to this issue in two decisions. In the first, *Canada Safeway Ltd. v. R.W.D.S.U., Local 454* (1998), 160 D.L.R. (4th) 1, the Court overturned the award of an arbitration board which had held that a mere reduction in *scheduled* hours — as opposed to *actual* hours worked — gave rise to a constructive layoff. (The employer reduced the grievor's weekly scheduled hours from 37 to a single four-hour shift. Because of "call-ins", however, the grievor's actual hours of work remained approximately the same.) In the Court's opinion, in the absence of a definition in the collective agreement, the term "layoff" generally refers to an interruption of work short of permanent dismissal. The possibility of a return to work may or may not materialize, but it is the *expectation* that the cessation will be temporary that results in the employment relationship being suspended rather than terminated. Consequently, the Court ruled, if an employee continues to work substantially the same number of hours as before, a layoff has not occurred (even though the employee may have cause for grievance under some other provision of the collective agreement).

Nonetheless, the Court acknowledged that a significant reduction in hours may, in certain circumstances, give rise to a constructive lay-off, entitling an employee to exercise his or her seniority rights under the collective agreement. Indeed, in the companion decision of *Battlefords and District Co-Operatives Ltd. v. R.W.D.S.U., Local 544* (1998), 160 D.L.R. (4th) 29 (S.C.C.), discussed in Chapter 20.2.3, the Court upheld an arbitrator's ruling to this effect.

In *Nova Scotia Power Inc. and I.B.E.W., Local 1928* (2000), 96 L.A.C. (4th) 257, Arbitrator Outhouse rejected the union's argument that the concept of constructive layoff approved in *Battlefords and District Co-Operatives* extends to situations in which the employer has significantly reduced the job responsibilities and pay of a number of its employees in the course of a workplace reorganization. The arbitrator held that, when *Battlefords and District Co-Operatives* was read together with the Supreme Court of Canada's decision in *Canada Safeway*, it was clear that the Court intended to limit the concept of constructive layoff to cases in which an employee's hours of work had been reduced, and that other disruptions of the employment relationship were not included.

In a number of cases, the employer has required that employees take vacation during periods when the plant is shut down for inventory reduction or maintenance purposes, and the union has challenged this practice on the basis that it is contrary to the layoff provisions of the collective agreement, particularly where senior employees with greater vacation entitlement have been compelled to use vacation time while junior employees remain at work during the shut-down. In *Altasteel Ltd. and U.S.W.A., Local 5220*, [2004] C.L.A.D. No. 225 (QL), a board of arbitration chaired by Allen Ponak dealt with a union grievance alleging that a partial shutdown, instituted to reduce inventories, constituted a layoff, and that the employer was therefore required to follow the layoff procedures prescribed by the collective agreement. After a comprehensive review of the authorities, the board provided the following summary of arbitral principles (at para. 30):

(1) Management has the right to schedule vacations during partial or full plant closures if vacation shut-downs are contemplated in the contract.

(2) A temporary shut-down can be construed as a layoff, potentially triggering contractual layoff provisions.

(3) Management's right to schedule vacations can be used to achieve a temporary shut-down, whether full or partial, without resorting to contractual layoff provisions. Management can choose whether to use layoffs or vacation scheduling rights to achieve a temporary workforce reduction.

(4) The scheduling of vacations to achieve a temporary shut-down is sub-
    ject to contractual constraints such as seniority-based vacation selec-
    tion, equitable vacation allocation, the explicit primacy of layoff
    procedures for workforce reductions, and union consultation.

(5) Contractual constraints on vacation scheduling, even where expressed
    in tepid or vague language, have been strictly enforced by arbitrators
    in a way that protects any rights enjoyed by employees in choosing
    their vacation times ... [S]uch provisions [have been held] sufficient to
    prevent the employer from placing employees on vacation in order to
    achieve a temporary workplace reduction because of the interference
    with employee vacation selection rights, however minor.

(6) Where the arbitrator concluded that management did not have unfet-
    tered discretion to place employees on vacation to achieve a temporary
    workforce reduction, and the workforce reduction could also be encom-
    passed by the contract's layoff procedures, it was concluded that the
    contract's layoff provisions were applicable.

Applying these principles to the case at hand, the arbitration board concluded that, although the employer had the right to schedule employee vacations and could use that right to achieve temporary workforce reductions, it had
violated two restrictions on vacation scheduling imposed by the collective
agreement. The first was a requirement that the employer meet with and advise
the union of the anticipated vacation schedule prior to March 1st of each year.
The second was a stipulation that vacation entitlement which remained unused
after plant shut-downs was to be scheduled between June and October on a
"rotational basis". While "rotational basis" was not defined in the collective
agreement, evidence of past practice showed that seniority had played a significant role in the scheduling of unused vacation time. In the board's view,
requiring employees to take vacation during a January shutdown, at a time
when employees with less seniority remained on the job, would interfere with
their vacation selection options, contrary to the "rotational basis" clause. However, the board noted that the result would have been different had all production employees been directed to take vacation during the January shut-down.

Additional Reading

G. Hopkinson, "Constructive Lay-Off in the Unionized Workplace: Assessing the
    Impact of the *Canada Safeway* and *Battlefords* Decisions" (1999), 7 Canadian
    Labour and Employment Journal, p. 297.

20.2.2   Layoff Distinguished from Discharge, Termination or Severance

Despite the Supreme Court of Canada's focus on the temporary nature
of a layoff, several arbitrators have held that a layoff may be temporary or

permanent, definite or indefinite. The best exposition of this perspective is found in *Artcraft Engravers Ltd. and G.C.I.U., Local 517* (1990), 12 L.A.C. (4th) 363, where Arbitrator Brent held that the key criterion in identifying a layoff is some initiative on the employer's part to reduce its workforce. If there is nothing in the collective agreement limiting such an initiative to temporary reductions, the character of a layoff may well be permanent. In the arbitrator's opinion, a layoff can be distinguished from a discharge by asking the following question: is the employer's professed need to eliminate a particular employee from the workforce or to reduce the workforce by eliminating a job? The former suggests a discharge, while the latter indicates a layoff.

Following amendments to Ontario's *Employment Standards Act* which took effect in 2001, a number of cases have raised the issue of when a notice of layoff will trigger statutory entitlements to termination and severance pay under the legislation. The statute has always allowed employers some leeway to use layoffs as a means of managing their labour needs by recognizing the concept of a "temporary layoff", which did not trigger the obligation to make termination and severance payments. Nevertheless, the regulations under the previous Act provided that notice of an indefinite layoff was deemed to be notice of termination of employment. In practice, this meant that a notice of indefinite layoff which did not specify a recall date triggered the statutory payment entitlement. The 2001 amendments reversed the presumed effect of an indefinite layoff by providing that a notice of layoff without a specific recall date did not have the effect of terminating the employee's employment, unless the actual period of layoff ultimately exceeded that of a temporary layoff, as defined by the Act: S.O. 2000, c. 41, s. 56(4). (Generally speaking, a temporary layoff for the purposes of the Act, where a collective agreement is in effect, is one in which the employee has been recalled within the time period set out in the agreement.) As a result, employers in Ontario may now be able to declare an indefinite layoff without incurring immediate liability for termination and severance pay. A comprehensive analysis of these changes is found in *Victorian Order of Nurses and O.N.A.* (2004), 134 L.A.C. (4th) 199 (Herlich).

20.2.3   Reduction of Hours Constituting Layoff

A decision by management to reduce the hours of work of its employees tends to give rise to grievances on two separate fronts. The first is a claim that the reduction violates a provision in the collective agreement specifying the "normal" or "regular" hours of work. The extent to which the employer's right to schedule work may be curbed by such provisions is reviewed in Chapter 21. Equally, though, a reduction in work hours may give rise to a separate allegation that the employer's action amounts to a layoff of the affected employees. The seminal award on this issue is *E.S. & A. Robinson (Canada) Ltd. and Printing Specialties & Paper Products Union, Local 466* (1976), 11 L.A.C. (2d) 408 (Swan). In that case, Arbitrator Swan held that a temporary reduction which applies uniformly to all employees in the bargaining unit generally represents a permissible exercise of management's right to schedule work and does not constitute a layoff. However, the employer cannot avoid the seniority provisions of the collective agreement by cloaking a layoff as a mere reduction in work hours. Thus, if there is to be any differential treatment of employees in effecting the reduction, the distinction must be drawn on the basis of seniority.

Arbitrator Marcotte's award in *Crown Ridge Place Nursing Home and U.F.C.W. (Leckey)* (1998), 72 L.A.C. (4th) 232 summarizes the consistent line of arbitral authority adopting the *E.S. & A. Robinson* approach. The arbitrator emphasized that, where an employer unequally reduces the hours of work of bargaining unit employees, it is the *unequalness* of the reduction that triggers a layoff, not the reduction itself.

In *Battlefords and District Co-Operatives Ltd. v. R.W.D.S.U., Local 544* (1998), 160 D.L.R. (4th) 29, the Supreme Court of Canada held that, where the collective agreement does not define the term "layoff", a substantial reduction in hours (if implemented unequally) can reasonably be considered a "constructive layoff", thereby allowing affected employees to invoke their bumping rights. In the Court's view, if a reduction in work hours arbitrarily singles out an employee without regard to seniority, it may be a legitimate interpretation of the collective agreement to characterize the reduction as a constructive layoff.

20.2.4   Layoff Distinguished from Transfer

In the absence of a severance or serious disruption of the employment relationship, arbitrators have generally been very reluctant to characterize as a layoff the reassignment of an employee to a different job classification, work location or shift within the bargaining unit. However, the result may be otherwise if, as a result of reassignment to a position excluded from the bargaining unit, an employee suffers a significant loss of status. The cases in which the distinction between transfer or reassignment and layoff has been applied are summarized in *York County Hospital and O.N.A.* (1994), 39 L.A.C. (4th) 398 (Knopf).

Although the prevailing opinion, as set out in *York County Hospital*, is that reassignment or transfer does not constitute a layoff unless it results in a reduction of hours, the specific wording of the collective agreement may dictate a different outcome. For example, following amendments to the definition of layoff in the collective agreement at issue in *York County Hospital*, expressly excluding reassignment for a partial or single shift, two arbitrators have ruled that reassignment of a nurse to a different unit within the hospital for two or more consecutive shifts does amount to a layoff: *Windsor Regional Hospital and O.N.A.*, unreported, July 18, 2003 (Etherington); and *Scarborough Hospital and O.N.A.*, [2004] O.L.A.A. No. 122 (QL) (Surdykowski). For a contrary view, see *Centre for Addiction & Mental Health and O.N.A.*, unreported, May 22, 2003 (Briggs).

20.2.5   Layoff Lasting Less than One Shift

In an early and often-cited decision, *Vaunclair Purveyors Ltd. and Amalgamated Meat Cutters, Local 633* (1963), 13 L.A.C. 369, Arbitrator Arthurs defined a layoff as any period in which employees are required to cease work, that could include being sent home 15 minutes before the end of a shift. Although most arbitrators have followed the Arthurs approach, there has been recurring controversy as to whether a cessation of work lasting less than one shift can be considered a layoff if the collective agreement contains a reporting pay provision (which typically guarantees payment of an agreed-upon number of hours' wages, at the basic straight-time rate, if an employee reports for work at the regular starting-time) or a provision requiring the employer to give advance notice of a layoff. *Phillips Cables Ltd. and Int'l Union of Electrical Workers, Local 510* (1968), 19 L.A.C. 185 (Christie) is a leading case in support of the principle that there is nothing inherently contradictory between the existence of a reporting pay clause and the application of the layoff provisions to an interruption of work lasting less than a full shift. For Arbitrator Christie, the overriding factor in reaching this conclusion was the contrast in employee interests which the two types of provision are intended to protect.

Peelle Co. Ltd. and U.S.W.A. (1986), 23 L.A.C. (3d) 1 (Burkett) represents the contrary view to the effect that the inclusion of a reporting pay clause indicates the parties' intention to distinguish between short-term layoffs and long-term layoffs. On the morning after a severe snowstorm, the employer closed the plant and sent home the 45 employees who had showed up, even though there would have been enough work to keep them occupied. All the employees were paid four hours' reporting pay, in accordance with the collective agreement. However, on the basis that work was "available" within the meaning of the reporting pay provision, the union claimed that the clause did not apply, and that the employees had been laid off. Accordingly, the union argued, the employees were entitled to pay in lieu of notice of layoff. Arbitrator Burkett denied the grievance, ruling that no layoff had occurred. Where the collective agreement contains both a general layoff provision and a reporting pay provision, he observed, it was appropriate to infer that the parties intended to distinguish between short-term layoffs occasioned by unforeseen circumstances and longer-term, planned layoffs. Thus, whenever the employer for legitimate business reasons decided to cease operations for part of a shift, the effect was to make work "unavailable", thereby triggering employees' entitlement to the reporting allowance.

More recently, in *Participating Hospitals and O.N.A.* (1993), 32 L.A.C. (4th) 24, Arbitrator Brent synopsized the conflicting arbitral jurisprudence on the impact of a reporting pay provision on an employee's ability to exercise seniority rights. In the result, the arbitrator opted for the *Phillips Cables* approach, holding that the mere inclusion of a reporting pay provision in the collective agreement should not preclude a finding that a layoff has occurred. However, it was also recognized that activating the full panoply of seniority rights, including chain bumping, would be impractical and unreasonable in light of the short duration of the layoff. Thus, the arbitrator ruled, where an employee is subject to a partial shift cancellation, the employer is entitled to designate the position into which the employee will bump for the remainder of the shift.

20.2.6   Requirement for Notice of Layoff

Often, the collective agreement requires the employer to provide advance notice of a layoff. There may also be provisions obligating the employer to investigate possible alternatives to layoff either prior to or following delivery of the notice. Such procedural requirements are enforceable at arbitration, and the employer's failure to comply may entitle the union to a compensatory order. However, where the collective agreement requires notice of layoff to be given to both the union and affected employees, arbitrators have held that the notices can be delivered at the same time (unless the agreement clearly specifies the union's right to be notified first). This approach was applied in *Kingston General Hospital and C.U.P.E., Local 1974* (1997), 66 L.A.C. (4th) 94 (Mitchnick). The arbitrator also ruled that the ordinary contractual principles of mitigation apply during the notice period, such that employees who are subject to layoff may be obliged to accept a reasonable offer of alternative employment at the same establishment, even though the notice period stipulated by the collective agreement has not yet expired. The fact that the notice provision in question referred to six months' notice of layoff "or pay in lieu thereof" did not derogate from the employees' duty to mitigate.

The decision in *Hamilton Health Sciences Corp. and C.U.P.E., Local 839* (2001), 94 L.A.C. (4th) 156 (Adams) exemplifies the arbitral rejection of "blanket" notices of layoff which fail to identify with sufficient specificity the positions to be affected and the timing of the layoff or elimination of positions. In the absence of such information, Arbitrator Adams noted, the parties were unable to engage in meaningful discussion and planning to deal with the consequences of the intended layoff.

20.3   BUMPING RIGHTS

Many collective agreements recognize the importance of seniority by providing for the exercise of displacement or "bumping" rights in the event of a layoff. Bumping refers to a process by which a senior employee subject to layoff has the opportunity to displace a junior employee in a job that will continue after the layoff. The collective agreement frequently includes detailed bumping procedures which define the respective rights of the "bumper" and "bumpee", the significance of skill and ability vis-à-vis seniority in determining an employee's entitlement to a particular position, and the scope of permissible bumping rights within the bargaining unit. However, where these contingencies are not clearly addressed in the agreement, arbitrators seek guidance in the established caselaw.

20.3.1 Is Chain Bumping Allowed?

Where the collective agreement does not specify the position or positions into which a laid-off employee may bump, the employer and the union often disagree as to whether "chain bumping" is permitted. Chain bumping enables a laid-off employee to choose the position of *any* junior employee that he or she is qualified to perform, which in turn gives the displaced employee a parallel right to choose the position of a still more junior employee, until the whole process has worked its way downward through the available positions. Employers have often contended that, unless the collective agreement states otherwise, an employee who is subject to layoff must displace the *most* junior employee in the relevant department or classification whose position he or she is capable of performing, as this would avoid unnecessary disruption. The prevalent position among arbitrators, however, is that chain bumping is permissible, and that it is up to the employer to secure specific restrictions in the collective agreement if it desires a more orderly procedure. In *Moloney Electric Corp. and U.E.* (1985), 22 L.A.C. (3d) 170, for example, Arbitrator Michel Picher expressed the view that there is a presumption in favour of allowing chain bumping unless the collective agreement imposes express restrictions. Arbitrator Burkett took issue with this conclusion in *York-Finch General Hospital and O.N.A.* (1993), 35 L.A.C. (4th) 258, arguing that there is no such presumption in favour of chain bumping. But the most comprehensive treatment of the jurisprudence is found in *Canadian Standards Ass'n and C.U.P.E., Local 967* (1995), 51 L.A.C. (4th) 105, where Arbitrator Swan reviewed the two opposing schools. In the arbitrator's opinion, in the absence of provisions delimiting the scope of bumping rights, every employee who is displaced, whether by the initial layoff or another employee's subsequent exercise of seniority, is entitled to select the best position that he or she can claim based on seniority and competence.

20.3.2 Scope of Bumping Rights

It is common for the collective agreement to define the group of employees within which bumping rights must be exercised, as, for example, within a particular job classification, department or working group. Although there were some early cases to the contrary, it is now widely accepted among arbitrators that, if the collective agreement is silent or fails to incorporate clear restrictions, bumping rights can be applied across the entire bargaining unit. This principle was applied in the leading case of *Western Grocers and R.W.D.S.U., Local 469* (1989), 6 L.A.C. (4th) 1 (Freedman). The approach taken by Arbitrator Freedman was adopted in *Nova Scotia (Department of Transportation & Communications) and C.U.P.E., Local 1867* (1996), 58 L.A.C. (4th) 11 (Veniot).

An issue which attracts somewhat less agreement among arbitrators is the extent to which an employee is permitted to choose not only the job title into which he or she will bump, but also the specific job assignment among several employees performing that job title. The award in *Hammond Manufacturing Co. Ltd. and Employees' Ass'n* (1992), 27 L.A.C. (4th) 218 (Brent) summarizes the arbitral authority. Arbitrator Brent noted that several decisions have recognized the right of an employee to choose the specific job assignment into which he or she will bump, provided there are provisions in the collective agreement which make one assignment more attractive than another. However, to the extent that the award in *Western Grocers*, *supra*, stands for the proposition that an employee may bump into any job assignment for which he or she entertains a merely subjective preference, she declined to follow it. In her view, if the employee's choice does not reflect a meaningful distinction grounded in the collective agreement, the employer should not be required to undergo needless complications and disruptions because of the displacement process.

The bumping rights of seasonal employees have been addressed in several decisions. Some arbitrators have held that, even where the collective agreement makes no distinction between seasonal employees and other members of the bargaining unit, seasonal employees' bumping rights are subject to implied limits. In particular, where there is a long-standing practice of hiring seasonal employees to work for a certain period and then laying them off at the same time each year, such employees may be precluded from bumping into other positions: see *Union Gas Ltd. and U.S.W.A., Local 2020*, [2004] O.L.A.A. No. 626 (QL) (Davie).

20.3.3   Bumping Up

The history of the debate as to whether, as a result of exercising seniority rights in a layoff situation, an employee may "bump up" into a position in a higher job classification or pay rate is detailed in *Canadian Broadcasting Corp. and N.A.B.E.T.* (1985), 17 L.A.C. (3d) 353 (M.G. Picher). In the view of early authorities, the absence of an express provision permitting bumping up should be taken to mean that the parties intended to limit seniority rights to lateral and downward bumping. The concern typically expressed was that allowing bumping up would have adverse and irrational effects on the job posting and promotion procedures, and would impair the exercise of management rights. However, beginning with the seminal decision of Arbitrator Christie in *York Gears Ltd. and U.A.W., Local 984* (1969), 20 L.A.C. 302, a consensus began to emerge to the effect that, where the collective agreement is silent on the issue, the right to bump up can be inferred as readily as the right to bump down.

However, despite widespread agreement that bumping up is not inherently objectionable, most arbitrators have inspected the collective agreement very closely for any signs of inconsistency between the recognition of a right to bump up and the operation of other provisions, most notably the job posting and promotion clauses, which would lower the standards of entrance into a higher, better-paying classification. The most common type of inconsistency is a discrepancy between the seniority clause applicable to promotions or job postings and that applicable to the displacement process. In *York Gears*, for instance, the grievance was in the end dismissed because the provision governing promotions was a "competition" clause, while bumping rights were premised on a simple "sufficient ability" or "threshold" clause. The right to bump up was also denied in *Canadian Broadcasting Corp.*, for similar reasons. For the purposes of promotion, Arbitrator Picher found, seniority was measured on the basis of functional group seniority, whereas for layoff purposes it was measured on the basis of corporation-wide seniority. In both cases, an inference that bumping up was permissible was precluded by the fact that it would permit employees to circumvent the job posting provisions.

Nevertheless, in recent years a number of arbitrators have held that permitting a laid-off employee to bump up would not be inconsistent with the promotion or job posting provisions of the collective agreement because the applicable language was similar. This was the case, for example, in *Stormont, Dundas & Glengarry County Roman Catholic Separate School Board and C.U.P.E., Local 1834* (1992), 28 L.A.C. (4th) 67 (Burkett), where both the promotion process and bumping rights were governed by a sufficient ability clause. The arbitrator also found that a 30-day trial period that was applicable to promotions, but not to bumping, did not create an inconsistency sufficient to preclude bumping up. Thus, he held, in the absence of an "irreconcilable conflict", there was no reason to restrict the otherwise unfettered bumping rights conferred by the collective agreement.

20.4   RECALL RIGHTS

20.4.1   Status of Employees on Layoff

In the earliest cases in which the employment status of laid-off employees came into question, it was generally held that they were not "employees" for the purpose of entitlement to benefits and other rights under the collective agreement (apart, of course, from the bare right to be recalled to work).

However, in the 1960s and 1970s, arbitrators gradually shifted to the view that the word "employee" as used in this context should not be restricted solely to active employees. The term thus came to include anyone who was in a legal employment relationship which had not been finally severed in accordance with the collective agreement. Accordingly, in the absence of clear provisions to the contrary, employees on layoff were held to be entitled to paid statutory holidays, the payment of premiums under a plan of insured benefits, and other benefits and perquisites granted to regular employees. In response, though, there arose a concern that such an approach was leading to unreasonably extended entitlements on the part of employees who had been out of the workplace for a long period of time, with little prospect of return. To avoid this problem, many collective agreements today contain detailed provisions specifying the status of laid-off workers. Where the parties have failed to address the issue, arbitrators now attempt to establish reasonable limits on entitlement to benefits conferred by the collective agreement, recognizing that they are intended as *compensation* for productive work performed on the employer's behalf. In other words, the question of whether an employee on layoff remains entitled to benefit payments involves the arbitrator in an inquiry as to whether it was within the parties' reasonable contemplation to confer the benefit in question, having regard to the necessity of preserving a reasonable connection between work done and the benefit claimed. The evolution of this approach to the status of laid-off employees is described in the decision of Paul Weiler in *Andres Wines (B.C.) Ltd. and United Brewery & Distillery Workers, Local 300* (1977), 16 L.A.C. (2d) 422 (B.C.L.R.B.).

More recently, the approach described by Weiler has been applied in *Atco Lumber Ltd. and I.W.A., Local 1-405* (1995), 49 L.A.C. (4th) 402 (Devine). By mutual agreement of the parties, all employees were required to take two weeks of vacation while the plant underwent its annual summer shut-down. The shut-down coincided with a period during which the grievor had been laid off due to a temporary shortage of material. In the union's view, the grievor should not have been compelled to take vacation at this time, since the right to paid vacation was a benefit associated with active employment. Disagreeing with the union's assessment, Arbitrator Devine ruled that the grievor's status was more akin to that of a regular employee than to that of a laid-off employee who has little prospect of recall. Accordingly, the grievor was bound by the obligations imposed by the collective agreement, including those relating to the summer shut-down. In the words of the arbitrator, at p. 408: "An employee on a temporary layoff can assert rights that may accrue under the collective agreement except for those rights, such as wages, which are associated with active employment. Conversely, an employee on a temporary layoff must also accept the obligations which attend by virtue of the continuing status of 'employee'".

The principles set out in *Andres Wines* were also applied in *Canada Brick and U.S.W.A., Local 225* (2002), 111 L.A.C. (4th) 220, where Arbitrator Briggs considered whether employees who had been given notice of permanent layoff due to the plant's closure (beginning December 14) were entitled to holiday pay for Christmas Eve, Christmas Day and Boxing Day on the basis that the employees retained recall rights under the collective agreement. It was held that, in the circumstances of a permanent layoff in which employees had received severance pay, there did not exist a subsisting employment relationship sufficient to require payment of holiday pay. However, in light of a provision in the collective agreement which entitled laid-off employees to holiday pay in respect of holidays that occurred not later than ten calendar days after the layoff, the arbitrator ordered the employer to pay holiday pay for Christmas Eve.

In addition, see *British Columbia (Public Service Employee Relations Commission) and B.C.G.E.U. (McGovern)*, [2003] B.C.C.A.A.A. No. 305 (QL), where Arbitrator Hope held that an employee continued to be eligible for long-term disability benefits, despite being laid off while she was still receiving short-term illness and injury benefits. The layoff occurred approximately two months prior to the expiry of these payments, and it was a condition of eligibility for long-term benefits that the claimant exhaust entitlement to short-term benefits.

20.4.2 Requirement for Notice of Recall

The collective agreement usually sets out procedures that govern the exercise of employees' right to recall following a layoff, including an obligation on the employer to give notice of recall. Even in the absence of express notice requirements, however, the arbitral caselaw imposes an obligation on the employer to do everything reasonable in the circumstances to notify an employee entitled to recall of the opportunity to return to work. This principle is set out in *Canteen of Canada Ltd. and R.W.D.S.U., Local 414* (1983), 9 L.A.C. (3d) 25 (Swan).

20.4.3 Triggering of Recall Rights

The collective agreement often outlines in general terms the circumstances in which a laid-off employee can exercise his or her right to recall, such as when work becomes available or when a vacancy arises in the employee's unit or job classification. In such cases, a decision by the employer to reassign work formerly done by the employee to other workers, particularly workers outside the bargaining unit, may well prompt a grievance alleging an improper denial of recall rights. As demonstrated by the award in *Fittings Ltd. and U.S.W.A., Local 1817* (1960), 10 L.A.C. 294 (Little), arbitrators at one time tended to deny such grievances on the ground that the collective agreement did not explicitly restrict management's right to assign work to employees outside the bargaining unit. More recently, however, arbitrators have recognized that the absence of an express restriction is not determinative, ruling that the existence of a negotiated job classification structure, seniority and recall rights, and job posting procedures all create an *implied* restriction on the employer's right to assign work in a layoff situation. In one of the leading decisions, *Irwin Toy Ltd. and U.S.W.A.* (1982), 6 L.A.C. (3d) 328 (Burkett), the issue was whether the employer had violated this implied restriction by assigning work normally performed by members of the bargaining unit to supervisors while employees remained on layoff. The board allowed the grievance in part, ruling that the disputed assignment violated the right to recall if it involved all or most of a full shift's work.

Arbitrator Haefling developed these principles further in *Drug Trading Co. and C.E.P., Local 11-0* (1994), 41 L.A.C. (4th) 140, ruling that the grievors' decision to bump into lower-rated positions did not bring to an end their right of recall from layoff. Accordingly, the assignment of work which they had previously performed to non-bargaining unit employees supplied by an outside contractor constituted a breach of the recall provisions of the collective agreement. Also important to this conclusion was the arbitrator's finding, on the basis of the employer's *de facto* control over the contract employees, that a valid contracting out of the disputed work had not been achieved.

Similarly, in *TRW Canada Ltd. and T.P.E.A.* (1992), 31 L.A.C. (4th) 203, Arbitrator Rose held that the employer's failure to recall a laid-off employee in the face of extensive overtime assignments was a violation of the collective agreement. The availability of overtime on such a scale, it was held, indicated that there were more than enough hours to occupy a full-time employee on an ongoing basis.

Nevertheless, the recall, contracting out and overtime provisions of the collective agreement may lead to a contrary result, particularly in the face of evidence of negotiating history or a consistent past practice. Thus, in *Freightliner (Sterling Trucks) and C.A.W., Local 1001*, [2003] O.L.A.A. No. 603 (QL), Arbitrator Burkett dismissed a union grievance alleging that the employer had violated the collective agreement by contracting out janitorial duties while 400 bargaining unit employees remained on layoff. The collective agreement prohibited the contracting out of bargaining unit work if it would have the "direct effect of causing a layoff of the affected bargaining unit employees". In this case, the arbitrator noted, the outsourcing did not result in an immediate layoff, as the janitors in question had been reassigned to other positions in the bargaining unit. Furthermore, he found, the union had agreed during collective agreement negotiations to withdraw a proposal expressly prohibiting the contracting out of janitorial services.

20.4.4   Recall Rights and Job Posting Provisions

The employer's decision to post a vacancy has often led employees on layoff to assert a pre-emptive right to be considered for the job. For the most part, however, this argument has been rejected. Arbitrators have repeatedly ruled that, unless the parties have specifically agreed otherwise, job vacancies must be posted in compliance with the procedures set out in the collective agreement, regardless of the fact that employees are on layoff. As articulated by Arbitrator Shime in *Metroland Printing, Publishing & Distributing and Southern Ontario Newspaper Guild* (1989), 4 L.A.C. (4th) 307, the rationale for this approach is to protect the integrity of the seniority regime. If employees on layoff were permitted to preempt vacancies as they occurred, he pointed out, applicants with more seniority would be denied the opportunity for advancement in accordance with the promotion provisions of the collective agreement.

See also *AGT Ltd. and I.B.E.W., Local 348* (1995), 51 L.A.C. (4th) 422 (Sims), where the job posting provisions specifically allowed the employer to accept applications from non-bargaining unit employees, and entitled applicants to assert company-wide seniority.

20.4.5   Bumping and the Retention of Recall Rights

Most collective agreements specify when an employee on layoff loses his or her status as an employee or the right to recall. An issue in respect of which the collective agreement is often silent, however, is whether an employee who has exercised his or her bumping rights and moved into another classification retains recall rights to the former classification. On the theory that recall provisions are generally intended to reverse the dislocations caused by a layoff, arbitrators have usually held that an employee does in fact retain the right to return to his or her previous position if a vacancy arises. As noted by Arbitrator Devlin in *Ottawa (City) and C.U.P.E., Local 503* (1990), 12 L.A.C. (4th) 138, to deny recall rights in such circumstances would be to penalize employees for taking advantage of their accrued seniority. Compare *Drug Trading Co. and C.E.P., Local 11-0* (1994), 41 L.A.C. (4th) 140, where Arbitrator Haefling ruled that an employee who bumps into another classification following layoff retains the right to be recalled to his or her former classification. However, he suggested, the result would be different if the collective agreement stated that employees who bump into alternative positions forfeit their right to recall.

20.4.6   Remedy for Breach of Recall Rights

In several cases, the employer and the union have taken issue with respect to the appropriate remedy for breach of an employee's right to recall. Whereas the employer normally advocates an in-kind remedy, that is, a future opportunity to work, the union has traditionally sought an award of monetary compensation on behalf of affected employees. Reflecting the influence of caselaw dealing with the loss of opportunities to work overtime (see Chapter 21), some arbitrators have ruled in favour of the employer on this issue. More recently, however, the trend has been in the opposite direction, as indicated by Arbitrator Kaplan's decision in *Domtar and C.E.P.* (1997), 65 L.A.C. (4th) 154. Since the employees in question should have been able to use their seniority to obtain the work available on recall in any event, the arbitrator held, an in-kind remedy is simply inappropriate. Once the work is lost, it is lost for good, and the missed opportunity cannot be recreated.

CHAPTER 21

HOURS OF WORK

21.1 SCHEDULING OF WORK WEEK

Arbitrators have generally held that the scheduling of work is an inherent management right. Subject, therefore, to any express restrictions found in employment standards legislation or the collective agreement, the employer is entitled to assign and to vary the hours and shifts of work. This principle was affirmed by the Supreme Court of Canada in *Air-Care Ltd. v. U.S.W.A.* (1974), 49 D.L.R. (3d) 467. The principles expressed by the Court were reiterated by Arbitrator Howard Brown in *Metropolitan Separate School Board and C.U.P.E., Local 1280* (1997), 68 L.A.C. (4th) 265. Nonetheless, the exercise of the employer's discretion to schedule work may be subject to an implied obligation to act reasonably and in good faith, and for legitimate business reasons, as discussed in Chapter 16.2.2.

In light of the necessity for an implied if not an express restriction, the vast majority of cases turn on the extent to which the language of the collective agreement can be said to limit the employer's authority to vary the days or hours of work, or shift schedules. In *E.S. & A. Robinson (Canada) Ltd. and Printing Specialties & Paper Products Union, Local 466* (1976), 11 L.A.C. (2d) 408, Arbitrator Swan held that the judgment of the Supreme Court in *Air-Care Ltd.* did not overrule longstanding arbitral principles with respect to collective agreement provisions which identify a "normal", "regular" or "standard" work schedule. Such clauses have generally been held to allow management to depart from the usual schedule on a temporary basis for legitimate reasons. However, most arbitrators have also ruled that the only way to give effect to *both* the management rights clause and a provision stipulating the normal or regular hours of work is to preclude the employer from unilaterally establishing a new norm or changing the hours of work on a permanent basis. In addition, as discussed in Chapter 20.2.3, the employer generally will not be permitted to use its right to schedule work as a means of avoiding or undermining the layoff and recall provisions of the collective agreement. These principles were reaffirmed in *Brampton Hydro-Electric Commission and C.A.W., Local 1285* (1994), 44 L.A.C. (4th) 1 (Brunner).

21.2   REDUCTION OF WORK HOURS

The employer's right to schedule production includes the right to shorten the hours of work, provided the reduction is not contrary to collective agreement provisions defining the "regular" hours of work or governing employees' rights in a layoff situation: unless employees' hours are reduced equally, the reduction will be held to constitute a layoff (for further discussion of the latter point, see Chapter 20.2.3). The decisions in *Air-Care Ltd. v. U.S.W.A.* (1974), 49 D.L.R. (3d) 467 (S.C.C.), and *E.S. & A. Robinson (Canada) Ltd. and Printing Specialties & Paper Products Union, Local 466* (1976), 11 L.A.C. (2d) 408 (Swan), discussed in Chapter 21.1, continue to be the leading authorities on the extent of management's right to curtail the usual work hours. While contract provisions which identify "normal" hours, or a "regular" or "present" schedule, do not represent a guarantee of minimum hours and will not preclude a temporary reduction, they do prohibit the establishment of a new norm by unilateral management initiative. The decision of Arbitrator Adams in *Ballycliffe Lodge Ltd. and S.E.I.U., Local 204* (1984), 14 L.A.C. (3d) 37 provides a concise summary of the principles relating to a reduction in work hours.

Similarly, in *Harvey & Co. Ltd. (St. John's Branch) and Transport & Allied Workers Union, Local 855* (1992), 29 L.A.C. (4th) 164, Arbitrator Alcock ruled that the employer was not entitled to reduce employees' "normal" hours of work from 40 to 37.5 per week pending an improvement in economic conditions.

21.3   VOLUNTARY AND COMPULSORY OVERTIME

Arbitrators have long held that, in the absence of an express provision in the collective agreement to the contrary, the employer may schedule and assign overtime within the limits prescribed by employment standards legislation. The employer's authority to assign compulsory overtime was recognized in the seminal decision of *Algoma Steel Corp. Ltd. and U.S.W.A., Local 2251* (1960), 11 L.A.C. 118 (Anderson), which has been widely adopted by other arbitrators. As a consequence, many collective agreements contain explicit provisions which limit management's right to compel employees to work overtime by making overtime voluntary or by imposing certain conditions on the right to resort to mandatory overtime. At the same time, the arbitration board in *Algoma Steel Corp.* recognized that the employer must accept a legitimate personal excuse from an employee who is unwilling to work overtime as scheduled.

The concept of a reasonable personal excuse exempting an employee from performing overtime was further elaborated in the leading case of *Cryovac*

Division, Grace Chemicals Ltd. and Printing Specialties & Paper Products Union, Local 466 (1972), 24 L.A.C. 127. Arbitrator Paul Weiler suggested that the reasonableness of an excuse should be interpreted very broadly where the employee has already put in his or her regular hours for the week. In such circumstances, he ruled, family and social obligations are entitled to greater consideration as reasons for not reporting for work. In *Canadian Timken Ltd. and U.S.W.A., Local 4906* (1994), 44 L.A.C. (4th) 252, though, Arbitrator Joyce pointed out that the employee has a positive obligation to communicate clearly and completely his or her excuse to the employer. Failure to do so may result in a ruling upholding the imposition of discipline for the employee's failure to work overtime as directed.

Collective agreement provisions which simply prescribe the "regular", "normal" or "existing" hours of work will not generally suffice to prevent the employer from assigning compulsory overtime. However, they will be effective to prevent the employer from compelling the performance of overtime for an indefinite term. In *Quebec & Ontario Paper Co. and C.P.U., Local 101* (1992), 24 L.A.C. (4th) 163 (MacDowell), for example, the collective agreement specified the start- and end-time of each of the three shifts in operation. The arbitrator ruled that, while the agreement authorized the employer to assign compulsory overtime in some situations, this right could not be exercised so regularly, routinely and predictably as to alter the negotiated work schedule.

Additional Reading

R. Venne, "Mandatory Overtime" in W. Kaplan, J. Sack, M. Gunderson & R. Filion, eds., *Labour Arbitration Yearbook 1998*, p. 231.

21.4   STATUTORY LIMITATIONS

Arbitrators have for some time recognized that they have the authority to apply general statute law, at least in cases where the provisions of the collective agreement are inconsistent with the statute. In some jurisdictions such as British Columbia and Ontario, the applicable labour relations legislation confers on arbitrators an express mandate to apply employment-related statutes to a dispute in the arbitral forum. Moreover, the Ontario *Employment Standards Act* provides expressly for the exclusive jurisdiction of arbitrators to apply and enforce its provisions in cases involving workers who are members of a bargaining unit that is subject to a collective agreement: S.O. 2000, c. 41, ss. 100-101. Whether or not there exists explicit statutory authority, the Supreme Court of Canada has held, in *McLeod v. Egan* (1974), 46 D.L.R. (3d) 150, that the enforcement of employment standards lies within the scope of an arbitrator's jurisdiction. More recently, arbitral jurisdiction to enforce employment standards legislation, even in the absence of a violation of an express provision of the collective agreement, was significantly enhanced by the Supreme Court of Canada's decision in *Parry Sound (District) Social Services Administration Board v. O.P.S.E.U., Local 324* (2003), 230 D.L.R. (4th) 257. In that case, the Court expressed the view that its previous ruling in *McLeod v. Egan* stood for the proposition that "the substantive rights and obligations of employment-related statutes are implicit in each collective agreement over which an arbitrator has jurisdiction" (at p. 271). On this basis, the Court concluded that arbitrators have jurisdiction to address alleged violations of such statutes, regardless of whether the collective agreement makes reference to the legislation or whether the legislation provides for its own enforcement mechanism: see the discussion of *Parry Sound* in Chapter 1.2.3. However, this decision is subject to an important qualification, namely, that only statutory provisions which are *compatible* with the collective labour relations scheme are incorporated in collective agreements: *Isidore Garon Ltée v. Syndicat du Bois Ouvré de la Région de Québec Inc.* (2006), 262 D.L.R. (4th) 385 (S.C.C.).

Federal employment standards legislation as well as that of some provinces sets out maximum daily or weekly hours of work which exceed the accepted norm of eight hours per day and 40 hours per week. Section 171(1) of the *Canada Labour Code*, R.S.C. 1985, c. L-2, provides generally that "the total hours that may be worked by any employee in any week shall not exceed forty-eight hours in a week". To the same effect, s. 9 of the Nova Scotia *Minimum Wage Order (General)*, N.S. Reg. 5/99, establishes a maximum work week of 48 hours.

The relationship between the standard 40-hour work week, the maximum hours stipulated by employment standards legislation, and the employer's right to exact compulsory overtime has been the subject of several court and arbitration decisions, all of which attempt to define the rights of individual employees in a unionized setting. Section 172(1)(b) of the *Canada Labour Code* provides that the scheduling of hours of work which exceed the statutory limit must be "agreed to in writing by the employer and the trade union". Similarly, Ontario's *Employment Standards Act* formerly provided that the employer was required to obtain a government permit authorizing the scheduling of work in excess of the statutory maximums of eight hours per day and 48 hours per week. The Act specifically stated, though, that the issuance of a permit did not have the effect of obligating an employee to work any additional hours "without the consent or agreement of the employee or the employee's agent", that is, the union. In *McLeod v. Egan, supra*, the Supreme Court of Canada ruled that a management rights clause that merely preserves the employer's right to schedule hours of work does not constitute the requisite "consent or agreement" of the employee or his or her agent. While the Court did not exclude the possibility that consent or agreement could be expressed through the vehicle of a collective agreement, it made it clear that the provisions on which the employer was relying must relate specifically to the performance of work by the employee beyond the statutory limit.

These principles were summarized and affirmed in *Ontario Hydro and Power Workers' Union* (1998), 74 L.A.C. (4th) 425 (Burkett). The arbitrator stressed that the collective agreement provisions advanced by the employer as constituting sufficient consent or agreement must evidence a clear intent to relinquish the right of employees to refuse hours of work beyond the statutory maximum. This intent may be demonstrated by language which refers to the statute, the permit, or the compulsory hours of work in excess of the statutory maximum. However, Arbitrator Burkett rejected the proposition espoused in a number of awards that nothing short of an explicit reference to the applicable legislation is capable of giving rise to consent.

In 2000, Ontario's Conservative government enacted the *Employment Standards Act, 2000*, S.O. 2000, c. 41, bringing about significant changes to many of the key components of its employment standards regime, including the hours of work and overtime provisions. The amendments, which took effect on September 4, 2001, eliminated the requirement for a permit authorizing hours of work that exceeded the statutory maximum, and enabled employees to agree to work in excess of the daily or weekly limits on hours of work, as long as they did not work more than 60 hours per week or exceed other limits prescribed by the regulations.

Although the reference to the "consent" of the employee's "agent" has been deleted, the Act continues to require the agreement of an employee to work hours exceeding the maximums prescribed by s. 17(1). However, s. 7 of the new Act provides that any agreement that can be made by the employee under the Act can be made by his or her agent, and s. 1 provides that trade unions with representation rights are agents. Section 1(3) specifies that agreements referred to in the Act must be in writing, unless otherwise provided by the legislation. Thus, it would appear that the existing caselaw will continue to be relevant in interpreting the new provisions.

In *Imperial Tobacco Canada Ltd. and B.C.T., Local 323T* (2002), 111 L.A.C. (4th) 434, Arbitrator Devlin held that s. 18(1) of the amended Act, which requires employers to give employees a period of at least 11 hours free from work every day, cannot be overridden by a collective agreement. In this regard, the arbitrator noted, an exception to the minimum hours of rest provision in s. 18(1) does not arise simply because the employer and an employee agree to extend the maximum hours of work pursuant to s. 17(2). The only available exceptions are those specifically enumerated in the Act: work performed during a call-in (s. 18(2)), or in connection with exceptional circumstances such as an emergency, potential disruption to the delivery of essential public services, or urgent repair work (s. 19).

Arbitrator Reilly has ruled that, for the purposes of the minimum rest period of 11 hours per day prescribed by the Act, the word "day" should be defined as the 24-hour period commencing with the beginning of a scheduled work day, not as a calendar day: *McKesson Canada and Teamsters, Local 424* (2004), 130 L.A.C. (4th) 34.

In 2004, the recently elected Liberal government in Ontario enacted significant amendments to the hours of work provisions of the *Employment Standards Act, 2000*, which came into force on March 1, 2005 (S.O. 2004, c. 21). The 2005 amendments attempt to answer criticisms that the Conservative amendments in 2000 failed to protect vulnerable workers from pressure by employers to agree to longer working hours. The amended legislation prohibits employers from requiring employees to work more than 48 hours in a week unless they have obtained approval from the Director of Employment Standards, as well as the employee's written consent. In addition, the Act now includes provisions intended to ensure that employees are fully apprised of their rights under the legislation before they enter into an agreement to work hours in excess of the statutory maximum. Overtime averaging arrangements, permitted under the Act, are subject to the same requirements — government approval and written agreement by the employee.

The employer's right to schedule hours of work may also be restricted by its obligations under human rights legislation. In *H.S.A.B.C. v. Campbell River & North Island Transition Society* (2004), 240 D.L.R. (4th) 479, the British Columbia Court of Appeal held that an employer's decision to change an employee's hours of work constituted discrimination on the basis of family status where it seriously impaired her ability to attend to the needs of her son, who suffered from a major psychiatric disorder. Accordingly, the revised work schedule was impermissible unless the employer could justify it as a *bona fide* occupational qualification.

21.5   ALLOCATION OF OVERTIME

It is very common for the collective agreement to contain restrictions on the employer's discretion to allocate overtime opportunities among its employees, both within and outside the bargaining unit. In the absence of express language, though, the distribution of overtime has been held to fall within the exclusive rights of management. In *Metropolitan Toronto Board of Commissioners of Police v. Metropolitan Toronto Police Ass'n* (1981), 124 D.L.R. (3d) 684, for example, the Ontario Court of Appeal quashed an award in which the arbitrator had inferred from a standard management rights clause an obligation on the employer to act fairly and reasonably in distributing overtime.

Where the collective agreement does restrict the exercise of management's discretion in the assignment of overtime, there has been considerable disagreement among arbitrators as to the appropriate remedy for employees who have been improperly denied an overtime opportunity. Many of the earlier decisions took the view expressed by Paul Weiler in *Canadian Johns Manville Co. Ltd. and Int'l Chemical Workers, Local 346* (1971), 22 L.A.C. 396 that an in-kind remedy of another overtime opportunity in the future was more consistent with a compensatory approach than a straightforward damages award to cover lost wages. In recent years, however, numerous arbitrators have held that an in-kind remedy will often be inappropriate because of its deleterious impact on other employees (who may *also* have a claim to the substitute opportunity in question), or because the original work was given to employees outside the bargaining unit or relevant classification, and was therefore "lost forever". The existence of substantial uncertainty as to when a replacement opportunity would arise has also been held to weigh against the granting of an in-kind remedy. A summary of the traditional approach, and the growth of arbitral reaction against it, is found in *Labatt's Ontario Breweries and Brewery, Malt & Soft Drink Workers, Local 304* (1993), 36 L.A.C. (4th) 289 (Gray).

The decision in *Bingo Press & Specialty Ltd. and Retail Wholesale Canada, Local 462* (2002), 107 L.A.C. (4th) 337 (Newman) contains a review of recent cases and confirms the existence of a trend among arbitrators to find that the presumption in favour of a "make-work", in-kind order is rebutted where the granting of such a remedy would adversely affect the seniority rights of other employees in the bargaining unit. The arbitrator commented that, in the absence of an overtime equalization scheme in the collective agreement, it will generally not be possible for the employer to provide bargaining unit work similar to that ordinarily performed by the grievor without violating other employees' seniority rights.

Additional Reading

M. Jackson, "Lost Overtime Opportunities: Cash or In Kind Remedies?" in W. Kaplan, J. Sack, M. Gunderson & R. Filion, eds., *Labour Arbitration Yearbook 1996-97*, p. 347.

CHAPTER 22
WAGES AND BENEFITS

22.1 WAGE RATES

22.1.1 The Job Classification System

The collective agreement usually identifies the job classifications found within the bargaining unit, and establishes a corresponding schedule of wage rates. The parties also commonly provide for periodic increases in the wage rates. In addition, the collective agreement may well prescribe procedures to govern the alteration or augmentation of existing classifications, or stipulate that an employee who, during a temporary transfer, performs the duties of a

different classification is entitled to be paid at the applicable higher rate. However, in the absence of express restrictions in the agreement, the mere existence
of a job classification scheme does not limit management's right to eliminate
classifications, to reassign duties from one classification to another, or to create new classifications. In *Windsor Public Utilities Commission and I.B.E.W.,
Local 911* (1974), 7 L.A.C. (2d) 380, the seminal decision on management's
right to reorganize the workplace, Arbitrator Adams emphasized the need for
management flexibility in this area. He noted, though, that even in the absence
of express limitations, arbitrators have implied a requirement that such decisions must be made in good faith, for a legitimate business purpose, and without arbitrariness or discrimination: see the discussion in Chapter 17.3.

Consistent with the award in *Windsor Public Utilities Commission*, arbitrators have recognized that the employer has the unilateral right to set the rate
of pay for a new job classification, unless, of course, the collective agreement
contains specific provisions to the contrary. This principle is set out in *British
Columbia Forest Products Ltd. and Pulp, Paper & Woodworkers of Canada,
Local 2* (1978), 20 L.A.C. (2d) 104 (Hope).

22.1.2   Work Performed in a Different Classification

There have been a significant number of cases in which an employee, for-
mally assigned to one job classification, claims that he or she is performing the
work of another, higher-rated classification, and should be compensated
accordingly. In the absence of contractual guidelines, arbitrators have articulated various tests to assess an employee's entitlement to a higher rate of pay.
The most frequently cited authority continues to be the decision of Arbitrator
Swan in *Metropolitan Toronto (Municipality) and C.U.P.E., Local 43* (1984),
13 L.A.C. (3d) 248. The arbitrator rejected the more traditional proposition
that, in order to succeed, the union was required to prove that the grievor's job
duties brought him or her "squarely" within the parameters of the higher-rated
classification. While acknowledging that classifications cannot be regarded as
water-tight compartments and that some overlap in duties is unavoidable, Arbitrator Swan held that the proper test simply involves demonstrating, on a balance of probabilities, which of the two classifications in issue is the better one
for the disputed job. Where the grievor performs the "central core" of a different classification, or that classification is revealed to be a "better fit", he or she
is entitled to be compensated in accordance with the higher rate.

Even where the more flexible approach advocated by Arbitrator Swan is
adopted, though, the union bears the burden of adducing satisfactory evidence
with respect to the nature of the job duties in each of the two disputed classifications. In *Long Packaging and E.C.W.U., Local 620* (1990), 10 L.A.C. (4th)
335 (Marszewski), the union alleged that 60 to 70 percent of the grievor's
duties lay within a higher-rate classification. The arbitrator concluded that,

even if she were to accept the union's evidence, this proportion was not high enough to enable the grievance to succeed, regardless of which test was applied.

A contrasting approach can be found in *Ontario Hydro and C.U.P.E., Local 1000* (1983), 11 L.A.C. (3d) 404 (Shime). Here, too, the amount of work performed by the grievors was insufficient to bring them within the scope of the higher-rated classification. Arbitrator Shime held, nevertheless, that they were entitled to be paid for any work assignments which did not pertain to their original classification, either at the rate prescribed for such work by the collective agreement, or, if the existing classification scheme was inadequate for this purpose, on a *quantum meruit* basis, *i.e.* what they reasonably deserved for the work.

In *Capital Health Authority and H.S.A.A.*, [2003] A.G.A.A. No. 94 (QL) (Moreau), an arbitration board dismissed a claim for temporary assignment pay on the basis that the grievors had not demonstrated that they performed the core duties of the higher classification for at least one full shift.

Additional Reading

P. Knopf, "Classification Disputes at Arbitration" in W. Kaplan, J. Sack & M. Gunderson, eds., *Labour Arbitration Yearbook 1993*, p. 75.

22.1.3   What Constitutes Compensable "Work"?

Unless there are provisions in the collective agreement to the contrary, employees are entitled to be paid only for hours actually worked. There are a large number of arbitration decisions on the issue of what constitutes "work" for the purposes of the collective agreement. Arbitrators have generally taken a fairly expansive and flexible view of the meaning of this term, holding that "work" may include activities other than those included in an employee's job description, or those which he or she is usually expected to perform. Work can thus encompass any time spent under the employer's control, such as attendance at a training course, lunch periods during which an employee is confined to the workplace, driving to a conference at the employer's request, or mandatory attendance at an after-hours health and safety meeting.

The fact that the employee has engaged in such activities on the understanding that participation was voluntary will not preclude a finding that he or she was "at work". The most frequently cited decision on this subject is *Steinberg Inc. and U.F.C.W., Local 486* (1985), 20 L.A.C. (3d) 289 (Foisy). In that case, while attendance was said to be voluntary, employees were "strongly encouraged" to be present at a meeting on store premises after working hours. During the meeting, the employer showed a video about the company's performance, and led employees in a discussion about workplace morale and customer service. Allowing the grievance, Arbitrator Foisy directed the employer to pay each employee who attended four hours' call-in pay. The fact that employees may have gone to the meeting voluntarily was not determinative, he noted, since the employer scheduled the event and openly encouraged staff to attend. However, in the more recent award of *MacMillan Bathurst and I.W.A., Local 1-830* (1998), 71 L.A.C. (4th) 368 (Bowman), the arbitrator rejected the union's claim that a voluntary familiarization session constituted compensable work. In this case, the employer had given advance notice in writing to all employees that attendance was "totally voluntary", and that those who attended would not be paid. According to the arbitrator, the activities at the meeting could not be considered training except "in the loosest conceivable application of that term".

22.1.4   Private Arrangements Prohibited

Some early awards seemed to uphold private arrangements which the employer had concluded with individual employees concerning wage rates or benefits, even if the arrangement conflicted with the collective agreement. More recently, however, arbitrators have consistently held that private understandings entered into without the union's consent violate the statutory principle of exclusive union representation as well as the union recognition clause in the collective agreement, and are unenforceable. For similar reasons, arbitrators have ruled that representations by an individual employee with respect to wages or benefits do not have the effect of precluding the union from enforcing the collective agreement at arbitration. In *Wiresmith Ltd. and U.S.W.A.* (1988), 34 L.A.C. (3d) 104, Arbitrator Brunner set out these principles and their justification in policy considerations.

The union's exclusive right to represent bargaining unit interests has also led arbitrators to hold that the employer cannot introduce a wage incentive or productivity bonus scheme without the consent of the union, unless the collective agreement contemplates such additional forms of compensation. *Alcan Building Products and U.A.W., Local 27* (1984), 14 L.A.C. (3d) 289 (Brunner) is an example of this line of cases.

22.1.5   Estoppel and the Right to Continuation of a Benefit

Traditionally, most arbitrators have refused to obligate the employer to continue making a payment or offering a benefit which is not contemplated by the collective agreement, as, for example, parking privileges, bonuses, or other perquisites. Union attempts to invoke the doctrine of estoppel against the employer have been rejected on the basis that the past practice of paying the benefit — often described as "gratuitous" — was not inconsistent with any specific provision of the collective agreement, and the employer had not represented that the practice would continue. Nevertheless, several arbitrators have held that the employer was in fact estopped from discontinuing the payment or benefit until the next round of bargaining. A summary of the conflicting caselaw on this issue is found in *Sterling Place and U.F.C.W., Local 175/633* (1997), 62 L.A.C. (4th) 289 (Pineau). Eleven months after entering into a first collective agreement, the employer discontinued a six-year practice of providing paid meals to employees whose working hours extended into a meal break. The arbitrator allowed the union's grievance, noting that the provision of meal benefits on a daily basis was a form of compensation, and that compensation was not normally subject to unilateral alteration during the term of a collective agreement. Furthermore, she held, the employer's silence at the bargaining table regarding the issue made it reasonable for the union to assume that the payments would continue at least until the expiry of the agreement.

However, other arbitrators remain of the view that the employer's long-term provision of a benefit not required by the collective agreement cannot, in itself, form the basis of an estoppel claim. As noted by Arbitrator Marcotte in *Coca-Cola Bottling Co. and U.F.C.W., Local 393W*, [2003] O.L.A.A. No. 181 (QL), it has often been held that a long-standing past practice does not give rise to an estoppel unless the practice was at odds with an express term of the collective agreement, or the employer has explicitly represented that the practice will continue.

In *Valspar and U.S.W.A., Local 3*, [2004] O.L.A.A. No. 627 (QL), Arbitrator Roberts held that one inconsistent incident did not defeat the estoppel asserted by the union, as there was an otherwise consistent practice of the employer paying the wages of union negotiators for time spent in collective bargaining with the company. It was held that, in order to preclude a finding of estoppel, the inconsistency must be recognized and knowingly acquiesced in by responsible union officials.

22.2 Premium and Overtime Rates

22.2.1 General

Employment standards legislation in Canada commonly fixes the maximum number of hours per day or per week that an employee can be compelled to work without his or her consent. Typically, the legislation also provides that a minimum overtime rate must be paid for all hours worked in excess of the prescribed number. Under the Alberta *Employment Standards Code*, S.A. 1996, c. E-10.3, the employer is ordinarily required to pay an employee an overtime rate of at least one-and-a-half times the regular rate for any hours worked in excess of eight in a day or 44 in a week, whichever is greater. Utilizing a somewhat different approach, s. 9 of the Newfoundland and Labrador *Labour Standards Regulations*, Reg. 781/96, establishes a schedule of dollar sums which represent the minimum overtime wage owing to an employee who works more than the "standard working hours", defined as 40 hours in a week. Some employment standards legislation permits the employer, usually only with the agreement of the employee, to average the number of hours per week over a period of several weeks for the purpose of determining entitlement to overtime pay. For example, s. 22(2) of the Ontario *Employment Standards Act, 2000*, S.O. 2000, c. 41, as amended, authorizes the employer, with the employee's agreement and the approval of the Director of Employment Standards, to average hours worked over a period of two or more weeks. In that province, the maximum hours of work permitted by the legislation are eight in a day and 48 in a week. In British Columbia, pursuant to the *Employment Standards Act*, R.S.B.C. 1996, c. 113, overtime must be paid "if the employer requires, or directly or indirectly allows, the employee to work more than 8 hours a day or 40 hours a week": s. 35(1).

Subject to such statutory requirements, the collective agreement may address a variety of issues relating to work performed on an overtime basis, including the allocation of overtime within the bargaining unit, the number of hours of work beyond which overtime becomes payable, notice requirements for the assignment of overtime work, and the applicable rates of pay. The agreement also frequently provides for premium rates of pay in respect of work performed on a Saturday or Sunday, or on days outside an employee's regular or normal work week. The allocation of overtime opportunities and the circumstances in which an employee can be compelled to work overtime are dealt with in Chapter 21.

22.2.2   Two Types of Overtime Entitlement

The way in which the parties frame an employee's entitlement to overtime pay generally falls into two patterns. Under one type of provision, overtime rates are payable only after an employee has worked a specified number of hours per shift or per week. Under the second type of provision, overtime is payable in respect of any hours worked "in excess of" or outside an employee's normal work day or work week, as set out in the collective agreement. As exemplified by the seminal decision of *Loblaw Groceterias Co. Ltd. and Int'l Mine Workers, Local 902* (1963), 14 L.A.C. 53 (Little), arbitrators have held that the words "in excess of" do not carry the same meaning as "in addition to", but rather denote *any* time worked outside an employee's regular or scheduled hours. Thus, in *Domglas Ltd. and United Glass & Ceramic Workers, Local 203* (1984), 19 L.A.C. (3d) 156, Arbitrator Kennedy held that the grievor was entitled to be paid at the overtime rate for all hours worked after the end of his regular shift, even though, having arrived at work late, he had not put in a full shift. See also *Longo Brothers Fruit Market Inc. and U.F.C.W., Local 633* (1995), 52 L.A.C. (4th) 113 (Solomatenko), discussed in Chapter 22.2.4.

Where the collective agreement contains both types of clauses, one entitling employees to overtime pay for working more than a specified number of hours in a day (typically eight), another defining the starting and stopping times of shifts, arbitrators have required the employer to pay overtime for all hours worked by an employee outside the contractually-stipulated periods. The rationale for this approach, it is said, is to preclude the employer from ignoring the regular hours of work clause and unilaterally changing shift times. However, if the employer schedules work at irregular times in order to accommodate a personal request by an employee, an arbitrator has the discretion to deny a demand for overtime payment. These principles are set out in *Dominion Bridge Co. Ltd. and U.S.W.A., Local 3390* (1980), 27 L.A.C. (2d) 399 (Adams).

22.2.3 What Constitutes Compensable "Work"?

Employee grievances concerning entitlement to overtime pay often arise from a dispute as to the meaning of the term "work" or "hours of work": see also the discussion in Chapter 22.1.3. In *Midland (Town) and O.P.S.E.U., Local 328* (1987), 31 L.A.C. (3d) 251 (Saltman), the employer instituted a new policy which restricted employees' freedom of movement during their unpaid lunch break. Because the change in policy effectively left the employees under the employer's direction and control, the arbitrator held that they were entitled to overtime pay for the break, even though their actual job responsibilities did not continue.

In *Petro-Canada Oil & Gas and C.E.P., Local 773*, [2003] A.G.A.A. No. 91 (QL) (Warren), the collective agreement entitled employees to premium pay if they were required to attend a course at a time outside their regular work schedule. Shortly before a mandatory course was to take place, the employer implemented a shift change in order to ensure that the grievor's attendance at the course coincided with his regularly scheduled hours. Arbitrator Warren ruled that, although the employer had the right to make shift changes, it must do so in good faith and without discrimination. In this case, because the employer had instituted a temporary shift change for the purpose of circumventing its obligation to pay compensation at a premium rate, the grievance was upheld.

However, in *Atomic Energy of Canada Ltd. and C.U.P.E., Local 1000* (2004), 129 L.A.C. (4th) 78, Arbitrator Devlin rejected claims for overtime pay advanced by employees who were periodically required to provide urine samples on Sundays while they were off duty, as part of a program to monitor radiation exposure in the workplace. The employees had previously provided the samples during regular working hours, but the collection of specimens was moved to Sunday, at least 24 hours after the workers' last shift. Rejecting the assertion that this obligation constituted "time worked" for the purposes of the collective agreement, the arbitrator ruled that the period of time required to take the samples was too inconsequential to form the basis for a claim to premium or overtime pay.

22.2.4   Only Part of Shift Worked on Premium Rate Day

The collective agreement may provide for the payment of overtime or premium rates for work performed on a Saturday or Sunday, or on a statutory holiday. Disputes as to entitlement often arise where an employee commences his or her shift on a regular working day, but finishes the shift on a premium rate calendar day. The wording of the collective agreement will always be determinative of whether the time worked qualifies for the premium rate. However, in the absence of express provisions to the contrary, many arbitrators have ruled that the entire shift should be viewed as falling on the day on which it began. In most of these cases, including the seminal decision in *Canada Cycle & Motor Co. Ltd. and U.A.W., Local 28* (1964), 15 L.A.C. 385 (Cross), evidence of past practice was also considered significant. The award in *Canron Inc. and Cement, Lime, Gypsum & Allied Workers, Local 494* (1987), 27 L.A.C. (3d) 379 (M.G. Picher) provides an overview of the traditional position.

More recently, though, some arbitrators have held that collective agreement language which simply refers to "work performed on Sunday" or "time worked on Sunday" is clear and unambiguous, and that an employee is therefore entitled to the premium or overtime rate for *any* hours falling on the named calendar day, without regard to the day on which the shift started or the fact that the hours were part of the employee's regular shift. Indeed, in *Cargill Ltd. and U.F.C.W., Local 1118* (1996), 54 L.A.C. (4th) 76 (Koshman), the arbitrator ruled that evidence of the parties' past practice was not admissible to override the plain meaning of the premium rate clause.

In a similar vein, in *Longo Brothers Fruit Market Inc. and U.F.C.W., Local 633* (1995), 52 L.A.C. (4th) 113 (Solomatenko), the arbitrator held that employees were entitled to be compensated at the applicable premium rate for any hours worked on Sunday. The collective agreement established a "basic" work week of five eight-hour shifts, which were to be scheduled between Monday and Saturday. In the arbitrator's opinion, the premium rate was payable in respect of all Sunday work, even if an employee had worked less than a 40-hour week between Monday and Saturday.

22.3   CALL-IN PAY

Most collective agreements provide for "call-in" or "call-back pay", also sometimes referred to as "call-out pay". Typically, this type of clause guarantees that if an employee is called in to work on short notice, outside of normal hours, he or she will receive not less than the minimum prescribed payment, regardless of the number of hours actually worked. The purpose of such a provision, arbitrators agree, is to compensate for the disruption to an employee's private life during non-working hours, and to deter the employer from resorting to the call-in mechanism unless there is enough work to justify the intrusion.

However, there has been a considerable amount of disagreement as to the circumstances which trigger entitlement to call-in pay. A number of arbitrators have espoused the principle formulated in *Webster Manufacturing (London) Ltd. and I.M.A.W., Local 49* (1971), 23 L.A.C. 37 (P.C. Weiler), to the effect that call-in pay is payable only if the employee is required to make an extra trip to and from work. Thus, where an employee is instructed in the course of the regular working day to report for work several hours after the shift has ended, eligibility for call-in pay has been established. By contrast, if the employee is still at work, or in the parking lot some time after the completion of his or her shift, and is asked to return to work at that time, the provision does not apply. More recently, the *Webster Manufacturing* principle was applied in *NTN Bearing Manufacturing Canada and U.S.W.A., Local 8890* (1995), 50 L.A.C. (4th) 289 (Kennedy).

At the same time, there is another group of awards in which the arbitrator has concluded that an extra trip from home is not the determining criterion for call-in pay (in the absence of express language to this effect). In the opinion of these arbitrators, call-in pay is owing whenever an employee is asked to perform unscheduled emergency work, and there is a break in time between the employee's regular scheduled hours and the work which he or she is assigned. A leading case in support of this view is *Shell Canada Ltd. and Oil, Chemical & Atomic Workers, Local 9-848* (1974), 6 L.A.C. (2d) 422 (O'Shea), where the grievor, having punched out, was recalled to work while in the company's parking lot. Arbitrator O'Shea ruled that, because the grievor had left the employer's control and supervision, he was entitled to call-in pay.

Finally, there is a third group of cases in which an employee has been called in on short notice several hours prior to his or her shift, and ends up working straight through to the end of the shift. Under the approach taken in both *Webster Manufacturing* and *Shell Canada*, the employer could argue that the requisite criteria have not been met, with the result that the employee would be entitled to payment at the appropriate rate (regular or overtime), but not to call-in pay. Nonetheless, several arbitrators have ruled that it is sufficient to establish entitlement if the employee has had little or no notice before being called in. In *Camp Hill Medical Centre and N.S.N.U.* (1994), 40 L.A.C. (4th) 381 (Rigg), for example, the arbitrator held that the purpose of call-in pay was to compensate an employee for disruption and expense, whether it was caused by the inadequacy of notice or by the necessity for an extra trip to work. Thus, if work performed on a call-in basis becomes contiguous with the employee's regular shift, call-in pay is payable, provided the employee was called in on short notice.

In *Health Employers Ass'n of British Columbia and B.C.N.U.* (1994), 43 L.A.C. (4th) 25 (Taylor), it was held that an employee who is required to work at home by responding to telephone calls from the employer, clients or customers may be entitled to call-in pay. In *University of Alberta Hospital and U.N.A., Local 301* (2000), 90 L.A.C. (4th) 328, Arbitrator Ponak also considered the issue of whether entitlement to call-in pay is triggered where an employee performs a telephone consultation while at home. On the basis of his review of previous awards, the arbitrator concluded that the result in each case depends on the precise wording of the collective agreement. Thus, the relevant inquiry is whether the call-in pay provisions of the collective agreement, properly construed, require the employee to return to the employer's premises as a precondition of entitlement, or merely to return to duty, whether in the workplace or at home.

The approach taken in *University of Alberta Hospital*, focusing on the purpose of the call-in provision at issue, was applied by the arbitration board in *Northeast Mental Health Centre and O.P.S.E.U.*, [2004] O.L.A.A. No. 673 (QL) (Whitaker). The trend in recent arbitral jurisprudence, the board noted, was to characterize the purpose of call-back pay as being to compensate for disruption to employees' personal time. Nevertheless, in the case before it, the board rejected a claim advanced by employees who provided services by telephone from their homes, ruling that the call-in provision in the parties' collective agreement was intended to compensate only for the inconvenience of having to make an extra, unplanned trip to the workplace.

It has been held that, in order to qualify for call-in pay, an employee must be obligated to work, rather than be given a choice whether to accept the assignment: *Lethbridge (City) and A.T.U., Local 987*, [2004] A.G.A.A. No. 29 (QL) (Warren). In that case, the arbitrator rejected a claim for call-in pay on the basis that the grievor had been asked (rather than ordered) on short notice to work additional hours after the end of his regular shift.

22.4   STAND-BY PAY

In addition to call-in pay, the collective agreement may provide for stand-by pay, which serves a different purpose than call-in pay. Stand-by pay is provided to compensate a worker for the general inconvenience of having to rearrange his or her life in order to be available to return to work immediately or on very short notice. The contrasting purposes of stand-by and call-in pay were explained in *Alberta and A.U.P.E.* (1986), 25 L.A.C. (3d) 276 (Elliott).

If, however, the collective agreement does not specifically provide for this form of compensation, arbitrators have declined to order the employer to pay stand-by pay. This was the position adopted in *Pembroke General Hospital and C.U.P.E., Local 1502* (1974), 6 L.A.C. (2d) 149 (H.D. Brown), where the collective agreement provided for call-back pay, but not stand-by pay. According to the arbitration board, "[t]he term 'call-back' presupposes that employees must be available to be called back and therefore must be readily available or on 'stand-by' to be called" (at p. 151). However, the board held, because the collective agreement was silent with respect to payment for time spent on stand-by, employees could not claim entitlement to such payment, and it would exceed the board's jurisdiction to award it.

Thus, unless the parties have specifically made provision for stand-by pay, the employer can require employees to carry a pager or radio during off-duty hours as a means of facilitating a potential call-in, without having to pay additional compensation: see *Maple Leaf Mills Inc. and U.F.C.W., Local 401* (1995), 50 L.A.C. (4th) 246 (Sims). However, where the employer goes further than this, and restricts employees' freedom of movement during an unpaid break (for example, by confining them to the work premises), arbitrators have generally held that the employees are "at work" for the purposes of the collective agreement and are therefore entitled to be paid at the appropriate rate. The cases are summarized in *Ottawa Civic Hospital and Retail Wholesale Canada, Local 414* (1996), 61 L.A.C. (4th) 101 (R.M. Brown).

22.5   HOLIDAY PAY

22.5.1   General

The collective agreement usually identifies a number of paid holidays to which employees are entitled during the course of the year. While employment standards legislation in every jurisdiction mandates the observance of certain holidays, the parties may augment the calendar of statutory holidays with additional paid holidays. The holiday provisions of the collective agreement may also stipulate a minimum period of service with the employer before an employee's entitlement accrues, provided the agreement is consistent with employment standards norms. Frequently, the agreement also establishes a "qualifying day" requirement, whereby an employee must attend at work on the day or shift before and after the holiday as a precondition to receiving holiday pay (see Chapter 22.5.4).

22.5.2   Holiday Falling on Non-Working Day

Arbitrators have often been called on to decide whether entitlement to holiday pay arises if the designated holiday falls on a non-working day. In the earliest cases, it was held that the purpose of holiday pay is simply to guarantee that an employee does not lose any pay on the holiday, and that this rationale necessarily precludes the payment of holiday pay on a non-working day. One example of such reasoning is found in *Steel Equipment Co. Ltd. and U.S.W.A., Local 3257* (1955), 6 L.A.C. 19 (Lane). It is now well established, however, that unless the collective agreement contemplates a more limited purpose, holiday pay is an earned benefit which forms part of the wage structure. Hence, employees should be presumed to be entitled to it, without regard to whether or not it falls on a regular working day. A seminal decision demonstrating the modern approach is *A. Silverman & Sons Ltd. and Sudbury General Workers' Union, Local 902* (1967), 18 L.A.C. 224 (P.C. Weiler).

A related issue which frequently arises is whether the collective agreement scheme governing holidays and holiday pay is consistent with applicable employment standards legislation. Collective agreement provisions which are inconsistent with such legislation are typically deemed null and void. At the same time, the legislation usually states that, where a collective agreement provides a greater right or benefit than an employment standard in respect of the same subject-matter, the collective agreement prevails: see, for example, the Alberta *Employment Standards Code*, R.S.A. 2000, c. E-9, s. 3(1)(b). In order to make the required comparison between the right or benefit conferred by the collective agreement and the minimum standard prescribed by the legislation, an arbitrator must consider, in their entirety, all the terms in the agreement respecting holidays and holiday pay. For an example of the type of comparison that is required under the Ontario *Employment Standards Act*, S.O. 2000, c. 41, see *Decor Entry Systems and I.A.M.* (2000), 92 L.A.C. (4th) 53 (Herman).

In several recent cases, the union has contended that the established approach is inconsistent with the ruling in *Parry Sound (District) Social Services Administration Board v. O.P.S.E.U., Local 324* (2003), 230 D.L.R. (4th) 257, where the Supreme Court of Canada held that the substantive rights and obligations of all employment-related statutes are implicit in every collective agreement (see discussion in Chapter 1.2.3). According to this line of argument, a "global" comparison between the provisions of the collective agreement and the employment standard is no longer appropriate, and should be rejected in favour of a more narrow focus on individual deficiencies in the agreement. So far, however, arbitrators have been unreceptive to this argument. See, for example, *Cascades Boxboard Inc. Folding Cartons and C.E.P., Local 341*, [2003] M.G.A.D. No. 54 (QL) (Hamilton).

22.5.3   Effect of Extended Absence on Entitlement

An issue which frequently recurs is whether an employee who has been absent from work because of layoff, sickness, compensable injury or paid vacation is entitled to holiday pay for holidays which occur during his or her absence. Once again, arbitral interpretation of the purpose of holiday pay can be critical. On the ground that the purpose of this benefit is to offer an indemnity against the loss of wages, many arbitrators in earlier years denied the union's claim, ruling that an employee who would have been absent from work in any event did not incur a loss. In accordance with the modern approach, however, most arbitrators have accepted that holiday pay is an earned benefit, *i.e.* additional payment for work already done, and is therefore payable during a layoff or leave of absence (even if sick pay or vacation pay may be payable as well). An intention by the parties to preclude entitlement in these circumstances, consequently, must find clear expression in the collective agreement. The leading case on the right of laid-off employees to collect holiday pay is *Andres Wines (B.C.) Ltd. and United Brewery & Distillery Workers, Local 300* (1977), 16 L.A.C. (2d) 422 (B.C.L.R.B.). In that decision, Chair Paul Weiler held that the applicable test was simply whether such employees were intended to enjoy the benefit of the provision.

The consequence of characterizing holiday pay as an earned benefit, one that continues during a period of involuntary absence from work, is that the employee's entitlement is exhausted at some point after the commencement of the absence. In other words, the required nexus between the benefit and work performed — for which the benefit represents additional compensation — will have disappeared. Most arbitrators have declined to define exactly when entitlement to holiday pay will be depleted, and some have suggested that an employee remains entitled to pay for *all* holidays which take place during an absence. In *T.C.F. of Canada Ltd. and Textile Workers' Union of America, Local 1332* (1972), 1 L.A.C. (2d) 382, though, Arbitrator Adell proposed a test whereby an employee must have worked at least one shift since the paid holiday prior to the one which he or she is now claiming. (Note that this test does not replace the customary "qualifying day" requirement, as reviewed in Chapter 22.5.4.)

For a review of the arbitral jurisprudence on this issue, see *Chelsey Park Oxford and London & District Service Employees Union, Local 220* (1989), 8 L.A.C. (4th) 1 (Mitchnick). On the question of the extent to which entitlement to holiday pay survives a permanent layoff due to plant closure, see *Canada Brick and U.S.W.A., Local 225* (2002), 111 L.A.C. (4th) 220 (Briggs), discussed in Chapter 20.4.1.

22.5.4   "Qualifying Day" Requirements

Almost invariably, the collective agreement stipulates that, as a prerequisite to receiving holiday pay, an employee must work on the days or scheduled shifts immediately preceding and following the holiday. The dominant arbitral stance with respect to "qualifying day" provisions, as they are known, was reflected in *Caressant Care Nursing Home of Canada Ltd. and London & District Service Workers' Union, Local 220* (1987), 29 L.A.C. (3d) 347, where Arbitrator Watters ruled that the purpose of the requirement is to deter unjustified absenteeism or "holiday stretching". In circumstances where that purpose will not be served, as where an employee is absent with permission of the employer, management itself has caused the absence, or the absence is involuntary (being due to illness, injury, pregnancy or other factors beyond the employee's control), absence on the qualifying days will generally not operate to disqualify the employee.

This purposive approach to qualifying day provisions was also applied in *Timmins (City) and C.U.P.E., Local 210* (1997), 66 L.A.C. (4th) 391 (R.M. Brown). The grievor had failed to give proper notice of his inability to report for work due to illness, prompting the employer to characterize his absence on one of the qualifying days as unauthorized. In the arbitrator's view, however, since the purpose of a qualifying day requirement is to discourage wilful absenteeism, not to encourage timely notice of absence, the grievor had not disqualified himself from holiday pay.

Nevertheless, certain awards have held that absence on one or both qualifying days does in fact disentitle employees from holiday pay, regardless of the cause of absence, as long as the agreement clearly indicates such an intention. Whereas some holiday pay provisions require that an employee work "his or her last scheduled shift" prior to the holiday, others impose a more general obligation to work "the last scheduled shift". For a number of arbitrators, use of the phrase "his or her" signifies a "subjective" qualifying day requirement, that is, one which permits consideration of the reasons underlying an individual employee's absence. Use of the definite article "the" in the phrase "the last scheduled shift", by contrast, is taken to imply an "objective" requirement that every employee must work the qualifying shifts, whatever the reason for the absence. The award in *C.W. Carry Ltd. and U.S.W.A., Local 5575* (1994), 42 L.A.C. (4th) 237 (Power) provides a concise example of this approach.

In *Aramark Canada Ltd. and O.P.S.E.U., Local 549*, [2001] O.L.A.A. No. 660 (QL), Arbitrator Devlin denied a claim for holiday pay on the ground that the grievor had missed her first scheduled shift after the holiday, even though the absence had been caused by a serious case of tonsillitis for which medical documentation was provided. Despite the fact that the grievor had an excellent attendance record, the qualifying day clause, which required employees to work "their complete scheduled shift" on the day before and after the holiday, and made no reference to any exceptions, was held to bar the claim. The arbitrator also rejected the union's argument that the qualifying day provision was inconsistent with the Ontario *Human Rights Code*, R.S.O. 1990, c. H.19, ruling that tonsillitis was not a handicap for the purposes of the *Code* and noting that, even if it were, it was not contrary to the *Code* to differentiate between employees based on their attendance at work when matters of compensation were at issue.

22.5.5 Holiday Pay and the Rule Against Pyramiding

As discussed in Chapter 22.7, the employer may object to the payment of holiday pay in conjunction with other collective agreement benefits such as sick leave benefits or vacation pay on the basis that it amounts to double payment, or an impermissible "pyramiding" of benefits. However, arbitrators who view holiday pay as an earned benefit for work previously done have frequently ruled that an employee is entitled to both types of payment. In the seminal decision of *North York General Hospital and O.N.A.* (1980), 27 L.A.C. (2d) 64, for instance, Arbitrator Shime held that sick leave benefits and holiday pay alike were earned benefits, and that both were therefore payable to the grievor in respect of the same day.

A different result may obtain if, in conjunction with an earned benefit such as holiday pay, an employee asserts entitlement to a collective agreement benefit aimed at providing indemnification against the loss of earnings. In *Unimin Canada Ltd. and Teamsters, Local 938* (1993), 37 L.A.C. (4th) 348 (Burkett), for example, the grievor challenged the employer's decision to suspend the payment of weekly indemnity benefits on days for which he had received holiday pay. The arbitrator dismissed the grievance, ruling that the employee's receipt of holiday pay rendered superfluous the wage replacement function fulfilled by weekly indemnity payments. See the discussion in Chapter 23.2.3.

A summary of the arbitral jurisprudence since *North York General Hospital* is found in *Atlantic Packaging Products Ltd. and C.E.P., Local 333* (2001), 96 L.A.C. (4th) 64 (Goodfellow). Characterizing the decision in *Unimin Canada* as representing a minority approach, the arbitrator identified the growing dominance of *North York General Hospital* on the issue of payment of holiday pay or indemnity benefits.

22.6   Vacation with Pay

22.6.1   General

The amount of annual vacation to which an employee is entitled under the collective agreement usually varies in accordance with the length of his or her employment or continuous service, calculated as of a specified calendar date or the employee's anniversary date. The same is true of vacation pay. In either case, an employee's entitlement cannot fall beneath the minimums stipulated by applicable employment standards legislation, which generally guarantees a stated period of paid vacation for each 12 months of employment, together with a basic rate of vacation pay. The British Columbia *Employment Standards Act*, R.S.B.C. 1996, c. 113, for instance, entitles employees to an annual vacation of at least two weeks after 12 consecutive months of employment, and three weeks after five consecutive years of employment; vacation pay must be not less than four percent or six percent, respectively, of an employee's total wages during the preceding year (ss. 57, 58). For another example of legislation which enhances the vacation entitlement of employees who have attained a particular level of continuous service, see ss. 183 and 184 of the *Canada Labour*

Code, R.S.C. 1985, c. L-2. The Ontario *Employment Standards Act*, S.O. 2000, c. 41, by contrast, simply provides for a minimum of two weeks' paid vacation after 12 months of employment, with pay at a rate equivalent to four percent of wages (ss. 33(1), 35.2).

22.6.2   Effect of Extended Absence on Entitlement

A dispute often arises as to what constitutes "continuous service", "continuous employment" or some similar term for the purpose of determining the period over which entitlement to vacation benefits has accrued. The arbitral jurisprudence has gradually come to accept that entitlement which is based on length of service or employment is not affected by an employee's involuntary absence, unless there is clear language in the collective agreement which indicates otherwise (such as a requirement for "active employment" or "attendance at work"). The caselaw underlying this position as it relates to absences due to disability or illness is summarized in *Kingston Regional Ambulance Service and O.P.S.E.U., Local 462* (1992), 22 L.A.C. (4th) 193 (Watters).

This approach taken by Arbitrator Watters is derived in part from the view that paid vacation is part of an employee's overall wage package, as contained in the parties' negotiated settlement. Accordingly, if an absence from work is intended to have the effect of reducing an employee's vacation benefits, there should be an express provision to that effect in the collective agreement. The same reasoning has been applied where an employee is on temporary layoff, with the result that service accrual does not cease. The arbitral approach to accrual of vacation benefits during a period of layoff is illustrated by *Selkirk Metalbestos Household Manufacturing Canada Inc. and S.M.W.* (1992), 27 L.A.C. (4th) 22 (Kates).

The importance of the precise language that is used to define the accrual of entitlement to paid vacation was emphasized in *David Thompson Health Region and U.N.A., Local 2* (1998), 76 L.A.C. (4th) 357 (Ponak). Vacation benefits were held not to accrue during an absence from work during a compensable injury because the collective agreement referred to the "position held" by an employee during the accrual period. In the board's view, the necessary implication of this phrase was that an employee must remain in active employment, *i.e.* "hold a position" as a prerequisite to accumulating vacation credits.

In Ontario, the *Employment Standards Act*, S.O. 2000, c. 41, has been amended to provide that absence on maternity or parental leave must be included in calculating the length of an employee's service or seniority for the purpose of the collective agreement. Thus, s. 52(1) of the Act provides that the period of an employee's pregnancy leave or parental leave is included in any calculation of his or her length of employment (whether or not it is active employment), length of service (whether or not it is active service) or seniority, for the purpose of determining his or her rights under a contract of employment.

Arbitrators disagree whether this provision precludes the pro-rating of *vacation pay* (as opposed to *vacation time*) due to absence on maternity or parental leave. Under the collective agreement at issue in *Algoma Health Unit and O.N.A. (Caughill)*, [2004] O.L.A.A. No. 227 (QL), for example, "vacation entitlement" was to be discounted on a pro rata basis where an employee had been absent from work for 20 days or more. Arbitrator Randy Levinson ruled that this provision permitted the employer to pro-rate the vacation pay of an employee who had been absent due to pregnancy and parental leave. In support of this conclusion, the arbitrator noted differences in the qualifying language under the Act for vacation time and vacation pay. Under s. 33, entitlement to the former is based on completion of one year's service, whereas under s. 35.2 entitlement to the latter is based on a percentage of wages earned during the period for which vacation is given.

However, in a contrasting decision, Arbitrator Knopf expressed the view that the amendments to the *Employment Standards Act* were consistent with a prior award between the parties holding that the employer was precluded from pro-rating entitlement to either vacation time or vacation pay: *Stoney Creek (City) and C.U.P.E., Local 1220* (1998), 71 L.A.C. (4th) 272.

In a recent Alberta case, Arbitrator Ponak ruled that where the collective agreement provides for vacation with pay based on years of continuous employment, service or seniority, and is silent with respect to the issue of pro-rating, the dominant view is that the employer cannot reduce entitlement to paid vacation because of absences due to parental or other authorized leaves: *Federated Cooperatives Ltd. and Teamsters, Local 987*, [2004] C.L.A.D. No. 234.

22.6.3   Vacation Scheduling

In the absence of an express provision in the collective agreement governing the scheduling of vacations, most arbitrators have held that management has an inherent right to schedule vacations at a time which best serves its business interests. This was the view adopted in *Mississauga (City) and C.U.P.E., Local 66* (1994), 43 L.A.C. (4th) 438 (O'Shea).

The right of an employer to schedule vacations at its discretion was also affirmed in *Brown Shoe Co. of Canada Ltd. and U.F.C.W., Local 175* (1998), 71 L.A.C. (4th) 19 (Starkman). In the absence of any collective agreement restrictions, the arbitrator upheld the employer's right to compel employees to take paid vacation during an annual summer shut-down, including employees who had hitherto been absent from work on sick leave benefits.

In *Ottawa Hospital and C.U.P.E., Local 4000* (2002), 113 L.A.C. (4th) 121, an arbitration board chaired by Russell Goodfellow extrapolated a number of principles concerning the employer's right to schedule vacations during a shut-down. In the board's view, the employer can require employees to take vacation time in conjunction with a partial or complete shut-down where the collective agreement expressly permits it to do so; the agreement is silent on the subject of vacation scheduling, and it is deemed to fall within management's rights; or the agreement contains a provision that clearly recognizes the employer's operational needs as the dominant factor in scheduling vacations. Where, however, the collective agreement makes employee choice the primary consideration, and the employee does not wish to take his or her vacation during the shut-down, the employer cannot compel the employee to do so, and will be required to apply the layoff and recall provisions in the agreement.

The collective agreement may require the employer to take into consideration the wishes of individual employees or their seniority rank in scheduling vacations. In such cases, unless the agreement clearly implies that the employee's wishes are to prevail, arbitrators have generally upheld management's right to make the final decision, provided the employer is able to demonstrate some legitimate business justification. The awards on point were succinctly summarized in *Hotel-Dieu Grace Hospital and S.E.I.U., Local 210* (1995), 48 L.A.C. (4th) 368 (Brandt). For a more recent summary of caselaw on this subject, see *Canada Safeway Ltd. and U.F.C.W., Local 832* [2003] M.G.A.D. No. 48 (QL) (Hamilton).

22.6.4   Calculation of Vacation Pay

Usually the parties to a collective agreement adopt a formula for calculating vacation pay which is based either on an employee's regular rate of pay for the period of the vacation, or on a percentage of the employee's "earnings", "total earnings" or "compensation" during a 12-month period prior to the vacation. A large body of arbitral jurisprudence has developed with respect to what amounts or payments must be included in the sum used as the basis for computing vacation pay. Prior to the seminal decision of Arbitrator Arthurs in *Pilkington Brothers (Canada) Ltd. and United Glass & Ceramic Workers, Local 295* (1966), 17 L.A.C. 146, there was considerable disagreement among arbitrators as to the proper approach. One group, who tended to regard vacation pay provisions as ambiguous, relied heavily on past practice in resolving the problem. For another group, a reference to "earnings" or "total earnings" was intended to cover all forms of compensation received by an employee. In *Pilkington Brothers*, Arbitrator Arthurs opted for the reasoning of the latter group, holding that an employee's vacation pay from the previous year had to be included in earnings for the purpose of calculating holiday pay in the current year. Similarly, other monetary benefits such as paid holidays also represented part of the compensation package which the union had bargained for, and should therefore be considered "earnings".

Almost 30 years later, in *Ipex Ltd. and Glass, Molders, Pottery, Plastics & Allied Workers Int'l Union* (1995), 52 L.A.C. (4th) 198 (Brandt), the arbitrator held that *Pilkington Brothers* was so widely accepted that any attempt to exclude the previous year's vacation pay would amount to an amendment of the collective agreement, regardless of seemingly anomalous results.

The extension of the rationale of *Pilkington Brothers* to encompass all earned benefits in the calculation of an employee's vacation pay was confirmed in *St. Raphael's Nursing Homes Ltd. and London District Service Workers' Union, Local 220* (1985), 18 L.A.C. (3d) 430 (Roberts). In the arbitrator's opinion, overtime pay, shift premiums, benefit allowances, holiday pay, uniform allowances and bereavement leave payments all had to be included in the calculation.

In *Union Drawn Steel II Ltd. and U.S.W.A., Local 2308* (1998), 71 L.A.C. (4th) 389, Arbitrator Gray ruled that payments derived from a profit-sharing scheme also constituted part of earnings or wages for the purpose of computing vacation pay. Indeed, the arbitrator held, a collective agreement provision that excludes profit share payments may contravene the minimum vacation pay provision in employment standards legislation.

By contrast, a number of arbitrators have held that workers' compensation benefits and income continuance payments provided by a third-party insurer while an employee is sick or injured do not constitute "earnings" for the purpose of determining vacation pay. The rationale for the exclusion is that such payments do not depend on the performance of work by the employee, and furthermore that they are furnished by a third-party insurance carrier, not the employer. An example of this reasoning is found in *B.C. Transit and I.C.T.U., Locals 1, 2, & 3* (1988), 3 L.A.C. (4th) 151 (MacIntyre).

At least one arbitrator has ruled that exclusion of workers' compensation benefits from the sum used to calculate vacation pay gives rise to adverse-effect discrimination on the basis of disability, contrary to the Ontario *Human Rights Code*, R.S.O. 1990, c. H.19: see *Clarendon Foundation (Cheshire Homes) Inc. and O.P.S.E.U., Local 593* (1996), 58 L.A.C. (4th) 270 (Craven). However, the precedential value of this award has been thrown in doubt by the decision of the Ontario Court of Appeal in *O.N.A. v. Orillia Soldiers Memorial Hospital* (1999), 169 D.L.R. (4th) 489, discussed in Chapter 18.2.1. In the Court's view, it is not discriminatory to withhold compensation-related benefits from an employee who is absent from work because of disability, and who is therefore not providing services to the employer.

In the absence of collective agreement provisions to the contrary, employees who cease to be employed before the end of the vacation year are entitled only to a pro-rated portion of their vacation pay. This was clarified in *Domglas Inc. and Aluminum, Brick & Glassworkers Int'l Union, Local 238G* (1986), 26 L.A.C. (3d) 29 (Kelleher).

22.7   THE RULE AGAINST PYRAMIDING

The ostensible purpose of what has come to be known as the "rule against pyramiding" is to preclude an employee from claiming two or more monetary benefits or entitlements for the same hours of work or for the same job. Common examples include overlapping claims for overtime and shift premium rates, overtime and weekend premium rates, overtime and statutory holiday premiums, and overtime and call-in rates. The employer may also invoke the rule against pyramiding in the context of an overlap between two different types of paid leave, as, for example, an overlap between sick leave and paid vacation or a statutory holiday.

It was suggested in some of the earliest awards that there exists an arbitral presumption against the pyramiding of benefits. In the frequently cited decision of *Ault Milk Products Ltd. and R.W.D.S.U., Local 440* (1962), 12 L.A.C. 279 (Anderson), the board ruled, at p. 282:

> If a contract is open to two interpretations and one interpretation involves the pyramiding of overtime and the other interpretation does not involve pyramiding of overtime, the board of arbitration, in the absence of specific wording in the contract, should accept the interpretation which does not provide for the additional penalty payments by reason of pyramiding overtime.

While most arbitrators may accept the legitimacy of some form of presumption against the pyramiding of benefits, the force of such a presumption has in practice been considerably undermined by two developments. First, in the face of ongoing disagreement about what constitutes pyramiding, a tendency has developed to define it fairly narrowly, thus restricting the concept to situations in which two types of premiums or benefits intended to serve the same purpose are being claimed in respect of the same period of work. Second, most arbitrators have recognized that any presumption can be rebutted fairly easily, especially where the underlying purpose of the disputed payments is different. This almost creates a reverse presumption in cases where such a difference can be established. An oft-cited decision that demonstrates these developments is *Associated Freezers of Canada Ltd. and Teamsters, Local 419* (1979), 23 L.A.C. (2d) 40 (Burkett), where the arbitrator stressed the contrasting purposes served by a statutory holiday premium and a premium offered for weekend work.

A decision which summarizes the arbitral jurisprudence on pyramiding is *Ault Foods Ltd. and Retail, Wholesale, Dairy & General Workers' Union, Local 440* (1994), 42 L.A.C. (4th) 289 (Fraser). While acknowledging that the caselaw discloses a variety of results in individual cases, the arbitrator identified four consistent elements in arbitral doctrine: the existence of a presumption against pyramiding; the rebuttable nature of the presumption; the relevance of the purpose of the benefit or premium in question; and the importance of paying close attention to the collective agreement itself.

In *Selkirk & District General Hospital and Manitoba Nurses' Union, Local 16* (1998), 69 L.A.C. (4th) 320 (Graham), the arbitrator applied the presumption against pyramiding to hold that several senior employees whose salaries had been red-circled were not entitled to a charge nurse premium when performing charge nurse duties. In the arbitrator's opinion, both the red-circling and the charge nurse premiums had the same underlying purpose, to provide extra compensation for increased responsibility. However, this award was quashed by the Manitoba Court of Appeal in *Manitoba Nurses' Union, Local 16 v. Selkirk & District Hospital* (2003), 235 D.L.R. (4th) 329. The Court ruled that the arbitrator's decision was patently unreasonable because the purpose of red-circling was to provide transitional salary protection to nurses who had been reclassified downward, whereas the purpose of the charge nurse premium was to compensate for increased responsibility. The Court's decision would appear to be more consistent than the original award with the prevailing arbitral viewpoint, as suggested by a similar ruling in *Overlander Extended Care Hospital and B.C.N.U. (Pflanz)* (2002), 105 L.A.C. (4th) 310 (Germaine).

In *Headwaters Health Care Centre and O.N.A.*, [2004] O.L.A.A. No. 332 (QL), Arbitrator Surdykowski provided a concise summary of the rule against pyramiding:

> . . . it is clear that in its modern form, the "rule" against pyramiding exists as a rebuttable presumption that is itself subject to the terms of the particular collective agreement. The presumption is that the parties did not intend that employees would receive more than one premium in addition to their regular wage rate for the same hours of work. To that end, arbitrators have distinguished between premiums that serve the same purpose, and premiums that serve different purposes. The former attract the operation of the presumption or "rule", and the latter do not . . . To put it another way, an employee is generally not entitled to more than one premium for the same hours unless the purpose of the premiums is different, or the collective agreement specifies otherwise. Conversely, where the underlying purpose of two applicable premiums is different, the presumption or "rule" does not apply and both premiums are payable unless the collective agreement specifies otherwise. (at para. 11)

22.8 RETROACTIVITY

The arbitral jurisprudence concerning the retroactivity of monetary and non-monetary provisions of a collective agreement has been in transition since the 1970s. For many years, arbitrators held that a typical back-dated duration clause (usually back-dated to the day after the expiry of the prior agreement) had the effect of making the monetary items of the collective agreement retroactive, but not the non-monetary items. In the seminal decision of *Penticton & District Retirement Service and H.E.U., Local 180* (1977), 16 L.A.C. (2d) 97, the British Columbia Labour Relations Board extended the presumption of retroactivity to encompass *all* the provisions of a collective agreement.

However, the Board pointed out, "this standard retroactive principle" did not apply where there was clear and specific language to the contrary, or where retroactivity would lead to impractical, unintended or unfair results. The Board noted that this approach was more consistent with the reasonable expectations of the parties in a long-term collective bargaining relationship. Employees frequently continue working during protracted negotiations for a new contract in the expectation that they will eventually receive any increase in wages or benefits. To hold otherwise, the Board observed, would result in an unexpected windfall for the employer.

The arbitral jurisprudence on retroactivity, including the decision in *Penticton*, is thoroughly reviewed in *Durham Memorial Hospital and London & District Service Workers' Union, Local 220* (1991), 19 L.A.C. (4th) 320 (Kaufman). In the arbitrator's view, all provisions in a collective agreement are to be construed as having retroactive effect unless the result would be absurd, impractical, unintended or unfair, or unless the parties have clearly indicated otherwise. Note that, in this case, the inclusion of a retroactivity clause which made specific reference to several provisions in the agreement was held *not* to rebut the general presumption in favour of retroactivity.

There continues to be some divergence of opinion as to whether former employees who leave the workforce prior to ratification of the new collective agreement are entitled to retroactive increases in wages and benefits. The traditional position, that there is a presumption against conferring on former employees a retroactive increase, is represented by the award in *Air Canada and C.A.L.F.A.A.* (1981), 1 L.A.C. (3d) 37, in which Arbitrator Howard Brown refused to follow a contrary ruling in *Penticton, supra.*

While *Air Canada* has had some adherents, the trend among most arbitrators is to adopt the *Penticton* approach, namely, that there is a rebuttable presumption in favour of retroactivity, even in respect of employees whose employment terminated prior to the ratification date. The Federal Court of Appeal has arrived at a similar conclusion in respect of federal employees governed by the *Public Service Staff Relations Act* (now the *Public Service Labour Relations Act*, S.C. 2003, c. 22). In the Court's opinion, withholding retroactive pay increases from former employees would lead to an absurd result, which the parties should not be taken to have intended in the absence of "very clear words" in their collective agreement: *C.A.T.C.A. v. Canada (Treasury Board)*, [1985] 2 F.C. 84 (C.A.). A thorough analysis of the conflicting jurisprudence, as well as the trend towards the reasoning in *Penticton*, is found in *Kitchener-Waterloo Record and C.E.P., Local 87-M*, [2003] O.L.A.A. No. 302 (QL) (Brent).

In *Tremblay v. S.I.E.P.B., section locale 57* (2002), 212 D.L.R. (4th) 212, the Supreme Court of Canada rejected claims by an employee that her former union had violated its duty of fair representation under the Quebec *Labour Code*, R.S.Q., c. C-27, and the prohibition against discrimination under the

Quebec *Charter of Human Rights and Freedoms*, R.S.Q., c. C-12. The union had negotiated a clause that restricted the right to retroactive pay increases to persons who had employee status on the date of signature of the collective agreement. In the Court's view, such a clause did not contravene any provisions of the *Code* or the *Charter*.

For additional commentary and cases relating to retroactivity, see Chapter 3.2.

CHAPTER 23

LEAVES OF ABSENCE

23.1 DISCRETIONARY LEAVES OF ABSENCE

The dismissal of an employee for failing to report for work often raises the issue of the employer's right to refuse a requested leave of absence. Where there is no specific contractual requirement to grant leave, arbitrators have adopted divergent views concerning the proper scope of review of management's decision. The traditional approach is that an arbitrator can interfere only if the decision was made in bad faith, or in an arbitrary or discriminatory manner. Another approach, which has gained increasing acceptance in recent years, is that an arbitrator also has authority to inquire into the reasonableness of the employer's decision to refuse leave. In accordance with this view, the employer is obligated to consider all relevant factors, and to balance the demands of production against the employee's interest in continued employment. The leading decision in support of this approach is *Alcan Canada Products and U.S.W.A.* (1974), 6 L.A.C. (2d) 386 (Shime), where the employer terminated the grievor's employment after he had been sentenced to a 41-day jail term because of a criminal conviction on motor vehicle offences. Taking into account the fact that the employer had not turned its mind to the impact of the grievor's absence on production, Arbitrator Shime upheld the grievance and ordered that the grievor be reinstated.

In *Alcan-Price Extrusions Ltd. and U.S.W.A., Local 6304* (1995), 52 L.A.C. (4th) 435 (Ponak), the arbitration board reviewed the two contrasting approaches to the scope of review, and listed a number of factors which are relevant to the balancing-of-interests approach. In assessing the reasonableness of the employer's decision to deny a leave of absence, the board ruled, an arbitrator should take into consideration the effect of the absence on the employer's business interests, the duration of expected absence, the employee's prior work record, and any misrepresentation by the employee.

In *Bombardier Transportation and C.A.W., Local 1075* (2003), 121 L.A.C. (4th) 84, Arbitrator Liang upheld a grievance challenging the employer's denial of a request for an indefinite leave of absence due to incarceration pending trial. The employer's main reason for refusing the request was its reluctance to set a precedent in other cases involving a leave of indefinite duration. In the arbitrator's view, the employer had acted unreasonably, given the grievor's 17 years of seniority and the fact that he could easily have been temporarily replaced during the period before his trial. The requirement that the employer exercise its discretion in a reasonable manner was also affirmed in *Uniroyal Goodrich Tire Manufacturing and U.S.W.A., Local 677*, [2003] O.L.A.A. No. 546 (QL) (Haefling). In that case, the collective agreement expressly provided that requests for an unpaid leave of absence, to a maximum of three months, were subject to the employer's approval. The arbitrator concluded that, where an employee had sought a six-month leave in order to accommodate his incarceration, this provision did not relieve the employer of its obligation to act reasonably in deciding whether to grant the request.

As the awards in *Alcan Canada Products* and *Alcan-Price Extrusions* illustrate, disputes respecting the denial of a request for leave of absence sometimes arise in the context of an employee's incarceration for a criminal or regulatory offence. A frequently arbitrated issue is whether the employer is required to participate in a so-called "temporary absence program", whereby the corrections authority permits offenders to continue working in their regular workplace during the sentence. Many arbitrators have held that the employer is not obligated to take part in a TAP program in the absence of an express or implied collective agreement obligation to do so. However, a number of arbitrators, adopting the principles expressed in the leave of absence cases, have stated that the employer must act reasonably and in good faith, and with due consideration for the employee's interests, in deciding whether or not to participate in such a program. The award in *Indal Technologies Inc. and U.S.W.A., Local 8848* (1992), 25 L.A.C. (4th) 436 (Simmons) summarizes the jurisprudence on this issue.

In *British Columbia (Human Rights Commission) v. British Columbia (Human Rights Tribunal)* (2000), 193 D.L.R. (4th) 488 (B.C.C.A.), the grievor was unable to report for work because he had been incarcerated following a criminal conviction for an off-duty offence. The British Columbia Court of Appeal held that the employer's refusal to grant the grievor an unpaid leave, and its subsequent decision to dismiss him for non-attendance at work, did not constitute employment discrimination on the basis of a criminal conviction, contrary to s. 13 of the British Columbia *Human Rights Code*, R.S.B.C. 1996,

c. 210. In the Court's opinion, the grievor had been dismissed, not because of the criminal conviction, but because he was unable to attend at work. Section 13 of the *Code* prohibited discrimination on the basis of a conviction that was unrelated to a person's employment, and this could not be said of a conviction that resulted in the person's inability to report for work.

The Supreme Court of Canada has endorsed this approach in a case involving a complaint under Quebec's *Charter of Human Rights and Freedoms*, R.S.Q., c. C-12. The complainant, who had been dismissed because of his absence from work while serving a term of imprisonment, invoked s. 18.2 of the *Charter*, which prohibits the dismissal of an employee "owing to the mere fact that he was convicted of a penal or criminal offence, if the offence was in no way connected with the employment or if the person has obtained a pardon for the offence". The Court concluded that the complaint was without merit. In the Court's view, where the differential treatment of an employee results from the civil consequences of the sentence, such as unavailability for work due to incarceration, rather than from the criminal record itself, there is no violation of s. 18.2: see *Quebec (Commission des droits de la personne et des droits de la jeunesse) v. Maksteel Quebec Inc.* (2003), 233 D.L.R. (4th) 385.

Where an employee seeks a leave of absence in connection with a personal religious observance, denial of the request may result in a finding of discrimination under the applicable human rights legislation. For example, in a key decision, the Supreme Court of Canada held that teachers of the Jewish faith must be permitted to observe Yom Kippur without loss of pay, and without performing another day of work to compensate for their absence: *Chambly, Commission scolaire régionale v. Bergevin* (1994), 115 D.L.R. (4th) 609. Similarly, an Ontario arbitration board has ruled that the employer's refusal to grant a paid leave of absence to members of the Greek Orthodox Church for purposes of religious observance was discrimination, given that the majority of Christian holy days occurred on statutory holidays for which leave was granted with pay: *Seneca College of Applied Arts & Technology and O.P.S.E.U., Local 561* (2000), 93 L.A.C. (4th) 355 (Whitaker).

However, while an arrangement which reduces the employee's earnings or benefits — such as forcing him or her to use vacation days — will not be considered a reasonable accommodation, except in rare cases of necessity, this does not necessarily mean that all religious leave must be paid leaves. Employers will not be required to put themselves out of pocket to accommodate religious leave if there is a feasible alternative, such as adjusting the work schedule. Thus, in *Ontario (Ministry of Community and Social Services) v. O.P.S.E.U.* (2000), 50 O.R. (3d) 560, the Ontario Court of Appeal concluded that making leave days available through scheduling changes (for example, the introduction of a compressed work week) was an acceptable form of accommodation.

In *Coast Mountain Bus Co. Ltd. and C.A.W., Local 111* (2004), 133 L.A.C. (4th) 77, the grievor's baptism fell on a work day, and Arbitrator Lanyon held that the employer's refusal to grant a day off raised a *prima facie* case of discrimination on the basis of religion. As a consequence, the employer was required to prove that its insistence on the grievor's attendance at work that day was a *bona fide* occupational qualification, and that it had accommodated his religious practices to the point of undue hardship. In the result, however, the arbitrator upheld a two-day suspension against the grievor for unauthorized absence from work, since the grievor failed to come forward with his request until the day before the ceremony, or to assist the employer by attempting to trade shifts with another employee. A claimant must act reasonably in seeking accommodation, the arbitrator noted, and the grievor had not done this.

23.2   Sick Leave Benefits

23.2.1   General

The rights of employees who are unable to attend at work because of illness or injury form one of the most important subjects covered by the collective agreement. Commonly, agreements provide for some form of short-term disability plan as well as a long-term disability plan. While the short-term plan is often self-funded by the employer, a widespread practice has emerged of arranging for the provision of long-term disability benefits through the purchase of a group insurance policy. In addition, or alternatively, the collective agreement may provide for some form of sick leave credit system, under which employees are entitled to accumulate credits for paid sick leave at the prescribed rate (for example, one-and-a-half days per month). The accrued credits remain at the employee's disposal in the event of sickness or injury. At one time, many collective agreements enabled employees to bank sick leave credits over the course of their employment, and to cash them in for some form of compensation upon retirement. With the growth in short-term and long-term disability plans of various models, and the provision of pension benefits, such arrangements have become more rare.

23.2.2   What Constitutes Illness?

The parties normally specify in the collective agreement any conditions to which a claim for sick leave benefits is subject. Such conditions may range from a right on the employer's part to request satisfactory proof of illness at its discretion, to a mandatory requirement for a medical certificate in respect of any absence which exceeds two or three days. In most cases, though, the collective agreement does not define what constitutes an illness or sickness for the purpose of establishing entitlement to benefits, and this has led to frequent disputes about the legitimacy of an employee's purported condition. While there appears to be little arbitral consensus, some general principles can be drawn from the jurisprudence.

First, it is generally accepted that the onus initially rests on the grievor to establish that he or she suffered from an illness or injury within the meaning of the collective agreement, whether or not the agreement requires that a medical certificate be provided. Normally, a note or certificate prepared by the employee's physician is sufficient to discharge this burden, thus shifting the onus to the employer to establish that the opinion is invalid or inaccurate. In the absence of a collective agreement right to have the employee examined by a physician of its own choice, the employer is generally limited to rebutting the certificate by calling the grievor's physician to testify or by adducing evidence of conduct that is inconsistent with the information provided. (However, see the award in *University of British Columbia and A.U.C.E., Local 1* (1984), 15 L.A.C. (3d) 151 (McColl), discussed in Chapter 4.5, which arguably expands the employer's right to have an employee submit to a medical examination.) These principles were applied in *Queen Elizabeth II Hospital and U.N.A., Local 37* (1998), 77 L.A.C. (4th) 170 (Moreau), where the arbitrator rejected a claim based on a doctor's note stating that the grievors had been too sick to attend at work. The grievors, operating room nurses, were allegedly too fatigued to work their regularly scheduled shift after being called in to assist with two emergency operations which had just ended. Cross-examination of the doctor at the hearing, the board found, revealed that he had not performed any medical examination of the grievors before writing the note, leaving their claim for sick leave benefits bereft of objective support.

There is a considerable body of arbitral caselaw on the extent to which an employee claiming sick leave can be required to provide detailed medical information as a precondition to qualifying for benefits. In *West Coast Energy Inc. (c.o.b. Duke Energy Gas Transmission) and C.E.P., Local 449*, [2004] C.L.A.D. No. 504 (QL), Arbitrator Hall provides a comprehensive summary of Ontario and British Columbia awards on this issue, which set out and apply the principle that the privacy rights of employees must be balanced against the employer's legitimate business interests in administering a sick leave plan. In general, the arbitrator observed, although an employee can be directed to provide enough information to justify a claim, privacy concerns may limit the amount and type of information that can reasonably be demanded. Thus, in the case before him, Arbitrator Hall overturned a requirement that the employee's physician disclose a specific medical condition or diagnosis (as opposed to a description of the general nature of the illness or injury, which was held to be permissible). A requirement that the employee sign an open-ended release form, authorizing plan administrators to obtain medical information directly from the employee's physician, was also struck down.

In *Ontario (Ministry of Housing) and C.U.P.E., Local 767* (1994), 39

L.A.C. (4th) 1, the Ontario Grievance Settlement Board upheld a claim for sick leave benefits based on evidence that the grievor had a severe hangover after a wedding. The Board rejected the proposition that self-inflicted illnesses did not qualify, noting that such a test was impracticable because it would rule out lung cancer caused by smoking, and illnesses related to a planned pregnancy. In the Board's view, entitlement is made out in any case where objective evidence establishes the existence of a physical (or possibly emotional) inability to work. The appropriate mechanism for dealing with underlying issues of employee misconduct is the disciplinary procedure under the collective agreement.

A focus on causation or fault in the assessment of whether an employee was ill for the purpose of obtaining sick leave was also rejected in *B.C. Cancer Agency and B.C.N.U. (Edwards)* (1997), 65 L.A.C. (4th) 380 (Larson). Noting a trend in the jurisprudence away from a fault-based approach, the arbitrator favoured instead an approach that focuses on an employee's symptoms.

The approach taken in *B.C. Cancer Agency* was affirmed in two recent arbitration awards in which it was held that an employee who was unable to work due to stress was entitled to short-term sick leave benefits: see *Sault Area Hospitals and S.E.I.U., Local 268* (2001), 94 L.A.C. (4th) 230 (Whitaker), and *Metrovalley Newspaper Group Ltd. and C.E.P., Local 2000*, [2001] B.C.C.A.A.A. No. 205 (QL) (Germaine). In both cases, the arbitrator concluded that the applicable test for determining entitlement was whether the claimant was incapable of working during the period in question due to injury or illness. In other words, the focus of the inquiry is the employee's condition, not the cause of that condition.

Another issue which frequently arises is whether an employee is entitled to sick leave benefits in respect of time taken off work in order to attend medical appointments for the treatment of illness or disability. A summary of the applicable principles is provided in *Baycrest Centre for Geriatric Care and O.P.S.E.U. (Phillips)*, [2002] O.L.A.A. No. 570 (QL) (Howe), where the board, adopting an analysis first developed by Arbitrator Burkett over two decades ago, distinguished between three different types of appointments: (1) following the onset of health problems which make it difficult for an employee to carry out his or her job functions; (2) in order to obtain an assessment of fitness to return to work after an absence due to illness; and (3) in the context of an ongoing health concern which requires periodic monitoring, even though the employee is otherwise well enough to work. In the first two cases, attendance at a medical appointment has generally been held to constitute an absence caused by sickness, and therefore to qualify for sick pay. In the third case, however, arbitrators have usually found that the employee's inability to attend at work was due to the fact that the appointment was scheduled during working hours, and not to illness or injury. Thus, entitlement to benefits was not established.

Finally, employers and unions must not run afoul of human rights legislation by improperly excluding certain types of illness or disability from the scope of coverage for sick leave or weekly indemnity benefits. In *Gibbs v. Battlefords and District Co-operative Ltd.* (1996), 140 D.L.R. (4th) 1, the Supreme Court of Canada held that a benefit plan provided by the employer pursuant to the collective agreement violated the prohibition against discrimination on the ground of disability in the Saskatchewan *Human Rights Code*, S.S. 1979, c. S-24.1, because the period for which indemnity benefits were payable was shorter in the case of employees suffering from a mental disability than in the case of employees suffering from a physical disability. In *Ontario Jockey Club and H.E.R.E., Local 75* (2000), 91 L.A.C. (4th) 146, Arbitrator Adams adopted the reasoning in *Gibbs*, ruling that a benefit plan which, while extending coverage to injuries caused by an "identifiable incident", disentitled employees whose disability had been caused by gradual onset or repetitive strain injury discriminated on the basis of handicap, contrary to the Ontario *Human Rights Code*, R.S.O. 1990, c. H.19.

23.2.3   Overlap Between Sick Leave and Other Forms of Leave

On the basis that the purpose of paid sick leave is to indemnify employees against the loss of wages, it has generally been held that such benefits are not available to an employee who was on paid vacation when the illness or injury arose. Frequently cited in support of this proposition is the award of Arbitrator Hinnegan in *VME Equipment of Canada Ltd. and C.A.W., Local 1917* (1990), 10 L.A.C. (4th) 348.

Similar reasoning was applied in *Unimin Canada Ltd. and Teamsters, Local 938* (1993), 37 L.A.C. (4th) 348 (Burkett), where the grievor was absent from work for an extended period as a result of illness. In the arbitrator's opinion, the grievor was not entitled to weekly indemnity payments on days for which he received statutory holiday pay pursuant to the collective agreement.

In addition, arbitrators have held fairly consistently that, in the absence of contract language to the contrary, an employee has no right to convert a vacation leave or other forms of paid leave to a sick leave simply because he or she fell ill during the leave. In *Unisource Canada Inc. and C.E.P., Local 1124* (1995), 47 L.A.C. (4th) 435, where the grievor was injured on the second day of a scheduled holiday leave, Arbitrator Blasina provided a thorough summary of the jurisprudence. Rejecting the union's argument that the grievor could reschedule his paid holiday leave and receive sick leave benefits instead, the arbitrator ruled that leave is generally characterized according to its fundamental and primary purpose, and that an employee has no general right to reschedule or to re-characterize a leave. The decision is also quite consistent with the nature of sick leave payments as an indemnity, since the grievor, being on paid leave, suffered no loss of wages.

However, the result may be different where the collective agreement expressly requires that the employer make reasonable efforts to schedule the leave in accordance with the employee's wishes. In *NAV Canada and C.A.W., Local 5454*, [2003] C.L.A.D. No. 538 (QL), Arbitrator Jones upheld a grievance against the employer's refusal to reclassify scheduled "lieu time" as sick leave. In that case, the grievor became ill and filed an official disability certificate along with his reclassification request several days before the lieu time was to commence. The arbitrator based his ruling on a clause in the collective agreement which required the employer to "make every reasonable effort to schedule lieu leave at times desired by the employee".

It is also the prevailing arbitral view that, in the absence of an explicit provision in the collective agreement, the employer cannot lay off an employee who is on paid sick leave at the time. In *Brown Shoe Co. of Canada Ltd. and U.F.C.W., Local 175* (1998), 71 L.A.C. (4th) 19 (Starkman), for example, the arbitrator adopted the principle that the status of an employee who is receiving paid sick leave or disability benefits is not affected by an intervening layoff or strike.

The rationale set out in *Brown Shoe Co.* was recently applied in a case where, after receiving a notice of layoff, an employee went on sick leave as a result of an injury sustained during an accident. The sick leave commenced a few days prior to the scheduled layoff date. The arbitrator ordered that the employer continue providing sick leave benefits to the employee, despite the notice of layoff. It was held that, in accordance with the arbitral jurisprudence, the characterization of a period of absence from work must be governed by the fundamental reason for that absence: *University of Manitoba and C.A.W.*, [2003] M.G.A.D. No. 72 (QL) (Jones).

Conversely, applying the same principle, an arbitrator has upheld the layoff of an employee who failed to report to work because of illness on the day on which the layoff notice was issued. Two days earlier, the grievor had discussed with a supervisor the likelihood that her position would be abolished and that she would be laid off. The arbitrator found that the absence was due to distress caused by the impending possibility of layoff, not to an independent and unrelated illness: *Keyano College and C.U.P.E., Local 2157*, [2004] A.G.A.A. No. 82 (QL) (Smith).

23.3   COMPLIANCE WITH EMPLOYMENT STANDARDS AND HUMAN RIGHTS LEGISLATION

23.3.1   Illness, Disability and Emergency Leave

Collective agreement provisions which govern the rights of employees absent from work because of illness or disability must comply with human rights and employment standards legislation. At common law, the employer was not permitted to treat an employee's disability as cause for dismissal unless it was serious enough to frustrate the contract of employment. In *Oxford*

Automotive Inc. and U.A.W., Local 251 (2004), 131 L.A.C. (4th) 84, however, Arbitrator Weatherill held that the common law doctrine of frustration cannot be invoked to terminate the employment of employees covered by a collective agreement who are absent for long periods of time due to workplace injuries.

Today, it is uncommon for employment standards legislation to address directly the rights of sick or disabled employees. Section 239 of the *Canada Labour Code*, R.S.C. 1985, c. L-2, which protects employees from discharge, layoff or discipline because of absence due to illness or injury for up to 12 weeks, is a rare exception. In September 2001, Ontario introduced new emergency leave provisions in s. 50 of its *Employment Standards Act*, S.O. 2000, c. 41. The amendments enable employees who work for an employer that regularly employs 50 or more employees to take up to ten unpaid days of emergency leave in a year for any of the following reasons: personal illness or injury; a medical emergency; the death, illness, injury or medical emergency of one of a defined group of relatives of the employee; or an urgent matter that concerns one of the above-mentioned relatives.

The rise of human rights legislation prohibiting unlawful discrimination in employment has led to numerous challenges to collective agreement provisions affecting employees who suffer from a disability or handicap. In the early 1990s, for example, the courts declared that so called "automatic termination clauses", which deem the employment of persons who have been absent from work to be terminated after a prescribed period, constitute discrimination, contrary to the Ontario *Human Rights Code*, R.S.O. 1990, c. H.19: see Chapter 14.3.1. The employer, it was held, did not have the right to discharge a disabled employee without first satisfying its statutory duty of accommodation to the point of undue hardship.

The extent to which this analysis can be extended to collective agreement provisions which, as a consequence of an employee's disability-related absence, limit or pro-rate the accrual of seniority or service, or the payment of employer contributions to a plan of insured benefits, has been a contentious issue. Some arbitrators have expressed the view that the suspension of seniority or service accrual, at any rate, is discriminatory and contravenes human rights legislation. Others, however, have adopted the analysis formulated by Arbitrator Richard Brown, who has drawn a distinction between what he calls "competitive seniority" (which affects the right of an employee to participate in or access the workplace), and "benefit seniority" (which determines the level of compensation or benefits to which an employee is entitled). This analysis rests on the premise that the Ontario *Human Rights Code* differentiates between the right to participation and the right to compensation. To the extent that a provision has the effect of curtailing or limiting the competitive seniority of an employee who is unable to attend at work due to disability, it gives rise to discrimination and calls into play the employer's duty of accommodation. However, where the disputed provision simply has a negative impact on remuneration or benefit entitlement, the Brown analysis holds that a disabled employee's only right is to be treated in the same way as any other employee. Thus, if other employees are not entitled to compensation or the continuation of employer benefit plan contributions during a prolonged absence, a disabled employee who is accorded identical treatment has no cause for complaint. This analysis was developed in Arbitrator Brown's decisions in *Versa Services Ltd. and Milk & Bread Drivers, Dairy Employees, Caterers & Allied Employees Union, Local 647* (1994), 39 L.A.C. (4th) 196, affirmed by the Ontario Divisional Court, [1995] O.J. No. 4931 (QL); and in *Porcupine & District Children's Aid Society and C.U.P.E., Local 2196* (1996), 56 L.A.C. (4th) 116.

The debate among arbitrators as to the correct approach appears to have been resolved, at least in Ontario, by the judgment of the Ontario Court of Appeal in *O.N.A. v. Orillia Soldiers Memorial Hospital* (1999), 169 D.L.R. (4th) 489 (leave to appeal to S.C.C. denied December 9, 1999). In *Orillia Soldiers Memorial Hospital*, the Court upheld an award in which Arbitrator Mitchnick, following the *Versa Services* dichotomy, ruled that a collective agreement provision which automatically suspends an employee's *seniority* accrual following a period of absence constitutes discrimination, contrary to the *Human Rights Code*. On the other hand, the arbitrator observed, provisions that restrict *service* accrual and payment of benefit plan premiums do *not* contravene the legislation, insofar as the collective agreement established service as a criterion in the determination of compensation levels.

Although the Court of Appeal disavowed the proposition, found in *Versa Services* and *Porcupine & District Children's Aid Society*, that a different standard applies to questions of compensation than to questions of participation in the workplace, ruling that the right to be free from discrimination is not subject to such distinctions, the decision appears to rest on largely the same reasoning as that advanced by Arbitrator Brown. In the Court's view, requiring work in exchange for compensation is a *bona fide* occupational requirement. The denial of service accrual, which under the collective agreement in question was linked to an employee's placement on the salary grid, did not therefore violate the *Code*. The same was true of employer contributions to a plan of insured benefits, which the Court characterized as a form of compensation. The accrual of seniority, by contrast, was triggered simply by the status of being an employee, and did not require the active provision of labour. Suspending an employee's seniority accrual, the Court held, put him or her at an unfair disadvantage in layoff or job posting situations, and could not be justified as a *bona fide* occupational requirement. Thus, while the reasoning may differ, the Court's judgment appears to maintain the *Versa Services* distinction between compensation and access or participation.

However, in *O.N.A. v. Mount Sinai Hospital* (2005), 255 D.L.R. (4th) 195, the Ontario Court of Appeal ruled that s. 58(5)(c) of the province's former *Employment Standards Act*, R.S.O. 1990, c. E.14, discriminated on the ground of disability, contrary to the *Charter of Rights and Freedoms*. The impugned provision created an exception to an employer's obligation under the Act to pay severance pay, in prescribed circumstances, by disentitling employees whose contracts of employment had been frustrated due to illness or injury. The Court found that the differential treatment of employees with disabilities, severe and prolonged enough to frustrate their employment, perpetuated negative stereotypes that such individuals were not likely to be members of the workforce in the future.

In *Canada Post Corp. and C.U.P.W. (Harriman)*, [2004] C.L.A.D. No. 512 (QL) (Jolliffe), it was found that the grievor's need to take four weeks of sick leave had been caused by sexual harassment and by the employer's failure to protect her from the harassment, contrary to the requirements of human rights legislation. Arbitrator Jolliffe ordered that the grievor's sick leave entitlement be fully replenished in order to put her back in the position she would have been in had the employer not breached its statutory obligations.

23.3.2 Pregnancy and Parental Leave

In *Victoria County Memorial Hospital and C.A.W., Local 607* (1994), 42 L.A.C. (4th) 194 (O'Connell), a Nova Scotia arbitrator ruled that the suspension of employer contributions to an insured benefit plan on behalf of an employee who was absent due to a pregnancy-related illness violated human rights legislation. In the arbitrator's view, this result followed from the Supreme Court of Canada's decision in *Brooks v. Canada Safeway Ltd.* (1989), 59 D.L.R. (4th) 321 that discrimination on the basis of pregnancy is a form of sex discrimination.

In Ontario, the issues raised by *Victoria County Memorial Hospital* have been addressed by legislative reform. Section 51(3) of the *Employment Standards Act*, S.O. 2000, c. 41, now requires the employer to continue making the requisite contributions to a benefit plan in respect of an employee who is absent from work on maternity or pregnancy leave. In *Kenora Ass'n for Community Living and O.P.S.E.U., Local 702* (2004), 124 L.A.C. (4th) 86, Arbitrator Roberts relied on the amendments to override provisions in the collective agreement which excluded time spent on pregnancy and parental leave in determining eligibility for participation in a pension plan.

However, in *Canadian Broadcasting Corp. and Canadian Media Guild*, [2004] C.L.A.D. No. 6 (QL), decided under federal legislation, Arbitrator Hornung held that it was not a violation of the *Canada Labour Code*, R.S.C. 1985, c. L-2, or the *Canadian Human Rights Act*, R.S.C. 1985, c. H-6, for the employer to require employees on parental leave to pay benefit plan premiums and pension contributions, even though the employer covered these costs in the case of employees who were receiving long-term disability benefits. After considering s. 209.21 of the *Code*, which entitles employees on parental leave to benefits "on the same terms as any employee who is absent from work for health-related reasons", the arbitrator ruled that, because employees on parental leave would qualify for the premium waiver if they became disabled, they already received benefits "on the same terms" as everyone else. Furthermore, he held, since employees on parental leave had to pay the same insurance premiums and pension contributions as those in active service, the employer's practice did not violate the anti-discrimination provisions of the collective agreement or the *Canadian Human Rights Act*. See Chapters 22.5.3 and 22.6.2 for a discussion of other decisions dealing with the effect of an extended absence on benefit entitlements under the collective agreement.

In *Kingston General Hospital and C.U.P.E., Local 1974*, [2005] O.L.A.A. No. 124 (QL) (Burkett), the employer had denied full-time service accrual and other benefits to an employee who, though commencing her maternity leave as a part-time technician, had successfully posted three months later into a full-time position as a nutrition assistant. The union asserted that, pursuant to Ontario's *Employment Standards Act* and *Human Rights Code*, the grievor was entitled to immediate accrual of full-time service and benefits, even though she did not begin working in the posted position until she had returned from maternity leave. An arbitration board chaired by Kevin Burkett dismissed the grievance, ruling that neither the part-time nor the full-time collective agreement contemplated a change in status until the employee had started work in the new position. Given this finding, the board concluded, there was no question of discrimination, since the grievor had received all the benefits provided by the part-time agreement throughout the period of her maternity leave.

With respect to eligibility for sick leave benefits, it has been held that the denial of a claim by an employee who is experiencing a pregnancy-related illness contravenes the prohibition against sex discrimination. In *O.S.S.T.F., District 34 v. Essex County Board of Education* (1998), 164 D.L.R. (4th) 455, the Ontario Court of Appeal concluded that, if an employer provides sick leave benefits, it is contrary to the *Human Rights Code* to deny such benefits to women for the period of disability following childbirth.

In *Peel Board of Education and O.S.S.T.F. (Bennett)* (2000), 92 L.A.C. (4th) 289, Arbitrator Kaplan upheld the union's argument that a six-week period of recovery from an uncomplicated childbirth should be recognized as a normative and practical standard, thus allowing employees to claim six weeks of sick leave benefits following childbirth without being required to attend at a physician's office to obtain a medical diagnosis of disability.

A benefit plan which provides for parental leave may also contravene human rights legislation if it makes improper distinctions between adoptive and biological parents. In *Ontario Hydro and Society of Ontario Hydro Professional & Administrative Employees*, [1999] O.L.A.A. No. 362 (QL), Arbitrator Michel Picher held that a collective agreement which provided greater benefits to adoptive parents than to biological parents in the context of parental leave gave rise to discrimination on the basis of family status, contrary to Ontario and federal human rights legislation. However, in a contrasting decision, an arbitration board chaired by Brian Keller has ruled that a collective agreement providing supplemental parental leave benefits to adoptive parents and biological mothers, but not to biological fathers, did not discriminate on the basis of family status: *Upper Canada District School Board and O.S.S.T.F., District 26* (2004), 126 L.A.C. (4th) 158. The board held that, since the purpose of granting supplemental benefits to adoptive fathers was to ameliorate their "special needs", the differential treatment was legal under the collective agreement, human rights legislation, and the *Charter of Rights and Freedoms*. In its award, the board adopted the analysis set out by the Supreme Court of Canada in *Law v. Canada (Minister of Employment and Immigration)* (1999), 170 D.L.R. (4th) 1, which emphasized the necessity of establishing an injury to the claimant's dignity when considering allegations of discrimination. The Ontario Divisional Court has affirmed the arbitration board's ruling: (2005), 260 D.L.R. (4th) 515, leave to appeal to Ont. C.A. denied January 20, 2006.

Finally, in *Carewest and H.S.A.A. (Degagne)* (2001), 93 L.A.C. (4th) 129 (Moreau), the grievor, having exhausted her maternity leave entitlement, sought an unpaid leave of absence in order to continue breast-feeding her child. According to the grievor, she was unable to attend at work because the child was having difficulty adapting to other sources of food and had to be breast-fed every three hours. The employer, while it offered to make a room available at the workplace to enable the grievor to express and store her milk, denied the request for leave. Arbitrator Moreau ruled that the denial constituted discrimination on the basis of sex, contrary to the collective agreement and the Alberta *Human Rights, Citizenship and Multiculturalism Act*, now R.S.A. 2000, c. H-14. The employer, it was held, had failed to accommodate the grievor to the point of undue hardship, and had not established that its insistence upon an immediate return to work constituted a *bona fide* occupational requirement.

The caselaw respecting the issue of whether an employee can be laid off while on a leave of absence was reviewed extensively by Arbitrator Dorsey in *British Columbia Public School Employers' Ass'n and B.C.T.F.* (2002), 108 L.A.C. (4th) 351. There was a general consensus, the arbitrator concluded, that the employer is not permitted to lay off an employee who is absent from work on pregnancy, parental, medical, or workers' compensation leave. However, a valid notice of layoff can be issued to an employee whose leave has not yet commenced as of the effective date of the layoff, even though the employee has already applied for and is otherwise entitled to the leave. The arbitrator also found that an employee who requests leave *after* receiving a layoff notice, but prior to the date on which the layoff takes effect, is not insulated from layoff during the leave (except in cases of pregnancy or parental leave, or medical or workers' compensation leave).

23.4   BEREAVEMENT LEAVE

Where the collective agreement provides for paid bereavement leave, commonly disputed issues include the duration of the leave, whether the deceased falls within the classes of person in respect of whom an employee is entitled to leave, and whether the employee is entitled to leave if the period of bereavement falls on non-working days. While questions relating to an employee's entitlement ultimately depend on the specific wording of the collective agreement, the arbitral jurisprudence discloses several overarching principles.

At one time, on the basis that the pyramiding of benefits should be avoided, some arbitrators construed bereavement leave provisions narrowly. In more recent years, however, this view has generally been rejected in favour of a more purposive approach that recognizes the extremely personal nature of such leave. The seminal decision in this regard is *Dominion Glass Co. Ltd. and United Glass & Ceramic Workers, Local 235* (1973), 4 L.A.C. (2d) 345 (Johnston), where the arbitrator applied a broad, purposive approach to the interpretation of the term "brother-in-law" in defining the scope of an employee's entitlement.

Nevertheless, there continues to be some divergence among arbitrators about the extent to which a broad and purposive approach (as opposed to a narrow or literal approach) should be adopted to the interpretation of bereavement leave provisions. This divergence is perhaps best represented by comparing two arbitral opinions as to whether the term "immediate family", when used in conjunction with "grandparents", extends to the death of an employee's spouse's grandparent. In *Montfort Hospital and O.N.A.* (1992), 28 L.A.C. (4th) 326 (M.G. Picher), the arbitrator refused to adopt a purposive approach, ruling that the collective agreement was "reasonably specific" as to the scope of entitlement. However, in the more recent decision of *Dominion Colour Corp. and Teamsters, Local 1880* (1998), 75 L.A.C. (4th) 364 (MacLean), after thoroughly canvassing the conflicting decisions on the interpretation of provisions similar to those found in *Montfort Hospital*, Arbitrator MacLean interpreted the term "grandparents" as including the grandparent of an employee's spouse, as, in his view, a liberal and purposive approach was more consonant with labour relations policy.

Another frequently encountered problem is whether an employee is entitled to paid bereavement leave if the death occurs while the employee is on vacation. Where the collective agreement does not deal with the problem of overlap between paid vacation and bereavement leave, a divergence of opinion has arisen. The more restrictive view is represented by the seminal case of *Gray Forgings & Stampings Ltd. and U.E., Local 557* (1980), 27 L.A.C. (2d) 61 (Shime). Arbitrator Shime was of the opinion that the purpose of bereavement leave is simply to provide time away from work without loss of pay, and that such leave is therefore not available to an employee who is already away from work. Moreover, the arbitrator commented, attending to a death in the family is not inconsistent with the purpose of vacation, which is to give employees time off for personal matters.

However, this restrictive approach has been rejected in a line of awards beginning with *Alcan Smelters & Chemicals Ltd. and C.A.S.A.W., Local 1* (1982), 5 L.A.C. (3d) 83 (Hope). Arbitrator Hope's approach is sometimes referred to as the "earned benefit" or "positive rights" approach, but it too is essentially purposive. According to this view, vacation with pay and bereavement leave are two separate and distinct benefits having different purposes. The purpose of vacation, specifically, is to provide an employee with time off which he or she has earned through work, and it is qualitatively different from other types of absence, such as sick leave. It is no more valid to say that an employee should use his or her vacation time in connection with a bereavement than to say that an employee who is actively working should use vacation credits to attend to a bereavement. Thus, in the absence of collective agreement provisions which clearly disentitle vacationing employees from paid bereavement leave, these rights should be viewed as co-existing. The two conflicting lines of jurisprudence are discussed in *Whitby Hydro Electric Commission and Power Workers' Union* (1997), 67 L.A.C. (4th) 20 (Stewart).

Applying a purposive approach may also have the effect of shortening the duration of leave to which an employee is entitled. In *Hamilton-Wentworth Police Services Board and Hamilton-Wentworth Police'Ass'n*, unreported, February 17, 1998 (Kirkwood), for example, the collective agreement allowed "not more than three (3) days or not more than five (5) days" [in the case of immediate family members] for the purpose of attending a family member's funeral. An employee was denied the maximum amount of compassionate leave. Arbitrator Kirkwood denied the grievance, ruling that entitlement to the maximum period of leave was not automatic, and that paid leave was specifically for the purpose of attending the funeral. Thus, funeral leave was to be distinguished from bereavement leave, which could be interpreted as having a broader scope and application.

An employee's right to bereavement leave, or to any of the benefits reviewed in this chapter, is subject to the rule against pyramiding and the arbitral principles governing retroactivity: see Chapters 22.7 and 22.8 for further discussion.

CHAPTER 24

RIGHTS OF TRADE UNIONS

24.1   UNION SECURITY CLAUSES

In Canada, unions and employers are free to include in the collective agreement one of a variety of union security clauses, providing for varying degrees of compelled support for the union by the members of the bargaining unit. Such clauses can range from a voluntary dues "check-off clause" (requiring the employer to deduct dues from the wages of employees who have opted in and to remit them to the union), to a "closed shop" or "hiring hall" clause. Where the collective agreement contains a "closed shop" provision, the employer is not permitted to hire anyone within the bargaining unit who is not a member of the union. Under a "hiring hall" provision, similarly, the employer is restricted to hiring employees who have been referred by the union's hiring hall. Other types of clauses are also common. A "union shop" provision requires that all employees in the bargaining unit must become and remain members in good standing within a fixed period of entering the bargaining unit. A somewhat less rigorous variation on this theme is the "maintenance of membership" provision, which stipulates that all employees who belong to the union when the collective agreement takes effect are obligated, as a condition of continued employment, to maintain their union membership. Finally, an "agency shop" provision — often referred to as a "Rand formula" clause — is one which makes all bargaining unit employees, regardless of whether they belong to the union, responsible for paying to the union an amount equal to regular union dues. In this situation, the employer usually makes the deduction at source.

Labour relations legislation often specifies that the parties to a collective agreement can agree to any of the various kinds of union security provisions without committing an unfair labour practice or violating the right to freedom of association: see, for instance, s. 15 of the British Columbia *Labour Relations Code*, R.S.B.C. 1996, c. 244, and s. 31 of the Newfoundland and Labrador *Labour Relations Act*, R.S.N.L. 1990, c. L-1. In some jurisdictions, the legislation provides that the employer must consent to the inclusion of a particular clause upon request by the union. This is true of agency shop provisions in Ontario, and maintenance of membership provisions in Saskatchewan.

A number of jurisdictions, including British Columbia, Ontario and the federal regime, have also enacted an exemption for employees who object to union membership or the payment of union dues on religious grounds. See, for example, s. 52 of the Ontario *Labour Relations Act*, S.O. 1995, c. 1, Sch. A, which limits the religious exemption to employees who were hired prior to the inclusion of the union security provision in the collective agreement, and states that the exemption applies only during the term of the first collective agreement in which the provision appears. Furthermore, since the enforcement of a union security clause may result in the discharge of an employee, the legislation of most provinces and the federal jurisdiction imposes certain limitations on the reasons for which an employee can be expelled from the union or denied membership (see s. 8(3) of the New Brunswick *Industrial Relations Act*, R.S.N.B. 1973, c. I-4, or s. 95 of the *Canada Labour Code*, R.S.C. 1985, c. L-2). Under s. 51(2) of the Ontario Act, the employer cannot be required to discharge an employee pursuant to a union security clause where expulsion or denial of membership was due to the employee's joining another union, opposing the union in a lawful manner, engaging in reasonable dissent within the union, or refusing to pay unreasonable fees, dues or assessments.

24.1.1   Enforcement at Arbitration

It has long been accepted that a union security provision is enforceable through the grievance and arbitration procedures. The union is thus entitled to request an arbitrator to order the employer to discharge an employee who has failed to become or to remain a member of the union, or refused to pay the requisite dues. These principles were applied in *Carrier Air Conditioning (Canada) Ltd. and S.M.W., Local 575* (1967), 18 L.A.C. 190 (Arrell), in the context of a union shop clause stipulating that every new hire was required to join the union as a condition of employment. It should be noted, though, that the result in *Carrier Air Conditioning* reflects the absence of any exemption in respect of religious objectors, such as has since been incorporated into most labour relations legislation.

Nevertheless, there is some disagreement in the arbitral jurisprudence concerning the precision with which the union security clause must address the consequences of failure to become a union member before it can create an enforceable obligation on the employer to discharge the offending employee. Many arbitrators have held that, in view of the severity of the consequences, the collective agreement should be construed strictly against authorizing the sanction of discharge unless the parties have clearly provided for it. A seminal decision representing the strict construction approach is *Joy Manufacturing Co. and U.S.W.A., Local 2871* (1955), 6 L.A.C. 149 (Anderson). The board ruled that a clause requiring all employees to remain union members in good standing during the life of the agreement was not sufficiently clear to justify an order for the dismissal of an employee whose membership had lapsed. In the board's opinion, only where the clause expressly states that membership in good standing is a condition of employment is the employer obligated to effect a discharge.

Other arbitrators have taken a broader, purposive approach to the interpretation of union security clauses. In their view, an employer obligation to dismiss should be inferred where it is necessary to give working effect to the clause. The seminal decision for this approach is *Northern Miner Press Ltd. and Toronto Printing Pressmen & Assistants' Union No. 10* (1958), 8 L.A.C. 251 (Laskin), where it was held that a provision that did not expressly make maintenance of membership a condition of employment nonetheless imposed an obligation on the employer to discharge an employee whose membership had been cancelled.

There is continuing ambivalence in the caselaw as to which approach — a "strict construction" approach favouring the employee or a "working effect" approach favouring the union — is to be preferred. In *Rogers Cable TV – Victoria and I.B.E.W., Local 230* (1987), 31 L.A.C. (3d) 62 (Munroe), for example, the union sought an order for the dismissal of an employee whose application for membership in the union had been rejected. The union security provision in question was a maintenance-of-membership clause, but it did not expressly make membership a condition of employment or require the dismissal of an employee who failed to maintain membership:

> All [employees] covered by this agreement shall, if not already members of the I.B.E.W., make immediate application for membership and assignment of dues and, if acceptable, shall become and remain members of that organization while employed under this agreement.

Arbitrator Munroe rejected the strict construction approach formulated in *Joy Manufacturing* as "unduly mechanical and legalistic", holding that a collective agreement should be interpreted so as to give effect, wherever possible, to its substantive content. Thus, in his view, the phrase "while employed under this agreement" indicated that the provision was intended to make ongoing union membership a condition of employment, the breach of which would subject an employee to dismissal at the instance of the union. However, the arbitrator also held that the words "if acceptable" gave rise to a serious ambiguity, since they were capable of being interpreted to mean that the requirement of union membership was not binding on an employee whose application had been rejected. Because an employee whose dismissal is sought pursuant to a union security clause is entitled to benefit from any ambiguities in the negotiated language, the grievance was denied.

An exposition of the purposive approach adopted in *Northern Miner Press* is found in *Windsor Regional Hospital and I.B.E.W., Local 636*, [2000] O.L.A.A. No. 500 (QL) (Levinson). In that case, the employee in question had been outside the scope of the bargaining unit when the maintenance-of-membership clause was first negotiated, but later came within the unit because of hospital restructuring. The arbitrator relied heavily on the purpose of union security provisions in holding that, as a consequence of the employee's refusal to become and remain a member in good standing, the union was entitled to require that she be dismissed, in accordance with the clause.

24.1.2 Requirements for Compliance with Union Constitution and Notice to Employer

Even where a collective agreement specifically provides for the discharge of an employee who breaches the union security clause, the obligation to discharge is not automatic upon bare notification to the employer that the employee is no longer a member of the union. Rather, recognizing the seriousness of the situation, most arbitrators have required the union to provide to the employer enough information to demonstrate that there was proper cause for expulsion under the union's constitution and by-laws, and that the expulsion was not contrary to common law or statute. There should also be sufficient information to show that the expulsion was carried out in accordance with due process, having regard to the principles of natural justice at common law and to internal union procedures. Finally, the by-laws or constitution pursuant to which the employee has been excluded from membership must be consistent with the collective agreement and with recognized public policy. All these principles were authoritatively established in *Orenda Engines Ltd. and I.A.M.* (1958), 8 L.A.C. 116, a seminal decision of Bora Laskin. Professor Laskin rejected the argument that it was beyond the jurisdiction of arbitrators to investigate whether the union's behaviour conformed to its own constitution and by-laws. Where union membership is made a condition of employment, he ruled, the union security clause has effectively projected the constitution and by-laws into the collective agreement itself.

The principles allowing arbitrators to test the conduct of a union against its constitution and by-laws were applied in *Dover Corp. (Canada) Ltd. and I.U.E.C., Local 90* (1974), 7 L.A.C. (2d) 398 (O'Shea). The arbitrator noted, however, that these principles did not entitle him to question the sufficiency of the evidence on which the union carried out the expulsion. Rather, he ruled, an arbitrator is limited to determining whether there was substantial compliance with the procedural requirements of the union's constitution and by-laws, and with common law and statutory norms.

Similarly, in *Pacifica Papers Inc. and C.E.P., Local 76* (2000), 94 L.A.C. (4th) 26 (Munroe), it was held that the principles expressed in *Orenda Engines* required the union to deliver particulars of the reasons why an employee was no longer a member at the time that the union requested the employee's dismissal pursuant to the union security clause. The provision in question stipulated that an employee who failed to maintain membership in good standing was to be discharged after seven days' written notice to the employer by the union of the employee's loss of membership. In Arbitrator Munroe's view, the clause could not be construed as compelling the employer to accept without question the assertion that an employee had ceased to be a member in good standing.

24.1.3   Constitutionality of Union Security Clauses

There have been numerous challenges to union security provisions of all types as being inconsistent with the freedom of association guaranteed by s. 2(d) of the *Charter of Rights and Freedoms*. However, none of these challenges has been successful, with the consequence that such provisions continue to be fully enforceable. In *Lavigne v. O.P.S.E.U.* (1991), 81 D.L.R. (4th) 545, for example, the Supreme Court of Canada affirmed the constitutional validity of a "Rand formula" or "agency shop" clause, pursuant to which employees who are not members of the union are nevertheless required as a condition of employment to remit to the union an amount equal to regular dues. In *Bhindi v. British Columbia Projectionists, Local 348* (1986), 29 D.L.R. (4th) 47 (B.C.C.A.), and *Arlington Crane Service Ltd. v. Ontario (Minister of Labour)* (1988), 56 D.L.R. (4th) 209 (Ont. H.C.J.), it was held that the *Charter* does not apply so as to prohibit the inclusion of a closed shop clause in a collective agreement between parties in the private sector. In *Arlington Crane Service*, moreover, the Court went on to rule that, even if the *Charter* did apply, the incorporation of a closed shop clause would not give rise to an infringement of any rights or freedoms guaranteed by the *Charter*.

Finally, in *R. v. Advance Cutting and Coring Ltd.* (2001), 205 D.L.R. (4th) 385, a majority of the Supreme Court of Canada held that a Quebec statutory provision which required workers to belong to one of five designated unions as a condition of employment in the construction industry did not violate the guarantee of freedom of association under s. 2(d) of the *Charter*. Although eight of the nine judges on the panel concluded that freedom of association included the freedom not to associate, only four of them held that a union security provision which compelled union membership represented impermissible coercive ideological association sufficient to constitute a breach of the *Charter*.

The five judges who rejected the challenge did so for different reasons. Justice L'Heureux-Dubé ruled that there was no constitutional right not to associate; Justice LeBel, along with two others, held that compelled membership in a union as a condition of employment did not result in coerced ideological conformity; while Justice Iacobucci decided that, although the legislation violated the freedom not to associate, it was justifiable as a reasonable limit under s. 1 of the *Charter*, because its advantages for employees in the construction industry as a whole outweighed the negative impact on their rights.

24.2   UNION ACTIVITY IN THE WORKPLACE

The right to engage in union activity in the workplace arises from three sources. First, labour relations legislation in Canada generally guarantees employees the right to join a trade union of their choice and to participate in its lawful activities. Typical provisions in this regard include s. 8(1) of the *Canada Labour Code*, R.S.C. 1985, c. L-2, and s. 5(1) of the Manitoba *Labour Relations Act*, R.S.M. 1987, c. L10. In addition, the legislation usually prohibits as an unfair labour practice any discrimination against employees on the basis of union activity, as well as employer interference in the administration of a trade union. Second, most collective agreements contain a provision protecting employees from discrimination, discipline or harassment because of their participation in union activity. The agreement may also recognize the right of union officials to engage in union business and to be given the necessary time off for such business. Finally, where there is sufficient government involvement in the collective bargaining relationship to attract the application of the *Charter of Rights and Freedoms*, certain forms of union activity may be protected under the constitutional guarantees of freedom of expression and freedom of association. Even if the *Charter* does not apply directly, an arbitrator may well look to *Charter* values to inform his or her interpretation of the collective agreement and statute law. For an analysis of the extent to which *Charter* protections of freedom of association and freedom of expression apply to union activity, see the Supreme Court of Canada's decision in *Dunmore v. Ontario (Attorney General)* (2001), 207 D.L.R. (4th) 193.

In *British Columbia Public School Employers'Ass'n and B.C.T.F.* (2004), 129 L.A.C. (4th) 245, Arbitrator Munroe upheld grievances against employer directives designed to prevent teachers from posting union notices on bulletin boards, discussing collective bargaining issues with parents during parent-teacher interviews, or providing parents with leaflets prepared by the union. In the arbitrator's view, the directives infringed teachers' freedom of expression, contrary to s. 2(b) of the *Charter*, and were not justified under s. 1 as reasonable limits on that freedom.

It has also been held that peaceful or "informational" leafleting at the employer's place of business constitutes legitimate expression to which

Charter protection attaches: *Sobeys Capital Inc. and U.F.C.W., Local 401* (2003), 98 Can. L.R.B.R. (2d) 1 (Alta. L.R.B.). Indeed, this protection extends to "secondary picketing" of suppliers or customers of a struck employer, provided the union has not engaged in criminal or tortuous conduct: *R.W.D.S.U., Local 558 v. Pepsi-Cola Canada Beverages (West) Ltd.* (2002), 208 D.L.R. (4th) 385 (S.C.C.). However, labour boards in Canada have generally upheld legislative bans on mid-term "political protest strikes" as a justifiable limitation on freedom of expression: see Chapter 13.10.1 for further discussion.

Additional Reading

B. Adell, "Secondary Picketing after *Pepsi-Cola*: What's Clear, and What Isn't?" (2003), 10 Canadian Labour and Employment Law Journal, p. 135.

M. Mac Neil, "Unions and the *Charter*: The Supreme Court of Canada and Democratic Values" (2003), 10 Canadian Labour and Employment Law Journal, p. 3.

P. Macklem, "Secondary Picketing, Consumer Boycotts and the *Charter*" (2000), 8 Canadian Labour and Employment Journal, p. 1.

24.2.1   What Is Union Activity?

Often, the first issue confronting the arbitrator is whether an activity to which the employer objects constitutes union activity for the purposes of the collective agreement or labour relations legislation. Arbitrators have generally taken a fairly broad and purposive approach to the definition of union activity or business. In *Air Canada and Canadian Air Line Employees'Ass'n* (1980), 27 L.A.C. (2d) 289, Arbitrator Simmons held that the distribution of partisan election pamphlets on the employer's premises during non-working hours was protected under the collective agreement as union activity. Nevertheless, the arbitrator observed, the right to participate in lawful union activity was not absolute. Union activity, even if lawful, can be limited where it would have an adverse effect on the employer's ability to control and direct the workforce.

In *Adams Mine and U.S.W.A.* (1982), 1 Can. L.R.B.R. (N.S.) 384, by contrast, the Ontario Labour Relations Board concluded that political canvassing on the job is not protected by the statutory right to engage in union activity unless the political controversy at issue is directly related to the workplace. It should be noted, however, that this more circumscribed view of union activity warranting protection has not been widely accepted by arbitrators. In *Canadian Broadcasting Corp. v. Canada (Labour Relations Board)* (1995), 121 D.L.R. (4th) 385, the Supreme Court of Canada also refused to adopt the narrow *Adams Mine* approach. In that case, the local union president published an anti-free trade article in the union newspaper, leading the employer to threaten dismissal if he did not give up union office. Upholding a ruling of the Canada Labour Relations Board to the effect that the ultimatum amounted to an unfair labour practice, the Court articulated views on the scope of protected union activity which are quite consistent with those expressed in *Air Canada.*

24.2.2   Distinguishing Between Protected and Unprotected Union Activity

Wearing union buttons or buttons with a political message has often been held to be union activity which is deserving of protection under the governing statute or the collective agreement. One of the most frequently cited awards on this issue is *Canada Post Corp. and C.U.P.W.* (1986), 26 L.A.C. (3d) 58 (Outhouse). In the view of Arbitrator Outhouse, where employees wish to pursue a lawful union activity on the employer's premises, the employer must show some legitimate business interest that justifies overriding the exercise of the employees' right to free expression. Such an overriding interest will frequently take the form of a disruption to production, harm to customer relations, or other demonstrable injury to the employer.

The Federal Court of Appeal has also interpreted broadly the parameters of permissible union activity. In *Quan v. Canada (Treasury Board)*, [1990] 2 F.C. 191, the union applied for judicial review of a decision by the Public Service Staff Relations Board dismissing the grievance of an employee whose supervisor had asked him to remove a button reading "I'm on strike alert". Allowing the application, the Court held that the wearing of the button during working hours constituted union activity which was protected by both the collective agreement and federal labour relations legislation. Rejecting a narrow interpretation of union activity which would cover only the *administration* of union business, the Court instead adopted a broader, purposive approach that is consistent with the legislative guarantee of the right to participate in lawful union activity. An employee's expression of his or her views on union matters should not be curtailed unless there is evidence of a detrimental effect on the employer's reputation or capacity to manage its business.

The outcome dictated by these principles, however, depends to a great extent on the context of the workplace, in particular the nature of the business, the duties of the employee, and the content of the union activity or expression at issue. In *Almeida v. Canada (Treasury Board)* (1990), 74 D.L.R. (4th) 674, for example, applying its ruling in *Quan*, the Federal Court of Appeal upheld an employer directive prohibiting customs officers from wearing a union button in protest against government cutbacks. The messages on the button included the statement "Keep Out Drugs & Porno". In the Court's view, in light of the officers' responsibilities and public visibility, the button had the clear potential to undermine the employer's reputation and its ability to manage the workplace.

In *National Steel Car Ltd. and U.S.W.A., Local 7135* (1998), 76 L.A.C. (4th) 176 (Craven), the question was whether a company directive prohibiting the wearing of union stickers and a T-shirt issued by the union constituted unreasonable interference with the right of employees to engage in union activity. Both items displayed the union name and logo, but the T-shirt also featured a drawing of a coiled cobra with its head reared, accompanied by the warning "If Provoked Will Strike". Arbitrator Craven ruled for the union on the sticker issue, but upheld the ban on the T-shirt on the ground that union expression may be restricted where its content is "offensive, provocative, embarrassing, disruptive, critical or insulting". However, it is unclear whether this is a separate ground for limiting union activity or simply an example of conduct which interferes with the employer's ability to manage and control the business. The award also stresses the importance of context in making the distinction between protected and unprotected activity. Thus, the fact that the union was not in a legal strike position when the T-shirt was being worn contributed to the arbitrator's finding that it was unduly provocative.

The accepted arbitral principles prescribing the limits of union expression in pamphlets or notices posted on bulletin boards in the workplace are summarized in *Metropolitan Toronto (Municipality) and C.U.P.E., Local 79* (1997), 68 L.A.C. (4th) 224 (Sarra). In Arbitrator Sarra's view, union officials are to be given fairly wide latitude in communicating criticisms of management to rank-and-file employees, and even (where the employer is a government institution) to members of the public. However, this right cannot be used as a vehicle for statements that counsel illegal behaviour; are knowingly or recklessly false, or malicious in nature; or that harass, degrade and vilify management or co-workers. At the same time, union-sponsored statements should not be held to the same standards of fairness and accuracy expected of more objective publications and, in the absence of malicious or recklessly false statements, the employer's only recourse against inaccuracies is to circulate a rebuttal.

24.2.3 Union Activity during Working Hours

Even where the collective agreement is silent on the issue, union members are entitled to engage in lawful union activity at the workplace during non-working hours, provided the activity does not interfere with the employer's business. The seminal decision demonstrating this principle is *Canadian General Electric Co. Ltd. (Peterborough) and U.E.* (1952), 3 L.A.C. 909 (Laskin).

Different considerations may apply to union activity conducted during working hours. Some arbitrators have suggested that, unless the collective agreement expressly restricts such activity, the principles outlined in *Canadian General Electric* continue to apply: see, for example, *Canada Post Corp. and C.U.P.W.* (1986), 26 L.A.C. (3d) 58 (Outhouse), discussed in Chapter 24.2.2. (Of course, it will often be much easier for the employer to demonstrate interference with production or its ability to manage where the disputed activity takes place during working hours.) However, the matter becomes more complex if the collective agreement purports to prohibit or to circumscribe the right to engage in union activity in the course of the working day. The legislation in many jurisdictions is silent or ambivalent on the issue. For example, s. 77 of the Ontario *Labour Relations Act*, S.O. 1995, c. 1, Sch. A, simply states that nothing in the Act authorizes any person to recruit members for the union on the employer's premises during working hours. At the same time, s. 5 provides that every employee has the right to participate in the lawful activities of a union. In the face of this ambivalence, some collective agreements include a prohibition against union activity on the employer's time. In *The Bay (Windsor) and R.W.D.S.U., Local 1000* (1990), 16 L.A.C. (4th) 298 (Shime), the employer defended its policy of prohibiting sales clerks from wearing union buttons opposing the legalization of Sunday shopping during store opening hours (but not during working hours *per se*). In Arbitrator Shime's opinion, the restrictive clause in the parties' collective agreement was not contrary to s. 5 of the Ontario *Labour Relations Act*, and the employer was within its rights to impose the prohibition.

In *Lapointe-Fisher Nursing Home Ltd. and S.E.I.U., Local 210* (1998), 79 L.A.C. (4th) 20, Arbitrator Brandt appeared to reach a different conclusion. The collective agreement, comparable to the one reviewed in *The Bay (Windsor) and R.W.D.S.U., Local 1000*, prohibited "union activity on the employer's premises except with the express permission of the [employer]". In the arbitrator's opinion, such a provision could only be said to exclude *unlawful* union activities, because a blanket restriction would contravene the statutory right to participate in lawful union activities.

In *Health Employers' Ass'n of British Columbia and H.E.U. (Davis)* (2004), 125 L.A.C. (4th) 145, Arbitrator Sanderson relied on *Lapointe-Fisher Nursing Home* and other awards to uphold the right of employees, during working hours, to wear stickers protesting against contracting out, despite a provision in the employer's code of conduct which prohibited the wearing of accessories that could have an adverse effect on its image.

24.3   DISCRIMINATION ON THE BASIS OF UNION ACTIVITY

In addition to the statutory prohibition against discrimination on the basis of union activity or union membership found in labour relations legislation, most collective agreements contain a similar prohibition. Arbitrators have recognized that the interpretation and application of such provisions should be informed by labour board rulings as to what constitutes anti-union discrimination, as well as by court rulings in human rights cases. Consistent with that approach, arbitrators have also ruled that the no-discrimination provisions of a collective agreement should be given a broad and purposive construction. Arbitrator McFetridge's award in *Alberta Hospital Ponoka and A.U.P.E., Local 42* (1994), 46 L.A.C. (4th) 231 provides an example of the modern approach.

Here, the arbitrator concluded that the collective agreement prohibition against discrimination on the basis of union activity encompassed discrimination of the kind recognized in the adjudication of human rights complaints. Accordingly, one of the grievors, who had been laid off partly because of his extensive involvement in union affairs, was found to have been discriminated against. Even more interestingly, the arbitrator held that the second grievor was also entitled to a remedy, even though he was *not* active in the union. In the arbitrator's view, since seniority principles required that the second grievor be laid off before the first, the employer's breach of the no-discrimination provision had an adverse effect on *both* of them.

Arbitrators have generally rejected the argument that the inclusion of a no-discrimination clause in the collective agreement precludes the employer from providing different terms and conditions of employment as between bargaining unit employees and non-bargaining unit employees. In *Ontario Hydro and C.U.P.E., Local 1000* (1994), 40 L.A.C. (4th) 135 (Swan), for example, union members were compelled to decide whether or not to accept a voluntary severance package at the same time as all other employees, despite the fact that employees outside the bargaining unit possessed more information concerning their susceptibility to layoff in the immediate future. The arbitrator rejected the claim that bargaining unit employees had been subjected to discrimination. Collective agreement provisions barring discrimination on the basis of union membership, he ruled, have never had the effect of preventing employers from offering different or even superior terms and conditions of employment to employees outside the bargaining unit.

In *University of British Columbia and Faculty Ass'n* (2004), 125 L.A.C. (4th) 1, Arbitrator Dorsey ruled that the employer had violated the union recognition clause in the collective agreement by negotiating directly with faculty members with respect to the assignment of copyright in an online course they had been assigned to develop. The arbitrator went on to hold that the employer's conduct also constituted discrimination on the basis of union activity, contrary to the collective agreement, because the one faculty member who refused to negotiate an individual agreement with the employer was excluded from participating in the development of the course.

CHAPTER 25

RESPONSIBILITIES OF TRADE UNIONS

25.1   GENERAL

In addition to their statutory responsibilities towards employees and the employer, a union may assume responsibilities to the employer under the collective agreement for which it can be held accountable through the grievance arbitration process. The most commonly arbitrated contractual obligation of the union is not to engage in an illegal strike or work stoppage. The labour relations legislation of every jurisdiction in Canada prohibits the parties from resorting to a strike or lockout during the term of a collective agreement. In some cases, as in Ontario, the legislation also requires that a no-strike, no-lockout provision be included in every collective agreement, and deems such a clause to be present if the agreement is silent on the issue. Whether or not the applicable legislation contains a deeming provision, the parties frequently replicate the statutory prohibition in their agreement, with or without additional restrictions. Furthermore, the decision of the Supreme Court of Canada in *St. Anne-Nackawic Pulp and Paper Co. Ltd. v. C.P.U., Local 219* (1986), 28 D.L.R. (4th) 1 made it clear that arbitrators have exclusive authority to consider claims for damages against the union for any breach of the collective agreement, including unlawful strike activity.

25.2   WHAT CONSTITUTES AN ILLEGAL STRIKE?

As discussed in Chapter 13.10.1, arbitrators have generally considered themselves bound by the broad statutory definition of "strike" found in the applicable labour relations legislation. Indeed, it has been held that arbitrators in Ontario are not at liberty to question or depart from decisions of the Labour Relations Board concerning the scope of prohibited strike activity. Aside from British Columbia, which, prior to 1987, had legislation stipulating that the work stoppage or slow-down must have a collective bargaining purpose, a purposive component has been absent from the definition of strike in Canadian labour relations legislation. For this reason, a stoppage or slow-down which is undertaken in the name of political protest or free expression will nevertheless be held to constitute impermissible strike activity if it has the effect of restricting or limiting output. The decision of Arbitrator Adams in *Kendall Co. and U.S.W.A.* (1978), 17 L.A.C. (2d) 408 established these principles in the context of the "National Day of Protest", an event organized by trade unions across Canada in 1976 to mobilize public opinion against the imposition of wage and price controls.

In *General Motors of Canada Ltd. and C.A.W.* (1996), 31 Can. L.R.B.R. (2d) 161, the Ontario Labour Relations Board affirmed these principles in the face of union arguments that they contravened the *Canadian Charter of Rights and Freedoms*. The union contended that the legislative prohibition against strikes during the term of a collective agreement infringed the *Charter* guarantee of freedom of expression. Although the Board accepted that the right to engage in a political protest strike was protected expression within the meaning of s. 2(b) of the *Charter*, it held that a blanket prohibition on strike activity during the currency of a collective agreement was a reasonable limit on this right. In a decision that split three ways, the British Columbia Labour Relations Board arrived at a similar conclusion, though leaving the door open to the possibility that a mid-term political protest strike might be justified in rare circumstances: *Health Employers' Ass'n of British Columbia and H.E.U.* (2004), 108 Can. L.R.B.R. 1.

At issue in *Green River Log Sales (1996) Ltd. and I.W.A., Local 1-3567*, [2003] B.C.C.A.A.A. No. 269 (QL) (Taylor) was the legality of the union's response to a proposal by the employer to eliminate part of its production process in the plant. At a meeting with management, a union official stated that the plan would be implemented only "over [his] dead body", and threatened to bring a grievance. Arbitrator Taylor held that, despite the harsh words used, the evidence fell short of establishing that employees refused to perform the work in question, or that the union threatened, declared, authorized, counselled or aided in an unlawful work stoppage. In the arbitrator's view, posturing, strong language or honest disagreement over a proposed course of action will not suffice. Rather, in order to constitute an illegal strike, the impugned comments must be followed by action.

The parties to a collective agreement cannot contract out of the statutory definition of strike. However, there is far less certainty as to whether a collective agreement provision which purports to give employees the right to refuse to cross a lawful picket line or to handle struck work from another employer is enforceable at arbitration. Several arbitration awards have implied that, notwithstanding the overarching prohibition against work stoppages, such a provision is effective to limit the employer's entitlement to damages arising from an unlawful strike where the impugned activity falls within the scope of the provision, or to shield employees from discipline for taking part in the strike. This view is perhaps best represented by the decision of Arbitrator Weatherill in

Toronto Star Ltd. and Toronto Photo-Engravers' Union, No. 35-P (1971), 22 L.A.C. 319. More recently, Arbitrator Dorsey has ruled that the inclusion of a "hot cargo" clause in a collective agreement does not violate the no strike/no lockout provision of British Columbia's *Labour Relations Code*, R.S.B.C. 1996, c. 244: see *Pacific Press and C.E.P., Local 2000* (2000), 86 L.A.C (4th) 1.

By contrast, the award of Arbitrator Howard Brown in *Kingston Whig-Standard and C.W.A., Local 204* (1995), 51 L.A.C. (4th) 137 asserts that struck work or picket line clauses are void *ab initio* and cannot be used by either party for any purpose. This view of struck work clauses was adopted by Arbitrator Beattie in *Labatt Alberta Brewery and Retail, Wholesale Canada, Local 250* (2004), 125 L.A.C. (4th) 96. For further discussion, see Chapter 13.10.1.

25.3 UNION LIABILITY FOR ILLEGAL STRIKES

The seminal decision on the nature and extent of union liability for violations of the collective agreement is *Polymer Corp. Ltd. and Oil, Chemical & Atomic Workers* (1958), 10 L.A.C. 31 (Laskin). Arbitrator Laskin began by rejecting the notion that a union can be vicariously liable for the actions of its members. As distinguished from its employees, agents and officers, members *simpliciter* have no capacity to implicate the union by their tortious conduct or breaches of a personal contract. Therefore, unless the union expressly accepts responsibility, the actions of its members do not constitute a potential source of union liability.

Arbitrator Laskin went on to outline the criteria by which the union's liability for an unlawful strike will be assessed. In his view, a common no-strike clause does not fix the union with absolute liability for illegal work stoppages. Rather, the import of such a provision is that the union will not, through its proper officers, sanction, direct, condone or encourage a work stoppage by employees. Thus, if the union leadership instigates an unlawful strike, say, by holding a strike vote, its liability arises the moment such official action is taken. In the case of unofficial action, such as a wildcat strike, whether or not the union is liable hinges on the sufficiency of its officials' efforts to get employees back to work. In general, union officials are obligated to promptly take all reasonable measures to end the strike. Depending on the circumstances, this duty may range from ensuring that no union steward or committee member is showing support for the stoppage or slow-down to taking disciplinary action against individual employees. Although for all intents and purposes steward action is union action for the purpose of determining the union's role in instigating or promoting a strike, *Polymer Corp.* suggests that different considerations may apply in the case of a spontaneous stoppage or workout. Here, a mere failure on the part of stewards to intervene may not be sufficient to make the union liable, since the authority and duty to end the disruption rests with higher-level officials.

The *Polymer Corp.* principles were affirmed and applied in *Riverside Forest Products Ltd. and I.W.A., Local 1-423* (1997), 70 L.A.C. (4th) 441 (Taylor). In this case, the failure of the union's executive officers to dissociate themselves decisively from a work stoppage was held to give rise to union liability.

In *Canada Forgings Inc. and C.A.W., Local 275*, [2003] O.L.A.A. No. 484 (QL), Arbitrator Surdykowski relied on *Polymer Corp.* to hold that the union was not liable in damages for a wildcat strike conducted by two employees, even though one of them was a union steward. The arbitrator found that the steward held no other position in the local or national union, and there was no suggestion that he was acting in his capacity as a steward or representative of the union, nor was he perceived by the employer to be acting in that capacity. It was also noted that, as soon as the slowdown was brought to the attention of a responsible local union officer, the plant Chair, he took reasonable and appropriate action to bring the strike to an end. Not every act of a steward, the arbitrator observed, can be attributed to the union.

"Union action" sufficient to ground liability is not limited to the conduct of union officials, where the rank-and-file membership adopts a course of "official" action without the sanction of elected officers. In *Hamilton Terminal Operators Ltd. and I.L.W.U., Local 1879* (1966), 17 L.A.C. 262 (Arthurs), for example, the responsible officers did everything reasonably possible to end an illegal wildcat strike. Nonetheless, the union was held liable for the damages suffered by the employer, since the members themselves had voted at a general meeting to initiate the strike.

25.4   MEASUREMENT OF DAMAGES

The leading case recognizing the authority of arbitrators to assess damages against a union which has engaged in an illegal strike is the second, remedial award of Arbitrator Laskin in *Polymer Corp. Ltd. and Oil, Chemical & Atomic Workers* (1959), 10 L.A.C. 51, reviewed in Chapter 7.4.1. The arbitrator rejected the argument that he lacked jurisdiction to award a remedy unless it was expressly set out in the collective agreement, ruling that the natural corollary of the statutory requirement for arbitration of grievances was the availability of remedial powers necessary to bring about a final and binding resolution of the dispute. However, in affirming the existence of arbitral authority to order damages, Arbitrator Laskin stressed that arbitrators do not exercise a punitive function or sit in a quasi-criminal capacity. Rather, the basis for an award of damages is compensatory, and the order should attempt to restore the innocent party to the position that it would have been in had the collective agreement not been breached.

While there was some suggestion in *Ontario Hydro and C.U.P.E., Local 1000* (1990), 16 L.A.C. (4th) 264 (Kates) that in rare cases arbitrators have authority to award punitive damages, the more recent decision of Arbitrator Williamson in *Waterloo (City) and C.U.P.E., Local 1542* (1995), 50 L.A.C. (4th) 197 maintains the traditional arbitral reluctance to grant punitive damages. The *Waterloo (City)* award also demonstrates that the *Polymer Corp.* principles for determining union liability apply as well to work stoppages which, though they fall short of the statutory definition of "strike", nevertheless violate a broadly worded no-strike provision in the collective agreement. Finally, *Waterloo (City)* illustrates that the employer's entitlement to damages depends on its ability to establish the existence of a loss and a sufficient causal connection between the union's breach of the agreement and the loss claimed.

As the party claiming damages for breach of the collective agreement, the employer is under a positive duty to take reasonable steps to mitigate losses resulting from an illegal work stoppage. Nevertheless, if the union wishes to assert that the employer has failed in this duty, it bears the burden of proving that the employer did not act in a reasonable and prudent manner, and that the damages claimed would have been reduced had the employer done so. These principles were applied in *MacMillan Bloedel Ltd. and I.W.A., Local 1-85* (1997), 65 L.A.C. (4th) 391 (Hope).

In *Durham District School Board and Elementary Teachers' Federation of Ontario* (2004), 131 L.A.C. (4th) 29 (Bendel), the employer alleged that the union had violated a memorandum of settlement for a new collective agreement by failing to end a "pink listing" boycott against the employer, and by imposing disciplinary measures against teachers who had not honoured the boycott. The remedies sought by the employer included an order that the union pay damages to those members who had been disciplined in contravention of the memorandum of settlement. Arbitrator Bendel, concluding that the allegations were substantiated, directed the union to provide financial compensation to the employer. However, he declined to issue an order requiring the union to compensate members who had been subjected to discriminatory treatment. In the arbitrator's view, it would be inconsistent with the labour relations regime enshrined in collective bargaining legislation to allow the employer to act as the agent for employees in championing their claims against the union.

INDEX

[Numerical references are to page numbers]